The International Encyclopedia of

SHOOTING

Contributors:

Terence Blank

Geoffrey Boothroyd

Michael Brander

C. L. Coles

William B. Currie

The Rt Hon. The Earl of Enniskillen

D. Green

Jeffery G. Harrison

R. B. Hungerford

Teppo Lampio

Pál Máriássy

W. A. Newlands

Wilson Stephens

Henry Tegner

C. A. Terry

C. W. Thurlow Craig

G. Kenneth Whitehead

P. H. Whitaker

The International Encyclopedia of

SHOOTING

Edited by Michael Brander

American Advisory Editor: Edward G. Zern

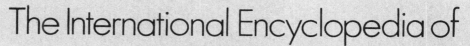

Pelham Books Ltd, London

This book was designed and produced by
Rainbird Reference Books Ltd,
Marble Arch House, 44 Edgware Road, London, w2,
for Pelham Books Ltd, 52 Bedford Square, London, wc1

House Editor: Peter Coxhead
Designer: George Sharp
Picture Research: Antoinette Moses

© Rainbird Reference Books Ltd, 1972
First published in 1972

SBN: 7207 0603 3

The text was photoset and the monochrome illustrations
were originated by Jolly & Barber Ltd, Rugby, England.
The colour plates were originated, and the book was
printed and bound, by Dai Nippon Printing Co. Ltd,
Tokyo, Japan

PRINTED IN JAPAN

Contents

List of Colour Plates

Preface

This encyclopedia has been compiled with the primary intention of gathering together concisely the more important information available about the fauna which may be hunted in each country, the conditions of terrain and climate likely to be encountered, the laws concerning game licences and import of guns, and details of the sporting methods employed by the hunters of that country. Apart from the intrinsic interest this must have for sportsmen the world over wishing to know how sport is conducted elsewhere, the sportsman in one country wishing to visit another country can quickly extract the salient features of interest to him. In each case addresses are given so that anyone wishing to do so may write for information on intended seasons, bag limits, licence fees and similar constantly changing data, although the most recent available figures have been included as a guide.

The season dates given for the United States and the Canadian provinces must only be taken as approximate, since seasons are set for each year, depending on the biologists' reports on game populations, split seasons, holidays (United States' seasons practically never start on Sundays and, indeed, Sunday shooting is illegal in several states) and other considerations. In the case of migratory birds, which come under Federal regulations, the states are annually given the choice of one relatively long season, or two seasons with a combined total of fewer days, but presumably a greater abundance of waterfowl, and the state's decision on which is preferred is sometimes not made until a few weeks beforehand. In these cases, as in other countries where dates of seasons, bag limits and licence fees are variable factors, the latest available figures have been given as a guide to the future, but the hunter should check with the competent authorities listed before embarking on a trip.

Among the many difficulties inherent in compiling an international work of this nature, the first of its kind, the worst problem of all is possibly that of language and meaning. For instance, between the English-speaking people on each side of the Atlantic there is a very considerable difference in the meaning of even such basic words as 'Hunting' and 'Shooting'. It must be made clear that this is a book on 'Hunting' in the broadest sense of the term as used in North America to describe hunting with dog and gun, including the pursuit of all birds and beasts hunted with firearms. Where there is any such distinction between meanings, as far as possible a 'mid-Atlantic' usage has been employed.

Technical language has been used only so far as it is intelligible to the average reader. In no sense is this a work of taxonomy or zoology. The matter of language apart, there is still enormous disagreement on even the basic facts concerning many quite common fauna between different schools of naturalists, zoologists, biologists, conservationists and hunters throughout the world, sometimes in the same country, let alone in neighbouring countries. However, the essentials of habitat, appearance, size, weight, breeding habits and other features of interest to the hunter are given on most of the birds and beasts commonly hunted. Under countries a standard format has been employed to show the general conditions, the terrain and climate, the relevant laws and the fauna which may be hunted.

The system of cross-referencing employed enables the reader to gather further information from other entries. In the lists of each group of animals, those species marked with an asterisk (*) have individual entries. Where fauna is listed under countries, though without individual entries, it may be taken that the species are hunted in those countries, but either not in sufficient numbers to warrant a separate entry, or else are not suitable quarries from a sporting viewpoint, either because they present no challenge to the hunter, or because they are endangered species.

It will be appreciated that many countries, for one reason or another, make little provision for visiting sportsmen. In cases where several countries can best be dealt with as a unit, as for example, parts of South America, West Africa, the Middle East and South-East Asia, this has been the method used. Where game regulations depend on a pattern of zones, or game management areas, or geographical divisions, it has been necessary to give a generalized rather than a detailed description. In all such instances the reader wishing to visit the areas concerned should consult the appropriate authorities beforehand.

This is the first attempt to consider hunting around the world from the hunter's viewpoint. It will be appreciated that in compressing so much information into one volume a large amount has had to be dealt with very briefly and much has had to be omitted. Various aspects such as the ballistics and theory of shooting have been ignored, since there are endless books on firearms which may be consulted on these subjects. Space has been found, however, to cover the importance of conservation and preservation of game against the pressures of population, pollution, and similar important international factors by including authoritative contributions on major points affecting hunters throughout the world. Acknowledgment should be made here, as well as separately, to the very considerable help and courtesy received from many countries and game authorities around the world without which the task of compiling this work would have been impossible.

Acknowledgments

A book of this kind, covering such a
wide field, could not have been compiled
without the generous assistance of many
people and organizations scattered
across the world. The editor is
particularly grateful to all those listed
below who freely supplied so much
information. However, full editorial
responsibility for the text is entirely his
own. Should there be omissions from the
list the editor tenders his sincere
apologies.

Afghanistan
Afghan Tourist Organisation, Kabul.

Australia
Norman Bartlett, Director, Australian
High Commission, London.
B. Hart, Chief Inspector of Wildlife,
Northern Territory Administration,
Darwin, Northern Territory.
A. N. Kavanagh, Secretary, Fisheries
and Wildlife Department, Melbourne,
Victoria.
L. J. Kelleher, Secretary, Animals and
Birds Protection Board, Hobart,
Tasmania.
L. J. McGovern, State Public Relations
Officer, Premier's Department, Brisbane,
Queensland.
D. G. McMichael, Director, National
Parks and Wildlife Service, Sydney, New
South Wales.
A. M. Olsen, Director, Department of
Fisheries and Fauna Conservation,
Adelaide, South Australia.
C. Roff, Fauna Officer, Department of
Primary Industries, Brisbane,
Queensland.
R. F. Ward, Department of Fisheries and
Fauna, Perth, Western Australia.

Austria
Herbert Durstberger, Vienna.
Carl Krois, Austrian National Tourist
Office, Vienna.

Belgium
P. Claus, Director, Belgian National
Tourist Office, London.
R. Laufer, Information Section, Belgian
Embassy, London.
William Ugeux, General Manager,
Institut Belge, Bruxelles.

Bolivia
Roberto Staszeski Lucero, Federacion
Boliviana de Caza y Pesca, La Paz.

Botswana
B. M. Setshogo, Botswana High
Commission, London.

Bulgaria
S. Charalambous, Bulgarian National
Tourist Office, London.
T. Damianov, Cultural Attaché,
Bulgarian Embassy, London.
M. Kossev, Chief of Section, and
M.Michailov, Director, 'Special Tourism'
Department, Balkantourist, Sofia.

Canada
Bruce Bailey, Public Relations Division,
Department of Tourism, Fish and Game,
Quebec.
John Bain, Director, Fish and Wildlife
Division, Department of Tourist
Development, Charlottetown, Prince
Edward Island.
F. G. Bard, Director, Department of
Natural Resources, Saskatchewan.
Madeleine Brock, Travel Counsellor,
Department of Tourism and Information,
Toronto, Ontario.
René Brunelle, Minister, Department of
Lands and Forests, Toronto, Ontario.
D. G. Dennis, Wildlife Biologist,
Canadian Wildlife Service, Aurora,
Ontario.
Director, Department of Indian Affairs
and Northern Development, Ottawa,
Ontario.
J. B. FitzGerald, Director of Game,
Government of the Yukon Territory,
Whitehorse, Yukon.
A. L. S. Hill, Consultant, Tourist
Branch, Saskatchewan Industry
Department, Regina, Saskatchewan.
Ann Holland, Travel Counsellor, Alberta
Government Travel Bureau, Edmonton,
Alberta.
H. Lyle Kohler, European Administra-
tion Officer, Canadian Government
Travel Bureau, Canada House, London.
E. Kuyt, Wildlife Biologist, Canadian
Wildlife Service, Fort Smith, North West
Territories.
P. A. Kwaternowsky, Superintendent of
Game, Government of North West
Territories.
D. J. Leger, Fish and Wildlife Branch,
Department of Natural Resources, New
Brunswick.
W. A. Morris, Wildlife Biologist,
Canadian Wildlife Service, University of
British Columbia, Vancouver, British
Columbia.

Stuart S. Peters, Executive Director,
Department of Lands and Forests,
Toronto, Ontario.
D. G. Pike, Director of Wildlife,
Department of Mines, Agriculture and
Resources, Government of Newfoundla
and Labrador.
Merrill Prime, Director of Wildlife,
Department of Lands and Forests,
Kentville, Nova Scotia.
Carol A. Scott, Wildlife Operations,
Department of Mines and Natural
Resources, Winnipeg, Manitoba.
C. E. Springstein, Director, Tourist
Branch, Saskatchewan Industry
Department, Regina, Saskatchewan.
Dan Wallace, Director, Canadian
Government Travel Bureau, Ottawa,
Canada.

Czechoslovakia
Miss V. Basetlikova, Assistant Cultura
Attaché, Czechoslovakian Embassy,
London.
Jírí Musil, Director, Czechoslovak
Travel Bureau, 'Cedok', London.

Denmark
Eiler Hansen, Danish Tourist Board,
London.
Kurt and Grete Bryde Nielsen, The
Danish Tourist Board, Copenhagen.
K. Plougmann, Assistant Press and
Cultural Attaché, Danish Embassy,
London.

Ethiopia
Zaudie Makuria, First Secretary,
Imperial Ethiopian Embassy, London.
Mulugeta Woldetsadik, Wild Life
Conservation Department, Imperial
Ethiopian Government, Addis Ababa.

Finland
Johannes Backstrom, Attaché, Finnish
Embassy, London.
Teppo Lampio, Director, Hunters'
Central Organisation, Helsinki.

France
M. J. Briens, Secretary, St Hubert of
France, Paris.
Christian Lepage, Services Officiels du
Tourisme Français, London.

Germany (Federal Republic)
Count Finck von Finckenstein, Press
Counsellor, Embassy of the Federal
Republic of Germany, London.
Dr Frank, Direktor, Forschungsstelle

für Jagdkunde und Wildshadenverhütung, Bonn.

Hungary
Joseph Gabor, Director General, 'Mavad', Budapest.
Ferenc Gal, Director, Tourist Information Service, Budapest.
Henry Schonthal, Director, 'Ibusz', Hungarian Travel Bureau, London.

Iceland
H. E. The Icelandic Ambassador, Icelandic Embassy, London.

India
N. S. Adkoli, Assistant Inspector General of Forests, Department of Agriculture, New Delhi.
A. C. Anand, Assistant Director, Indian Government Tourist Office, London.
A. G. Raddi, Special Officer Wildlife, Department of Tourism, New Delhi.
H. H. Rajadhiraj of Shahpura, Raytiabagh, Shahpura, Rajasthan.

Iraq
T. M. Makki, Acting Cultural Attaché, Iraqi Embassy, London.

Ireland, Republic of
P. Callanan, Game and Wildlife Branch, Department of Lands, Dublin.
N. Kavanagh, Irish Tourist Board, Dublin.
B. C. Thornberry, Field Officer, Irish Tourist Board, Dublin, Eire.

Israel
Ari Avnerre, Embassy of Israel, London.

Italy
F. Donini, Cultural Attaché, Italian Embassy, London.
Marino Moricci, Federazione Italiana della Caccia, Rome.

Japan
Taizo Watanabe, Japanese Embassy, London.

Kenya
F. A. Njiri, Office of the Director, Kenya National Parks, Nairobi.
T. K. Ngaamba, Ministry of Tourism and Wildlife, Nairobi.
S. L. Muhanji, Kenyan High Commission, London.
Tippett's Safaris, P.O. Box 43806, Nairobi.

Malaysia
Rashid Bin Mat, Ministry of Information, Kuala Lumpur.

Mexico
H. Guterriez Vega, Cultural Counsellor, Mexican Embassy, London.

Nepal
M. B. Busnyat, General Manager, Nepal Wildlife Centre, Katmandu.

Netherlands
H. K. Michaelis, Director, Netherlands Hunters' Association, The Hague.
D. J. van Wijnen, Counsellor for Press Affairs and Information, Royal Netherlands Embassy, London.

New Zealand
W. F. Bern, Travel Commissioner, New Zealand High Commission, London.
Rex Forrester, Fishing and Hunting Officer, Government Tourist Bureau, Rotorua.

Nigeria
A. P. Leventis, Leventis Stores Ltd., Lagos.

Norway
Torleiv Anda, Press Counsellor, Norwegian Embassy, London.
A. K. Andersen, Manager, Norwegian State Railways Travel Bureau, London.
Erik Myhre, Director, Erik Myhre Travel Bureau Ltd., Oslo.
Hjalmar Pavel, Direktoratat for Jakt, Trondheim.
Dag Mork Ulnes, Press Attaché, Norwegian Embassy, London.

Pakistan
M. Nurul Islam, Department of Tourism, Karachi.
Abdul Quayyum, Press Counsellor, Pakistan High Commission, London.

Peru
Ricardo W. Stubbs, Minister, Peruvian Embassy, London.

Philippines
H. E. Jaime Zobel de Ayala, Ambassador, Philippines Embassy, London.

Poland
P. Cieslar, Counsellor, Polish Embassy, London.
N. Grzechowiak, First Secretary, Polish Embassy, London.
Mrs. I. J. Pedzich, Deputy Manager, Polish Tourist Information Centre, London.

Portugal
M. Jorge G. Dias, Director, Portuguese National Information Office, London.
Salvador Hassan, Consulet de Portugal, Genève.

Rhodesia
B. P. M. O'Donoghue, National Parks and Wildlife Management, Salisbury.
Reay H. N. Smithers, Director of Museums, Salisbury.

Rumania
Mrs M. Gustea, Cultural Department, Rumanian Embassy, London.

South Africa
R. M. Breach, Director of Nature Conservation, Capetown.
D. C. Hills, Secretary, Natal Parks, Game and Fish Preservation Board, Pietermaritzburg.
John W. Shilling, Anglo-American Corporation Ltd, Johannesburg.
W. van der Westhuizen, Secretary, South African Hunters' and Game Preservation Association, Pretoria.

Spain
A. Vasquez de Prada, Director, Spanish National Tourist Office, London.

Sweden
Mrs Gudrun Boström-Murphy, Royal Swedish Embassy, London.
Mona Östling, Swedish National Travel Association, London.
Bo Thelander, Svenske Jagareförbundet, Stockholm.

Tanzania
D. N. M. Bryceson, Minister of Agriculture and Co-Operatives, Dar es Salaam.
Peter O. Oyoyo, Ministry of Natural Resources and Tourism, Dar es Salaam.

Turkey
Mustafa Erturk, Assistant Cultural Attaché, Turkish Embassy, London.
Munci Giz, Director, Turkish Tourism Information Office, London.

United Kingdom
W. G. Dallas, Divisional Forest Officer, Ministry of Agriculture, Belfast.
Miss P. Trohear, Northern Ireland Tourist Board, London.

Uganda
F. D'Mello, Uganda Wildlife Development Ltd, Kampala.
Lamech E. Akongo, Ugandan High Commission, London.

U.S.A.
Rod Amundson, Chief, Educational Division, Wildlife Resources Commission, North Carolina.
Dan C. Armbruster, Chief, Division of Wildlife, Department of Natural Resources, Ohio.
G. Ray Arnett, Director, Department of Fish & Game, California.
William R. Barbee, Director, Game & Parks Commission, Nebraska.
E. Kliess Brown, Chief Information Department, Fish & Game Department, Idaho.
George W. Bucknam, Commisioner,

Acknowledgments – continued

Department of Inland Fisheries & Game, Maine.
Farrell Copelin, Director, Department of Wildlife Conservation, Oklahoma.
Bernard W. Corsob, Director, Fish & Game Commission, New Hampshire.
Henry L. Diamond, Commissioner, Department of Environmental Conservation, New York.
Frank H. Dunkle, Director, Fish & Game Department, Montana.
John L. Farley, Director, Fish & Wildlife Service, U.S. Department of Interior.
Woodrow Fleming, Director, Fish & Game Division, Department of Natural Resources, Indiana.
O. E. Frye, Jr, Director, Game & Freshwater Fish Commission, Florida.
David M. Goodrich, Director, Game & Fish Commission, Tennessee.
John S. Gottschalk, Director, Bureau of Sport Fisheries & Wildlife, Department of the Interior.
Carl M. Grouse, Director, Department of Game, Washington.
Richard L. Hall, Supervisor Game Management, Department of Natural Resources, West Virginia.
Ralph C. Hammer, Chief of Extension Services, Fish & Wildlife Administration, Maryland.
Edward L. Hanson, Chief of Wildlife Section, Department Natural Resources, Indiana.
Austin N. Heller, Secretary, Department of Natural Resources, Delaware.
Andrew H. Hulsey, Director, Game & Fish Commission, Arkansas.
Franklin F. Jones, Director of Game, Board of Fish & Game, Alaska.
Tom Knight, Information Officer, Department of Game, Washington.
Harold C. Lacaillade, Game Biologist, Fish & Game Department, New Hampshire.
Ira S. Latimer Jr, Director, Department of Natural Resources, West Virginia.

John W. McKean, Director, The Game Commission, Oregon.
Ralph A. MacMullen, Director, Department of Natural Resources, Michigan.
Joseph H. Manning, Director, Fish & Wildlife Administration, Maryland.
George W. Bucknam, Commissioner, Department of Inland Fisheries & Game, Maine.
George C. Moore, Director, Fish & Game Commission, Kansas.
Carl L. Noren, Director, Department of Conservation, Missouri.
Clyde P. Patton, Director, Wildlife Resources Commission, North Carolina.
George M. Purvis, Chief, Information Department, Game & Fish Commission, Arkansas.
Chester F. Phelps, Director, Game & Inland Fisheries Commission, Virginia.
Robert L. Salter, Director, Fish & Game Department, Idaho.
M. Sawyers, Chief Information Officer, Game & Fish Commission, Wyoming.
Keith Severin, U.S. Department of Agriculture, Washington, D.C.
David A. Watts, Game Biologist, Department of Natural Resources, Ohio.
James B. White, Commissioner, Game & Fish Commission, Wyoming.
H. G. Williamson, Staff Biologist, Department of Wildlife Conservation, Oklahoma.
24, 205, 252
Also the Directors of:
Division of Game & Fish, Albama Department of Conservation.
Arizona Game & Fish Department.
Colorado Game Fish & Parks Department.
Connecticut Board of Fisheries & Game.
Georgia State Game & Fish Commission.
Division of Fish & Game, Hawaii Department of Land & Natural Resources.
Game Division, Department of Conservation, Illinois.

Fish & Game Division, State Conservation Commission, Iowa.
Division of Game, Kentucky Department of Fish & Wildlife Resources.
Division of Fish & Game, Louisiana Wildlife & Fisheries Commission.
Massachusetts Division of Fisheries & Game.
Division of Game & Fish, Minnesota Department of Conservation.
Mississippi Game & Fish Commission.
Nevada Fish & Game Commission.
Division of Fish & Game, New Jersey Department of Conservation.
New Mexico Department of Game & Fish
Pennsylvania Game Commission.
Rhode Island Department of Natural Resources.
Division of Game & Boating, South Carolina Wildlife Resources Commission
Game Division, South Dakota Department of Game Fish & Parks.
Texas Parks & Wildlife Department.
Utah State Department of Fish & Game
Vermont Fish & Game Board.
Game Management Division, Wisconsin Conservation Department.

U.S.S.R.
N. Pleshanov, Assistant Agricultural Counsellor, Embassy of the U.S.S.R., London.
I. Zavorin, Intourist Moscow, London.

Yugoslavia
Milan Zupan, Counsellor, Yugoslav Embassy, London

Zambia
Z. J. Kafulubiti, Press Attaché, Zambia High Commission, London.

Certain phrases in the entry 'Dog Breeds for Hunting' are reproduced from *The Complete Dog Book* by kind permission of The American Kennel Club.

Picture Credits

Page numbers in *italics* refer to colour plates

13

Introduction

No doubt man first hunted animals for food but the true hunter's attitude to his quarry has always had an undertone of respect, of reverence, even worship, in it. Without this element there is little to distinguish man the hunter from his ancestor the ape-man. Many early cave paintings had a strong magical or religious significance and almost all early pagan religions had a close link with animals through hunting. Records of the early Persian and Chinese civilizations demonstrate this, as did the Egyptians with their animal-headed deities. Both Greek and Roman mythology continued the theme. The lion and the unicorn of heraldry are but one obvious instance of a modern survival of these beliefs.

The early hunter, who depended on killing his quarry to live and was constantly aware that he might himself be killed, skilfully delineated the antelope, the auroch, the bison and the mammoth among many other animals on the walls of his cave dwelling. While in some cases this may simply have been a record of the hunt in other instances he was clearly trying to establish a mystical relationship with his quarry. A belief in the resurrection of the hunter's spirit after death in the shape of the quarry he hunts is still the basis of many primitive religions. The American Plains Indian held this anthropomorphic belief in various forms well into the last century and many primitive tribes today share similar convictions.

This respect, amounting to reverence, for the quarry is to be found in the custom, not yet extinct among modern European hunters, of communing silently for a few moments beside the body of the shot stag before placing a sprig of greenery between its jaws representing its last meal on earth, or possibly food for its journey into the next world. A twig dipped in the blood of the quarry is then placed in the hatband of the successful hunter. Clearly these are survivals of the earliest primitive pagan rites of man the hunter.

When the British huntsman 'bloods' the novice follower of hounds by daubing his brow with blood from the severed brush, or tail, of the fox after a successful hunt, he is unwittingly acting the part of the priest in a pagan religious ceremony. The sounding of the horn, or horns, at the successful conclusion of the hunt fulfills the twofold function of summoning the laggards, both hounds and hunt followers, as well as saluting and honouring the passing of the quarry. Each is undoubtedly a modern survival of a much older ceremony dating back to the days of early man.

With the exception of the mating instinct the impulse to hunt is the oldest of man's natural instincts. Neither of them are anything to be ashamed of, although some people, whose own instincts are often debased or atrophied beyond recognition, would have it so. In modern man, inevitably, these instincts have become less keen, in some cases altered, even twisted, but this is no matter for pride.

The modern opponent of hunting generally lays claim to a civilized attitude. He implies, rightly, that he cannot understand the attitude of the hunter. He has himself generally lost the reverence for the quarry inherent in the true hunter. It would however be wrong simply to accuse him of lack of reverence or of atrophied instinct. It is merely understanding that he lacks. Reared from childhood on Bambi or Beatrix Potter, he often suffers from a twisted anthropomorphic belief that animals feel pain and reason like humans. Mistakenly he equates himself with hunted animals and credits them with his imaginary fear and pain. Such reasoning, of course, bears no relation to the realities of the Chase or of Nature.

It is very understandable that the modern town dweller, born and bred in unnatural concrete surroundings, knows nothing of the delicate balances of life in the wilder countryside. He does not appreciate that the sufferings of the lame calf striving to keep up with the herd are abruptly and mercifully stilled forever by the jackals hovering on their trail. The game preserver who strives to understand his quarry, who admires its struggles to survive, who culls the animals which are past their prime and saves them from the defeats of old age, the rebuffs by younger animals, the final ostracism from the herd and a lingering death, is to be applauded not censured.

The opponents of hunting generally know little, and care less, about the background. They know nothing of the cold wet dawns, or long freezing evening vigils, or even of the heat and flies of summer, when any movement betrays the hunter's presence. Nor can they, generally, understand that very often it is reward enough merely to watch the quarry in its wild state, to see the delicate courtships, the fond maternal care of the mother, or the playful antics of the young.

By imbibing knowledge of every aspect of his quarry's way of life the hunter naturally increases his admiration of it. As well as a hunter he becomes a game preserver. Awareness of its courage in defence of its young, knowledge of its mating displays and ceremonial, experience of it at every season of the year, all these add up to essential hunter's knowledge. They also add up, inevitably, to understanding, respect and even worship of a worthy adversary.   M.W.B.

Contributors

The initials after contributors' names are those used
at the end of their entries

TERENCE BLANK — TB
Research Director, The Game Conservancy,
Fordingbridge

GEOFFREY BOOTHROYD — GB
Author of books on firearms

MICHAEL BRANDER — MWB
Author of books on hunting, shooting, and fishing

C. L. COLES — CLC
Director, The Game Conservancy, Fordingbridge

WILLIAM B. CURRIE — WBC
Writer on field sports

THE RIGHT HON. THE EARL OF ENNISKILLEN — E
Ex-Honorary Game Warden, Kenya

D. GREEN — DG
Hunter and journalist

JEFFERY G. HARRISON, O.B.E. — JGH
Honorary Director, Conservation and Research, and
Vice-chairman, The Wildfowlers' Association of
Great Britain and Ireland

R. B. HUNGERFORD — RBH
Australian hunter and Editorial Manager of
Sporting Shooter Magazine

TEPPO LAMPIO — TL
Director, Hunters' Central Organisation, Helsinki

PÁL MÁRIÁSSY — PM
Organizer of hunting tours

W. A. NEWLANDS — WAN
Writer and aviculturist

WILSON STEPHENS — WS
Editor, *The Field*

HENRY TEGNER — HT
Author and roe-deer stalker

C. A. TERRY — CAT
Hand-loading expert

C. W. THURLOW CRAIG — CWTC
Hunter and journalist

G. KENNETH WHITEHEAD — GKW
Author and expert on deer

P. H. WHITAKER — PHW
Editor, *Country Landowner*

A

Abyssinia *see* Ethiopia

Aden *see* Middle East

Afghanistan
Afghanistan is a country of about 250,000 square miles lying to the north-west of West Pakistan, with Russia to the north and Iran to the west. Three-quarters of the country is mountainous and the elevation is generally over 4,000 ft, but the Hindu Kush, the chief mountain range, rises to over 24,000 ft in the north-east. There are three great river basins: the Oxus (Amu Darya), Helmand and Kabul. The land is much flatter towards the south-west, with all-year heat. Elsewhere the winters can be very cold, and there is snow for nine months of the year in the north, though the central Kabul plains are pleasantly mild. Rainfall is nowhere heavy.

Agriculture and sheep raising are the principal industries, mineral wealth being as yet undeveloped. Areas such as the Kabul plains can produce two crops a year, one of wheat or barley and the other of rice or millet. Sugar beet, cotton, and many fruits are also grown, but agriculture is generally not far advanced as the country is still being 'opened up'. Few of the roads are metalled, and pack horse is still the most common form of transport. Visitors wishing to hunt should not, therefore, expect easy access or modern facilities, but the corollary to this is that a variety of otherwise shy and fairly uncommon species are available and the hunting can provide good rewards.

Afghanistan can offer most of the upland deer, mountain sheep and mountain goats that are found in the western Himalayas. Among the most common are ibex, urial and markhor. There are many other non-trophy animals, and fox, wolf and ermine are hunted widely for their pelts. Shooting, game and firearm regulations are very few and visitors may import two sporting guns and 100 rounds of ammunition duty free.

Further Information
Afghan Tourist Organization, Ministry of Press and Information Building, Kabul.

Agouti *(Dasyprocta aguti)*
Agoutis are guinea-pig-like rodents about the size of a rabbit with a button tail, slender legs and short coarse hair, found in colonies in the West Indies, and, in different forms, in South America. They are nocturnal, forest dwellers, able to move fast in a series of swift bounds and they can swim well. They feed on fruits, roots and berries, causing

The agouti is common over a wide range of South America and parts of the West Indies.

considerable damage to sugar and banana plantations. The commoner species, found throughout much of Brazil and the Guianas, has an orange coloured, erectile, rump patch and similar, but differently coloured erectile rump patches are a feature of the other species. Taking to water readily, they are commonly shot by beating an area near a river with hounds and shooting them as they bolt for the water. Vulnerable to predators they are also much hunted, being considered very good eating. *See also* South America, Shooting in.

Alabama (U.S.A.)
One of the Gulf states, Alabama covers about 51,000 square miles. It is principally an agricultural state, with very fertile land in the north and centre, broken up by the ridge and valley landscape of the southern tip of the Appalachian Mountains. In the south the land is low lying, heavily wooded, and sparsely populated. The climate is warm, but with very cold spells in some winters.

The state is famous for its excellent deer and quail hunting. Most of the quail land is in private hands, but there are extensive Game Management areas, either owned by the Department of Conservation, or run by it in agreement with private owners or Federal service departments. In these management areas hunting is by permit and the bag is limited. Besides deer and quail, wild

Seasons and Limits—Alabama

Game	Period	Bag Limits	Notes
White-tailed deer	13 Nov-11 Jan	1 per season	antlered buck only; state-wide
		3 per season	Game Management areas
Cotton-tailed rabbit	15 Oct-28 Feb	8 per day	
Gray & fox squirrel	15 Oct-11 Jan		
Wild turkey	13 Nov-11 Jan	1 per day 5 per season	autumn season in some counties; gobblers only
	20 Mar-26 Apr		spring season in all counties; gobblers only
Racoon, opossum, bobcat	15 Oct-28 Feb	none	
Bobwhite quail	20 Nov-27 Feb	10 per day	

Licence Fees—Alabama			
Status	Type	Period	Fee ($)
Resident	all-game	1 year	$3.15
Non-resident	all-game	1 year	$85.15
		7 days	$10.15
	small-game	1 year	$10.15
		7 days	$7.15

Obtainable from : Office of the Judge of Probate at county seats ;
from sports shops and agents elsewhere.

Big Game Inventory—Alabama		
Species	Shot	Est. pop.
White-tailed deer	68,000	300,000
Wild turkey	40,000	225,000

Barren ground caribou, found in Alaska and other parts of the North American tundra, move around in search of food more than any other caribou species.

Licence Fees—Alaska			
Status	Type	Species	Fee ($)
Resident	hunting/fishing		$12.00
Non-resident	hunting/fishing		$20.00
Non-resident	tags	black bear	$10.00
		brown bear	$75.00
		grizzly bear	$75.00
		polar bear	$15.00
		bison	$50.00
		caribou	$25.00
		deer	$10.00
		elk	$25.00
		goat	$25.00
		moose	$50.00
		musk ox	$1,000.00
		sheep	$50.00
		walrus	$100.00

turkeys, rabbit, squirrel, opossum, raccoon and waterfowl are shot.

Further Information

Division of Game and Fish, Department of Conservation, Administrative Building, Montgomery, Alabama 36104.

Alaska (U.S.A.)

Covering nearly 600,000 square miles it is very much the largest state in the U.S.A., and occupies the extreme north-west of the continent. It is only scantily settled, and that mainly in the south-west.

Alaska is famous for its big game hunting. It has the largest bear population, and the biggest bears in the world; Dall sheep, Sitka black-tailed deer, giant moose, caribou and mountain goats are also found. Buffalo, introduced from the south, and musk ox, another introduced species, have multiplied sufficiently to need annual culling, and white mountain goats are fairly abundant. There are polar bears and walrus to be hunted in the Arctic north. Upland game birds are confined to ptarmigan and grouse. There is excellent goose shooting, especially in the breeding grounds around the Yukon-Kuskokwin delta. Wild duck have generally migrated southwards before the season starts, but some resident duck are found in the south-west. Non-residents must be accompanied by a licensed guide when shooting big game, and, if hunting polar bear, he must be a qualified Arctic guide. The state is divided into twenty-six Game Management Units, with different game, limits, and seasons. There are large areas of national parks and game reserves where hunting is prohibited.

Further Information

Department of Fish and Game, Subport Building, Juneau, Alaska 99801; Licensing Section, Alaska Department of Revenue, 240 South Franklin, Juneau, Alaska 99801.

Alaskan Brown Bear (*Ursus kidderi, U. townsendi, U. sitkensis, etc.*)

Although a giant bear has certainly lived along the Alaskan coast since prehistoric times, it remained unknown until the coastline and islands became accessible less than a century ago. There is some doubt whether it constitutes a single species, for there is considerable size and colour variation, and some sixteen species or sub-species have been recognized and named. The fact that it lives on widely separated islands may account for this variation. The largest of all, the Kodiak bear, may weigh up to 1600 lb, but the average weight throughout its range is probably no more than 800 lb, the female always weighing less than the male; the cub takes several years to reach full size.

The pelt, always rare, was once fashionable for carriage robes until a Federal law prohibited trading in them. The beast's great size is certainly due to the abundant runs

Seasons and Limits—Alaska

Species	Period	Bag Limits	Comment
Black bear	1 Sept-30 June; no closed season in some units	1-3	No females with cubs may be shot
Brown bear and Grizzly bear	1 Sept-30 June; autumn and spring seasons in some units	1 every 4 years	
Polar bear	15 Feb or 1 March-30 April	1 every 4 years	
Bison	Announced according to cull required	1 every 4 years	
Caribou	Some units have no season, some have no closed season, some Aug-March	Vary from 1 to no limits	
Deer	1 Aug-Nov or Dec, shorter for antlerless deer	1-4	Season only in the southern units
Elk	Kodiak Island only 1 Aug-31 Sept	1	At Commissioner's discretion
Mountain goat	In 7 units only. Aug-31 Dec or 31 Jan	1. Permits can be issued in Unit 8 for up to 15	
Moose	Aug and Sept; also in Nov in some units	Limited, especially for antlerless moose	
Musk ox	Sept and Oct by permit only Feb and March	Limited to a total of 50 bulls in each season	
Dall sheep	10 Aug-20 Sept	1 ram with $\frac{3}{4}$ curl horns or larger	
Grouse (spruce, blue, ruffed or sharptail)	Aug-April or May	Either 5 per day and 10 in possesion or 15 per day and 30 in possesion	According to Unit
Hare	1 Sept-30 April in units 1-5, elsewhere no closed season	5 per day No limit	
Ptarmigan (willow, rock or whitetail)	Aug-April or May	20 per day and 40 in possession	
Seals	In units 17-26 no limit season No open season anywhere for elephant seal	No limits anywhere Non-residents: 1 adult bull walrus at any time in units 18, 22, 23 and 26	

Big Game Inventory—Alaska

Species	Shot	Est. pop.
Moose	6,000	140,000
Caribou	33,000	600,000
Black bear	1,200	
Brown and grizzly	637	
Black-tailed deer	14,000	
Elk	72	

of salmon in the area. Although it is omnivorous, eating kelp, grasses and berries, it relies on the spawning salmon to provide it, throughout the summer, with the unlimited supplies of protein and oil-rich food with which to prepare for hibernation. Prior to hibernating it stops eating and purges itself, before moving to a solitary den on the mountainside in late autumn.

The female breeds once every two years, in May and June, the cubs being born the following winter during hibernation. They are normally twins, though singles and triplets are common, and remain with the dam until she breeds again in the second summer. The male is solitary, and seeks out the female only at breeding time, when he will drive the cubs away.

In summer they are to be found near rivers where the salmon run, and their habitat is generally confined to the coastline and islands of the Alaskan Peninsula. There is a certain overlapping of terrain and interbreeding with the grizzly bear (q.v.), and a rough and arbitrary classification is that any bear found more than 75 miles inland is a grizzly, and any found closer to the coastline is an Alaskan brown bear. (Some taxonomists, in fact, deny that these are separate species.)

The bear is hunted normally in spring, when the pelt is in best condition. The hunter must, by law, be accompanied by a guide. The best method is to stalk the beast upwind; still-hunting along a known path, or even 'spooking' it downwind to the waiting gun may be necessary. A heavy bullet and high velocity rifle are almost essential, as are telescopic sights. In the case of a wounded animal, either charging or attempting to run, a shoulder or forearm shot is recommended.

Alberta (Canada)

This is the most westerly of the three great Prairie Provinces, covering some 240,000 square miles. Except where it runs up, in the south-west and west, towards the Rockies the land is flat and undulating. There are many lakes, some of them very large, in addition to the wet weather sloughs and potholes found on most prairie steppes. There are also three great river systems — those associated with the Milk River in the south, the Saskatchewan River in the centre, and the Athabaska and Peace Rivers in the north.

The climate varies, as one would expect in any land mass covering eleven degrees of latitude, but is, on the whole, extreme, being hot in the short summers and very cold in the long winters. There are about 70 million acres of farmland, a third of it under plough and producing, mainly, cereals. The rest is ranched. Much of the north of the province is covered with forests.

The ecosystems may be described as Alpine Barren in the higher Rockies above the

The largest deer in the world, the moose, by a lakeside in Alberta

timberline, Montane just below it, and Foothill all along the approaches to the mountains. In varying degrees these provide the principal habitats for bighorn sheep, mountain goat, elk, mountain caribou and the grizzly bear. Much of the north of the province is occupied by a mixed wood system that merges, in the far north-east, into the muskeg and rocks of the Great Canadian Shield. Here the heaviest populations of moose and woodland caribou are found. The centre and the central south of the province are occupied by parkland, whose rich, black soils give way, in the south-east, to the more arid soils of a sagebrush prairie. This is deer country, both white-tail and mule, with antelope surviving in the south-east, though no longer in sufficient numbers for an open season.

Mountain-goat numbers have also so decreased, under pressure from hunting, that an open season is no longer possible, and there is an open season for caribou only, in the far north-west. Moose, elk and deer, however, seem to maintain fairly stable populations under present harvesting methods. The province is divided, for purposes of game management, into sixteen Big Game Zones, and no one is allowed to hunt game of any sort in any of these without a valid Wildlife Certificate, which costs $3.

Further Information

Fish and Wildlife Division, Department of Lands and Forests, Natural Resources Building, Edmonton, Alberta.

Alligator *see* Crocodiles and Alligators; South America, Shooting in

American Brant *(Branta bernicla hrota)*
One of the black geese, closely resembling

Waterfowl Inventory—Alberta		
	Shot	
Duck	459,000	Mallard 60% Pintail 11% Gadwall 8.5% American widgeon 8.5% Others 12%
Geese	59,050	Canada 58% Whitefront 20% Lesser snow 19% Others 3%

both the black brant *(B. nigricans)* q.v. of the Pacific coasts and the Brent goose *(B. bernicla brenta)* q.v. Like them it is a small, completely maritime goose breeding high inside the Arctic Circle. Except for Ross's goose *(Anser rossii)* it is the smallest of all the geese, weighing, at between three and four pounds, little more than a mallard, and measuring between sixteen and seventeen inches. It has a black bill, face and neck, the stocking ending well down, with only a small crescent of white under the throat. The upperparts and wings are brownish-gray and the underparts are light gray, turning white towards the tail. The feet are black and, on the water, the white undertail coverts are prominent, since the tail is carried elevated. Flight is usually in line abreast, low over the sea, somewhat higher over land.

The main breeding ground is on Ellesmere Island, though they also nest in Greenland and on other islands bordering Baffin Bay. The nest is a down-lined depression in the ground; the normal clutch is from three

Seasons and Bag Limits—Alberta

Big Game
The limits on all big game, for residents and non-residents alike, is one, but a resident with an elk licence is also permitted to take a cougar, and one black or brown bear, and, with a black bear licence, may take two black or brown bears in the spring season.

White-tailed Deer
There are open seasons for stags in all 16 zones, and shorter seasons for does in all except two of southern zones. The earliest opening date in any zone is 8 September and the latest closing date 12 December. These are also the dates for the doe season in the mountainous south-western zones, but elsewhere the doe season last no more than five or ten days in either October or November. In two zones the doe season lasts only one day. (Note that 'doe' includes, for this purpose, males with antlers less than 4in. long.) Best areas : the central and eastern parklands.

Mule Deer
There are open seasons for stags in all zones except one in the south-east. The earliest and latest dates are the same as for white-tail. There are also open seasons for does in the western and northern zones. These last, at their longest, for ten days in November. Best areas : the foothills of the Rockies.

Moose
There are open seasons for bulls in the western and northern zones. The earliest opening date is 8 September and the latest closing one 12 December. There are open seasons for cows in the northern and moun-tainous south-western zones, with the same earliest and latest dates as for bulls.

Elk
There are open seasons for bulls in the western and northern zones, with the same earliest and latest dates as moose. The open seasons for cows in four of the western zones generally run for two days in November. Best areas : the foothills of the Rockies.

Sheep (trophy or non-trophy)
There are open seasons in the moun-tainous south-western zones and one in the north-west. They run mostly from 29 August to 31 October. Best areas : the Rockies. Licences for non-trophy sheep are available for residents only.

Caribou
There is only one complete zone in the north-west with an open season for caribou, and that runs from 8 September to 31 October. There are, however, 'extended seasons' in certain parts of the northern-most zone, lasting from 8 September to either 31 October or 12 December.

Black bear
There are open seasons in all zones except those of the north and the south-east, and they run from 8, 9 or 26 September to 14 November. In addition there is a spring season from 1 April to 31 May, but during this season females with cubs, as well as the cubs themselves, are protected.

Grizzly bear
There is an open season that runs from 1 April to 31 May in certain parts of the northern and central western zones. Females and cubs are protected in the spring season. Best areas : the foothills of the Rockies and around the Peace and Smoky Rivers.

Cougar
May be shot from 1 October to 31 December, and may be hunted with dogs from 1 January to 31 January, but only by a hunter holding a valid elk licence.

Wolf, coyote, wolverine, fox, porcupine, rabbit and hare
All may be shot without a licence on private land in certain districts. In other districts, and on all Crown lands they can only be hunted from 8 September to 30 April by the hunter holding a valid big-game licence.

Upland Game Birds
For the purposes of game-bird manage-ment the province is divided into five zones that do not correspond with the 16 big-game zones. A game-bird licence costs a resident $3.50 ; a Canadian non-resident $5 ; and an alien non-resident $50. Game birds shot must have their wings left on until the birds have been cleared by a wildlife officer or brought back to the place of residence. Not more than 65 birds may be exported free of charge in any one year, of which no more than 15 should be pheasants.

Pheasants
The season, in all five zones, runs from 9 October to 5 December. The bag limit is 3 per day, 9 in possession, between 9 October and 31 October, and 5 per day, 15 in possession for the rest of the season. Hens may be shot in some very restricted areas in the south, where there may be 2 hens in the daily bag and 3 in possession.

Hungarian partridge, sharp-tailed, ruffed and spruce grouse
The season usually runs from the end September or early October to early December, except in the extreme north and central western mountains, where it runs from early September to early December. Bag limits in all zones are 10 per day, 30 in possession.

Blue grouse
The season runs from the beginning or end of September to early December, in the extreme north and the central western mountains ; Bag limits are 5 per day and 25 in possession.

Willow ptarmigan
In parts of the northern half of the country there is a season that runs from 2 November to 27 February. Bag limit is 5 per day and 25 in possession.

Sage grouse
There is a season for these in parts of the south-east that runs from 23 October to 31 October. Bag limit is 2 per day, 2 in possession.

Waterfowl and other migrants
The province is divided, under the Migratory Birds Convention Act, into seven zones, which differ from both the big-game and the game-bird zones. The seasons generally run from the beginning of September to early December, or from middle or late September to late December or early January. Some zones have special geese seasons. The bag limits for duck are 8 per day, 16 in possession, and for geese 5 per day, of which not more than 2 may be whitefronts, and 10 in possession, of which not more than 4 may be whitefronts. For rails and coots, the limit is 8 per day and 16 in possession, but there are no limits for Indians, Eskimos and professional trappers. The Wilson's snipe limit is 10 per day, 20 in possession.

---

to five eggs; incubation takes around twenty-eight days. The gander remains in attend-ance during nesting and rearing. Immature brant are more gray than adults and the white crescent on the throat is often missing. They are ready for the flight south within three months, which is important, since migration must start early in those latitudes to escape the freeze-up. They leave early in August, and return from the wintering grounds along the Atlantic coast from New Jersey to North Carolina in March and

April, to arrive back at the nesting grounds in June.

Their main food on the wintering grounds is eel-grass *(Zostera marina)* and their numbers always reflect the supplies of this grass in the area. They pull it up by the roots, tipping to do so. Since this can only be done at low tide they then pull up more than they can eat, leaving it to float and be eaten later. Having eaten they leave the sandbanks to rest well out at sea, hardly ever coming in to land or grazing like other geese. During the long period when eel-grass blight hit the Atlantic coasts of America and Europe, brant fed on the so-called 'bay cabbage', a seaweed which imparted an unpleasant flavour to the meat, and many hunters ceased shooting brant. As a result the birds multiplied dramatically, but since the eel-grass beds have recovered the bird is once again a favourite of east-coast hunters, and the population has been considerably reduced, although it is still high.

They nearly always have to be approached and shot over water, which means using a punt, or sneak float, or else a blind and decoys. They are less wary when feeding than most geese, and they also decoy more readily.

American Coot *(Fulica americana)*
Coots are not, of course, true ducks, but members of the *Rallidae*, a family that includes the rails and gallinules. They are, however, often confused with scoters, which are true ducks, partly because they, also, are largely black, and partly because they carry, in America, popular nicknames such as bald-headed coot, old gray coot and so on.

The American coot resembles very closely the coot *(Fulica atra)* of Europe, Asia and Australasia, and differs mainly in having a brown, rather than white, crown-plate. This is a toughened area supposed to enable the bird to push its way through the sharp-edged grasses and reeds of its marshy habitat. The bird, though it runs like a chicken, has a duck-like appearance, and is, roughly, of mallard size. It has a white bill and a black head and neck. The rest of the body is slaty-gray, darker on top than underneath; the tips of the secondary wing-feathers are white, and show as a white border in flight; the undertail coverts are also white. The legs and feet are green, and the toes are long and lobed, with no webbing, which distinguishes them from the gallinules. However, like the gallinules, they can move around on the vegetation on top of a marsh, but, unlike them, they swim and dive readily. They take wing with some difficulty, needing to splutter over the water using both feet and wings. There is no apparent difference, other than size, between male and female, but the young coot, in the downy stage, has a red bill, a bald head, and bright, orange, hair-like feathers scattered along the head and neck. After the downy stage they assume adult plumage which is, at first, lighter coloured.

American coots nest throughout North America on fresh-water marshes. The nest is built of grass and reeds, anchored to the surrounding vegetation. The clutch consists of from eight to fifteen eggs and incubation starts as soon as the first egg is laid, with the consequence that the young hatch out one by one. The male bird looks after those that have hatched early and already left the nest. Many coots winter on their nesting grounds, but those nesting in the far north will move south, and there are large, wintering colonies along the Gulf of Mexico.

Coots are principally vegetarian, and are, perhaps, only marginally edible. When they add small fish and crustacea to their diet this is no longer true, since the skin, during cooking, gives out an oil with a fishy taste and smell. Since they are reluctant flyers they provide indifferent sport and are rarely hunted.

American Goldeneye *(Bucephala clangula americana)*
One of the diving ducks of America, closely related to the goldeneye of Europe *(B. clangula clangula)* q.v. and to another American duck of the same genus, Barrow's goldeneye *(B. islandica)* q.v. It is a medium-sized bird, the duck being smaller than the drake, which has an average weight of around 2 lb and measures between 17 and 19 in, with a wingspan of between 27 and 30 in.

The adult drake in full winter plumage is predominantly white, with the back, tail and parts of the wings black. The head is a glossy green, with a prominently rounded forehead and an oval white patch between the black bill and the bright yellow eye. The legs and feet are orange. In eclipse the plumage becomes duller and more like the ducks'. The eclipse moult begins in July and the autumn one in September, full winter plumage reappearing by December. The adult duck is brownish-gray above and white below, with a white collar under her chocolate-brown head. In the breeding period the nail of her black bill turns yellow. Young ducklings resemble the duck in plumage, differentiation not beginning until the second year. Both the drake and duck are generally silent, though the drake may use a two-note call during courtship, which consists of the customary plumage and swimming display, during which the head is jerked backwards and forwards. The 'whistling', from which its popular name of 'Whistler' derives, come from the rapid beat of its wings. It is a good diver, diving both for food and to escape danger, and it frequently feeds underwater rather than bring its food to the surface. It rarely, however, stays underwater for much more than half a minute.

The nesting grounds stretch over most of

One of the many North American waterfowl, the American goldeneye has a wide distribution.

Canada and Alaska, and as far south as North Dakota and Minnesota. Unlike other diving ducks, they generally build their nests in trees, often high up, the ducklings fluttering to the ground on the second day after hatching. The average clutch is eight to twelve, and incubation is short, taking only twenty days. Winter migration, down the Atlantic coast as far south as North Carolina, and down the Pacific coast as far as California, does not take place until October; the spring migration, back to the breeding grounds, begins in March. They migrate in small flocks, flying very fast and at high altitudes. Principally maritime ducks, they do show some preference for such localities as estuaries, where salt and fresh water may be found in proximity to each other.

Like most diving ducks they have a varied diet, including fish, molluscs and crustacea, as well as vegetable matter. The degree of edibility depends on the amount of fish they have been eating, and is never as high as that of surface feeding ducks. They are wary birds, suspicious of decoys and never easy to shoot.

American Pintail (Anas acuta tzitzihoa)

This is probably the third most important of the surface-feeding ducks, coming only after the mallard and black duck in numbers, palatability, and popularity with hunters. It is a sub-species of the pintail of Europe (Anas acuta acuta) q.v. The duck closely resembles the mallard, but it is a darker brown and has greenish-gray, rather than orange, legs and feet, and the speculum is dark brown. The drake is larger than the duck, and weighs, on an average $2\frac{1}{4}$ lb. It has a dark brown head and upper neck, with a pronounced white stripe running up from the white of the breast along the side of the neck to the rear of each eye. The back and flanks are vermiculated gray, the scapulars black and buff, and the underparts white. The characteristic long tail is further elongated by the two central feathers projecting some three or four inches beyond the others, so giving a long, sharp point to the tail. In eclipse plumage the drake closely resembles the duck, except for the speculum, which is an iridescent green, with buff in front and black behind. Ducklings all resemble the female until the end of the year, when the young drakes begin to assume the male plumage.

Courtship generally involves aerial display and pursuit of the duck by several drakes at once. There may also be display and pursuit on the water. Nesting, which takes place principally in Alaska and the Yukon, though it may extend as far south as Oregon and South Dakota, is done on the ground, a depression being lined with grass and down. The clutch of 6 to 12 eggs takes around 23 days to incubate, and the drake stays for part of this period before leaving

at the start of the eclipse moult. Ducklings are generally able to fly within 10 weeks. Pintails are among the earliest of the ducks to migrate to and from their breeding grounds, and they winter along the Atlantic coast from Maine to Florida, along the whole of the Gulf of Mexico and south, almost to Panama, and along the Pacific coast from Washington to Costa Rica. They seem to prefer swampy ground slightly inland from the coast.

The pintail is largely vegetarian, living on pond weeds, water plants and grasses, and only a small proportion of insects and molluscs, which is probably why it makes such good eating. It is one of the fastest-flying ducks, and is extremely cautious, being wary of decoys and difficult to approach. Since its breeding grounds lie in the undisturbed country of the far north, where there is little ploughing and less draining, and since it is rather more difficult to shoot than either the mallard or the black duck, its numbers have kept well up.

American Ring-necked Pheasant
(Phasianus colchicus torquatus)

Although the Latin name is that of the Chinese ringneck, it is rare, now, to find a pure Chinese bird in America. The native American pheasant is, in fact, a stabilized hybrid resulting from repeated importations of, and subsequent interbreeding between, Chinese, English and Mongolian pheasants.

The pheasant, in the collective sense, is one of the few game birds that always benefits from its contacts with man. As a grain and seed eater it flourishes wherever

A bird of hybrid origin, the American ring-necked pheasant is intelligent and wary.

American pintail in one of the waterfowl refuges established throughout the United States

grain is grown. It is easily reared artificially, though it is sometimes difficult to turn a hand-reared bird into a successfully breeding wild one. Because the cock pheasant is both polygamous and conspicuously different from the hen, it can be heavily shot without damaging the breeding population, and this is not possible with many other game birds. But, when pheasant shooting started in America, at the end of the last century, and after a hundred years of importations, America was particularly suited to its rapid spread. Forests were receding, and with them native game birds were also receding. The forests were being replaced by arable farms, and these particularly suited the pheasant. Hunting pressures were mounting, and there was a particular need for a bird whose numbers could be easily increased and whose shooting could be very simply controlled. Consequently, within fifty years of the first open season (in Oregon) being declared, the pheasant population in the country has become capable of supporting an annual harvest well in excess of 10 million birds. Only in the southern states has the pheasant failed to establish itself successfully, a fact attributed to the unsuitable local soil conditions. The Iranian black-necked pheasant, however, is now becoming established in the southern states.

The American ringneck, though slightly larger, is very similar in appearance and characteristics to the English (common) pheasant (see Pheasants). Young birds attain sexual maturity within one year. The cock, having established crowing territory, will mate with from two to five hens. Nesting is on the ground, usually in long grass or other crop cover, and it will start in April and continue, with re-nestings, where first broods have been lost, until August, and even September. Peak nesting period is from 10 June to 25 June, which is later than in Europe. The average clutch is 12, with a range of from 6 to 18, and incubation takes 23 days. The chicks begin to fly at 10 days, and reach adult size within 15 weeks. The average survival to 15 weeks and beyond is expected to be five per brood, and the average life expectancy is 14 months. Birds will range within a half-mile radius for food and cover, and well over that distance for breeding. They feed in the morning and evening on grass and weed seeds, cereal grains, mast, berries, fruit, clover and other green foods, and on insects. They roost either in thick cover on the ground or in trees.

At least 18 states now have open seasons, and these include, in descending order of annual harvest, South Dakota, Minnesota, Nebraska, North Dakota, Iowa, Wisconsin, Illinois, Pennsylvania, New York, New Jersey, Connecticut and Massachusetts.

Pheasants are seldom driven, as they are in Europe. The usual method of shooting them is walking them up in grain fields, preferably with some of the guns forward. Hunting them in thicker cover with or without dogs is also common, but pheasants do not hold well to pointers, being inclined to run ahead. A less free-ranging flushing dog, such as a springer, or even a cocker, is probably to be preferred. There are also, of course, large numbers of pheasant farms where 'put and take' shooting is practised.

American Woodcock *(Philohela minor)*

A member of the *Scolapacidae*, or snipe family, the American woodcock is smaller than, but otherwise very similar to, the European woodcock *(Scolapax rusticola rusticola)* – *see* Waders. Its numbers were, at one time, greatly reduced by over-hunting, market hunters being allowed to shoot it during the summer, but it is now protected under the Federal Migratory Birds Act.

It is almost impossible to distinguish the sexes, though the female's bill is supposed to be up to one-quarter of an inch longer than the male's. Both are small birds, mottled rufous, black and gray on the upperparts, and pale reddish-brown on the underparts, a colouring that creates an excellent camouflage effect against the dead leaves which form their customary background. The long, grooved bill is flesh coloured, the upper mandible can be moved independently of the lower, and both are provided, towards the tip, with an elaborate nerve system that enables the bird to identify food inside the ground.

One of America's most important game birds – the American woodcock

The woodcock is largely nocturnal, flying to its feeding ground at dusk and returning to its home cover at dawn. Unless flushed, it will not fly during the day. It depends largely on camouflage and 'freezing' for protection. When flushed, it generally adopts a twisting, pitching form of flight, weaving in and out of the trees, often quite low. If driven into the open it may, however, fly fairly straight.

The males are believed to be monogamous, and indulge, either singly or in twos and threes, in roding, a flight display that is part of the courtship procedure. This takes place in April, and nesting follows in May. Nesting probably occurs in each of the states east of the Mississippi, but principally in Nova Scotia, New Brunswick, Maine, Ontario, and Pennsylvania. The nest is built on the ground, generally near water, and the clutch, generally of four, takes 20 to 21 days to incubate. The young leave the nest soon after hatching, but need to be brooded for some days. They mature rapidly, are able to fly within a fortnight and remain as a family until autumn. The migration south begins in September, and most woodcock, ultimately, winter in Louisiana, East Texas, Florida, Mississippi and Alabama. During the migration, however, the resident population will suddenly be vastly increased by a 'fall' of woodcock. This will happen, most commonly, in places where woodcock have always been found – generally fairly open stands of not very heavy timber, often alder and willow near to water, and with bushes, or pollarded and stooled timber to give shelter. They may also be found in derelict orchards and on deserted, over-grown farmlands.

They need a constant supply of worms and soil insects, and soft soil in which they can probe for them. Because of this they must always move south in front of the frosts that will harden the topsoil, and they like damp soils close to water, and soils kept warm by fallen leaves.

Since the bird tends to sit close, it is an ideal one for pointers, and it is certainly best shot over dogs. It is often flushed accidentally whilst hunting for ruffed grouse.

Antelopes (Bovidae)

The so-called antelope of North America or pronghorn is not a true antelope. Antelopes are only found in Africa and Asia. Their size may vary from that of a hare to that of an ox. The larger antelopes generally have tremendous vitality and speed, and if not killed outright may often be lost to the hunter and the bag. They require heavy calibres and accurate shooting, more especially as they can often be dangerous when merely wounded and should always be approached with care, even when apparently dead. The smaller species are often encountered, unexpectedly, when game-bird hunting and can generally be shot with

a shotgun. In some species both males and females carry horns, in others only the males are horned. The meat is generally good eating and the horns and hides may form a valuable trophy.

Antlers *see* Trophy Measurements

Aoudad (Ammotragus lervia)

The Barbary sheep or maned sheep is the only wild sheep found in Africa in the rocky, sandy districts, from Morocco through to Egypt. It stands about 40 in at the shoulder, with curving horns which measure up to 30 in, those of the female slightly shorter than the male's. The adult rams have a fringe of long hair which hangs from the throat and chest down to the front legs. Their colour is best described as a uniform tawny. They usually travel in family groups of 10 to 12, but old rams are often solitary. One or two lambs are born to each ewe annually, generally in the spring. The sheep do not require much water and are principally grazers. They are extremely wary and since they roam considerable areas, not easy to find. Considerable persecution by nomadic Arabs has sharpened their naturally acute senses and any hunter who obtains a good head of this animal has earned it.

Arctic Hare (Lepus arcticus)

Largest of all American hares it can weigh to 12 lb and measure over 2 ft. The coat is brownish-gray in summer and white in winter, except for black tips to the ears. It is solitary, except in the mating season during April and May.

Gestation takes 30 days and the litter, usually five to seven, is dropped in the open. Within a few weeks the breeding groups have dispersed and the hares revert to their solitary habit. The Arctic hare is found, never in very great numbers, all along the Arctic Sea and Bering Sea coasts.

Argali *see* Great Tibetan Sheep

Argentina

Argentina is the second largest country of South America, with an area of just over 1,000,000 square miles, occupying most of the southern end of the continent, together with the eastern half of the island of Tierra del Fuego. In the west the land rises to the Cordillera de los Andes, along which runs the border with Chile. Elsewhere the country is almost entirely a succession of vast level plains. Those in the north-east are heavily wooded and known as El Gran Chaco. The rest of the plains consist mostly of the treeless pampas. The chief rivers, all flowing east, are the Colorado, the Rio Negro, and the Parana and its tributaries. The climate ranges from cold temperate to sub-tropical.

Agriculture is the basis of the economy. The chief crops are cereals, alfalfa, sugar

---

Antelopes

Beira
Blesbok
Bluebuck
Bushbuck*:
    common (harnessed), menelik
    (Natal)
Chiru
    (Tibetan)
Chousingha
Dibitag
Dik-dik
Duiker:
    blue, common, Natal, red bush
Eland*
Gazelle*:
    Dama, Dorcas, Grant's, Haughlin's,
    Indian (Chinkara), Pezeln's
    Soemmering's, Speke's,
    Thomson's, Tibetan
Gemsbok
Gerenuk
Gnu*
Grysbok
Hartebeest*:
    Lelwell's, Neumann's, red,
    Swayne's
Impala*
Klipspringer*
Kob
Kudu*
Lechwe*
Nilgai*
Oryx*
Puku*
Reedbuck*:
    Chandler's, common (bohor),
    mountain
Roan*
Sable*
Saiga
Sitatunga*
Springbok*
Steinbok*
Suni (Livingstone's)
Topi
Tsesseby*:
    (bastard hartebeest, sassaby)
Waterbuck

and cotton, but more important is the livestock rearing.

For game *see* South America, Shooting in.

Special Regulations
Permission to import firearms should be obtained from the Military Attaché in Buenos Aires.

Further Information
Direccion General de Parques Nacionales, Santa Fe 690, Buenos Aires.

Club de Caza y Pesca General San Martin, Ayasucho 181, San Martin, provincia Buenos Aires.

Club de Cazadores, San Huperto, Artoino 430, Ramos Mejia, provincia Buenos Aires.

Licence Fees—Arizona

	Residents	Non-residents
Hunting licence	$7	$30
Valid hunting/fishing licence	$12	$45
Game tags :		
Javelina	$3	$20
Turkey	$2	$10
Bear	$2	$25
Deer	$3	$30
Antelope	$20	$50
Elk	$20	$75
Bighorn	$50	$250
Lion	$1	$10

Seasons and Bag Limits—Arizona

Species	Seasons	Bag Limits	Comment
Bighorn	12-19 April	1 bighorn with at least ¾ curl horns in a lifetime	Only 10% of permits may go to non-residents. (In 1971 22 units open and 84 permits issued)
Buffalo	1971 hunt held at House Rock Ranch from 8-11 Oct	Annual cull of the state's two herds	There were 80 permits in 1971. Permits may be drawn only by residents
Elk	Bulls only in early season except in unit 1a—24-29 Sept. Late season—27 Nov-5 Dec for bulls only in some units and any elk in others		Permits may be applied and drawn for, every three years. In 1971 5,000 permits allowed for 20 different units
Deer	Special area hunts. General Deer Hunt in 1971, for buck only, 29 Oct-14 Nov	1 deer per year	81,000 permits issued for 55 different units
Javelina	In 1971 from 19-25 Feb	1 per year of any age or sex	26,000 permits issued for 29 different units
Bear	Opens 1 Sept or 1 Oct ending everywhere 31 Dec	1 of any sex per season	No draw. No special permit needed
Turkey	In 1971, except for some units, 2-11 Oct. Spring season	1 of any sex 1 bearded turkey	
Mountain lion	No closed season or area	1 per calendar year	
Tree squirrel	1971 season was from 1 Oct-26 Nov in 52 units	5 per day or in possession	
Cottontail	No closed season or area	10 per day or in possession	
Quail	1971 season from either Oct, Nov, Dec 1 ending 31 Jan	15 per day in the aggregate	In some units only Gambel's and scaled quail may be shot—in others any quail
Blue grouse	In units 1a, 1b and 25 only was from 4-12 Sept	3 per day or in possession	
Chukar partridge	In units 12a and 12b only from 1 Oct-31 Jan	8 per day or in possession	

Big Game Inventory—Arizona		
Species	**Shot**	**Est. pop.**
White-tailed deer	3,000	35,000
Mule deer	13,000	220,000
Elk	1,400	9,000
Antelope	369	6,000
Javelina	5,200	17,000
Bighorn sheep	47	3,000
Buffalo	75	300
Black bear	242	1,500
Wild turkey	1,600	35,000

Above, the viscacha is a fur-bearing rodent, which lives on the Argentine pampas. Below, there are two herds of bison in Arizona, which allows an annual cull.

Arizona (U.S.A.)

The fifth largest state in the Union, it covers 114,000 square miles, and lies in the far south-west. It consists, in the south and south-west, of largely desert plains, and in the north and north-east, of a plateau broken by mountains up to 12,000 ft. In the west the rainfall is less than 10 in, and crops depend almost entirely on irrigation. In recent years, extensive water impoundment schemes have been completed, supplying irrigation to over one and a half million acres, mainly in the Colorado and Gila valleys. The most important crops are cotton and cereals, and there is large-scale ranching on the drier lands. Forests cover over 13 million acres.

There is a varied big-game population which includes mule and white-tailed deer, javelina, bear, elk, antelope, bighorn, buffalo, mountain lion and wild turkey. Game birds and waterfowl are less numerous, water, food and cover for them being scarce. They have, however, increased in numbers since the large irrigation schemes were undertaken, and wild duck and Canada geese are now found on some of the waters, as well as increased numbers of Gambel's and scaled quail and mourning and white-winged dove, which are native birds, together with the chukar, pheasant and blue grouse which may be shot in some of the Game Management Units. The state is divided, for purposes of game management, into 60 units, and the game, seasons, bag and sex limits vary from one to the other. There are certain hunting regulations in force.

Further Information

Arizona Game and Fish Department, 2222 W. Greenway Road, Phoenix 85023.

Arkansas (U.S.A.)

A southern central state. Rich, flat, alluvial lands in the south give way, in the north-west, to the Boston Mountains and the Ozark Uplift. There are several large rivers, in addition to the Mississippi and the Arkansas, and the annual rainfall is heavy, averaging between 45 and 55 in. Cotton and rice are the most important crops.

The existence of many river valleys and irrigation impoundments, as well as the fact that the state lies along the Mississippi Flyway make it an excellent centre for duck,

Licence Fees—Arkansas	
All Game	**Small Game**
Resident $3.50	
Non-resident $30	Non-resident $20
Licences can be bought from county clerks and licensed dealers throughout the state	

Big Game Inventory—Arkansas		
Species	**Shot**	**Est. pop.**
White-tailed deer	20,000	300,000
Wild turkey	1,129	30,000

Seasons and Bag Limits—Arkansas		
Species	**Seasons**	**Bag Limits**
White-tailed deer	Split season. 9-14 Nov and 14-19 Dec	1 in each period— 2 per season
Turkey	Split season. 5-25 Oct and 4-14 April	1 gobbler per year
Cottontail rabbit	1 Oct-15 Feb	8 per day
Bobwhite quail	7 Dec-mid Feb	8 per day

goose and coot shooting. There is still good bobwhite quail shooting in the Ozarks and in the south-west of the state. Wild turkey are found in the Ozarks and in the national forests. Re-stocking has brought the deer population to over a half million.

Special Regulations

Dogs may be used when hunting deer or game birds. Rifles may not be used on turkey, and no rifle of .22 calibre or using rimfire cartridges may be used on deer.

Further Information

Game and Fish Commission, Game and Fish Building, State Capitol Grounds, Little Rock, Arkansas 72201.

Asiatic Ibex (Capra ibex)

Found generally in the higher areas throughout Central Asia and the Himalayan region from Gilgit to Nepal, its average height, at the shoulder, is 40 in and the average weight will be around 200 lb. The colour varies from brownish to gray, and it is somewhat stout and cobby in appearance: possessed of fine eyesight and scenting abilities and extremely active. The mature buck has massive, curving annulated horns measuring, on average, about 35 in. With their long, shaggy, black beards and fine horns they present a memorable picture. The female ibex has very poor horns only 9 to 11 in long, and seems possessed of even sharper sight and watchfulness than the male, often proving exasperatingly patient in watching for danger at the only possible approach for the stalker. Principally grazers, they have one young in the spring. Since they come down from the heights in winter, and retreat upwards with the first melting of the snows, it is advisable to get after them as early as possible before other hunters have made them even warier than normal. Stalking them in May can prove a fascinating sport; all the features of picturesque mountain scenery are present in suitable ibex country: rugged cliffs of rock, shale and snow on either hand. Since ibex tend to stick firmly to the same feeding grounds it is advisable to avoid firing unless certain of a good head, so as not to disturb the herd. When alarmed, they prefer to move upwards, and by remembering this, it is sometimes possible to ensure the chance of a second shot before they are out of range. One feature of the ibex should not be overlooked: in the pure air of the mountains their strong smell is quite unmistakable and with the wind in the right direction it is possible to ascertain their whereabouts. Once within range, they are not difficult to bag; a bullet in the ribs will generally be sufficient and it is as well to remember that a wounded ibex will almost always try to work its way uphill, and the presence of lammergeyers and other birds of prey wheeling above the spot will give away its position.

The Asiatic ibex used to inhabit the European Alps, but apart from re-introductions, it is now found only in Asia.

Australia

Firearms Licensing Laws

The State Houses of Parliament, like the governments of many countries, have their current policy of firearms licensing under review. At present by Act of Parliament each state within the Commonwealth dictates and polices its own laws on the use of firearms within the state boundaries. In general, a responsible applicant has little difficulty in obtaining a licence where required. By this means the state authorities have a measure of control, ensuring that weapons do not fall into the hands of irresponsible individuals and, at the same time, revenue is obtained for conservation and for biological studies of fauna.

To this extent no legitimate sportsman would find fault with the act, in that he is as keen as the state authorities to prevent irresponsible and unsporting shooting, unfortunately sometimes evident in damaged road signs and dead farm animals. In other respects the results of the act are anachronistic and confusing, even undesirable from a sporting viewpoint. For instance, in Western Australia it is necessary to submit a strong case in order to obtain any calibre heavier than a .22. One result of this is that rather than be deprived of their sport, most owners of this calibre will tackle almost any game with it, from a rabbit upwards. It also leads to wildcat experiments with .22 projectiles and necked down .243, .270 or .303 cases, which have been used successfully on such game as dingo, fox, wallaby, kangaroo, wild pig, wild goat and deer, sometimes at extreme ranges.

Various shooting organizations and sporting bodies are urging Parliament to review this outdated act. Bodies such as the Australian Conservation Foundation are also being regularly lobbied by shooting clubs, to urge the Commonwealth Government to legislate in this matter, providing laws on the use and ownership of firearms common to all states. Unfortunately, it is acknowledged that such legislation would create an undesirable precedent and the only alternative is to urge all state Governments to act in unison and produce laws common to all. The responsible ministers in each state are examining this question, but it is doubtful if they will act on their own initiative and agree to common legislation without further concerted pressure from the sportsmen themselves.

Sporting Facilities

It is not necessary to travel great distances for sport with either rifle or shotgun. Good sport with the rifle, from rabbit to deer shooting, can generally be had a few hours drive from most capital cities. Advice on where to go and how to set about obtaining sport can usually very readily be obtained from a local shooting club. There are many of these and their activities are by no means restricted to range-shooting. Members are instructed in the care and safe use of firearms and occasional hunting trips are also organized. The city shooter, especially, is taught always to ask the property owner for permission to shoot on his land and to respect his wishes.

In the interior the property owner may have paddocks extending to several hundred square miles, largely unfenced, where it takes him several months merely to round up his stock. Very often in the same area, herds of brumbies (wild horses), wild goats, kangaroos or even camels may also be grazing and breeding unmolested to the detriment of the stock and such fences as there may be. In these circumstances shooters who are prepared to rough it may be paid for their successes and the rewards may be well worthwhile. Using a Landrover and operating from a base camp, re-loading their own ammunition to keep down costs; such an expedition can provide good sport and good rewards, financially, to the experienced hunter. The property owner is likely to welcome any approach on these lines, but it is advisable to know the terrain and the hazards before embarking on such a venture.

For the shotgun there is plenty of variety during the season, which varies considerably from state to state, as do bag limits and protected birds. The ubiquitous stubble quail, the commonest of the three types of quail found in Australia, provides the best sport. The swamp or brown quail found respectively in grasslands and swampland are the next commonest. The king quail, the smallest of the four, is a native of New Guinea and is neither as widespread nor as sought after as the others. Three types of snipe are represented by the Jack, or Australian, the pin-tailed and the painted snipe. The two former are Asian summer migrants and are found chiefly in boggy areas near the coast.

Duck shooting is also popular and in parts of Victoria and New South Wales, especially, there is very good sport to be had during the season. Rice growers in the Murrumbidgee Irrigation area in the south of New South Wales, one of the principal duck breeding areas of Australia, particularly welcome the opening of the season as the prospect of some relief from the depredations of thousands of ducks which cause heavy damage to their growing crops. The principal ducks shot are black duck, gray teal, chestnut teal, wood duck, maned geese, mountain duck, freckled or monkey duck, hardhead or white-eyed duck and widgeon, while in the north, magpie geese provide good sport. The black duck is generally regarded as the favourite of most hunters both because of its size and numbers. The gray teal, which is also found in abundance throughout Australia, taking as readily to salt water as to fresh, is another strong favourite.

One of the hazards in duck shooting is the number of snakes in certain areas, although it is possible to shoot year after year without ever seeing one. Along the border of New South Wales and Victoria, which is one of the best breeding grounds for duck, snakes can be encountered at any time and care must be taken to avoid stepping on them. Generally, most snakes will move away, or remain still if not disturbed.

In the south of Australia the most aggressive and venomous is the tiger snake, which is generally found around the swamps, rivers and lagoons. This snake will attack when provoked, whether accidentally disturbed, or in defence. They strike very hard and generally hang on to the victim, injecting large quantities of their highly lethal venom. If a dog is bitten, death can be expected in half-an-hour to an hour unless treated with anti-toxin. This can be carried, but it is very expensive, should be kept in a thermos flask or an ice box, and injection is a job for a veterinary surgeon.

There are also many other snakes in the south, such as the brown, the king brown, the copper head and the black snake in descending order of venomousness; the brown snake is quite dangerous but the black seldom causes death. Surprisingly, although snakes are quite numerous, reports of hunters and dogs being bitten are rare. Nevertheless, care must always be taken and dogs should not be let off a chain, when camped in snake-infested areas, and at other times should work or hunt close to the hunter.

The Australian black duck is a favourite with Australian wildfowlers because of its size and numbers.

There are open seasons for various species of pigeons and doves, but they are scarce and no one is likely to go out specifically to shoot them, more especially as the topknot, which is easily the best to eat, is strictly protected. Scrub turkeys are shot, but as they tend to fly from tree to tree do not provide very sporting shooting. The emu, where not protected, is not regarded as a game bird since its inquisitive nature frequently causes it to walk right up to the hunter and its flesh is coarse and unpalatable. For the rest there are several varieties of eagles, hawks and birds of the crow family, as well as smaller birds such as finches, which are rightly regarded as pests to be shot with shotgun or rifle throughout the year. Foxes, too, may provide good sport for shotgun or rifle when whistled within range by imitating a rabbit squealing. Rabbits themselves, are another ubiquitous pest against which all-out war with shotgun, rifle, poison or other means is waged around the year.

Wild pigs, mainly feral domestic pigs, are both shot and hunted. Shooting a three hundred-pound boar requires accurate aim and a calibre such as .243 with an open nosed bullet since they are tough-skinned, fast and extremely fierce when wounded, or roused in defence of their young. Their tusks are capable of causing severe injury or even death to both dog and man, and if only wounded, they may end by treeing the hunter. An experienced pack is required for hunting, and the hunter must be fit enough to follow them across rough country at speed, then capable of providing the quietus with his knife. Anyone wishing to reduce the pig population by any means is likely to be welcomed by the property owner and shown the best areas.

Although deer are both hunted with hounds, and stalked and shot with a rifle, the latter is generally considered more sporting due to the difficulties experienced in following hounds through the forests. There are six species of deer in Australia, the chital, or spotted deer, the fallow deer, the hog deer, the red deer, the sambar and the rusa. Unfortunately, little research has been conducted into their habits and indeed it is only within the past five years that the sixth of these species was recognized. They range throughout Australia, but the greatest concentration is in New South Wales and Victoria. The methods of stalking must vary with the terrain, which may be forest or rocky hillside. They are not generally regarded as a pest, unlike in New Zealand, for compared with the kangaroo they represent no serious problem.

Despite its place in the Australian coat of arms the kangaroo has been, and in some areas still is, a menace to the nation's economy. Professional cullers are permitted to take out special kangaroo licences and landowners provide them with every assistance on their properties. Although this government action has given rise to protests and deputations, biologists have proved conclusively that kangaroos could never be wiped out by this method. Commonsense indicated that cullers only operate while the harvest is profitable; as soon as the numbers are sufficiently thinned to make further culling in that area unprofitable, the professionals move on to more profitable areas, leaving the remainder to breed and increase in numbers.

From the sporting shooter's viewpoint the kangaroo is a difficult proposition. It is shy and will stand erect with ears pricked at the slightest sound. Generally one or more act as guardian to the herd and a sudden departure by the sentinel will act as a danger signal causing them to scatter, not necessarily in a single group, but in separate, open flight to rejoin later. Calibres for roo-shooting are generally .222 or .270. A rimfire .22 is frowned on by the sportsman as more likely to wound than kill.

Kangaroos are still sometimes hunted with hounds, though the old breed of roo-hound, a cross between a greyhound and a Scottish deer-hound, is becoming scarce.

Typical Australian fox country. The hunter, with the wind in his face, makes for a gulley, where he will whistle the foxes to him.

When driven hard, the old-man kangaroo will sometimes stand at bay in a water hole. He is then capable of drowning any dog rash enough to approach him, by holding it underwater. The coup de grâce in such cases should be delivered by shooting.

Although the old, large-scale, kangaroo drives are generally a thing of the past, sometimes small-scale drives are carried out by property owners where there is a massive concentration and severe action is required. Generally they are driven forward by beaters on horseback or in Landrovers. The guns lie in wait, behind shrubs and trees, armed with shotguns; any which have been merely wounded are despatched with .22s.

Inevitably, the spread of civilization, in particular new mining ventures and industrial progress, also the draining of swamps and modern farming methods, have affected Australian wildlife. Yet there is a vast area still available for the sportsman and his quarries. Waterfowl in particular have adjusted themselves so that their breeding rate continues to be maintained and their flight lanes from north to south in summer, and south to north in winter remain unimpaired. Quail in particular are being carefully supervised and biological experiments are being conducted by the Fauna Departments of the various states, also by the Commonwealth Scientific and Industrial Research Organisation, which operates independently, but contributes most to the understanding of the bird behaviour patterns. RBH

See also New South Wales, Northern Territory, Queensland, South Australia, Tasmania, Victoria, Western Australia

Australian Quail *(Coturnix pectoralis)*
A common quail of the eastern and southeastern parts of Australia, and Tasmania. Found on open grassy plains and cultivated land, it feeds on seeds and insects, and gets its alternative name of stubble quail because of the great numbers that visit the fields for grain after the harvest.

It closely resembles the quail of Europe (*Coturnix coturnix*) q.v., only differing in that the cock has the sides of its head, chin and throat a dull brick-red, and the hen has the feathers of the chest and breast longitudinally barred with black, the bars being interrupted with a buff interspace.

It is a good flyer, lies well to a pointer, and makes good eating.

Australian Swamp Quail *(Coturnix australis)*
Also known as the brown quail, this is found in south-eastern New Guinea, Australia and Tasmania, generally in damp, overgrown spots close to water. It resembles the common partridge in being found in coveys of up to eighteen which flush and pitch together.

A feral pig crashing its way through scrub near a waterhole in north-western New South Wales.

The upperparts are reddish-brown, mottled with black, the sides of the head and throat are dull gray, and the underparts are buff with almost no black cross-bars. About 7½ in long, it weighs about 4¾ oz. The female has the sides of her crown black and heavier black markings on the upper- and underparts. The call is very similar to that of the partridge.

The Australian swamp quail sits extremely close, and often needs to be pressed hard before it will flush. It lies, therefore, excellently for a pointer. It makes excellent eating.

Austria
Austria is a landlocked central European state of over 32,000 square miles. The proximity of the Adriatic means that the climate is not markedly continental, though the western half of the country is completely alpine. The eastern half mostly consists of the wide Vienna plain, stretching towards the Danube and forming a fertile triangle between the Alps and the Carpathians. Although there are heavy industries and some mining, agriculture is still very important, with stock on the alpine pastures, and mixed arable farming, including vineyards, on the plains. There is also an extensive timber industry with over a third of the country under afforestation. With such a varied and relatively unspoilt terrain Austria offers a good selection of sport, and has always been classed among the best hunting areas in Europe.

Seasons
Seasons vary, sometimes considerably, from area to area, usually depending on the altitude. Where there is such variation dates are given between which the season opens or closes.

Special Regulations
All hunting is privately owned, and visitors must arrange their sport with the owners of hunting preserves (several tourist resorts and some special hotels have their own hunting preserves, a fact noted in their brochures). Hunters can establish contact with preserve owners by advertising in one of the three main Austrian hunting magazines. Upon agreement with a preserve owner, a hunter must deposit half of the relevant shooting premium in advance.

The premiums (in Austrian schillings) for shooting and keeping the trophy are shown in the table.

The hunter keeps the trophy, but the game usually remains on the preserve. On paying the premium the hunter is brought as close as possible to the quarry and within shooting distance (up to 200 metres in mountainous areas). Depending on any previous agreements reached, the premium may be payable in full, or in part, for game shot at but not retrieved, or for several obvious misses.

Shooting rights for an entire preserve (usually for one year), or 6 – 12-year leases can be arranged. The Austrian Federal Forestry Commission also occasionally grants hunting leases.

Licences

Visitors may import, duty free, two shotguns or rifles, together with 100 rounds per gun, and do not require a small-arms certificate. However hunters require a shooting licence, issued by the local district authorities, for which they must produce identification, an Austrian third-party hunter's insurance certificate, and some proof of hunting ability, in the form of either an earlier Austrian shooting licence, or a certificate from a hunting organization in their own country. Without these, hunters must obtain a membership card of an Austrian provincial hunting organization, or pass the hunting examination. In addition to the shooting licence, hunters must hold a shooting permit from the owner of the preserve where they intend to shoot. The necessary documents may usually be obtained from the preserve owner, for a fee, varying from province to province of between 350 and 1,120 schillings for a complete season; in several provinces it is possible to obtain a temporary visitor's hunting card at a reduced rate.

Seasons—Austria		
Game	**Season opens**	**Season closes**
Roe (buck)	mid May-mid June	end Sept-end Oct
Chamois	Aug	mid Dec-end Jan
Mouflon	Aug	end Dec-end Jan
Red deer	Aug	end Dec-end Jan
Snipe	Sept	end March-end May
Blackcock	mid April	end May-mid June
Capercailzie	mid April	end May-mid June
Marmot	Aug	end Oct
Partridge	mid Aug	end Sept-end Dec
Pheasant	Sept-mid Oct	end Nov-end Dec

The following may be shot all year round:
Wild boar, fox, polecat, wild rabbit, weasel, sparrow-hawk, hawk, heron (except when breeding)

Further Information

Bund Osterreichischer Jagdvereine, Weiringergasse 38, 1040 Vienna. (Association of Austrian Hunting Societies.)

Verband Osterreichischer Armbrustschutzen, per Adresse Herrn Georg Windhofer, 5600 St Johann im Pongau, Salzburg. (Austrian Archers.)

Austrian National Tourist Office, Hohenstaufengasse 3 – 5, A-1010 Vienna 1.

Austrian hunters (left) giving thanks to St Hubert, the patron saint of hunting, for their successful kill.

Barnacle geese are seldom found inland, preferring tidal mud-flats and estuaries.

Trophy Fees—Austria	
Species	**Austrian Schillings**
Blackgame and capercailzie	3,000-5,000
Roe (buck)	1,500-5,000
Warrantable stag	3,000-30,000
Royal stag	up to 50,000
Lesser stag	from 1,500
Hind	from 1,000
Marmot	from 1,000
Chamois (buck)	2,000-8,000
Chamois (doe)	1,000-3,000
Mouflon (ram)	3,000-15,000

B

Baldpate *(Anas americana)*
Also called the American widgeon, it is similar to, though larger than, the widgeon of Europe *(Anas penelope) q.v.* but it breeds only on the American continent, the breeding grounds stretching from Alaska to as far south as northern Nevada, Utah and Nebraska and as far east as Minnesota. Its wintering grounds lie along most of the Pacific and Atlantic coasts of North America and all of Mexico and as far south as El Salvador.

A surface feeder, it often feeds with diving ducks, stealing the water-celery roots they bring up to the surface. It feeds mainly at night, and frequently grazes in grain and corn fields rather like a goose. A restless, nervous bird, it will rise straight off the water at the slightest alarm, and is liable to disturb other ducks by its movements. It is found on larger bodies of water and along the coast, rather than on the ponds and potholes generally frequented by other surface feeders, and it seeks a more southerly, and warmer wintering ground than most other North American ducks.

The drake and duck are of similar size, weighing about 2 lb and about 20 in long. The duck is grayish-brown with white underparts and a gray-white head and neck speckled with black. The drake, in eclipse plumage, resembles the duck, but in full winter plumage, which is assumed by December, has a buff forehead and crown and neck with a glossy green patch on the side of the head. The upperparts are pinkish-brown, the breast pink, there is a conspicuous white patch on the wings and the speculum is dark green. The bill and feet in both sexes are bluish-gray.

Mating probably takes place after arrival at the breeding grounds, and nesting is on dry ground. Laying is seldom completed until after the middle of June, and the clutch of 9 to 11 eggs takes 24 to 25 days to incubate. The young drakes resemble the duck in plumage until September, when male wing colours begin to appear. Adult winter plumage is fully assumed by December. Migration to the wintering grounds usually starts in September and is completed by November. Because the nesting grounds lie, on the whole, outside the ploughing and land draining areas of America, baldpate numbers remain fairly constant.

The baldpate comes readily to decoys, and, although extremely nervous, and with an erratic flight, it is shot in great numbers. It is one of the most edible of ducks.

Band-tailed Pigeon *(Columba fasciata)*
A migratory pigeon found on the western side of America from British Columbia to Central America. It was, at one time, in considerable danger of being wiped out, as the passenger pigeon was, by market hunters, for its habit of concentrating into large flocks when feeding make it particularly vulnerable to over-shooting. Greatly shortened seasons, and, when necessary, no open season at all, have restored its numbers, and it is still a highly favoured bird for pass shooting in California and other western states.

It is rather larger than the domestic pigeon, being some 16 in long and 16 in from wingtip to wingtip. The upperparts are brown and gray, the underparts and head purple. The neck is iridescent with a white mark or collar at the nape. There is a band of darker gray across the light gray tail which gives the bird its name. It is a gregarious bird, except during the breeding season, when breeding pairs will disperse. A strong, fast flyer, it will spiral and plane as well as fly straight at up to 40 miles per hour. Take off is noisy, with a great deal of wing flapping. When a flock is disturbed the birds take off a few at a time, rather than as a flock. Roosting is in tree tops, preferably on dead branches to allow rapid take off. Male and female look identical.

The male is monogamous and helps in nest building and incubating, as well as producing pigeon 'milk' as much as the female. The nest is a crude affair of twigs and may be in a tree, hedge, bush, or on the ground. The clutch is usually only one egg and incubation takes from 18 to 20 days. The young are helpless and have to be fed on pigeon milk for about 20 days, and after that on regurgitated and partially digested seeds and corn.

The birds migrate from north to south and during these migrations, pass shooting, along the flyways, is popular.

Bangladesh
Now an independent state, this country has been treated under Pakistan. Due to the change in administration, all regulations should be checked in advance.

Barbary Red-legged Partridge *see under* Reg-legged Partridge

Barnacle Goose *(Branta leucopsis)*
A brent goose that breeds in Greenland and Spitzbergen, and winters on the Baltic, North Sea and Atlantic coasts of Germany,

American black bear, Tennessee

Holland, Denmark and Great Britain, with accidentals as far afield as Italy and the United States.

It is larger than either the brent goose or the American brant, and has a white head, broken only by a black streak running from bill to eye, and a black strip running from the neck, over the crown to the forehead. The neck itself is black, the upperparts are gray barred with black and white, and the underparts are light gray fading into white. The tail, bill and legs are black.

Barnacle geese are extremely gregarious, feeding in flocks, on the tidal flats, on maritime grasses. They breed in colonies on the ledges of steep cliffs, returning from their winter feeding grounds to the same nesting site year after year.

Barrow's Goldeneye (Bucephala islandica)

A diving duck that is almost identical with the American goldeneye (B. clangula americana) q.v., and often mistaken for it. The drakes can be distinguished from each other by the fact that the Barrow's goldeneye has a crescent-shaped, instead of circular, white face patch. The ducks, however, are almost impossible to distinguish from each other, except by a difference in bill length and colour.

This duck is considerably rarer than the American goldeneye, largely because it is more localized. It is very much tamer and less alarmed by man, more of a fish eater, and consequently, even less edible than B. clangula.

It has two well defined and quite separate ranges, with no cross migrations between them, but on each range there is a considerable overlap between breeding and wintering grounds. The eastern range has its breeding grounds from eastern Greenland to Labrador and its wintering grounds along the Atlantic coast from Labrador to New York. The western range has its breeding grounds along the Rocky Mountain range from British Columbia to Colorado, and its wintering grounds westwards along the Pacific coast.

Bartavelle see Chukar Partridge

Bean Goose (Anser fabalis)

A gray goose almost as big as the graylag (Anser anser) q.v., but darker coloured and with a longer bill coloured orange and black. Its nesting grounds lie along the the shores of the Arctic Ocean and Barents Sea from Lapland to Siberia, and its wintering grounds lie as far south as the Black and Caspian Seas and the Mediterranean. It winters in some parts of Scotland and along the east coast of England. In habits it is very similar to the graylag.

Bears (Ursidae)

Bears are to be found throughout most of the world with the exception of Australasia. Generally either forest or mountain dwellers, they are true hibernators and are usually solitary. As they tend to breed only every second year they are becoming increasingly rare in areas subject to the pressures of expanding civilization. Careful conservation is required and in the case of the polar bear complete protection is desirable. Although generally shortsighted, most bears have extremely keen powers of scent and hearing. They may be stalked, tracked in suitable conditions, or still-hunted, depending on the terrain and the hunter. They may also, very occasionally, still be hunted with hounds and treed. A heavy bullet and calibre is generally desirable since if not killed outright they may require considerable stopping. The meat is sometimes eaten, but the skin is usually regarded as the only trophy.

There is considerable disagreement among zoologists as to the number of true species, especially in North America, but

A flock of barnacle geese on the shores of the Solway Firth, Scotland. Some of the birds were ringed in Spitzbergen, where they breed.

The spectacled bear, which inhabits the Andes from Ecuador to Chile, is so called from the fawn-coloured ring encircling its eyes.

Bears
Axis *
Alaskan brown *
Grizzly *
Himalayan black *
  (Asiatic black ; moon)
Kodiak
Malayan
Honey (sun)
Polar
Sloth *
Spectacled (Andean)

those shown in the table are distinct from the hunter's viewpoint.

Beisa *see* Oryx

Belgium

Belgium is a small country of about 12,000 square miles, situated in north-west Europe. It consists of a fairly flat, well cultivated plain, protected from the sea and the Lower Scheldt by dykes. The south-eastern portion is broken up by the streams, rivers, valleys and hills of the Ardennes, and is rather less fertile than the rest of the country.

The two principal rivers are the Scheldt and the Meuse, both of which flow northwards. The climate is temperate, except in the south-east, where the winters are colder and longer. Although heavily industrialized, Belgium has approximately 4 million acres of cultivated land, and about one and half of forest. The farming is intensive, but the farms mostly small.

The table shows the chief game species, their seasons (liable to variation), and their average annual bag where available.

Small game is found all over Belgium, except in the Ardennes, where there are only a few grouse. It is only in the Ardennes that red deer are found in any numbers. Roe are also particularly common there, but can be found all over the country, as can wild boar, with the exception of Flanders and Antwerp. Waterfowl are particularly numerous in the marshes of Camoine and the Yser valley.

Belgium was the home of St Hubert, the 'Apostle of the Ardennes' and the patron saint of all hunters, and it has always been traditionally well stocked with game and hunting grounds. However, the pressures of civilization and population have left little shooting available for the foreigner who is not a guest or member of a syndicate. On private land the sporting rights go with ownership, or are leased out, usually for periods of nine years. Common land is let by the commune at a public auction. The Administration of Water and Forests, a department of the Ministry of Agriculture, which exercises a general control over all hunting, controls the management and letting of sporting rights in all the state forests and along all river banks. The letting of sporting rights over other state lands, military and coastal areas, etc., is dealt with by the departments concerned, as is the case with lands owned by local government authorities, provinces, communes, etc.

Licences

Gun licences are a necessary precondition for the issue of hunting licences, and may be obtained from the Commissaire de l'Arrondissement for 3,920 Belgian francs plus a provincial tax. Hunting licences must also be obtained from the Commissaire on the presentation of a passport photograph, character reference and insurance certificate. Those writing from abroad should apply to the Commissaire de l'Arrondissement de Bruxelles, enclosing additionally a birth certificate and references from two Belgian citizens. Special five-day licences may be obtained by Belgians for foreign guests for a fee of 1060 francs.

Special Regulations

Shooting in snow is prohibited, as is all night shooting except for flighting duck. Game laws are enforced by the police, by keepers of the Administration of Water and Forests, and by private keepers. Finally the Royal St Hubert Club of Belgium, to which most Belgian hunters belong, maintains an inspector and 16 wardens who help to carry out one of the club's principal objects, the suppression of poaching.

Further Information

Institut Belge d'information et de documentation, 3 rue Montoyer, Bruxelles 4.

Royal St Hubert Club de Belgique, Place Jean Jacobs, Bruxelles 1.

'The Vision of St Hubert', a woodcut by Albrecht Dürer (1491–1528). Belgium was the home of the patron saint of hunting.

Seasons—Belgium		
Species	**Season**	**Comments**
Red deer Stags (with more than ten points)	1 Oct-30 Nov	Certain stags, age and no. of points fixed annually, may be still-hunted only between 15 Sept and 30 Sept
doe	15 Oct-30 Nov	Annual bag : 1,800
Roe deer bucks	1 Oct-30 Nov	Bucks with more than six points may be still-hunted only from 15 July to 15 Aug
doe	15 Oct-30 Nov	Annual bag : 6.500
Wild boar	All year	Annual bag : 2,000
Pheasant cocks hens	15 Oct-31 Jan 15 Oct-31 Dec	
Partridge	First Saturday in Sept to 30 Nov	
Hare	20 Sept-31 Dec	
Blackbird, Turtle dove, Thrush	1 Oct-15 Nov	
Waterfowl and Migratory birds	21 July-28 Feb	But woodcock and snipe 21 July-15 March
Rabbit and Wood-pigeon	All year	
Protected species	Fallow deer, black game and all birds of prey	

Bharal *(Pseudovis nayaur)*

Also known as the burrel or blue wild sheep, it is found above 10,000 ft in the Himalayas, frequently even above 17,000 ft on the slopes below the snow line. The height of a full grown male is from 30–36 in. The average measurement of the horns is from 22–24 in, exceptionally over 30 in. The ears are short and the horns are set close together, springing outwards from the head, the points then curling backwards and upwards. The animal is intermediate between goats and sheep, but looks distinctly sheep-like, and has no ruff or mane. The coat is browny-gray in summer and slate-gray in winter. The male has a black face and chest, and a black stripe down the front of the limbs and sides of the body. The female is smaller, with rudimentary horns. Their sight and scenting powers are good and since there is little cover they are nearly always in sight, making a stalk difficult. Like most wild sheep they are hard to kill and must be shot in a vital spot, but the mutton is excellent.

Bighorn *see* Mountain Sheep

Bison *(Bison bison)*

This North American member of the Bovidae is commonly called Buffalo, though it differs considerably from the true Buffaloes of India *(Bison bubalis)* and Africa *(Syncerus caffer)* in size, habits and appearance. It is, in fact, closely related to the now almost extinct European Bison *(Bison banasus)*, and probably first crossed into North America, via the Bering Straits, in the mid-Pleistocene period.

There were, at one time, three recognized sub-species, of which two still survive. The wood bison, which is darker and larger than the plains bison, is not now, in spite of its name, a beast of the forests, but it will browse in addition to grazing. At one time bison were found all over North America from Alaska to Mexico. The economy of the plains Indians depended on them. Now, as everybody knows, over-hunting has reduced them to a few herds, mainly in National Parks and Wildlife Refuges, though some are also in private hands. There are probably fewer than 10,000 in the United States, and a few more in Canada. Attempts to commercialize them as meat producers, or to use them for hybridizing domestic cattle have proved failures economically. The American Bison Society has, however, ensured their survival, and there is a possibility that they will, once again, be hunted, though under very strict controls and limitations, as they are now, in Texas, Arizona, and the Northwest Territories.

The body colour is dark brown, almost black in front, and the humped shoulders, neck and head are covered with long hair. There is a beard hanging from the chin which may be a foot long. Both sexes are horned, the horns being short, thick, and

'Catlin the Artist Shooting Buffalos with Colt's Revolving Pistol'. One of four lithographs by J. M. Chester after George Catlin (1794–1872).

pointing outwards and upwards. The cow is considerably smaller than the bull, standing about 5 ft high and weighing about 800 lb; the bull may stand 6 ft high and weigh between 1,800 and 2,000 lb. They are selective grazers, preferring the shorter grasses, which make it easy for them to over-graze their range. The rut occurs in July and August, and the calves are generally dropped in April and May. They are able to follow the herd soon after birth.

There are, at present, so few hunting permits issued and these only in order to cull the herds and prevent over-grazing, that it is not necessary to discuss methods of hunting. In the old days bison were hunted on horseback, with bow and arrow by the Indians, with a broad-headed lance by the Mexicans, and with a carbine by the market hunters. The greatest slaughters, however, were carried out when the hunters dismounted, approached the herd under cover until within close range, and then fired, steadily, from cover, into the dense mass, the other animals hardly moving as the dead dropped among them.

Black Bear *(Eurarctos americanus)*

An essentially American bear, quite different from the Alaskan brown bear and the grizzly, which, it is argued, are sub-species of the brown bear of Europe and Asia. The black bear, which may be other colours than black, once found throughout North America, is still widely distributed, though often in small numbers. Only eleven states have no black bear population at all, and five have populations estimated to be above 20,000, with an estimated total population in the United States of quarter of a million.

It is found in wooded areas close to its

food supply. Since the beast is omnivorous this may mean fruit, berries, nuts, honey, rodents, and, on occasions, farmstock, carrion and fish. In the more northerly states where the growing season is short the tendency to be carnivorous is more pronounced.

Smaller than the brown bears, the black weighs between 150 and 600 lb, the body is about 5 ft long, and the height at the shoulder about 25 in. Colours range from black to cinnamon, and may reflect different races. The curved claws and shoulder hump of the grizzly are missing. They are solitary, except at breeding time. The cubs remain with the dam until new cubs are born, normally after two seasons. They possess poor sight but keen powers of scent; hearing is moderately good. The life span may extend to 25 years, sexual maturity and breeding start at about three years. Range extends to about 30 miles. The animals hibernate in solitary dens, in which the cubs, generally twins or triplets, are born, with their eyes open and weighing about 5 lb by the time hibernation is broken in April.

In most states the black bear has probably passed the point of being considered a predator to being thought of as an increasingly rare game animal, and its protection has been extended. Some states have an autumn and a spring season during which it may be hunted. In some of the southern states this can still be done with dogs, though this method has, quite rightly, been made illegal in most states. The bear, though capable of short bursts of speed, is certainly not a beast of chase, and the target it offers, once it has been bayed or treed, is not a sporting one. In the western states a horse is sometimes killed for bait, with the hunter concealed down wind. This is a method that can only be condoned when used by a rancher protecting stock from further attacks, but it should not attract the sportsman.

The black bear is hunted and shot, in most cases, as a secondary quarry, met during the course of a deer hunt. It can, and frequently is, stalked for itself – a method requiring some skill, and, for a short period after the first snows and before hibernation, can be tracked down. There is a small element of danger in all bear hunting, and casualties are reported every season. It is probable, however, that no black bear ever deliberately charges a hunter, even when it has been wounded. What it may well do, however, is to run, shortsightedly, on to a hunter who has got in his way.

Most rifles normally used for deer hunting will be adequate for bear, which are easily killed, but they must not, of course, be the high-velocity, low-calibre ones generally used on vermin. At the ranges general in forest hunting a 12-bore shotgun with rifled slugs will also be adequate.

A fine example of the cinnamon-coloured black bear

Black Brant (*Branta bernicla orientalis*)
This brant of the Pacific coast is similar, in all except distribution and colouration, to the American brant (*B. bernicla hrota*) *q.v.* It is a small goose, no larger than the cackling goose (*B. canadensis minima*), and has a black head, neck and breast, with a white collar around the sides and front of the neck, and grayish-white sides and flanks.

Its breeding grounds lie along the coast of the Arctic Ocean from Siberia to Western Canada, and it winters along the Pacific coast of the United States, gathering, especially, in the larger bays of the Californian coast, where it provides excellent sport especially after the duck season. For other details *see* American brant.

Black Duck (*Anas rubripes*)
A bird of the Atlantic Coast and the eastern United States, it is considered, in those regions, to be one of the most important of all surface feeding duck, and is even more eagerly hunted than the mallard it so closely resembles. It is a bird of the coastal marshes rather than of the prairies, and has not therefore, been so badly hit by the draining of potholes and wetlands that has taken place. On the other hand there are signs that it is suffering from the effects of D.D.T. and of the general pollution of the Atlantic coastline, and there is strong evidence that it is now being over-hunted.

It is a large duck, weighing up to 4 lb and, even in winter plumage, there is some difficulty in telling the drake from the duck. Both are brownish-black in overall plumage, with lighter head and neck colouring, and purplish-blue speculum. In winter plumage, the drake has U-shaped buff markings on the breast and his feet and bill are orange and yellow. The duck has V-shaped markings, her bill is greenish, and her feet are duller and more brownish. In summer the bills and feet of both sexes are almost green. The eclipse moult is generally in June and the autumn moult in September, full winter plumage being assumed in October.

Courtship is usually by pursuit through the air and on the water, with two or three drakes competing for a single duck. The breeding grounds stretch from Labrador and Newfoundland as far south as North Carolina, and overlap considerably the wintering grounds, which stretch from Maine to the Gulf of Mexico. Nesting is usually near woodland lakes and streams, though the nest may sometimes be well away from water. It is made of twigs and grass and down, and the clutch of from 6 to 12 eggs takes up to 28 days to incubate. The ducklings are led immediately to water and remain with the duck until their flight feathers appear, at which stage she withdraws into cover to moult. Migration starts as the freeze begins, and is done in small groups.

In the course of the migration they learn

to avoid decoys, blinds and calls, and spend much of the day in 'rafts' far out on large bodies of water, coming back to the marshes to feed only at dusk. During this period they add crustacea to their normally vegetable diet, then becoming considerably less edible. Nevertheless since there is, along many parts of the southern Canadian and northern United States coastline, a blind to every hundred yards, they are probably, in spite of all their caution, still being over-shot.

Blackgame *see* Black Grouse

Black Grouse *(Lyrurus tetrix)*

Blackgame, as they are also known, are found throughout Scandinavia and much of central Europe, even as far as Siberia; in Britain they have a wider range than that of the capercailzie, *q.v.*, though no longer as common in many areas as they once were. They are found on the edges of moors, in marshy ground with scattered trees, or on rocky heathland or near plantations. They will perch in trees and are nearly omnivorous, eating berries, insects, heather shoots, corn and conifer buds. The male or blackcock is about 21 in long and weighs from 3½ to 4 lb. He is easily distinguished by his shiny blue-black plumage and notable, lyre-shaped tail with very conspicuous white under-tail feathers, also by a noticeable white bar on the wings. The female or grayhen, is much smaller, being only about 16 in long and weighing from 2¼ to 3 lb. At first sight it is easily confused with the red grouse, *q.v.* though distinctly larger in size and not so brown. It may also be confused with the female capercailzie, which is, however, larger and more boldly marked. It is differentiated from each of these by the white bar on the wings and the lyre-shaped tail, although neither of these are always easily seen, especially when the bird is approaching head-on. Both sexes have a scarlet wattle over the eye. They are more gregarious than the capercailzie, and polygamous. In the spring the blackcocks establish communal mating grounds, known as 'leks', on which they perform elaborate mating dances to attract the hens. This involves much display of spread tail and half-opened wings combined with a very vocal bubbling mating song. At the end of the display the blackcocks will fight, the victor taking the hens. Thereafter, the hen goes off on her own to nest, very often merely a scrape in the ground, generally choosing a grassy stretch of moorland or similar surroundings.

The clutch varies from 5 to 10 and the incubation period is from 24 to 26 days. The young tend to remain in family groups during the summer and are generally found in groups of from 10 to 20 throughout the early part of the autumn.

They may be shot over dogs, but a cunning old blackcock or grayhen may run a very considerable distance before taking flight and it needs a good dog to find and hold them pinned on point. They are quite commonly driven, especially in Britain. In parts of Europe and Scandinavia they may be stalked, or still-hunted in the woods with a light rifle, sometimes with the aid of a barking dog such as a Finnish spitz. They tend to fly silently and with a slower wing beat than the red grouse, but as much as twice, or perhaps even three times as fast. They are liable to fly very much higher and will sometimes turn back and circle over the same ground. Since they are frequently encountered in the same habitat in Britain it is easy to mistake the grayhen for a red grouse before the blackgame season has begun, the penalty for which varies from place to place, but usually amounts to a bottle of whisky. Confusing hybrids with both red grouse and capercailzie do occur, making matters rather more difficult, even for the experienced sportsmen. Their flight appears deceptively slow and due to their size it is very easy to underestimate their speed and shoot behind them. It is necessary to swing fast when shooting and heavy shot such as 4s or 5s is also desirable. It is very easy to take overlong shots and this also should be avoided. Their lyre-shaped tail feathers are often regarded as a trophy. The flesh, especially of the young, is excellent. *See also* Grouse.

Black Rhinoceros *(Diceros bicornis)*

At one time found throughout Africa, is now only found in a few areas in Central and East Africa. Due largely to senseless persecution for the believed aphrodisiac value of their horn, their numbers are annually decreasing and they may soon have to be protected like their close relations, *D. simus*, the white or square-lipped rhinoceros of Africa and *Rhinocerus unicornis*, the great Indian rhinoceros, which has only one horn, was once found throughout Nepal, Bengal and Assam, but is now very scarce. The black rhinoceros, when mature; stands over 5 ft at the shoulder and is about 11 ft long, weighing well over a ton. The tough gray-brown hide may vary greatly in colour due to the fact that with frequent wallowing it tends to take on the shades of the various mud baths. They live in the open plain and thin bush and are browsers, feeding mostly on leaves and the shoots of shrubs. Both sexes are horned with a front horn of from 24 to as much as 36 in and a rear horn of less than 12 in, both composed of closely packed fibre. They are shortsighted, have keen scenting powers, and a largely undeserved reputation for bad temper.

Licences to shoot them may be obtained in Tanzania, Remza and Ethiopia and probably certain other parts of Africa. They may occasionally wreak havoc around a native village and sometimes a rogue has to

A male black grouse, or blackcock, displaying its conspicuous white feathers.

be shot, but shooting them for their trophy head seems entirely unjustifiable. Despite their size and their tough hide they are easily stalked and shooting them is a comparatively simple matter. As with any other potentially dangerous big game, however, it should not be underrated. A charging rhinoceros is a fearsome enough spectacle and with the head down it is easy to find the bullet deflected by the horn, thus a heavy calibre is desirable.

Black-tailed Deer
(Odocoileus hemionus colombianus)
A deer of the Pacific coast, it has never, apparently, been seen east of the Rockies. It is found from south-eastern Alaska to as far south as the Santa Barbara country of California. Very similar to the mule deer, *q.v.*, it is argued that it is no more than a sub-species of the mule deer. The chief differences are that the mule is heavier, both in body weight and in rack, though the blacktail has the same bifurcated type of antler as the mule. The blacktail has, as one would expect, a black tail, bushier and wider than the mule's, and white underneath. It is held either erect or slightly drooping whilst running, but not pressed against the body like the mule's. In coat colouring it is more like the white-tailed deer, *q.v.*, than the mule; the summer coat is yellowish-brown and the winter one brownish-gray, in both cases with a black stripe running down the back. The average length of the metatarsal gland is 3 in.

Blesbok *see* Tsesseby

Blinds
A form of hide generally of permanent or semi-permanent nature, sometimes on stilts, or on a promontory in a regular flight line used by migratory wildfowl. Most commonly found on the west coast of France or the coasts of the United States. Most are simple lined pits, sunken barrels or brush-camouflaged floating boxes, but they may be luxurious in concept and execution, providing heating, sanitation and sleeping quarters for the hunters. Their effectiveness is a matter of location and the skill with which decoys are set out, and most of the wildfowl shot in North America are killed from such hides. The term may also be used to describe more temporary erections. *See also* Hides and Decoys.

Bluebuck *see* Duiker

Bluebell *see* Nilgai

Blue Goose
(Anser caerulescens caerulescens)
One of the brent geese, it is considered by most biologists to be a dominant colour phase of the lesser snow goose, and many experts believe that eventually the white phase (snow geese) will disappear altogether, as the blue phase has a higher survival rate, and tends to occur more often in early clutches, with better prospects of surviving adverse weather. Both snows and blues may

The blue goose is a dominant colour phase of the lesser snow goose, and is likely to replace the latter.

Although their numbers are decreasing, it is still possible to shoot the black rhinoceros in some parts of Africa.

41

occur in a single brood, but studies show the percentage of pure white birds to be decreasing significantly.

It is medium-sized, with a white head and neck and bluish-gray body, the underparts being lighter than the rest. The bill is red, with a whitish nail and black cutting edges, and the feet change from pink to orange in winter. There is considerable colour variation, especially in the wavy lines on the back and sides.

The breeding grounds are on the tundra on certain of the islands in Hudson Bay and in parts of the Northwest Territories and Baffin Island, and until recent years the wintering grounds were within a limited area of coastal marshes along the Gulf of Mexico. Since 1960 blues and snows have begun to winter in man-made water impoundments far north of their traditional wintering areas and, as with the Canada goose, new migratory patterns are being established.

Blue geese are voracious feeders, pulling the marsh and tundra grasses up by the roots. They begin migrating southwards in late September or October, and return to the breeding grounds in late March, in an almost uninterrupted flight from Vermillion Bay to Hudson Bay. Mating is generally completed before arrival and the nests are built, of grass and moss, on high tussocks of tundra grass. The clutch of from three to five eggs takes around 24 days to incubate, the gander remaining in attendance. The goslings can fly within five weeks and are nearly full grown within eight weeks. Their heads and necks remain brownish-gray, instead of white, until they reach maturity.

Blue geese are seldom hunted largely because both their breeding grounds and their wintering grounds are difficult to reach, and they have few halts in their migrations backwards and forwards. At James Bay, an extension of Hudson Bay, there are about twenty commercial hunting camps reached by bush plane. All of the camps employ Cree Indians as guides, and several camps are entirely operated by Crees, under government auspices. Hunting starts in September, when the geese gather on the marshland 'staging areas' to feed and gain strength for the non-stop flight to Louisiana or Texas. The young birds come readily to crude decoys made of lumps of mud, or pieces of white paper, but mature adults are warier. Hunting continues into late October, when most flocks have headed south, and although hunting is not difficult, a trip into this area is memorable.

Blue Grouse (*Dendragapus obscurus*)

Like so many of the North American grouse, this western species has a wide range of alternative names, including: dusky grouse; gray grouse; mountain grouse; pine grouse; and along with one or two other varieties, fool hen.

Also known as the dusky grouse, the blue grouse of North America, in spite of its trusting nature, is still found in considerable numbers.

This variety of blue hare, found in Scotland, turns completely white in winter.

It is the largest of the woodland grouse, and second in size only to the sage grouse q.v. It is found, in the summer, in fairly open pine woods, and, in the winter, moves up to the thicker woods on the ridges. In summer it eats insects, fruit, berries and leaves, and in winter the buds and leaves of conifers, during which period its flesh becomes largely inedible. It is a bird of the coniferous and evergreen forests of the Rocky Mountain ranges from the Yukon to Arizona and from Alaska to California.

The average weight lies between $2\frac{1}{2}$ and $3\frac{1}{2}$ lb and the average length between 15 and 19 in, the cock being longer than the hen. The head, neck and upperparts of both the male and female bird are grayish-black, blending to light brown on the shoulders and secondaries. The underparts are bluish-gray. The cock has an orange-red comb and air sac, and its broad tail is dark brown, ending in a wide band of light gray. The hen has no comb or air sac, and its narrower tail is mottled brown, white and black.

The cock claims territory in the spring, which he defends by making hooting calls to warn intruders away. He is polygamous, and courtship consists of a series of strutting dances, in the course of which the air sacs are dilated so that the feathers surrounding them are puffed up. The sudden expulsion of air from the sacs produces a booming noise, rather similar to the 'drumming' of the ruffed grouse. The hen nests on the ground, making a crude nest of grass and pine needles. The clutch of five to seven eggs takes 24 days to incubate.

Where it has not been heavily hunted the blue grouse is remarkably unalarmed by man, and it gets its name of fool hen from the calm manner with which it allows hunters to come up to its perch and shoot it sitting. In spite of this it is protected by the inaccessibility of the forests, and is still found in fair numbers.

Blue Hare (*Lepus timidus*)

Also known as the varying hare and mountain hare, there are a number of closely related sub-species typical of which are the Scots mountain hare (*L. timidus scoticus*) and Irish mountain hare (*L. timidus hibernicus*). They are gray-blue with small differences. The Scots sub-species turn completely white in winter whereas the Irish only turn partly white. Much more finely boned than the brown hare, q.v., the blue weighs only 5 to 7 lb, being generally a good deal smaller. Their habits are similar to those of the brown hare, except that they are as their secondary name implies, found at a good deal higher level on mountainous moorland, or stony hillside. When chased they take cover in a hole or under rocks, which the brown hare is hardly ever known to do. Like the brown they are generally shot by driving, or over dogs, but are seldom coursed as they will merely take cover.

Boar *see* Wild Boar

Bobcat *(Felis rufa)*

Smaller than the Canadian lynx, *Felis lynx* *(q.v.)*, which, in North America, is found only in the wilder parts of Canada and which it otherwise resembles, the bobcat is found almost everywhere in North America, from Nova Scotia to Mexico, and seems at home in any environment, whether mountain, forest, desert or swamp.

Entirely carnivorous, it lives close to its food supplies, which range from rodents and rabbits to lambs, poultry, and even full grown does. Treated, in most of the states, as predators, they may be hunted at any time.

The bobcat weighs around 20 lb, the female rather smaller than the male, but specimens weighing up to 50 lb have been reported. The coat is generally pale or reddish-brown, and the underparts are lighter. The tail is striped black on top and is lighter coloured underneath. The ears are tufted.

Mating takes place usually in January or February, but may occur later. The kittens, usually between two and four in number, are born in March or April. The den is usually situated under a windfall, or in a natural cavity such as a rocky ledge or cave.

The bobcat stalks its prey by both sight and smell, and is best hunted by hounds. This may be done by just one or two, the hunter waiting, with a rifle, for the bobcat to circle, but the best method is to use a fast running pack, preferably of foxhounds, which will run the bobcat until it is either pulled down or treed. Since they leave only a light scent, hunting is best in the early morning, or at night, when the dew helps to hold the scent.

Although its pelt is of less value than that of a Canadian lynx's, it is still frequently trapped or hunted.

Bobwhite Quail *(Colinus virginianus)*

This is the best known of the American quail and probably still the most frequently shot bird in North America. It is, essentially, a bird associated with arable and open farmland, and it depends on the right balance between food and cover crops for survival. It is, therefore, primarily a bird of eastern and southern North America, and its range stretches from Manitoba to Texas. It is, however, most abundant in the southeastern states of the United States, where, in spite of hunting pressures, mechanization, 'clean' land farming, and the destruction of hedges and cover, it still survives to be hunted.

The bobwhite is a small, plump bird, with an average weight of five to six ounces, and an average length of 8 to 10 in. Male and female have similar plumage, but the cock can be distinguished by white markings on the head and throat. There are several subspecies including the southern bobwhite *(C. virginianus floridanus)*, the western, Texan, or Mexican bobwhite *(C. virginianus texanus)* and the masked bobwhite *(C. virginianus ridgwayi)*. Essentially terrestrial birds, they all run well, and rely on freezing and camouflage for protection. If flushed they rise rapidly in whirring flight, but will not fly far. They are gregarious and are found in coveys, which begin to 'pack' in autumn. They roost on the ground, in circles, heads outwards. The winter coveys average about 15, and the average life expectancy is little over a year. The covey ranges over about a quarter of a mile, and feeds morning and evening on a variety of cereal and grass seeds, berries, insects, mast and weeds. Population densities vary, but a bird every four acres is the norm, and one every acre would be the maximum. Populations depend far more on soil condition, soil use, and weather than on pressures from predators, including hunters.

It is monogamous; pairing occurs in early spring and nesting from May to September, with a peak in June and July. Re-nesting occurs only when an earlier nest or clutch has been destroyed. The average clutch is 15 and incubation takes 23 days. The chicks are precocious and first flight takes place at about fourteen days. Full adult plumage is assumed after 16 weeks.

Because of its tendency to freeze and rely

A female bobwhite quail incubating its eggs

on camouflage effects for protection, the bobwhite is one of the best birds for dogging, especially with pointers. In those states where coyotes are common predators, however, quail will no longer lie tight to dogs. In shooting this bird, the object must be to split up the coveys, and so leave single birds for the dog and hunter to deal with. In some parts of the United States it is customary to use horses so as to follow more closely the work of the pointers. Unfortunately wild quail populations are decreasing as habitat shrinks, and today most bobwhite are shot on shooting preserves, as they are easily reared artificially.

Bokor *see* Reedbuck

Bolivia

Bolivia is a landlocked South American state of about 420,000 square miles. The main chains of the Andes run through the western part, enclosing a great tableland with an average elevation of over 12,000 ft, within which lie Lake Poopo and part of Lake Titicaca. This region is, therefore, comparatively cold, but there is a temperate region formed by the valleys between 4,500 and 7,500 ft. In the east lie hot plains, densely wooded and sparsely populated.

Agriculture is also important: cereals and potatoes are grown, and the eastern regions are being increasingly developed for rice, sugar and cotton.

Further Information
Federacion Boliviana de Caza y Pesca, Av. Camacho 1377, La Paz.

Boschvark *see* Bushpig

Botswana

Botswana is a republic of south-central Africa, with an area of about 275,000 square miles. A plateau, about 4,000 ft high, divides the country into two distinct regions. In the east the land slopes downwards and provides a watershed for the Marico, Notwani and Limpopo rivers. West of the plateau lies a flat region consisting primarily of the Kalahari Desert and the Okavango swamps. The latter lie in the north-west corner of Botswana, and with the Chobe river (a tributary of the Zambesi) in the north and the Limpopo in the south are the only source of permanent surface water in the country. Between the swamps and the desert are the Northern State Lands, an area of forest and dense bush. As the varied terrain indicates, although the climate is generally subtropical it can vary widely with latitude and altitude: the rainfall is also very irregular, the south-west being particularly dry.

Field crops are undependable owing to the irregularity of the rainfall, thus cattle rearing is the main occupation. Botswana's game is one of its more important assets since large parts of the country can support

nothing else. The government consequently controls and organizes all non-resident hunting, and though there are no particularly special or unique species, most common African game may be shot.

Licences
Holders of a general game licence, which costs 150 Rand, may purchase supplementary licences for the animals shown in the table.

A package game licence may be obtained for R.550 and entitles the holder to shoot one each of the species listed under the supplementary licence, plus leopard.

Holders of a package licence may shoot a male sable (R.150) and a male roan (R.100). Holders of a general or a package licence may shoot a male eland (R.100) and a male lion (R.200).

There are three bird licences: one week (R.3), one month (R.10) and one year (R.15). They entitle the holder to shoot all duck, geese, francolins, guinea-fowl, quail, sand grouse, snipe, turtle-doves and greenpigeon, but excluding pygmy goose and fulvous tree duck.

All licences include export fees (except ivory). They must be obtained from the relevant licensing officer the day before hunting. The details given above are for the 1971 season. They may vary slightly from year to year.

Special Regulations
All hunting in Botswana is controlled by the Department of Wildlife and National Parks, and visitors may only hunt in the Controlled Hunting Areas. Visitors wishing to hunt should send the appropriate application form to the Department before 15 January, and should receive notification of the areas they have been allocated and the animals they may hunt by 15 February. On acceptance, the permit fee for the Controlled Hunting Area or Areas must be remitted by postal order, cash, or bank guaranteed cheque, the fee being non-refundable. Permit fees are, in most cases, R.50 per hunter per week. Visitors will be informed beforehand as to whom they should apply for game licences. Each controlled hunting area has an annual quota of animals that may be hunted. In any area each visitor will be allocated certain animals, and having accepted this allocation it may not be changed. The only change that may be permitted is in the personnel of the party. Game scouts will be provided to accompany each party to advise on the law and the boundaries of the area; they are not guides, cooks or skinners. Trackers and guides may also be hired separately, usually for about R.1 per day. All controlled hunting area permits must be returned, properly endorsed, to the issuing officer, within 48 hours of completion of hunting.

Two rifles and one shotgun may be im-

The warthog is still common in open woodland areas of south and east Africa. It is one of the many animals that may be shot in Botswana and other parts of Africa.

ported for hunting, provided a firearms-import application form has been forwarded to the department at least two months before entry. No pistols, revolvers, automatic weapons, .303, .22, or .222 calibre rifles may be imported.

There are certain regulations concerning the movement of trophies, skins, meat, etc. within Botswana; these should be checked beforehand. Permits are, for instance, required to move trophies from Ngamiland and the Northern State Lands to the east of Botswana. They are obtainable from the Veterinary Department Offices.

Visitors are advised not to drink water without boiling it, and not to bathe in pools and dams as there is bilharzia. An anti-malarial prophylactic should also be carried, and if ill after visiting a tsetse fly area a doctor should be advised of the possibility of sleeping sickness.

Further Information
The Chief Game Warden, Department of Wildlife and National Parks, P.O. Box 131, Gaborone.

Brant *see* American Brant; Black Brant

Brazil
Brazil is an extremely large South American country covering more than 3,000,000 square miles. Most of the country consists of plains and plateaux. The three chief plains are those of the Parana-Paraguay rivers, the

coastal lowlands, and the immense Amazon river system. There are several chains of mountains, averaging 3,000 to 5,000 ft in the north, and a great system of scarps and plateaux along the south east coast. Lying on both the equator and the Tropic of Capricorn the whole country is very hot. The Amazon basin, in particular, is famed for its permanently hot, wet climate and dense jungle growth.

Brazil is largely agricultural, with a very large production of coffee, castor oil beans, cocoa, sugar and tobacco. Cattle and sheep rearing is also extensive and very successful. Much of the interior, and consequently the game, is unmapped, unexplored and unexploited.

Anything may be shot, including feral species, except animals used for agriculture, carrier pigeons, ornamental birds, small birds not harmful to agriculture, and some rare species. A list of the rare species is drawn up annually by the Diviseo de Caca e Pesca of the Ministry of Agriculture. This department also decides open and closed seasons. Generally the closed season lasts for about seven months. However, animals considered harmful may be killed at any time.

There is considerable hunting and shooting in Brazil, but it is largely private, conducted on private estates, which demands the landowner's permission and co-operation.

Visitors must obtain two permits in order to shoot: the first is an import licence for sporting guns (this excludes automatics and machine guns) issued by the civil police, which is valid for a year throughout Brazil; the second is a shooting licence, issued by the Caca e Pesca department on production of the first licence. Neither will be issued to anyone under 18.

For game *see* South America, Shooting in.

Further Information
Diviseo de Caca e Pesca, Departmento Nacional da Producae Animal, Ministero da Agricultura, Largo da Misericordia, Rio da Janeiro GB.

Brent Goose *(Branta bernicla bernicla)*
Almost identical with the American brant *(B. bernicla hrota) q.v.,* it breeds in the European and Asiatic tundras, and winters on the North Sea and Atlantic coasts of Europe, and on both sides of the Pacific as far south as China and Japan. It is a winter visitor to many of the coasts of Great Britain.

British Columbia (Canada)
This, the most westerly of the Canadian provinces, covers an area of 366,000 square miles, including Vancouver Island and the Queen Charlotte Islands, and consists, basically, of two great mountain ranges – the Rocky Mountains and the Coast Range – with intervening valleys, basins and

45

Seasons and Limits— British Columbia

Big Game

Mule and Columbian black-tailed deer
Open seasons in all M.A.'s. The earliest starts 15 August, and the latest finishes 31 December. Limit: Queen Charlottes none; elsewhere, maximum seasonal bag is three, of which two may be antlerless; in some areas the limit is two, of which one may be antlerless. Tag licence fee: 50c; trophy fee: $25. Best areas: mule, in the south; blacktail, Vancouver Island.

White-tailed deer
No open season in the western M.A. In other areas the earliest starting date for bucks is 5 September, and the latest finishing date is 31 December. Bag Limit: generally two, of which one may be antlerless; in some M.A.'s the limit is one. Tag and trophy fees: as for mule. Best areas: in the east, especially the extreme south-east.

Moose
No moose may be shot in certain southern M.A.'s, and in addition cows may not be shot in others. The earliest opening date for bull moose is 15 August and the latest closing date 31 December. The earliest date on which cows may be shot is 3 October, and the latest date 31 December. Bag Limit: in all areas, one, with a choice of sex in those areas where antlerless moose may be shot. Tag fee: $6. Trophy fee: $60. Best areas: in the centre and the north of the province.

Elk
There is no open season for elk in several scattered M.A.'s. Bull elk may be shot in the other areas, but cows may only be shot in certain eastern M.A.'s and the Queen Charlottes. The earliest opening date in any area for bulls is 15 August, and the latest closing date 13 December. The earliest date for antlerless elk is 29 August and the latest closing date 13 December. Bag Limit: one, with a choice of sex only in those areas where cows may be shot. Tag fee: $5; trophy fee: $60. Best area: East Kootenay in the extreme south-east.

Rocky Mountain goat
There is no open season in Vancouver Island, the Queen Charlottes and parts of a few other M.A.'s, mostly in the south west. All other areas have open seasons, the earliest of which starts on 1 August and the latest closes on 13 December. Bag limit: two, one of each sex if hunter wishes to shoot nannies. Tag fee: $2; trophy fee: $60. The northern and some of the south central M.A.'s have open seasons. The earliest this season opens in any area is 1 August and the latest it closes is 1 November. Limit: one ram per season. Tag fee: $5; trophy fee: $75.

Grizzly bear
Vancouver Island and the Queen Charlottes are the only areas with no open season. The earliest opening of the season in other areas is 29 August, and the closing date for all areas is 31 December. Baiting is prohibited in most areas. Bag Limit: one of either sex. Tag fee: $10; trophy fee: $60.

Black bear
There is an open season in every M.A. in the province. In most it runs from 29 August to 31 December, but it may start a little later in a few of them. Bag Limit: in one or two south-central areas, none; in all others, two of either sex. Tag fee: 50c; trophy fee: $5.

Cougar and Coyote
Except in Vancouver Island and the Queen Charlottes there is no closed season, for either. Coyotes may be hunted by non-residents without a guide, and there is no bag limit. Bag Limit for cougar: varies from one to five of either sex, and in some south-central M.A.'s, none. Cougar tag fee: $5; trophy fee: $60. There are no extra fees for hunting coyote.

Timber wolf
The open season in the south-eastern M.A.'s runs from 15 September to 31 March. There is no closed season in the other areas. Bag Limit: south-west and the north, none; in other areas it varies from one to three of either sex. Tag fee: none; trophy fee: $40.

Small Game   Tag and trophy fees: none

Raccoon
Hunted in the Queen Charlottes and some south western M.A.'s. In those areas there is no closed season. Bag Limit: none.

Skunk
Can be hunted everywhere except the Queen Charlottes and Vancouver Island. There is no closed season. Bag Limit: none

Bobcat
Can be hunted everywhere except Vancouver Island, the Queen Charlottes and the north-west. There is no closed season. Bag Limit: none.

Fox
Hunted in Vancouver Island and the south-west only. There is no closed season. Bag Limit: none.

Wolverine
There is no open season in Vancouver Island, the Queen Charlottes and the M.A.'s on the centre of the southern border. The earliest opening in any of the other M.A.'s is 15 August, and the season closes everywhere, except in the south-west where it continues until 31 March, on December 31. Bag Limit: one, in all areas.

Lynx
Hunted only in the south central M.A.'s from 1 November to 28 February. Bag Limit: one.

Game Birds

Blue grouse
May be shot in all areas. The earliest start in any is 5 September, and the latest finish is 13 December. Bag Limit: 10 per day.

Spruce and Franklin grouse
May be shot in all M.A.'s except Vancouver Island and the Queen Charlottes. The earliest date is 5 September, and the last date 13 December. Bag Limit: 10 per day.

Sharp-tailed grouse
Shot in about a dozen scattered M.A.'s The earliest date in any area is 5 September and the latest date 13 December. Bag Limit: 6 per day.

Ruffed grouse
May be shot everywhere except in the Queen Charlottes. The first date anywhere is 29 August and the latest 13 December. Bag Limit: 10 per day.

Ptarmigan
Can be shot throughout the province except in the Queen Charlottes and the Okinagan Valley, which runs down the centre of southern B.C. The earliest date anywhere is 15 August, and the latest 13 December. Bag Limit: 10 per day except in one or two M.A.'s, where it is 6 per day.

Pheasant
Shooting cocks is allowed, generally, only between 8 a.m. and 4 p.m., in all or part of most of the less mountainous southern M.A.'s. The earliest date is 10 October, and the latest 29 November. In Vancouver Island and the Queen Charlottes there are also two-day seasons for hens. Bag Limit: 2, either sex, per day in the two named areas; 3 cocks per day in other areas.

Hungarian partridge
These can be shot, generally only between 8 a.m. and 4 p.m., in a few of the less mountainous south central M.A.'s. The earliest opening date is 5 September, and the latest closing date 31 December. Bag Limit: 10 per day.

Chukar partridge
May be shot in almost all the same areas as Hungarian partridge. The earliest and latest closing dates and the bag limits are also the same.

Quail
May be shot, in most places only between 8 a.m. and 4 p.m., in rather fewer of the same areas as partridge. The season, in every area, opens on 10 October and closes on either 15 or 22 November. Bag Limit: in Vancouver Island and around the Okinagan Valley, 10 per day; elsewhere, 3 per day.

plateaux. There are some great rivers, including the Fraser, Columbia and Peace Rivers, and many lakes. Much of the north is covered with boreal forest but, in the valleys, and in the south, much of the land is extremely fertile. There are over 800,000 acres under the plough, mixed farming, dairying and fruit growing being the principal forms of agriculture. Lumbering is the greatest industry of all, British Columbia having the largest stand of softwood in the whole of the Commonwealth.

It is also reputed to have the greatest variety, quantity, and quality of big game in North America. The province is divided, for the purpose of game management, into 28 areas, with seasons, bag limits, and game available varying from one to the other, and from year to year.

Licences

These can be obtained from the Fish and Wildlife Branch in Victoria, or from a number of local centres, and cover big and small game and upland game birds. They cost: resident $4, non-resident Canadian $15 and for a non-resident non-Canadian $25. There are, in addition, Tag Licence fees to be paid for most forms of big game, and non-residents must also pay Trophy fees for most big game they shoot, whether the carcass is removed or not. Should waterfowl be shot a federal Migratory Game Bird permit ($2) is necessary. Except when shooting game birds or waterfowl, non-residents must employ a licensed guide. Lists of guides are issued by the Department of Recreation and Conservation, Victoria.

The arrangement of the Management Areas (M.A.'s) is such that they cannot be understood in detail without the help of a map. Where groups of M.A.'s are mentioned, therefore, they are classed together under a rough description of their position in the province, as, for instance, the central part of southern B.C. (south central), the southeast, the north-east, etc. If a number of M.A.'s are not classifiable into such a group it is simply mentioned that a certain number of M.A.'s are distinguished in a particular respect. Two areas stand out as being frequent exceptions to the general rule: Vancouver Island and the Queen Charlotte Islands; they are mentioned by name.

Waterfowl and Migratory Birds

The province is divided, for the purposes of the Migratory Birds Convention Act (*q.v.*), into six districts, each containing at least one provincial management area. The northern part of the province is largely covered by boreal forest, and does not have many waterfowl, but Canada geese nest in the far north-east and fly in great numbers down the centre of the province during the spring and autumn migrations. The Peace River area, further south, is more open, and produces a variety of ducks, especially mallard, widgeon and pintail. The central area,

Bag Limits (Waterfowl and Migratory Birds)— British Columbia	
Species	**Bag Limits** (all districts)
Duck	8 per day, 16 in possession
Geese	5 per day, 10 in possession, of which not more than 4 and 8 respectively may be black brant
Snipe	10 per day, 20 in possession
Coot and Rail	8 per day, 16 in possession
Band-tailed pigeon	10 per day, 20 in possession
Mourning dove	10 per day, 20 in possession

The coyote is often shot in British Columbia, as elsewhere, while hunting other game animals.

With a range extending from British Columbia to Mexico, the raccoon is generally hunted with coon dogs.

Seasons (Waterfowl and Migratory Birds)—British Columbia

District	Species	Season
1. Vancouver Island and the Queen Charlottes	Duck	10 Oct-10 Jan
	Black brant	26 Dec-10 Mar
	Geese	24 Oct-10 Jan
	Snipe	24 Oct-10 Jan
2. West coast	Duck	10 Oct-10 Jan
	Black brant	5 Dec-10 Mar
	Snow goose	10 Oct-6 Dec and 6 Feb-10 Mar
	Other geese, and snipe	10 Oct-10 Jan
3. All south-central M.A.'s	Duck	19 Sept-20 Dec
	Geese and snipe	19 Sept-20 Dec
4. South-east	Duck, snow goose and snipe	12 Sept-13 Dec
	Other geese	1 Sept-7 Dec
5. North-central	All migratory birds	12 Sept-13 Dec
6. North-east	All migratory birds	1 Sept-29 Nov
South-central and south-east	Mourning dove	1 Sept-29 Nov
All except south-east and north-east	Band-tailed pigeon	1 Sept-25 Oct

The European brown hare is generally a solitary animal, and prefers rough country.

with its many lakes and open grassland, is especially rich in Canada geese and puddle ducks. In the south-central area there is much dry, fairly open forest, with mourning doves, as well as ducks and geese. The wetlands in the south-east provide good wildfowling, as does the coastal area, though this is often inaccessible. Vancouver Island and the Queen Charlottes are famous for sea duck, black brant and other wildfowl.

Further Information

Director of Fish and Wildlife Branch, Department of Recreation & Conservation, Parliament Buildings, Victoria, B.C.

Canadian Wildlife Service, University of British Columbia Campus, Vancouver 8, B.C.

Western Guides and Outfitters Association, P.O. Box 2629, Williams Lake, B.C.

Brocket *see* Deer of the World and their Hunting

Brown Hare *(Lepus europaeus)*

The familiar, long-eared, brown-furred mammal famed for its speed is found in many parts of Europe. With its long, powerful hind legs and delicate fore legs it is capable of leaving most dogs far behind. Its strange walking gait and wary movements are sometimes curiously cat-like and its common country nickname is 'Puss'. It weighs 6 to 7 lb in some areas, and in others may be as much as 11 or 12 lb, varying so much in size as to seem almost a sub-species, but the difference is probably merely due to habitat and feeding. It is vegetarian, a grazer and occasional browser. The hare lives above ground in a 'form' or freshly scratched-out hollow seat or bed, in the ground, in which it will spend a period of rest. Their generally accepted breeding season is from February to August, during which period they may not be legally sold in Britain. They may, however, breed several times a year and three to four litters annually are not uncommon. Like the rabbit (*q.v.*), the phenomenon of double oestrus or second fertilization is not uncommon. The young are born furred with their eyes open and the litters may vary in number from 2 to 5. They are soon moved to separate forms and the doe then makes the rounds feeding them. The leverets, as they are termed, mature within six months and are themselves capable of breeding within nine months.

They may be hunted with harriers or beagles, coursed with greyhounds, driven to waiting guns or shot over dogs. Due allowance should be made for their speed and size, and long shots should always be avoided. Number 5 shot is advisable and they should be shot well forward. The flesh is dark coloured with a strong flavour.

Brush Rabbit *see under* Cottontail and other American Rabbits.

Buffalo *(Syncerus caffer)*

The African buffalo or wild ox is common throughout Central Africa, where it is found in all types of country, though only sporadically in mountainous regions, preferring to remain in the vicinity of swampy land. The herds may often number several hundreds, but the bulls are frequently solitary or in small groups. They stand about 4 ft 6 in with a powerful body covered with sparse, black hair, large ears, long, tufted tail and massive horns. Those of an average bull measure about 36 in across the widest part and 25 in from tip to tip with 14 to 15 in of palm at the base, protecting the forehead. Principally grazers they also browse and the cows may produce a single calf at any period of the year, with the peak calving period during the dry season. They are easily stalked in fairly open country despite their acute sense of smell. They should be shot broadside on, the best place to aim being low down behind the shoulder, although if this is not possible, due to the length of grass, the neck shot is next best. Great caution should be always be exercised when approaching a fallen beast, for as long as there is the slightest sign of life it is capable of staggering to its feet and annihilating the hunter. Though not generally pugnacious, unless a cow with calf or an old bull driven from the herd is encountered, when it may charge without provocation, a wounded buffalo is notoriously cunning and ferocious. It does not charge blindly, but with the head only a few degrees off horizontal, dropping it for a sidelong thrust at the last moment. Consequently, it offers little to shoot at, for the massive horns will deflect most bullets. The point to aim at then is the nose, since even if the bullet does not strike the brain it will stop the charge by penetrating the vital parts of the neck and chest. When a wounded buffalo has disappeared into thick grass it is advisable to allow time for it to stiffen up before following it as it is liable to lie in wait for the hunter, or even double back and track him by scent. Heavy calibres are thus necessary.

Bufflehead *(Bucephala albeola)*

This is an American diving duck, similar to the goldeneye but smaller, being very little larger than a teal. The drake weighs about 1 lb and has a wingspan of around 22 in. It is a coastal species, eating only a small proportion of weeds and aquatic plants in addition to its principal diet of fish, crustacea and molluscs. It breeds in the north from Alaska to Hudson Bay and from British Columbia to Manitoba. It winters in the south of its breeding range, and in all the western, southern and eastern states. It is a rare vagrant visitor to Europe.

Like the goldeneye, the bufflehead has a markedly round head, this roundness being emphasized by its habit of fluffing up its head feathers. The drake has a black head with a broad white V across the top, white neck and underparts, and a black back and wings, with white patches. The female is a drab brown, with white patches on the cheeks and wings. Unlike other diving ducks, the bufflehead can spring straight off the water, and can emerge from under the water into direct flight. When pursued it frequently dives into the water from a considerable height.

Courtship involves flight displays, fights with other drakes, and a considerable amount of feather puffing and neck stretching. It is one of the last ducks to migrate northwards, and nesting is usually done in trees not far from water. The normal clutch of 8 to 10 eggs takes about three weeks to incubate. The young flutter to the ground after very few days. They resemble the duck in plumage, differentiation not occurring until the second autumn.

They come readily to decoys, but dive under water at the flash of a gun. Although they become, as their popular name of 'Butterball' indicates, very fat, they are hardly worth shooting, since their fishy diet makes their flesh inedible.

Bulgaria

Bulgaria lies in south-east Europe, covering an area of approximately 43,000 square miles. It is generally hilly, with the Balkan mountains forming the backbone of the country. In the south-east, between the Balkan and Rhodope Mountains, there is a

The sight and hearing of the African buffalo is poor, but its power of scent is well-developed, and when grazing in herds, sentries give warning of impending danger.

Bag Limits, Licences and Charges—Bulgaria

There is a bag limit of 14 per day per person (average figure for the whole stay) on pheasants, hares and partridges. On other small game there are no bag limits but an additional fee of $20 per day is required.

Shooting hen pheasants is not permitted, and a fine of $10 is charged for each one shot. There is also a fine for shooting the female and young of red deer and wild boar. A separate fee is set for wounding or missing deer and boar. There is a charge of 20% of the sum payable for small game shot, to cover those wounded or not picked up. When wild boar hunting nothing else may be shot except wolf and fox.

In addition to the charges for shooting outlined above, guides, dogs, carts (or sledges), and transport have to be paid for separately. An interpreter is free but obligatory, though it is unnecessary for him to accompany visitors in the hunting ground. Hunting may only proceed with a stalker/guide ($3 per day without dog, $6 per day with dog).

A licence is required for shooting small game: $3.50 for one day, $4 for up to three days, $6 for over three days; each licence is valid for only one hunting ground, the fee must be paid anew at any other hunting ground. Third party insurance is compulsory: $2 for 10 days; $5 for 30 days.

stretch of flat land where the river Maritsa drains into the Black Sea. It has two distinct climates: south of the Balkan Mountains the climate is Mediterranean with dry summers and mild winters, while north of the mountains it is continental, with severe frost. The mountains themselves are naturally colder all the year and also have a higher rainfall.

Despite the mountainous terrain the soil is generally good, and the country is still predominantly agricultural, the climate being particularly good for cereals, though other crops are grown. Timber is also important: over a third of the country is afforested.

Although there is an important tourist industry, this is concentrated on the Black Sea resorts, thus leaving much of the hinterland unspoilt. However, because of the climate, terrain and economy the variety and number of game shot are limited.

Shooting methods are to some extent dictated by the hilly terrain and limited game. There is, for instance, no driven shooting of small game. Deer are stalked or called, and boar are shot by hunting parties, not driven.

Seasons
As in most European countries the hunting seasons may vary from year to year, and should always be checked in advance. The animals in the table may be shot between the dates given.

Special Regulations
Guns, cartridges, cameras, binoculars and any other hunting equipment may be taken in and out of the country free of charge on completing a simple declaration. Deer and boar may only be shot with rifles of over 6mm calibre; soft-nosed rounds are illegal, as are shotguns that accept more than two cartridges. It is recommended that hunters use rather heavier shot than normal; number 3 for hare, number 5 for pheasant, and number 7 for partridge and quail. Cartridges for 12-bore are easily obtainable (10 for $1), but anything else is uncommon, and the hunter is advised to take his own rifle ammunition.

Deer and boar trophies, and small game belong to the hunter, and may be exported free of charge. There is no reduction for small game should the hunter not wish to keep it. Big game meat must be bought at $1.50 per kilogram. The hunter is under an obligation to show his trophies in at least two international exhibitions should the Bulgarian government make this request. Awards gained belong to the hunter.

All shooting is arranged through Balkantourist, the Bulgarian travel bureau. Visiting hunters must make a deposit of $50, or the equivalent in any free currency, at least 30 days before their date of arrival. Balkantourist cannot guarantee any shooting unless they have received the deposit. If trips

Seasons—Bulgaria			
Species	**Season**	**Fees**	**Comment**
Red deer, stags only	1 June-30 Nov	$50 upwards depending on weight	Best: 20 July-30 Aug
Wild boar	1 Oct-31 Jan	$20 upwards, depending on length	Best: Dec and Jan (varying with snow cover). Trophies are weighed and measured 24 hours after boiling and cleaning
Hare	5 Oct-15 Jan	$4	
Pheasant, cock	13 Sept-29 Dec	$3	
Partridge	4 Oct-30 Nov	$3	
Rock partridge	4 Oct-30 Nov	$5	
Turtle dove	9 Aug-27 Dec	$1	By special arrangement only
Quail	10 Aug-28 Dec	50c	Best: Sept
Snipe and jacksnipe	9 Aug-31 Mar	50c	Best: mid-Nov to mid-Dec
Duck	1 Sept-31 Mar	$1.50	Best: Dec-Mar
Goose	1 Sept-31 Mar	$3	

are cancelled Balkantourist will refund the deposit, less $2 per person, provided they receive notice of cancellation at least 7 days before the date of arrival. Those cancelling after that date will have their deposit refunded less $16 per person.

Further Information
Balkantourist, at one of their European agencies, or at the following address: Balkantourist, Section 'Hunting', 17 Slavyanska Street, Sofia.

Burma *see* South East Asia

Burrel *see* Bharal

Bushbuck *(Tragelaphus scriptus)*
The common bushbuck, or harnessed antelope, is a medium-sized African antelope found generally in forests and thick bush, sometimes in mountains, but never far from water and cover. It stands about 2 ft 8 in at the shoulder and is about 5 ft long. The males have rather small, spiral horns a little over 1 ft long, about 4 in round at the base and 6 in apart at the tips; the females are hornless. Although usually solitary, they may be found in twos and threes, or in groups of about six. The coat is reddish, marked with white lines and spots and the

Great bustard, Portugal

tail is bushy. Principally browsers, they sometimes graze a little. A single lamb may be born at any period of the year. Albinos have been recorded but are very exceptional. They are generally shot with a shotgun when the hunter is after feathered game, although they may be driven past the hunter during organized drives in the bush.

Menelik or Natal bushbuck (*Tragelaphus scriptus meneliki*), found in Ethiopia, is a very handsome black sub-species with few markings, but rarely shot. *See also* Sitatunga (*Tragelaphus spekei*).

Bushpig (*Potamochoerus porcus*)
Found throughout Africa in almost any densely forested regions, but seldom far from water, it stands about 30 in at the shoulder, but is of rather heavier build than the warthog and frequently weighs over 200 lb. The colouration is usually dark brown or black with lighter markings around the head. The body is covered with coarse hair and the tail is straight and thin. The tusks are generally about 6 in long. It is shy and retiring and mainly nocturnal, rooting in herds of up to about twenty and at times causing considerable damage to crops. During the day it generally lies up in thick grass or reed cover. It is an excellent swimmer, taking readily to water when pursued, but it is a fierce fighter when cornered and in such circumstances can be dangerous. The sow farrows in a burrow, generally having an annual litter of five or six. The young have very pronounced striping.

Though seldom specifically hunted for sport the bushpig can be a pest near cultivated land and organized drives are sometimes arranged to keep their numbers down. Otherwise they are generally only encountered during a drive for other animals. A medium calibre is sufficient to kill them if hit in the head or behind the shoulder. As a wounded boar can be dangerous, light calibres are not recommmended for this form of shooting. The flesh is good eating.

A sub-species known as the red river hog is found in West Africa and has a reddish body, white dorsal crest and long ear tassels. Yet another sub-species is the southern river hog or boschvark, found in South Africa, but this is now less common.

Bustards (*Otidae*)
These are members of a family of large, cursorial, upland birds found in rapidly decreasing numbers, on open grassy plains in Europe and Asia and on bush savannahs in Africa. They include the great bustard (*Otis tarda*), the little bustard (*Otis tetrax*), both of Europe and Central Asia; the great Indian bustard (*Choriotis nigriceps*) and the floricans and houbara of India; the 'wild turkey' (*Otis australis*) of Australia, and the various bustards, houbara, gorri-paaver and koorhaan of Africa. There are, in all,

English springer spaniel with rabbit (left)

Although a shy animal, the bushbuck will defend itself if attacked (above, right).

The great bustard was once widespread in Europe, but hunting pressures have considerably reduced its range (right).

thirty species of bustard, of which two are resident in Europe, five are resident in Asia, twenty-two are resident in Africa and one is resident in Australia.

The different species vary in size, but the females are always smaller than the males except in the case of the floricans, where the reverse is the case. They are all wary, keen-sighted, fast-running birds of the open country, relying, in the first instance, on their sight and their speed across country for their defence. They are reluctant, but very strong, flyers, and many of them are either migratory, or semi-migratory, undertaking long flights in typical crane style and formation, with head and neck straight out in front and legs trailing behind. They are extremely wary of man and, if approached on foot will run immediately; surprisingly, they show little alarm at the approach of a man on horseback or in a cart or other vehicle. They are, by preference, graminivorous, but will also eat other seeds as well as insects, snakes and small birds. They roost and nest on the ground, the nest being little more than a hollow in the ground with a little grass in it. The clutch usually consists of a single egg, though two may sometimes be laid, and some of the smaller African bustards may lay up to five. Since nesting occurs only once a year, it is plain that these are birds of low reproductive capacity.

They are usually found in pairs or small groups of no more than ten or twelve, and even the smallest species is conspicuous, because of size, occupation of an open habitat, and habit of either running or else flying close to the ground.

The great Indian bustard *(Choriotis nigriceps)*, which is protected, is probably the largest flying bird normally to alight on land. The paauw or kori bustard *(Otis kori)* of South Africa and the great bustard *(Otis tarda)* of Europe and Central Asia are nearly as large. Other Indian bustards include the Bengal florican *(Otis bengalensis)*, the lesser florican *(Otis aurita)*, and the eastern ruffed bustard or houbara *(Otis macqueeni)*. These are all smaller birds, ranging between 19 and 28 in in height.

The male great bustard of Europe *(Otis tarda)* stands about 40 in and weighs up to 36 lb. It is distinguished by its 'whiskers' – tufts of long, bristly white feathers growing from each side of the throat just under the chin. These give it its popular Spanish name of 'barbones'. Its upperparts are rufous-buff barred with black, and its underparts are white, with a chestnut breast and, in full breeding plumage, a ruff. It is found on grassy plains and steppes and in large fields of grain and maize. It was once found and hunted in Britain, especially over the Norfolk brecks and the Wiltshire Downs (the last British bird was killed in 1838). It is still found and hunted on the Danubian Plain, that is, in Czechoslovakia, Rumania and Hungary, as well as in Spain and Portugal and along the southern shores of the Baltic. The little bustard *(Otis tetrax)* is similar except for some details of plumage, but is half its size, and is found as a resident in Spain, Portugal, Sardinia, southern Italy, Albania, Greece, Asia Minor and northern Africa, and as a summer visitor, in France and along the Danubian Plain and Delta.

The houbara bustard of Africa *(Chlamydotis undulata)* is a desert bustard, halfway in size between the great and little bustards, sometimes found, as a vagrant, in Europe. In Africa there are still sometimes found, in addition to the kori bustard, Stanley's bustard *(Otis caffra)* and Ludwig's bustard *(Otis ludwigi)* as well as the many species of more numerous and smaller bustards generally referred to as 'koorhans'. The Australian bustard or 'wild turkey' is now a protected bird and, being a reluctant flyer, it never provided good sport for discerning hunters.

In many parts of the world the bustard is now a protected bird, but its numbers decline almost as much where it is not hunted as where it is.

Where it is still-hunted, this is done in a variety of ways. The larger bustards may be stalked and shot with a rifle, and if cover is not available, it is sometimes possible to get within range by going round the birds in decreasing circles. They may be stalked, also, from behind a stalking horse and use is made of the fact that it rarely is alarmed by the approach of a horse, a cart or car, thus allowing a man on horseback or hiding inside a cart to get within range. They may be driven over guns, either by a line of beaters or else by three mounted beaters – one behind and two flankers. The guns may crouch on the ground or be behind butts or over the brow of a hill, but they must remain quite motionless if the birds are not to swerve away from them. In Spain the peasants sometimes shoot them when they come to water at known watering holes, or put them up from their roosts on the ground at night, shooting them by artificial light. In South Africa the paauw and other large bustards used to be ridden down on the open veldt. The little bustard may even be walked up, as is sometimes done in France and Portugal, though a successful shot got in this way can never be anything more than lucky, for the bird when flushed, which generally happens early, soars to a great height.

Altogether, there are too many ways in which the bustard may be hunted and killed, and it is quite possible that many, if not all the species of this fine bird will, sooner or later, be seen only in aviaries and zoos. It can be bred in captivity, so that it might be possible to restock areas from which it has disappeared. But its habitat is disappearing also, and this cannot be so easily reconstituted.

Wild turkey are now well enough established in California for there to be two seasons in certain counties.

C

Cactus Buck *see* Mule Deer

Caiman *see* Crocodiles and Alligators

California (U.S.A.)

A large, Pacific coast state covering 159,000 square miles. Two great mountain ranges run along it, with the Central Valley of the Sacramento and San Joaquin rivers in between them. In the north the climate is cool and the rainfall heavy; in the south it is warm and semi-arid. There is a considerable amount of ranching, but not a great deal of intensive cultivation. What there is, is devoted to fruit and cotton growing.

There are over 25 million acres of forest.

Because there is little cultivation, a great deal of the state is open for hunting, and there is an unusually varied big game population, including mule deer, bear, antelope, bighorn, wild pig, mountain lion, wild turkey and elk. Of these bighorn is completely protected, and there are only three hundred permits each, for elk and antelope, issued to residents only. Small game includes brush, cottontail, snowshoe and jack rabbits; pheasant, chukar, grouse, quail, band-tailed pigeon and doves.

Cougar, coyote, raccoon, wildcat, and wolf may be shot at any time.

Licence Fees—California

Resident $4. Deer tag $2
Non-resident $25. Deer tag $10
Bear and Lion tags $1 each
Pheasant stamps $2
All can be bought from stores and agents throughout the State.

Big Game Inventory— California

	Shot
Bear	638
Turkey	50
Wild boar	800
Mule deer	1,700
Black-tailed deer	34,668
Pronghorn antelope	189

Seasons and Limits—California

Species	Seasons	Limit
Deer	According to county. Early season from about 7 Aug-26 Sept; main season from 25 Sept-26 Oct in most counties	From 1 buck with at least three points to 2 bucks with at least two points
Mountain lion	May be shot in certain counties only from 15 Nov-28 Feb or until 50 have been taken	1 adult lion per season
Bear	In certain counties only from 16 Oct-2 Jan	1 per season
Wild boar	All year round	None—except in Monterey County
Pheasant	State-wide from about 13 Nov-5 Dec	In some counties, 2 birds of any sex per day, 10 per season. Elsewhere 2 cocks per day for first 2 days, 4 cocks per day thereafter and 10 for the season
Quail	According to county but generally from 30 Oct-2 Jan. Additional early season for mountain quail	10 per day, 10 in possession
Chukar partridge	30 Oct-30 Jan	8 per day, 8 in possession
Ruffed and Sierra grouse	Shot in some counties only from about 4 Sept-26 Sept	2 per day, 2 in possession
Sage grouse	4 Sept-6 Sept in four counties only	2 per day and per season
Turkey	Nov 20-28 April 22-30	2 per season of any sex 1 bearded bird per season
Rabbit	3 July-30 Jan	8 per day and in possession

Further Information
Department of Fish and Game, 1416 Ninth Street, Sacramento, California 95814.

Canada *see* Alberta; British Columbia; Manitoba; New Brunswick; Newfoundland; Nova Scotia; Ontario; Prince Edward Island; Quebec; Saskatchewan; Yukon Territory; Northwest Territories

Canada Goose (*Branta canadensis*)
This is the best known and most eagerly hunted of all the North American geese. The familiar, V-shaped flights of the 'Honkers' herald, for many Americans, both the beginning and the end of winter.

There are several recognized sub-species. Since almost the only important differences between them are those of size and distribution, a description of the common Canada (*B. canadensis canadensis*) will be sufficient.

The only apparent difference between the goose and the gander is that the goose is slightly smaller. The gander averages between 9 and 10 lb, though specimens of up to 20 lb have been known. The body length varies between 35 and 40 in, and the wingspan is up to 6 ft. The stocking is a lustrous black with a sharply defined white band stretching from behind one eye round under the throat to behind the other eye. The stocking ends in a sharp line at the ash-gray of the upper chest, which is barred, wavily, with white. The flanks and belly are white, the rump black, and the tail coverts white. The bill has a wide nail and is black, as are the legs and feet.

Although excellent swimmers they spend a considerable time on land, grazing, and they are good walkers. But, above all, they are superb flyers, averaging migration flight speeds of 50 mph. They generally fly in V-formation, but this may change to an oblique line abreast. Whilst flying they produce the loud honking that gives them their nickname.

Canadas are almost entirely vegetarian, though they will eat a certain proportion of insects, molluscs, and small crustacea. When feeding on the water they frequently up-end themselves like ducks. On land they can crop grass and green corn closer than sheep and, since they also foul the land they feed on, farmers generally seek to drive them off. Their normal feeding times are early morning and late evening, but when they are feeding on the stubbles they will sometimes come in during the day.

They are not only monogamous, they are reputed, like swans, to mate for life. However, when in captivity, they will take another mate if the first mate dies, and it is probable that this happens in the wild. The nest is a depression in the ground lined with grass, moss and down, and the clutch of five to six eggs takes from 28 to 30 days to incubate, the gander remaining in attendance during this time, and assisting with the

Canada geese flying above Kingsville, Ontario

subsequent brooding. The parents moult at midsummer, during which time they remain under cover in reedbeds until they are once more able to fly. Migration starts at the end of August, and the family stays together for the rest of the year.

There are several sub-species, including:
The western Canada goose (*B. canadensis occidentalis*): a goose of the same size as the common Canada, but with a restricted range from Alaska to Vancouver Island, inside which it is a partial migrant.
The lesser Canada goose (*B. canadensis leucoparia*): a smaller and shorter-necked goose, commonest of all the Canadas, found along the western coast. It breeds along the Arctic coast and winters on the Pacific coast to as far south as Mexico. It is seldom, if ever, seen along the Atlantic coast.
The cackling goose (*B. canadensis minima*): the smallest of all the Canadas. It is like the western Canada in all but size, and its cry is a shrill 'luk-luk' that gives it its name. It breeds in the Aleutians and winters from British Columbia to California.
Richardson's goose (*B. canadensis hutchensii*): this is like the common Canada in all but size and call. It rarely exceeds 6 lb and, instead of a 'honk', its call is a trilling 'k.r.r.r.'

The common Canada has the widest range of them all. Its nesting grounds lie in the northern marshes of the Canadian Prairie Provinces, and its wintering grounds depend on the Flyway followed. Those using the Pacific Flyway summer in Alaska and winter along the Pacific coast to as far south as Mexico. Those using the Central and Mississippi Flyways summer in the central Canadian provinces and winter along the shores of the Gulf of Mexico. Those using the Atlantic Flyway summer along the shores of Hudson Bay and in Labrador and the Maritimes, and winter along the Atlantic coast from Chesapeake Bay to Florida. The Canada has also been imported, at various times, to Europe, normally as a park bird, but has escaped and established itself as a feral bird, breeding in Britain and Sweden, and possibly also in Ireland, Norway, Denmark, Holland and France.

Methods of shooting the Canada goose vary from area to area, but all methods must take into consideration its habit of returning, regularly, to the same feeding ground, its extreme wariness – it posts sentries while grazing – and its ability to spring straight into the air like a mallard, when alarmed. In Canada it is most often shot from pits dug during the day in the stubble fields. Along the Atlantic coast it is more usually shot from a more elaborate and permanent blind with the aid of block or profile decoys. The heaviest bags are obtained on the wheat fields of the Prairie Provinces early in the season, and in Illinois, California, and North Carolina later.

The Canada goose often feeds in pastures, and may damage immature crops considerably.

A cock capercailzie, displaying on a log. Such displays generally begin at dawn, or even earlier, and may continue well into the day.

Canvasback *(Aytha valisineria)*

A large, American diving duck, it is highly esteemed by both sportsmen and epicures. Its Latin name connects it with the wild celery – *Valisineria speralis* – on the roots of which it feeds, and from which it is popularly supposed to acquire its excellent flavour. It was once so highly valued as a table bird that market hunters were paid a high premium for it, and it was in some danger of being exterminated. The market hunters have disappeared, but now the draining and ploughing of the Prairie Provinces in which it breeds are a threat to its numbers. In spite of this it is still found over a wide range, breeding in eastern Alaska and over a wide belt from Alberta to Utah and east as far as Minnesota; it winters along the whole length of the Pacific coast from Washington to Mexico, and along the Atlantic coast and the Gulf of Mexico.

The drake has a rusty red head and neck, black breast and hindquarters, and a pale gray back, finely vermiculated with black, which gives it its name. Its sloping forehead and black bill distinguish it from the red-head drake *(q.v.)*. The duck is pale slaty-brown with a reddish-brown head, neck and chest, and is slightly smaller than the drake, weighing just over 2 lb and measuring about 20 in; the drake weighs over 3 lb and measures nearly 22 in. The drake resumes full winter plumage in November, after the eclipse summer moult. The canvasback is largely vegetarian, but about one fifth of what it eats may consist of fish, crustacea etc. It experiences some difficulty in taking off from water, and has to skip along the surface for some way before becoming airborne. Once in flight, however, it is extremely fast and, during the migrations, will fly in large V-shaped formations.

There are normally more males than females, and courtship consists of a vigorous pursuit of a single duck by two or more drakes indulging in various forms of display, all of which may last for several days before the duck finally chooses a mate. The nest is built in shallow water among reeds and sedges which anchor it. The clutch of seven to nine eggs takes 24 to 28 days to incubate. The young drakes resemble the duck in plumage until late autumn, when differentiation begins.

Capercailzie *(Tetrao urogallus)*

Also called capercaillie or more familiarly capper, the 'Cock of the Woods', is the largest game bird of the grouse family. It is found throughout most of Scandinavia, a large part of Europe, especially central Europe even as far as Siberia and the north of Spain, also in Scotland, where it was supposed extinct in the early nineteenth century and was re-introduced by Lord Breadalbane and Sir Thomas Fowell Buxton in 1837 and is now quite common. It is strictly a bird of the pine woods, although often found on the edges of forests and moors. Its chief food is the shoots and buds of conifers, although like black grouse *(q.v.)*, it is almost omnivorous, eating blaeberries, corn, bracken, insects etc. The cock is a large bird of about 34 in from beak to tail, weighing up to 12 lb. The hen averages about 24 in and weighs from 7 to 8 lb. The cock is greeny-black on the breast with an olive-brown back and has a prominent patch of white where the wings join the body. With a powerful beak and scarlet eye wattle he is quite unmistakable when full grown, but when young may be mistaken for a cock pheasant except for the square tail. The hen is similar to the red grouse and greyhen, but larger, with rounded tail and rufous red patch on the chest. A notable feature is its silence both in flight and at rest. Only during the mating season does the cock give a call rather like the sound of a cork being pulled. Despite its size it can gain speed and height with deceptive ease. They are polygamous and the cock will court his hens with a solitary display similar to that of the black cock; in certain countries it is sometimes stalked and shot during this mating period. The hen will sometimes move a considerable distance away to nest on her own, usually in a scrape in the forest undergrowth. The number of eggs may vary from 5 to 10, generally laid in early May with an incubation period of from 26 to 29 days. Hybrid crosses with pheasant and blackgame are not uncommon due to their similar polygamous habits.

When shooting them it is as well to

remember that the bird may burst out of cover very noisily with a clatter of wings and breaking twigs, or alternatively may take wing quite silently from a bare branch. A form of still-hunting is the only way for a single gun to hope to shoot them in thick woods. Alternate fast wing beats and glides can prove deceptive in flight as it is generally travelling a good deal faster than it appears and a quick swing-through is required. Number 4 or heavier shot is desirable in a shotgun. In Britain it is generally shot by driving with beaters pushing the birds out of the woods over the waiting guns posted at strategic flight points, within gunshot of each other. In Scandinavia it is generally stalked or still-hunted, frequently with a light rifle. The spitz is used to find the birds and bay them sometimes, his barking bringing the hunter to the scene. In parts of Europe they are stalked in spring during the mating season when the sound of the cock's mating song can be heard and will attract the hunter to the mating area. An approach can only be made when he is actually calling, for at this point his head is back and he is no longer alert. The moment he stops the approaching hunter has to freeze and can only advance again when the cock starts to call once more. Those who have done this claim that it is an exciting sport, but other opinions are that no bird should be shot when mating or during the spring. Due to the very strong turpentiney taste of an old bird's flesh, acquired from its diet of conifers, it is almost uneatable; the flesh of the young birds, on the other hand, is very good. They are, therefore, best shot in the early part of the season when the hens and young birds can often be shot over pointers and provide good sport. As a driven bird, however, they probably furnish the most sporting shooting. *See also* Grouse.

Capybara *(Hydrochoerus hydrochoeris)*
The carpincho, as it is also known, is the largest living rodent and is found in South America. It looks like an enormous guinea pig, standing about the height of a sheep, measuring about 4 ft in length and 21 in at the shoulder and weighing about 100 lb when adult. Covered with short coarse light brown bristly hair and found singly or in herds on the river banks, it is a water-loving herbivore which lives on the lush riverside grasses and aquatic vegetation. The usual method of hunting them is to beat the river bank with hounds and drive them into the water where they are shot from boats. If hit the body sinks, but after a while rises to the surface. The hide is valuable and the fat is said to be good for rheumatism. *See also, South America, Shooting in.*

Caribou *(Rangifer tarandus)*
This is a deer of the American Arctic, regarded by some zoologists as the same

A bull barren ground caribou shedding velvet from its antlers

species as the reindeer of Lapland and Siberia. There are several recognized subspecies, the most important are the barren ground caribou *(R. tarandus arcticus)*, woodland caribou *(R. tarandus caribou)* and mountain caribou *(R. tarandus montanus)*.

Of these the barren ground caribou are the smallest but by far the most numerous. They are distributed in a circumpolar pattern from Alaska to Labrador and Newfoundland, and there are probably still half a million of them in Alaska alone. The Eskimo and Indian economy in the circumpolar regions is largely a caribou economy, depending on the hunting of the barren ground caribou during their migration south to the forest line. At the turn of the century, in an attempt to bolster this economy, reindeer were introduced from Siberia, but a reindeer culture was never established, such as there is in Lapland. Reindeer, however, may have hybridized with the barren ground caribou.

The woodland caribou were once common in the forests of many of the northern states of the United States, and especially in Maine and New Hampshire. As virgin forests were felled, however, open, secondary forest growths more suitable for whitetailed deer than for caribou developed, and there are probably no more than 100 woodland caribou left in the United States outside Alaska, though they are still found in many parts of Canada. The mountain caribou, which is the largest of them all, is also the scarcest, and is now only found in the Rocky Mountain and Selkirk Range areas of British Columbia and Alberta.

The main differences between these subspecies are those of size and range. They are all polygamous, the bull collecting a harem of up to twenty cows. The rut is in September, though it may start as early as July in Alaska, and the young are usually dropped in June, and are able to follow the herd within a few hours. They are all extremely gregarious, feeding and migrating in large herds. They are the only deer to have the females as well as the males antlered. The cows carry a rather smaller rack then the bulls and shed them, as do the young bulls, in May. The old bulls, however, shed their antlers in late autumn. The antlers are semi-palmate, the palmation varying with the species. The main beam is normally flattened, and bends backwards and then forwards and upwards, ending in a palm with small tines. The brow tine forms a massive 'shovel' projecting out over the face. The general body-colour is brown, with seasonal variations, with white on the belly, neck and muzzle. The coat is hairy, each hair being hollow, which makes the animal buoyant when swimming. The hoof is especially wide, with hollow centre, and it spreads easily, so giving support in swampy ground and snow.

In summer the caribou grazes on grasses and plants, but in winter it is dependent on browsing on the lichens it travels widely to find. The barren ground caribou is migratory, moving south from the arctic tundra towards the northern forests. It is at this time that the Eskimos hunt it. Being a herd animal it has little caution and the herd will continue to move steadily on while animals are shot in the middle of it. There is, of course, little sport involved in this, and the shooting is largely restricted to the Eskimos whose existence depends on it.

The mountain caribou is both less gregarious and less migratory, moving down from the higher forests to the lower ones in winter in small groups of a dozen or so, rather than in herds of thousands.

Caribou hunting must always be difficult if only because of the inaccessibility of the terrain. The barren ground caribou does not offer any sport. Both forest and mountain caribou, where they may be shot, need to be stalked, and this will involve flying to an outfitter's camp and setting out, from there, with packhorse or boat, and guides. The caribou's powers of scent are keen, and the stalk will often prove difficult. *See also* Deer of the World and their Hunting.

Carpincho *see* Capybara; South America, Shooting in

Catamount *see* Cougar

Cats *(Felidae)*

Wild cats vary in size from that of the domestic cat to the tiger or lion and are found throughout the world except in Australasia. Generally nocturnal carnivores and polygamous, they are mostly holding their own with such notable exceptions as the cheetah, the tiger and the Asiatic lion, the last having been reduced to a small group, strictly protected. The

The chamois, although a European animal, has been introduced to the South Island of New Zealand, where this picture was taken.

Cats
Bobcat*
Cougar*
(catamount, mountain lion, painter)
Jaguar*
Jaguarondi
Leopard*
Lion, African*
Lynx
Ocelot (ring-tailed cat)
Puma
Serval
Snow Leopard (ounce)

---

larger cats are capable of attacking and killing man, and man-eating leopards are still quite common in India. Hunting the larger cats by stalking, still-hunting, driving or baiting can prove a hazardous business even when armed with a high-powered large-calibre rifle. Some of the smaller cats can, of course, be easily killed with a shotgun in suitable conditions. Some, such as the cougar, are still occasionally hunted with hounds. In most cases the skin provides a good trophy, but the meat is not edible.

Cavy *see* Paca

Chamois *(Rudicapra rupicapra)*
This largely European 'antelope' is found in the Pyrenees, the French, Italian and Jugoslavian Alps, the Jura, the Tatra and Carpathian Mountains, the highlands of south-east Europe and south-west Asia. They have also been introduced, with great success, in the South Island of New Zealand. They are generally found between the 5,000 and 8,000 foot levels, descending lower in winter, to below the treeline.

They are moderately sized, deep-chested beasts with sturdy limbs, admirably built for alpine life. A full grown male may weigh 100, or even 120 lb; the female will generally weigh about 20 lb less. Both sexes are horned, the male's horns being thicker, wider apart, and curving backwards more strongly. Females, however, can provide good trophy heads, and one was recently shot in New Zealand with 12-in horns. Behind the horns lie the two scent glands, which are particularly active during the rut, when a heavy, musk-like smell is given off. They show two coats – a reddish, smooth summer coat, and a thick, long-haired, black winter one.

They are, primarily, browsers, and eat leaves, twigs, bark, and ivy when in the forest. During the summer, however, when on the upper slopes, they graze the alpine grasses and weeds. They are generally to be found in small family groups, the young of the last two seasons accompanying the dams. The males are sexually mature at three years, the females at about 19 months. They breed polygamously, the rut starting in November. Gestation takes between 160 and 170 days, the young, generally singles, but occasionally twins, being dropped in June. Before parturition the dam leaves the herd and finds a sheltered hiding place in which to give birth. The young chamois can stand and even walk before its coat is dry, and begins to graze at about 10 days. Average life expectancy in the wild is about 10 years. Besides their quasi-migrations to the lower slopes the chamois range very widely during the summer, shifting from pasture to pasture.

They are probably the most agile of all mountain game, and hunting them requires fitness and climbing skill to a far greater degree than stalking red deer. With keen powers of sight and scent, and inhabiting a terrain in which approach will always be difficult, stalking success depends more than usual on observation, not merely in order to pick a beast, but to establish the herd movements and routes, for they are very much creatures of habit. They have, unusually, the habit of always running away into wind, instead of running away from the direction from which scent came. This sometimes allows the hunter who has been winded still to come within range of the beasts, especially if he can place himself directly into the wind. Chamois need to be shot with a flat trajectory, high-velocity rifle, preferably equipped with telescopic sights. Since a great deal of climbing will be involved, the weight of the weapon must also be a consideration.

Chamoix were once hunted, commercially, for 'shammy' leathers, but these are now produced from domestic sheep and goats, and chamoix are now hunted almost solely as trophy animals.

Cheetal or **Cheetul** see Chital

Chile

Chile is a long narrow country running down the southern end of the coast of South America, with a total area of about 290,000 square miles, including the very numerous islands off the coast. Almost the entire mainland lies on the western slopes of the Andes and faces the Pacific Ocean. The country can be divided into three strips: the mountainous Andean area in the east, mostly between 5,000 and 15,000 ft, generally lower towards the south; the coastal chain of mountains; the central valley or tableland between the mountains. Rivers are short and unimportant, but there are several lakes in the south. The climate varies widely with the latitude as well as the altitude. The north is rainless desert. The south is cold, wet and heavily forested. Between them the centre has a Mediterranean-type climate.

Agriculture is not particularly important; the chief crops are cereals, vegetables and European fruit and vines. Forestry also is limited, because of high production costs. For game see South America, Shooting in.

Further Information

Consult initially the nearest Chilean conulate. Those wishing to import firearms should write to the Ministry of Defence, Santiago, with details of firearms, the game to be shot, and the length of stay.

Chinkara see Mongolian Gazelle

Chital (*Axis axis*)

Sometimes spelled Cheetal or Cheetul, this animal is perhaps better known as the spotted deer of India or axis deer and is found throughout southern Asia, as well as being now established in Australia. It prefers more or less open jungle which provides them with good grazing and water, and so is particularly numerous in the sub-Himalayan tract, especially in the Terai-Bhabar area. It is common where deep shade, long grass and water are readily available. Although generally found in small herds of 7 to 8 animals, considerable gatherings of several hundred beasts are sometimes seen in June in the Terai forests. They greatly resemble the European fallow dear, being similar in coloration, a light fawn with considerable spotted marking on back and sides, but they are slightly smaller, being only about 32 in at the shoulder and weighing around 200 lb. The essential difference, however, is in the antlers, which are not palmated. The stag has three distinct points on each curved antler, often with one or two short snags above each brow antler. The average length is about 30 in with a beam of about $3\frac{1}{2}$ inches. The span may vary from around 20 to 24 in. The chital is not as nocturnal in its habits as the sambar and is found in the early part of the day and in the evening in its favourite areas. They are companionable animals and interbreed with hog deer so that occasionally one of the latter may be found in their company. They may also be found grazing with domestic cattle in the forests, eating fruit and leaves dropped by monkeys. In such circumstances and where there is fair cover it is not difficult to stalk them. Sometimes the hunter will hear the clash of rival stags' horns as they fight and will be able to approach unheeded by the combatants. The only sporting method of hunting them is by still-hunting. They should not be driven as in these circumstances they stand virtually no chance of escaping the gun. The venison is good eating and the skin and antlers make a good trophy. *See also* Deer of the World and their Hunting.

Chousingha *see* Four-horned Antelope

Chukar Partridge *(Alectoris graeca chukar)*

This is a red-legged partridge, originally from the foothills of the Himalayas, that has now been successfully introduced into the United States, and more especially into the drier, prairie and mountain areas west of the Mississippi. It is very similar to the French partridge *(Alectoris rufa)* and the Bartavelle *(Alectoris graeca saxatilis)* of Europe and the Mediterranean basin. Indeed both the Bartavelle and the French partridge are being introduced as further exotics into America, while the French have introduced the chukar into France, not from its original Nepal, but from the United States.

The chukar does best in the fairly open, hilly country and semi-arid conditions that best reproduce the prevailing factors of its original habitat. Its food consists largely of green stuff, and grass and weed seeds, though the chicks need insects early in life. In winter the coveys may need to come down to farmlands and feed off spilt corn and in pastures. Normally they concentrate around water holes but, after the rains, they disperse. The bird is an extremely strong runner and flies as well as the bobwhite quail, but for longer distances. It has not done well in the humid condition of the eastern seaboard, but has flourished in the western Great Plains and in the Rocky Mountain and Cascades areas.

The chukar is a plump, small bird, only 13 to 15 in long; a cock weighs 1½ lb and a hen 1 lb. Apart from weight, and a blunt spur found in the cock but missing in the hen, it is difficult to tell the sexes apart. The birds roost and nest on the ground. Pairing takes place early in March with nesting in April and May. The clutch of 10 to 15 eggs takes 23 days to incubate, and the coveys will remain together until the following spring.

Although they tend to run on in front of the guns, chukar will lie well to pointers, and so they are best shot over them in the same way as quail. It will be found, however, that, when the covey is first split up, the individual birds will fly on for much longer distances than the bobwhite quail would. *See also* Red-legged Partridge.

Collared Peccary *(Tayassu tajacu)*

The collared peccary, or javelina as it is more commonly called, is a vaguely pig-like animal peculiar to the Western Hemisphere. It is found throughout South America, and the northern limits of its range include the

Introduced into California from India in 1928, the chukar partridge is a popular upland game bird there, and in other American states (top).

The collared peccary is found in the south-western states of North America as well as in parts of Central and South America.

south-western states of the United States, most notably Texas, Arizona and New Mexico. In the more southerly parts of its range there is another species of peccary, the white-lipped *(Tayassu albirostris)*, but only the collared is found in the United States. Peccaries are distinguished from members of the *Suidae* (Old World pigs) by the fact they never produce more than two in a litter, the upper tusk turns downwards, and the hind foot has only three toes.

There was a time when javelina were badly over-shot by market hunters for their hides, which make the best of all pigskin, but now protected by the game laws of the various states, their numbers are recovering. It is estimated that there are now nearly 150,000 in the three North American states in which they principally survive. Peccaries are extremely adaptable, flourishing in such different habitats as the rain forests of Central America, the coastal swamps of Texas, the deserts of Arizona and the mountains of northern Mexico. They may be found in mountains, up to about 6,000 ft, but lower, warmer terrain is their preferred habitat. They are gregarious, and run in herds of a dozen or more, generally led by an old boar.

They are, like most pigs, omnivorous, and will eat anything from berries, roots and nuts to toads, snakes, earthworms and even carrion. Like wild boar they root up the ground where they feed. In appearance they look like small, very lean pigs, with little difference in size between the sexes. The average weight lies between 50 and 70 lb; they stand about 2 ft high and measure about 3 ft overall. The coat, black at a distance, is a dark gray, with a pepper and salt effect produced by the lighter banding on the hairs. The collar is a narrow, lighter band running across the shoulders and down each side of the neck, rather as though it were the start of a saddle in a saddle-backed pig. The tail is vestigial, and the large musk gland that gives the animal its characteristically rank smell lies on the back, between the hips. The long snout covers the tusks, two on each side, which are razor sharp and between 1½ and 2 in long.

It is customary to hunt javelina with a pack of dogs. Though fast over a short distance, it has little endurance and will soon turn at bay. This is when the need arises for the dogs to be well trained, content to ring the animal until the hunter comes to kill it. If they rush in, or if the hunter only wounds it, the dogs may well be severely damaged. A neck or head shot is recommended. A more sporting method, perhaps, is to stalk a herd. This has to be done upwind, not only because otherwise the herd will catch the scent and disappear, but also because the hunter, in his turn, will be able to scent the herd before he can see it. There are not many animals that man can hunt by smell, but this is one of them.

Seasons—Colorado

Colorado operates an elaborate system of varying seasons and bag limits for deer, designed to encourage hunting in over-stocked regions, and giving a choice between antlered- and non-antlered deer. The whitetail season runs from about 18 Oct to 28 Oct, and the mule deer season from about 17 Oct to 6 Nov.
The season for bear coincides with that for deer and the hunter may take one on his deer or elk licence. The elk licence has to be drawn for.
Antelope are shot from about 26 Sept to 28 Sept with special drawing for permits.
Bighorn sheep are shot from 15 Aug to 7 Sept after special drawing by residents only.
Lion are shot from 1 Sept to 31 Dec; limit one of either sex.
Cottontail and snowshoe rabbit are shot from 1 Oct to 28 Feb.
The season for all grouse starts about 12 Sept, as does the season for chukar partridge and ptarmigan.
The season for Gambel's quail starts about 12 Nov and for bobwhite and scaled quails about 21 Nov.
Closing dates are usually announced well in advance of the season, but may be postponed if surveys have not been completed.

Colorado (U.S.A.)

A Rocky Mountain state, it covers 105,000 square miles, and the Rockies run through it from north to south. The climate is dry, with extremes of heat in summer and of cold in winter. Of its 66 million acres, 26 million are dry grazing, 20 million are forest, and over 3 million are irrigated farmland. The chief crops are cereals, lucerne (alfalfa) and vegetables.

The state is unusually rich in both big and small game. Big game includes whitetail and mule deer, antelope, elk, black bear, bighorn, mountain lion and wild turkey. There is some of the best pheasant shooting in America in the agricultural areas of the north-east, and other game birds include sharp-tailed, sage and blue grouse; ptarmigan; bobwhite, Gambel's and scaled quail; and chukar. Cottontail and jack rabbits are abundant.

Special Regulations
A licensed guide is recommended for non-resident big-game hunters, but is not obligatory. No big game may be hunted with a rifle firing a bullet of less than 70 gr or with a rated energy of less than 1,000 foot-pounds at 100 yards.

Further Information
Game, Fish and Parks Department, 6060 North Broadway, Denver, Colorado 80216.

Colombia

Colombia lies in the north-west corner of South America, covering about 440,000 square miles. The country is traversed from north to south by three great ranges of the Andes, the Western, Central and Eastern Cordilleras. East of the Andes the terrain is predominantly heavily wooded plains, or jungle, watered by the Amazon and Orinoco river systems. There is one important, completely Colombian river, the Magdalena, which flows into the Caribbean. Though a tropical country, the climate varies considerably with the altitude.

Agriculture is still very important. Coffee and bananas are notable exports, and cotton, rice, tobacco and sugar are also grown on a large scale. The extensive forests have much valuable wood, which is only now being developed.

For game *see* South America, Shooting in

Further Information
Consult initially the nearest Colombian consulate.

Connecticut (U.S.A.)

One of the smaller New England states, covering 5,000 square miles. The west and north are moderately hilly and the best farmland lies in the south. Dairy farming, tobacco and fruit growing are the most important forms of agriculture. The climate tends to extremes of hot and cold. There are some 2 million acres of forest land.

The state is too thickly settled and too heavily industrialized to have a large big-game population. There are some white-tailed deer, but no bears except those that stray in from other states. Most of the land is posted, but the state maintains several regulated shooting areas open, by permit, to the public. There is also a hunter-land-owner co-operative system operating over 200,000 acres of game land. Both the Department and the co-operatives release pheasants every year, and ruffed grouse are found in some woodlands, but most of the state-owned coastal land is managed for waterfowl, which provide what is possibly the best shooting of all in the state.

Special Regulations
No rifle may be carried that uses ammunition heavier than .22 long rifle.

Further Information
State Board of Fisheries and Game, State Office Building, Hartford, Connecticut 06115.

Coot *see* Waders; American coot

Corncrake *see* Waders

Cottontail and other American Rabbits
(Sylvilagus species)
The true rabbit, *Oryctolagus cuniculus cuniculus*, was never imported into America, whose indigenous rabbits are members of the genus *Sylvilagus*. These differ from the European rabbit in being solitary and in nesting above, rather than below, ground. They differ from hares in having shorter ears and hind legs, and young that are born blind and naked.

Cottontails (*Sylvilagus floridanus*) are found over the whole of the United States, though their numbers fluctuate, not in a regular cycle, as with grouse or snowshoe rabbit, but unpredictably, in response, probably, to the effects of the disease known as tularemia. They are, primarily, animals of farmland, feeding on short grasses, clover and shrubs, though in winter they will be driven to eating bark and twigs of the smaller bushes.

The sexes look alike, with brown coats and white bellies and scuts. Size depends largely on food supplies, but the average cottontail will weigh between 2 and 3 lb and measure about 13 in. They breed for most of the year in the warmer states, and throughout the summer elsewhere, producing several litters with an average of four per litter. The young are born above ground in a depression scraped out of the earth and lined with the doe's fur. After a few days the blind and naked litter is able to see and follows the doe. The brush rabbit (*Sylvilagus bachmani*) lacks a white scut and is smaller and darker. It avoids open country and lives in thick brush. The marsh rabbit (*Sylvilagus palustris*) is similar to the

Seasons and Limits—Connecticut

Species	Season	Limit
Deer	On private land by permit signed by owner	1 per permit ; 2 per season
Cottontail rabbit	17 Oct-Jan	3 per day ; 25 per season
Gray Squirrel	17 Oct-Jan	8 per day ; 40 per season
Pheasant	17 Oct-Jan	2 per day ; 10 per season
Ruffed grouse	17 Oct-Jan	2 per day ; 10 per season
Bobwhite quail	17 Oct-Jan	2 per day ; 10 per season
Snowshoe hare	May be shot between about 20 Nov-10 Jan	

cottontail, also lacks the white scut and is smaller and darker. It is, perhaps, the only rabbit to live alongside water, for it inhabits the swamp areas of south-eastern United States. The hind feet are webbed and it is an excellent swimmer.

Rabbits are normally shot with a shotgun, usually over dogs, though they may also be walked up by two or more hunters without dogs. The best dogs to use are beagles, bassets, cockers or dachshunds, since all are possessed of good noses and able to follow fairly cold scent, but none are fast enough to push the rabbit so close and fast that shooting would be impossible.

Cougar (Felis concolor)

The cougar has several popular names, including mountain lion, panther, puma, painter and catamount. At one time its range extended from British Columbia to the Straits of Magellan, but now it is only found in small, isolated pockets across the North American continent, mainly west of the Rockies, and in southern South America.

A carnivore, fourth biggest of all the cats, and second only to the jaguar among American cats, its principal prey is deer, but it is also liable to attack farm stock, and most especially young colts. It is, however, extremely reluctant to attack man.

A big male cougar may reach a maximum weight of 200 lb, though the average weight is nearer 140 lb. Overall length may be between 8 and 9 ft, of which one-third will be tail. Colour can vary from gray to almost red, and there is a Florida sub-species that is chocolate-brown. There is no mating season, and the cubs may be born at any time of the year. The litter usually consists of two or three, and the cubs are spotted, losing these markings with age. They are, very largely, nocturnal as well as being partially arboreal.

The only successful way to hunt them is with a pack of cougar hounds. These need to be highly specialized hounds, able to work from a cold scent and to ignore all other scent; there are few such packs, all of them belonging to professional guides. The cougar is extremely fast over about 100 yd, but has no stamina, and is fairly quickly treed. It can then be shot out of the tree, and, since this will be from close range, a rifle of no larger calibre than a .30-30 will suffice. This animal can even be shot with a hand gun.

Coyote (Canis latrans)

The coyote is a small wolf-like wild dog found all over the western half of North America from Alaska to Mexico. Although it occasionally attacks and kills poultry,

The cougar is a great hunter and needs to kill, on average, one deer a week.

sheep and calves as well as game birds and small game it plays a useful role in controlling destructive mice, gophers and jack rabbits. It has been attacked as vermin with poison, traps and gun for well over a century, but still maintains a fairly stable population, and the only effect of all the attempts to destroy it seems to have been to disperse it more widely over areas not previously colonized.

A carnivore with a wide range of appetite, it will eat carrion, insects, birds, rodents, reptiles, farm stock, and as a member of a pack, it is capable of pulling down a deer trapped in heavy snow. It sometimes hybridizes with domestic dogs to produce the 'coydog', a predator of formidable size and cunning.

It is, in appearance, not unlike a small German sheep dog, but its ears are permanently pricked, the face is fox-like, and the brush is long and heavy. The coat is gray with light tan underparts, but it becomes lighter in winter. Weight, for an adult male, may be as much as 35 lb, and length is around 4 ft including the brush. Mating is normally in January and February, and gestation takes about nine weeks. The litter, which will average around seven, will be born in a den similar to that of the wolf.

Coyotes are primarily hunted not for sport but as vermin, and for their pelts and the bounty attached to them. They are often shot when hunting for other game, but some hunters set out specially to hunt them. They generally do this in winter, using either a motor-car or a horse to bring them up with such a fast moving quarry. They can be coursed, but only with something as fast moving as a greyhound. To shoot them a very accurate, high velocity rifle with telescopic sights is recommended.

Crakes *see* Waders

Crocodiles were once pests in the north of Australia but they are now partly protected. A large specimen is shown below, and, at the foot of the page, a professional crocodile hunter with an aborigine ready to thrust a harpoon into the reptile as soon as it is shot, to prevent the body from sinking.

Cranes (*Gruidae*)

There are fourteen different species of cranes in the world, all of them in some danger of disappearing. They have, since the days of Ancient Egypt at least, been steadily hunted by man with arrows, nets, guns and hawks. Since they are birds of very low reproductive powers they have failed to resist hunting pressures, and now are either protected completely or else hunted under strict limitations.

They are found everywhere except in South America, Malaysia, the Pacific Islands and New Zealand. They are all gregarious, and usually migratory, flying in V-formations at great heights for long distances. Principally vegetarians, they will also eat insects, rodents, and other small mammals and occasionally fish. Following a courtship involving elaborate dances, they nest on the ground, and the clutch seldom exceeds two. They are among the most long-lived of birds. Species include the common and demoiselle cranes that breed in Europe and winter in Africa, the crowned and wattled cranes of Africa, the white-naped cranes and the sarus crane of Asia, and the very few survivors of the Japanese crane, now only found in Hokkaido, and the whooping crane, which has dwindled to 43 birds outside captivity, that breed in Wood Buffalo Park in Canada and winter in the Aransas Refuge in Texas.

One species is still legally hunted in North America – the sandhill crane (*Grus canadensis*). There are five sub-species of this, of which by far the most numerous is the lesser sandhill (*G. canadensis canadensis*), which breeds in the tundras of northern America, from the Aleutians to the Northwest Territory, and winters in the southern tier of American states from California to Texas. It is still shot for 12 days in Saskatchewan and for 14 days in

The common crane of Europe

Czechoslovakia is famed for its red deer (right), especially in the Carpathian Mountains.

Manitoba, although in each case only inside the province's Crane Management Area, and shooting has to stop immediately if whooping crane are reported anywhere in the province, to prevent the possibility of mistake. They are also shot in New Mexico, Texas and Colorado.

Crocodiles and Alligators (*Crocodilia*)
These reptiles are found in parts of North America, notably the Everglades of Florida, also throughout South America, Africa and Asia, as well as in the Northern Territory of Australia. Due to unrestricted commercial trapping and hunting they are now becoming scarce in most areas and in general they are either protected or only shot under strict controls. The Nile crocodile, *Crocodilus niloticus*, may be shot in Ethiopia and other parts of Africa. The spectacled caiman, *Caiman crocodilus*, may be shot almost everywhere in South America. The marine crocodile in the Northern Territory of Australia is partly protected and may only be shot under licence. None of these are likely to be much over 12 ft in length and, indeed, the spectacled caiman only attains a length of 8 ft.

Shooting them between the eyes is comparatively simple. Using a torch at night from a steady boat is one method very commonly practised. From a rocking canoe it might be more hazardous and more difficult, but in general none of the crocodilia can be regarded as providing very rewarding sport. The trophy is, of course, the skin.

Curlews *see* Waders

Cushat *see* Woodpigeon

Czechoslovakia
Czechoslovakia lies in the centre of Europe, covering an area of 49,700 square miles. The country is divided vertically by the valley of the River Morava. The area to the west (Bohemia), in which lies Prague, is heavily populated and comparatively flat, except along the borders where the terrain is more hilly. The eastern region (Slovakia) is sparsely populated, comparatively backward, and much more mountainous – the western arm of the Carpathian range runs along the centre of the country, rising to over 8,300 ft. The eastern region also has a much more continental climate.

Agriculture is highly developed in the country, with several dependent industries, and some regions are among the most heavily afforested parts of Europe.

Because of its abundant game Czechoslovakia has been renowned for hunting since the early Middle Ages, and the construction of large ponds in southern Bohemia has resulted in a bird-life unusually varied and prolific for such an inland country. A policy of careful game preservation applied throughout the country ensures that Czechoslovakia maintains its ancient reputation and can still provide some of the best sport in Europe.

Seasons
All seasons tend to vary annually. They have, therefore, only been specified to the nearest half-month (inclusive) in the table, which should be treated as a rough guide.

Hunts for most big-game are organized individually, with the hunter allotted his choice of shooting ground, unless it has already been reserved. The only big-game that are normally driven or shot by groups of hunters are wolf and wild boar. The latter, together with bear, is also commonly shot from a stand, while other big-game, though it can be shot this way, is usually stalked. Red deer and roe may be called, and bustard, capercailzie and blackgame

Seasons—Czechoslovakia

Species	Season	Annual Bag	Trophy Fee
Roe deer	Mid-May to Sept	Approx 75,000	$15 upwards
Carpathian (red) deer	Aug-Dec, longer in game preserves. Best: mid-Sept to mid-Oct	Approx 15,000	$85 upwards
Fallow deer	Oct-Dec, longer in game preserves	Approx 1,500	$50 upwards
European mouflon	Oct-Dec, longer in game preserves	Approx 1,000	$90 upwards
Bezoar goat	Oct-Dec only in Southern Moravia. Special authorization		
Chamois	Oct and Nov. Only in 3 preserves. Special authorization		
Wild pig	Boar: all year Sow: Aug-Dec	Up to 10,000	$70 upwards
Bear	All year. Best: Feb-April and Oct-Nov. Old or dangerous animals only to be shot. Special authorization	Approx 10	$1,000 upwards
Lynx	All year	Approx 100	
Wolf	All year. Best during snow	Approx 50	
Wild cat	Oct-Feb	Approx 1,200	
Capercailzie	Mid-March to mid-May. Cocks only	Approx 1,000	$75 per bird
Blackgame	Mid-March to mid-May. Cocks only	Approx 5,000	$40 per bird
Bustard	April to mid-May Cocks only. Special authorization		$160 per bird
Fox	All year		
Hazel grouse	Mid-Aug to mid-Oct. Cocks only		
Hare	Mid-Oct to Dec	Approx 1,000,000	
Partridge (gray)	Mid-Aug to Sept	Approx 500,000	
Pheasant	Mid-Oct to Dec. Best Nov and Dec	Up to 700,000	
Rabbit	All year. Shooting prohibited in some areas	Approx 30,000	
Snipe	Oct-Dec	Approx 10,000	
Duck	Aug-Nov	Up to 120,000	
Geese	Oct-Nov	Approx 2,000	
Woodcock	Shot when flighting in the spring and in the autumn during driven shoots for other game		

ing up, driving, or for various types of battue, though partridges and snipe are usually only shot walking up. Hunters are recommended to make up their own groups for this sort of shooting. For those unable to do so, 'collective' hunts are organized in which hunters are registered in the order their applications for individual places are received.

Special hunting areas, as distinct from game preserves, are run by both the state and independent hunting societies. In all of these the same rules for seasons, etc, apply, with exceptions such as rabbit, noted above.

Fees

All shooting trips are ultimately arranged through the Czechoslovakian Travel Bureau, 'Cedok', though any travel agency may be used as an intermediary. Orders for hunting trips should be made well in advance, in particular for those wishing to shoot fallow deer, chamois, moufflon, wild boar, blackgame, capercailzie and wild geese. The shooting fees for the various types of game are detailed in a price list available from 'Cedok', who will confirm all arrangements for hunting trips. No agreement is binding, however, until 'Cedok' have received a deposit, which must amount to at least 50% of the fee stipulated in the price list. If the fee is dependent on the trophy, the deposit is based on the fee for one of average quality, which, for example, would be about $200 for fallow deer or mouflon, $300 for red deer, and about $50 for roe. The balance is payable immediately after the conclusion of the hunt. Because of the varying circumstances that can affect the hunting of hoofed animals, the fee is paid only if the animal is actually killed. Otherwise the hunter has only to pay the expenses, which are about 30 Korunas per day. The costs of driven shooting for small game are based on a fee per head of game shot that varies with the total bag. There is a picking-up fee of between 10% and 20% of the total bag. Hunting fees include guide, drivers, porters for the game, transport of the game, and a simple preparation of the trophy.

Licences

Entry permits must be obtained, along with the visa, for all rifles, shotguns, telescopes and ammunition (two guns are recommended for those shooting extensive bags of small game). Ammunition is easily obtainable, and other equipment may be hired if necessary. Shooting licences and third-party insurance (compulsory) may be obtained for a fee of $15 per month, or $35 per year.

Further Information

'Cedok' offices throughout Europe and in New York, or from 'Cedok', Hunting Branch, Prague 1, Na prikope 18.

are all shot by calling or stalking, or a combination of the two.

While ducks and geese may be shot by individuals, on the Danube, in southern Slovakia only, small game is generally shot by groups of 10 or 15 (even 20 for hare in Slovakia). Dogs, and as many as several hundred beaters, are used, either for walk-

D

Decoys *see* Hides and Decoys

Deer *(Cervidae)*

Deer may vary in size from the giant moose to the tiny muntjac or barking deer of Asia and are now spread throughout the world except for Africa. Principally browsers rather than grazers they are antlered, not horned. Some species are closely bound up with primitive economies and some can be domesticated, viz the reindeer, the only species to have antlers in both sexes. While rightly regarded as worthwhile sporting game in most regions, in others, even though an introduced species, as in New Zealand, they are regarded as pests. The flesh is generally edible and the hide and antlers are regarded as good trophies. They may be shot by stalking, still-hunting, or from high seats. In some areas they are still hunted with hounds, either followed on foot or on horseback. *See also* Deer of the World and their Hunting.

Deer of the World and their Hunting

There are some forty different species of deer which the zoologists have divided into over 190 sub-species. Generally speaking, the sportsman – as distinct from the professional hunter who is probably killing for gain – is only interested in game animals that carry some trophy – the bigger and more spectacular the better, for there is, and always has been, the challenge to obtain a 'record' trophy. From a trophy point of view, therefore, a number of species have no great appeal, and these include the muntjacs and tufted deer of Asia, and the pudu and brockets of South America, all of which have insignificant antlers of but a few inches in length, the last three mentioned having no branching tines whatsoever to the single spikes. To this list should be added the Chinese water-deer and musk deer – the sole representatives of the living *Cervidae* in which neither sex develop any antlers. Instead, the males of each species, as also the tiny muntjac, are furnished with long upper canines which are used as weapons of aggression. The possession of these tusks, however, does not seem to arouse the same interest in sportsmen as does a good pair of canine tusks from a red deer stag, which are much valued by European sportsmen for conversion into brooches, cuff links etc.

The musk deer, however, has a commercial value as a producer of musk, a strong smelling perfume which is contained in a bag situated on the belly. Each bag of musk weighs about one ounce and as removed

---

Deer

Black-tailed*
Brocket
Caribou* (reindeer)
Chital* (axis)
Fallow*
Hangul
Hog
Huemul (guemal)
Marsh
Moose*
Mule*
Muntjac (barking)
Musk
Pampas
Pudu
Red*
Roe deer*
Rusa
Sambar*
Shou
Sika*
Timor
Wapiti* (elk)
White-tailed* (Virginian)

The 18-in musk deer, found in Central Asia, unlike most other deer, does not develop antlers but has long canine tusks.

---

from the pouches, is worth about £100 per pound. However, when purified after extraction, their value can be as much as £500 per ounce. Musk deer are taken chiefly by driving them into nets placed across the end of a valley or by snares set up in their trails. Hunting with gun and dog is less productive.

Mention is made elsewhere of the methods normally employed in hunting red deer (*see* Red and Fallow Deer Stalking) on the mountains of Scotland or in the forests of Europe. Further east, in Caucasia and Asia Minor, the European red deer is replaced by the maral, and in the steep forest-clad hillsides, the most successful method is to go out at dawn or dusk during the rut and take up a position overlooking some clearing where the deer can be expected to come out. An imitation roar, which some of the local hunters are most adept in producing with the aid of a horn, will often invite an answering roar from a stag, and so reveal its presence.

In the Far East and North America, the red deer's counterpart is the wapiti (*q.v.*) – which is called elk in America – and here again, the most productive time to shoot a good bull is during the rut either by stalking their rutting call, or spotting them as they feed out of the timber on to an open clearing. With wapiti, as well as with reindeer, caribou, elk and moose, it is usual to refer to the male and female as bull and cow respectively. One of the most thrilling ways of coming to terms with a bull wapiti is by calling or bugling during the rutting season. The wapiti's bugle is a challenge to other bulls in the area, and if the deception is well executed, very spectacular results can be achieved. The successful 'bugler' must know the time of day when the bull is most likely to challenge, the correct weather conditions for bugling, and length and variation in tone. Bamboo is as good as anything to make a bugle, but many other materials have been used.

In North America, when anyone speaks about 'deer' it is assumed that he is referring to white-tailed or mule deer (*q.v.*). Otherwise the particular species is generally referred to by name. The largest of the North American deer – indeed the largest deer in the world – is the Alaskan moose, good specimens of which may stand as high as 78 in at the shoulder, and weigh up to 1,500 lb.

Hunting moose in North America – as indeed other game animals as well – is by permit and whilst some states reserve the greater proportion of permits for resident hunters, a number are always available for non-residents, who the law requires should be accompanied by a guide. If the guide knows his country well, and his game, this will facilitate the bagging of a good trophy.

The usual method of hunting is to get into good moose country and spy from some advantageous position along the timber line edge, especially near water. Once having sighted the animal, and decided that the trophy is worth going after, a conventional stalk is then made.

Another method is calling but it must be done by an expert, imitating the call of the cow, either through the cupped hands, or using a horn made of dry birch bark. Calling should be done from some concealment near water, or from a canoe along lake shores. A clear, calm morning or evening is best for calling, when the sound may carry a mile or more. As with other 'deer calling', it is a waste of time to try it during periods of high wind.

In Europe the moose is referred to as elk, and is well distributed throughout Scandinavia, northern U.S.S.R. and eastwards into Siberia. In Scandinavia the elk enjoys one of the longest closed seasons extended to any deer, and in both Sweden and Norway the official hunting season only lasts about three to ten days during September and October, the actual dates varying from one district to another, the more northerly ones having an earlier one than those in the south. It is the practice, however, for owners of large estates to apply for a special licence that will enable a specified number of elk to be killed which would not be possible during the short season. This special season will be granted after the termination of the official short open season, and this is done to prevent owners of small farms on the perimeter killing animals that are driven out of the large estates during the shooting period.

Three methods of hunting elk are employed in Scandinavia – namely: driving, tracking with hound-on-leash and hunting with loose-hound. Elk driving, particularly on some of the larger estates, requires a considerable amount of organization, but it is the only practicable method that will produce a large cull in a minimum time. As a sport, however, it cannot compare to hunting with hound-on-leash or with the loose-hound, both of which offer not only excitement but can be a real test of physical endurance – particularly the latter. Moreover, hunting with such a highly intelligent animal as the elkhound adds greatly to the enjoyment.

A good loose-hound (lös-hund) will not necessarily make a good leash-hound (bind-hund) but it is certainly more likely to be useful in this role than a leash-hound running loose. Whatever its role, it is essential that the hound must have a good nose, for the hunter relies solely on this to bring him in contact with his quarry. It is essential

A good bull moose shot in British Columbia

that a hound running loose must give tongue only when it has brought the elk to bay. Then it should keep up an incessant barking until such time as either the hunter, attracted by his noise, has arrived on the scene or the elk has moved off, when the whole procedure of running the animal and bringing it to bay again will have to be repeated. A hound-on-leash, however, should always remain silent, even though an elk may be standing in full view only a short distance away.

Hunting with loose-hound can only really be successful in fairly thick cover, otherwise the elk may run completely off your hunting ground before standing at bay. As soon as baying is heard, the hunter must run with all speed to the spot which may be a mile or more away. Should the bay be down wind, a detour will have to be made to avoid the chance of any human scent being carried to the elk. Whatever animal your hound is baying, it is prudent to shoot it so as not to discourage the hound for future hunts. Undoubtedly the best way to obtain a big bull is to work with a leash-hound, for one does not have to shoot every beast that the hound has followed. One can, therefore, be more selective.

The caribou (q.v.), a very close relative of the Old World reindeer, has a wide range in North America, with an overall distribution which includes practically all of northern Canada, most of Alaska and the principal islands off Hudson Bay and the northern Arctic coast line, including western Greenland. Two main types are recognized, the tundra caribou in the more northernly parts, and the woodland caribou in the southern part of its range.

Hunting for sport mostly takes place during September, though animals may be killed by the Indians and Eskimos throughout the winter months of the year for their livelihood.

In good caribou country it is not difficult to make a kill, but to acquire an outstanding trophy requires patience and a good know-

A pack-horse loaded with caribou trophies in British Columbia

ledge of the quarry, for most caribou antlers look, when seen at a distance, better than they really are. A knowledge of shoulder height is a good guide from which to estimate antler length.

Since most caribou hunting is carried out in open country, the game will have to be stalked, with full use being made of what little cover or dead ground is available. However, the caribou is an inquisitive animal, and provided no *direct* approach is made, it is often possible to ride up on horseback to within range of a beast.

In the Old World, the reindeer replaces the caribou, and although the species is well distributed throughout much of northern Europe and Siberia, the only truly wild animals in the west of its range are in Norway, those in Sweden, apart from straying animals, being under the control of Lapp herdsmen.

Reindeer are protected throughout most of the year in Norway, the shooting season lasting for about three weeks in September, during which time hunters will only be permitted to kill the number of deer for which a licence has been granted. Very little stalking or selective shooting is done by the majority of peasant hunters, whose main concern is venison for the winter. Many hunters, therefore, as soon as it is light, make for some favourite pass in the mountains, and there they will wait until sooner or later a herd will pass their way. To avoid a number of animals being wounded if a herd is fired at indiscriminately, it is illegal to use an automatic rifle, and any magazine has to be sealed off officially, by the police prior to the hunt.

Stalking a big bull in the middle of a herd, which may be a thousand strong, can be highly exciting, and if the animals are on the move, it is also extremely arduous. On the other hand, reindeer hunting is a chancy affair, for the herds move and feed continuously into the wind, and should this change, all the animals may leave the district you are hunting, never to return until the season is over.

In hunting mule (*q.v.*) and white-tailed deer (*q.v.*), the best advice is to be out of camp before dawn, and try to reach some ridge or point where as much open country as possible can be viewed at first daylight before the deer have retired to cover where they will remain for most of the day. The same advice goes for the evening, but results are never so rewarding for although just as many deer may be seen from your spy point, the day is rapidly shortening and insufficient time may be available before darkness falls if a lengthy or difficult stalk has to be undertaken to get within range. Moreover, all deer are more nervous when venturing out in the evening, because they expect to find danger, whereas in the morning, well fed, their senses seem less alert. Still-hunting during the morning or late afternoon along a ridge top looking for deer will give better results than keeping to the valley bottoms, but one should hunt upwind and avoid skylining one's self; it is best to proceed along one side or the other, making use of any cover. Go very slowly – in fact one cannot go too slowly when still-hunting deer.

Apart from the hangul and shou which frequent the western and eastern parts of the Himalayas respectively and are now so rare that they should not be considered as a game animal for hunting, the main habitat of most of the other Indo-Malaysian deer is in the forest or plain, which makes hunting difficult during the dry season. Of these, the sambar has a wide distribution, being found in all large forest tracts and upon many hill ranges from well within the Himalayas to the extreme south of India, and eastwards through Burma, Malaya, the Philippines and south China. Sambar may be stalked in the hills or by still-hunting in the plains, as well as by beating patches of cover.

The chital or axis deer is also well distributed in India and Ceylon but is not as common as formerly. In an indigenous state it occurs nowhere else. In some parts of India, particularly in the south, when the grass is not too high, it is possible to catch them out feeding at dawn and dusk by still-hunting open forest glades and likely feeding grounds, but when the height of the grass and undergrowth renders shooting on foot impracticable, they can be shot from elephants.

Hog deer (*q.v.*) is another little deer which owing to its habitat in high grass, is usually shot from elephant. It does not occur in southern India, but is plentiful in the low alluvial grass plains of the Indus and Ganges valleys. Its range also includes Ceylon, Burma and Thailand.

All these last three mentioned species are

characterized by a six-point head. Another typical six-pointer is the rusa deer of Indonesia – a deer which has also been introduced to New Guinea and North Island of New Zealand. It offers similar hunting to sambar.

Both the swamp deer of India and Eld's or brow-antlered deer of India, Burma and Thailand carry rather distinctive antlers which are undoubtedly attractive to the serious trophy hunter, but both deer are rare and on the endangered list, so should not be shot.

In eastern China, Indo-China, Korea, Manchuria, Formosa and on many of the Japanese islands there are a number of different races of sika deer – but although somewhat similar in habit as red deer with which they will inter-breed – are more nocturnal, and can be best stalked at dawn and dusk. This deer has been introduced to many alien countries, including Great Britain, and in some areas are hunted in similar fashion to roe and fallow deer.

The deer of South America, which includes the huemul and pudu of the Andes as well as the marsh deer and pampas deer of the plains, offer a wide variety of hunting country, ranging from the marshy ground of southern Brazil and north-east Argentina, which is the home of the marsh deer, to the high Andes of the western seaboard where the huemul is seldom found below 13,000 ft. The lower Andes is the home of the small spike-antlered pudu, whilst in the low pampas zones of northern Argentina, southern Brazil, Paraguay and southern Bolivia is found the most elegant of all the South American deer – the six-tined pampas deer, which spends most of the day lying up in long grass. Unfortunately this deer is now rare. At one time the 'gaucho' used to race after this deer on horseback, catching them by lariat. When within range of the deer they hurled their *bolas* – or balls – which consisted of three stones, about the size of a man's fist, attached to strong cords, about a yard long and united to a common centre. The bolas would become entangled around the head or antlers of the deer, causing it to stop, thus affording an opportunity for the lariat to be thrown about their necks. Red deer have been introduced into several South American countries and are well-established, providing excellent trophies.

Another deer typical to Central and South America is the spike-antlered brocket, a small species generally hunted only for meat.

Despite the wealth of deer throughout the Far East, it is surprising to find that not a single species of indigenous deer exists in the whole of Australia and New Zealand.

During the past century and half, however, many exotic species of deer from both western and eastern hemispheres have been introduced, and in New Zealand the following have firmly established themselves in the wild state. In the North Island, red deer, fallow deer, sika deer, rusa deer and sambar, whilst in the South in addition to red and fallow deer there are also wapiti and white-tailed deer from North America, the latter also occurring, along with red deer, on Stewart Island. Moose have also established themselves in South Island but are barely holding their own. Whilst fallow, sika, rusa, sambar and white-tailed deer are found mostly in scrub-land at lower altitudes, red deer and wapiti, particularly in South Island, are found in steep mountainous country, much of which is heavily afforested on the lower slopes, and so offers a variety of hunting conditions, from still-hunting to pure stalking in the tussocky country above the timber line.

In Australia at least six species have established themselves in the wild state and these include red deer, fallow, rusa, axis and hog deer, and sambar. Although the last two are restricted to Victoria and south-east corner of Australia, and axis and rusa to Queensland in the north-east, both red and fallow occur in four of five states. The last named species is also present in Tasmania.

In the majority of areas the deer inhabit dense bush and in consequence dogs are often used to drive them out. This is particularly the case with the sambar, where one hunter in Gippsland recently accounted for about 500 deer in five years. GKW

Delaware (U.S.A.)

The second smallest state in the Union, covering 2,000 square miles. The climate is mild and oceanic, and much of the state is intensively farmed for market garden crops. There are large swampy areas along the coast.

Although a small state with a growing population, much is done to provide hunting

A fine fallow deer buck photographed in Denmark, one of several countries in Europe where this species is hunted.

Licence Fees—Delaware	
Residents	$5.20
Non-residents	$25.25

Seasons and Limits—Delaware

Species	Seasons	Limits	Comments
White-tailed deer	2 days in early Nov. A few days longer in Kent and Sussex Counties	1 of either sex	887 shot from est. pop. of 3,500 in 1968
Pheasant	In state areas from about 10-17 Oct. In New Castle County from about 20 Nov- 2 Jan	2 cocks per day	
Quail	20 Nov-28 Feb	8 per day	
Cotton-tailed rabbit	20 Nov-3 Jan		
Raccoon	1 Sept-28 Feb. No closed season in New Castle and Kent Counties		

for the public. The waterfowl shooting is good, as is dove-shooting, and deer populations have been restored. There is a farmer-hunter co-operative system, under which the state stocks private land provided it is opened to hunters asking permission to hunt.

Special Regulations
Deer may be shot only with shotguns larger than 20 gauge using single slugs or buckshot. Otherwise it is illegal to have shotguns in the field with shot larger than number 2. Hunting on Sundays is forbidden, except for red fox and woodchuck. Bells, or other noise producing devices may not be used on hunting dogs.

Further Information
Board of Game & Fish Commissioners, Box 457, Dover, Delaware 19901.

Licences—Denmark

All game rights belong to the landowner, but they may be leased out for life, or for maximum periods of 10 years. Shooting is free in Danish territorial waters, but only open to Danes. Otherwise the same conditions for game licences apply to both foreign nationals and Danes. Game licences are compulsory and automatically serve as third-party insurance policies. A 5 kroner licence entitles the holder to shoot on his own land and where the shooting is free ; a 25 kroner licence entitles the holder to shoot anywhere provided he holds the game rights.

Denmark

Denmark is a small country of north-west Europe, the southernmost of the Scandinavian countries, with a total area of about 17,000 square miles. The country is extremely flat, rarely rising over 500 ft above sea level, and the climate temperate, though the winds can be extremely strong.

Though there are few industrial raw materials the soil is very fertile. This factor, combined with the climate and the flat terrain has resulted in intensive cultivation and a highly advanced co-operative system of agriculture based on the small-holdings and small farms that are much the predominant element in Danish agriculture. Altogether nearly three quarters of the total land area is agricultural, with only about 10% afforested. Nevertheless, despite the intensive agriculture, small areas of wooded land, and relatively high population, Denmark is able to support a fair variety of game. However concentration of the population in the south means that sport is only readily available to the visitor in the north of Jutland.

Special Regulations
Falconry is completely prohibited. Shooting is prohibited before sunrise and after sunset, except for flighting duck, which may be shot an hour and a half before sunrise and after sunset. The use of traps and guns is strictly controlled. Sporting guns may be imported for a stay of under three months provided the visitor has a fire-arms certificate from his native country, or a declaration stating that such a certificate is not required. The appropriate ammunition may also be imported with the gun or guns.

Organizations
There are three important shooting associations: The Danish Game and Wildfowl Association (Dansk Jagtforening), with a membership of about 27,500, the National Game and Wildfowl Association (Landsjagt-forening), with a membership of about 32,000, and the Danish Inshore Wildfowl Society (Dansk Strandjagtforening) with a membership of about 6,000. Between them these organizations have about 1,300 local branches, and the two large associations have representatives on the Game Council (Jagtradet), which assists the Ministry of Agriculture in distributing the resources of the Game Fund (collected from the licence fees), fixing the seasons and dealing with other game questions, including reserves. There are at present over 50 reserves, mostly for ducks and waders, though there are only one or two moorland reserves, principally intended for black-game.

Further Information
Dansk Jagtforening, Bredgade 47, DK 1260 Copenhagen K.

Jagtradet, H. C. Andersens Boulevard 40, 1553 Copenhagen V.

Game and Seasons—Denmark

Seasons are occasionally reviewed and should be checked in advance. The dates can be altered, and species may be removed from, or added to, the list of those protected the whole year. Special local seasons are fixed in the islands of Als and Bornholm and sometimes in other parts of Denmark

Seasons (months inclusive) :—
○ Open
● Closed
◑ Mid-month

Species	Jan	Feb	Mar	Apr	May	Jun	Jul	Aug	Sep	Oct	Nov	Dec	Comment
Mammals													
Badger	○	○	○	○	○	○	○	○	○	○	○	○	
Elk	●	●	●	●	●	●	●	●	●	●	●	●	protected
Fallow deer, bucks	○	○	●	●	●	●	●	●	○	○	○	○	occasionally starts earlier
Fallow deer, hinds and young	○	○	●	●	●	●	●	●	●	○	○	○	
Fox	○	○	○	○	○	○	○	○	○	○	○	○	
Hare	○	○	○	●	●	●	●	●	○	○	○	○	
Hedgehog	●	●	●	●	●	●	●	●	●	●	●	●	protected
Mole	○	○	○	○	○	○	○	○	○	○	○	○	
Otter	○	○	○	○	○	○	○	○	○	○	○	○	
Pine-marten	●	●	●	●	●	●	●	●	●	●	●	●	protected ; occasional all-year season
Polecat	○	○	○	○	○	○	○	○	○	○	○	○	
Rabbit	○	○	○	○	○	○	○	○	○	○	○	○	
Red deer, stag	○	○	●	●	●	●	●	●	●	○	○	○	occasionally starts earlier
Red deer, hinds and young	○	○	○	○	○	○	○	○	●	●	○	○	
Roe deer	●	●	●	●	◑	○	○	◑	●	●	●	●	
Seal	○	○	○	○	○	○	○	○	○	○	○	○	
Sika deer	●	●	●	●	◑	○	○	◑	●	●	○	○	
Squirrel	○	○	○	○	○	○	○	○	○	○	○	○	
Stone-marten	○	○	○	○	○	○	○	○	○	○	○	○	
Weasel	○	○	○	○	○	○	○	○	○	○	○	○	
Birds													
Ducks													
Common scoter	○	○	●	●	●	●	●	●	○	○	○	○	
Eider	○	○	●	●	●	●	●	●	●	○	○	○	
Gadwall	●	●	●	●	●	◑	●	○	○	○	○	○	
Garganey	●	●	●	●	●	●	●	○	○	○	○	○	
Goldeneye	○	○	●	●	●	●	●	●	○	○	○	○	
Long-tailed	○	○	●	●	●	●	●	●	○	○	○	○	
Mallard	●	●	●	●	●	●	●	○	○	○	○	○	
Pintail	●	●	●	●	◑	●	●	○	○	○	○	○	
Pochard	●	●	●	●	●	●	●	○	○	○	○	○	
Merganser	○	○	●	●	●	●	●	●	○	○	○	○	
Red-crested pochard	●	●	●	●	●	●	●	●	●	●	●	●	protected, occasional all-year season
Scaup	○	○	●	●	●	●	●	●	○	○	○	○	
Shoveller	●	●	●	●	●	●	●	○	○	○	○	○	
Teal	●	●	●	●	●	●	●	○	○	○	○	○	
Tufted	●	●	●	●	●	●	●	●	○	○	○	○	
Velvet scoter	○	○	●	●	●	●	●	●	○	○	○	○	
Widgeon	●	●	●	●	●	●	●	○	○	○	○	○	
Geese													
Barnacle	●	●	●	●	●	●	●	●	●	●	●	●	protected
Bean	○	○	○	○	○	○	○	○	○	○	○	○	
Brent	●	●	●	●	●	●	●	○	○	○	○	○	occasional all year seasons
Graylag	●	●	●	●	●	●	●	○	○	○	○	○	occasional all year seasons
Pink-footed	○	○	○	○	○	○	○	○	○	○	○	○	
White-fronted	○	○	○	○	○	○	○	○	○	○	○	○	
Other Birds													
Avocet	●	●	●	●	●	●	●	●	●	●	●	●	protected
Birds of prey	●	●	●	●	●	●	●	●	●	●	●	●	protected : occasional winter seasons
Bittern	●	●	●	●	●	●	●	●	●	●	●	●	protected
Blackgame, cocks	●	●	●	●	●	●	●	●	◑	○	○	○	occasional all-year seasons
Black guillemot	○	○	●	●	●	●	●	●	○	○	○	○	
Black-headed gull	●	●	●	●	●	●	●	●	○	○	○	○	
Bustard	●	●	●	●	●	●	●	●	●	●	●	●	protected
Capercailzie	●	●	●	●	●	●	●	●	●	●	●	●	protected
Common gull	●	●	●	●	●	●	●	●	○	○	○	○	

Species	Jan	Feb	Mar	Apr	May	Jun	Jul	Aug	Sep	Oct	Nov	Dec	Comment
Coot	●	●	●	●	●	●	●	○	○	○	○	○	
Cormorant	○	○	○	○	○	●	●	○	○	○	○	○	
Corncrake	●	●	●	●	●	●	●	○	○	○	○	○	
Crane	●	●	●	●	●	●	●	●	●	●	●	●	protected
Crow	○	○	○	○	○	○	○	○	○	○	○	○	
Cuckoo	●	●	●	●	●	●	●	●	●	●	●	●	protected
Curlew	●	●	●	●	●	●	○	○	○	○	○	○	
Dotterel	●	●	●	●	●	●	●	○	○	○	○	○	
Dunlin	●	●	●	●	●	●	●	○	○	○	○	○	
Fulmar	○	○	●	●	●	●	●	●	●	○	○	○	
Gannet	●	●	●	●	●	●	●	●	●	●	●	●	protected
Godwit	●	●	●	●	●	●	●	○	○	○	○	○	
Golden plover	●	●	●	●	●	●	●	●	○	○	○	○	
Grayhen	●	●	●	●	●	●	●	●	●	●	●	●	protected
Greater black-headed gull	○	○	○	○	●	●	●	●	○	○	○	○	
Grebe	●	●	●	●	●	●	●	●	◐	○	○	○	
Grouse	●	●	●	●	●	●	●	●	◐	○	◐	●	
Guillemot	○	○	●	●	●	●	●	○	○	○	○	○	
Heron	○	○	○	●	●	●	●	○	○	○	○	○	
Herring gull	○	○	○	○	●	●	●	●	○	○	○	○	
Jackdaw	●	●	●	●	●	●	●	●	○	○	○	○	
Jay	●	●	●	●	●	●	●	○	○	○	○	○	
Kittiwake	●	●	●	●	●	●	●	●	○	○	○	○	
Lesser black-backed gull	○	○	○	○	●	●	●	●	○	○	○	○	
Little auk	○	○	●	●	●	●	●	●	●	○	○	○	
Little gull	○	●	●	●	●	●	●	●	○	○	○	○	
Magpie	○	○	○	○	○	○	○	○	○	○	○	○	
Moorhen	●	●	●	●	●	●	●	●	○	○	○	○	
Owl	●	●	●	●	●	●	●	●	●	●	●	●	protected
Oyster catcher	●	●	●	●	●	●	●	○	○	○	○	○	
Pallas's sandgrouse	●	●	●	●	●	●	●	●	●	●	●	●	protected
Partridge	●	●	●	●	●	●	●	●	◐	○	◐	●	
Pheasant, cocks	●	●	●	●	●	●	●	●	●	○	○	○	hen season, if any, within cock season
Puffin	○	○	●	●	●	●	●	●	●	○	○	○	
Quail	●	●	●	●	●	●	●	●	◐	○	◐	●	
Razorbill	○	○	●	●	●	●	●	●	●	○	○	○	
Ringed plover	●	●	●	●	●	●	●	●	●	●	●	●	protected
Rook	○	○	●	●	●	●	●	●	○	○	○	○	
Ruff	○	○	○	○	●	●	●	●	○	○	○	○	
Shearwater	○	○	●	●	●	●	●	●	○	○	○	○	
Skua	○	○	●	●	●	●	●	●	●	○	○	○	
Snipe	●	●	●	●	●	●	●	●	○	○	○	○	
Sparrow	○	○	○	○	○	○	○	○	○	○	○	○	
Spoonbill	●	●	●	●	●	●	●	●	●	●	●	●	protected
Stock dove	●	●	●	●	●	●	●	●	○	○	○	○	
Stork	●	●	●	●	●	●	●	●	●	●	●	●	protected
Stormy petrel	○	○	●	●	●	●	●	●	○	○	○	○	
Swan	●	●	●	●	●	●	●	●	●	●	●	●	protected
Tern	●	●	●	●	●	○	○	●	●	●	●	●	protected
Thrush	○	○	●	●	●	●	●	●	○	○	○	○	
Turnstone	●	●	●	●	●	●	●	●	●	●	●	●	protected
Turtle dove	●	●	●	●	●	●	●	●	●	●	●	●	protected
Water rail	●	●	●	●	●	●	●	●	○	○	○	○	
Woodcock	○	○	○	◐	●	●	●	●	◐	○	○	○	
Woodpecker	●	●	●	●	●	●	●	●	●	●	●	●	protected
Woodpigeon	●	●	●	●	●	●	●	●	○	○	○	○	
Wryneck	●	●	●	●	●	●	●	●	●	●	●	●	protected

The Danish Tourist Board has offices throughout Europe and in New York and Los Angeles. The address of the head office is: Danmarks Turistrad, Banegardspladsen 7, DK 1570 Copenhagen V.

Denmark, Hunting in

Immediately on entering Denmark there is the feeling that this friendly land of highly developed agriculture must be an exceptional habitat for game, both fur and feather. The terrain is mostly flat with a few nicely undulating hills here and there, but no mountains and few forests. Yet there is ample cover for game and the Danish hunter has plenty of variety.

The shooting rights belong to the landowner and the best shooting is to be had on the large estates. The few woods or afforested areas, mostly hardwood rather than softwood, are virtually all in private hands. There are deer for the rifle, red, fallow and roe, also hares, foxes, partridges, pheasants, pigeons, wildfowl and last but not least, woodcock for the shotgun.

In the spring the discriminating Danish sportsmen are particularly fond of shooting woodcock over pointing dogs. Since there are few wooded areas, spread over different parts of the country, it is easy for the gun to know and find the places where the woodcock like to rest for a few days on their spring migrations to the breeding areas in the north. If there is a 'fall of cock' an experienced hunter may shoot as many as 15 to 20 in a day. The spring season is short, from 1 March to 7 April, but the cock rarely arrives before 15 March.

Spring woodcock shooting has been criticized by conservationists as being damaging to the woodcock population. The argument was that both cocks and hens were shot, whereas, if the shooting is restricted to 'roding' flights in the evening, only the males would be shot. Statistics over the past years, however, show that the number of woodcock in Denmark has actually increased. More birds are shot during the autumn, when woodcock are encountered in almost any cover.

Partridge shooting over pointers is also very popular. There are more gundogs, both pointers and retrievers, in Denmark than in the other three Scandinavian countries. The Danish hunter likes to go out with his dog after working hours every day during the season and shoot a few birds, hares, or ducks for his larder. Driven pheasant shooting, when the bags are as high as 1,000 a day, are now mostly syndicated to Danish or foreign guns.

Wildfowling from a boat, or punt, was once much more popular, whereas shooting from blinds, or hides, with decoys, was less common than it is now. However the diving duck and geese have become scarce and the open season has consequently been shortened. Pigeon shooting is also a popular sport and on August 1st, the opening day, everyone is out shooting them. The Danes however are not as skilled in decoying pigeons, or in camouflaging their hides or their person, as the average pigeon shooter in Britain.

Throughout Denmark, roebuck are only shot with the rifle and the methods used are stalking and the use of the high-seat. The peak of the open season is from 16 May to 15 July, though culling and minor trophy shooting is carried on from October to the end of December. The red stag is mostly shot during the rut, whereas fallow bucks are often taken before the rut. This is because there have been many casualties amongst fighting bucks. The landowners frequently sell their stags or fallow bucks to foreign trophy collectors for quite high fees. Although the red stags seldom reach medal class, Denmark has produced fallow trophies amongst the highest CIC point score; however most fallow deer, as well as some sika, are found in deer parks.

For those interested there is also seal shooting, which may be carried out on the shores practically anywhere in Denmark. The season is from mid-June, through to the end of February, and for harbour seal it continues until the end of May.

In many ways Danish hunting is closer to that of central-European hunting and shooting traditions and customs than that of the other Scandinavian countries. The Dane is also more trophy-conscious and cosmopolitan and likes to go shooting abroad and to have foreign sportsmen as his guests. PM

Desert Quail (Lophortyx gambelli)

There are several sub-species of this quail. The most important is Gambel's quail (L. gambelli gambelli) but there are also the larger Olathe variety (L. gambelli sanus) in the eastern parts of the range, and the fulvous-breasted (L. gambelli fulvipectus) along the west coast of Mexico. The differences are only those of size and colour.

Their diet consists of mesquite beans and various grass and weed seeds during the dry season, and of green food and fruit during the rains. The young also need an insect diet. When there is green food the need for free water is less urgent, and birds can disperse from the water holes. Otherwise they must drink once a day, which controls their distribution. Their range includes parts of Utah, Arizona, California, New Mexico and Mexico, and they have recently been introduced into Idaho.

They are talkative birds, with a clear, metallic whistle of 'killink-killink' during the mating season, and a scatter call of 'quirrt'. They run well, and fly in short but fast bursts. They live in coveys, which merge into flocks in the autumn. The flocks pack in the spring, just before pairing starts. Afterwards the pack breaks up and the pairs disperse to their original covey territory.

When there is no rain and no green, pairing does not take place, and the birds remain in coveys.

The birds are monogamous, average five to six ounces in weight and are between 10 and 11 in long. The cock has a red cap and black crest made up of six feathers about one and a half inches long. The throat is black with a white border, the breast gray, with a black patch, and the flanks are chestnut streaked with white. The hen resembles the cock but lacks the black throat and black stomach patch. The nest is a scrape in the ground lined with grass, and the clutch of 10 to 15 eggs takes 22 days to incubate. If the rains are plentiful there may be a second brood.

Desert quail are great runners and, unless in thick cover, they tend to run on in front of a dog rather than hold to a point. It may also be necessary to run the coveys down and break them up before it becomes possible to use a dog effectively.

Dibitag *see* Gerenuk

Dingo *see* individual Australian States

Dog Breeds for Hunting

BASSET HOUND. A breed of medium-sized hounds that originated, probably, in Flanders, and was first introduced into Britain in the early seventeenth century. They were primarily used for hunting the hare, with the field following on foot, a function for which their persevering but slow natures well suits them. They are not, however, as small as the beagle or as fast as the harrier. The head is long, narrow, and slightly domed, with considerable resemblance to a bloodhound's because of the wrinkles and deep flews. The eyes are sunken and show haw. The ears are long and set very low. The muzzle is powerful. The body is long in proportion to its height and heavy in the bone. The back is straight, wide and strong, the chest wide and round with the breast bone prominent. The legs are short, thick and slightly crooked, with wrinkled skin. The feet are large, open, and well padded. The coat is short, smooth, and of any hound colour. Height to shoulder about 13 to 15 in. Weight about 45 lb.

BEAGLE. An English breed of hound used for hare hunting that probably descends from the old southern hound which descends, in its turn, from the Talbot hound of the Normans. They are not unlike small harriers to look at, and there is considerable variation in size and coat inside the breed. They are justly noted for their powers of scent, endurance, and intelligence.

The head is moderate in length and width, with a slight dome and a well defined stop. The ears are long, thin, pendant, and set low. The muzzle is fairly long but must not be snipy. The body is muscular and deep

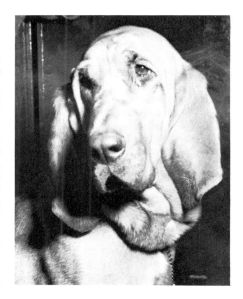

Bloodhound

Bassett hound

with a shorter back than the basset. The chest is deep and the legs strong and straight with round, compact feet. The stern is high-set, thick, and fairly long, and is carried high, but not curled. The coat is short and smooth, the colour the usual hound tri-colours and also lemon and white. Heights vary from 13 to 16 in, but the best height is thought to be about 14 in. The weight is around 35 lb.

BLACK AND TAN COONHOUND. These have only been recognized as a seperate breed in America comparatively recently. For at least two centuries any hound that would follow and tree a raccoon or opossum was entitled to be called a coonhound. But many of them could not breed coonhounds, even though they themselves carried some of the foxhound or bloodhound blood necessary. The black and tan coloured coonhounds have always been preferred to all other colours, probably because it pointed to their descent from the old Virginia black and tan foxhound. In addition to the foxhound blood, there was introduced, at some time or other, bloodhound blood, and this can be seen not only in their looks but also in their working methods. The now standardized black and tan is a big dog with an excellent nose, great determination and a good note. He is alert, powerful, enduring, and covers country well.

The head is clean cut and narrow in proportion to its length, the skin on it is thin and loose but without wrinkles or excessive dewlaps. The flews are well developed, and the ears are very long, low set, and hang in folds. The neck is medium long, the chest deep and the ribs well sprung. The back is level and the stern long, tapering, and set lower than the backline. The legs are long and large in the bone. The coat is short but thick and the colour black with tan markings. Height varies from 22 to 26 in.

BLOODHOUND. Sometimes referred to as sleuth hound. Its name derives from its power to pick a wounded deer out of a herd and track it down by scent. It has always been used to track either animals or men, and all other hounds are probably descended from or connected with the breed. They are the closest descendants of the original Talbots which descend, in their turn, from the St Hubert hounds. They will follow a scent slowly but unremittingly and if checked will cast back until it is found again.

The head is long and narrow and much domed on the top with the skin loose and wrinkled between and above the eyes. The eyes are medium size, sunken and show haw. The ears are pendant and long and set very low. The muzzle is powerful with large open nostrils and deep flews and dewlaps. The body is long and strong with the neck set in almost a straight line with the back. The chest is deep, the loins muscular, the legs heavy and straight, the feet large. The stern is set fairly high and is long and thick, and it is carried high when in action. The coat is short and close, and the colours are black and tan, red and tan, red, copper, mahogany, black, puce or tawny. Height is between 23 and 27 in and weight between 90 and 110 lb.

BRITTANY SPANIEL. These are the only spaniels born with a strong pointing instinct and with little or no tail. They look and behave considerably more like setters than spaniels, and it is thought by some that they are descended from Irish setters. They originate from the town of Pontou in Brittany, supposedly from a crossing of a local bitch and a lemon and white spaniel brought there by an Englishman for the woodcock shooting. They were later outcrossed with the braque de Bourbonnais, from which cross the short or absent tail and the pointing instinct probably come. They make useful working dogs since they possess the retrieving instinct of the spaniel and the pointing instinct of the braque.

The head is rounded with a medium long, rather pointed muzzle, and short rather than long ears set fairly high. The stop is well defined but sloping and the eyes are deep amber. The medium neck is light and clean, and runs down to a deep-chested, short-backed muscular body. The tail, if there is one, is no more than four inches long and is carried low. The legs are straight, rather finely boned, and muscular, with lightish fringes, and the toes are close and with little hair between them. The coat is fine, flat, and smooth or slightly wavy, and its colours are liver and white or orange and white with or without roan ticking. The height varies between 17 and 19¾ in.

CHESAPEAKE BAY RETRIEVER. A water dog used on a limited scale in the United States but tending, both there and in the rest of the world, to be replaced by the Labrador. The breed is supposed, like the Labrador, to be descended from the Newfoundland dog, in this case from two Newfoundland puppies rescued from the wreck of a brig off the Maryland coast in 1807. It is not certain whether coonhound or water poodle blood was introduced but, by the middle of the last century the Chesapeake was beginning to emerge as an outstanding dog for use in water, performing best in heavy seas and freezing temperatures. The breed has four outstanding characteristics: – its love of water, its very oily, water-resistant coat that dries with a couple of shakes, its great endurance, and its powers of memory that allow it to mark every duck that has been shot and to pick out those which fell only wounded, so that they might be retrieved first. These are the qualities that made the Chesapeake the market hunters' favourite dog. The market hunter, in his turn, ensured that the Chesapeake should enjoy the reputation of being a 'sharp' dog – one that

shows friendliness to no other dog and no other man. It is, perhaps, this reputation that has prevented them from enjoying some of the popularity of, say, the Labrador.

The head is broad, round, with a medium stop and a medium short nose ending in a pointed, but not sharp muzzle. The ears are small, pendant, and set high. The eyes are of a medium size and a clear yellow colour. The body is powerful, straight backed, with a deep chest and flanks well let down. The legs are strongly boned, and the feet are harelike, large and webbed. The tail is medium long, thick at the root, tapered, and is carried horizontally or lower. The coat is thick, short, remarkably oily, and has a dense, fine, woolly undercoat. The coat should not curl, but a tendency towards waviness on the neck and back is permissible. Colour varies from brown to a pale straw, and a white spot on the chest or toes is allowed. Heights and weights vary from 21 to 24 in and 55 to 65 lb for bitches and from 23 to 26 in and 65 to 75 lb for dogs.

CLUMBER SPANIEL. One of the oldest of British spaniels, it takes its name from Clumber, near Worksop, a seat of the Dukes of Newcastle. It is traditional to accept that they descend from four dogs given to the then Duke of Newcastle in 1770 by the Duc de Noailles. It has also been suggested that they have basset blood in them. Certainly, they are unlike other spaniels, and the old saying that 'in almost any litter of spaniel puppies there will be three kinds – cocker, springer and Sussex' has never been extended to them. They have lost much of their former popularity in the shooting field, largely because they are so much slower than springers or cockers.

The head is large and massive, round above the eyes, flat on top, with a furrow between the eyes and a marked stop. The jaw is long, broad and deep, with the lips of the upper jaw overhung. The nostrils are large, open, and flesh or cherry coloured, and the eyes are large, hazel, and show haw. The ears should be long and vine shaped, set low, and feathered only on the forward edge. A long, thick, powerful neck should lead into a very long, low and powerful body – a good dog covers two and a half times his height. The legs are short, straight and heavy in the bone with thick hair on the back just above the feet, and the feet themselves are large and compact with plenty of hair between the toes. The coat should be silky, straight and thick, with abundant feather, and colour white and lemon or white and orange, though orange is not greatly liked. The height is 17 to 18 in and the weight is 55 to 65 lb.

COCKER SPANIEL. This is probably the world's most popular breed, even though its popularity among shooting men is now declining. Though, in the early days, all spaniels were probably differentiated from each other by size rather than by breed, there has always been a small, short-legged, 'springing' spaniel used for work in close cover and in woods, and especially useful for springing woodcock – hence a 'cocking' or 'cocker' spaniel. It may well be descended from Blenheim spaniels, but it was firmly established as a separate breed by the end of the last century, when J. J. Farrow did a great deal of work in standardizing it.

It is a neat-headed, short-bodied, powerful little dog, showing great intelligence, and quick and merry at work. The skull is domed and there is a clearly defined stop. The eyes ought to be full, round and brown, the muzzle short, rather square and strong, and the ears long, low set and covered with long, straight, silky hair without either curls or ringlets. A muscular neck, free from throatiness, and long enough to allow the nose to reach the ground easily should lead to a short, cobby body. The legs are short, straight, and well boned and muscled, whilst the feet are round and firm with deep pads and plenty of hair between the toes.

Curly-coated retriever

The tail, which is docked, should be set low and carried level with the back, and it should move continually while the dog is at work. The coat which is flat and silky, should be longest on the ears and the backs of the legs and shortest on the head and the fronts of the legs. The colours are various – all black, all red, all golden, all liver, blue roan, red roan, red and white, black and white, but not all white. Whole colours should not be faded or 'washy'. Height is between $15\frac{1}{2}$ and $16\frac{1}{2}$ in at the shoulder, and weights vary from 28 to 30 lb for dogs and from 25 to 28 lb for bitches. In America, where the Cocker is altogether a smaller dog, the weight requirements are not under 18 or exceeding 24 lb.

CURLY-COATED RETRIEVER. This is one of the older specialized retrieving breeds and it resembles the Chesapeake except for being covered with a mass of tight curls. Like the Chesapeake it is probably descended from the St Johns Newfoundland though whether it also has Irish water

spaniel, or poodle, or setter blood is a matter for argument. Its outstanding characteristic, as a working dog, is its eagerness to retrieve both on land and water. Chief criticisms of it are that it is slow and tends to be hard mouthed, and it is seldom seen, nowadays, on the shooting field, having been replaced, like the flat coat retriever, by the Labrador, a lighter and faster dog.

It is a rather square-built dog, with the head wide at the ears, long and tapering to a pointed muzzle. The eyes should be black or brown, but never yellow. The ears are small, pendant and low set and should be covered with curls. The body is straight backed and deep chested, rather short and muscular, with straight legs ending in round, compact feet with well arched toes. The tail is moderately long, tapering towards the point, covered with curls and carried horizontally. The coat is a mass of characteristic curls from the occipital crest to the tip of the tail, and the colour is either jet black or liver. A white patch is undesirable. Height and weight have not been standardized, but about 22 in at the shoulder and between 65 and 75 lb are normal.

DOBERMANN PINSCHER. This is one of the many European pointer breeds, and it was evolved, at the end of the last century, by Herr Dobermann, from pinscher, Weimaraner and vorstehhund blood. It is, primarily, a gundog, but it is now widely used, throughout the world, as a police dog.

It is a striking, square-looking dog, whose body is as long as its height. The head is long, clean cut and free from wrinkles, and is set on a powerful neck leading to a short backed, deep chested body. The legs are long and end in small, compact, cat-like feet. The tail is docked at the first or second joint. The coat is smooth, hard and thick and is coloured, black, tan and blue. The height is 25 to 26 in, and the weight between 60 and 65 lb.

ELKHOUND. A Norwegian dog that looks very much like a smaller Eskimo husky. It is used, primarily, for hunting elk and bear, but it also can be used on small game and game birds, and can be trained to point and retrieve admirably.

The head should be broad between the ears with a marked stop and a moderately long muzzle. The body is compact and short-coupled, with a wide, straight back and a broad chest. The tail is bushy and the coat thick, with a full undercoat, and forms a ruff round the neck and chest. Colour can be of various shades of gray, always darker on the back. Height varies between 19 and 21 in and the weight between 45 and 55 lb.

ENGLISH POINTER. Whether all pointers are descended from the perdiguero – the Spanish partridge dog – or not is always something that can be argued about. Certainly there have been pointing dogs in Britain for a very long time, though they only emerged as a distinctive breed in the nineteenth century. They are short haired dogs, better able to stand up to hot weather than the setter, but less suitable for cold and thick cover. They are, however, rugged and hardy dogs with the desire to hunt and the pointing instinct deeply ingrained.

The head is long, moderately wide, with a marked stop and a slight furrow between the eyes. The muzzle is long, square and straight. The nose is black or brown except in the white and orange or white and lemon coats, when it may be flesh coloured. The ears are thin, silky and pendant and should hang to just below the throat. Eyes are of medium size, full, and black or brown in colour. The neck is long, clean cut and arched, leading to a strong, well muscled body that slopes away slightly from croup to stern. The chest is deep and well ribbed but not excessively wide. The tail should be straight, strong, tapered, and carried level with the back. The legs should be moderately short with plenty of bone, and the feet should be round, deep, and well padded. The coat should be short and smooth, and colours should be either self coloured, or white with black, lemon, orange, or liver, or tricoloured. Height is around 24 in and weight varies from 50 to 55 lb.

ENGLISH SETTER. Setting dogs, i.e. ones that crouched in front of game, were especially useful when netting birds, for the nets could be cast over dog and bird alike. Gervase Markham mentions a 'setting spaniel' from Spain, and it is probable that setters are descended from these. The English setter came into prominence after Edward Laverack had improved it, probably using Irish setter blood, and it is still a popular gundog, especially in America.

The head is long and lean, with a well defined stop and well domed between the ears. The muzzle should be long and fairly square and quite straight, with no suggestion of a dishface or Roman nose. Jaws should be of equal length, and ears should be set low and close to the head, be moderately long and covered with silky hair. The neck should be long and lean and lead to a medium long body that slopes slightly down from the shoulders to the loins. The chest should be deep, but not especially wide, and the legs long and muscular ending in closely set strong feet, well rounded and with hair between the toes. The tail should be of medium length, straight, set low, and taper to a fine point and the feather should be straight and silky without any suggestion of bushiness, and should never curve above the backline. The coat should be flat, fine and silky, and of moderate length, with considerable feathering on the backs of the legs and thighs. Coat colours are white flecked with blue, liver, orange, tan, lemon or black. The markings should be small flecks and not large patches. Height varies from 23 to 25 in and weight from 50 to 70 lb.

ENGLISH SPRINGER SPANIEL. From early times spaniels were split up into setting spaniels and springing spaniels. The duty of the springing spaniel was to spring game – i.e. cause it to spring up into the air – a very different activity from either pointing or setting it. Spaniels used for springing were, at one time, known as starters, and some, like the cockers, were given the name of the bird they were most used for. But, though not necessarily a separate breed, there were always numbers of larger, longer legged, springing spaniels which, whether they were selected by size alone or not, came to be known as springers. They were particularly popular in East Anglia, where a black, or liver and white springing spaniel, bred, originally, by the Duke of Norfolk, gave rise to the Norfolk spaniel, a breed that has now disappeared into the ranks of the English springer. On the other hand the Welsh springer has kept its separate identity. English springers first emerged, as a

English springer spaniel

distinct breed, in 1903, but the Boughey family of Aqualate in Shropshire had been keeping a pure line of springer spaniels since 1812. They are fast working, active, enduring dogs, good in the water as well as on land. They will quarter their ground within gunshot, flush, drop to shot, mark, find, and retrieve to hand. They therefore provide a very useful general purpose dog, especially suited for walking up pheasants. They have become steadily more popular in the United States as pheasant has replaced quail as the most important of the upland game birds. Whilst a pointer or setter would probably be a more useful bird on quail, the springer is more useful on pheasants, since they, generally speaking, will always run on in front of a point or set.

The head is relatively long, rounded over the eyes, but flat rather than domed on top. The stop is defined, but not so markedly as with a clumber. The muzzle is fairly long and rather square and the eyes are of medium size, dark, and show no haw. The ears, which are set fairly low at eye level, are long, wide at the end, and covered in-

side and out with fine hair, which ought not to curl. The tail is set low and docked, and moves continually when the dog is at work. The body is compact and muscular, with a straight, fairly long back and powerful hind quarters. The legs are straight, short in the pastern, and end in round, compact feet with plenty of feather between the toes. The coat should be short and fine on the head and the front of the legs, and longer on the rest of the body. It should be either flat or wavy, but never curly, and thick enough to hold out thorns and the weather. There should be a fringe of wavy hair on the throat, brisket and chest. Colours vary, but black and white is most common, though black and tan, liver and white, tan and white and roans of these colours are also common. Height should not vary very much from 18 in and the weight should be about 45 lb for dogs and 40 lb for bitches.

FIELD SPANIEL. This is a spaniel that was specifically developed as a cocker substitute when something both stronger and shorter legged was required. It is a product of cocker and Sussex spaniel crosses. There was, unfortunately, a period during which its legs were progressively shortened until it became useless in the field. Saner breeding practices are now, fortunately, restored.

The head is moderately long, with a slight dome and a marked stop. The eyes are full and dark and the ears low set, wide, long and with profuse feathering. The muzzle is fairly long and neither square nor snipy. The body is of good length, but must not sag. The chest is deep and well ribbed, sometimes making the forelegs look shorter than they actually are. The tail is docked, set low, and carried horizontally or lower. The coat is flat, soft and of fair length, with, perhaps some waviness on flank, brisket and breeching. The feathering on the legs and ears is long and silky, but there must be no tendency to curls. They are normally self coloured, or self coloured with tan. The average height is about 18 in and the average weight about 40 lb.

FLAT-COATED RETRIEVER. This is a breed that was finally fixed in the last half of the last century, but is now largely replaced, as the curly-coated retriever has been, by the Labrador. Like the Labrador it has Newfoundland and, perhaps, Chesapeake blood, but this was probably crossed with Gordon setter.

The head should be long, wide between the eyes, and tapering to the muzzle, with a perceptible stop. The body is short, square, straight-backed with deep chest and well sprung ribs. The legs are strong and the feet large. The tail is long, tapering, and feathered. The coat is dense, fine, and flat, not wavy. The usual colour is black, though liver sometimes occurs. Height varies between 22 and 24 in, and the weight between 60 and 70 lb.

FOXHOUND. One of the most versatile of all hounds, for, though in Britain it is only used, in packs, on fox, in America it may be used, singly, in couples, or in packs, on anything from deer to rabbit, can be turned into a 'tree' dog for raccoons, or can be used along a trapline.

The head is moderately broad and rather long with a well defined stop. The eyes are of medium size and dark hazel to brown. The ears are fairly high set, of medium length and pendant. The muzzle is strong and deep. The neck is moderately long and slightly arched and is set on a broad body of moderate length with a deep chest and straight firm back. The legs are straight, well boned, and muscular, with round, not over compact feet. The stern is set high, is strong at the root, and is carried gaily. The coat is short, close, and smooth. The colours are various, the most common being black and white, tan and white, tricolour, badger pied, hare pied, or fawn with or without white points. The height should be between 23 and 24 in for dogs and 22 to 23 in for bitches. The average weight is around 70 lb.

GERMAN SHORT-HAIRED POINTER. This is another of the many Central European pointers and, perhaps, the only one with any right to claim to be a pointer-retriever. It is a most versatile gun dog, and is well suited for the rough or mixed shoot and for the one man hunter, since it will quarter, point, drop to shot, retrieve fur and feather and takes well to water. It has also been used on wild boar and deer. It is not as fast, perhaps, as the ordinary pointer, but it is considerably more versatile. The breed originated in Germany, probably from a cross of the bloodhound on the old Spanish pointer. Both foxhound and English pointer blood were also used.

The head should be long and broad, only slightly rounded and with a distinct stop and a slight furrow between the eyes. It is not as domed as the English pointer's head, and it runs more smoothly into the neck. The muzzle should be long enough and strong enough to allow game to be carried for some distance. The nose is solid brown. The ears are high set, of medium length, slightly folded, and hang close to the cheek. The eyes are of medium size, soft, and of any shade of brown or olive. The lips are well developed and slightly pendulous. The neck is moderately long, arched, and larger towards the shoulders, and the body is short and strong, sloping away slightly from the shoulders. The loins are slightly arched and the hips rather wide, falling slightly towards the tail, which is docked at two thirds of its length. The legs are straight, muscular and well boned, and the feet round, deep, and well padded, with arched and heavily nailed toes. The coat is short, flat and firm, and the only permitted colours are liver and white, though in many combinations, i.e. solid

German short-haired pointer

liver, liver and white spotted, liver and white spotted and ticked, liver and white ticked. Dogs should weigh between 55 and 70 lb, and bitches 45 to 60 lb. Height varies between 21 and 26 in.

GOLDEN RETRIEVER. These are the only retrievers not to claim American, i.e. Newfoundland, ancestry. The tradition is that they are all descended from a troupe of Russian circus dogs of the Russian Tracker type, bought from a circus in Brighton by Sir Dudley Marjoribanks in 1860, and that the only other blood used in them came from a single bloodhound outcross. They were recognized as a separate breed by the Kennel Club in 1911. As a breed they possess stamina, a good nose, a good mouth, and are intelligent and easily trained.

The head is broad, with a good stop and a wide powerful muzzle. The eyes are dark with dark rims, the ears small and well set on. The nose should be black, but light colours are allowed. The body is deep, short coupled, well muscled, with a level back and the flanks well let down. The legs are straight and with good bone and the feet round and catlike. The tail is thick at the root and tapering, and must not be curled at the tip or carried over the back. The coat is flat or wavy, dense and water resisting, and with a good undercoat. The colour will range from cream to almost Irish setter red, but should be a rich gold with lighter feathering. Dogs should weigh 65 to 68 lb and bitches 53 to 60 lb, and heights vary between 23 to 24 in for dogs and 20½ to 22 in for bitches.

GORDON SETTER. These probably descend from the old black and tan setter mentioned by Gervase Markham, though they were first established as a breed by the Duke of Richmond and Gordon at the beginning of the nineteenth century. They are extremely elegant dogs, but are not now in great favour as gun dogs, possibly because they are rather slow as compared with both the English and Irish setters. They are strong, moderate sized dogs of rather racy build.

The head is deep rather than broad, with a rounded skull and a good stop and lean above and below the eyes. The muzzle is long but not pointed, the lines running almost parallel. The nose is large, with open nostrils and black. The eyes are of fair size and dark brown in colour, and the ears are fairly large, thin and set low on the head. The neck is long and lean and runs into a deep but not broad chested body, slightly heavier than an English setter's. The legs are big boned and straight with deep, compact feet and plenty of hair between the toes. The tail is short, thick at the root and tapering to a point, and is set in line with the back and carried below the horizontal. The feather starts near the tail root and grows quite straight, getting uniformly shorter as it gets nearer the tip. The coat is soft, silky and glossy, short on the head and

Gundogs

Setters
English
Gordon
Irish

English Pointers

Pointer—Retrievers
German Short-Haired Pointer
Magyar Viszla
Weimaraner

Retrievers
Curly-haired
Flat-haired
Golden
Labrador
Interbred
Chesapeake Bay

Spaniels
Clumber
Cocker
Field
Irish
Water
English springer
Welsh springer
Sussex

on the fronts of the legs, but longer and feathery on the ears, chest, belly, backs of the legs and tail. The hair on these may be wavy but should never be curly. The colour is black with bright, clearly defined, chestnut marking over the eyes, on each side of the muzzle, on the throat and chest, on the legs and round the vent. Height should be around 26 in for dogs and 24½ in for bitches. Average weight is around 70 lb.

GUNDOGS. The classification for gundogs laid down by the Kennel Club is shown in the table.

HARRIER. Hare hunting hounds are among the oldest of the working dogs. Originally, they were probably slow animals to be followed on foot or used for working the hare into nets as in classical Greece. Gradually, however, they were bred faster so as to provide a chase to the kill, with the hunt mounted. This produced the harrier, the fastest of all the hare hunting hounds. Their speed undoubtedly stems from an infusion of foxhound blood, and their appearance shows considerable variation, depending on the amount of foxhound blood that has been used.

The head resembles a foxhound's, except that the skull is broader. The ears are high set, pendant, and wide at the base. The muzzle is deep and the nose broad and black. The body is muscular, compact, and of moderate length, with a straight, firm back and deep chest. The legs are straight, well boned, not too long, and with reasonably large, open, feet. The stern is set high, thick at the root, and carried gaily. The coat is short, dense, and harsh, and the colours vary from tricolour to white flecked with lemon. Heights are rather variable, but the truest types stand about 18 to 19 in, and they should never exceed 21 in. The weight should be between 50 and 55 lb.

IRISH SETTER. This is, possibly, the oldest setter breed, a similar dog being mentioned in early Irish history. At one time, however, it was not entirely red, but red and white, whereas now white is only allowed on the brisket, feet and tail tip. It is no longer as popular as a shooting dog as it once was, for it has a reputation, probably quite undeserved, for flightiness and unsteadiness. The trouble is more likely to be that it has, because of its good looks, become a show dog rather more than a gundog, and breeding has tended to reflect the fact.

The head is long and lean, rather narrower than the English setter's, with an oval skull and a pronounced stop. The muzzle is moderately deep and square, with considerable length. The nose is dark mahogany or chocolate and the eyes hazel. The ears are low set, moderately long, pendant, and hang close to the head. The neck is long, slightly arched, muscular, but not thick, and leads into a moderately long, deep, rather narrow body, though with well sprung ribs and muscular, slightly arched loins. The legs are long and straight, with rather small, firm feet. The tail is moderately long, set low, and is strong at the root, tapering to a fine point. It is carried either straight, or in a slight curve, just below the horizontal. The coat is short and fine on the head, front of the legs and tips of the ears, and of moderate length and flat elsewhere. There is feathering on the ears, backs of the legs, tail, belly, chest and throat, and the feet are feathered between the toes. The colour can vary from a golden chestnut to a mahogany red. The average height is 26 in and weight 60 lb.

IRISH WATER SPANIEL. This is the largest of the spaniels and is used almost entirely as a retriever, generally on waterfowl, though it may also be used for flushing upland game. It is one of the oldest of the Irish breeds, and is probably, like all spaniels, of Iberian origin, though it is thought to be descended from the Portuguese Cao d'Agua rather than from the Spanish setter-spaniel. It has been argued that it may be of poodle descent, but the absence of curls on its face and most of its tail seems to contradict this. As a working dog it is now almost entirely used for wildfowling, its hardness, liking for water, and good retrieving capabilities suiting it well for that sort of sport.

The head is fairly long and wide in the skull and well domed. The topknot, which consists of a cluster of long, loose curls, grows down into a well defined peak between the eyes, but the hair on the rest of the face is short and smooth. The eyes are set almost flush and are generally hazel, and the ears are low set, long and abundantly covered with curls. The neck is long, arching, and muscular, and the body is of medium length with deep chest and well sprung ribs. The loins are short, wide and muscular, and the flanks well let down. The tail is set low, so giving a rounded appearance to the hindquarters. The legs are straight, well boned and muscular and covered with curls, which are shorter on the fronts of the legs. The feet are large and spreading, with plenty of hair between the toes but no feather. The tail is short and thick at the root, tapering to a fine point to produce the 'rat-tail' characteristic of the breed. This is emphasized by the fact that the first three inches of tail are covered with curls, and the rest with short, smooth hair, giving a clipped appearance. Except for the face and this part of the tail, all the rest is covered with tight, crisp ringlets. The colour is solid liver. Height for dogs varies between 22 and 24 in, for bitches between 21 and 23 in. Weights for dogs vary between 55 and 65 lb and for bitches between 45 and 58 lb.

LABRADOR RETRIEVER. This is, perhaps, the most popular and the most useful of

Labrador with pink-footed goose

modern gundogs. It can quarter its ground, if trained to do so, and flush game within gunshot. It can even achieve a rudimentary point. But both pointers and setters can do these things better. But the Labrador is, par excellence, a retriever, both on land and water.

The breed is, by tradition, descended from the St Johns Newfoundland, though it is said that these, in their turn, were first brought to Newfoundland by Devon fishermen going out to the Banks in the late sixteenth century. The breed in Britain is commonly believed to stem from dogs landed at Poole harbour from a Newfoundland fishing boat in 1793. The breed was not, however, recognized by the Kennel Club until 1903. Since then they have, very largely, supplanted the flat and curly-coated retrievers in this country, and the Chesapeake in America.

It is a strongly built, short coupled, active dog, capable of more speed than other retriever breeds, fond of water, and with excellent powers of nose, sight and memory. The head should be wide, with a slight stop, the muzzle moderately long, powerful, square rather than pointed, and free from snipiness. The nose is wide, with well developed nostrils, the ears small, set well back and low, and hanging moderately close to the head. The eyes, which are of medium size, show great intelligence and can be any colour from yellow to black. A moderately long and powerful neck runs into a close, coupled, deep, wide body, with well sprung ribs and powerful loins. The legs are straight, with short pasterns and compact feet with well arched toes and deep pads. The tail is otter-like, being thick at the root and tapering to the tip. The hair on it is thick, but there must be no suggestion of feathering, nor should it curl over the back. The coat is short and very dense, without any suggestion of wave. The colour is black, though yellow often occurs. It is sometimes argued that yellow Labradors are a distinct breed and, indeed, they come close to being one. But all Labradors carry the yellow colour gene, and yellow and black puppies will frequently occur in the same litter. The average height is about 22 in and the average weight about 65 lb.

PLOTT HOUND. This is still a highly localized and specialized breed, even though it is no longer bred and owned solely by the Plott family. Jonathan Plott, when he emigrated to North Carolina and the area of the Great Smoky Mountains in 1750, brought with him a number of boar hounds. These he continued to breed and, in the absence of wild boar, used them for bear hunting. The family has continued with the strain ever since, and, now that wild boar may be hunted in that part of the world, the Plott hounds have reverted to their original purpose. They are not only courageous but hardy, general purpose dogs, ready to follow any game that will either run or fight. Although they are too slow to use as foxhounds, they possess a good note and have been successfully used on such different quarry as wolf, mountain lion, coyote, deer, and small game. They are medium sized hounds, weighing no more than 60 lb, and are generally a brindled brown with white or black points.

SUSSEX SPANIEL. This is a breed developed from a strong, liver coloured spaniel found in Sussex in the eighteenth century, and known as Relf spaniels. There was then, though there probably is no longer, a need for a specially powerful, short legged spaniel to meet the special conditions of the county as it was at the time, that is, heavily wooded and with a wet and heavy soil. The Sussex spaniel is the only spaniel to give tongue – a practice not altogether without its uses in thick country as Sussex once was. They are slow, if conscientious, workers, and, because of their slowness, are now seldom used in the shooting field.

The head is moderately long and fairly wide with a well marked stop. The ears are set low, pendant, long, thick, and lobe shaped. The muzzle is fairly long and square. The neck is thick, strong, and slightly arched and leads into a deep chested, long backed body. The legs are short, strong, and with good feathering, and the feet are large and round. The tail is docked, thickly feathered and carried low. The coat is thick, flat, and short, except for the feathering on legs and tail. The colour is a golden liver. Height is around 16 in for dogs and 15 in for bitches. Average weight is 42 lb.

VIZSLA. Reputedly of very ancient origin, the Magyar Vizsla or Hungarian pointer is said to descend from the hunting dogs brought into the Carpathian mountain region by the migrating Magyars in the 9th century. During the Turkish occupation, which lasted for 150 years, they were freely interbred with the yellow Turkish dogs and other breeds, but by the 16th century the name Vizsla seems to have been in common usage. Subsequently, in the great days of the Austro-Hungarian Empire, they were crossed by the Hungarian nobility with braques, beagles and German short-haired pointers and towards the end of the 19th century an attractive cross was stabilized which was expected to retrieve hares and foxes, point and retrieve woodcock, quail and other feathered game, as well as track and pull down deer, or bay wolves or wild boars. They were also used extensively on the Hungarian marshes to retrieve waterfowl. It was only in the 1950s, following World War Two that they were introduced to Britain and the U.S.A. They are handsome pointer-type dogs of a russet-red colour with fine shorthaired coats. Their eyes are deep amber and the nose, lips and toenails are the same colour as the coat. The tail is docked by a third to avoid injury in cover. They weigh between 50 and 60 lb, standing 21 to 25 in at the shoulder.

WEIMARANER. A breed that originated, as its name suggests, at Weimar at the beginning of the last century. The desire was to create an all-purpose dog that could hunt, point, retrieve and trail. It is probable that a great deal of red Schweisshund blood was used but, as soon as the desired result was achieved, the stud book was closed and the breed has been kept under very careful control ever since, and, even now, although the breed has achieved some popularity in America, there are not a great many Weimaraners outside Germany. It is difficult, therefore, to estimate how good they are in the shooting field, but they do excellently in obedience trials. They are striking looking dogs, with silver gray coats and blue gray eyes. Males weigh from 65 to 95 lb and bitches from 55 to 75 lb. Heights vary between 24 and 26 in for dogs and 22 and 25 in for bitches.

WELSH SETTERS. These, if they formed a different breed, are now extinct, except, perhaps for the Llewellin strain of English setter that was at one time extremely fashionable in the United States.

WELSH SPRINGER. Red and white spaniels were mentioned in ancient Welsh history, that were unlike any others in Britain. They were once called Welsh cockers, but were recognized, in 1902, as a separate breed under their present name. They look very much like a smaller edition of the English springer.

The head is moderately long, broad in the skull, and with a prominent stop. The eyes are hazel and the ears, which are set low, are pendant, small, and pear shaped, with no fringes longer than the leather. The muzzle is fairly long and rather more pointed than the English springer's. The neck is strong and slightly arched, the shoulders long and sloping, the back of medium length and with no sag, the chest deep and the ribs well sprung. The legs are straight and only slightly feathered, the feet round and with thick pads. The tail is docked, carried low, lightly feathered, and moves gaily whilst the dog is at work. The coat is short, flat, and smooth, with only light featherings on ears, legs and tail. The colour is red and white, the red varying from orange to chestnut. The height is around 17 in, and the weight between 33 and 40 lb.

WIRE-HAIRED POINTING GRIFFON. This is a completely man-made breed evolved, in the second half of the last century, by a Dutchman called Korthals, and, in France, where much of the later development was done, it is still called Korthals' griffon. It is

Weimaraner

probable that spaniel, setter, otterhound and German short-haired pointer blood were all added to the original griffon to produce the ultimate pointer, but, even then, it was a slower dog than existing pointing breeds and, outside the marshy country it was bred for, it has never been very popular. It has the distinction, however, of being the only wire-haired pointer. It is a strong, short-backed and short-legged dog, with a harsh, bristly coat.

The head is long, and the long coat provides what look like moustache and eyebrows. The eyes are large with a yellow iris, and the ears are of medium size, set rather high and slightly hairy. The nose is brown and the neck rather long. The legs are straight, muscular, and covered with short, wiry hair. The feet are round, well formed and firm. The tail is generally docked to one third of its length, and is carried gaily. It has no feathering but is covered with harsh hair. The coat is hard and stiff, and the undercoat is downy. The colour is steel gray, gray white, or chestnut, the first two with chestnut splashes. The height varies between $21\frac{1}{2}$ and $23\frac{1}{2}$ in for dogs and $19\frac{1}{2}$ and $21\frac{1}{2}$ in for bitches.

Dogs with the Gun

Four categories of dog serve the gun. They are the pointers and setters (colloquially known as 'bird dogs'), the retrievers, the spaniels and, in North America, the hounds, particularly the beagle, over which more ground game is shot than over any other breed. A sub-category, the pointer-retrievers developed to meet shooting requirements in central Europe, cover in non-specialist ways the functions of all these, and a little more.

Bird dogs range wide tracts of open country to find winged game; unlike other gundogs, their work excludes ground game. They indicate the bird's position, when found, but refrain from flushing it until the shooter has taken up position and gives the order. In Europe and Britain they have no further duty after the shot is fired, but in America are commonly taught to retrieve on command.

Retrievers, when used in the traditional manner, have no duty until a shot is fired. Prior to this, they are required to walk at heel awaiting their moment. When game (either winged or fur) is down they are sent to retrieve it in the many situations which the shooter himself cannot meet. For example, birds falling in thick cover; in or beyond a river; or, if winged, running long distances (pheasants often go half a mile). In finding wounded quarry, perhaps their most important single function, retrievers must distinguish between the bloodscent of the pricked bird and the body scent of unshot game which is to be left undisturbed until later. In the United States retrievers, especially Labrador, are frequently used as game finders when hunting woodcock, ruf-

fed grouse and pheasant, much as spaniel would be used and are preferred by many upland hunters for their endurance and versatility.

Spaniels operate both before and after the shot is fired. Their work is to hunt thick cover closely, always within gunshot; to flush birds and ground game alike; to drop and remain motionless whenever game is moved to avoid distracting the shooter; and, when ordered, to seek out and retrieve whatever has been shot, acting in this respect exactly as a retriever would.

The foregoing are all used specifically for small game shooting. The pointer-retrievers from central Europe have been evolved to cope also with the larger game commonly taken there. They may be required to track wounded deer or wild boar, or to retrieve fox.

Though their functions differ widely, the object of all categories of gundog is identical – to bring game quickly and mercifully to the bag. The use of efficient, well-trained gundogs has a humanitarian aspect. This manifests itself not merely in prompt retrieving of the wounded but, in the cases of bird dogs and spaniels, in the presenting of game to the shooter so as to give him the maximum chance of killing cleanly.

Though many breeds, briefly noted below, compose these categories, most of them originated as strains evolved to meet local requirements of terrain, climate or usage. Only two main tap-roots of the world's gundogs are discernible. The origins of both are lost in antiquity, and their modern products diverge widely.

One original was the primeval spaniel, known to the Romans (and nobody knows for how long before that), from which derive all spaniels and setters. The other was an unknown progenitor of hound type from which descended the 'southern hound' of France (chief ancestor of foxhounds and beagles), the old English talbot (extinct except on coats-of-arms and inn signs), the modern pointer, and his collaterals.

So pointers, setters and spaniels as pure breeds selectively nurtured by knowledgeable persons, antecede by many centuries the use of firearms in sport. They were used for 'springing' birds to be taken by hawk (hence the springer spaniel), 'pointing' birds at a distance to which a horseman could fly his falcon (hence pointers), and 'setting' game which medieval fowlers then took by net (setters).

From the dogs' viewpoint the supersession of these ancient practices by the gun did no more than alter a detail in their lives. Their pattern and purpose remained unchanged. From the concentration of inherited characteristics fostered by falconers and fowlers across the centuries derive the gentle yet ardent temperaments, the uncanny perceptions of the nose, the chain-reactions of nerve reflexes set in action by

The African elephant provides exciting and often dangerous hunting

the analysis of deflected drifts of wind. This legacy from the past has made setters, pointers and spaniels creatures of air as well as earth. Though dissipated by the show-ring's inversion of breeding priorities, these inherited capacities are preserved and made still more perfect by field trials.

In one sense retrievers form an exception to this. Though their genetic components are ancient, their evolution is recent. It falls substantially within the last century, deriving from the introduction of the breech-loading shotgun. This led to the practice of driving game rather than walking-up over dogs and, by greatly increasing the amount of game shot, created the need for single-purpose retrieving dogs. Previously it had been taken for granted that pointers and setters would retrieve when necessary, the attitude being comparable to the modern estimate of a spaniel which will not retrieve as only half a spaniel.

Bird dogs comprise English, Irish and Gordon setters and the pointers. The English setter achieved pre-eminence last century. This it largely retains, though its spaniel-orientation does not give it the physical durability of the hound-orientated pointer, especially in hot climates and on rocky terrain.

The Irish setter's development in sparse game country has given it long-lasting optimism. In parts of Ireland a day may yield only one find, and this is as likely to happen in the last ten minutes as in the first. So the Irish setter is renowned for keeping going when the rest have stopped. The Gordon setter, always black-and-tan, was bred by successive Dukes of Richmond and Gordon to work in the high heather of the Scottish Cairngorms, and is taller than other bird dogs.

The five retriever breeds have five different genetic backgrounds. Consequently, their temperaments and styles of working also differ. Now numerically the most popular, the Labrador shares the hound-orientation of the Spanish black pointer which was used in the mid-nineteenth century to improve the strain of black, close-coated dogs thought to have reached Europe from Newfoundland. From this speculative fusion of blood the present breed emerged. For decades it remained in the hands of a few British landowning families, achieving public recognition in the early 1900s.

Probably the Labrador is in fact European in origin, and was first valued for its swimming powers. Certainly it was introduced to Britain by Portuguese fishermen returning from the Newfoundland cod banks, giving rise to the belief that this was where the breed came from. It is equally probable that these dogs or their forbears had first crossed the Atlantic in the opposite direction from Portugal. Significantly, in the Portuguese language the word 'labrador' (small 'l') means 'the worker' and is a more apt title

for the breed than Labrador (large 'L') now (but not then) designating a territory on the Canadian mainland.

The first retriever breed to achieve recognition had been the curly-coat. It shares not only its coat but other characteristics with the standard poodle. The word poodle comes from the German 'pudel', meaning water. Standard poodles are good swimmers and are trainable. Probably they are now used as shooting dogs as often as curly-coat retrievers, which are more often seen in the show ring. Their upstanding good looks catch the eye there.

But the curly-coat had never dominated the sport. Until general recognition of the Labrador the flat-coated retriever had been unrivalled for half a century. Its derivation was almost certainly based on the same fisherman's dog as produced the Labrador, but in this case the 'improving' blood was that of the black setter, a few strains of which are still jealously guarded in Western Ireland and the Hebrides, and for which flat-coats are often mistaken. The flat-coated retriever is nearer to a retrieving setter than to any of the other four retriever breeds. It owns scent at bird-dog range, quests with a high head until hitting the line, and has the verve of the galloping breeds.

The golden retriever, evolved from a strain of English water spaniels now extinct, has a more deliberate, less adventurous outlook than the others. (For another theory of its evolution *see* Golden Retriever, in the entry: Dog Breeds for Hunting). It has a particular appeal to ladies. The fifth, the Chesapeake Bay retriever, the only pure retrieving breed to be evolved outside Britain, is a robust, aggressive, courageous dog with Labrador-like characteristics evolved primarily for foreshore work by commercial duck hunters and baymen on the Atlantic seaboard of North America.

There are seven British sporting spaniel breeds, one French and one German. The English springer, tallest and raciest of them all, is the world's most popular all-purpose practical shooting dog. Its adaptability makes it as popular in India, Africa and Australia as in Britain and North America. It represents the counterpart in the setter/spaniel complex to the English setter. While Purcell Llewellin, Edward Laverack, and more recently William Humphreys were developing the then run-of-the-mill gundogs into the English setter as a work of art for aristocrats shooting in the grand manner, others were making a second version as the man-of-all-work for rough-shooters. The result, the English springer, has now achieved as patrician a status as the setter. He can do everything except work in small spaces, for which the cocker exists – so named because its traditional use was to push woodcock out of low-growing rhododendron thickets.

Grant's gazelles, small antelopes found in the open plains and bush country of east Africa

The careful, unhurrying Clumber is, in Britain, the senior shooter's friend; keeping pace with him poses no problems. The field spaniel, now rare but a breed of high quality, is a less high-powered counterpart of the English springer and rather easier to handle. The low-slung Sussex is designed to work on the steep slippery chalk slopes of the English Downs.

The Welsh springer, bottomless in stamina and courage, is generally a better hunter than retriever; the Irish water spaniel, an evident offshoot of the curly-coated retriever – standard poodle family, is effective if sometimes happy-go-lucky in rugged conditions. The Brittany spaniel is the French answer to the English springer, and is popular in the United States for the ease with which it can be trained to point birds and hold a point. It is especially well

A golden retriever marking high pheasants

liked by grouse and woodcock shooters. The admirable Munsterlander has been bred true to type in Germany for many generations and may represent the norm in dogs which worked to the falcon before sporting guns impelled a deviation between setters and spaniels.

Of the pointer-retrievers, the German short-haired pointer has well made its mark outside its native area; surprisingly, its wire-haired counterpart has not. The Weimaraner and the charming Hungarian Vizla have also established themselves, especially in America where the sporting canon is less rigid than in Britain.

In most countries the years since World War Two have seen a blurring in gundog functions. In the United Kingdom bird dogs have been less used. In Britain and America retrievers have been increasingly used for hunting-up, which is properly spaniel work. Among the spaniels themselves four of the seven breeds have been increasingly unemployed in active shooting. The reasons are inter-related.

Bird dogs reached peak popularity in an age of leisure when sportsmen were home-based and had few other pre-occupations. The training and handling of high-mettled dogs then came easily to them. The contrary is the case now, when the country-side is less and less a way of life, and more and more a place of resort for those whose day to day interests are far away.

In countries of sparse game populations pointers and setters are used as much as ever, simply because sport would be impossible without them. Examples include upland North America, Scandinavia, Italy and France. Their wider use in Britain could enable shooters operating in pairs as distinct from parties to enjoy sport in smaller areas, especially near towns.

Retrievers do spaniel work because of two combining influences. Breeding for show has dissipated most of the working potential of Welsh springers, Sussex, Clumbers and field spaniels. Breeding for trials has produced a type of English springer and cocker which is too much of a handful for average shooters. They have therefore come to regard the working strains with misgivings as great as those held towards show strains, though different. Hence the trend towards the supposedly less headstrong retrievers.

Some Labradors take kindly to the change, though they are naturally less methodical in ground treatment and less adaptable in cover than spaniels whose job it is. Golden retrievers are specially favoured for this work by British gamekeepers who declare them to be easily controlled, courageous in cover and tireless. Flatcoats tend to setter-like ranging. To use each breed for its proper purpose seems the best policy, or else an all-rounder from among the pointer-retrievers. ws

Dotterel *see* Plovers

Doves *see* Pigeons

Ducks *see* Waterfowl; *also* Hides and Decoys; Waterfowl Flighting Ponds; Wildfowl and Wet Gravel Pits; Wildfowling Round the World.

Duiker (*Cephalophus* species)

Duiker is a name derived from the Dutch 'duiker', or diver, which has been used loosely to describe various fairly closely related species of small antelopes found either singly or in pairs throughout Africa south of the Sahara. The name indicates their preference for diving into cover and squatting rather than running to avoid danger, although generally they do have a good turn of speed and staying power when chased. They are generally encountered and shot with a shotgun when the hunter is after game birds. Their flesh is considered moderately good to eat. Most of the species commonly shot are of the genus *Cephalophus*, which have rounded ears, both sexes horned and no inguinal pouches, with the notable exception of the common duiker (*Sylvicapra grimmia*) or duikerbok, which is common in many parts of south and central Africa, generally found in woodland, forest margins, scrub and the deep, jungly ravines of the mountain ranges, sometimes in the open or cultivated land. It stands 26 in at the shoulder with pointed ears and a characteristic tuft of hair between them. The female is hornless; the male has short, sharp horns averaging 4½ in long and inguinal glands are present. Coat colour may vary considerably, even in the same locality, from greenish-yellow to reddish-brown. A grazer and browser, it will eat any vegetation and may lamb at any time of year, generally only one, though two is not uncommon. Albinos and horned females have been recorded, but are exceptional.

Other species of duiker shot are:
Blue duiker (*Cephalophus monticolus*) or blue-buck, also known as *C. caerulus*, is found in parts of central Africa, especially in forests and thickets in mountainous country. It is a slaty blue colour and rather smaller than the common duiker. It is a browser and in a suitable habitat not uncommon; thought to breed one or two young between August and December.

Red duiker (*C. natalensis*) or Natal redbuck, a small, bright bay species found in South Africa, notably Natal; both grazer and browser.

Yellow-backed duiker (*C. sylvicultor*) found in central Africa, especially Zambia, is not uncommon though local in distribution. This rather larger beast has a notable yellow dorsal crest, which is erected under stress. Principally a browser it also grazes, and is thought to breed in December.

The common or gray duiker is widely distributed in Africa, in a large range of habitats, from the Cape to Ethiopia.

E

Ecuador

Situated on the west coast of South America, Ecuador is about 226,000 square miles in area. It falls into four distinct regions: the Andean regions or Sierra, composed of the Eastern and Western Cordilleras, and the inter-Andean valleys, cooled by the altitude; the tropical coastal region; the Oriente, stretching eastwards from the Andes to the Amazon basin, and consisting largely of undeveloped tropical forest; the Galapagos islands (twelve large and several hundred small) which lie about 500 miles off the coast. The mainland is watered by the upper Amazon in the east and several short rivers in the west.

Crocodiles and other reptiles may be hunted in the Amazon regions. In the mountains there is deer hunting on horseback as well as the best bird shooting. Pigeons are the chief species shot, but condors are perhaps of most interest to the visitor. Large game, such as jaguars and pigs, are hunted in the jungle along the Amazon. For further information on the game *see* South America, Shooting in.

Hunting in Ecuador is mostly private, but there is the occasional organized public hunt, especially along the Amazon.

Further Information

Consult initially the nearest Ecuadorian consulate.

For an import permit for firearms visitors should write, before entering the country, to the Secretary, Ministerio de Gobierno, Quito, Ecuador, giving details of firearms, length of stay, etc.

Egypt *see* Middle East

Eiders *(Somateriini)*

The eiders form a group of northern, maritime, diving ducks of considerable ornithological and even commercial interest, but they ought not to interest us very greatly as hunters. Even the southerly limits of their wintering ranges fail to bring them sufficiently south for wildfowlers to have frequent contact with them; as maritime ducks they spend most of their time out at sea; they live almost entirely on molluscs, crustacea and echinoderms, and their flesh, as a consequence, is inedible to anyone except an Eskimo. Their down, of course, has considerable commercial value, and in Iceland and Norway there are eider farms where great batteries of nesting boxes are set up so that the down may be taken, daily, from the nests. All of these factors explain why, in most European countries, the eider is a protected bird and nobody particularly wants to hunt it.

The eiders breed in the American as well as the European Arctic, and their wintering grounds bring them down as far as the New England coast, where so much waterfowl hunting takes place. They are not, in America, protected birds; the Eskimos shoot and enjoy them in the north, and in the south they have to take some of the pressures that arise from too many hunters and too few birds to hunt. The situation is a well known one. The comparative scarcity of game birds diverts hunting attention to the waterfowl. The comparative scarcity of the more edible waterfowl diverts attention to the less edible, and, in the end, the inedible ones. Eiders are shot in America because they are ducks, because they fly, and because there are a great many American hunters.

There are several species of eider. Most of them are larger and more heavily built than other diving ducks. They all have long, rather than round heads, with sloping foreheads merging into prominent, high-based bills. They are essentially marine ducks, and only come ashore to nest, to rest, and to preen. Even then they seldom go inland, but to islands and the foreshore. They fly close to the water, generally in Indian file, with a slow wingbeat and their heads held low. They nest, generally in colonies, close to the water, the clutch of four to six eggs being covered with down, and taking 28 days to incubate.

Five different sub-species of the European eider *(Somateria mollissima)* are recognized, among them being the American eider *(S. mollissima dresseri)*, and the northern eider *(S. mollissima borealis)*. The drakes all have black bellies, and white backs, pinkish breasts and green bills and legs. The head has a black crown and a green nape. The duck has uniformly brown plumage barred with black. The drake weighs about 4 lb and measures between 22 and 24 in, the duck is about one pound lighter. The Pacific eider *(S. mollissima v-nigra)* resembles these except that the drake has a black, V-shaped marking on the throat with the point at the base of the bill. It is also the largest of all the eiders. The European eider breeds in Iceland and from north Scandinavia east to Novaya Zemleya, and winters on the shores of the North Sea and on the west coast of France. The American eider breeds along the coast of Hudson Bay, Labrador and Newfoundland and winters from Newfoundland to Long Island. The northern eider

A European eider drake photographed on a rocky seashore

nests and winters in Arctic waters, from Iceland to Baffin Bay. The Pacific eider nests along the Alaskan and Yukon coasts and winters as well as nests in those regions.

The king eider *(Somateria spectabilis)* resembles the European eider. The drake is strikingly coloured, being largely white in the foreparts and black elsewhere. The head is blue-gray with light green cheeks, and there is a broad orange shield at the base of the bill. There is a prominent white patch on the forewing, and the speculum is blue. It breeds along the Arctic coasts of Europe and Asia and winters principally along the southern limits of its breeding grounds.

The spectacled eider *(Somateria fischeri)* is a rare bird, with an extremely limited range in Siberia and Alaska. It has suffered from over-hunting by the Eskimos. The duck resembles the European eider duck, but has feathers growing over the top of the bill, as has the drake. The drake has the light upperparts and the dark underparts of the other eiders, and the 'spectacles', a black rimmed white circle round the eyes, are distinctive.

Steller's eider *(Polysticta stelleri)* a comparatively rare bird, is placed in a different genus, seldom found outside western Alaska and eastern Siberia. The drake has a white head with a black throat, black collar, and black ring around the eye. The duck has deep brown plumage and a blue speculum edged with white. It is a partial migrant, coming south as far as the Aleutian Islands only when driven there by storms.

Eire *see* Ireland, Republic of

Eland *(Taurotragus oryx)*
This is the largest of the African antelopes and is found singly or in small herds in the thornbush cover on the edge of grasslands throughout south and east Africa. Standing 6 ft high at the shoulder the eland weighs upwards of 1,500 lb with horns present in both sexes and a noticeably heavy dewlap

A gregarious animal, the Cape eland has been found up to 14,000 ft.

and a hump on the shoulders. The horns are heavy and screwlike rather than spiralling, averaging about 28 in in length; the female's being slightly thinner than those of the male. The body colour is light fawn to brown with a black dorsal stripe and tail tuft and there are a series of narrow white stripes or vertical markings most noticeable behind the shoulder but fading towards the hindquarters. They are mainly browsers and probably calve throughout the year with a tendency for several cows to calve at the same time and a preponderance between October and November. Twins occur, but usually only a single calf is born. Although greatly reduced in many places their numbers remain quite good. They are surprisingly inconspicuous for such a large animal and are probably more plentiful than might be thought. In spite of their considerable size and weight they are surprisingly active and have been seen to leap thorn-bushes as much as six feet in height. The head of a good bull eland makes an excellent trophy, but they are generally so easily stalked and shot that no sportsman would wish for more than one. The sub-species, *T. oryx livingstonei*, is found in small to large herds in central Africa and is very similar. The giant eland, another species, *T. derbianus*, is found only in west Africa and is even larger than the other two sub-species, also having longer horns. It is strictly protected.

Elephants *(Elephantidae)*
The African elephant, *Loxodonta africana*, is the largest land mammal in the world, found in many parts of central Africa south of the Sahara. They stand on average about 10 ft 3 in at the shoulder. The tusks of a male seldom weigh less than 30 lb, averaging from 5 to 6 ft long. The tusks of the female are much smaller, averaging about 15 lb and nearer 3 ft long. Tusklessness occurs in both sexes. They feed on fruits, leaves, grass and roots. Wild fruits may cause seasonal movements of the herds which

vary in size from five to a hundred. The bulls may be either solitary or in small groups. Single calves may be born at any time of year but twins have been recorded. They have very keen senses of smell and hearing, and can move extremely fast, so that hunting is by stalking from downwind and a heavy calibre is required. It is a good plan to study a skeleton so that the size and position of the brain may be noted from all angles. A bullet at the nasal base of the skull, just below the bump over the trunk is the frontal shot for the brain; halfway between the eye and the ear from an angle will also hit the brain. From sideways on, a bullet just in front of the earhole will kill the elephant, which is also easily killed by a heart shot behind the elbow and level with the girth. When the elephant is down it is advisable to run up and put another bullet

into the back of the neck, for a beast that is merely stunned can be up in an instant and move as fast as a polo pony. A wounded elephant charging is not only a frightening spectacle, but also exceedingly dangerous – in this situation cool nerves are essential.

The Indian elephant, *Elephas maximus*, slightly smaller than the previous species, is found in Mysore, Travancore, Nilgiri, South India and forests of Assam and Bengal. Only proscribed rogues may be shot by sportsmen. The average height at the shoulder is 9 ft 9 in and the length of tusks under 6 ft. Many of these rogue elephants are tuskless males, but none the less dangerous for that. Hunting and shooting methods are much the same as for the African elephant.

Elk *see* Moose; Wapiti

It has been estimated that a charging African elephant can reach a speed of 25 m.p.h.

Emperor Goose *(Anser canagicus)*
A goose of limited distribution which is becoming increasingly rare, largely because the Eskimos have over-hunted it. Its breeding grounds lie around the mouths of the Yukon and Kuskokwim rivers, and it migrates no further than to the western end of the Alaskan Peninsula, and out to the Aleutian Islands.

Although, by the nature of its habitat, it is of little interest to hunters, it is a beautiful bird of medium size, with a scaly gray appearance, white head, pink bill with white nail and a 'grinning' patch on the lower mandible.

Emu *see* Australia

England *see* United Kingdom of Great Britain and Ireland

Ethiopia
Ehiopia covers approximately 450,000 square miles in north-east Africa. Most of the country consists of a large mountainous plateau, deeply intersected by important valleys, such as the Blue Nile and the Rift Valley. The plateau is surrounded by desert and semi-desert areas at a much lower altitude, which, with the valley gorges, are very hot. The higher plateaus, however, are well watered and have a pleasant climate with two distinct seasons: a dry winter from October to May, and a wet summer from June to September, though there is also a season of 'small rains', usually in March.

The country has a considerable physical range: from mountains over 15,000 ft, to areas below sea level, with accompanying extremes of heat and cold. The ecology of the different areas is naturally very varied. Agriculture and cattle breeding are the main occupations, the crops ranging from sugar cane, tobacco, cotton and coffee, to cereals, potatoes, citrus fruits, and many others. The forests are fairly extensive, but remain a largely untapped source of wealth. The type of fauna is considerably affected by the varying environments, to the extent that while there are many species common to the neighbouring countries of Kenya, Somalia and the Sudan, there is much that is uniquely Ethiopian. The resulting choice of game and hunting conditions is almost bewildering, but should provide something to suit nearly any sportsman's taste.

The main areas of wildlife are in the western half of the country, in particular the Gambella enclave in the Nile basin, probably the richest game area in Ethiopia. However, the Omo river drainage further south, the other side of the great mountain spur that extends south-west towards the Sudan, is also notable, especially for its eland, buffalo and elephant.

The eastern side of the main north-south mountain axis has a more desert environment, and less plentiful wildlife, the Somali wild ass being the most notable species. To the south of this area the land becomes richer, with typical African plains' fauna, though giraffe, buffalo and elephant are not common.

There are many varieties of gazelle in the arid border of the east and south-west, including Soemmering's, dorcas, Houghlin's, Eritrean, Grant's and others. There are two species of ibex, the walia ibex, of the high Simian massif in the north, which is completely protected, and the Nubian ibex for which a limited number of licences is issued each year. The latter is found on the Red Sea coast of northern Eritrea. There are also three species of hartebeest: Swayne's, found in the east and south-east, the tora of the north-west, and the lelwel, or Jackson's hartebeest of the south-west.

A representative bag of the most commonly sought species is easily obtained, and would include, elephant, buffalo, lion, leopard, zebra and a wide variety of antelopes. Of the latter the greater kudu provides perhaps the most satisfying hunt, together with good trophies, but good heads of lesser kudu, gerenuk, roan and eland are also relatively abundant. To some, however, Ehiopia's greatest attraction is the possibility of acquiring unique trophies that may be obtained nowhere else in Africa. Such, for instance, is the mountain nyala, much larger than the lowland nyala of southern Africa, with horns measuring up to 45 in; the black leopard, a melanistic variety of the common leopard, is comparatively common in the highlands; and the menelik bushbuck, the male of which is all black and which is quite abundant in Ethiopia.

Ethiopia has a varied big-game fauna, and one of the most attractive is the leopard, shown here with a recently-killed monkey.

Protected Species—Ethiopia

Mammals
Aardwolf
Beira
Antelope
Cheetah
Dugong
Pelzeln's gazelle,
Speke's gazelle,
Gelada
Giraffe
Swayne's hartebeest
Tora hartebeest
Pangolin
Black rhinoceros
Simian fox
Walia ibex
Wild ass

Birds
Lammergeyer
Waldrapp.
White-winged dove
Scarce swift
Prince Ruspoli's turaco
Taita falcon

Special Regulations

Visitors must employ a licensed professional hunter who knows the country and the game, and they are advised to contact one before arriving, particularly as all the necessary arrangements can be made beforehand. Every visitor must moreover be accompanied by a game guard, for which there is a service charge of $10 per day, and for which a deposit is required, based on the expected duration of the stay. At the end of the stay both the professional hunter and the game guard submit a list of the number and type of animals shot for calculating the capitation fee.

Sporting firearms and ammunition must be imported as accompanied baggage. One hundred and twenty rounds of ammunition per weapon is permitted, and although ammunition for shot guns and the more common calibres of rifle is usually available in Addis Ababa, visitors are recommended to take their own. No firearms may be cleared through customs without permission from the Security Department. The most convenient procedure is to apply to the Wildlife Conservation Organisation who will inform the Security Department so that the weapons may be cleared with the least possible delay. The total fee for the import and re-export of firearms is $22, to be paid to the Security Department. Self-loading and automatic rifles are prohibited, and .22 rifles and shotguns may only be used for birds and wounded big game. For buffalo and elephant, rifles must have a larger calibre or more muzzle energy than a .375 magnum.

Hunting is prohibited at night, as is shooting from, or in close proximity to, a vehicle. No hunting is permitted in National Parks, Game Reserves and Sanctuaries. Hunting is allowed in controlled hunting areas with a permit issued by the Wildlife Conservation Organisation. A list of the species available in each area may be obtained from the organization. The table gives the controlled hunting areas, the season they are available, and the recommended duration of the hunt:

Further Information

The following names and addresses are of professional hunters in Ethiopia, who can arrange everything for a hunting trip, from outfitting, stuffing and export of trophies to hunting and firearms' licences.

Ted Shatto, P.O. Box 1745, Addis Ababa.

Thomas Mattanovich, P.O. Box 2444, Addis Ababa.

Karl Luthi, P.O. Box 2787, Addis Ababa.

Major Gizaw Gedlegiorgis, P.O. Box 2183, Addis Ababa.

Lieutenant Getachew Tefera, P.O. Box 2183, Addis Ababa.

The Wildlife Conservation Organisation, P.O. Box 386, Addis Ababa, deals with all shooting, conservation, licences, etc.

Controlled Hunting Areas—Ethiopia

Area	Season
Danakil and Southern Eritrea	All year, 10-21 days
Ogaden	October-June, 10-21 days
Borana	July-March, 21-30 days
Omo valley and south west Kaffa	July-March, 21-30 days
Gambela	Dec-May, 15-25 days
Mizan Tafari (montane forest areas of Kaffa and Illubabor)	Oct-May, 12-21 days
Bale, Arussi and Chercher mountains	Nov-April, 15-25 days
	Nov-May, 15-25 days

Licences—Ethiopia

There are six categories of game licence:

The general hunting licence is compulsory for everybody hunting game, but without a supplementary licence it only confers the right to hunt bushbuck, bushpig, dik-dik, hare, and warthog, with a limit of 2 per day, except for hare and warthog, limited to 3 per day. Licence fee: $50 (Ethiopian dollars).

The game-bird licence applies to duck, quail, sand grouse, geese, francolin, guinea fowl, speckled pigeon, red-eyed dove and ring-necked dove with a bag limit of 10 per day, except for sand grouse (30 per day). Licence fee: $30.

The snipe licence covers all snipe except the painted snipe. Licence fee: $25.

The supplementary game licence is available to holders of the general licence. This licence is issued, subject to the availability of the desired game, on an annual quota and a 'capitation fee', varying with the species, is charged per head shot. The licence covers the following game (capitation fee, in Ethiopian dollars, in brackets): buffalo ($200), common bushbuck ($40), menelik bushbuk ($70), bushpig ($30), crocodile ($60), blue duiker ($30), common duiker ($20), eland ($200), elephant ($750), dorcas gazelle ($50), Grant's gazelle ($50), Heuglin's gazelle ($60), mongalla gazelle ($50), Soemmering's gazelle ($40), gerenuk ($50), giant forest hog ($100), hare ($5), lelwel hartebeest ($100), hippopotamus ($300), Nubian ibex ($750), klipspringer ($20), white-eared kob ($60), greater kudu ($500), lesser kudu ($300), leopard ($400), black leopard ($500), lion ($300), Nile lechwe ($1,000), mountain nyala ($1,500), oribi ($20), oryx ($150), Chandler's reedbuck ($80), common reedbuck (bohor) ($50), roan antelope ($200), topi ($80), warthog ($30), waterbuck ($100), common (Burchell's) zebra ($150), Grevy's zebra ($300).

A special permit may be issued to holders of a general licence. Capitation fees are determined by the Wildlife Conservation Organization. This permit covers aardvark, bat-eared fox, bush baby and galago, caracal, civet, elephant (young and female), genet cat, Neumann's hartebeest, hunting dog, hyrax, monkeys, otters, pectinator, ratel (honey badger), serval, spring hare or gerboa, striped hyena, immature game animals and pregnant females or females with young; blue-winged goose, pygmy goose, ruddy shelduck, Harwood's francolin, vulturine guinea fowl, monitor lizard, python, tortoise.

Certain animals may be captured under a game capture permit (fee determined by the game capture organization). They are the vervet monkey, all animals not mentioned elsewhere, and corvids, white-vented bulbul, Swainson's sparrow, gray-headed sparrow, white-browed sparrow or weaver, black-headed sparrow, baglafecht weaver, red bishop, bronze mannikin, cut throat, red-billed fire finch, waxbill and red-cheeked cordon bleu. (The capitation fee for the birds is about $0.20)

The following birds and animals are classified as vermin and may be hunted or shot without licence or permit: common baboon, spotted hyena, mole-rats, porcupines, rats, and mice, red-billed quelea, red-headed quelea, mouse birds.

There is a standard form for application for a hunting licence. This requires the visitor's full name and address, nationality, passport number, age, dates of stay in Ethiopia, type of licence required, and type and date of any Ethiopian licence previously held, particulars of firearms and ammunition, name of professional hunter employed, proposed hunting areas and species, signature and countersignature of professional hunter.

F

Fallow Deer (*Dama dama*)

Originally introduced from the Mediterranean area, the fallow deer has been common in British and European parks and forests for centuries, and is now common in many parts of Britain, Europe, N. Africa and Asia. The summer coloration is fawn with white spots distributed over the upper half of the body, turning in winter to a uniform gray. Due to inbreeding in parks there are many variations on this natural coloration, running the whole gamut from white to black. They usually stand about 36 in at the shoulder; the bucks averaging about 100 lb and the does about 50 lb. Only the bucks have antlers, which are characteristically handsome and palmated, averaging from 24 to 30 in long. They are always found in herds, although during the summer months the old bucks are generally found away from the young bucks and does. The mating season begins about September and the gestation period is eight months, after which the doe may have from one to three fawns. Although basically grazers they may often eat the leaves of trees, standing on their hindlegs for this purpose.

Shooting may be by stalking in suitable surroundings, though still-hunting is the method most generally employed; they may also be shot from a high seat. The venison is generally regarded as preferable to that of red deer, and the hide and horns make a handsome trophy.

See also Red and Fallow Deer Stalking.

Feral Animals

Any animal which has at one time been domesticated and then reverted to the wild state, is termed a feral animal. Very often such animals can become pests, even more of a nuisance than truly wild animals of the same species. Australia is particularly rich in such animals, including feral camels, which are on the list of pests which may be shot, in some states, throughout the year. Feral cats, pigs and goats are extremely tiresome there, causing much damage to game stock and poultry.

Ferrets and Ferreting

Ferrets belong to the *Mustelidae* or weasel family, whose members are to be found in every country of the world except Australia and Madagascar. It includes badgers and bears as well as polecats, stoats and weasels. All are more or less aggressive and tough fighters when cornered. Distinctive features are five toes on each foot, a pronounced bony ridge running the length of the skull and an automatic locking of the jaws when shut which almost defies dislocation without bone damage.

Originally bred from polecats, ferrets, in spite of their domestic strain, are probably the most cold-bloodedly efficient members of this family, hunting purely for pleasure. They share most of the attributes of their kind, but unlike stoats and polecats, cannot climb trees. Two colour variations are common: one known as the 'polecat ferret' is similar to its namesake in markings; the other is the albino strain, with a cream or white coat. The first is generally regarded as being the 'sharper' of the two, but the second is often preferred by sportsmen because it is easier to see against a background of earth and foliage.

Of all the sportsman's allies ferrets are far the most poorly documented. Pliny

Two fallow deer bucks with their palmated antlers interlocked in combat

refers to Roman legionaries hunting with ferrets in apparently similar fashion to hounds. It is reasonable to assume that the development of the ferret and ferreting followed hard on the exploitation of rabbiting for food or for sport; presumably, therefore, ferrets were in use on the European continent before they made an appearance in Great Britain, for it is known that rabbits did not occur in the British Isles before the Norman Conquest. The use of ferrets is common to the countries of central and eastern Europe and the British Isles, but elsewhere is seldom practised. In the United States ferrets are sometimes employed for hunting rats but in many states their use is prohibited by law.

Male ferrets are known as hobs; the females as jills. Both sexes may be kept together and should only be separated when the jill comes in season unless it is planned to breed from them. It is often said that a jill ferret will die if she is not mated in her second season. Although this is not strictly true, the females, like those of other species, are usually healthier and live longer for having a litter in their youth.

A jill may come into season at any time during March, April or May. Once a year is the general rule, but a ferret from which the young are taken at birth, or which is not allowed to breed, may come into season more than once. When the hob has been left with the jill for 24 hours and his interest has declined, he should be removed, although some ferret keepers, who have developed a special bond of confidence between themselves and their animals sometimes leave both sexes together throughout the gestation period and even after the young are born. The safer rule is to part them, in case the hob or jill disturb each other's peace of mind and eat the young.

The period of gestation is six weeks, during which the jill should be well fed on raw flesh and milk. A week before the young are due the sleeping compartment of the hutch should be cleaned, provided with fresh bedding in the shape of short hay or straw and it should then be closed to all except the jill and not disturbed again for six weeks.

The average litter is from 6 to 10, born blind, their eyes opening after about six weeks. Two weeks later they start to leave the nest and may be safely handled. They are weaned at eight weeks and can be removed to their own hutch a fortnight later. The more handling they receive at this time, the more manageable they will become.

By nature ferrets are clean animals and should be kept in clean hutches with plenty of room to exercise themselves. They need a sleeping compartment and one in which they can be fed and where they can relieve themselves. They are thirsty creatures. Their diet should be one of flesh and water, with bread and milk given only if no fresh flesh is available. The old idea of starving them for

24 hours to make them work more keenly is a bad one, only likely to encourage them to kill a rabbit and lie up with it.

Ferret hutches should be dry with an airy daytime compartment, but protected from draughts. Straw in the sleeping compartment and sawdust on the floor of the outer compartment are recommended. Feeding and drinking utensils should be heavy enough so that they cannot be upset and must be kept scrupulously clean. If ferrets are greeted with a familiar call or whistle at feeding time, they will be encouraged to leave rabbit burrows later in response to the same sound.

Similar methods of working ferrets are universal. The principle is to cause the rabbits to bolt at the approach of the ferret, either into the open where they can be shot, or into purse nets set at the mouths of the burrows. Large ferrets, therefore, which can catch hold and kill a rabbit, are not required. Smaller bolters which an adult rabbit can shake off and escape from are preferable, but it is useful to have a large hob ferret in reserve which will work on a line to locate a bolter which has killed, or caught and laid up with a rabbit. The kill can then be located by digging along the line and following the hole.

It was once a common practice to muzzle ferrets with soft string or a special metal muzzle and in earlier, less enlightened days warreners used to stitch their bolters' lips together, or break off their teeth with a key. With properly fed, trained and handled ferrets none of this is necessary and a muzzle can cause a ferret to die a lingering death from starvation. In any event lost ferrets do not usually take kindly to a life in the wild and will generally not survive for long. Although they are fearless and will, for example, bolt foxes, they will often come to grief in a burrow of old rats. Bolting rats with ferrets was once a country pastime,

Ferret being introduced to a burrow

which has declined with the increased efficiency of modern rat poisons. Ferrets are still sometimes used to decoy crows and magpies within shot, for these predators are quick to spot and mob a tethered ferret placed in a ride or on the edge of a wood in the early morning.

Quietness is the essence of successful ferreting; noise and heavy footed movement above a burrow are to be avoided. Rabbits bolt best in dry, frosty weather, although frozen ground magnifies the movement on the surface. Windy days make it difficult to hear the movement of ferrets and rabbits below ground and mask the footfalls of ferrets which leave a burrow unnoticed, while rabbits dislike facing a wind. Snow hides treacherously large warrens, and rainy days are out of the question.

The use of purse nets with ferrets is common practice. First the holes are carefully covered with purse nets pegged in position. The ferret is then inserted in the principal hole. After a short while rabbits will be heard moving below ground and will be seen suddenly bolting from the holes. They then become entangled in the purse nets, which, as their name implies, operate like a purse with a draw string opening so that the force of the rabbit entering the net causes the string to pull tight behind it.

Ferreting provides good sport, in that there is always an element of uncertainty about where and when a rabbit will bolt. Frequently a rabbit will suddenly appear from a concealed hole which has not been noticed. For this reason it is important to try to locate all the holes beforehand. When several rabbits are bolting together in a crowded warren the fun can be fast and furious. Unless each rabbit struggling in a purse net is at once removed and the net replaced, another rabbit may bolt from the same hole and escape, so that it is generally wise to have at least one gun available for such occasions.

In close country it is advisable to use a light gun, such as a ·410, so that rabbits shot at close range are not hopelessly mangled by a heavy charge of shot so as to be uneatable. A half charged cartridge in a twelve bore is an alternative, but a lighter gun has the advantage of being easier to handle and more suitable for the sport.

When guns are used dogs are best left at home, unless well trained and accustomed to ferrets. Care must also be taken that shooters on either side of a hedge or ditch know each other's precise whereabouts. Rabbits should never be shot actually in the mouth of the hole in case the ferret is right behind them. Ferrets not being used are best kept well out of the way in a carrying box where they are not only out of the line of fire, but far enough from the burrow not to alarm rabbits by their sctratching on the box side. PHW

Top, the reason for the ferruginous duck's other name of white-eyed pochard is clearly seen in this picture.

Bottom, Finland is one of the European countries where brown bear are shot, generally at the end of May.

Ferruginous Duck (*Aythya nyroca*)
Also known as the white-eyed pochard this is a diving duck, very similar to, though less common than the Pochard (*Aythya ferina*) q.v. The drake has white eyes, dark chestnut head, neck and breast, white underparts and white wing patch. The female is similar, but with duller colouring and brown eyes.

It breeds in the Mediterranean basin, southern Siberia, Persia, northern India and Tibet and winters south of its breeding range in Nigeria, Sudan, southern India and Burma.

Finland
Bounded on the north-west by sections of Norway and Sweden. Finland is the most eastern, and certainly the coldest of the Scandinavian countries. Its total area is over 130,000 square miles, over a third of which is north of the Arctic Circle; 72% is afforested, but only 9%, in the south, under cultivation. Another 9% is lakes, and the rest waste or urban. As these figures indicate, there are vast tracts of unspoilt country, with population levels sinking to as low as ·2 per square kilometre in the north; towns and farming are concentrated in the south. The lakes form the principal means of communication, whether by water or by ice (even the harbours are mostly icebound for at least five months of the year).

Always famous as a source of furs Finland has attracted hunters from Roman days. The fur-bearing animals that exercised this attraction, though now hunted for sport rather than for their pelts, all, naturally, belong to the northern game element, which has a considerable bearing on the type and availability of shooting and the Finnish attitude towards it. Despite the vast areas of unspoilt countryside, the game population is not as high as might be expected, mainly because the Northern game predominant in Finland is always strictly limited in its density. Even more southerly game that is found in Finland is operating at the extreme of its range, and is consequently not as numerous as elsewhere. All this means that the Finnish hunter generally adopts a very sporting attitude towards his shooting, works hard for his game, and is more concerned with quality than quantity.

Game Population
Finnish game is particularly distinguished by the continuous change in the game populations from year to year. The table of game therefore includes total bag figures for average and peak years.

As the statistics indicate hunters have to work for their game in Finland. Visiting hunters should be aware of this and should have taken it into account before deciding to shoot in Finland. It is quite possible to walk 10 or 20 miles without once firing a shot. An indication of the sort of conditions

Total Annual Bag—Finland

Game	Average year	Peak year
Blackgame	160,000	350,000
Capercailzie	110,000	175,000
Hazel grouse	75,000	120,000
Partridge	4,000	25,000
Pheasant	1,000	3,500
Pigeon	3,000	12,000
Ptarmigan	50,000	100,000
Wildfowl	240,000	263,000
Ermine	5,000	30,000
Brown hare	20,000	100,000
Fox	18,000	28,000
Marten	500	1,600
Mink	1,000	2,300
Moose	5,000	8,500
Muskrat	170,000	603,000
Seal	2,500	5,000
Blue hare	170,000	250,000
Squirrel	1,000,000	2,500,000
White-tailed deer	400	not available
Other mammals	1,000	2,000

There are no statistics for the annual bag of wolf, wolverine, bear and lynx, but very few are shot.

Licences—Finland

Visitors may import their own rifle, shotgun, and the necessary ammunition, on a two-month permit. This also qualifies as a game licence. The permit can be obtained at any major airport or point of entry at a cost of 14 Finnish marks: the applicant must produce his home-country licence. At these points of entry that have no immediate permit service, the firearms must be deposited at the customs office, and the permit obtained from the local police station. In all other respects visitors are bound by the same rules and laws as the Finns.

prevailing is given by the average annual bag per Finnish hunter, which is only five birds, hares or moose, and five fur bearers, despite a considerable number of hunting trips. If, nevertheless, a hunter decides to shoot in Finland, it is probably easiest to obtain shooting on state-owned property in Lapland and the north. Shooting in the south and centre of the country is mostly owned by hunting clubs, so the chances of sport there are limited. Parties will usually have to be specially made up for visitors, even so the cost tends to be very reasonable.

Rubber or waterproof boots are nearly always essential, but snow does not start until late September in Lapland, with permanent snow cover from about mid-October, the respective dates for south Finland being November and as late as Christmas.

Finnish hunting methods are dictated almost entirely by the low density of game. There are few shoots involving large parties of guns, and practically no driven shooting, except for pheasant. One of the most typical forms of hunting is shooting tetraonids or forest game birds with a barking dog, such as the Finnish spitz, or the black and white Karelian spitz. To shoot them while calling in the spring is illegal and is considered an unsporting violation of the breeding season. Moose are also often hunted with barking dogs. Pointers are used for partridge and ptarmigan, and also, on occasion, for pheasants and tetraonids. Snow hares, and foxes, are hunted by groups of sportsmen and a single Finnish hound (bred specially for the purpose), which pursues the quarry for hours until it passes within gunshot of one

of the hunters. White-tailed deer are usually still-hunted at their feeding places.

Special Regulations

Hunting rights belong to the landowner, with a few exceptions, such as the right of locals to hunt on state lands in northern Finland. Rights are leasable. Shooting within 150 metres of courtyards and gardens is forbidden without the consent of the owner, and shooting in fields and meadows before the harvest is also forbidden. Those carrying a firearm, or equipment for trapping, snaring, etc, may not enter an area where they have no right to hunt unless they have a legitimate purpose, the firearm is unloaded, and any dog or dogs are on the leash.

Rifles may be used only if they fire a half-mantled bullet, weighing at least 10 grams, and have a minimum striking energy of E25 (250 kilipondimeters). Any bore of shotgun may be used, but not one that can load more than three cartridges. Air rifles and guns are completely prohibited, and small calibre rifles may only be used on squirrels and ptarmigan.

The direct use of a motor vehicle, or the employment of a mechanical sound-making device is prohibited in hunting. All firearms in a motor vehicle must be unloaded and cased. No animal may be shot over, or on, a road or railway. Game driven into an area by a dog being used for hunting on another property may not be shot while it is being driven or barked at, unless this has been going on for over half an hour.

Third party insurance follows automatically on the acquisition of a shooting licence. All new hunters who have not previously paid the game management fee must first pass a hunter's examination, though foreign visitors are considered to be experienced sportsmen and this requirement does not apply to them.

Administration and Control

The administration and control of shooting and wildlife management is divided between governmental agencies (in particular the Bureau of Fisheries and Game, which is a branch of the Ministry of Agriculture) and the Hunters' Central Organisation. The latter consists of all those who possess a shooting licence, about 170,000 people, divided into 14 game management districts and 300 game management associations, with a representative power structure working upwards from the associations through the districts to a general assembly of 70 members that meets every three years. It works in the field of wildlife education and training, and the practical aspects of shooting and wildlife management, and publishes a magazine six times a year.

Hunting clubs provide the other controlling force in Finnish shooting affairs. In the heavily settled provinces of the south they have acquired the shooting rights of nearly all the available land. Up till 1962 when the Hunters' Central Organisation was founded, the Finnish Hunters' League, an association of hunting clubs, was as powerful as the Central Organisation is now. The Hunters' League still excercises considerable influence, as does the newer and smaller Finnish Hunters' and Fishermen's League.

Further Information

Bureau of Fisheries and Game, Ministry of Agriculture, Aleksanterinkatu 10, Helsinki.

Forest Service, Erottajankatu 2, Helsinki.

Hunters' Central Organisation, Fredrikinkatu 47, Helsinki.

Finnish Hunters' League, Vanrikki Stoolinkatu 8 A 4, Helsinki.

Finnish Hunters' and Fishermen's League, Tuomiolirkonkatu 34 A 8, Tampere.

Finland, Hunting in

The Finnish scenery is different from that of Norway, but the landscape nevertheless offers the full beauty of an autumn day with the birch leaves red and golden and the birds turning white. There are thousands of lakes, forests and mountains. Here the Lapps shoot wolverine, lynx, bear and even wolves whenever they stray in from Russia. (The resident wolf population of Finland is not more than 4-6 animals). Bears are legal between 20 May and 15 October and between 40 and 70 are shot annually, mostly by the Laplanders. They are generally hunted at the end of May when there is still snow on the ground and they can be tracked and pursued on skis; the use of sno-tracs is illegal. As in northern Norway wolverine and lynx are very seldom encountered and are mostly shot by the Lapps, who are always willing to take along a non-resident hunter on such forays provided he is fit and well trained, and able to keep up with them on skis. Such a chase is a unique experience and quite a challenge.

In the north there is a vast area of forests, consisting of pine, birch and dwarf birch, where moose as well as the predators are found. Lapps may be found to act as guides for foreign sportsmen and the method is to spend 10 to 12 days in the open, often sleeping under the sky, stalking or pursuing moose. All moose in Finland are shot under licence and between 5,000 and 6,000 are shot annually. Further south they are hunted with dogs and beaters. Although there are no roe deer in Finland the white-tailed Virginian deer has been introduced and is well established. About 400 are shot annually under special licence.

A favourite sport is upland game bird and willow grouse shooting. Capercaillie and blackgame are mostly shot over the Finnish spitz and willow grouse mostly over pointers. Over the years capercaillie and blackgame have decreased in numbers, but the numbers

The annual kill of red squirrel in Finland is often over one million.

of willow grouse and ptarmigan have remained fairly constant.

Hare hunting with drever is also popular, and as in Norway the quarry is the mountain or blue hare. The patience of the Finnish shooting men is admirable – they are willing to listen for hours on end to the bark of their driving dogs and more than satisfied if, at the end of the day, the bag is one hare. Often hunters in the north shoot only 4 to 6 hares in a season and consider this more than satisfactory. Foxes are taken both from their earths with dachshunds, and shot in drives with braques or harriers, the latter method being the more popular.

On the west coast of northern Finland wild-fowling is quite good near the Baltic and it is also regularly practised on the many lakes. There are less mallard than further south, but more tufted duck, goldeneye and scaup.

Although hunting is a long-standing tradition, the Finnish hunter is not a formalist and does not hold to rigid rules or rites in the field as some of the Central European hunters do; however, he is very strict on discipline and gun safety. When the shooting is over he is gregarious and likes to spend the evening with his companions. Over good food and good company he spins good hunting yarns. In spite of the language barrier hunters usually get along well with the Finns. PM

Seasons—Finland

These vary from year to year and should always be checked in advance. They are usually regulated through the closing date, the opening date remaining fairly static. The pigeon season generally opens in the south on 10 Aug but elsewhere at the same time as the duck season, i.e. 20 August at 12 noon. The season for grouse and hares usually opens on 10 September, but in the provinces of Culu and Lapland in the north, 1 September is more normal. The ptarmigan season also starts 1 September in those two provinces ; elsewhere this bird is entirely protected. A special licence is required for moose hunting and is valid from 16 October to 30 November, extending to 15 December in the northern province. Bear is only shot in very limited numbers in the summer ; lynx only in the eastern communes. Wolf, wolverine and seal are entirely unprotected, as are the goshawk and sparrowhawk and, in Lapland, the Arctic buzzard. In exceptionally poor years, and in areas where a particular species shows a marked decline, the season may be cancelled altogether. Local game-management associations may impose additional variations. Such rigorous control of the seasons tends to render bag limits unnecessary. Certain hunting clubs, nevertheless, impose bag limits or close a proportion of their grounds each year. In any case, whatever control is imposed, it is always based on calculating the number of young of each species each fall.

Firearms

History

An effective firearm requires a suitable chemical propellant, and in an intimate mixture of saltpetre or nitre (potassium nitrate, KNO_3), sulphur (S) and charcoal (C) such a chemical propellant can be found. A great deal of time and effort have been expended in the hope of being able to state that gunpowder or black powder was discovered by such a person on such a date. Regrettably no such statement is possible, but modern scholarship now believes that a knowledge of how to make gunpowder became known in Europe about the middle of the 13th century.

The earliest firearms were developed from artillery, the hand cannon or powder shaft consisting of a tube closed at the rear and mounted on a long shaft. The tube or barrel was provided with a touchhole or vent at the top near the closed or breech end and the charge, consisting of propellant and projectile, was introduced into the barrel from the front or muzzle end.

Such weapons were in use in Italy and, although early documents provide little information, some illustrated documents do exist which can be dated and which illustrate how these early portable firearms were employed. Actual examples are rare. One of the oldest, the 'Tannenberg' gun, was discovered under the ruins of the Castle of Tannenberg which was destroyed in 1399.

Two important developments followed. The first was the modification of the shaft to permit the gun to be fired from the shoulder, and accurately aimed. The second was the invention of a mechanical device to fire the gun. Pictorial evidence suggests that firearms with a stock, which permitted the weapon to be aimed, had appeared by the second half of the 15th century but the equally important 'serpentine' or pivoted clamp, which held the glowing match or touche, is to be seen illustrated in a document dated 1500. The serpentine was the first step towards a gunlock; it permitted the firer of the weapon to look at the target at the moment of discharge instead of having to locate the touchhole and bring the touche to the priming powder. The ability to aim the weapon was aided by the appearance of rudimentary sights but nevertheless for effective military and sporting use the bow and crossbow had not been replaced.

The term 'arquebus' in one or another of its variant spellings was used to describe light portable firearms with stock and serpentine, and these weapons were to be fitted with the first true gunlocks. The flashpan was moved from the top of the barrel to the side and a sliding cover was provided. The serpentine, with its adjustable jaws to hold the match, was now mounted on a lock plate and provided with a trigger and sear and instead of the weight

of the lower limb of the early serpentine causing the match to move away from the touchhole this function was now performed by a spring. The 'matchlock' had much to commend it, the principal virtues being low cost; simplicity and ease of operation allied to ease of repair, vital for military weapons. The chief disadvantage was the need to employ the lighted match: this means of ignition was liable to go out and if the weapon were kept in a state of readiness the match was being consumed and required constant adjustment and replenishment. A stealthy approach presented some difficulties particularly at night when the glow-worm's light from the match could alert both man and beast to your approach. The alternative was the more costly and complicated wheellock, the origin of which is somewhat obscure. The earliest dated specimen is to be found in the Royal Armoury in Madrid, the date, 1530. The earliest wheel-locks which can be dated with some degree of certainty are all well developed, they are not 'first attempts' by any means and it is reasonable to believe that earlier examples once existed and may in fact still exist although at present they are unrecognized for what they are. The wheel-lock dispensed with the lighted match and therefore the danger presented by having lighted match near gunpowder. A wheel-lock could be loaded and carried ready for instant use without any adjustment, and the speed of ignition of the charge was also superior. The priming in the pan was ignited by the spark pro-

A late 16th century finely-engraved wheellock rifle, showing (top) obverse and (bottom) reverse views

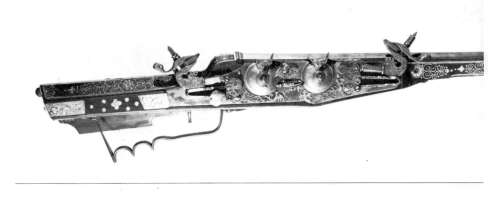

duced when a piece of iron pyrites was held in contact against the serrated edge of a rotating wheel. The impression gained is that the wheel was spinning around but, in fact, on most wheel-locks the wheel turned less than a complete revolution, but it did this very quickly under the influence of a powerful spring. The wheel-lock was a far more efficient weapon than the matchlock but mechanical knowledge was needed to repair any breakage or damage. For this reason it did not supplant the matchlock as the standard weapon for infantry, as it did for sporting and personal use.

The first of the flint and steel-locks, the snaphance, appeared about the middle of the 16th century and simulated the action of making fire with flint and steel, the flint secured in the jaws of a pivoted cock, the steel attached to a swinging arm beneath which was a pan containing the priming. The snaphance employed a separate steel and pan cover, the later flintlock combined the steel and pan cover and in so doing simplified the mechanism. Flintlock weapons reached the peak of their development in the opening years of the 19th century and accurate and effective shotguns, rifles and pistols had been developed, the majority of which were still loaded from the muzzle. Multi-barrel weapons had been made from almost the earliest times but weight and complexity restricted their adoption. The appearance of a new system of ignition, percussion ignition, the invention of a Scottish clergyman, the Rev Alexander Forsyth, greatly improved the reliability of firearms and paved the way for the next major step forward – the cartridge breech-loader. In the past one hundred years, the significant advance has been the application of machinery to the production of firearms, both military and sporting. At the beginning of the 19th century wars were fought with muzzle-loading flintlock muskets and by the end of that quite remarkable century, full automatic weapons, mass-produced by sophisticated machine tools, were in use. G B

The Modern Rifle

The rifle of today can be classified according to the use to which it will be put; sporting, target or military; or by type; single-shot, double-barrel, bolt-action, lever-action, self-loader and so on. There is also a further and quite simple classification based on the type of ammunition used, rim-fire or centre-fire.

To reduce the subject to dimensions with which we can deal in brief compass, two complete classes of rifle must be ignored, the target and the military. It must be remembered, however, that both types of rifle have contributed towards the development of the sporting rifle, many of which are based on military actions and whose accuracy has been greatly improved by reason of the work done by target riflemen.

A study of the rim-fire rifle scene is made very much easier by the fact that we are dealing with but one type of ammunition, the .22 rim-fire. Today, there are four different varieties of .22 rim-fire ammunition, the .22 short, the .22 long, the .22 long rifle and the .22 rim-fire magnum. There are other .22 rim-fire cartridges which may be encountered, such as the .22 BB and the .22 CB, but they are outclassed by the .22 short. This cartridge first appeared in the mid-19th century and today it is loaded in both standard and high velocity loads with solid or hollow-point bullets. The high velocity version will penetrate two inches of soft pine so, although this cartridge looks innocuous, it can at the extreme range of one mile, seriously wound or kill a person. The .22 long appeared in the 1870's and today has largely outlived its usefulness being replaced by the .22 long rifle which was first introduced in the late 1880's. This cartridge is extremely accurate and in high velocity, hollow-point loadings, will handle rabbit-sized animals up to 75 yards. Of the .22 rim-fire special cartridges, the .22 Winchester Magnum Rimfire differs in that it employs a 40 grain thin-jacketed hollow-point bullet and at 2,000 feet per second it has just about double the velocity of the standard .22 short. This is a very effective 125-yard small-game cartridge, first introduced by Winchester in 1959. Although the range of cartridges is commendably narrow the rifles are made in many different types, styles and with a wide price range.

One of a pair of 12-bore double-barrelled hammerless shotguns, built in 1932 by J. Purdey, with fine game engraving; below, a double-barrelled flint-lock fowling piece, built about 1830 by Samuel and Charles Smith.

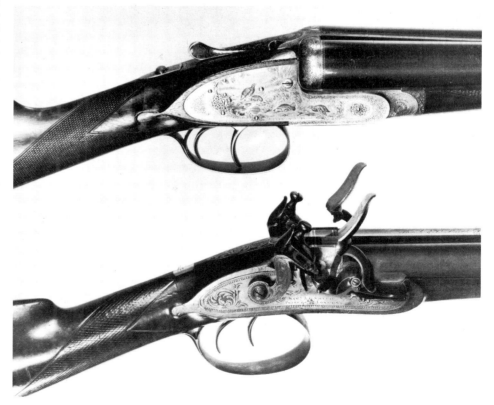

The traditional .22 rifle in the United States is the single-shot bolt action; in Europe, falling block actions of the Martini pattern were popular. Such rifles have been re-introduced but today their styling follows that of the Winchester lever action and is obviously aimed at a section of the American market. Most of the single-shot .22 rifles sold today are bolt action and the significant feature of this type of rifle in more recent years has been the availability of 'man-sized' weapons. This tendency is particularly noticeable in the bolt-action repeating .22 rifles. Box magazines appear to predominate but there is still a market for repeating rifles with tubular magazines under the barrel, and most of the better quality weapons now have integral provision for mounting telescopic sights. The fastest growing section of the .22 field is that of the .22 automatic. The variety presently obtainable is quite remarkable: from the .22 Armalite 8-shot autoloader with a steel-lined alloy barrel and alloy receiver, the fibreglass stock housing the barrel and action when dismounted, to, on the other hand, the traditional Browning Lightweight model with the magazine in the butt stock and built to the standards of the 19th century with solid machined forgings. 'Full sized' rifles can again be found in the auto-loading range. The idea of a 'family' of rifles of different calibre but sharing the same basic handling characteristics was pioneered by Remington, and their current 552A rifle matches the Remington 742 'Big Game' rifle both in style and handling. At the other extreme the Remington Nylon 66 employs solid nylon as the main structural material and represents a possible future trend in rifle styling and manufacturing techniques.

In centre-fire rifles the task of examination and investigation is more complicated because of the vast range of ammunition available and the fact that there is a wider range to choose from. There is also an additional complication, that of cartridge availability.

If properly cared for, rifles have an almost indefinite life when used for normal sporting purposes. Many rifles which have survived into the second half of the 20th century use cartridges which are no longer made. The reasons which dictate the popularity, and consequently the economics of continued manufacture, almost defy rational explanation, but we have to accept that certain very satisfactory rifle cartridges are obsolete and others which leave quite a lot to be desired, are for some unaccountable reason, still in production. This is mentioned because of the possibility of buying what appears to be a second-hand bargain, only to find that ammunition to fit the rifle cannot be obtained. If the rifle is so attractive and you *must* have it, cartridges may be able to be adapted to fit or the barrel can be rechambered to take another cartridge, or, if this is not possible, the rifle can be re-

The Ruger No 1 light sporter is a single-shot falling block rifle chambered for most modern cartridges.

barrelled in another, available calibre. To make any sense out of the complicated and illogical maze of calibre and nomenclature, we again have to resort to classification. The classes are arbitrary but they are of some value in bringing reason to chaos.

A word first of all on nomenclature. If we look at an ammunition catalogue we will find such descriptive terms as .22 Hornet, .25-20 Winchester, 7mm Mauser, .30'06 Springfield, .300 H & H Magnum and so forth. The .22 Hornet is typical of such cartridges as the Swift, Bee and Zipper, where the name is not descriptive and the bullet diameter is not .220 of an inch but .225. The .25-20 Winchester tells us a little

Detail from the German painting 'Trierer Jagdgesellschaft', 1845, by Friedrich Anton Wittenbach

more. We know that it was developed by Winchester and that the '20' refers to the original charge of black powder. Today, the cartridge is still loaded, but with smokeless rather than black powder, and the .25-20 is still a useful small game cartridge. With the 7 mm Mauser we come to another problem, the use of metric dimensions for certain cartridges. The .25-35 Winchester, the larger brother of the .25-20, was known in Europe as the 6·5 × 52R mm, but the 7mm Mauser has never been described by decimal inch units, always metric. The 6·5 mm Mannlicher-Schonauer was, on the other hand sometimes described as the .256 M-S. The 7 × 57 mm Mauser, although originally a military round, has proved to be one of the most successful all-round sporting cartridges ever developed. In common with other German cartridges the second set of figures, × 57, refer to the case length. There is, for example, another 7 mm cartridge with a case length of 64 mm known as the 7 × 64 mm. With equal commonsense it is German practice to indicate whether or not the cartridge is rimmed by placing the letter R behind the cartridge dimensions as in the case of the .25-35 Winchester or 6·5 × 52R mm. The .30'06 Springfield is yet another example, but here the second group of figures is not a nostalgic memorial to an almost forgotten black powder charge, nor is it the case length. The '06 is the contraction of the year of adoption of the service cartridge for the Model 1903 Springfield rifle. The original 1903 cartridge used a 220 grain round-nosed bullet with a muzzle velocity of 2300 f.p.s. This was changed to a 150 grain pointed or 'spitzer' bullet with a muzzle velocity of 2700 f.p.s. and this was the cartridge which was adopted in 1906. The last example is of a cartridge designed by the British firm of Holland & Holland in 1920 which accounts for the letters 'H & H' and the term Magnum indicates that the cartridge develops more power than one would normally expect from a cartridge of given dimensions.

There is no short cut through the jungle of cartridge specifications, the choice is often a personal one and may be backed up by personal experience, serious technical investigation, or perhaps the man in the gunshop advised it, or because of a recommendation from a friend. Paper ballistics do help, but nothing can outweigh practical experience of what the cartridge/rifle/man combination can do under actual conditions in the field.

The mention of one particular cartridge as being the most suitable for a specific task in say, the correspondence columns of a sporting paper, is sure to bring a shoal of letters contradicting everything, except the name and address of the foolish man who was rash enough to state his preference. For this reason, few will dare to put forward

one cartridge; they propose a class or group and you make your own choice. One such such series for European hunting would be for small deer: the 5·6 × 52R or the .222 Remington; deer and chamois: .245 Winchester, 6·5 × 57R, 7 × 57 and ending with the 7 × 65R. For the above, plus occasional big game, the 8 × 57 would be included and for what the Europeans class as big game, the list would extend to include the .30'06 and the 9·3 × 74R. If we are to include African big game, then the picture alters somewhat, and the large bore cartridges and Magnums have to be considered. Possibly one of the best 'all round' big game cartridges, is the .375 Holland & Holland. Overpowered for American big game, except perhaps for Alaska (moose and grizzly), it is the best of the medium bores for African hunting. An American cartridge in this class is the .458 Winchester and for the man who wants the biggest and the mostest, the .460 Weatherby Magnum fills the bill.

Many of the large calibre British sporting cartridges are still on the selling range and there are several masquerading under different versions of the same name due to the policy of British makers producing 'special' cartridges for their own rifles. Many, such as the Holland & Holland series, gained world-wide acclaim, others remain to clutter up the catalogues and confuse the beginner. With this class of cartridge it is essential to check on future availability; otherwise you have a fine rifle and nothing on which to feed it!

There is, as one might expect, a greater variety of rifles available in the centre-fire calibres than we found in the rim-fire. Single-shot rifles are again appearing, using modernized falling block actions, and styled in the tradition of the late 19th century. Dominating the entire field are those rifles based on the Mauser bolt action, from re-worked military actions to new, modified Model 98 actions manufactured in Spain, Belgium, Germany, Czechoslovakia and elsewhere. With an incredible variety of styles and calibres, the choice largely depends on what you have in your pocket and whether or not you wish to buy a re-worked military rifle, the standard factory product or a special 'custom' rifle made by one of the 'riflesmiths' who will be found in most countries of the world – his approach varying from that of a gifted amateur to a highly specialized factory, drawing on supplies from the world over. British steel made into barrels on Austrian machine tools and attached to Spanish-made actions based on a German design with the stocks made in Italy and Japanese telescopic sights for the market places of North America. As well as single-shot and bolt action systems, centre-fire rifles are still produced with lever and slide actions. The lever action is a predominantly American design; Winchester, Marlin and Savage still produce such rifles

ifficult to stalk, the giraffe is easily shot, nd makes excellent eating.

105

adapted to American needs and yet they have been carried for one purpose or another in most parts of the globe. Less popular, are the slide-action rifles, well liked in .22 calibre but less so in the heavier centre-fire calibres. Latest on the scene is the self- or auto-loading rifle. Largely inspired by the wider military use of auto-loaders, several are sporting versions of military self-loading rifles; others, such as the Browning, are new designs and, in the case of the Browning Magnum Auto Rifle, as yet the only self-loader which can handle the 'Magnum' sporting cartridges.

Acclaimed as 'The King of Rifles', the sporting double rifle is still made although, with the passing of the years, the cost, both new and secondhand, has risen astronomically. Considered by many to be the *only* rifle for dangerous game its high price is due to the high content of hard labour: no one yet has discovered how to automate the manufacture of a high grade sporting double. Probably if it were done, the loss of the very qualities which make it desirable would doom such an experiment. The enormous variety of cartridge and rifle currently available to the sportsman cannot help but encourage the natural desire for acquisition and experiment. This is a most enjoyable pastime but for results which count, knowledge of the rifle and ammunition it uses are of paramount importance.
GB

The Modern Shotgun
The modern sporting shotgun in its widest and most acceptable form is a side-by-side double barrel 12 bore, self cocking and with automatic selective ejectors. Such a weapon is extremely sophisticated, extremely expensive and represents the absolute pinnacle of over a century of intensive development.

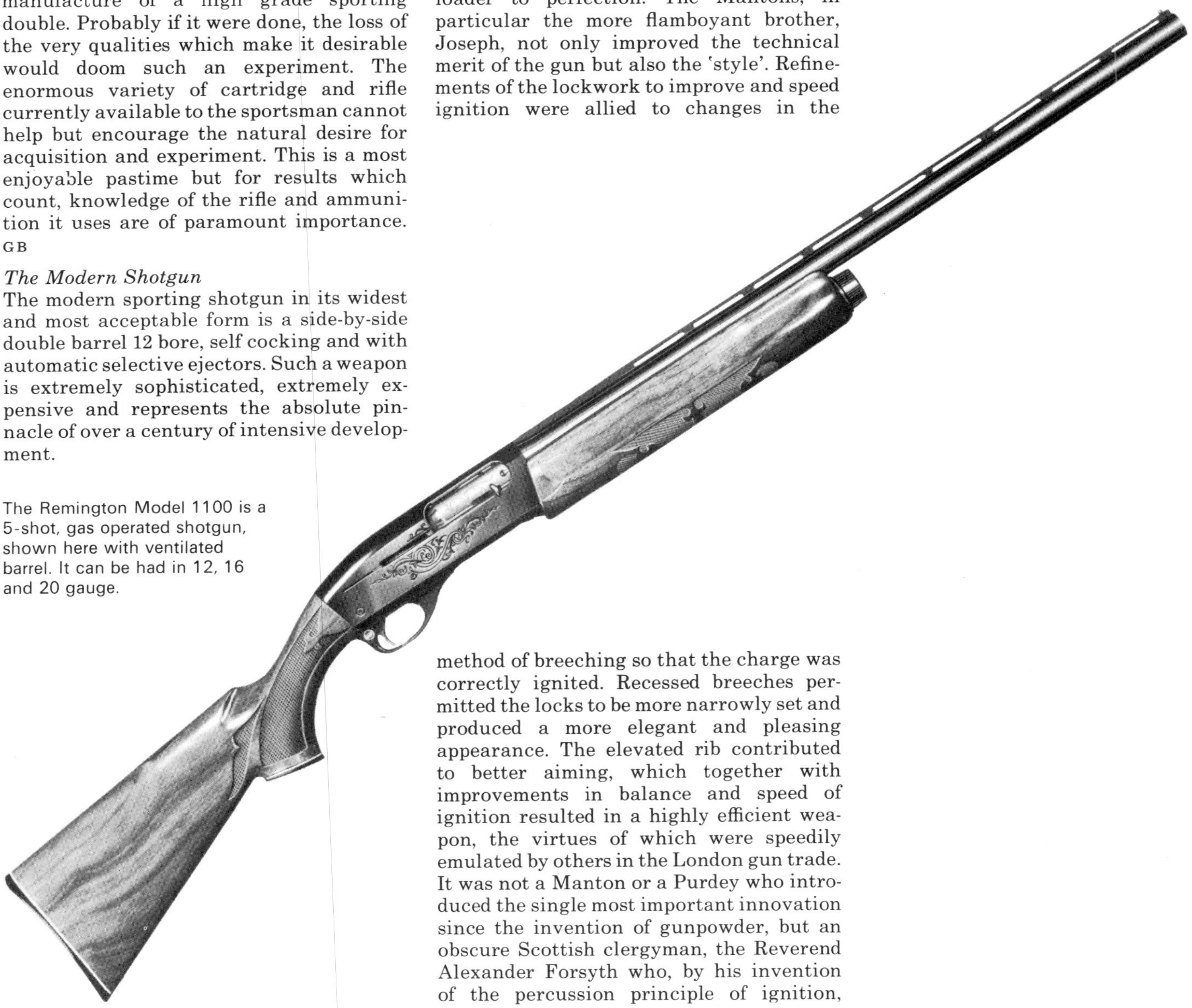

The Remington Model 1100 is a 5-shot, gas operated shotgun, shown here with ventilated barrel. It can be had in 12, 16 and 20 gauge.

Originally, game was stalked on the ground with the aid of a stalking horse or it was taken with nets, snares, or bird lime. The shooting of flying game was introduced to Britain by the returning exiles at the time of the Restoration during the second half of the 17th century. The exiles brought with them not only the technique of 'shooting flying' but also fine French flintlock sporting guns and, spurred by example and necessity, the British gunmaker sought to surpass his French rivals, and by the early 19th century had in fact done so.

The European sporting gun of the 18th century of good quality was likely to have a Spanish barrel, the qualities of which were greatly esteemed, and the stock would be decorated by the use of inlaid silver wire. By the second half of the century double-barrel guns had become more popular but it was left to the genius of the brothers Manton of London to bring the flintlock muzzle loader to perfection. The Mantons, in particular the more flamboyant brother, Joseph, not only improved the technical merit of the gun but also the 'style'. Refinements of the lockwork to improve and speed ignition were allied to changes in the

method of breeching so that the charge was correctly ignited. Recessed breeches permitted the locks to be more narrowly set and produced a more elegant and pleasing appearance. The elevated rib contributed to better aiming, which together with improvements in balance and speed of ignition resulted in a highly efficient weapon, the virtues of which were speedily emulated by others in the London gun trade. It was not a Manton or a Purdey who introduced the single most important innovation since the invention of gunpowder, but an obscure Scottish clergyman, the Reverend Alexander Forsyth who, by his invention of the percussion principle of ignition, revolutionized firearms making possible the introduction of a practical method of breech loading. The first percussion or 'detonating' shotguns that were made by Forsyth in London had one undoubted advantage, speed of ignition. The improvements, laboriously achieved by Manton's mechanical genius, were surpassed by the chemical agency of fulminating powder and by 1830 few flintlock guns were used by leading sportsmen.

No sooner had the percussion muzzle loader gained an ascendency than its position was challenged by a newcomer from across the English Channel. Considerable work had been done by the French on the development of cartridges and the complacent arrogance of the British gunmaker was shattered by the appearance at the famous Great Exhibition of 1851 in London of a breech-loading shotgun by the Paris gunmaker, Lefaucheux. If Manton can be said to have established the shape, form and style of the sporting shotgun, Lefaucheux introduced the principle of the drop down barrel, hinged in a manner similar to that employed today for modern side-by-side guns. The French breechloader employed a gas-tight paper-cased cartridge with its own means of ignition developed by the Paris gunmaker Houllier. Although many considered that the ease and speed of loading and unloading the pin-fire breechloader were enough to outweigh its disadvantages, certain opponents to the new system were quite vociferous in their condemnation. Loudest of the critics was the renowned Birmingham gunmaker W. Greener, who pointed out, with some justification, that the pin-fire was heavier, not as well balanced, required more powder to achieve the same result and had a heavier recoil than the muzzle loader. Also it was weaker!

One by one these faults were rectified, the first real advance being the substitution of central-fire cartridges for pin-fire; the invention was again French but the significant advances in the construction of the gun were made in Britain. The reasons are not difficult to discover, in Britain there was an unrivalled market for best quality shotguns and the gunmakers of London and Birmingham sought to capture it. The strength of the breech closure was improved by the introduction of the rotary underlever and this was followed by snap actions which closed and locked automatically when the barrels were returned after being loaded. The most famous of these snap actions was that invented by James Purdey, and originally operated by a lever in front of the trigger guard. Later, this type of lever was replaced by the top lever which became almost universally adopted for double guns. Improvements in the lock work followed, the most important being the development of the rebounding lock. This greatly facilitated the opening and closing of the gun

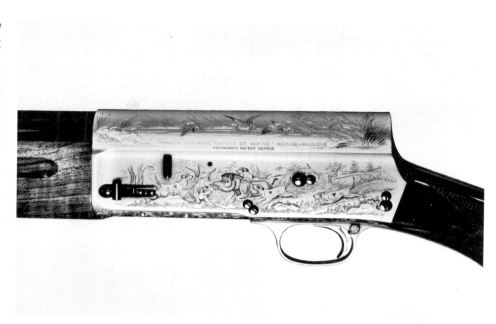

The classic Browning automatic shotgun. Made by Fabrique Nationale, this example is engraved with a fine quality sporting scene.

since the hammers 'rebounded' to half cock. The only two operations which were not made automatic were the cocking of the hammers and the removal of the fired empty cases. The gunmakers of Victorian Britain soon rectified these oversights. The first 'hammerless' gun was that introduced by Murcott in 1871. The internal hammers cocked by the under-lever which operated the locking bolt. A number of 'lever cocking' guns appeared but all suffered from the same defect – the force needed to operate the lever. A much longer lever was needed and in fact was available, the barrels themselves and the first hammerless gun which employed the fall of the barrels to cock the action was that invented by Anson & Deeley. The A & D action was not just an adaptation of a previous design, rather it was a radical and entirely new approach and probably more double shotguns have been made on this system or a variation of it than on any other. There are only three main limbs in each lock and, as originally made by the famous firm of Westley Richards, locking was by the 'doll's head' extension to the top rib. Later the bolting was improved by employing a Purdey double-bite bolt. In order to remove the fired cartridge ejector systems were introduced, the earliest being due to Joseph Needham in 1874. Selective ejectors are rather ingenious; the gun is opened and if both barrels have been discharged the two empty cases will be ejected from the gun. If only the right-hand barrel has been fired only the right-hand case will be ejected, the cartridge in the left-hand chamber being slightly withdrawn but not expelled from the gun.

In addition to the Anson and Deeley or 'box lock' action, sidelock guns continued to be built, the last 'improvement' being the fitting of a single trigger or a single selective trigger which eliminates the need to move the trigger finger from one trigger to another when firing both barrels. The most recent innovation has been the reintroduction of the 'over and under' principle where the barrels are placed one on top of the other, instead of side-by-side. British makers did not enjoy the same degree of success with this configuration and many of the designs which were produced have that curiously unsatisfactory appearance peculiar to many old-fashioned 'patent' devices which were never quite successful. Much of this was due to the use of conventional locking with lumps and bolts under the barrels which made the action inordinately deep and produced guns which were lacking in those desirable attributes of grace and line, which had become the enviable heritage of British gunmaking.

Two over and under guns surmounted this difficulty; the Boss, for which patents had been obtained in 1909, and the Woodward. In both cases the bottom lumps had been discarded and locking was achieved by bites located on each side of the barrel group.

Elsewhere in Europe, over and under guns had appeared with unusual and for the most part short-lived bolting systems, such as the Stendebach and the Schuler. Those which have withstood the test of time are the Kersten, which can be regarded as a double Greener, and locking systems employed by the over and under guns made by Breda and Beretta in Italy.

One of the most successful of all the over and under guns is the Browning, a unique combination of the gunmaking skills of the old and new worlds. Designed by one of the most remarkable gun designers of all time, John M. Browning, and production-engineered and built by the famous firm of Fabrique Nationale in Liège, Belgium, the Browning 'Superposed' has received the final accolade – it has been extensively copied! American gunmakers have been rather neglected for, unlike the gunmakers of Birmingham or Brescia, London or Liège, those of the Eastern seaboard of America did not come into their own until the appearance of the repeating and the semi-automatic gun.

Repeating guns have been made employing most of the available systems, revolving, bolt action, slide action, lever action and so on. One of the earliest to achieve commercial success was the American Spencer which set the fashion for the slide or 'tombine' action. Winchester introduced their first shotgun, predictably a lever action, the Model 1887 and this was followed by one of the most successful repeating shotguns ever made, the Winchester Model 1897, a

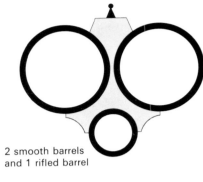

2 smooth barrels and 1 rifled barrel

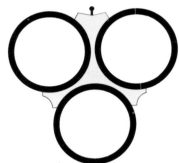

3 smooth barrels

An early Drilling made by G. F. Störmer, Germany, with two side-by-side shot barrels and a third, rifled barrel.

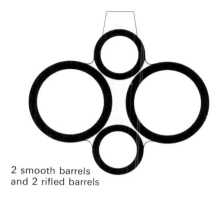

2 smooth barrels
and 2 rifled barrels

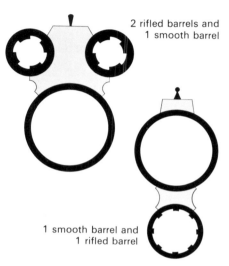

2 rifled barrels and
1 smooth barrel

1 smooth barrel and
1 rifled barrel

2 rifled barrels

1 smooth barrel and
1 rifled barrel

2 smooth barrels

slide-action hammer gun with a tubular under-barrel magazine which continued in production until 1957. Enjoying equal popularity was the Winchester Model 12 introduced in 1912, and by 1943 one million had been made. Although currently superseded by the Winchester Model 1200, the Model 12 can still be obtained. Remington were slightly later in the repeating shotgun stakes, introducing their hammerless slide-action gun in 1907. This design is today represented by the Ithaca Model 37. As with the slide action the self-loading or 'automatic' shotgun was primarily an American invention and although used for 'hunting' in the States it is mainly to be seen on clay bird shooting grounds in Europe and is rarely encountered in the field. The first autoloader was the Remington Model 11, designed once again by John Browning, and in Europe this Browning design was made, under licence, by Fabrique Nationale and it is still on their selling range.

Over half a century had to go by before there was any significant and basic design change. This took place in 1954 when Winchester brought out their Model 50 autoloader. The traditional auto-shotgun such as the Browning and its many variants is of the long recoil type; the Model 50 introduced the short recoil system and in 1956 Remington brought out the Model 58 featuring their contribution to the new shotgun technology, gas operation. The current version of this model is the Remington Model 1100 which together with the Winchester Model 1400 and the Ithaca Model 51 represent the gas-operated brigade. Which you prefer is largely a matter of personal choice, a softer recoil is claimed for gas and short recoil systems, and certainly they don't take quite as much getting used to as does the long recoil system gun. Today, the purchaser of a shotgun has a wider variety of choice than ever before.

The British now make only quality shotguns and this is largely true of the Liège gunmakers. A wider quality range is available from both Spain and Italy, the Spanish maker depending on the traditional side-by-side double and the Italian makers also offering over and unders and self-loading shotguns. A feature of the American market has been the introduction of shotguns which bear world renowned names like Winchester, but when you look a little closer you find that one Winchester model has three little words, 'Made in Japan'. Today, the Japanese industry is still largely in the copyist phase; what will happen tomorrow when new and unusual ideas are produced gives rise to perhaps one of the most interesting lines of speculation in the shotgun world. GB.

Shotgun and Rifle Variations
The British gun trade expanded and developed to meet the requirements of the

'Grand Victorian Sportsman' and since a well known British characteristic is the ability to compromise it is remarkable that neither the sportsman nor the gunmaker showed much inclination to do so in the matter of firearms. Both the user and the maker kept rifle and shotgun as quite separate entities. This attitude even extended to the man's ability: if you were good with a rifle you despised the shotgun (*anyone* could hit *anything* with a scattergun – taking good care not to disprove this theory by handling the offending shotgun yourself) and, of course, as a shotgun man the fact that most rifle shots were taken at *stationary* targets was enough to bring the whole clan of riflemen into disrepute.

More thoughtful people took a slightly different point of view, and whether on a crow shoot in rural England, or in pursuit of dangerous game in India or Africa, the moment would come, sooner or later, when they wished their shotgun was a rifle or vice versa. Once a need was established there were many people ready to fill it, and to fill it by various ingenious means.

The easiest solution is to carry a shotgun and to have a supply of rifled slugs which can be used when required. The use of ball loads in smooth bore barrels is not new; most of the wars fought with firearms were fought with smooth bore weapons and round ball, and round ball is still used although even under ideal conditions only moderate accuracy can be expected. It is also important to ensure that *solid* round ball is no larger than the minimum diameter of a choke-bored shotgun barrel in order to prevent damage.

Due to the inherent inaccuracy of round ball, even when wadded or patched, a number of special shotgun slugs were developed for use with smooth-bored barrels. In Britain there was the Rotax Patented Bullet, the Lyons Lethal Bullet and the Kynoch Destructor. In Germany, the equivalent of the Rotax was the Stendebach slug and a similar design by von Witzleben and the famous Brenneke. The latter's original design was introduced by Wilhelm Brenneke in 1898. Some of these slugs, such as the Model 1930 Brenneke, had body ribs or 'rifling' and tests which have been carried out show that this rifling does result in a slow rotation, although such a rotation will not ensure adequate spin stabilization. In general, shotgun slugs are what is called 'arrow-stable' and are kept 'point-on' by the trailing skirt and general weight distribution. Wilhelm Brenneke in fact described his early slugs with the screw attached wad system as being 'designed according to the arrow principle, forward heavy, rear light'.

Today Winchester offer rifled slug loads in 12, 16, 20 and .410 as do Remington. The Remington muzzle velocities for all calibres except the .410 are 1,600 feet per second and 1,830 f.p.s. for the smallest calibre. Muzzle energy with the 12-gauge 1 oz Remington rifled slug is 2,485 ft/lb, more than the commercial loading of the .303 British with a 215 grain bullet. In Europe rifled slugs are available by Hubertus and Brenneke, and in Britain round ball loads and rifled slug from Eley. Sellier & Bellot offer their 'S-Bal' rifled slug load and of course the re-loader can also load his own with the aid of a bullet mould, which will cast a smooth hollow-based slug, but lacking the factory 'rifling' or slanted ribs. Lyman, in America, did at one time supply a special die set, which would cut the ribs on the cast slugs but the improvement in accuracy obtained did not merit the extra effort needed, and the die set has now been discontinued.

The rifled slug, when used in a single-barrel smooth-bore gun, preferably cylinder bored and fitted with *accurate* rifle-type sights, can then be employed against small game animals up to about 80 yards and against deer-sized targets up to 125 yards. For a variety of reasons (not the least important being legal restrictions) the use of special slug barrels or guns for use with rifled-slug loads, 'deer guns' or 'deerslayer' guns is now fully recognized and slide, automatic and single-barrel 'deer' guns are to be found in the pages of most gun catalogues of the United States.

This situation is again, not a new development. Special guns were made in Britain, where the accuracy potential was built into the gun rather than the projectile. Known as 'ball-and-shot' guns, they are now no longer made and perhaps the most famous was the 'Paradox' made by Holland & Holland based on patents obtained by Lt Col G. V. Fosbery, who was also responsible for the Webley-Fosbery 'automatic revolver'.

Ball-and-shot guns could be regarded as a sort of half-way stage between double shotguns and double rifles.

The bores were provided with a long choke at the muzzle into which fairly deep rifling was cut. The Paradox ball-and-shot gun proved to be extremely popular in the years before World War 1, and in black powder days it was made in a wide range of bore sizes up to 8-bore. In the larger sizes the Paradox was not intended for use as a shotgun, being regarded rather as a heavy big-game rifle. The success of the Paradox led to other ball-and-shot guns being introduced, some of which had a very fine rifling for the whole length of the bore, enough to spin a conical bullet without unduly affecting the pattern of a shot charge. Besides the Holland & Holland Paradox, Westley Richards had their 12-bore 2½ in Explora and a 2¾ in 12-bore, the Super Magnum Explora and, in 20-bore, the weapon was known as the Fauneta. Most British makers employed special cartridges of the 'collar-button' type with two bands separated by a wide waist and offered in a variety of special types, metal-based, steel-pointed, hollow-nosed, copper-tubed, split-cap and so on, each with some real or imagined benefit and only to be obtained from the one maker or patentee.

The system offered a powerful and sufficiently accurate double rifle for the ranges at which one would normally expect to use it, and a close range shotgun which could deliver improved cylinder patterns at about 30 yards. Yet another attempt at this compromise was the so-called 'Cape Rifle', which had a smooth-bore barrel fully choked for shot and a single barrel rifled for a common rifle cartridge, which could be .303. The Cape 'combination gun and rifle' was, on the whole, less popular than the ball-and-shot gun and although the term 'Cape Gun' seems to have been made popular by the London firm of Thomas Bland, who offered .577/.450 and 12-bore shot; .500 Express and 12-bore shot; .450 Express and 16-bore and .400 Express and 20-bore shot. The term 'Cape' came to be used generically for what the German sportsman would call a 'Büchs-flinte'.

It is with the German and Austrian gun-makers that the combination rifle-gun system has been brought to the greatest peak of perfection. The side-by-side rifle/shotgun was made in both hammer and hammerless systems with 12-bore shot barrels and the rifle barrel chambered for cartridges ranging from the German equivalent of the .25-35 Winchester, the 6·5 × 52R up to the 9·3 × 72R or .360 Express. A variant form was the 'Bochbüchsflinte', or over and under configuration, with the shot barrel on the top and the rifled barrel underneath. The over-under system was one of the few which has been manufactured outside Europe consistently, and in the form of the Savage Model 24, it is still the only rifle/shotgun currently produced commercially in the United States. This gun performs remarkably well considering its low cost – some unbelievable shooting has been done with the .410/.22 version. Also available in 20 and 22 RF Magnum or .222 Remington, the consistent up-dating of the rifle calibre should ensure that this quite remarkable little gun stays on the selling range for many more years.

Of all the combination guns the most famous is the Drilling. This is the German for 'triplet' and, as the name suggests, there are not two barrels but three. Usually, two are smooth bore and the third, underneath, is rifled. The first successful breech-loading Drilling was patented by Peter Oberhammer of Munich, in 1878. His patent covered the use of a special hammer arrangement so that the right hammer would fire the right shot-barrel or the under rifled barrel merely by the movement of a small attachment to the striker. With the appearance of hammerless actions, the problem became somewhat more complicated, and one of the best solutions was the use of a trigger-plate action made popular by Krieghoff. Such systems incorporated automatic erection of the rifle sights and, since the changeover to the rifle barrel is made by moving a tang-type catch, the safety is of the Greener pattern and is on the side of stock.

A rather rarer version of the Drilling is where the shot barrel is mounted above a 'big game' rifled barrel with a small game rifled barrel for the .22 rim-fire or .22 Hornet to one side. In Austria, a double rifle with under shotgun barrel is still made, the Doppelbüchs-Drilling, but perhaps the ultimate in the combination shotgun/rifle system is the Vierling, a gun with four barrels, two shot and two rifled.

The two shot barrels are of the same calibre, 12, 16, or 20 gauge side-by-side with the small calibre rifled barrel above, chambered for the .22 rim-fire or perhaps the .22 Hornet or .222 Remington. The lower rifled barrel could be chambered for 7 × 65R or perhaps the 8 × 57IRS. With four barrels it is necessary to have four locks, and apart from the understandable complexity of the Vierling, weight is also a problem. To some extend this has been countered by the use of a light-alloy action and the modern four-barrel gun is not very much heavier than a robust side-by-side double shotgun.

The Vierling does not, by any means, exhaust the German gunmakers' ingenuity Available some years ago, the Repetier-Büchsflinte was a conventional repeating bolt-action rifle, such as the Mauser 98, but with an additional smooth-bore barrel under the rifle barrel and made as part of the fore-end. As an alternative to a smooth-bore barrel a supplementary small calibre rifle barrel, chambered for the .22 rim-fire might be fitted, the supplementary barrel having its own lock and extraction system.

The extra barrel was built as part of the rifle and offered an immediate choice of cartridge. An alternative consisted of using 'adaptors', which allowed the conversion of a large rifle calibre into a small calibre rim-fire such as the standard .22 rim-fire. Such adaptors were available for the Mauser-system repeating rifles and others could be had to convert the shotgun into a rifle.

In the 1920's the British firm of Parker-Hale introduced a line of rifled adaptors for shotguns which were made for the .25 ACP automatic pistol cartridge and also for a .22 centre-fire cartridge of special design. To avoid the need to use special cartridges, a modified form of adaptor was then brought out for the .22 rim-fire, overcoming the need to position the barrel eccentrically to permit the rim-fire cartridge to be fired. Such adaptors were mainly used to check on shooting ability because without satisfactory sights the accuracy potential was slight. Still made are the .410 adaptors for 12- and 16-bore shotguns; now in light metal,

Top, sectioned cartridges using (left), fibre and card wads with roll closure, and (right) plastic wad/shot cup with crimp closure

Centre, reloaded cartridges showing, left to right: roll top with overshot card; 6-pleat crimp; 8-pleat crimp

Bottom, a comparison of fibre and card main wads (left), with a plastic wad/shot cup (right)

two adaptors can easily be carried in the pocket.

These compromise solutions are interesting, and do make the guns more versatile.

Hand-loading Shotgun Cartridges

Shotgun cartridges have been hand-loaded, to some extent, since the times when muzzle loaders were being superseded by cartridge-loading guns. In the days of muzzle loaders, sportsmen were accustomed to trying their guns with various loads until the best result for a particular purpose was obtained. It was natural, then, that at least some users of the 'new' cartridge-loading guns would wish to continue this practice and retain the choice of loadings open to users of muzzle loading guns. As long as black powder was freely available, cartridges could be loaded to give satisfactory results with a variety of loads and a careful hand-loader could produce cartridges tailored to his own needs, regular in performance and cheaper than the proprietary cartridges of the day.

With the coming of smokeless powders the situation changed somewhat. These powders did not ignite so readily as black powder and often required more powerful and more regular primers for the best results. The ratio of shot to powder, the ramming pressure and the closure strength of the cartridges were all found to be more critical than with black powder. The greater care and knowledge needed for successful loading and the availability of cheap factory loaded cartridges, resulting from increased mechanization, reduced the popularity of home-loading which, for many years, was carried on by only a small minority.

Since World War 2 the increase in cartridge costs and the popularity of clay pigeon shooting have made hand loading an attractive proposition for many shotgun users. The demand for hand-loading tools has been met, particularly in the United States, by the production of hand-loading presses designed for the domestic user. These presses enable hand-loading or, more usually, hand reloading to be carried out more rapidly and consistently than with the simpler hand tools of former years.

An important function of a hand-loading press is its capacity for restoring a fired case to approximately the dimensions it had before firing. Re-sizing is necessary because, on firing, a cartridge case expands and distorts due to the gas pressure and can no longer be easily loaded into a standard gun chamber. After re-sizing a fired case may again be used in any gun of appropriate gauge and chamber-length.

The problem of re-sizing has been reduced by the advent of the plastic-tubed cartridge case: the plastic tube reverts, after firing, to virtually the same size as before. It is therefore only necessary to re-size the metal cartridge base.

In fact, even the best re-sizers have little effect on swollen paper tubes, particularly when these have been damp, and some degree of selection is always necessary when using paper-tubed cases. Whichever kind of case is used, all damaged cases should be discarded.

On a typical hand-loading press all the following operations may be carried out, not necessarily in the exact order shown.

1 Re-sizing of fired cases
2 Removal of fired primers
3 Insertion of new primers
4 Loading of measured quantity of powder*
5 Loading of wads
6 Application of correct ramming pressure to wads and/or powder as applicable
7 Loading of measured quantity of shot*
8 Closing of cartridge

Although hand-loading presses make loading easier it is still necessary to follow certain rules if safe, effective cartridges are to be loaded. Only loads recommended by competent authorities, or found to be safe by properly conducted proof tests, should be used. Any deviation from a recommended load can affect performance.

High chamber pressures may result from the use of too powerful a primer, too fast burning a powder and/or too heavy a charge, a change in wadding, ramming pressure, shot load, shot size or closure strength. It is essential, therefore, that any change in components or loading technique is followed by test firings of the modified load in a pressure gun, to check for safe pressures before the load is adopted for normal use. The exceptions to this rule are when expert advice is available or when a small change in shot size is made, say from No 7 to No 6 or No 5 in an otherwise identical load. If, however, a load is known to give normal pressures with a large size of shot such as BB, then a change to very fine shot such as No 9 will certainly call for a reduced powder load and perhaps a change to a slower burning grade of powder, to keep within safe breech pressures and normal velocities.

Powder loads should be kept as close as possible to the weight recommended. A small percentage increase in powder load produces about $2\frac{1}{2}$ times that increase in breech pressure, i.e. a 4% increase in powder will increase breech pressures by about 10% in a properly loaded cartridge. For safety, then, powder changes should be within 2% of the correct load and, for the most regular ballistics, should not vary by more than 1 or even $\frac{1}{2}$% from the nominal loading. The use of the wrong grade or type of powder may be extremely dangerous and can easily produce breech pressures high enough to burst a normal gun.

From the safety aspect, shot weight is less critical than powder weight but, even so, the shot charge should not exceed the nominal load by more than 5% and for regular ballistics should be within 2% of the nominal load.

Where fixed shot and powder measures are provided on a press, adjustment of loads can be achieved by choosing slightly larger measures than required and reducing the volume by sticking smooth-backed adhesive tape inside until the precise load required is thrown.

Powder and/or wad ramming pressures should be applied as recommended using the pressure gauge fitted to the press.

Perhaps the most critical single operation in cartridge loading is the making of the closure. This has to be strong enough to resist movement of the wads until the powder is properly ignited, a function vital to good ballistics. Apart from this requirement the closure has to be able to retain the shot load in the unfired cartridge when one barrel of a double-barrelled gun is fired. The recoil of the gun causes the shot in the unfired cartridge to push against the cartridge closure. The pressure is brief but is of the order of 40 lb for a typical gun and cartridge.

Although powerful primers can ensure good powder ignition with closure strengths lower than 40 lb, this figure, for the reason quoted, may be taken as the practical minimum for a 12-gauge cartridge or perhaps a little less for 16 and 20-gauge. Factory closures are seldom less than 50 lb on paper tubes and about 60 to 100 lb on plastic cartridges.

Too strong a closure may cause an increase in breech pressure, but the increase is seldom significant when using paper or plastic tubes unless an abnormal method of making the closure is employed. If, however, a crimp is pushed in too deeply so that pressure is transmitted to the wads and powder via the shot, then the combination of strong closure and increased loading pressure may cause a marked increase in breech pressure on firing.

The appearance of modern hand-loading presses coincided, particularly in the U.S.A., with the general adoption of the crimp-closed cartridge. This type of closure can be re-closed with a crimping tool using linear movement only, although factory crimps are always finished with a rotating chuck. These chucks operate on exactly the same principal as the hand turnover chucks formerly used for roll-top closures.

A turnover chuck is a valuable loading accessory, whether mounted on the press or separately as it enables the loader to make a closure similar in strength and appearance to that on factory loaded cartridges. It allows the loader, moreover, to use a rolled closure if desired, an option which is useful for rare cartridges such as the 2 in 12-gauge.

Until recent years the wads between powder and shot in a cartridge were of card and felt or a felt substitute. These wads are now being superseded by plastic wads which offer the advantage of combining the function of over-powder card, main wads and undershot card in a single unit. In addition, plastic wads incorporate a shot sleeve which protects the shot during transit up the bore. It is probable that this type of wad will eventually replace the older form as loading is simplified and accurate control of wad compressibility and obturative properties are possible, offering the prospect of very regular ballistics. These wads, however, have not yet reached the limit of development and new forms are still appearing. The effect of replacing felt or fibre wads by plastic wads differs from type to type so it is particularly important that proper tests are carried out when a substitution is tried. Typically, a 10% reduction in powder may be needed to keep within safe breech pressure limits and, in some instances, a change of powder grade may be advisable. This can only be determined by proof testing.

In the U.S.A. some manufacturers of plastic wads publish recommended loads utilizing readily available primers, powders and cases from other sources. Where this custom prevails the handloader's choice is made wider, safer and easier. CAT

Loading Tools and Accessories for Brush Hunting

The bench-rester and international target shot has to work to the finest tolerances, and gauge his bullet and powder weights – not to mention the cubic capacity of each shell – down to one four-thousandth of an inch; and this means very heavy, costly equipment impossible to tote around in the wilds. It is also inconvenient to carry a large quantity of loaded shells. However, the brush-hunter can resort to what is nowadays derisively referred to as 'kitchen-sink' hand-loading. Modern smokeless powder is easily carried and so are primers. Every rifle shell used only with such powders and non-mercuric non-chlorate primers will take 60 or more loads in perfect safety. Lead and solder for hardening are easily obtainable. Hard bullets, preferably gas-checked, should always be used in hot countries – particularly in very dry weather – to prevent leading.

Tong-tools are readily available and the complete outfit – tool, bullet mould and all necessary dies – weighs around 3 lb and can easily be carried in a small saddle-pocket. Lead, powder, etc will be left at base. They are the cheapest tools on the market, they are reliable, and are quite capable of loading ammunition that will put every bullet, from 30·30, 32 Spl or 44 Ruger carbine into less than a five-inch group at 100 yards. For this type of hunting, a mould casting a flat-nosed bullet is preferable. In the rifle calibres quoted above, a gas-check should always be used on the base of the bullet, and the bullet-alloy cast hard, i.e. about 90% lead and 10% tin. This, with the gas-check, cuts down leading possibilities to the minimum.

In the case of the hunter using a smooth-bore slug repeater the procedure is a little different. His old-fashioned shotgun-reloading tools weigh almost exactly the same as the rifle tong-tool and accessories and can be easily packed away. There are also tools for making excellent rifled slugs – but they weigh as much as the bench-rester's equipment and are out of the question. He will therefore take a supply of rifled slugs; but he will also take a mould casting a spherical ball of his chosen calibre, 12- or 16-gauge. This ball should be a fairly tight push-fit all the way down the barrel of his gun; say .731 in for a 12-gauge, .663 in to .664 in for a 16-gauge. Many years ago in the British weekly, *The Field*, there was an article on the shooting of round ball in rifles and well-bored smooth-bores. It was found that rifling only came into its own after the 100-yards range had been passed; that up to 100 yards round ball, fired from a smooth-bore, was virtually as accurate as that fired from a rifled barrel. Also, the modern smooth-bore slug-gun hunter will be astonished at the accuracy possible with spherical ball fired from his single-barrelled repeater. The solid round ball is of course somewhat heavier than a modern rifled slug; the 12-gauge ball weighs about 510 grains, the 16-gauge about 390 grains. It is excellent in brush and a real killer; moreover, it is far cheaper than any rifled slug. The only danger is that it should never be fired out of a choked barrel as the area of greatest diameter (just where it bears on the barrel) is also the area of its greatest density. It should be cast in the same way as the gas-check rifle bullets mentioned above, 90% lead to 10% tin, as leading in a smooth barrel is nearly as bad for accuracy as in a rifle – and just as annoying for the owner to remove.

As to the actual casting of bullets one point should be remembered. The important thing is to throw the first half-dozen bullets back into the pot and keep none until they come smooth from the mould; this indicates that the mixture is hot enough. If it starts slagging too much on top, it may be too hot and the tin will burn away.

The old frontiersman in the days of the flintlock muzzle-loader used to chop up chunks of lead with his belt-axe and throw it into a small iron cooking-pot on three legs. He ladled it out with the family lipped soup-ladle, the handle conveniently lagged with an old sock or something. Cursing and swearing and hopping about (for the transaction was a warm one) he cast bullets fully capable of bringing down his enemy at ranges up to 400 yards. CWTC

Glossary

ACTION. The part of the gun, screwed to the stock, that contains all the mechanisms necessary for the attachment of the barrels and for the firing of the cartridges.

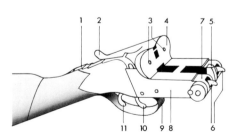

Action. 1. safety catch; 2. lever; 3. stikers; 4. action face; 5. extractor cam; 6. cocking levers; 7. knuckle; 8. side plate; 9. trigger guard; 10. right trigger; 11. left trigger.

ACTION BODY. The steel housing that actually contains the various moving parts of the action. The body is stamped out and then worked up from a solid bar of carbon steel, and consists of three different sections:

(a) the bar, which is the bottom part and lies under the barrels and engages with them

(b) the face, which is the vertical part that seals the breech when the gun is closed

(c) the strap, which is the top part that extends into the stock and is screwed to it, so holding the action body to it.

ACTION BOLT. A moving part of the action that slides forward to engage with the grips in the lumps (q.v.) in order to secure the barrels to the action. The bolt is actuated by the lever which, when moved, actuates a cam working in an elliptical slot cut in one side of the bolt.

ACTION PIN see CROSS PIN

ARQUEBUS. An early type of gun whose name is probably derived from hackbut (q.v.) but refers, primarily, to a light type of gun that could be fired from the shoulder or chest and required no rest. Later the name was sometimes used to distinguish a wheel-lock from a matchlock.

AUTOMATIC. A rifle or other gun that continues to fire for so long as the trigger is pulled. Such guns are more relevant to warfare than to sport. The term is often used for a gun that is not, properly speaking, automatic, but merely self-loading: that is, it will fire each time the trigger is pulled.

AUTOMATIC SAFETY. The automatic locking of the triggers by the safety stop that occurs whenever the action lever is moved and the gun is opened and cocked.

BAKER EJECTOR. A not commonly used type of ejector. A rod held under tension by a coiled spring is released, by a tumbler, when the gun is fired. When the gun is opened this rod is then free to slide forward and strike the extractor leg.

BAKER RIFLE. The first rifle to be made for, and submitted to, the British Ordnance Board. It was selected and issued to rifle regiments and used during the Peninsular War. It had seven-grooved rifling that made only a quarter turn, which made it easier to ram the patched ball home. Without the patch the ball could be dropped in and the rifle used as a smooth bore musket that could be rapidly reloaded for close action.

BALANCE (of a shotgun). It is commonly accepted that the actual point of balance of a gun should lie slightly in front of the trigger guard. But balance, in the more general sense of handling well, is probably best ensured by having as much of the total weight of the gun as possible concentrated between the two hands of the man holding the gun.

BALLING. This occurs when pellets of the shot charge jam together in clusters of up to six or eight. Balling is to be avoided for it ruins the pattern, damages the game, and can be dangerous to beaters and bystanders because of the greater carrying power of the balled pellets. It is caused by a faulty cartridge, that is one in which either the pressure has been excessive or the felt wad has been faulty.

BAR. See ACTION BODY

BARREL. That part of the shotgun which contains the bore, cone, chamber and lumps, bolt loop, top extension etc.

BEND (of stock). The amount by which the stock is dropped below the barrels in order to bring the eye smoothly along the line of the barrels. It is measured by the distances between a theoretical continuation of the top rib and the comb and the heel of the stock.

BENT. A notch cut in the lower end of the tumbler. When the gun is opened and cocked the nose of the sear engages in this notch, and so holds the gun in the cocked position even after the gun has been shot and the cocking levers withdrawn.

BITES see GRIPS

BLACK POWDER. The trade name for gunpowder, which has been used as a propellant for many centuries until replaced by smokeless powders. The composition of gunpowder is: potassium nitrate (saltpeter) 75%, charcoal 15%, sulphur 10%.

BLANKS. The circular bars of steel, approximately three feet long and less than one and half inches in diameter, from which tubes, and so, eventually, barrels, are made by drilling and shaping.

BLOWN PATTERN. A pattern in which, because of excessive pressure, the pellets have been unduly scattered. The greater the amount of choke in a gun the smaller the probability of a cartridge producing a blown pattern.

BLUEING. The colouring of the metal work of a gun by the process of painting it repeatedly with a blueing solution. Once a gun has been blued it passes from being 'in the white' to being 'in the black'.

BORE. That part of the inside of the barrel which is entirely filled and sealed by the shot charge and wads on firing. Often used, loosely, instead of gauge when referring to the size of a shotgun, e.g. 12-bore.

BOLT LOOP see LOOP

BOTTOM PLATE. The plate that is screwed over the bottom of the action in box lock guns. It serves to cover the locks and to protect them from moisture.

BRAZING. The method by which barrels, ribs, lumps, etc, are generally joined to-

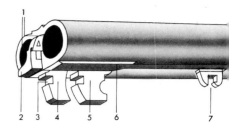

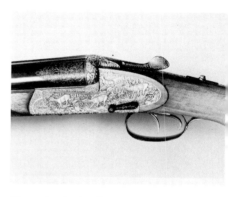

Barrels. 1. breech; 2. extractor; 3. bite; 4. rear lump; 5. hook; 6. flat; 7 bolt loop.

The action body of this modern German Drilling is engraved with an attractive hunting scene.

gether. It involves using spelter, at a high temperature, with borax as a flux.

BREECH. The chamber end of the barrels. (The face of the action body is also sometimes referred to as the standing breech.)

BREECH PIN. The main pin holding stock, action and trigger plate together.

BRIDLE. The small plate on the inside of a side lock action that carries the inner end of the tumbler axle.

BUTT. The bottom end of the stock, which is held against the shoulder at firing.

CALIBRE. The measurement of the bore of a rifle, expressed in decimal points of an inch for British and American guns, and in millimetres for Continental guns. It is not the measurement of the bullet, but of the inside diameter of the barrel before rifling. The bullet is actually made slightly larger to provide good obturation (*q.v.*).

CALIVER. A light form of arquebus (*q.v.*).

CAP. The part of the cartridge that can provide, because of the properties of fulminating compounds, the means for igniting the powder charge. As a working unit it consists of:

(*a*) the cap, which is a small copper capsule, open at one end, and about one fifth of an inch in diameter. The cap composition, which is usually composed of a mixture of fulminating compounds, is placed on the floor of this capsule.

(*b*) the cap chamber into which the cap is fitted. The chamber itself is then fitted into the base of the cartridge in such a way that the gases from the explosion of the cap composition can shoot through the small hole in the cap chamber and ignite the powder charge.

(*c*) the anvil, which is a thin, sharp-pointed piece of brass so placed that, when the cap has been struck by the striker the blow causes the cap composition to be compressed between the cap and the anvil, so providing sufficient friction and heat to ignite the cap composition.

(*d*) the cap composition, which is, generally, a mixture of three different fulminating compounds, which may vary, slightly, from maker to maker, but produce the three-element cap which is now almost universal.

CARBINE. A firearm with a shorter barrel. Originally a short-barrelled musket, the name was later used of short-barrelled rifles. These were issued to mounted troops, who needed a weapon short enough to fit into a saddle holster that would not be so long as to bang against the horse's shoulder or quarter and so chafe it. The handling advantage of such a weapon in thick cover, soon became apparent, and sporting carbines were developed for forest shooting.

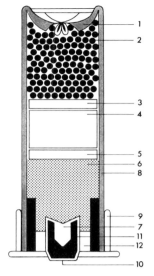

Cartridge. 1. crimp closure of case; 2. shot charge; 3. card wad; 4. felt, fibre or plastic wad; 5. card wad; 6. powder charge; 7. anvil; 8. waterproofed paper case; 9. brass head; 10. cap; 11. cap compound; 12. base wad.

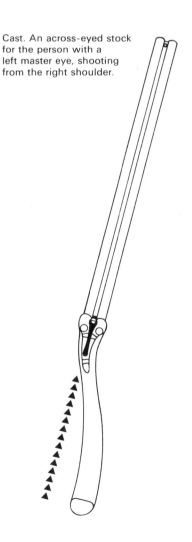

Cast. An across-eyed stock for the person with a left master eye, shooting from the right shoulder.

The most famous of these was, perhaps, the Winchester 30–30 carbine, used by generations of deer hunters in the woods of the United States.

CARTRIDGE. The shotgun cartridge consists, essentially, of:

(*a*) the tube, which may be made of paper, plastic, metal, or combinations of any of these.

(*b*) the head, which is of brass and contains the cap.

(*c*) the powder charge.

(*d*) the wads.

(*e*) the shot charge.

CARTWHEEL PATTERN. This is becoming increasingly rare, since it cannot occur with crimped cartridges. A pattern is said to have cartwheeled when the pellets are found to have scattered round the circumference of the pattern instead of being distributed more or less regularly all over the circle. Cartwheeling is thought to be caused by the over-shot wad (*see* Wads) tilting after firing, so distributing the shot column moving behind it.

CASE HARDENING. The process by which the action body is hardened off by heating it in a furnace in the presence of bone ash. This causes it to absorb carbon, which produces an outside layer of steel of great hardness without impairing the elasticity of the underlying metal.

CAST. The amount by which the stock needs to be bent, laterally, to bring the barrels into the natural line of vision. A right-handed shot will normally need cast-off, and a left handed shot cast-on, which means, in both cases, that the barrels will be closer to a centre line than the butt. The actual amount of cast required will differ from person to person, and is determined by build, master eye, shooting habits, etc.

COMB. This is the part of the stock at which the butt dips down to the hand, or grip.

CHAMBER. That part of the inside of the barrel into which the cartridge is loaded. It must, because of the thickness of the cartridge case, always be of a larger bore than the rest of the barrel.

CHAMBER CONE. That part of the barrel which connects the front end of the chamber to the rear end of the bore. Since the one is wider than the other it must, of necessity, taper. In most British guns the length of the cone is between three eighths of an inch and one inch.

CHASSEPOT. An early breech-loading, bolt-action rifle invented in France in 1866 by Antoine Alphonse Chassepot and named after him. It was, for some time after, the standard French Army rifle.

CHAUMETTE. A Huguenot gunsmith, working in the early eighteenth century in both

France and Britain, who produced an early form of breech-loading gun. Its action depended on unscrewing a plug that passed right through the barrel and whose base formed the trigger guard.

CHOKE. A system of finishing the boring of the barrel so as to leave a constriction of the bore near the muzzle end. This constriction acts to prevent the shot charge from spreading as quickly as it would otherwise have done, which has the effect of improving the pattern at a distance. Choking normally starts about one to one and a half inches from the muzzle, tapers for about half an inch, and then runs parallel once more. The tapering part is known as the cone, and the rest as the parallel. The degree of actual constriction can vary from three to 40 thousandths of an inch, and each thousandth of an inch is known as a point of choke. A full choke, therefore, is one of 40 points, a half choke is one of 20 points, and so on.

COCKING LEVERS (or dogs). These both pivot in a peg running right through the action body. Their fronts protrude through slots in the knuckle of the action and fit into slots in the fore-end. When the gun is opened the drop of the barrels depresses the front end, and elevates the rear end of each cocking lever. This lifts the front end of each tumbler, which then pivots on its pin until the bent comes opposite to the sear. The pressure of the sear spring then forces the sear to engage in the bent, which holds the tumbler back even when the pressure of the cocking lever is removed as the gun is closed.

CORNED POWDER. A better, milled gunpowder, which was produced by damping the unimproved meal powder, and forcing the resultant paste through a series of sieves to produce, when dry, small hard grains that would not cake like meal powder and would burn faster.

CRIMPING. A method of closing the top of the cartridge other than with a turnover and over-shot wad.

CROSS BOLT. A common form of top extension (q.v.).

CROSS PIN (action pin). The large screw across the front end of the bar on to which the barrels are hooked. In cheaper guns there is not, generally, a separate pin but a solid cross joint cut out as part of the action body. The advantage of having a cross pin instead of a solid cross joint is that a pin can be adjusted and so allow the barrels to be brought back 'on-face'.

DAMASCUS (TWIST) BARRELS. An early method of barrel manufacture. The tubes were made, not by boring or drawing steel, but by forming a ribbon made of alternate strips of steel and iron welded together and rolled out, and then twisting this ribbon to form a barrel, the twists being welded to

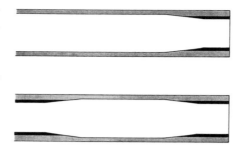

Types of choke: top, ordinary, with the constriction at the end of the barrel; below, recess, which is made by boring out a section of the barrel.

each other. This method is no longer used even in the manufacture of the cheaper guns.

DEELEY EJECTOR. This ejector consists of what is, essentially, a miniature lock placed inside the fore-end. It is cocked by the closing of the gun and released by its opening.

DICKSON ROUND ACTION. Invented by Scottish gunsmiths, this is to all intents and purposes a sidelock action, except that these locks are mounted on one central plate and due to this design the action is particularly strong and is therefore particularly suitable for a light-weight gun.

DOG LOCK. An early lock in which the cock was held safely at half cock by a small hook that engaged in its rear.

DOGS see COCKING LEVERS

DOLL'S HEAD. A common form of top extension (q.v.). It is the simplest and, perhaps, the best form because it consists of no more than a partially circular extension, wider at the top than the bottom, that fits tightly into a correspondingly shaped recess in the action. Because of its shape it requires no extra bolt to secure it.

DOUBLE. The name commonly given to a double-barrelled sporting rifle. Such a rifle will, like a shot gun, have either a box or a side lock and will open and be loaded in the same way as a shotgun. It has largely been replaced by the single barrelled repeating rifle. Nevertheless, its advantages are that it is a better balanced weapon; the second shot can be got off quicker than with a bolt or lever action, and without the noise caused by reloading; it is more reliable since there is no magazine, bolt, slide or lever to jam. Its disadvantages are largely cost and weight, though a double is also probably less accurate at ranges over 100 yd.

DRAWN TUBES. Drawing is a rather cheaper method of forming tubes, and so, eventually, barrels, than the more usual one of boring blanks.

EJECTOR. A mechanical device for flinging a fired cartridge out of the gun by giving it extra momentum after primary extraction (q.v.). There are several ways of doing this but nearly all depend on a miniature lock housed inside the fore-end, whose tumbler strikes the long arm of the extractor and drives it violently forward. Since, in ejector guns, both the extractor and the long leg of the extractor are split in two, only the cartridge in the fired barrel gets ejected, even though there is always primary extraction of both barrels. The two commonest types of ejector are the Deeley and the Southgate, though well known variants are also produced by Boss, Dickson and Greener.

EXTRACTOR. A mechanical device for partially withdrawing fired and unfired cartridges from the chambers. A segment of the

Typical of the double rifle of the mid-19th century, this 10-bore for round ball was made by McLauchlan of Edinburgh.

breech end of the barrels is separated from them in such a way as to be able to slide in and out on one or more guides known as legs. As it slides out it pushes against the rim of the cartridge and so carries it partially out of the chambers. The extractor is caused to slide out by the action of opening the gun, when the extractor cam (*q.v.*) forces it outwards. If the gun is not also an ejector (*q.v.*) then the cartridge is only partly pushed out of the chamber, and has to be removed by hand. This partial withdrawal is known as primary extraction. In non-ejectors the extractor is in one piece and works on both barrels whether they have both been fired or not. In ejectors the extractor is divided in two to allow ejection of the fired cartridge only.

EXTRACTOR CAM. A fixed projection from the knuckle of the action that, when the gun is opened, pushes against the leg of the extractor and drives it forward.

EXTRACTOR STOP PIN. The screw that runs through the forward lump and holds the extractors in position.

FACE (STANDING BREECH). See under AC-TION BODY.

FINE BORING. The process of finishing the manufacture of the barrels by forming the chambers, choke, etc.

FIRING LEVER *see* SEAR

FLATS. The flat-shaped parts at the rear ends of the barrels that fit against the flats of the action.

FLATS OF THE ACTION. The flat, upper surface of the bar on which the flats of the barrels lie when the gun is closed.

FLINTLOCK. A lock that gradually replaced the matchlock and survived for almost all forms of guns, until the emergence of the percussion cap. Its essential action consisted of causing a flint to strike a steel bar in such a way that sparks were struck over a pan containing priming powder. In its final form it was developed by the famous French gunsmith Marin le Bourgeoys early in the seventeenth century, who combined the internal spring and tumbler of the snaphaunce (*q.v.*) and the combined steel and pan cover of the Miquelet to produce the lock used on most firearms for the next three centuries.

FLIP. This is the name given to one of the movements that occur in a gun barrel when the gun is fired – in this case a slight bending downwards that has some small effect on shot path and pattern. Flip varies, though only slightly, from gun to gun, depending on the length and strength of the barrels involved. In the over and under, flip is almost entirely eliminated, because of the reinforcing effect of the barrels on each other.

FORE-END. The largely wooden part of the gun that fits on to the barrels at one end and the knuckle of the action body at the other and has three main functions:

(*a*) To prevent the barrels slipping off the cross pin whenever the gun is opened.

(*b*) To act as a grip and guard for the forward hand whilst shooting.

(*c*) To contain the ejector mechanism and to receive and depress the front ends of the cocking levers.

The fore-end is held in place by a snap spring bolt that engages in the barrel loop. It may simply snap into place, or it may be of the Anson type where the spring bolt extends beyond the fore-end as a small stud that has to be pushed, or the Deeley type, where a small loop near the tip of the fore-end has to be lifted in order to engage the bolt in the loop.

FORSYTH. Alexander John Forsyth, 1768–1843, a Scots clergyman who first took advantage of the explosive qualities of fulminates to produce a percussion lock.

GAUGE. The measurement of the bore of a shotgun (and occasionally, still, of an artillery piece), not in decimals of an inch, but in terms of the number of spherical balls of pure lead, each exactly fitting the bore, that would go to the pound. Shotgun bores smaller than 32 are, however, measured in decimals of an inch, e.g. .410.

GRIPS (BITES). Slots in the lumps (*q.v.*) into which the action bolt slides so as to hold the barrels securely in place.

HACKBUT. A very early form of hand gun which did away with the need for a rest by having a hook or projection from the underside of the barrel that could be hooked over a wall, and so take up some of the recoil on firing. *See also* Arquebus.

HALL RIFLE. An early, breech loading rifle invented by J. H. Hall, born 1778, and adopted by the United States Army in 1819. The whole breech block tipped up to allow loading when a spring catch was released.

HAMMER GUNS. Guns in which the hammers (or tumblers) fit on to the tumbler pin outside the action body, forming visible hammers. The action is a normal side action except for the absence of cocking levers. The gun is cocked by pulling the hammer back by hand until the sear engages with the bent in one of two positions. Hammer guns are not now made, even in the cheapest ranges.

HAND (or GRIP) of Stock. The thin part of the stock where it is held by the trigger hand. On a good gun it is chequered and made diamond shaped, rather than round to prevent the hand from slipping.

IMPROVED CYLINDER. A barrel bored with the smallest amount of choke possible, i.e. three to five points.

INTERCEPTING SAFETY STOP. A safety device, found in the best sidelocks, that is additional to the normal safety stop.

IN THE WHITE. The state in which the unfinished gun is sent for proofing. Both wood and steel are still in their natural colours. *See* Blueing.

KNUCKLE. The rounded end of the bar, on to which the fore-end fits, and through which the cocking levers protrude.

LEGS. (Of the Extractor). The extractor usually works on two legs – the long and the short leg – that slide in and out of holes drilled between the barrels at the breech end.

LENGTH (of stock). This is an important consideration for the 'fit' of the gun. The most important length measurement is that from the centre of the front trigger to the centre of the butt, but the measurements from that trigger to both the toe and the heel of the butt are also considered.

LEVER. The arm that operates the mechanism for opening and closing a gun. It is most commonly placed on top of the strap, in which position it is called a top lever, but it can be placed on one side of the action body, when it is a side lever, or under the trigger guard, when it is a bottom lever. It turns a cam which moves the action bolt backwards, so allowing the gun to open and the barrels to drop. At the same time it actuates the safety mechanism, usually by moving a stop into position above the trigger blade.

LEVER ACTION. A rifle action in which the breech bolt and carrier mechanisms are operated by opening and closing a finger-lever trigger guard. It is used in such rifles as the Winchester, Savage and Marlin.

LOAD. The particular combination of powder and shot that is put into any particular type of cartridge.

LOCK. The mechanism that causes the gun to be fired. In the modern gun, the mechanism that causes the cap of the cartridge to be struck. There are two types of lock in use in the modern shotgun – the box lock and the side lock.

LOOP (BOLT LOOP). The projection beneath the barrels, some way up from the breech, to which the fore-end fastens.

LUMPS. These are the two large metal projections from the underneath of the breech end of a pair of barrels that serve to attach those barrels to the action body and stock. They are known as the forward and rear lumps, and the bottom part of the forward lump, which is the part that hooks on to the action pin when the gun is put together, is known as the hook of lump. Lumps can be formed in two ways: they can be forged in one piece with the tube, in which case they are known as chopper lumps, (these are the

most reliable, but are expensive in labour and are only found in the best guns); alternatively, they may be brazed into position, either between the barrels or merely under them. In the back of each lump is the grip (or bite) in which the action bolt engages. *See* Action Bolt; Grip.

MAGNUM. When applied to a gun, it means one chambered to fire a load heavier than those normally associated with guns of that bore. Thus a shotgun may be chambered to fire a three, or two and three quarter inch cartridge instead of the more normal two and a half inch cartridge. The effect of this is to allow, within the limits of safety, a lighter gun to be used than would otherwise be normal for that charge or, alternatively, a higher muzzle velocity than would be normal for that gun.

MAINSPRING. A powerful flat spring, inside the action, that is connected, at one end, to the upper edge of the tumbler. When the gun is opened the cocking lever forces the tumbler to rotate and this, in its turn, compresses the mainspring. This compression is maintained as the bent of the tumbler engages with the sear. When the trigger is pulled the sear disengages, the tumbler is released, and the tension on the mainspring is also progressively released. This produces sufficient force to drive the tumbler violently round until the striker (pin) is pushed through the action face sufficiently far to strike and explode the cap.

MARTINI. A rifle action based on the falling block system that is now largely obsolete, except for certain .22 rimfire rifles. Frederich von Martini, a Swiss, did not invent the falling block breech system but improved on Henry Peabody's invention to produce the Peabody-Martini breech that was used in so many European army rifles during the second half of the last century. His particular contribution was to substitute an internal, self-cocking striker for Peabody's external, hand-cocked hammer.

MATCH. This was, originally, a slow burning device carried separately from the gun but used for igniting the charge and so firing it. Its invention allowed the gunner, for the first time, to move away, with his gun, from a source of fire and yet carry a glowing coal with him. It consisted of a loosely twisted rope of hemp that had been dipped into saltpeter and spirits of wine to make it burn steadily and hold a glow that could be blown on.

MATCHLOCK. The first gun in which the match – that is, the firing mechanism – was successfully made an integral part of the gun. This allowed the gunner to hold his gun with both hands and to take aim without having to look up to see where the match and the touchhole were. This was achieved by clamping the match into the top end of

Diagram to illustrate the principle of the muzzle brake

An over and under shotgun made by Fabrique Nationale of Belgium

an s-shaped piece of metal called a serpentine which was able to swivel round a pin driven through its centre and into the stock. When the lower end of the serpentine was raised its top end would be lowered, with no need for further guidance, onto the powder in the pan. When the matchlock was fully developed the lower end of the serpentine was abolished and a trigger, sear and spring were introduced, instead, for lowering and lifting it.

MAUSER. A bolt action still much used in single-barrelled sporting rifles, that was first perfected by the German designer Peter Paul Mauser, and that has been used, at various times, for many military rifles. The British P'14 Enfield and the American Springfield M'03 are developments of the original Mauser design.

MINIE. A hollow based rifle bullet designed, in 1849, by the Frenchman, Captain Minie, in an attempt to find a bullet that would fit tightly enough for a rifle and yet not need hammering home. It was found that, with or without pegs or cups inside the hollow base, it would expand sufficiently on firing, to give obturation and fit the rifling. Variations of the Minie ball were quickly adopted by many armies, and the smooth bore musket was quickly abandoned as a weapon of war.

MUZZLE BRAKE. A device fitted to the end of a rifle barrel to reduce recoil by diverting the escaping gases at right angles through slots in the brake. The action of the escaping gases on the forward edges of these slots appreciably reduces recoil.

MUZZLE VELOCITY. This is the velocity with which the shot charge leaves the barrel, and this, in its turn, depends very largely on the progressive nature of the powder used.

OBTURATION. The sealing of a bore to prevent the gases of an explosion from escaping prematurely. In a shotgun the action of the gases on the felt wad cause it to spread laterally and provide obturation.

OFF-THE-FACE. When a gun has become so worn that light can be seen between the ends of the barrels and the face of the action, then it is said to be 'off-the-face'. *See also* Cross Pin.

OVER AND UNDER. A shotgun whose two barrels are fitted in a vertical plane (one under the other) instead of in a horizontal plane (side by side).

PACKING. In a shotgun this consists of the supports placed between the barrels to hold them in correct alignment and to strengthen the joins. It is usually, but not always, composed of four pieces of steel shaped to fit the curvature of the barrels, and placed at equal intervals between the muzzle and the bolt loop.

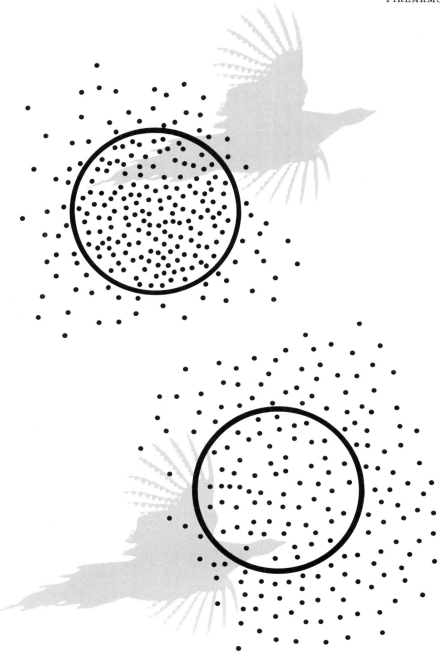

Top, the pattern of full choke at 40 yd. The pheasant missed, behind and below. Bottom, the pattern of improved cylinder, also at 40 yd, and well placed above the bird.

PAN. This was the small receptacle next to the touch hole that held the priming powder needed to fire the main charge in the days before Forsyth invented the percussion lock.

PATTERN. This is, in the first instance, thought of as the number of pellets to be found inside a 30-inch circle when a 12-bore, firing a cartridge loaded with one and one sixteenth ounce of No. 6 shot and 33 grains of smokeless diamond powder is fired at the plate from 40 yd. This number will vary with the points of choke of the gun as well as with the charge. It is possible to work out theoretical values for all these, and to measure any gun and any cartridge against these values.

PEPPERBOX. The popular name given to any multi-barrelled gun whose barrels were made to revolve round a single chamber so that each could be fired in turn. This is the opposite principle to the revolver.

PETRONEL. An early hand gun, light enough to be fired with the butt held against the chest. The name is derived from the French *poitrine* (breast).

PILL LOCK. An early form of percussion lock. The fulminating compound was bound with gum arabic and rolled into small pills which could be inserted into a special touch hole, in which they could be exploded by a pointed hammer.

PIN. In gunmaking, a screw is always referred to as a pin.

PINFIRE. An early form of self-contained cartridge in which the cap was mounted sideways inside the base, with a pin above it whose head protruded through the cartridge case. A blow from the hammer drove this pin into the primer and exploded the cartridge.

POINTS (of looseness). The degree to which the chambers of guns have to be made slightly larger than the minimum cartridge size in order to accommodate slight variations in manufacture, dampness, etc. *See also* Choke.

POWDER. The material whose ignition supplies the energy that propels the shot. Modern powders are double based and depend on combinations of nitro-glycerine and either gelatinous or fibrous nitro-cellulose.

PRESSURE. In ballistics, the force generated by the combustion of powder. Such combustion liberates gas with great rapidity and at very high temperatures. Hot gases expand immediately they are generated, and this expansion produces considerable force or pressure.

PRIMARY EXTRACTION. *See* EXTRACTOR

PROGRESSIVE POWDERS. Those powders that burn to produce, as nearly as is possible, constant pressure.

PROOF. The official proving of all shotguns, in Britain either by the Gunmakers Company or by the Birmingham Proof House, that is required by law. If the gun passes, it is stamped with the necessary proof mark. There are two separate proofs:
  (a) the provisional, which is of the barrels only, to save the gunsmith from working on flawed material.
  (b) the definitive, which is of the completed gun, even though it is still in the white.

REBOUND LOCK. A lock in which, after firing, provision is made for moving the striker automatically off the cap. This is important in rifles where pressure may have driven the cap hard back on the striker. It used, also, to be important in the case of hammer guns, where the strikers point slightly downwards and are not easily pushed off the cap. But in modern, box lock guns, where the striker is integral with the tumbler and moves back with it as the gun is opened, the rebound principle is no longer important, and rebound locks are seldom fitted.

RECOIL PAD. A rubber pad added to the butt of a gun, either to lengthen the stock, or to reduce the recoil, or to do both.

REVOLVER. A gun, normally a handgun, with a cylinder containing several chambers, each of which revolves into place in line with the barrel. The revolving principle, both single and double action, had been used for centuries by various gunsmiths trying to produce weapons capable of firing several shots without reloading, but Samuel Colt, 1814–62, produced the first really popular revolver.

RIFLING. The spiral grooves in the barrel which impart a high rotational velocity to the bullet, so ensuring that it maintains equilibrium during flight. It is these grooves that, primarily, distinguish a rifle from a shotgun or any other smooth bore weapon.

RIMFIRE. Cartridges in which the cap composition occupies the whole of the base of the cartridge, instead of being concentrated into a central cap. The cap composition, therefore, constitutes a larger proportion of the total charge than in capped cartridges. The striker need not strike the centre of the cartridge to explode it. Such cartridges are now almost confined to .22 'Vermin' rifles, which exist in great numbers and many makes.

ROLLING BLOCK. A breech system developed by the Remington Arms Company towards the end of the Civil War. The breech was opened by cocking the hammer and rolling the breechblock back with the thumb. A locking lever held the hammer back whilst the cartridge was inserted, and then held the block closed.

SAFETY STOP. A device in the action of a shotgun that automatically slides forward as the gun is cocked and locks the triggers, but not the tumblers and sears. It is actuated by the action lever, and it is released by moving the safety catch forward.

SEAR (FIRING LEVER). A lever that pivots about a peg that goes right through the action. When its front end is lifted by the sear spring so as to force it to engage with the bent the rear end is depressed, which allows it to press down on the trigger.

SERPENTINE *see* MATCHLOCK.

SHARPS. Christian Sharps, an American gunsmith who, in 1848, designed the Sharps'

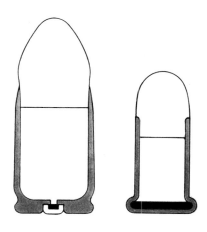

Cross-sections to illustrate the difference between centrefire and rimfire

The gray partridge, one of the most popular game birds of western and central Europe (right)

rifle and carbine. These had actions that employed the falling breech block principle, later taken up by Winchesters.

SHOT. The shot in a shotgun cartridge consists of spherical pellets made of lead to which a little arsenic or antimony has been added as a hardening agent. The spherical shape is obtained by dropping the molten lead down a shot tower into a tank of water. After this the pellets are checked for roundness, polished, and then graded into different sizes by passing through a series of screens. Different names or numbers are given to different sizes of shot, and the number of pellets in one ounce of any given size of shot is known.

SIDE LOCK. A gun where the locks are let into the side of the stock, behind the body of the action, instead of being completely housed inside the body as in the case of box locks.

SIDE PLATE. The outside plate that carries the outer end of the tumbler axle in a side lock.

SIGHTS. On a sporting rifle these may consist of a bead or blade foresight with a V, or aperture, or leaf backsight, or it may be a telescopic sight, or it may consist of various combinations of these, together with adjustments for windage and so on. It is desirable, however, not to use sights that need constant adjustments to be made, since it is nearly always quicker to use the existing sights and aim either high or off. In this respect game shooting with a rifle differs from target shooting. A shotgun, of course, requires no sights, since aim is never consciously taken.

SINGLE-TRIGGER GUNS. These are guns in which the normal trigger arrangement has been altered so that, instead of having a separate trigger for each action and each barrel, one trigger fires them both by separate, and normally consecutive pulls. Certain single-trigger guns, however, are so designed that the barrel to be fired may be selected.

SNAP ACTION. The action that drives the action bolt of a shotgun further home, once the gun has been closed, and after the bolt has engaged with the bites in the lump. The additional motive force for this is supplied by the spring on the action lever.

SNAPPING LOCK. This was any of the locks on early guns in which a pivoting arm holding a flint clamped to its end was driven forward by a powerful V-spring in such a way as to strike against a steel bar that was either above the pan or part of it, and shower sparks over the powder in the pan.

SNAPHAUNCE. An early type of flintlock, first developed in the Low Countries in the sixteenth century. It had a snapping lock, and the action of the arm holding the flint

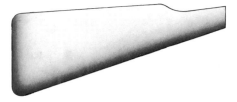

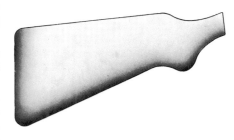

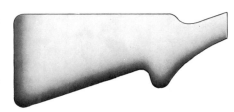

Types of stock; from top to bottom: straight hand, Monte Carlo, half pistol grip, full pistol grip.

The grizzly bear (left) is now largely protected but can still be hunted in parts of northwest Canada and Alaska.

driving forward was thought to resemble the action of a pecking cock. The Dutch, therefore, called it *snaphaan*, from which comes the name snaphaunce, and the name cock for the metal arm holding the flint.

SNIDER. Jacob Snider, an American, who invented a method of converting muzzle loaders to breech loaders to which his name was given. The Snider-Enfield was, for many years, the standard British Army weapon. The conversion consisted, in essence, of a hinged breechblock that would swing to the right for loading.

SOFT NOSE. A bullet whose lead core is allowed to protrude through the jacket of harder metal in such a way as to form a soft nose that will spread on impact. The amount of lead that protrudes will control the amount of expansion the bullet will provide on impact. If the soft nose is split, that is, has longitudinal splits cut in the nose end of its jacket, then there will be more expansion than is possible with a simple soft-nosed bullet.

SOLID. A bullet designed for use on thick-skinned big game where what is needed is not expansion, but penetration. It is completely jacketed, and the jacket is made of steel with a gilding metal to prevent fouling.

SOUTHGATE EJECTOR. One in which the ejector tumbler works on the 'over-centre' principle.

SPENCER. Christopher Spencer designed the Spencer Rifle, a magazine repeater that preceded the Winchester Henry and the Winchester 1866. It was used extensively during the Civil War, but it was of a larger calibre and lower velocity than the Winchester and carried only seven shots in the tubular magazine in its stock, so it found little favour in peacetime, and the Spencer Repeating Rifle Company went bankrupt in 1869.

STANDING BREECH *see* FACE

STOCK. The wooden part of the gun into which the action body and trigger plate fit, and on to which the barrels fasten. *See also* Butt; Hand.

STOP PIN. A pin inserted through the forward lump and fitting into a slot in the extractor long leg. It serves to stop the extractor from being pushed out too far.

STRIKER. That part of the action that hits the cap. In most box locks the striker is integral with the tumbler, but in side locks it has to be a separate part.

STRINGING (of shot). The spacing out from front to rear, as opposed to the lateral scatter, of the pellets of a shot charge. This stringing out is due to inevitable small variations in the size, weight and shape of the pellets in any charge. These variations produce different air resistances, and so different speeds through the air. Modern grading methods in the production of shot have done a lot to reduce stringing, and probably only 15% of the charge now strings out appreciably. That is, 85% of the shot forms a shot column as long as the tail formed by the remaining 15%.

SWIVEL. A device commonly used in side locks which acts between the mainspring and the tumbler and, in theory at least, helps to maintain the velocity exerted by the mainspring when first released.

TOP EXTENSION. A projection from the top of the breech end of the barrels which acts as an additional connection between the barrels and the action body. Its function is to relieve some of the strain put on the bar of the action body every time the gun is fired. There are several different designs of top extension, and some guns do without one. *See* Doll's Head.

TOUCH HOLE. The small hole in the breech end of all muzzle loading guns through which the main charge is ignited.

TRAJECTORY. The curve described by a projectile in its flight through the air. In shooting, trajectory becomes important when firing a rifle at ranges of 300 yd and more, since at such distances the drop of the bullet may amount to 9 or 30 in. That is why for shooting at such distances a rifle and cartridge giving a flat trajectory are preferred. A flat trajectory is, of course, the product of a high muzzle velocity.

TRIGGER. A lever hinged, at its front end, on a peg. The upper part of the trigger is the trigger blade, and it is this part that is in contact with the sear, moving the sear out of the bent at firing, and being itself pressed down by the sear at cocking.

TRIGGER BOX. A projection from the trigger plate carrying the peg on which both the triggers are hinged.

TRIGGER GUARD. A steel plate, screwed into the trigger plate at one end and the stock at the other, that curves round under the triggers and prevents them from catching in anything. A properly shaped trigger guard helps to prevent any damage being done to the trigger finger.

TRIGGER PLATE. A steel plate let into the stock in such a way as to form a continuation of the bar of the action body, although it is not integral with the action body but merely screwed to it. The trigger plate carriers the triggers, and also serves to strengthen the stock a little at its weakest point.

TRUE CYLINDER. A barrel that has been bored without any points of choke. Such barrels are now uncommon, having generally been replaced by improved cylinders, which are barrels bored with no more than five points of choke.

TUMBLER. That part of the action which drives the actual striker forward. In box locks the striker is generally an integral part of the tumbler. The rotation of the tumbler at cocking compresses the mainspring, thus providing the energy the tumbler will eventually impart to the striker.

TUMBLER PEG. The screw on which both tumblers pivot. In a box lock this peg has to go through the bar of the action close to the angle, which is, perhaps, the main demerit of such locks, since this involves weakening the bar at a point of maximum pressure.

TWIST BARRELS *see* DAMASCUS BARRELS

WADS. Discs of cardboard or plastic and felt that serve to hold the shot charge together whilst it is still inside the barrel. More important than this is the fact that the felt wad provides a certain amount of essential obturation (*q.v.*), sealing the bore between the escaping gases and the shot charge. Most ordinary cartridges contain four wads:

(a) the over-powder wad, which is normally made of cardboard one twelfth of an inch thick and glazed to protect the powder from the grease on

(b) the felt wad. This is the wad that acts as a seal because of its ability to spread laterally after firing. It is greased to lubricate its passage up the bore. The quality of felt used is important, and many synthetic felts and substitutes have proved to be less efficient.

(c) over-felt wad. This is another cardboard disc that serves to prevent the bottom layers of shot from sticking to the greased felt wad, and also prevents the felt wad from being destroyed by the shot as it is forced up the bore.

A simple, yet well-made hide among rushes

(d) the over-shot wad. This is another cardboard wad that serves to hold the shot firmly inside the cartridge case. It is itself held in place by the turnover. Both the over-shot wad and the turnover are left out in crimped cartridges, which are rapidly replacing all others.

WALNUT. The wood from which most stocks and fore-ends are normally made in European countries. The best walnut comes from the South of France and Italy, but wherever it comes from it needs to be completely and carefully seasoned before it is used if a tight fitting gun is to be made.

Flighting Ponds for Duck
A small pool or splash can often be found more than half made in a marshy undrained corner, but where unavailable one can be easily excavated with a spade or digger. It need not contain more than a few inches of water; anything over a foot is quite unnecessary since duck should be encouraged to dibble for their feed around the edges and into the centre. If it can be sited so that it is naturally fringed with rushes or long grass so much the better, since this will give feeding duck the illusion of privacy and security, and will also make the siting of the butts, or blinds, which should be covered with similar material, that much easier.

The whole should be fenced off from cattle or sheep, as they will quickly ruin the butts and may eat the feed. Note should be taken of the prevailing winds and the background when siting the butts round the pool; it is desirable to avoid any danger of the guns firing into each other. Ideally, matters should be so arranged that whichever way the ducks approach, they will automatically give two or more guns the chance of a shot. The number of butts must, of course, depend on the size of the pond, but it may, in any case, be advisable to ring the pond, so that from whichever angle the wind may be blowing, two or more of the butts will provide suitable shooting. An additional touch to any flighting pond is some tame call-ducks (although in North America these are illegal), or three or four decoys may be mounted on a light, floating crosspiece with a string leading to the nearest butt causing one of the decoys to upend realistically at the critical moment to attract the attention of approaching duck at the same time as a decoy call is sounded. Such refinements are, however, unnecessary providing the pond is well sited and well fed with rotten potatoes or corn tailings (also an illegal procedure in America). Once the duck learn of the feed they will come in regularly. Shooting should not be more than once a fortnight, and in suitable conditions, with a good cloud background and high wind, excellent sport may be had. Two or three flighting ponds of this nature can liven up an otherwise dull shooting area. Duck should always be reared to make up for those shot.

Florican *see* Bustards

Florida (U.S.A.)
The most southerly state, of 58,000 square miles, it seldom rises more than 200 ft above sea level. There are lakes and swamps in the centre, and the south of the state consists largely of submerged forests called 'Everglades'. The main industry is agriculture, and the principal crops are citrus and other fruits. The increase in cattle has led to the closing of much formerly open hunting land. Large areas are under forestry, much of which is opened to the public for hunting. The climate is sub-tropical.

The Game and Fish Commission maintains a million acres of hunting grounds open to the public, and manages even larger areas for various Federal departments. Deer, turkey, and quail are the most important game. There are also large populations of mourning doves, large wintering colonies of geese, especially blue geese along the coastal marshes, as well as duck, rail and snipe.

Special Regulations
No shotgun larger than a 10-bore may be used, and rifles firing .22 rimfire cartridges

Big Game Inventory—Florida		
Species	**Shot**	**Est. pop.**
White-tailed deer	45,000	450,000
Black bear	20	1,000
Wild turkey	20,000	60,000

Licence Fees—Florida	
Resident	$7.50
Non-resident	$26.50
10-day permit	$11.50
Aliens	$50.00

Seasons and Limits—Florida			
Species	**Season** (earliest and latest dates)	**Limit**	**Comment**
White-tailed deer	31 Oct-24 Jan	2 bucks per day 3 per season	There are three zones, southern, central and western
Bear	31 Oct-24 Jan	1 per season	
Turkey	31 Oct-24 Jan (Autumn) 6 March-4 April (Spring)	1 gobbler per day, 2 per season	
Bobwhite quail	31 Oct-7 March	12 per day	
Feral hog and wild boar	31 Oct-24 Jan		A special licence is needed to hunt wild boar in the Eglir Airfield area
Gray and fox squirrels	31 Oct-7 March		

may not be used on deer. Night hunting and baiting are illegal. Panthers, alligators, Key deer, axis deer and all birds of prey are protected. Dogs may be used for hunting all game except turkey.

Further Information

Game and Fresh Water Fish Commission, 620 South Meridian, Tallahassee, Florida 32304.

Fool Hen *see* Blue Grouse

Four-horned Antelope
(Tetracerus quadricornis)
Also known as chousingha, they are found in localized areas in southern Asia, and are small antelopes standing only 30 in at the shoulder and weighing no more than 50 lb. They are the only antelopes to have two pairs of horns, the front pair of which are always shorter than the rear pair. The length of the rear pair may be as much as 7 in and that of the front pair about 3 in. Grazers rather than browsers, they are generally found either singly or in pairs in grassy areas near to water, seldom in open country or forest.

They are not easily found, tending to lie close in cover, but they are seldom intentionally hunted. They have the odd habit, similar to the chital and the nilgai, of depositing their droppings regularly on a pile in a chosen area, from which their presence in any locality may be detected. They are most frequently bagged with a snap shot, with the shotgun, when the hunter is after game birds, in the same way as the smaller bush-loving antelopes of Africa. They are good eating.

Fox *see* Gray Fox; Red Fox

Fox Squirrel *see under* Gray Squirrel

Shelduck are among the many waterfowl shot in France.

Right, the European rabbit is a pest but is also a popular small-game animal in France, as elsewhere.

France

France, the largest of the west European countries, has a total area, including Corsica, of 212,000 square miles. The east and south-east are mainly mountainous, with the Vosges and Jura mountains in the north, the Cevennes and the Central Massif in the centre, the Alps in the south-east and south and the Pyrenees in the south-west. The country is watered by several great rivers: the Seine and the Somme running into the English Channel; the Loire, Garonne, Dordogne and Adour running into the Bay of Biscay; the Rhône emptying into the Gulf of Lions.

In the north-east of the country the climate is continental with long, cold winters like those of central Europe. Elsewhere it is more moderate and maritime, with a rainfall that rarely exceeds 20 in, moderate winters and little snow except in the mountainous regions. In the south the climate is of the Mediterranean type.

Much of the land is very fertile. Out of a total area of some 55 million hectares, 35 million are farmed, 25 million of which are under the plough. The principal crops are cereals, roots, grape vines, oilseeds, tobacco and flax, and the country is famous for its fruit, vegetables and cattle. There are 12 million hectares under forest, mainly in the mountainous regions of the east and south, and in the poor, sandy areas of the south west. Although France is a heavily industrialized country it is not, by Western European standards, thickly populated. Administratively it is divided into 90 departments, which are further divided into arrondissements, cantons and finally communes.

Hunting Methods

The standard methods, such as still-hunting and stalking for the larger animals, and driving and walking up, with or without dogs, for the smaller species, are widely employed. In addition, deer may be hunted with a pack of hounds; red deer in particular afford good sport this way. Roe will not run so readily, and fallow are too few for many to be hunted by any means. Wild boar and brown hare are also still pursued with organized packs of hounds, a very wide

Chief Game—France	
Red deer	Throughout the country except the south, south-east and Corsica
Roe deer	Throughout the country up to 2,000 metres ; thinly distributed in the south and south-east
Fallow deer	Found only in, or around, two parks in eastern France
Brown hare, rabbit	Throughout the country, especially the east
Pheasant	Throughout the country, but not in large numbers except on well-keepered shoots
Partridge	Gray : throughout the country, especially the plains in the north Red-legged : Brittany and the Loire basin Rock : Midi Greek or bartavelle : Alpine areas Chukor : being introduced
Quail	Migratory. On arable land in the summer
Woodcock	Mostly migratory. Resident in the west
Snipe	
Pigeon	Throughout the country. Both resident and migratory
Corncrake, Water rail, Golden plover, Norfolk plover, Lapwing	Found and shot in many parts
Passerines	Both resident and migratory. Shot throughout France for the table. The most popular are larks, song and missel thrushes, blackbird and ortolan (bunting).
Mountain game	Brown bear : In the Pyrenees between 1,500 and 2,000 metres Ibex : found, but rarely seen, on the Italian border Chamois : in the Jura, French Alps, and Pyrenees Mouflon : in Corsica and introduced to parts of metropolitan France. Varying hare : in the Alps, but rarely seen Capercailzie : in the Jura, Vosges parts of the Alps and Pyrenees Blackgame : in the Ardennes, and between Lake Geneva and the Mediterranean Ptarmigan : high in the Alps and Pyrenees, but rarely seen Hazel grouse : throughout the mountains and hills of eastern France
Waterfowl	Shoveller, teal, widgeon, pintail, sheldrake, mallard, pochard, scaup, goldeneye, scoter, and tufted duck ; merganser ; graylag, bean, pinkfoot, white-fronted and brent goose.

Seasons—France

Hunting is controlled by the Ministry of Agriculture, and in principle all seasons are decided by the minister and announced at least 10 days before the opening date. In practice the dates for the general season are now fairly well established in the various regions. In most departments in the north the general season opens on the second Sunday in September, in the west on the third Sunday in September, and in the south on the last Sunday in August, closing, in each case, on 31 December.

Alsace-Lorraine has its own local laws and seasons. However, the general season has a variable application.

Pheasant shooting usually starts two weeks after partridge shooting.

Many birds only pass through France on their way north or south, such as migratory woodcock; others, like corn-crake and ortolan, summer briefly in France; both categories may have special seasons.

Some animals, notably rabbit and pigeon, are classed as harmful and these may be hunted until 31 March.

Wild boar, are a pest and have an all-year season.

Mountain game, deer and waterfowl have their own seasons. The usual waterfowl season runs from 14 July to 31 March, but in certain departments it may start on the same date as the general season.

The particular species of migratory birds, waders and waterfowl that may be shot are determined by the minister. Prefects can vary the opening dates, and thus lengthen the closed season, for deer and chamois if requested by the local Conservator of Forests and the president of the local Hunters' Federation. The minister, however, determines the closing dates and by this means can severely restrict the seasons for red deer, chamois, mouflon and bear.

Hunting with hounds has its own season for each species, usually starting at the same time as the shooting of the species, but continuing rather longer, often to the end of April.

variety of the smaller breeds being used for hare. Boar can also be driven, but this is a process that requires some skill. Driving is sometimes used for culling deer herds but is inevitably unselective.

The mountain species pose their own special problems. Bear, though numbers are very limited, are still-stalked in the morning or evening, or tracked in the snow. Large drives are occasionally organized when a particular animal is reputed to have become dangerous. Chamois can only be stalked and obviously require mountaineering skill. Capercailzie are also stalked, in the spring, during their courtship display, because if shot over dogs in the autumn, the cocks will not hold to the point and only the hens and the young will be shot. Blackgame may not be shot in the spring, but will hold to the point if hunted in September when the heat of the sun makes them torpid.

Of unusual interest, however, are the methods of hunting the passerines, in particular the non-migratory skylark of the south and west. This is shot with the aid of mirrors, which are attached to pieces of wood that revolve round a peg (controlled by clockwork or a length of string). The peg is set in open ground, near suitable cover for the hunter (who should have his back to the sun) and the flashing mirrors then attract the skylark, which will plummet down to within gunshot. The best time of day is the early morning. No 9 shot is normally used.

Special Regulations
The use of greyhounds or greyhound crosses is prohibited, as are air rifles, nightlights and shooting from cars. Waterfowl may only be shot in certain specified places.

Further Information
The organization of hunting is officially on three levels. At the departmental level there are Hunters' Federations, at the regional level there are Hunting Zones and at the national level there is the National Council which advises the minister and acts as liaison between him and his departmental Hunters' Federations. Also useful and influential, although not at an official level, is the French St Hubert's club, and it is probably the best source of further information. St Hubert Club de France, 21 Rue de Clichy, Paris 9.

Francolins
The genus *Francolinus* contains 44 species which range over most of Africa and Asia and parts of the Mediterranean region. The species vary in size from being no larger than quails to being as big as red-legged partridges. Most of them have sharp spurs and they are fierce fighters during the breeding season. They generally nest on the ground, under cover. The clutch may consist of anything up to 10 eggs, but coveys are, on the whole, small, often not exceeding three.

Francolins, like most partridges, are primarily birds of cultivated land and are found, in many parts of the world, in all the crops, but especially in wheat, rice, mustard, hemp and newly planted cotton fields. Some, however, are found in the brush or in apparently completely barren land and desert. Their diet includes grain, various seeds, young leaves, fruits, berries and insects.

Not only size, but colour and plumage vary from species to species. The general effect is one of barring and mottling carried out in various combinations of brown, black, buff and white, designed to allow the bird to blend with its own particular background. The underparts may also be broken black and buff, or entirely buff or pale gray, or buff, barred with black, and the head and throat are often more brightly coloured. In some species both sexes are spurred, in some only the cocks, and in some the spurs are rudimentary, or entirely lacking.

Licences—France

No one may hunt or shoot without a permit. The national permit is valid for the whole of France, including Corsica, for an entire year, and costs 200 French francs. This includes all stamp duties and membership of the local Hunters' Federation.

Departmental and regional permits may also be taken out, costing Fr60 and Fr90. respectively.

Foreigners must obtain their permits from the local Prefect, but residents may apply to the mayor of the appropriate commune. Applicants must sign a declaration that they do not belong to any of the categories to whom it is illegal to issue a permit, and must produce an identity card, an insurance certificate and two photographs. Foreigners must also produce a 'Certificat d'Honorabilite', which will be issued by the French consulate on production of evidence from the police that the applicant has no convictions.

The permit, in itself, does not confer the right to shoot anywhere. Only those who are landowners, tenants, shooting tenants, guests, or members of a private or communal syndicate may shoot. Sporting rights go with the land and may not be alienated in perpetuity. Landowners may, however, lease the shooting rights for a set term of years, subject to every tenant's and sharecropper's inalienable right to shoot on the land they lease. Shooting rights in State forests must be put up to public auction, generally for 9-year periods, but in default of that for one year at a time. Communes may let their shooting rights without an auction, except in Alsace-Lorraine; there, all sporting rights are taken over by the commune for a rental (only those holding over 50 acres may reserve their shooting) and are then let by public auction.

All the francolin are hunted, and some make extremely good shooting, especially those that live in open country, for they rise faster and fly more swiftly than the gray partridge, and take a great deal of shot. Some of the bush francolin, however, tend either to run on or to fly up to perch, which makes shooting more difficult. Most francolin will lie well to pointers, and in most areas where they are shot dogs are almost essential. Francolin are generally white fleshed, even down to the thighs, and are thought to be good, though perhaps slightly dry, eating.

The most important species are:

Common (black or Asiatic) francolin (*F. francolinus*):
An excellent game bird, with a length about 13 in, it is also easily tamed, and is often kept as a call-bird. It used to range as far west as Cyprus and as far east as northern and central India and Assam, but it is very seldom seen, now, in the Mediterranean, and it has been over-shot in India.

Chinese francolin (*F. chinensis*):
With a length $12\frac{1}{2}$ in, it is found in southern China and south-east Asia down to Burma, and it has been introduced to Mauritius and Réunion.

Painted francolin (*F. pictus*):
A rather more arboreal species than most francolin it roosts on trees and bushes. It is known to hybridize with the common francolin. It is found in western and central India and Ceylon, but it is very locally distributed, being found, generally, only where there are trees or scrub jungle.

Gray francolin (*F. pondicerianus*):
Its length is $12\frac{1}{2}$ in. Found in south-western Asia from Arabia to India and Ceylon, generally in hedges or scrub close to cultivations, though they may also be found on completely barren land, it is difficult to flush, but flies excellently once in the air.

Coqui francolin (*F. coqui*):
About 11 in long. This is a small francolin, widely distributed throughout east, south, and south-east Africa. It is a bird of the open grasslands, and is often found in coveys, like the European partridge. It is a ground rooster, which makes it particularly prone to predation.

Rüppell's francolin (*F. gutturalis*):
Found in north-east Africa, notably in Somalia and Ethiopia, it is $12\frac{1}{2}$ in long. It is found in small coveys, and looks remarkably like a gray partridge, but its flesh, in the summer months, is almost uneatable, because of its diet of beetles at that time of the year.

Pearl-breasted francolin (*F. africanus*):
Found in eastern South Africa it is principally a high-ground bird. It is a particularly fast runner, and a fast flyer, though only for short distances; 13 in long.

Levaillant's francolin (*F. levaillanti*):
13 in long, is found in South Africa, where it frequents river valleys, being found in rushes or thick grass; it is difficult to flush it from such cover. It flies extremely well.

Indian swamp francolin (*F. gularis*):
This bird is found in northern India, where it is also known as 'grass chukor' or kyah. It is 13 in long and is commonly discovered in low jungle or reed beds close to water, but visits paddy fields and other cultivations not more than half a mile from water.

Shelly's francolin (*F. shelleyi*):
Found in eastern South Africa and as far north as Malawi; 13 in long.

Close-barred francolin (*F. adspersus*):
With a length of $12\frac{1}{2}$ in, this is the most common species to be found in western South Africa. It is not a particularly good game bird, for it tends to run on in front, and if flushed, flies straight into the thickest tree in the vicinity.

Double-spurred francolin (*F. bicalcaratus*):
Found in west Africa from the Niger to Morocco; $12\frac{1}{2}$ in long.

Cape francolin (*F. capensis*):
This large, 16-in long francolin is found in many parts of South Africa, where it is commonly called 'Cape pheasant'. It is not much use as a game bird since it tends to perch on bushes out of reach of dogs, and if disturbed will always run rather than fly.

Natal francolin (*F. natalensis*):
Found in wooded country near water or the sea in eastern South Africa, it is $13\frac{1}{2}$ in long. Like the Cape pheasant it is reluctant flyer.

Jackson's francolin (*F. Jacksoni*):
A particularly large francolin found in Uganda; $15\frac{1}{2}$ in long.

Swainson's bare-throated francolin (*Pternistes swainsoni*):
With a length of 14 in, this bird resembles the Cape francolin and, like it, is referred to as 'pheasant'. It is found in coveys, which are difficult to flush. It roosts in trees at night and spends the day in open country close to streams.

Sclater's bare-throated francolin (*Pternistes afer*):
About 14 in long and found in south-west Africa as far north as Angola. Also known as 'partridge' or gray-wing, it is a favourite game bird.

Long-billed francolin (*Rhizothera longirostris*):
With a length of $14\frac{1}{2}$ in, it is one of the two species with strong, curved bills and only twelve tail feathers. Found in the Malay Peninsular, Sumatra and Borneo.

French Guiana

For a description of the country *see* Guyana.

Further Information
Consult initially the nearest French consulate.

G

Gadwall in flight

Gad *see* Red Sheep

Gadwall *(Anas strepera)*
A surface-feeding duck breeding in northern Europe, Asia and America, and wintering in Africa, India, southern China, California, Mexico and the south-eastern states of the United States. It is both resident in, and a winter visitor to, the British Isles, breeding especially on the east coast.

The duck is distinguished from the mallard by its smaller size and white speculum. The drake is mainly gray, with a fine brown speckling on the head and neck, black tail coverts, white belly, a chestnut patch on the forewing and a white speculum, bordered, in front, with black. The legs and feet are orange to yellow. Average weight for the drake is around 2 lb. It is a good walker, often being found inland on stubbles, and a fast flyer, with a particularly rapid wingbeat that produces a whistling sound. Primarily vegetarian, it can not only scoop and tip for water plants but also, unusually for a surface feeder, dive for them. In summer it is liable to eat tadpoles, fish and worms, and at these periods it is less edible than in winter. It is a shy bird, seldom seen on open water, and its numbers, in America, seem to be declining, probably because its breeding range on the Canadian and American prairies has suffered from draining policies.

Courtship involves a simple display of bobbings and jerkings and some flight pursuit. The nest is generally built away from water, and the clutch of 7 to 13 eggs takes 28 days to incubate. The eclipse moult occurs between June and August and, unusually, it is a complete one, all feathers being lost from the tail and wing. By November the second moult is completed and full winter plumage is resumed.

Gallinules *see* Waders

Game Feeding *see* Pheasant Management

Garganey *see* Waterfowl

Gaur *(Bos gaurus)*
The Indian bison, found in Assam, the Central Indian Provinces and Mysore, also Malaysia and Ceylon, is a fine dark brown ox standing an average of 5 ft 9 in at the shoulder, and the horns average 30 in from tip to tip. A mainly nocturnal herbivore, it is usually found in herds of around ten, or as a solitary bull. It is necessary to rise early to hunt them, as during the day they tend to retire to the shade of the jungle. They may however sometimes be seen on the grassy slopes of hills when they can be stalked, but more commonly they are tracked and the best time for this is just before the rainy season starts. They mate in the winter and produce a single calf in August or September. The cow's horns are smoother and more upright than the bull's, which tend to become chipped and corrugated. The head of the gaur is usually the first part seen, but as it is carried with nose in the air a head shot is very uncertain and it is better to wait for the chance of a neck shot or one behind the shoulder. Wounded gaur can be dangerous and also show considerable vitality. If a beast is wounded it is advisable to leave it to stiffen up for half an hour or so, before following it.

Gazelles *(Gazella)*
Gazelles are small antelopes, seldom standing more than 2 ft 6 in and often even smaller, found throughout Africa and parts of Asia. They mostly prefer the open plains or desert regions where only their wariness and fleetness can preserve them from danger. They are generally sandy in coloration, with dark and light markings on the face and frequently a dark band on the flanks. Their horns are generally lyrate and developed in

Grant's gazelle is about 34 in at the shoulder. It inhabits open plains and semi-desert country.

both sexes. Almost all are grazers, though sometimes occasional browsers, and usually only one young is born annually. They are generally found in small herds and their flesh is mainly well flavoured, although a little dry. *See also* Antelopes.

Geese *see* Waterfowl; *also* Hides and Decoys; Wildfowling

Gelinotte *see* Hazel Hen

Gemsbok *see under* Oryx

Georgia (U.S.A.)

A state of about 58,000 square miles, its coastal area is swampy and extremely fertile – all American crops except tropical fruit can be grown there. The interior is more hilly and ascends, in the north, towards the Appalachians. The climate varies from sub-tropical along the coast to extremes of heat and cold in the north. Much of the state is covered by forests.

Quail provide the best sport, but cotton-tail and dove shooting are also good. There is an increasing deer herd, but much of Georgian hunting is made difficult by posting, and there is little sportsman/farmer co-operation. The state is zoned for deer hunting, as for rabbit and squirrel, and seasons and limits differ from zone to zone.

Further Information

Game and Fish Commission, 401 State Capitol, Atlanta, Georgia 30334.

Gerenuk (*Lithocranius walleri*)

This creature, also known as giraffe antelope or Waller's gazelle, is found in East Africa and Somaliland. It is chestnut coloured with fawn sides and white belly and stands about 39 in at the shoulder with an elongated slender neck and legs. Only the buck has horns, which are about 15 in long and curve backwards for most of their length with a forward turn at the tips. A browser, it is found in bush country generally far from water, which it does not require, in pairs or family groups. It has a peculiar method of running from danger, crouched down in elongated form with neck stretched forward.

Its nearest relative, which is intermediate between it and the gazelles, is the dibatag, *Ammordorchas clerkei,* which is found in the same habitat. It also has a long neck and the short horns with upward and forward curvature are found only in the bucks.

Germany, Federal Republic of

The Federal Republic lies in northern Europe and has a total area of nearly 96,000 square miles. It is geophysically divided into three parts. In the extreme south the Bavarian Alps and their foothills lead up to the Austrian border; to the north of these lie the central mountains such as the Harz

range; the northern section of the country is the North German Plain, which is traversed by two ranges of low hills. The chief rivers are the Rhine, Ems, Weser, Elbe (lying partially in the German Democratic Republic) and Danube; there are not many lakes except in southern Bavaria.

The Federal Republic is the leading industrial power in Europe, but despite this there is still much agriculture and forestry. The agriculture varies widely: mixed arable and/or stock farming is widespread; many areas specialize in wines, tobacco, potatoes, market gardening or sugar beet. About 30% of the country is afforested, especially the south. The climate is temperate.

Organization and Further Information

Control and organization of shooting and hunting rests, to a large extent, with the authorities of the eleven districts into

Licence Fees—Georgia

Resident, hunting/fishing	$5.25
Non-resident	$25.25
10-day licence	$12.50

Sold at camps, court houses and sporting-goods stores.

Big Game Inventory—Georgia

Species	Shot	Est. pop.
Deer	22,000	130,000
Bear	200	6,000
Turkey	3,000	21,000

Seasons and Bag Limits—Georgia

Species	Season	Bag Limit	Comment
White-tailed deer	15 Oct-5 Dec	2 per season	Generally bucks only but in some counties either sex
Black bear	7 Nov-2 Jan	1 per season	
Cottontail rabbit	20 Nov-30 Jan or 27 Feb	5 per day in north and 10 per day in south	
Bobwhite quail	20 Nov-27 Feb	Limits variable	
Ruffed grouse	16 Jan-27 Feb	3 per day	
Turkey	Spring season—dates variable	1 gobbler per season	
Squirrel	Mainly 15 Oct-28 Feb		

A female gerenuk and young standing in shade under a thorn tree

131

Seasons and Bags—Federal Republic of Germany

Species	Season	Bag 1969/70
Red deer	1 Aug-31 Jan	27,171
Fallow buck Fallow doe and fawn	1 Sept-31 Jan 1 Aug-31 Jan	6,850
Sika stag hind and fawn	1 Sept-31 Jan 1 Aug-31 Jan	
Roe buck doe and fawn	16 May-15 Oct 1 Sept-31 Jan	550,757
Chamois	1 Aug-15 Dec	1,643
Mouflon	1 Aug-31 Jan	893
Boar	All year	27,917
Hare	16 Oct-15 Jan	1,136,180
Marten	1 Dec-31 Jan	12,519
Badger	1 July-15 Jan	5,964
Rabbit	All year	567,123
Fox	All year	114,398
Polecat and Weasel	All year	98,479
Seal	16 July-31 Dec	
Capercailzie (Cocks only)	20 April-31 May	145
Blackgame (Cocks only)	20 April-31 May	465
Hazel grouse	20 April-31 May	
Pheasant	1 Oct-15 Jan	983,375
Partridge	1 Sept-30 Nov	445,564
Turkey, cock	1 April-15 May and 1 Oct-15 Jan	
Hen	1 Oct-15 Jan	
Pigeon	16 Aug-30 April	421,727
Snipe	16 Oct-15 April	29,331
Woodcock	1 Aug-31 Dec	
Heron	1 Sept-31 Jan	
Sea-gull	1 Aug-31 March	
Buzzard, Hobby hawk, Sparrow hawk	1 Nov-end Feb	
Corvidae	All year	568,063
Geese	1 Oct-15 Jan	4,213
Duck	1 Aug-15 Jan	386,907

which the Federal Republic is divided. The following organizations relate to the whole country and may be useful:

Forschungsstelle für Jagdkunde und Wildschadenverhütung, 53 Bonn-Beuel, Forsthaus Hardt.

Deutscher Jagdschutz-Verband e.V., 53 Bonn, Schillerstrasse, 26.

Above, a red fox, and right, a roe deer; both animals are popular game in Germany. Roe deer are either still-hunted, or shot from a high seat.

Below, the common snipe is a popular game bird of the German marshlands.

Licences—Federal Republic of Germany

All visitors must obtain shooting licences at the Under Shooting Office (Untere Jadgbehörde) of the district in which they wish to shoot.

A licence is valid for one shooting year (1 April-31 March), though in certain areas a 5-day licence may be obtained. Applicants must have passed the Hunter's Examination—a test in German hunting customs, regulations, practices, safety rules and the biology of game species, and must produce a recent photograph (6 x 4 cm), a previous shooting licence or proof of shooting ability, and insurance.

The minimum permitted cover is 250,000 Deutsche Marks for injury to persons, and DM.25,000 for injury to property. The premiums are usually up to about DM.25 for a 1-year shooting licence, and up to DM.15 for a 5-day licence.

The licence fees vary, depending on the district, between DM.50 and DM.250 for a 1-year licence, and from DM.6 to DM.50 for a 5-day licence.

The fees are determined by such varying factors as the game available in the district, and the licence conditions prevailing in the applicant's native land.

Germany, Democratic Republic of

The G.D.R., with an area of over 41,000 square miles, lies in northern Europe. Most of the country consists of the North German Plain, traversed only by the northern and southern ridges, but in the south the plain gives way to the Erzgebirge range of the central mountains of Germany. The two chief rivers are the lower reaches of the Oder, on the Polish border, and all except the lower reaches of the Elbe. The climate is generally temperate.

The country is not as highly industrialized as the Federal Republic and the fertility of the plain means that agriculture is very important. Nearly 30% of the country is under forest. There is less high ground than in the Federal Republic of Germany, and consequently fewer mountain species.

Further Information

Oberste Jagdbehörde beim Staatliches – komitee für Forstwirtshäft, Berlin Karlshorst, Königswinter Strasse 36.

Seasons—German Democratic Republic		
Species	**Season**	**Bag 1967/68**
Red deer, stag hind and fawn	16 Aug–31 Jan 16 Sept–31 Jan	} 6,400
Fallow, buck doe and fawn	1 Sept–31 Jan 16 Sept–31 Jan	} 1,750
Mouflon, ram ewe and lamb	1 Aug–31 Jan 16 Oct–31 Jan	} 230
Roe deer	16 Sept–31 Jan	127,250
Boar	All year	37,800
Hare	1 Oct–15 Jan	160,000
Rabbit	All year	11,822
Fox	All year	8,400
Badger	1 Aug–15 Jan	1,500
Marten	1 Dec–31 Jan	30,000
Polecat and Weasel	All year	18,000
Pheasant, cocks only	1 Oct–31 Dec	76,000
Partridge	1 Sept–30 Nov	126,000
Pigeon	1 Aug–15 April	
Snipe	1 Sept–31 Jan	
Woodcock	15 Aug–31 Dec	
Duck Geese	1 Sept–15 Jan 16 July–31 Jan	} 32,500
Heron	1 June–15 March	
Crested diver	1 July–31 March	
Corvidae	All year	275,000

Licences and Fees—German Democratic Republic

Permission to import and export hunting weapons must be obtained from the Soviet Ministry of the Interior. The control system and the organization of shooting is the same as in other Soviet states. Shooting trips must be booked in advance through the state travel bureau, with a deposit.

The fees are fixed in advance for accommodation and organization, but vary depending on what is shot, on the standard of the trophy, or, in the case of small game, on the number shot.

The only particularly notable feature is that visitors from other Soviet states may obtain their shooting licences from the district authorities, while those from other countries must apply to the Oberste Jagdbehörde (the overall hunting authority).

Germany, Hunting in

The systematic organization of hunting in Germany is done with truly Teutonic thoroughness and efficiency. The game belongs to the landowner but an overall shooting plan *(Schussplan)* is prepared on a national basis, by which seasons and numbers of game to be shot are decided in advance each year for each area. In a country which is intensively farmed by traditional methods of agriculture, resulting in small fields, hedges and woods, providing a diversity of wildlife food and cover, it is necessary to plan on an overall scale to obtain maximum game production. Selective shooting of poorer stock is encouraged, as is winter feeding of game stocks. Should wild game, such as boar, stray from a wood and damage the crops of a neighbour, that neighbour is entitled to sue and obtain redress from the landowner if he can prove that the damage was due to beasts from the land concerned. The landowner is entitled to lease the right to hunt game on his land to hunters if he so wishes.

Hunters must first take the Huntsman's Examination (see under Licences in the previous entry). Only then may he apply to a landowner for permission to shoot so many head of game, or for a lease of some shooting. Poaching, illegal shooting or trapping of game, is regarded as a serious offence and a landowner is entitled to shoot a poacher who will not stop when ordered to do so. This makes poaching uncommon! Dogs or cats found roaming in hunting areas may also be shot on sight. Both big and small game are harvested systematically like any other crop on the land. The general German hunting garb is of loden cloth, a dark green cape of this material being a favourite garment, nearly waterproof and useful camouflage, at the same time allowing the arms free for shooting. Leather knickerbockers and stout boots for stalking are also common and a loden green hat with black game feathers or boar tuft in the hatband, and several badges of hunting clubs or awards is also customary. The traditional drilling or double-barrelled shotgun, with additional rifle barrel carried on a sling over the shoulder, is the favourite form of sporting gun and is useful in a country where pheasant, black game, boar or deer may all be encountered during the course of a single drive.

The German methods of hunting are adapted to their country. Deer are generally either still-hunted, or shot from a *Hochsitz* (high-seat), placed at the intersection of two rides in the forest. Sometimes large drives are organized, when considerable areas may be driven by a circle of hunters closing gradually into the centre, with beaters interspersed between them at intervals between the guns. As the circle closes in the guns halt and face about, shooting only away from the centre so that there is no danger to each other or to the beaters closing in towards the centre. Driving also takes place towards guns posted at a gun shot or so from each other in rides or in line. All German hunting, however, is extremely formalized in that bugles and horns are blown to let the hunters know what is happening at each stage. The organizer of the hunting day will first instruct the assembled hunters in what game is to be shot and what the meaning is of each horn or bugle call he will hear; for instance, one blast: the drive is about to start; three blasts: the beaters are approaching within shot; and, perhaps, four prolonged blasts: the time has come to move on to different ground, and so on. The customary greeting of one hunter to another is *Waidmannsheil* and the customary and indeed only reply is *Waidmannsdank*. Whenever a hunter has been successful, the other hunters solemnly shake him by the hand and greet him in this way, as is also done at the start and end of the day. Much of the customary hunting language in Germany belongs to a specialized vocabulary which is apart from the German language itself. This formality in hunting extends to the hunting customs in particular; thus, when a hunter has killed a deer by still-hunting it is customary to commune briefly with the animal. This is known as the *Totenwache* or death watch.

The use of small branches and twigs, taken from oak, spruce, pine, alder or silver fir and no others, is another integral part of German hunting lore. A 'shot branch' is thrust into the ground where the animal is shot. An 'ownership branch' is placed on the animal after it has been laid out on its right side to indicate a legal kill and, if the animal is male, the broken end of the branch should lie towards the head but, if female, it should be the other way round. The capercailzie or *Auerhahn*, and blackgame or *Birkhahn*, and all cloven hoofed game are customarily provided with a small branch or twig placed crosswise in their mouths to signify their last bite on earth. Whenever any of these or a fox are killed, a small twig is dipped in their blood and presented to the organizer of the hunt who, in turn, presents it to the hunter responsible. After the hunt the game is laid out with great ceremony, the best of each being prominently displayed in the order of red deer, fallow, wild boar, roe, fox, hare, rabbit, capercailzie, blackgame, pheasants and other game birds. The hunter must be careful never to step over the game, but always to walk round it with due solemnity.

When the game has been duly laid-out the hunters all take their places, at attention, in front of it and a final blast, the *Halali,* is blown on the horns as a last salute to the game. All this elaborate ceremonial is a little difficult for those who are unaccustomed to it or those who do not take it quite as seriously as do the Germans or, indeed, most Central Europeans, but it does add a touch of formality which may perhaps be lacking in some other countries and for which they might be none the worse. As sportsmen and hunters the Germans are thorough and knowledgeable.

Giraffe *(Giraffa camelopardalis)*

This, the tallest living mammal, is found in many parts of Africa, south of the Sahara; several races, which differ slightly, have been described. It is generally found in light woodlands or on the plains, in herds of around 15 to 20, though the bulls are sometimes solitary. The bull stands, on average, 19 ft high; the female around 16 to 17 ft. Calving may take place at any period of the year and one calf is normal, though twins are not unknown. They are browsers and have a long prehensile tongue used for plucking down the leaves and branches of acacia and other trees on which they live. They have keen sight and scenting powers and are extremely shy. Apart from flight, their only means of defence is their forelegs with which they can repel an attacker, quite effectively, striking out dangerously with their large hooves. They have an extremely tough skin, so a heavy calibre is required, but they are easily enough shot when a successful stalk has been completed. The flesh of the young, especially the cows, is excellent and the huge marrow bones, sawn in half and roasted, are considered a great delicacy.

Giraffe Antelope *see* Gerenuk

Gnu *(Connochaetes* species)

The brindled gnu or blue wildebeest (*C. taurinus*) is a form of antelope peculiar to Africa and still found in fair numbers in parts of central, east and south Africa, in herds varying from 15 to 100, either in open plains, scrub or thin woodland. Solitary males are sometimes found alone, or attached to herds of other species, particularly zebras. The body colouring is dun, heavily marked in the forepart with dark stripes, hence the name brindled. They average about 52 in at the shoulder, with a heavy buffalo-like head, the front and chin covered with shaggy black hair, which also hangs from the dewlap and breast. They have a long, upstanding black mane and a flowing, black tail. The horns, shaped like those of a buffalo, average about 24 in and are a formidable defence. Their legs are slender and well shaped so that while appearing lumbering at a gallop they can move

The brindled gnu covers large distances in search of food and water

135

quite fast. Although chiefly grazers they do browse a little. Calving varies from August to December, depending on the locality, and although usually restricted to one calf, twins are not unknown. Albinos have been seen, but are exceptional. The flesh is poor and unpalatable and they should only be shot for culling or trophy purposes. They are not usually hard to stalk and when in full flight can frequently be turned by firing a bullet into the dust, in front of them. When wounded, however, they can be dangerous and care should be exercised.

Another species, the white-tailed gnu (*Connochaetus gnu*), also known as black wildebeest, once common throughout South Africa, was threatened with extinction due to unrestrained slaughter, but saved by careful conservation. Though now rare and protected in most areas, it can still be shot in a few places in south-west Africa. In appearance, it is similar in many ways to the previous species, except for white hairs on the upper lip and round the eyes. Additionally, it has a light coloured mane and, as the name implies, a flowing white tail. The horns extend downwards over the eyes and then upwards in a formidable hook and it is extremely dangerous when wounded. It is exceeding fast and active, and of a very wary, suspicious nature.

Goats and Sheep (*Caprini* and *Rupicaprini*)

Goats and sheep are active and hardy mountain-loving grazers and browsers, depending largely on their keen sight and scenting powers as well as their formidable climbing abilities for protection from predators and man. Where not indigenous, as in Australasia, they have been introduced by man and have rapidly become acclimatized. They are, however, not found in Africa, with the exception of north Africa and east Africa, where the Masai tribe have large herds of goats, nor in South America, where both climate and predators are against them. Wild sheep were formerly found in Ecuador, although rare or extinct now, and goats are found on the Argentine estancias. Hunting them generally calls for mountaineering ability and a head for heights. The trophy is the horns, frequently found in both male and female. The hides are also valued but, with exceptions such as the bighorn, whose flesh is considered to be the finest of all North American game, their flesh is often poor eating.

Godwits see Waders

Goldeneye see American Goldeneye; Barrow's Goldeneye; Waterfowl

Gooral see Goral

Goosander see Waterfowl

Goral (*Nemorhoedus goral*)

Sometimes spelled gooral and known in Kashmir as the Himalayan gray goral and in Nepal to Burma as the brown goral, this goat has a short rough coat of brownish gray and a white throat patch. It is found on precipitous hillsides and in rocky forests above 4,000 ft to as high as 10,000 ft. It stands about 27 in at the shoulder and weighs about 60 lb. Both sexes have short black horns the doe's being thinner and generally shorter. A good buck's horns average about 7 in with a slight backward curve and are about 4 in at the base. It has been thought by some biologists to be a connecting link between goat and antelope. A single young is generally born in the early summer months.

It feeds in the morning and evening and its powers of hearing, sight and scent are acute, but although timid and wary it will frequently perch on a prominent rock even after being shot at, giving its alarm call and usually returning to its favourite haunts after being driven from them. A good head for heights and an ability to climb well is required to hunt goral; it has been understandably called 'The Himalayan Chamois'.

Gorri-Paaver see Bustards

Gray Fox (*Urocyon cinereoargenteus*)

The gray fox of the United States and South America is not, like the red fox (*Vulpes fulva*) q.v., a member of the genus *Vulpes* but nevertheless closely resembles it in both appearance and habits. There are small skeletal differences between them, and the gray is generally rather smaller than the red. Their ranges, also, are similar, and there is considerable overlapping, though the gray reaches further into the southern states and the red further into the northern ones. Both gray and red are native to North America.

The arrangement of guard hairs on the brush is different from that of the red fox and it is, of course, a grizzled gray in colour, with pale underparts.

The gray fox weighs between 7 and 11 lb, and dens not underground, but generally among rocks or in a hollow tree. Mating seems to be at least semi-permanent, and the dog helps the vixen with rearing and feeding the cubs, which are born in the spring and stay with the dam until autumn.

It is hunted in a variety of ways in addition to being trapped and hunted with hounds, although it does not give hounds nearly such a good run as the red fox. It can be hunted on foot, with hounds; still-hunted; tracked in the snow.

Graylag Goose (*Anser anser*)

This gray goose is the direct ancestor of the domestic goose, and the only wild goose to nest in the British Isles. It does this, in small numbers, in the extreme north of Scotland and the Hebrides; attempts are

---

Goats

Asiatic ibex*
Markhor
Nubian ibex*

Note : the chamois, Rocky Mountain goat and serow are not true goats.

Sheep

Aoudad* (Barbarry or maned)
Bharal* (burrel or blue)
Great Tibetan sheep* (argali, Marco Polo)
Mouflon*
Mountain*: bighorns (Californian desert or Cimarrone)
thinhorns (Dall or white, black or stone)
Red (gad, shaper, urial)
Takin

~~CHASE~~

HECHINGERS
PAINT IS IN

50 45 35 25 0

being made to breed it in other parts of
Scotland and the Wildfowlers' Association
of Great Britain and Ireland (WAGBI) has
re-established it, for the first time in two
hundred years, in England. In spite of all this,
it is still the rarest wild goose found in
Britain, and those seen are more likely to be
migrants from Iceland than home-bred.

They are vocal birds: their cackle, closely
resembling that of the domestic goose, can
be clearly heard when a gaggle flies over-
head in formation. This is either in line or in
V-formation. They are diurnal, spending the
night on sandbanks or islands and flying in
to graze early in the morning. Highly gregarious, they nest socially, on the ground
near water. The nest is made of heather or
other local material lined with down, and
the clutch of four to seven eggs is laid in late
April and May. It takes about 27 days to
incubate, during which period the gander
remains watching over the nest and helps,
later, to rear the goslings, which are able to
fly in about eight weeks. Graylags are fond
of grazing, and are sometimes found on
winter corn, which they badly damage. They
also graze meadows and sometimes come in,
after harvest, to the stubbles.

There are two European races – the
Western and the Eastern, the former with
an orange and the latter with a pink bill. In
both the bill has a white nail and no markings. The legs and feet are pinkish; the
upperparts are gray, barred brown, and with
light gray shoulders. The underparts are
plain gray with no barring, though there
may be some black spots on the breast of the
adult bird. Average size is between 33 and
35 in, and average weight around 10 lb.

The graylag's breeding grounds lie in
northern Europe and Asia from Iceland to
Korea, and, generally, are slightly to the
south of the breeding grounds of other wild

The common, or gray partridge is known as
the Hungarian partridge in the United
States.

The graylag is the only wild goose to breed
in Britain

geese. They are partial migrants, wintering
in the more southerly parts of their breeding
range, as well as in Holland, Belgium, and
parts of the Mediterranean basin.

Although a fairly scarce bird, the graylag
is highly prized by the wildfowler, and hunted in a variety of ways. One of them is
pass-shooting, the hunter placing himself
along a known flight path, and hoping to get
a shot at the geese as they fly over, morning
or evening, to or from their feeding grounds
– a difficult method because they generally
fly too high to be within shot. A more productive method is to conceal oneself on or
near a known sleeping ground, but this
cannot be done very often or the geese will
change their sleeping grounds. They can
sometimes be stalked on the stubble or
grass they happen to be feeding on, but this
is rarely successful, even with a stalking
horse. They can be driven, but this is a
delicate exercise, since it involves position-
ing the guns upwind of the geese, who will,
of course, take off into wind when they are
put up. Graylags, like other gray geese, will
come readily to decoys, and can be called
down by those skilled enough to do it. It is
never easy to get close enough to them with
a punt or small boat since, unlike the
barnacle goose, they do not lie out on the
estuaries and off the coastline. Fairly heavy
shot should be used, No 4 at the very least,
and most hunters use only BB. Deplorably,
some shoot them on the ground with .22
rifles, and there seems to be no law or regulation in Britain against doing so.

Gray Partridge *(Perdix perdix)*
The gray partridge was, and possibly still is,
the principal native game bird of western
and central Europe. It is found in those
regions that lie between the grouse and
ptarmigan populations of the north, and the

quail, francolin and redleg of the south. Its recent decline in numbers has undoubtedly impoverished sport throughout that area. Nevertheless, the gray partridge still ranges from the British Isles and southern Sweden in the west and north to the Altai Mountains and Asia Minor in the east and south. Introduced to the United States and Canada, it is known there as the Hungarian partridge (q.v.).

Both sexes look alike, being small, plump, chicken-like birds of a general brownish-buff colour, with chestnut heads, gray necks and gray underparts. Their flanks are barred boldly with chestnut, and the cocks, and some of the young hens have chestnut horse-shoe markings on the breast. Older hens have scattered chestnut splotches. The hen can only be distinguished from the cock by examination of the wing coverts and scapulars. These are crossed by wavy bars of buff in the hen which are absent in the cock. Birds of the year can generally be recognized by their having the first flight feather pointed, rather than rounded, as in the adult. The legs are yellowish-brown, rather than gray-blue, until late in the autumn, and the mandibles are pliable and less horny.

Gray partridge are declining in Europe at a varying rate, and though some of that variation is due to the vagaries of weather affecting the hatch in different ways in different countries, there can be little doubt that some of the variation is due to different methods of land use and agriculture. It may well be that Czechoslovakia and Hungary and other eastern European countries continue to possess large partridge populations because there are no landowners there except the State, and farmers experience few of those economic pressures that drive western landowners and farmers to utilize every inch of their farms, and to practise with an almost religious fervour, the rituals of clean farming. It is an odd outcome, but it now seems probable that the last flourishing partridge manors will not be in East Anglia or Wiltshire, England, the Beauce or Aisne, France, but in the Socialist republics of eastern Europe.

The entry on Partridge Biology (q.v.) discusses methods of game management that will help to slow, if not arrest, the decline in partridge populations. There are some techniques of shoot management that might also help. Because of the scarcity, and variability, from year to year, of partridge populations, it is quite possible that the old practice of dogging for partridge, that had been so largely superseded by driving, will come back a little. There are several reasons why this might help with maintaining partridge populations. Dogging allows shooting to be more selective, and this in its turn, will allow emphasis to be laid on the shooting of old birds, something that must improve the partridge holding capacity of any shoot. Dogging is less likely to produce pricked birds, or to allow wounded birds to be lost. And dogging, in most cases, must produce smaller bags than driving will.

On the other hand, driving partridges, and shooting driven partridge, must count among the highest pleasures of sport, and there is no reason why dogging and driving should not be practised on the same shoot. Dogging will have shown the owner where his coveys are and which way they will next want to fly, knowledge that will be useful to him when it comes to driving. It will, in addition, have helped him to get rid of old birds and have taught the young birds how to fly. The large partridge drives using dozens of beaters, flankers, markers, in double gangs will probably never come back to western Europe, though they may still be found in eastern Europe. Drives, now, will need to be smaller, less killing affairs, with comparatively few acres being driven at any one time, and little attempt to drive the same birds backwards and forwards. The pleasures of driven partridge do not, after all, lie in the number of birds put over the guns nor the ease with which they may be killed; they lie, surely, in having however few birds put over the line in steady sequence and at heights and speeds that demand skill of the guns.

If the present scarcity of partridges teaches us to make partridge shooting a more skilful and less wasteful sport, then all will not have been lost. For the rest, Europe needs, above all, a sequence of good hatching years, and a greater realization that efficient farming need not necessarily mean the end of the gray partridge. It is, after all, a bird of the arable lands, and the fact that much of Europe is experiencing the biggest expansion of arable farming since Napoleonic days ought to have brought it increase, not destruction. It need not be inefficient farming so to arrange the rotations and the total land use that there will always be undisturbed areas for nesting, that stubbles are not all burnt, that not all insect life is destroyed, and that, once the corn is taken, there shall still be cover somewhere.

Gray Squirrel (Sciurus carolinensis)

The various species and sub-species collectively known as the gray squirrel are natives of North America. Some, however, are now found in Europe, where they are thought of, and treated, as vermin, largely because they are thought to do damage to forestry, and to drive out the native red squirrel (S. vulgaris). In North America, however, squirrels are thought of as small game; they are both hunted and eaten, and there are, in most of the states, closed and open seasons for them. By a queer reversal it is the red squirrel that is thought of as an aggressor and predator upon the much larger gray squirrel, chasing it and, tradition has it, castrating it by biting it in the scrotum. It is as a popular small game

Above, 'Pigeon Shooting', 1813 by Robert Pollard; below, 'Grouse Shooting' 1830 by James Pollard.

animal in North America, rather than as a pest in Europe, that it will be described.

The common gray squirrel is an arboreal animal found in all the suitably forested areas of the United States and Canada. Local populations, however, may fluctuate, largely because squirrels will undertake mass migration in response to pressures arising from over-population or a drop in food supplies. Squirrels are, normally, entirely vegetarian, depending on buds and leaves of trees in spring and summer and on bark, nuts, mast etc. in autumn, storing some of these in caches for the winter. They may, however, attack and eat songbird nestlings and eggs.

There are considerable colour and size variations through the various species and sub-species. The general colour is gray, with white underparts and tan markings on cheeks, muzzle, ears and paw, but black, red and buff are common colour variations. The average weight is around 1 lb and length about 19 in, half of which will be tail. The fox squirrel *(S. niger)*, however, is very much larger, weighs up to 3 lb, and is gray in its upperparts and a reddish fox colour in its underparts.

Mating starts in January, the male staying with the female for very few days. Gestation takes about 44 days, and the first litters appear in February. Second litters may start to appear in July. The young, seldom more than four, are born blind and hairless. Their eyes open at five weeks, and they begin to emerge from the drey a week later. By nine weeks they are able to feed themselves. They are mature by the end of the year, and the life span is thought to be about 15 years.

Squirrels are generally shot with a .22 rifle, the hunter either walking through the wood and hoping to pick a squirrel out on a branch, or else standing still in a likely spot and waiting for the squirrel to move. A dog can be useful because by standing at the bottom of a tree it can, even if it does not bark, attract the squirrel's attention and allow the hunter to approach and get his shot in. Skilled shots may still try that legendary test of frontiersman marksmanship, 'barking'. This consists of firing into the branch so close to the squirrel that it is concussed by the impact whilst, at the same time, the bark is pushed up and dislodges the squirrel, which falls to the ground unconscious and unmarked.

Great Tibetan Sheep
(Ovis ammon ammon)

The argali, as it is also called, is found in Siberia, Mongolia and Tibet, and the uplands of Ladakh in Kashmir. The true argali stands approximately 48 in at the shoulder and weighs upwards of 350 lb, its massive, annulated horns making nearly a complete turn and measuring over 50 in on the curve. The winter coat is lightish brown growing

paler in the summer. There are fifteen closely related sub-species of *O. ammon* found in southern Asia, including the Marco Polo sheep, *O. ammon polii*, which is a paler colour and has slightly longer but more slender horns. All the species have notably slender legs contrasting with their heavy, sturdy bodies. Most commonly found in the Himalayas is *O. ammon hodgsonii*. The full grown ram is dark brown on the back, has a noticeable white ruff at the throat, while the neck of the female is distinctly darker and her horns are much thinner and shorter, seldom exceeding 20 in. There is little trouble in distinguishing the rams due to their white ruff and the darker colour of their bodies, but there is generally considerable difficulty in establishing the length of the horns, due partly to their colour, which merges with the background, but also to their peculiar curving shape.

Stalking a herd is likely to be extremely difficult as their senses of smell and sight are both acute and there is invariably one of the flock on guard. They will scent the hunter at a distance of half a mile should the wind be wrong, and at 17,000 ft or so, especially near the snow line, the wind is very changeable. Nor must the immense vitality of these sheep be forgotten. Although a

mortally wounded beast may soon leave the flock, a sure sign that it is seriously wounded, cases have been known of a ram travelling eight miles or more over rough ground before expiring from a shot close to the heart. Obtaining a fine head of this species is proof that the hunter has endured and overcome arduous stalking conditions. It has been described as 'The Blue Riband of Himalayan Sport'.

Greece

Greece is the southern part of the Balkan Peninsula jutting into the Mediterranean, with an area of about 51,000 square miles. It is a varied and very rugged country and shooting takes place in some of the finest Mediterranean scenery. The most popular sport is to be found in the extensive olive groves in Attica and the Peloponnese, where hunters with cars drive out on Sunday and shoot missel thrushes. Woodcock are found in the pine woods and bushy country of central Greece, but, being migratory, are likely to be taken on flight routes anywhere, and they are often shot within ten miles of the centre of Athens. Olive groves and the low, dry hills of coastal areas are the easiest shooting country; elsewhere, one encounters some exciting but arduous ground. Typical is the steep stony mountainside with thorny shrubs and occasional stunted trees. This is very uneven terrain with boulders ranging in size from scree to clusters of very large rocks. Birds, such as partridges, are hard to flush from these stones and once shot are often impossible to find even with good dogs. Waders and duck are shot on marshes at the mouths of certain rivers but these wetlands are now seriously diminished because of drainage schemes and water extraction for irrigation. In Macedonia, boar may be shot in the fir forests, occasionally bear and wolves, and, in extreme contrast, partridges and quail are hunted both on the mainland and the Aegean islands.

Shooting is the largest participant sport in Greece; it is estimated that up to 250,000 Greeks go hunting on any given Sunday in the shooting season. There is a tremendous keenness apparent in their sport; it is practised continuously throughout the legal seasons and a very wide variety of game is sought. Clubs and associations hire coaches to take them to shooting areas each Sunday and many others travel long distances and stay overnight in their search for game. It is not only in the remote areas that the sport is carried on; in the olive groves of Attica, within ten miles of Athens, many hunters find their sport, and a typical Sunday in these areas is punctuated with gunfire from the earliest light.

Although the range of game is wide, covering both resident birds and ground game as well as migrant birds, small bags are typical – a brace or so of woodcock, three or four brace of migrating doves on a lucky day, or three or four thrushes. Further, the State attempts to conserve its low stocks of game by imposing variable restrictions, both on the species one may shoot and to the days in the week, or the season of the year in which that species may be taken.

Seasons and Game
The main season begins on 20 August with migratory and resident pigeons and doves and quail; and for normal shooting ends on 10 March with woodcock and missel thrushes. Extensions of the season may be allowed on special licences after this date if there are large numbers of doves still migrating, but it is impossible to predict this arrangement.

Doves (Trigonia). Season: 20 August to March, plus extensions. There are migratory doves, for the most part collared doves and two main periods of migration are noted. The first begins about the first week of September and may last for more than a month. The return is in early spring but the birds are thinner and the migration is more fickle. The best places are the staging points on the route, for instance the southern headlands of the Peloponnese, Sounion, and the main line of flight from Missolonghi up through Agrinion to Arta.

Quail (Ortika). Season: 20 August onwards, closing date varies. There are good stocks of resident quail in the plains of Attica, Boeti and Thessaly and numerous islands have birds. They are usually pointed and flushed by dogs from long grass (often head high) and although the numbers are now down there are still village stories of quail being netted and snared in large numbers, much in the manner described by Homer. This is now illegal. Migrant quails also appear in Greece from about 20 September onwards.

Partridge (Perdika). Season: 1 October to 3 November. Restricted to Tuesdays, Thursdays and Saturdays; bag limit: 4 partridge each day to a licence holder. The Greek partridge (the red-legged or French partridge) lives in stony, shrubby country and is very hard to locate without pointers. Coveys are quickly broken up and one is lucky to see more than a brace flushed at a time, except on the first day or so of the season.

The field partridge of Greece, which is similar to the gray partridge, is completely protected. It is (or was) widely distributed over the wheat and olive areas of central Greece, and because such territory is accessible to casual shooters the bird has been virtually lost.

The Greek partridge (rock red-legged partridge or bartavelle) is a big handsome bird, perhaps the finest sporting prospect in the country. It takes refuge in the high stony hills during the day and, like Scottish grouse, may fly down to grain fields in the evenings. Apparently the Greek partridge can exist without water, relying only on berries for moisture.

In Greece, the collared dove is one of several birds shot while migrating.

Duck (Papies). Season: 10 September to 10 March. They are found on marshes with large winter migrations in from other parts of Europe. The main wetland area is near Alexandroupolis where the Evros river forms a fine habitat. Most species from central Europe arrive here in the autumn, including mallard, teal and widgeon. But there are also migrations from the Black Sea and Caspian areas. While conservation authorities say the numbers of migrants have been drastically reduced in the Evros wetlands there seems to be a steady annual supply. Their remoteness does not prevent large numbers of Greek hunters from going there; in the past few years there have been 'festivals' of duck shooting there. Duck elsewhere in Greece are severely reduced in numbers and on inland lakes tend to be harried in and out of season.

Geese. Season: as for duck. The Evros is the only place to which geese migrate and bags are largely a matter of luck.

Woodcock (Begatses). Season: 9 September to 10 March. These birds are all migrants and there is no restriction on numbers shot. The mountains of central Greece, including Parnassos above Delphi are most productive.

Pheasants. There are no pheasants in Greece except for a few winter strays from Bulgaria. A pheasant in the bag would be a great curiosity and reported in the press.

Thrushes (Tsaikles). Season: 10 September to 10 March. Found in the olive groves of central Greece, these are the most usual quarries of hunters. Bag limit: none.

Blackbirds (Kotsifas). Season: as for thrushes; usually no restrictions. Occasionally in cold winters the bird is protected by special laws.

Hares (Laghi). Season: 20 September to 1 January. Like partridges, these may only be shot three days in each week; bag limit: one per day. WBC.

Licences—Greece

Hunting licences are designated for different species and for various areas (nomarchies). Greek hunters pay 125 Drachmas for each nomarchy, and Dr.600 for all Greece. Foreigners, pay Dr.2,000 per month for all Greece, Dr.3,000 for two months and Dr.4,000 for the whole season.

Further Information

The Ministry of Agriculture, Dasarcheion, Athinon, Agion Constantinou Street, Athens.

Greek Partridge *see under* Red-legged Partridge; *also* Greece

Grey *see* Gray

Grizzly Bear *(Ursus arctos horribilis)*
An American bear that was once common throughout the western part of North America, from northern Mexico to Alaska, especially in the foothills of the Rockies. Civilization and hunting have now compressed it, in the United States, into a very few pockets, mainly in National Parks and Wildlife Refuges. Almost all the grizzly now hunted are to be found in Alaska, British Columbia and the other provinces of northwest Canada. The 1964 World Wildlife Fund inventory suggests a continental population of about 36,000, of which 35,000 probably live in Alaska and western Canada. The Mexican grizzly *(Ursus arctos nelsoni)* is reduced to a population of about twenty animals, all occupying a limited range north of the city of Chihuahua. Wyoming has between 100 and 200, Montana 350, Idaho 50 and Colorado and Washington about 10 each.

The grizzly is essentially an animal of the forested wilderness, within which it changes its range to meet the seasonal food supplies. Being omnivorous, it will probably feed on southward facing slopes in spring on newly sprouted vegetation, shift to open country for berry-bearing plants and marmots in the summer, and descend to salmon-spawning streams in the autumn. During the winter it will hibernate, generally retreating to a den in November and emerging in March and April. It is a creature of crepuscular, if not nocturnal habit, feeding early and late, and avoiding, especially, the midday sun of early summer.

There are a great number of variations within the species, which has led to an elaborate system of sub-species. The differences are mainly those of size and habitat, but there is also considerable colour variation, from cream to black, the whitish tipping to the hairs giving the grizzled appearance. The weight for a mature bear can vary from 350 to 1,000 lb, which makes it larger than the black bear, from which it can also be distinguished by its prominently humped shoulders and long claws. A grizzly will not reach full size until after three years, nor full maturity until after seven. Average life span in the wild is around 20 years.

They normally breed in June and July, and the young, usually twins, but ranging from one to four, are born from January to March whilst the dam is hibernating. She cannot ovulate whilst suckling, and breeding, therefore, is biennial. An animal of

A grizzly bear photographed in Alaska in October. This Toklat bear has a well-defined 'hump'.

enormous strength, it is not, normally, dangerous to man unless either wounded or surprised. It can, however, be dangerous to farm stock, and it will attack and kill any animal whilst defending its range. Unlike the young bear, the adult is unable to climb trees because of a stiffening of the wrist.

There are few places left where a grizzly may be specifically and legitimately hunted. Normally it will be met and, perhaps, shot, in the course of hunting for deer, elk, or other animals. The normal method of hunting is to stalk it, which requires great skill and endurance, because of its great powers of scent and hearing. The best time for stalking is during the spring, just after the

bear has come out of hibernation when it will be feeding in the open on a mountain slope. It can also be tracked in autumn, after the first snows but before hibernation. This could be, however, a more dangerous undertaking. Finally, it can be baited, with the carcass of a horse or deer. It is a difficult animal to kill with a single shot, the brain being small and the skull thick. If a spine or brain shot is impossible, then one that smashes the shoulder and goes on towards the heart is probably best. If the animal charges, a shot at the shoulder or foreleg is recommended, rather than an attempt at a brain shot. A high-velocity rifle firing a heavy bullet is essential.

Grouse

The 15 species of grouse found in the northern hemisphere are outstandingly important in their contribution to sport hunting, both in quantity and quality. Many of the species, in both Old and New Worlds, are highly specialized and provide sport in regions where no other gamebird can survive – for example, the sage grouse in arid brushland and the red grouse on open moorland. This specialization has enabled grouse to occupy most of the available natural habitats in northern Europe, Asia and America, but they are not opportunists and have been unable to take advantage of agricultural changes, except on the fringes. There are grouse on the tundra, in wet forests, dry desert scrub and on mountaintops.

Two species, the rock ptarmigan and the willow grouse, are circumpolar. Of the remainder, seven are found in North America and eight in Europe and Asia.

The ruffed grouse *(Bonasa umbellus)*, a plump bird with a 2 ft wingspan, weighing about 1¼ lb, is one of America's best-known gamebirds, originally found in all wooded areas from Arkansas and Georgia, to Alaska. It has receded from parts of its south-central range owing to interference with its forest habitat, but is still common over most of this vast range.

There are red and gray phases of the plumage, which is mainly barred brown and buff, with a wide dark stripe on the fan-shaped tail. The ruff which gives the bird its name is a fringe of black feathers at the back of the neck, spread by the male in display. One of the species' most distinctive features is its spring display, when the male drums by standing vertically on a log, braced back against his tail, and thumps the air with his rapidly beating wings.

Most puzzling feature of the ruffed grouse's ecology is its boom-and-bust cycle of abundance, which takes approximately 10 years. This is most noticeable in the northern forests, less so in the bird's southern range, and tends to coincide with population changes in another northern species, the snowshoe hare. A decline occupies 2 to 3 years of the cycle, followed by 3 to 4 years of recovery and good hunting for another 3 to 4 years. Theories for the switchback are many and varied – ranging from ozone levels to predator-prey relationships – but it remains one of the unsolved riddles of the wildlife world.

Ruffed-grouse shooting consists of walking up the birds in dense cover, usually calling for a 12-bore or 20-gauge with open boring. Dogs such as pointers, setters and even retrievers are often used, with many hunters favouring the Brittany spaniel. Season length and bag limits vary from state to state, but tend to be most restrictive in the south and east of their range and more liberal in the north and west.

During the shooting season, ruffed grouse are found as singles or small groups, often in the thickest undergrowth, near their sources of food: birch, aspen buds, wild grapes and the fruits of sumac and blueberry in particular.

The Old World equivalent of the ruffed grouse is the hazel hen *(Tetrastes bonasia)*, found in timbered country and thickets from France and Norway in the west, to Korea and Japan in the east.

Most famous of the Eurasian grouse, however, is the red grouse *(Lagopus lagopus scoticus)* found on heather moorland in northern England, Wales, Ireland and Scotland. Unlike the willow grouse or willow ptarmigan of Scandinavia, northern Asia, Canada and Alaska, this race does not turn white in winter.

During the breeding season this powerful, dark rufous-brown bird (weight, 1½ lb) is monogamous and highly territorial – cocks defending their patch of heather against all comers. In autumn, the family groups or coveys form into large packs, although the strongest birds continue to hold territories at all seasons. This complex social behaviour has been studied in detail by a unit of the Nature Conservancy, based at Banchory, near Aberdeen, Scotland.

Research at the unit has proved that shooting, predation, parasites and disease are not important in controlling populations. The stock on a moor is governed by the basic fertility of the soil, which affects growth and nutritive value of heather, the bird's food plant. Annual variations in numbers can be caused by bad weather which affects heather growth. In the long term, the burning of patches of heather to give a varied pattern of ages and heights of the plant increases the stock.

About 5,000,000 acres of the British Isles is statistically regarded as grouse moor and on the best of this land, the population may reach a density of one grouse per acre in late summer. Shooting traditionally opens, in Britain, on 12 August ('The Glorious Twelfth') and continues until 10 December.

In the early days of the season, red grouse may be shot over pointers, but this species is mainly famed as a driven bird, shot by 8 to 10 guns from concealed butts as coveys are driven forward by a line of beaters crossing the moor. The fast-moving birds, which may travel up to three miles after being flushed, offer unparalleled targets. At Littledale and Abbeystead moors, Lancashire, on 12 August, 1915, eight guns killed 2,929 grouse. On 20 August, 1888, Lord Walsingham killed 1,070 grouse to his own gun on a Yorkshire moor.

Among North American grouse, sport hunting is also provided by blue and spruce grouse of the northern conifer forests, sharp-tailed grouse of the prairie fringe and sage grouse of the West and Inter-mountain regions. The prairie chickens have greatly

Top, the spruce grouse, which inhabits the wooded areas of Canada and Alaska.

Above, the male black grouse, or blackcock, is found in northern and central Europe on moors and heather-covered hills.

Grouse

Black *
Blue *
Capercailzie * (capercaillie)
Dusky (gray, mountain, pink)
Hazel hen *
Pinnated * (prairie chicken)
Ptarmigan * : rock, white-tailed and willow
Red *
Ruffed *
Sage *
Sharp-tailed *
Sharp-winged
Spruce *

decreased owing to the destruction of their natural grassland habitat and are now protected. Rock and white-tailed ptarmigan are hunted in tundra and mountain habitats from Alaska to New Mexico.

In the Old World, sharp-winged grouse are a favourite quarry in northern and eastern Asia, ptarmigan on mountains and tundra from Scotland and the Alps to Kamchatka, while the huge (12 lb) cock capercaillie and the lyre-tailed blackcock are regarded among the finest of field sports trophies in Scandinavia, Britain and eastern Europe. The latter two species are often shot while displaying in spring. WAN

Grysbuck (bok) *see* Steinbuck

Guemal (or Huemal) *see* Deer of the World and their Hunting

Guineafowl *(Numididae)*
These are fowl-like birds found, in various forms, in most countries of east, west and south Africa. They include the helmeted guineafowl *(Numida)* one species of which, *N. meleagris*, is the familiar, domesticated guineafowl of Europe. Other genera include the turkey-like guineafowl *(Agelastes)* the crested guineafowl *(Guttera)* and the vulturine guineafowl *(Acryllium)*.

They are all fairly large birds, measuring around 20 in, and with plumage that is predominately speckled black and white. The head and upper neck are usually bare, sometimes highly coloured, and there may or may not be a crest or helmet. They are reluctant flyers, and roost in trees to avoid predators. They are generally found in coveys or even flocks, and they live principally on seeds and fruit.

When flushed from cover, the plumed guineafowl, shown here in a Congo forest, flies noisily into the trees.

They are among the most edible of African game birds, and are hunted primarily for the pot, rather than for sport, since they are very poor flyers. The Africans sometimes hunt them with dogs, which tree them and engage their attention until the hunters come up and either shoot them or pull them off their perch.

Guns *see* Firearms

Guyana
Guyana is the largest of the three states in the north-east of the South American continent, north of Brazil and east of Venezuela. From west to east they are Guyana (about 83,000 square miles), Surinam (a Dutch territory of about 55,000 square miles) and French Guiana (about 34,000 square miles). All three countries share a low coastal belt with a higher hinterland to the south. There are also some hills in the centre of Surinam and the west of Guyana. All have dense forest and jungle growth except for the higher parts of the hinterland, which are savannah. There are two dry seasons: mid-February to April, and mid-August to November. The climate, though not pleasant in the interior, is much better on the coast, particularly in Guyana.

The timber resources are being utilized, especially in French Guiana. The other countries grow sugar and rice in considerable quantities, as well as coffee, coconuts and bananas, but French Guiana has only a very small area under cultivation.
For game *see* South America, Shooting in.

Further Information
Consult initially the Ministry of Information, Georgetown, Guyana.

H

**.and-loading Rifle and Shotgun
.artridges**
.e under Firearms

.ardhead *see* Waterfowl

.ares *(Leporidae)*
.he difference between hares and rabbits
. that, generally, hares have longer ears
.d legs, and their young are born furred
.d with their eyes open. Also they usually
.ve in the open rather than in burrows.
.part from South America they are native
., or have been introduced into, most con-
.nents. Although generally shot over dogs
.ey are also sometimes driven, and are
.equently hunted with hounds, either with
.eyhounds coursing by sight, or by scent-
.g hounds, working as a pack, such as
.agles or bassets. They provide sport for
.e shotgun or light rifle. Their flesh is dark
.d strong tasting.

.artebeest *(Alcelaphus busephalus)*
.here are several closely related species of
.ese antelopes found throughout Africa as
.r north as the Sudan, but mainly south of
.e Sahara. In general they stand about 48
. at the shoulder, sloping somewhat towards
.e hindquarters and weighing in the region
.‛400 lb. Their heads are generally long and
.arrow with rugged, corrugated, lyre-
.aped horns, carried by both sexes, which
.se upwards from a high frontal bone and
.nd abruptly backwards towards the tips;
.ose of the southern species are generally
.rger than those of the northern species.
.oloration also tends to vary considerably.
.heir legs are slender and shapely and their
.eed and staying powers are exceptional.
.hey can generally run clean away from
.anger, and also have the ability to last
.ithout difficulty for several months in
.esert surroundings without water. Mainly
.azers and only occasional browsers, they
.rop one calf a year, though twins are not
.nknown. In common with many other
.ntelopes they have largely forsaken the
.ains in favour of thin scrub or woodland
.d they may often be found in mixed herds
.ith zebra and gnu. Their own herds are
.enerally small, from 10 to 20 beasts, led by
.n old bull. Their immense vitality makes it
.ssential to use a heavy calibre to ensure a
.ill, as they will run for great distances, even
.hen mortally wounded, and may be lost to
.e hunter. Another common species is the
.ichtenstein hartebeest. *A. lichtensteini,*
.und throughout parts of central Africa,
.otably Zambia, in herds of from 15 to 20,

Hares

African grass
Alaskan
Arctic*
Blue* (varying, mountain,
  snowshoe rabbit)
Brown*
Jackrabbit*: antelope, black-tailed
  white-sided, white-tailed
Japanese
Natal red
Rand red

The European brown hare

---

often associating with other species such as
zebra or roan antelope. Their coloration
is a yellowish-dun and they stand about 50
in at the shoulder with an average horn
measurement of about 18 in. The Cape
hartebeest or red hartebeest, once common
in south Africa, is a bright bay colour with
slightly larger horns and is now very limited
in numbers being strictly protected in most
areas of south Africa, although still shot in
the south-west. Other hartebeests commonly
shot are Lelwell's, in Ethiopia, and Voke's
in Tanzania.

Hawaii (U.S.A.)
A chain of islands (once known as the
Sandwich Islands) in the north Pacific.
There are twenty in all, eight of them in-
habited. Most of them are extremely fertile,
and the climate is mild, with no cold season.
All tropical and sub-tropical crops are
grown, and there are extensive forests.

Hunting depends on introduced species,
there being no native mammals or game
birds, and the native waterfowl – nene
goose, Hawaiian duck and Laysan teal – are
all protected. Some of the introduced mammals are now numerous enough to be hunted,
others are still becoming established. There

Seasons and Limits—Hawaii

Species	Season	Comment
Axis deer	21 March-12 May on Lanai 9 May-21 June on Molokai	
Black-tailed deer	1 Oct-31 Oct on Kuai only	120 permits drawn for
Feral sheep	1 Aug-30 Sept	Weekend shooting only
Feral goat	All year round in Lanai and parts of Hawaii	Elsewhere according to island
Mouflon	16 Aug-23 Aug	80 permits issued for Sunday only
Wild boar	All year round	
Pheasant ring-necked Japanese	7 Nov-17 Jan	
Quail Japanese Californian Gimbel's	7 Nov-17 Jan	
Chukar partridge	7 Nov-17 Jan	
Francolin gray black	7 Nov-17 Jan	
Turkey	7 Nov-17 Jan	

Licence Fees—Hawaii

Resident	$7.50
Non-resident	$15.00
Big-game tags	Free

are 22 game management and public hunting areas, but most of the hunting is on private land.

Further Information

Division of Fish and Game, 400 South Beretania Street, Honolulu, Hawaii 96813.

Hazel Hen (*Tetrastes bonasia*)

This is a small, rather handsome grouse, also sometimes called hazel grouse or gelinotte that is found in secluded, and highly localized, communities in many parts of Europe and Asia. Its range stretches, in the north, from Norway to Kamchatka, and reaches as far south as northern Spain and Transylvania in Europe and Japan and northern China in Asia.

It is an elusive bird, found only in the wilder and more mountainous regions, and almost always in pine or beech woods, hazel copses or young plantations of beech and oak. It is, unusually for a grouse, white-fleshed, and it makes excellent eating. Indeed, some epicures consider it the finest of all game birds. Because of this it has always been heavily shot, and its numbers have suffered accordingly. Brunius calculated, in 1798, that some 60,000 hazel hen were eaten annually in Stockholm alone. In th[e] past ten years the average number of haze[l] hen shot each year in the whole of Swede[n] has been 12,000. The inference is a plain on[e] but it should be remembered that there ar[e] nearly always more hazel hen than peopl[e] imagine: they are merely hidden.

Their flight is generally noisy and sho[rt] and, when flushed, they nearly always f[ly] into the nearest tree and perch halfway u[p] it. They are rarely found in open country, [or] outside a forest, but they do change habita[t] in winter, deserting hazel copses and ope[n] deciduous tree stands for thick pine forest[s] where the cover, and protection from pre[-] dators, will be better. They begin to pair [at] the end of March; courtship is largely b[y] song, the cock's call consisting of a lon[g,] sharp, whistle, ending in a sudden chir[p.] Nesting is on the ground, the clutch vari[es] between 8 and 12 eggs and the hen si[ts] extremely tight during incubation, so e[x-] posing herself to attack by predators. Th[e] young are able to fly very soon, when the[ir] wings and tail are only partly feathere[d.]

The cock measures about 14 in and weigh[s] less than 1 lb, the hen being slightly small[er] and lighter. In both sexes the upperpar[ts] are rufous and gray barred and speckle[d] with black. The underparts are grayis[h] white with a chestnut-coloured, horsesho[e-] shaped mark on the chest and a black breas[t] with the breast feathers outlined in whit[e.] The cock has a small buff crest and his ch[in] and neck are black, whereas the hen has n[o] crest and is largely white around the ch[in] and throat. The legs are only partly feat[h-] ered, the lower part and the feet bein[g] naked. The tail is long and square an[d] consists of 16 feathers.

Although small, the hazel hen is a[n] excellent game bird. It is sometimes sho[t] over pointers, but it does not hold well [to] the point and tends to run on; as this will b[e] into thick cover or will end in its flying up[a] tree, shooting becomes difficult. The stan[-] dard method, now illegal in some countrie[s,] is to call it, using an easily made whist[le] and imitating the cock's courting call in th[e] spring and in autumn, when the cove[ys] first break up.

The subspecies include: *T. bonasia rup[e-] stris*, the hazel hen of central, southern an[d] and south-western Europe; the gray-belli[ed] hazel hen (*Tetrastes bonasia griseiventri[s]*) inhabits eastern Russia; Severtzov's haz[el] hen (*Tetrastes bonasia severtzovi*) is foun[d] in north-eastern central Asia.

Hides and Decoys

Before the development of the art of shoo[t-] ing birds in flight, when the sitting, and [if] possible the flock-shot was every hunter['s] aim, a hide or some sort of ambush was th[e] first requirement for success. Although th[e] efficiency of guns and the accuracy of the[ir] users have increased considerably sinc[e] those days, a suitable hide, or blind, and i[ts] correct use are no less important in many forms of modern shooting. Basically, there are two types of hide; the static and the mobile, or portable. Examples of the first include grouse butts built of turves or stone, duck flighting platforms built on stilts, familiar on Dutch waters, sink boxes or circular concrete pits found on some American, German and Scandinavian flyways and pigeon platforms and high seats for deer shooting, built high in the trees of many European forests. The second category is larger and varies according to the ingenuity of the hunter.

In Britain portable hides for use against duck and woodpigeon are generally homemade from materials such as wire netting interleaved with foliage or double-folded to form a sandwich that is packed with straw; camouflaged netting or hessian painted ingeniously to represent straw bales, the type of hedge, or fence with which it must blend, and even artificial grass matting. In the mobile category, the American sneak-boat or variations on a floating, camouflaged raft theme, like the British gunning-punt, both used for duck and goose shooting; the white screened sled pushed across the Baltic ice by prone seal-shooters; the artificial stalking horse still in occasional use on the plains of Europe and in England, the Hungarian hunting cart and even the motor car suitably screened, are just some that come to mind.

A combination which can be either static or portable is the camouflaged clothing, adopted by many hunters, which may be complete to the extent of face mask, gloves, leafy headgear and painted or cloth-wrapped gun barrels. Whether a hide is static or portable, permanent or temporary, and wherever it is sited, similar rules apply to its construction. It must blend with its background and be roomy enough to accommodate its occupant, or occupants, without interfering with a free and all round use of the gun. Wherever possible a seat for the gunner can be installed with advantage and anyone anticipating long waits in shooting ambushes should accustom himself to shooting from a sitting position.

In ideal situations material for speedy hide building can be collected on the spot and an ambush improvised with only a knife or small axe and some pieces of string. But the builder should avoid spoiling hedges or trees, or siting his hide where it may interfere with farming operations or attract the unwelcome attentions of inquisitive cattle. On his departure the site should be left tidy.

However much effort is spent on building any sort of hide, it will be to no avail if the occupant cannot remain patient and still, free from fidgeting for long periods. Needless to say, the hide must also be in the right place. If it is not, the hunter must be prepared to move until he has found the best

Four well-made decoys: From top to bottom: black duck by Charles Hart, Gloucester, Mass., *c.* 1900; Canada goose by Joe Lincoln, Accord, Mass., *c.* 1905; Yellowlegs by unknown maker, Eastham, Mass., *c.* 1890; Canada goose by unknown maker, Chatham, Mass., *c.* 1885.

position, which is a good reason for keeping the hide simple.

For maximum efficiency, hides are always best used in conjunction with decoys. In Great Britain and in America the use of tethered, live decoys is prohibited by law, but in other parts of Europe, notably in France, the indiscriminate slaughter of birds of prey lured to a tethered, live eagle owl decoy has long been practised to the concern of international conservationists. The use of an owl for luring birds within range of gun or trap is based on the habit of most birds to harass owls and hawks. Another use for owl decoys, live or inanimate, is to attract members of the crow tribe within gunshot, a method universally popular with game preservers. Stuffed cats and foxes also will attract crows, magpies, rook and jackdaws within range of a gun hidden nearby.

On the continent of Europe small live birds are also used to decoy hawks into special cage traps and wildfowlers in Holland train duck, and sometimes geese, not only to call out to attract passing fowl, but even to fly out to meet them and lead them within range of a hide or catching net.

The most popular use of decoys, however, is by the shooters of wildfowl and woodpigeon. The two countries in which they are most commonly used for these purposes are the U.S.A. and Britain, although naturally their use at times is virtually worldwide. The employment of duck and other wildfowl decoys in the United States dates from the practices of the American Indians, whose only weapon was the bow and arrow. It followed that wildfowl had to be attracted within close range; hence the need for effective decoys. That is why in America the decoy is unique in being a true form of primitive art. Amongst the earliest examples of wildfowl decoys are some canvasback and merganser imitations discovered in Lovelock Caves, Nevada, which are about 2,000 years old.

Decoy making is pure sculpture, and just as an artist's work can be identified by his style and method, the decoy sculptor's art can be recognized. It is also possible to tell where the decoy originated from its type of construction, and the collection of hand carved wildfowl decoys of all sorts is widespread in the United States. The popularity of wildfowl decoys in the States owes its origin to the market gunning days of the last century. Nowadays conveniently light decoys are mass-produced in a variety of materials, but most American wildfowlers prefer carefully carved wooden models.

There are a few rules which apply to the use of all decoys. They must not shine in the sun; they should resemble their live counterpart as closely as possible, although there are occasions when pieces of newspaper, for instance, will attract widgeon on the fore-

A simple hide made from bales of straw

shore, and corked beer bottles bobbing in the sea will bring in sea-going duck, such as scoter. Lumps of mud are often enough to fool wildfowl in the half light of dawn or dusk and combined with a small cleft stick and a strip of white paper wedged in it, are effective decoys for blue geese. As a general rule, however, all decoys should be set out head to wind or tide and the more the better. Usually the hide is best placed upwind or to one side of the decoys, and there is a school of thought which prefers larger than life-size models in the belief that they are more easily seen from a distance and have a better drawing power.

Some enthusiasts use mechanical wood-pigeon decoys which move or flap their wings, powered by pulleys and cords or an electric battery powered motor. The objection is sometimes made that the extensive use of decoys simplifies wildfowl shooting to the extent of seriously diminishing stocks. But where market gunning does not exist and wildfowlers know and accept the principles of sportsmanship and conservation, the dangers of over-shooting are negligible. *See also* Blinds; Flighting Ponds for Duck. PHW

Himalayan Black Bear *(Selenarctos thibetanus)*

The Asiatic black bear, or moon bear as it is also called, is found in Kashmir and other parts of the Himalayas. Standing about 30 in at the shoulder, it is, as the name implies, black in colour, with a pale V-shaped white mark across the chest. It is omnivorous, eating fruits, acorns, and crops, doing considerable damage to maize in particular. Though mainly vegetarian it will sometimes kill cattle or other animals when hungry. It measures up to 7 ft and weighs between 380 and 400 lb when adult. It spends the winter in the foothills, but in the summer is often found as high as 12,000 ft. It is

Below, the Himalayan black bear is a good climber, and is found up to 10,000 ft.

Bottom, the Himalayan thar is beardless and has comparatively short horns.

Right, a bull hippopotamus

said to hibernate chiefly in hollow trees about 15 ft above ground.

One or two cubs are born in the spring and by the following autumn are generally able to fend for themselves, although not fully mature for another two years. Their eyesight and hearing are poor, but their acute sense of smell makes them difficult to hunt. They are frequently found in trees, but should not be shot when above the hunter. Though not generally pugnacious they are capable of charging the hunter and a heavy calibre is advisable. The subspecies found in Japan is much smaller, but the subspecies found above the snow line, the Himalayan snow or Isabelline bear, *U. thibetanus isabellinus,* may be even larger. The females, however, are smaller and should not be shot. Their pelts are in good condition in the autumn and sometimes in the spring up to May, although generally better in the winter.

Himalayan Thar *(Hemitragus jemlahicus)*

Found south of the Himalayas from Kashmir to Bhutan, it is also established in New Zealand in the South Island mountain ranges. This large goat has a thick, soft furry coat; the head is long, narrow and finely furred without a beard. Standing about 3 ft high and reddish-brown in colour, it has a heavy body and long legs; its horns average from 12 to 14 in and are almost semi-circular in shape. Like most goats it feeds in the morning and evening, and shelters beneath rocks during the day. It prefers steep forest-covered slopes to rocky precipes where it is sometimes found. The young are generally born in June or July. As its sight and scenting powers are very highly developed, stalking is a difficult task. The sight of a thar perched on a pinnacle with its hair down to its knees is, however, one which makes any stalk worthwhile.

Hippopotamus *(Hippopotamus amphibius)*

This large mammal is found in many parts of Africa south of the Sahara in herds of from 4 to 30 living in lakes, swamps and rivers, except during the rains, when it may be found far from water. Males are occasionally found alone. The skin colour of these nocturnal grass eaters may vary from reddish-pink to gray-blue. Though standing only 5 ft high they may be 13 ft long and weigh from 2,000 to 3,000 lb. A single calf may be born at any time of the year, rarely twins. Both sexes are pugnacious, and an enraged hippopotamus may charge a canoe or small boat and upset or damage it, which adds an element of risk to this form of shooting. In spite of their size, their head presents a very small target when they are swimming and it is not easy to hit a vital spot. On shore they are easily killed and no sportsman would shoot at that time unless their flesh, which is excellent eating, was required for the camp.

Hog *see* Bushpig

Hog Deer *(Axis porcus)*
These are relatives of the chital and are found in southern Asia. The species has also been introduced into Australia and is firmly established there. Hog deer are common in the sub-Himalayan tracts, particularly in the Terai jungle, where some of the best trophies have been obtained, and they are also found in Assam, north of the Brahmaputra river. They are somewhat smaller and heavier in build than the chital *(q.v.)*, having a long body, and legs rather short for their size. The name is probably derived not only from their somewhat pig-like build and appearance, but from their habit of running or scuttling, with their head held low, rather than bounding in the characteristic manner of most deer. The antlers are set on boney pedicels of 1 or 2 in in length, and are seldom much above 16 in long. Although hog deer are usually found alone or at most, in groups of two or three, they are occasionally found in Assam in herds of as many as 18 or more. Normally they will not be found grazing far from cover into which they disappear at the first sign of danger, but as they interbreed with chital, a stag may sometimes be found grazing in company with them and in such circumstances is almost invariably a good beast. Their somewhat secretive habits tend to make them a difficult animal to still-hunt, except during the early morning or late evening round the edges of open spaces. When suddenly put up by the hunter, however, they sometimes have a habit of stopping and standing after running only a very short distance and may then provide a simple shot. A very easy method of calling the stags, which is also very successful with barking deer, is often used by Burmese poachers. A piece of grass placed between the thumbs and blown on closely resembles the sound of a small deer in distress. Should any hunter be tempted to use this method it is as well to remember that it sometimes has the effect of attracting a prowling panther. *See also* Deer of the World and their Hunting.

Holland *see* Netherlands

Houbara *see* Bustards

Hounds *see* Dogs

Huemal (or Guemal) *see* Deer of the World and their Hunting

Hungarian Partridge *(Perdix perdix)*
This is the name given in the United States and Canada to the European gray partridge *(q.v.)*. It was first introduced from Hungary and now, almost inevitably, bears the popular name among shooting men of 'Hun'. Its habits and appearance are discussed under its European name.

It was originally imported in an attempt to provide a replacement for the disappearing sharp-tailed grouse. It flourished, most of all, in the arable and grain-growing states, as well as in the west, but it has never established itself strongly in the eastern states. Nonetheless, its numbers are increasing every year, as is its popularity with the American hunter, who is discovering what his European counterpart has always known, that the gray partridge is the most sporting of all the game birds. There are now open seasons for it in the following states and provinces: Idaho, Indiana, Iowa, Montana, Colorado, Ohio, Minnesota, New York, North Dakota, Nevada, Washington, Oregon, South Dakota, Wyoming, Wisconsin, British Columbia, Alberta, Ontario, Nova Scotia, Prince Edward Island, and Saskatchewan.

In America pairing and nesting take place a little later than in Europe, with the peak of the hatch occurring about a fortnight later. They are never driven, as they generally are in Europe, but walked up behind dogs, which is a return to the traditional practices of Europe in the days of the muzzle loader.

Hungary

A republic in central Europe, with an area of about 36,000 square miles. Hungary consists almost entirely of the plains of the middle Danube. The river runs down through Budapest and the centre of the country, with the Great Hungarian Plain in the East, watered by the River Tisza and its tributaries. West of the Danube is the Little Hungarian Plain, and west of that, Lake Balaton, largest of the central European lakes. North of Lake Balaton lies the mountainous Bakony forest, the highest ground in Hungary, which stretches north and then east along the northern frontiers.

The climate is variable but never particularly extreme. The soil is generally fertile. Most of the Great Hungarian Plain, once almost entirely pastures, is now under cultivation, and over half the total area of the country is arable land. The timber industry is also important, so there is plenty of unspoilt country and cover for game, despite the flatness of the terrain. Hungary has long had a reputation for its hunting, particularly round the turn of the century. World War 2 was a setback, but the stock has now been amply restored.

Generally speaking the game is fairly evenly distributed throughout the country. However, mouflon only inhabit the highest parts of the mountainous regions in the north, and there are few red deer towards the south-east. Fallow deer, in particular, abound (Hungary holds the world record head). Bustard may be found wherever the terrain is particularly open and flat and there are large numbers of pheasant, hare and partridge in the plains. Wildfowl, though widely distributed, are particularly strong in the grass and fishponds of the Hortobagy region, one of the best wildfowl areas in Europe.

There are two types of hunting area: the big game hunting grounds, in which boar and deer live permanently, and the small game grounds, which these animals occasionally visit. In the latter boar may be shot, but not the deer. The State manages only 18% of the hunting grounds, the rest being leased out to hunting associations. All such associations operate under the auspices of the National Association of Hungarian Huntsmen, and no one may join an association without passing the National Association's examination for professional huntsmen. By this means the number of those allowed to hunt is restricted to under 20,000. Tourists, however, are offered some of the best hunting available in the State hunting grounds.

Seasons are variable and should always be checked in advance; those given in the table are only approximate, and are the longest likely ones.

The pricing is complex and a price list should be obtained before a trip. The charge for deer trophies rises with the weight of the antlers, but for mouflon and boar it is based on the length of the horns and tusks, respectively. For big game there are also charges for wounding (usually 50% of list price), for a miss, and for shooting the female and young of the species. Wild boar may be driven for an additional fee. The fees for small game given above are for walking up. There is an entirely different pricing system for small game when driven. Board, accommodation, transport, insurance, and interpreter are all charged separately.

Seasons and Fees—Hungary

Species	Season	Best	Fee (minimum)
Red deer	Sept-Jan	Sept	$110.00
Fallow deer	Sept-Jan	Oct	$137.00
Roe deer	May-Sept	Aug	$8.20
Mouflon	Nov-May		$164.00
Wild boar	all year	Sept-Feb	$68.30
Bustard, cock culls only	April-May		$328.00
Pheasant	Oct-Jan		$1.70
Partridge	Sept-Nov		$1.70
Brown hare	Sept-Jan		$1.70
Geese	mid-Oct-Nov		$2.20
Duck	mid-Aug-Nov		$2.20

Licences—Hungary

All hunting trips must be organized through 'Mavad', the Hungarian Game Trading Co-operative Company, which will obtain visas, accommodation, and the shooting required. On request Mavad will send two visa application forms, together with a document to ensure free import of guns, rifles and ammunition. One completed application form, plus photograph, must be sent to Mavad; the other, plus photograph and passport, to the Hungarian Embassy. After permission is granted, usually in 8-10 days, the embassy will deliver the visa and firearms permit. The visa is valid for 14 days from date of entry, but may be prolonged for another 14 days, in which case another two photographs are required.

Further Information
'Mavid', Budapest 1, Uri u. 39.
For initial enquiries the Hungarian travel Bureau, with offices throughout Europe, may also be useful.

Hunting and Land Use

It is now commonly agreed that the world is over-populated, since it contains insufficient available land to provide all the foods, houses, roads, reservoirs, airports, etc that modern civilization appears to need. It might seem slightly difficult, therefore, to justify hunting as a method of using land, especially since it is rarely – in Britain at least – a people's sport, and its efficiency as a food-producing industry is, by modern standards, rather low.

But it is important to realize that hunting, whether it be for rabbits or elephants, is seldom an exclusive user of land, and rarely shuts out the possibility of that land being used for other purposes as well. Any discussion of hunting today is necessarily a discussion of how hunting can best fit in with those other purposes, for the days when the New Forest, in England, had to be enclosed, solely to allow William Rufus to shoot a stag, or the Highlands of Scotland had to be depopulated solely to allow the Victorians to stalk one, have long since gone. Even the splendidly self-indulgent days of the squirearchy, when a wood might be planted principally for the pheasants and a spinney principally for the foxes, have passed away. Modern landowners have to make their landowning and farming and forestry pay, or come as near to paying as is possible in a town-controlled civilization. Hunting, therefore, has to be carried on without interfering at all, or at least only a little, with the serious business of making a profit.

There are, it is true, large areas of the world where hunting is the only possible, or only economic, form of land exploitation, and in such areas it becomes justified as part of the tourist industry. Much of Africa, for example, will grow game better than it will grow anything else. Game, however, is a crop that can be harvested by hunting. (It is true that professional game wardens can

Roe deer, depicted here in velvet, may be shot in Hungary from May to September. The best time is during August.

In Scandinavia reindeer provide both stock and sport.

be employed to do this, but it cannot be good business management to pay government officials to do jobs that other people would pay quite large sums to do for them).

Game is an important part of the African tourist industry, for tourists pay large sums to travel in Africa solely to look at it. Hunters, however, will pay even more in order to hunt it, and their hunting, if properly controlled, will actually improve and increase the game populations, so increasing the attractions of the continent to tourist and hunter alike. In this way an entirely beneficial spiral is created, and land that is intrinsically unproductive is made to produce at least three crops – tourists, hunters and meat, with a few by-products such as trophies, hides, ivory, and elephant-foot umbrella stands.

This is an example of hunting as a form of exclusive and beneficial land use, but the position in other parts of the world is not, unfortunately, so simple. Ours is a world in which millions of people are quite plainly under-nourished. As a consequence, it is considered immoral not to produce food wherever it can possibly be produced. The sentiment is an admirable one, but the food produced rarely, if ever, finds its way to the people who are under-nourished. All that happens is that local surpluses build up to

make food unnaturally cheap to the alread well fed and well paid industrial population Although everyone knows that this is wha actually happens, sentiments about th morality of food production still prevail, an no government in any civilized country wi ever dare to take land out of farming i order to allow it to be used for huntin, though it may, of course, be taken out i order to build more motorways, holida camps and airports. It is true that farmer sometimes decide to abandon farms tha have been producing food they have bee unable to sell, or to sell economically, an where this has happened – pricipally in th New England states and in the dust-bow areas of the Middle West of the Unite States – the derelict farms have rapidl gone back to scrub and trees, attractin back the grouse and the deer the plough ha originally driven away. But this is rarel allowed to happen; farmers are kept pro perous enough to continue farming, an modern hunting has to exist alongside th moral imperative that any land that possibl can be farmed must be farmed.

This, generally speaking, it is able to d The hunting of certain animals fits rath awkwardly into patterns of modern agr culture and has to be reserved for area where the farming pressure is low. Red dee and red grouse, for example, are only possible in the setting of the primitive, inefficient, and entirely pastoral agriculture of the Scottish Highlands, just as deer and wild boar are only possible inside the forest, rather than the farm, economies of continental Europe. However, the traditional game animals of an arable countryside – pheasant, partridge, duck, hare, rabbit, quail, woodpigeon – can all, with little extra effort, and with varying degrees of success, be accommodated inside modern farming. They provide another, second harvest that can be taken from the land without really damaging the primary, agricultural harvest. Each may slightly reduce the efficiency of the other; good game management may, for example, require less than the optimum use of poisonous sprays, and good farm management may require less than optimum game populations, but it is probably that we are producing food rather too efficiently already. Nor can there by any doubt that the two activities combined will produce a greater return from the land than either could have done alone.

Farming is not the only form of land use to which hunting must accommodate itself. Land is increasingly needed for the officially recognized recreations of the population. Now in the United States, and in some of the countries of Western Europe, and, perhaps, even in some of those of Eastern Europe, hunting is recognized as a people's sport and is therefore not only respectable in itself, but may also be respectably in occupation of land. In Britain, however, largely because there is so little land to go round, hunting has never been a people's sport. Indeed, for a long time now, it has been politically useful to represent it as a class symbol, rather than as the recreation it so plainly is. 'Grouse-moor' is still the dirtiest adjective one politician can use to describe another, which is a pity, if only because it has made it socially and politically difficult to give hunters the help and facilities given to other recreational users of land. It is plainly absurd to suggest that the hunting instinct is found only in the rich: it is found in all men alike, and those who possess it strongly ought to be given some opportunity, however limited, to exercise it. It is logical to believe that the suppression of an instinct so fundamental, and, in some men, so strong, can only be dangerous.

However, in Britain the pressures of opinion and population alike are opposed to any process of bringing hunting to a wider public. Opinion can be and should be changed, but the physical limitations are immutable. None the less, something may be learnt from practice in the United States, where hunting is, in the fullest sense of the word, a popular sport. There the State and National Forests are made available to the public as hunting grounds, with the State providing keeping and control. The posi-

Ringing wildfowl, in this case a swan, is a very valuable method of investigating their migratory patterns. Such scientific work is part of an international programme to rationalize wildfowl hunting.

tion in Britain is by no means analogous, since our population pressures are far greater, but we do possess National Forests of a sort. These are administered by the Forestry Commission, which is now the largest landowner in the country and continuing to expand. Forestry and hunting go hand in hand, and the Commission has recognized the fact to the extent of letting the sporting rights on some of its lands. But it insists that its prime and only important duty is to produce timber. It is possible that the Commission would be of greater service to the nation if it were turned into a Hunting and Forestry Commission, with a duty to provide hunting, and training in hunting to people who could not, otherwise, have any access to it. It would be idle to pretend that hunting would, in this way, be made available on an American scale, but it would, at least, be made more available than it is at present.

The opportunity to travel the world is being offered to more and more people. More and more people will be brought into contact with game and with hunting. Few, however, will themselves be able to afford the costs of hunting in foreign countries. It is increasingly important that their own countries, should, so far as they can, offer them hunting opportunities at home. If it is complained that this is too expensive it might be worth looking at another useful American practice. There, all the proceeds from the sales of gun and game licences are hypothecated to the hunting services and used by them to provide better facilities for hunters everywhere. It seems an intelligent use of both land and money. D G

Hunting Dogs *see* Dogs

Hunting Rationalization Research Group (HRRG)

Reports from different countries indicate that wildfowl populations have decreased recently, at least locally. This may be caused mainly by a reduction of living conditions, such as deterioration of habitats, loss of important feeding areas, or pollution, but there is also full reason to ask whether, and to what degree, hunting is responsible for the decrease. Even if we assume that hunting under earlier conditions was not a factor in reducing wildfowl populations, shooting may become disastrous under the changed circumstances, unless controlled so that it does not exceed the populations' carrying capacity.

Based on these viewpoints, the International Wildfowl Research Bureau established the Hunting Rationalization Research Group in 1969 to study different aspects of wildfowl hunting in Europe, Asia and Africa. For practical reasons the group has been divided into the following six regions, the Co-ordinators being given in brackets: The Northern European Region

(Teppo Lampio, Finland; also the Co-ordinator of the Research Group), The Western European Region (H. Michaelis, Holland), The Eastern European Region (S. Priklonski, USSR, and E. Nowak, Poland), The Southern European Region (S. Valentincic, Yugoslavia), The Asian Region (E. Nayebi, Iran), and The African Region (M. Fesseha, Ethiopia). Each region has a network of national contacts.

Though the diversity of hunting regulations, established customs, etc in the different countries is well known, there has been no detailed information on these aspects. As all plans and conclusions must be based on reliable facts, the HRRG organized a 40-page questionnaire to solve the present situation concerning regulations. With three exceptions all (39) European countries and areas with separate game legislation answered the questionnaire before the end of 1971. In Asia and Africa, however, work was at that time only in the initial state.

The analyses of the questionnaire indicate that all wildfowl species are protected for part of the year throughout Europe, except in Malta, where no wildfowl are ever protected, and Scotland, where the red-breasted merganser and goosander are not protected. Some wildfowl species are protected all year around. This applies to swans practically everywhere, except in a few southern European countries. The number of fully protected wildfowl species is highest in the northern and some western European countries, lower in eastern Europe and zero in southern Europe. Woodcock and snipe are hunted nearly everywhere, but all or almost all other waders are fully protected in half of the areas.

The open seasons for wildfowl are fairly reasonable in the northern and eastern European countries but considerably longer in central, western and particularly southern Europe. In these parts of Europe the seasons often begin in late July or early August, whereas in the eastern and northern European countries they begin in the middle of August or later. In northern and eastern Europe the seasons close before the end of the year but in central, western and southern Europe seldom as early as December or January.

To protect wildfowl from over-shooting, most countries regulate hunting by prohibiting hunting circumstances and methods which are too disastrous to the populations, e.g. shooting by night is prohibited in most European countries. Though shooting at dusk and dawn is commonly allowed, many countries have regulated it through various restrictions. Shooting from motor boats is usually but not always prohibited. Nowhere is wildfowl hunting practised from aircraft. There are common restrictions as to the maximum calibre of shotguns, but the maximum permitted number of cartridges loaded into the shotgun or the use of rifles is limited in only a very few countries. The use of live or dead decoys is only seldom prohibited. The use of nets or artificial lights is illegal in most European countries.

Bag limits are prescribed in the legislation in the USSR and locally in Yugoslavia only. Most countries stated that bag limits are considered impractical, unnecessary or uncheckable.

The number of wildfowl lost as cripples is reduced in the different countries in various ways, e.g. through retriever dogs or avoiding shooting into flocks or at swimming birds. In order to save wildfowl populations, selling the bags is regulated in many countries. Selling is, however, very common in several western and southern European countries. The unusual number of wildfowl hunting violations observed in some countries is believed to be caused by sportsmen's inability to identify wildfowl species.

In order to be able to improve hunting rationalization, we must know how wildfowl hunting is practised in different countries, not only in Europe but also wherever the wildfowl populations breed, migrate through or spend the winter, i.e. also in Asia and Africa. The next phase in the work of the HRRG is to find out which hunting methods are too dangerous for the wellbeing of the wildfowl populations. A study should also be made as to whether and to what extent wildfowl populations really have decreased and whether hunting is responsible for the reductions. For this purpose annual censuses must be carried out regularly at the breeding, migrating and wintering areas. As many countries lack reliable and comparable hunting kill statistics at present, methods for securing them must also be developed and put into practice.

The purpose of the HRRG is to improve rationalization of wildfowl hunting, step by step, by stopping hunting methods too harmful for the survival of the populations. The Research Group can only point out such methods and make proposals for recommendations, but not decide about adopting or implementing them. Adopting the proposals is the job of the representatives of the different countries at international meetings, and implementing adopted recommendations that of the sportsmen's organizations and authorities making the rules and regulations.

As wildfowl are the common property of a large number of countries, hunting should be correctly regulated in all of them. This means that the open seasons should also be adjusted by the countries in accord, due regard being paid to the carrying capacity of the wildfowl populations. It is quite possible that the final goal of the work of the HRRG will prove to be an international convention on the rationalization of wildfowl hunting. TL

Ibex *see* Asiatic Ibex

Iceland

Iceland is a large island, of about 40,000 square miles, situated in the North Atlantic just south of the Arctic circle and about 230 miles south-east of Greenland. It consists primarily of a plateau of volcanic rock, about 2,500 ft high, although in places the island rises to nearly 7,000 ft. Short turbulent rivers and waterfalls abound, and there are numerous hot springs and active volcanoes. The climate is mild and wet, but three quarters of the island's area is unproductive, wild and inhospitable.

There is only one native wild mammal, the Arctic fox. Rats and mice, inevitably, are now fairly common, as is mink. Reindeer have also been introduced, and are numerous enough in the eastern highlands for about 600 to be shot a year. Their hunting is strictly controlled by the reindeer inspector, from whom a special permit must be obtained, with the total bag limit established according to the conditions prevailing each year. In bad years hunting may be banned altogether.

Birds, by contrast, are extremely numerous. The island is a great flyway stopping place, and about 75 species actually nest there, in most cases in great abundance.

Further Information

Iceland State Tourist Bureau, Laekjargata 3, Reykjavik.

The ptarmigan is found throughout the high mountain slopes in northern Europe and Iceland, where it is hunted. The North American rock ptarmigan is a closely related species.

Idaho (U.S.A.)

The Rocky Mountain state, Idaho is largely mountainous, with areas of desert and sagebrush in the south, and is, for that reason, ranch rather than farm country, but sugar beet, potatoes, cereals and fruit are grown, and there is extensive irrigation. There are 21 million acres of state forest, and 64% of the state consists of public lands.

Idaho is famous for its big game, but pheasant are also abundant in the farming areas, as are mallard, and the lakes and irrigation waters attract large numbers of

Species	Season	Limit	Comment
White-tailed deer	Varies between 19 Sept-13 Dec	one per year either sex, 2 in some units	
Mule deer	Varies between 19 Sept-13 Dec	one per year either sex, 2 in some units	
Elk	Varies between 19 Sept-19 Dec	one per year either sex	
Antelope	No general season		Controlled hunts with special drawings
Black bear	5 Sept-30 May in some parts, open in others	one per year	
Grizzly bear			Protected
Bighorn sheep	5 Sept-18 Sept 19 Sept-31 Dec		General hunt. Controlled hunts with drawing for $25 permits in some units
Mountain goat	5 Sept-13 Dec		By special drawing in some units
Moose	Various lengths between 19 Sept-6 Dec		Antlered moose only
Cottontail rabbit	1 Sept-28 Feb	5 per day	
Snowshoe hare	open		
Jack rabbit	open		
Pheasant	Oct-Nov, varying	varies	
Ruffed grouse Sharp-tailed grouse Spruce grouse Blue grouse Hungarian partridge Chukar partridge Bobwhite quail California quail Mountain quail Gambel's quail	Starts 21 Sept, length varies according to population		

The pronghorn, which inhabits Idaho and other western states, has no near relative elsewhere in the world.

Canada geese and duck. Most public land are open to hunting, and the Fish and Game Commission is active in game management and habitat improvement. The state is divided into Game Management Units with season and bag variations from one Unit to the next.

Special Regulations
No rifles may be used when shooting game birds, and only .22 centre-fire or larger rifle may be used on big game. Dogs may be used to hunt bear and predators, but not other big game. No animal may be shot with flashlights or at a salt lick.

Further Information
Department of Fish & Game, Box 25 Boise, Idaho 83707.

Illinois (U.S.A.)
A highly industrialized, mid-west state, of 56,000 square miles, it lies in the valley of the Mississippi and the basin of the Great Lakes. It consists largely of a flattish, fertile plain, next only to Iowa in importance as a cornbelt state. Fruit and cotton are also grown and large numbers of livestock reared.

Pheasant, quail and waterfowl offer most of the sport available. There is an established deer population, but this may be hunted by residents only, drawing for permits on a county basis. The Division of Game operates seven pheasant shooting areas and two goose shooting areas, but apart from these, posting makes hunting difficult for the average man.

Further Information
Division of Game, State Office Building, Springfield, Ill. 62706.

Impala (*Aepyceros melampus*)
Found in many parts of south and east Africa in the open plains as well as in light woodlands or scrub, the palla, as it is also known, stands about 36 in at the shoulder and weighs as much as 80 lb. It is perhaps the most familiar and typical of antelope, being characterized by its lyrate horns

Licence Fees—Idaho

Type	Status	Fee	Comment
Hunting/Fishing	Resident	$6	Necessary for all permits and tags
	Non-resident	$135	
Upland game birds and small game only	Non-resident	$35	

Permits:

Moose	$25
Bighorn	$25
Mountain goat	$5
Antelope	$3

Tags:

Moose	$10
Bighorn	$10
Mountain goat	$10
Antelope	$5
Turkey	$5
Elk	$3
Deer	$2

Big Game Inventory—Idaho

Species	Shot
Antelope	1,292
Bighorn	47
Black bear	2,597
Deer (white-tailed and mule)	78,441
Elk	17,064
Moose	53
Mountain goat	161
Wild turkey	9

Licence Fees—Illinois

Resident	$3.25
Deer permit	$5.00
Non-resident: reciprocal with his state of residence, with a minimum of	$15.00

Seasons and Limits—Illinois

Species	Season	Limit	Comment
Deer	3 days in Nov 3 days in Dec	one per season	Residents only
Cottontail rabbit	14 Nov-31 Jan	5 per day	
Squirrel, gray and fox	1 Aug or 1 Sept (depending on zone) -15 Nov	5 per day	
Pheasant	15 Nov-31 Dec	2 per day	
Bobwhite quail		8 per day	
Hungarian partridge		2 per day	

averaging about 20 in and by a pair of glands with black tufts of hair on the hind feet, just above the heel. The females are hornless. The colour varies from reddish-brown upperparts to white below, with a fawn band along the flanks. They are a most elegant and attractive medium-sized antelope. They are gregarious and are found always in herds varying from ten to several hundred

on occasions, sometimes with the males in separate groups. They are often found associating with other species such as puku (*Kobus vardoni*), also zebra and gnu. Each herd is led by an old male and several young males are reputed to act as sentinels; their sneezing alarm call will set the entire herd in flight, with leaps as much as 10 ft high and 30 ft in length. Browsers and grazers, they have a sharply defined breeding season, varying with the locality from September to November, generally bearing one young, sometimes twins. Stalking can prove difficult but they are good eating.

India

The Republic of India (1,261,816 square miles) comprises the bulk of the great south Asian peninsula, or Indian sub-continent, that lies between the Himalayas and the Indian Ocean. It falls into three distinct geophysical units: the Himalayas, the Indo-Gangetic Plain, and the Deccan. These three areas are so markedly distinct in terms of terrain, climate and game that it will be convenient to discuss them separately. Under these three headings are given the most common or noted types of game in each area. The political divisions obviously affect the shooting laws, and it should not be assumed that every type of game listed may be shot, even when protection is not specifically noted.

The peninsula is subject to monsoons from both the Arabian Sea and the Bay of Bengal. The south-east monsoon strikes between June and October, the south-west in November and December. January and February are cold months, and March, April and May hot. Although the south-west monsoon lasts slightly longer in the Deccan it is much heavier further north, Bengal and Assam having particularly heavy rainfall. The climate in the south is fairly equable, but in the north continental.

The Himalayas

One of the greatest mountain ranges in the world, the Himalayas effectively cut India off from the rest of Asia. They stretch in a shallow arc of about 1,500 miles from the gorge of the Brahmaputra in the east to the gorge of the Indus in the north-west, where they culminate in the Pamir plateau. The range gets progressively narrower and higher to the east, with the highest peaks in the world, including Mt Everest, in Eastern Nepal and the Protectorate of Sikkim. Snow-fed rivers emerge into the Indo-Gangetic plain all along the range, and provide convenient axes of reference, forming three distinct regions: the Indo-Sutlej or Western Himalayas, the Sutlej-Gandak or Central Himalayas, and the Gandak-Brahmaputra or Eastern Himalayas.

Both monsoons strike the south face of the Outer Himalayas (the southernmost chain of the whole system). Generally speaking, however, the rainfall is much heavier towards the east. Srinagar in Kashmir has 30 in per year, while Cheerapunji in the Khasi hills of Assam has about 430 in. The whole of the southern edge of the Himalayas is fringed by heavy jungle growth, and there are many fertile valleys cradled amidst the mountains.

The following species are common to the Indo-Sutlej, the Sutlej-Gandak, and the northern side of the Outer Himalayas in the Gandak-Brahmaputra region: wild yak, wild ass, bharal, Tibetan antelope, brown and black bear, thar, Kashmir stag (hangul), barking deer, snow leopard and clouded leopard, serow, goral, sambar, musk deer and great Tibetan sheep. Markhor and ibex are found on the northern side of the Outer Himalayas in both the Gandak-Brahmaputra and the Indo-Sutlej regions. Panther and tiger are only found in the Sutlej-Gandak and southern side of the Outer Himalayas in the Gandak-Brahmaputra. The latter area also has many goral, sambar, barking deer and black bear, some Mishmi takin, and even the occasional great one-horned rhinoceros. The shapu is confined to the Ladakh mountains of Jammu and Kashmir, but has close relatives in the urials of the Punjab and Afghanistan and the gad of Baluchistan.

The Western Himalayas (the Indo-Sutlej) probably provide the best opportunities for sport, as they combine accessibility with a wide range of game. Hunting is, unlike other areas, well organized and the sportsmen will find everything laid on: mule transport, guides, shikaris, servants and accommodation.

The Indo-Gangetic Plain

This plain is based on three river systems, the Indus, the Ganges and the Brahmaputra. It forms a moat to the wall of the Himalayas, stretching all the way across the Indian peninsula from the Naga hills in the east, on the border between Burma and Assam, to the Baluchistan mountains of West Pakistan. The whole area is very flat (rising only 60 ft in 800 miles) and the climate is generally mild, although the areas towards the Indus basin in the west are arid, particularly so in the Thar desert that lies on the West Pakistan-India border, between the rivers feeding the Ganges system and those feeding the Indus. Elsewhere the combination of fertile alluvial soil, flatness and climate make the Gangetic basin the most densely populated area of India. This has had its inevitable repercussions on the wildlife of the area, with forest cover destroyed by the cow and plough, and game driven to the more inhospitable tracts such as the Terai jungle at the foot of the Nepalese Himalayas, the Aravallis hills on the eastern edge of the Thar desert, or the southern highlands that lead up to the Deccan plateau.

The game of the Indo-Gangetic Plain is

Protected Species—India

Blackbuck
Brow-antlered deer
Caracal
Cheetah
Clouded leopard
Crocodile
Easter pangolin
Four-horned antelope
Golden cat
Golden langur
Great Indian bustard
Indian elephant
Indian python
Indian swamp deer
Indian wild ass
Kashmir stag
Lesser panda
Lion
Marble cat
Markhor
Mongolian gazelle
Musk deer
Peacock
Pygmy hog
Pink-headed duck
Rhinoceros
Rusty spotted cat
Snow leopard
Spotted lisang
Takin
Tiger
Tragopans
Urial
White tiger
White-winged wood duck
Wild buffalo

A drawing by an Indian artist of the muntjac, or barking deer, which inhabits thick cover in India and other parts of southeast Asia.

distributed on roughly the following lines:

The Himalayan foothills: tiger, panther, sambar, bear (sloth, Himalayan, and, on the Burmese border, Malayan), barking deer, elephant, buffalo, rhinoceros (in Assam and Bengal), chital, hog deer, swamp deer, four-horned antelope.

The central plain: black buck, nilgai, pig, porcupine and chinkara (Indian gazelle) can be found in the west; desert cat, desert fox, desert hare and species of desert gerbils in the Thar desert; and rhinoceros, buffalo, Indian bison (gaur) and swamp deer in the moister regions of the east, with thamin on the Burmese border.

The Aravallis and southern highlands: tiger, panther, sambar and barking deer, while the urial is found in the Kala Chitta hills of the Punjab.

The Deccan

This is the great tableland to the south of the Indo-Gangetic plain, that forms the bulk of the Indian peninsula proper. The northern edge of the plateau is formed by the Vindhya, Satpura and Kaimur hills, which rise from the plain in a series of terraces. The two other sides of the triangle are flanked by the Eastern and Western Ghats, which converge to an apex in the south. The tableland of Mysore is about 3,000 ft above sea level, but the Deccan's average elevation is about 1,500 ft, with a slope down towards the east. The Eastern Ghats are not above 1,000 ft, while the Western Ghats rise to 8,000 ft or more in the Nilgiris (Blue Mountains). The south-west monsoon lasts rather longer in the Deccan than elsewhere, but it is not so heavy.

The Deccan is divided into three distinct regions:

1 The west coast area, including the Western Ghats and other smaller ranges, with a rainfall of 80 in per year or more, and

consequently luxurious vegetation, providing very good cover for game.

The east coast, including the Eastern Ghats, and most of the plateau south of the river Godovari, which have a limited rainfall (rarely exceeding 40 in), averaging between 20 and 40 in per year, because the Western Ghats form a barrier against the south-west monsoon; the vegetation is consequently dessicated, low and thorny. The central plateau, north of the river Godovari where the Western Ghats are much lower and the south-west monsoon can get through, has a rainfall varying between 25 in and 80 in with mixed forest and grassland.

Wildlife in the Deccan is as varied as the diverse terrain and climate indicate. In the open savannah lands many small animals can be found, such as mongoose, common fox, palm squirrel, hare and rodents, gazelle antelope, jungle cat, hyena and Indian wolf. Bison (gaur), sambar, spotted deer, mouse deer (not usually shot), sloth bear and wild dog inhabit the deciduous forests, except in the humid zone that receives both monsoons, where the forests have swamp deer, buffalo and elephant. The evergreen forests of the Western Ghats and the ranges in the south-west also boast elephant, bison, Nilgiri langur, lion-tailed macaque, Nilgiri brown mongoose and Malabar civet. The higher regions of these hills, however, have

climate similar to that of the lower Himalayas, and consequently repeat some of the Himalayan species such as the thar, pine marten and European otter. Additionally and to be particularly noted are sloth bear, spotted deer and three species of antelope: the nilgai, the black buck and the four-horned antelope, which are common in the Deccan, but are not found at all outside the Indian Peninsula.

Feathered Game

The distribution of feathered game is generally much less marked by sharp regional patterns, and many species can be found all over the peninsula and far into the Himalayas, providing much good shooting. The following are the chief species:

Wildfowl. Includes many species, but particularly common are the white-eyed pochard, Brahminy duck, Cowls duck and bar-headed goose; black partridge, painted partridge, gray partridge, chukor partridge; common or gray quail, black-breasted or rain quail, jungle bush quail, bustard quail; red jungle fowl, gray jungle fowl, red spur fowl; painted snipe, common or fan-tailed snipe, pin-tailed snipe; common sandgrouse, imperial sandgrouse; common green pigeon.

Licences and Special Regulations

There are obviously variations from state to state with regard to the game laws. Different game, different habitat, different seasons and conditions, even within the three geophysical divisions outlined above

The ratel or honey badger (drawn by the same artist), is often seen during the day, although it is a nocturnal animal. It also inhabits Africa.

are bound to affect the shooting and hunting regulations. The details of the variations are too numerous to list so visitors are recommended to apply to the Conservator of Forests, or equivalent officer, of the area they wish to visit for further details regarding rules, regulations, restrictions, shooting permits, fees, roads, seasons, etc. Nevertheless many of the game laws are common to most of the states, or at least very similar.

A 'Possession Licence' must be obtained by all those importing firearms or ammunition from the Commissioner of Police, or District Magistrate, at the point of entry. Applications for such licences may be submitted in advance through recognized travel agents. Certain bores used by the army and police are strictly prohibited to visitors, e.g. .303 rifles, .410 smooth bores, and .38, .441 and .445 pistols and revolvers. All firearms and ammunition are liable to a duty, seven-eighths of which will be refunded if re-exported within two years. Arms not covered by licence will be cleared from the Customs House only on production of the necessary licence and payment of duty.

In October of each year the Conservators of Forests list certain forests as sanctuaries in which shooting and trapping are strictly prohibited except with a special licence issued by the appropriate Conservator of Forests. Viewing and photography, within sanctuaries, is permitted on payment of a prescribed fee.

Those forests not classed as sanctuaries are then organized on the shooting block system. This involves the separation of Forest Divisions, by the Divisional Forest Officers in charge of them, into shooting blocks of various sizes, for which shooting licences are issued for certain limited periods, on payment of a prescribed fee. Lists of shooting blocks are displayed in the Offices of Conservators and Divisional Forest Officers and copies may be obtained for a small fee. There is a prescribed application form for shooting and fishing licences

The Himalayan brown bear, which is not uncommon in Kashmir.

which requires the full name and address of the applicant, occupation, reasons for application (e.g., sport, defence of property, etc.), areas in which the applicant intends to hunt or shoot, species of big game he particularly wishes to shoot, period for which licence is required, signature, and date of application. Applications usually have to be made between one month and three months before the commencement of the licence. The local forest officer requires 24 hours' notice before a visitor enters any forest or block, and in most states a report of all game killed or wounded has to be made to the Forest Ranger in charge of the range (Divisions are sub-divided into ranges).

The following are prohibited within all forests:

Shooting roosting birds.

Driving or destroying of birds or animals in snow.

Shooting animals or birds by artificial light, or from a wheeled vehicle, or at night from half an hour after sunset to half an hour before sunrise, except with special permission from the competent licensing authority, usually only granted for man eating tigers, cattle lifters, predators and vermin.

Further Information

The Department of Tourism approves a number of 'Shikar Outfitters', who organize hunting trips in various parts of the country. A list of the Shikar Outfitters may be obtained from the Government of India Tourist Offices throughout the world or from the head office at the following address: Department of Tourism, Government of India, Transport Bhavan, 1, Parliament Street, New Delhi-1.

More information on wildlife and shooting may also be obtained from: The Inspector General of Forests, Government of India, Ministry of Food, Agriculture, Community Development and Co-operation, Krishi Bhavan, New Delhi-1.

Fees—India

The fees vary between Rs (Rupees) 5 and Rs 200 depending on the importance of the block, the game to be shot, and the period covered by the licence.

Big Game Inventory—Indiana

Species	Shot
Deer	6,500

Licence Fees—Indiana

Type	Status	Fee	Comment
Hunting/Fishing	Resident	$4.00	Sold by county
	Non-resident	$16.00	clerks and their
Deer	Resident	$3.00	agents
	Non-resident	$25.50	

Seasons and Limits—Indiana

Species	Season	Limit
Deer	21 Nov-2 Dec	1 buck per season
Rabbit	10 Nov-21 Jan	5 per day
Squirrel, gray and fox	15 Aug- 15 Oct	
Pheasant Bobwhite quail Hungarian partridge	10 Nov or 20 Nov -21 Dec or 31 Dec depending on zone	
Ruffed grouse	24 Oct-14 Nov	

Licence Fees—Iowa

Type	Status	Fee
General	Resident	$3
General	Non-resident	$20
Special deer		$10

Seasons and Limits—Iowa

Species	Season	Limit	Comment
Deer	5 Dec-7 Dec	1 buck per season	Residents only, by special drawing
Rabbits, jack and cottontail	12 Sept-Feb	10 per day	
Squirrel, gray and fox	12 Sept-31 Dec		
Pheasant	starts 14 Nov	3 cocks per day	The annual kill is the biggest in the country
Bobwhite quail	24 Oct-Jan	8 per day	

Indiana (U.S.A.)

A thickly populated, highly industrialized state lying in the basin of the Great Lakes and the Mississippi Valley, its 26,000 square miles consist, mainly, of well watered prairie land and form part of the cornbelt; more than 90% of its area are farmed. The climate provides extremes of both heat and cold.

Apart from deer, which have been re-established, there is no big game, and over-drainage of the heavy, 'day-pan' soils has reduced the wetlands and the waterfowl. Rabbits and squirrels are shot in large numbers, and there are good pheasant populations in the north and quail in the south. Partridge and ruffed grouse are scarce and turkey, prairie chicken and mourning dove are protected.

Further Information

Division of Fish and Game, 605 State Office Building, Indianopolis, Ind, 46204.

Indian Bison *see* Gaur

Iowa (U.S.A.)

An important agricultural state of the mid-west, it lies mainly between the Mississippi and Missouri rivers, consisting principally of a rolling alluvial plain of great fertility. Ninety per cent of it is farmed and 65% is under the plough. The climate is one of great extremes, and the rainfall varies between 26 and 36 in.

As there is little forest big game is scarce. A deer population has been re-introduced, and there is now a buck season, for residents only, with special drawing. Duck and geese are plentiful, even though land drainage has reduced the resident population. Mourning dove is protected.

Special Regulations

Rifles may not be used on deer, only shotguns with rifled slugs. Dogs may not be used on deer.

Further Information

Division of Fish and Game, State Conservation Commission, E.7th and Court Avenue, Des Moines, Iowa 50308.

Iraq *see* Middle East

Ireland, Republic of (Eire)

Eire consists of the bulk of Ireland, which is in the Atlantic Ocean, separated from Great Britain by the Irish Sea and St George's Channel, while Northern Ireland (part of the U.K.) is separated from Scotland by the North Channel. Ireland covers 26,600 square miles. The Central Plain is the most dominant characteristic of the country, only varying between 50 and 350 ft above sea level. The mountains are low, rarely rising above 3,000 ft, ringing almost the entire coastline, especially in the west. The climate is generally more temperate than that of Great Britain, but rainfall can be very heavy, particularly in the mountains on the west coast, where it exceeds 100 in per year, though in the east it drops to below 30 in per year. Much of central Ireland is covered by lowland bogs, important for peat, but there is also plenty of fertile limestone

Shooting in County Wicklow, Ireland.

farming land. Agriculture is still the most important industry and Ireland is famed for its unspoilt countryside. However, game is not as plentiful as might be expected, because of the relatively unchecked hunting that has been pursued through the centuries, and game preservation policies are only just beginning to take effect. Shooting for migratory wildfowl, therefore, offers better and more easily available sport than shooting for native gamebirds.

Wild birds, other than those already listed as game birds, are not generally shot, and sportsmen in Ireland are particularly requested not to shoot the following: blackbirds, thrushes, fieldfares, redwings, larks, pipits, buntings, finches, swans, herons, king-fishers, grebes, divers, mergansers, birds of prey and owls. However, birds regarded as pests such as hooded crows, wood pigeons and magpies may be shot.

Organization

All shooting rights in Eire are privately held, and are mostly in the possession of the landowners, from whom prior permission for shooting should always be obtained. There are, however, 19 preserves spread around the country, mostly in the more mountainous regions near the coast, which are privately run specifically to offer occasional or visiting shooters a selection of sport at a fixed charge per day or per week. A list of these preserves is obtainable from the Irish Tourist Board. A typical entry gives the name of the shoot; the name, address and telephone number of the agent; the type of shoot, whether it is walk-up and/ or rough, and how large it is (shoots vary between 1,000 and 120,000 acres); the shooting available, i.e. a list of the birds likely to be shot; the season for the shoot, which will, of course, be listed per gun and per species (in many cases a typical bag is also quoted); the total number of gun-days shooting available, which is usually between 100 and 200 (lowest 42, highest 500); the number of guns per day, varying between 4 and 12; the daily charge, which is variable. It always gives a charge per gun, but there may be a reduction for parties. The charge always includes the services of a guide, or ghillie, and dog(s), and it may also include transport, light refreshment, lunch, or full board and accommodation. Certain hotels are also able to make shooting arrangements for their guests. There is, however, no guarantee that shooting facilities will be available from any hotel at a given time, so applications should be made to the proprietors (or agents) well in advance.

Further Information

Bord Failte (Irish Tourist Board), Baggot Street Bridge, Dublin 2.

Seasons—Ireland

Species	Season	Comment
Wild duck	1 Sept-31 Jan	except brent, barnacle and
Wild geese		graylag
Plover		except green plover
Snipe		
Woodcock		
Grouse	12 Aug-30 Sept	Cork, Kerry and Mayo
	1 Sept-30 Sept	All other areas
Pheasant, cock	1 Nov-31 Jan	
Partridge	1 Nov-15 Nov	
Hare	26 Sept-28 Feb	May not be shot in Cork, Meath, Waterford, Kerry, Clare, South Tipperary and lands preserved by hare hunting clubs
Fox	all year	Except in hunting districts
Gray squirrel	all year	
Mink	all year	Escaped from breeding centres
Rabbit	all year	

Licences—Ireland

Visitors must have an Irish firearms certificate; applications, with the appropriate fee, to the Secretary, Department of Justice, 72 St Stephen's Green, Dublin 2. The applicant should give his name and address, type of weapon, the maker's name and serial number, the port of entry and his Irish address.

Certificates are valid for one year from the date of issue. The fees are £1.50 per rifle; and £3.25 for the first and 75p for each additional shotgun. Only double-barrelled shotguns may be used. Repeaters may only be loaded with two cartridges. All shooters must carry third party insurance.

Licences—Israel

All hunters in Israel must have firearms and hunting licences. The former are issued by the Ministry of the Interior, Jerusalem, and the latter by the Ministry of Agriculture, Jerusalem. Visitors must have an import and export licence for their firearms. Import and export licences are obtainable from Israeli embassies.

Licences and Fees—Italy

Hunting fees for the preserves are usually about 3,000 lire a day (including guide). A hunting licence is required and is obtainable from Italian consulates. The fee is about $8, the licence is valid for 30 days, and it permits the import of one gun and 200 rounds of ammunition.

Israel

Israel is a republic lying along the south-eastern seaboard of the Mediterranean and stretching down to the top of the Gulf of Aqaba. Nominally Israel covers nearly 8,000 square miles, but is, at present, in possession of large areas of territory formerly under the suzerainty of the neighbouring Arab countries. Physically, Israel proper is divided into four parts: the hill country of Galilee, Jordan and Samaria, rising to nearly 4,000 ft; the coastal strip and the plain of Esdraelon which cuts the hill region in two; the Negev, the semi-desert area in the south; and the River Jordan valley. The winter is rainy, especially in January and February. The summer is hot but tempered by winds from the Mediterranean.

Large areas of the country are fertile and produce cereals, citrus fruits, cotton, tobacco, vegetables and livestock. However, the infertile areas such as the Negev are also being developed by means of irrigation. This development in particular has given a new lease of life to species such as the gazelle which was in danger of extinction in the area.

The chief game species are leopard, wolf, wild boar, gazelle, sugar or rock partridge (red-legged), quail, rock pigeon, band-tailed pigeon, waterfowl and snipe.

Leopard and wolf are not at all common now and usually are only hunted when they have become a menace. Wild boar, on the other hand, are quite numerous in the hill region to the north of the Sea of Galilee (Lake Tiberias). Gazelle are also found in the Galilee hill region as well as the northern Negev, but despite their recent comeback they may only be shot under a special licence and the annual bag is rigidly controlled. There is no bag limit on any game birds but there is a season for partridge from September to January and for pigeon from September to February. Partridges are most common in the hills round Lake Tiberias, and are usually shot over pointers, as are quail. Both quail and waterfowl are shot while passing through on their migrations between Europe and Africa.

There is at present no established organization through which visitors may arrange hunting, but the Israeli Government Tourist Corporation will put interested parties in touch with Israeli hunters who are willing to take visitors hunting and impart the benefits of their experience.

Further Information
Israeli Government Tourist Corporation in Jerusalem.

Italy

Italy consists primarily of a long narrow peninsula stretching south-east into the central Mediterranean, the island of Sicily at the foot of the peninsula, and the island of Sardinia to the west of the centre of the peninsula. There are several other smaller islands, and the whole has an area of about 130,000 square miles. The Apennine mountain range forms the backbone of the country, rising to about 9,000 ft, but there are two extensive low-lying areas, the Po valley, between the Apennines and the Alps, and Apulia, the 'heel', in the extreme south-east. On the west coast there are confined fertile areas around Naples and Pisa. The south is generally much hotter than the north, though the Po valley plain has a continental climate, not common to the rest of the peninsula because of the proximity of the sea. Rainfall is between 30 and 50 in, falling mostly in February and March.

Agriculture is important, though employing a decreasing share of the population. Wheat, olives, vines, sugar beet and citrus fruits are the chief crops, while cattle are of increasing importance.

The chief game species are red deer, roe deer, chamois, ibex, wild boar, wolf, marmot, fox, hare, pheasant, partridge, and woodcock; waterfowl are not particularly plentiful.

Italy is not renowned for its hunting, but there are several hunting preserves, the most important of which are the Capalbie preserve, near Grosseto, which is on the west coast about half way between Pisa and and Rome, and the Matruneto del Serino preserve, near Benevento, which is in the hills above Naples. Both are heavily wooded and offer wild boar, hare, woodcock, pheasant and partridge. It is, perhaps, surprising that there is not another hunting area of equal importance for the Alpine species, in particular chamois and ibex. One way of shooting these is in the National Parks, in which hunting is not normally permitted, but culling licences are sometimes issued. Three of the four parks have chamois and one has ibex.

Organization
The Italian Federation of Hunting (FIDC), with a membership of 900,000, is the main organization for Italian hunters. It is responsible for conservation, restocking, etc, where necessary, and at present is reintroducing partridges (gray), pheasant and hares to the game-depressed zones of southern Italy.

The Ministry of Agriculture and Forestry publishes, each year, a booklet giving details of the hunting season, game laws, firearms regulations etc. This is only published in Italian, but for visitors staying for any length of time it is extremely useful.

Further Information
Federazione Italiana della Caccia, Viale Tiziana 70, Rome.

This federation will accept bookings for the hunting preserves.

Ministry of Agriculture and Forestry, Via Venti Settembre 20, Rome.

J

Jack Rabbits (*Lepus* species).

Although always called rabbits, the various species of America's jack rabbit are all, in fact, hares. Included among them are the white-sided jack *(Lepus alleni)*, one of whose sub-species is the antelope or burro jack. The one name commemorates the animal's speed, the other the length of its ears. The white-sided jack, whose coat is white from shoulder to rump, is among the largest of the hares, weighing up to 10 lb and measuring 24 in. Other species include the white-tailed jack *(Lepus townsendi)* and the black-tailed jack *(Lepus californicus)*.

These are all large, long-eared, rather heavy hares, found throughout the west of America from Canada to Mexico. They feed on all greenstuff, cactus, and the bark and the leaves of trees. They are gregarious, living in groups of 15 or more. In times of food shortage they will concentrate, in great numbers, in such areas as alfalfa fields and young orchards, where food is available. The consequent damage can be considerable, and because of this they are treated as pests.

Individually, they are shy creatures, depending on camouflage and speed to protect them. When crouched in their forms they are difficult to pick out, and when flushed they are almost impossible to follow. They are, next to the antelope, the fastest wild animals in America. They run in a series of bounds, which may be well over 10 ft, punctuated by very high jumps which allow them to look around for danger. In areas with severe winters some of the Jacks will, like the snowshoe and arctic hares, adopt a white winter coat during the snows. The number of litters born per year varies with the latitude. At the northern extreme of the jack's range only one litter may be born; at the southern extreme it may be three; the gestation period is 30 days and the young are weaned within five weeks.

Hunting Jack rabbits is not a simple occupation. Their wariness and speed make a shotgun useless in most cases. A high velocity, low trajectory 'varmint' rifle is a useful weapon, but the hunter must be prepared to take snap shots, with little opportunity for using telescopic sights. On the flat, no dog except a greyhound would be any use, and even then, two greyhounds are better than one when coursing Jacks. In hill country a fast running pack of fox-hounds could provide some sport and have some hope of keeping up, but this would only be over broken ground and uphill. Jacks are not highly edible, but they are

A white-tailed jack rabbit in Alberta

pests, and hunting them provides exercise either for the rifle or for the greyhounds.

Jaguar *(Felis onca)*

This, the largest of the American cats, is also the third largest cat in the world, being smaller only than the lion and the tiger. It looks rather like a leopard, but is considerably heavier, and has a more massive head. The spots are not really spots, but rosettes enclosing black dots. There is a melanistic phase, called, in Brazil, *Onca Prieta*, in which the spots can only be seen against the light, rather as though they were watermarks in paper. No less than 16 sub-species, or geographical types have been recognized, and there are considerable size variations. The largest jaguars may exceed 300 lb in weight, but the average is considerably less.

Jaguars were once found in several states of the United States, including New Mexico, Texas and California, but now they are only occasionally found in the south-east of Arizona. They are still numerous, however, in Central and South America, being especially plentiful in the Matto Grosso jungle of Brazil. They show considerable adaptability, being able to live in both jungle and desert, and they can take to mountains as easily as they can take to water. Carnivores, they will eat anything from turtles to tapirs, but they are especially fond of peccary, and can acquire a damaging liking for farmstock. They appear to possess no definite breeding season and the young, which number from two to four, will be dropped at any time of the year after a gestation of approximately 100 days.

Since they are nocturnal, they are difficult animals to hunt, and the only really constructive method of hunting them is with a pack of hounds. These are best used in the early morning, when the scent is fresh and the dew still lies, and they may be followed, if the terrain permits, on horses. Hounds need not be fast, so long as they have a good nose, for the jaguar, though fast over short distances, will not run far. The dogs should, however, be trained not to run in on the quarry when it checks, for the jaguar will not necessarily take to a tree as a cougar would, but might turn and attack the hounds, wounding and even killing several. Nor should they run in on a jaguar that has been wounded, for it possesses great vitality, and even when shot through the heart or lung can still inflict damage. A heavy rifle and a head- or neck-shot are recommended if hounds are to be spared. The Brazilian Indians are sometimes able

call jaguars down to the water by imitating their breeding cry on birch trumpets, while waiting, in canoes, for a shot. *See also* South America, Shooting in.

Japan

Japan consists of over a thousand islands, with a total area of more than 142,500 square miles, in the north Pacific Ocean. Four principal islands make up the bulk of the country; from north to south they are: Hokkaido, Honshu (the mainland), Shikoku and Kyushu.

The climate varies from cool temperate in northern Hokkaido to sub-tropical in the southernmost islands. Generally the Pacific coasts, warmed by the Japan current, are warmer than the western coasts, which in Hokkaido and Honshu are liable to frequent snowfalls. Rainfall is plentiful, lakes numerous, and the rivers are mostly short and swift-flowing.

The coastline is deeply indented, particularly on the Pacific shore, so that few places are far from the sea. A range of mountains, with numerous volcanoes, runs down the centre of the country, and the interior is generally extremely hilly (the highest point is Mount Fujiyama (12,390 ft), about 60 miles from Tokyo in Honshu). Extensive well-watered plains divide the mountains and form the main farming areas, though the terrain prevents more than a sixth of the country from being under cultivation. There is plenty of unspoilt country which can provide varied and strenuous sport.

A jaguar, photographed in the Matto Grosso, Brazil

Hunting in Japan is generally confined to the hilly and mountainous areas. Consequently the going is difficult, and a fair standard of fitness is called for, particularly if hunting copper pheasant or wild boar, both of which are usually hunted on steep hillsides. A minimum of 10 miles a day may well be necessary, and tough footwear is an essential.

Licences
There are three types of hunting licence: for nets and snares; for hunting firearms; for air guns. To obtain a licence a hunter must be over 20, and must attend an orientation course in the prefecture in which he intends to hunt. The fee (in yens) for the course is Y500, but the licence itself costs Y200 and is only granted after payment of a variable tax of about Y2,500. Moreover the licence is only valid for the prefecture in which it was issued, and the procedure has to be repeated by those who wish to hunt in more than one prefecture.

All those possessing or carrying guns must have a licence issued by the Public Safety Commission of the appropriate prefecture. Visitors importing guns, therefore, must leave them with the police chief at the point of entry, apply for a licence, and show it to the police chief in order to reclaim their guns. A permit is required to import explosives, so much the same procedure must be followed by those entering Japan with their own ammunition.

There are hunting areas which specialize

A Japanese green pheasant hen

Bag Limits—Japan	
Species	**Limit per day**
Birds:	
Asiatic goosander	
Bamboo partridge	5
Common snipe	10
Coot	5
Copper pheasant	2
Eastern bean goose	2
Green pheasant (cock only)	2
Hazel grouse	3
Jungle Crow	
Kamchatkan raven	
Korean ring-necked pheasant	2
Latham's snipe	10
Moorhen	5
Night heron	
Quail	10
Red-breasted merganser	
Rook	
Russet sparrow	
Smew	
Swinhoe's snipe	
Tree sparrow	
Turtle dove	10
White-fronted goose	2
Wild duck (except mandarin duck)	10
Woodcock	10
Mammals:	
Badger	
Chipmunk	
Deer (bucks only)	
Feral cat	
Feral dog	
Formosan squirrel	
Fox	
Giant flying squirrel	
Hare	
Japanese mink (males only)	
Marten	
Nutria	
Raccoon dog	
Wild boar	

Seasons—Japan	
Species	**Season**
Badger	Hokkaido:
Deer	15 Nov-31 Jan,
Fox	Honshu:
Giant flying squirrel	1 Dec-15 Feb
Japanese mink	
Marten	
Raccoon dog	
Squirrel	
All other species	Hokkaido: 1 Oct-15 Feb Honshu: 1 Nov-15 Feb

in providing specific game animals. The admission fees vary from ground to ground as do the bag limits, which are set by the management of each hunting ground and do not necessarily conform to those listed above. Whether shooting in a hunting ground or not, a guide is recommended. Guides may be hired simply by application to the office of the hunting ground. In other areas those needing a guide should either enquire at the office of the local hunting association, or the Japan Hunters' Association, who will recommend a good guide in the relevant locality.

Special Regulations

The following are prohibited:

The use of explosives, drugs, poisons, placed guns, dangerous traps, and dangerous snares.

Shooting before sunrise and after sunset or in a thickly populated area. Shooting towards a person, or cattle, houses, or any means of transportation, including trains, streetcars, ships, boats, aeroplanes, etc.

Hunting in a wildlife protection area, game reserve, public road, park, temple, shrine premises, or cemetery.

Further Information

Japan Hunters' Associations, 2 Kudan 3-chome, Chiyoda-ku, Tokyo.

Javan Rusa (*Cervus timorensis*)
A deer, related to the sambar, although smaller, inhabiting the islands of Timor, Java, Borneo and adjacent areas. A mature stag stands on average about 42 in at the shoulder and weighs between 150 and 200 lb. The hinds average about 38 in and weigh around 90 to 120 lb; both sexes have powerful legs.

Their seasonal coloration varies from reddish-brown in summer to a darker gray-brown in winter. Their tails grow to nearly a foot long and are thin and somewhat brush-like. The antlers are restricted to six points, but are longer, more slender and less rugged than those of the sambar, making an attractive trophy. Their gait and movements are similar to those of the hog deer – they run stiff-legged with their heads held close to the ground – making tunnels in thick undergrowth. They move extremely quickly and, like the sambar, they are entirely nocturnal in habit, feeding only at night, lying up very tight in fairly thick cover during the day.

Javan rusa are difficult to hunt; they are sometimes hunted with hounds; alternatively they may be driven, if the cover is suitable, although this is seldom easy; much must depend on the local terrain. The best method is probably still-hunting, although they are extremely hard to find and when disturbed, usually bolt for cover at high speed. Their venison is excellent.

Javelina *see* Collared Peccary

Jordan *see* Middle East

Jungle-fowl *(Gallus* species*)*
Jungle-fowl, having been domesticated in prehistoric times, became one of the ancestors of modern poultry. They are found in India, Ceylon, the East Indies, Indo-China, Malaya, the Philippines and Hainan, generally in bamboo jungle, forest or brush, though often in close proximity to cultivated land, for, though omnivorous – eating grass, leaves, buds, seeds, worms, grasshoppers, beetles and other insects – they are, by choice, graminivorous, and will feed in the open on stubbles or in cornfields, and have been known to come out of cover on to roads to pick grain from cattle droppings. In the autumn, when the corn has ripened and been harvested, they grow fat on the gleanings, and at that time their flesh is superior to that of the native domestic fowls; at other times there is little difference between them. They are the only pheasants to possess comb and wattles, and their tails are carried in a higher arch. The cock's fine feathers are replaced during a second moult.

They are extremely pugnacious birds, and where they are numerous, have regular fighting grounds where the cocks battle. Some species are gregarious, gathering in groups, and some, like the gray jungle-fowl, are solitary. They are wary birds, although living on the fringes of cultivated land, and it is almost impossible to approach them in cover. They can, however, quite easily be called, the cocks answering readily anyone successfully imitating their crow. They, themselves, not only crow at dawn and dusk, but will stand in the fighting ground and crow challenges.

They are thought to be polygamous, the nest is usually a hole scraped in dead leaves, and the clutch varies from three to six. Breeding occurs from about January to July. They all roost on trees at night, generally on the lower branches.

They may be shot in a variety of ways. When they can be found in small, detached clumps of jungle they may be driven out with beaters and dogs; they can be walked up, in the open, on stubbles and roads, with a dog; or be shot out of trees into which they will probably fly when alarmed. Inside cover, however, it is very difficult to come up with them, even with good dogs. Once shot over they are also difficult to approach in the open; they will run on in front until they think they are out of shot, and then rise, fly for several hundred yards, come down, and start running again. The natives sometimes call them by striking the thigh with the open hand, reproducing the sound of a cock flapping his wings in challenge.

Jungle-cock are best shot from October till the end of May, when in full breeding plumage. The first moult begins in June, and the second in September; by October full plumage is resumed. The following species of jungle-fowl are common:

Red jungle-fowl *(Gallus gallus)*
The long hackles covering the mantle and rump are orange-red before the summer moult, and black between that and the second moult in September. The comb and wattles are red, the sides of the face, chin and throat are naked, and there are long, sharp, curved spurs. Plumage colour varies from bird to bird. The hen has a red head, yellow neck and mantle with the rest of the upperparts reddish. Underparts are light red, browner on belly and flanks. The cock measures about 29 in overall, the hen about 16½ in. The red jungle-fowl is found in central and north-eastern India, south through the Malay Peninsula to Sumatra, and east through Siam to Indo-China. It is also found in the East Indies and the Philippines, but it is probable that they were introduced. All domestic fowl are said to descend from the red jungle-fowl, which was disseminated throughout most parts of the world as a fighting cock, in the first instance, and only secondarily as an ancestor of egg layers and meat producers. If domestic poultry, even now, are allowed to escape into jungle conditions they will, in a very few generations, develop a jungle-fowl appearance.

Ceylon jungle-fowl *(Gallus lafayetti)*
The adult male has golden-orange hackles with a black band down the middle, lower mantle, chest, breast and sides orange-red with a dark maroon stripe – the belly is black, mottled with chestnut. Length 30 in. The female resembles *G. gallus*, but the secondaries are black and chestnut, barred with buff, the chest and sides mottled black and buff, the breast white fringed and marked with black. Length is 17 in. It is found only in Ceylon.

Gray jungle-fowl *(Gallus sonnerati)*
The hackles of the male adult are black fringed with gray and with a yellowish spot at the ends. The lower back and underparts are black glossed with purple and edged with gray. Length 28 in. The hen resembles the *G. layfayetti* hen. It is found in western, southern, and central India.

Javan jungle-fowl *(Gallus varius)*
The adult male has an unserrated comb and a single wattle down the middle of the throat; the back of the neck and upper mantle are purplish blue, the lower mantle is golden-green shading into violet-bronze, the hackles of the lower back are long and black, margined with yellow; wing coverts are orange-red and underparts black; length 28 in. The female has a sandy-brown neck and upper mantle, with the rest of the upperparts black, slightly glossed with green and barred with buff. The underparts are buff, and the length is 15 in. It is found in Java, Lombok and Flores.

K

Kangaroos and Wallabies
(Macropodidae)

These are amongst the best known of Australian fauna. There are over forty known species, amongst which the largest and perhaps the best known of all is the red kangaroo, *Macropus rufus*. A mature 'red' can stand about 7 ft tall and weigh over 200 lb. It may clear 25 ft at a bound, leaping as high as 10 ft and attaining a speed of 30 m.p.h. When cornered it can defend itself formidably with its hind feet, rearing up on its large tail. Principally a browser, it is found on the plains, but other species are adapted to living in almost every habitat available in Australia. 'Roo coursing with dogs was once considered a typical outback sport in Australia, but due to the damage both wallabies and kangaroos do to both grazing and fences they were generally regarded as a pest rather than a sporting proposition. They used to be driven into large pens or similar culs-de-sac where they were shot or mercilessly clubbed. Due to public outcry this form of mass slaughter has now been banned and licences to shoot either kangaroos or wallabies are generally only issued to officially approved cullers, who travel from district to district. 'Roos are stalked with rifles and shot by these cullers and when the numbers are reduced the cullers move on to another area. Stalking can be a difficult proposition as the animals are alert and generally not easy to see, frequently closely resembling the stones amongst which they are often found. At the first sign of danger they will scatter and travel considerable distances before stopping. They are mostly protected.

A kangaroo in flight is a difficult target.

Kansas (U.S.A.)

A Great Plains state, there are no mountains but a plateau rises from the east towards the High Plains in the west. The soil is a rich loam of the highest agricultural value, and the state is a great wheat-growing area. It is sparsely wooded.

Kansas was once rich in big game, but was stripped of these by market hunters. Deer, antelope and turkey have been reintroduced, and there is now hunting, for residents only, for both white-tailed and mule deer. Pheasant and quail are the most plentiful game birds, and duck and geese are widely distributed, as are migrating woodcock and snipe. The Game Commission follows an aggressive policy of habitat restoration, lake construction, and game management, partly financed by the Upland Bird Stamp that all game bird hunters must buy.

Seasons and Limits—Kansas

Species	Season	Limit	Comment
Deer, white-tailed and mule	5 Dec-9 Dec or 13 Dec	One per season	Residents only, by special drawing
Rabbits, cottontail and jack	15 Dec-15 Oct	10 per day	
Squirrel, gray and fox	1 Aug-31 Dec		
Pheasant	13 Nov-Dec	2 cocks per day	
Prairie chicken	5 days in Nov	2 per day	Some areas only
Quail, scaled and bobwhite	20 Nov-Dec	8 per day	

Big game Inventory—Kansas		
Species	Shot	Est. pop
Deer	1,924	24,000

Big Game Inventory—Kentucky		
Species	Shot	Est. pop.
Deer	8,000	65,000

Licence Fees—Kansas		
Type	Status	Fee
General	Resident	$3
General	Non-resident	$15
Deer		$10

Further Information

Forestry, Fish and Game Commission, Box 1028, Pratt, Kansas 67124.

Kentucky (U.S.A.)

A central state, the east of which is mountainous, being crossed by the Alleghenies. The land here is poor and farming is more or less on a subsistence level. In the west is the famous 'bluegrass' country of fertile limestone. Here stock and bloodstock are reared. Principal farm crops are tobacco, cereals, maize and potatoes. Nearly half the state is wooded, and the climate tends towards extremes of heat and cold.

Licence Fees—Kentucky			
Type	Status	Fee	Comment
General	Resident	$4.25	On sale at county
General	Non-resident	$25.50	court houses,
Deer tags		$10.50	sporting-goods
			and hardware stores

Seasons and Limits—Kentucky			
Species	Season	Limit	Comment
Deer	14 Nov-18 Nov	one buck per season	Except in certain counties
Rabbit	19 Nov-21 Jan	8 per day	
Squirrel, gray and fox	15 Aug-21 Oct, and 19 Nov-31 Dec	6 per day	
Ruffed grouse	19 Nov-28 Feb	4 per day	
Bobwhite quail	19 Nov-21 Jan	10 per day	
Wild turkey	26 April-4 May	one bird	Only birds with visible beard
Red fox	18 Nov-31 Jan		
Gray fox	all year round		

Deer have been re-established most successfully, and are now hunted in most counties. Squirrel, fox, turkey, quail and ruffed grouse are all shot, grouse and turkey being subject to restocking programmes. Waterfowl are fairly plentiful on state and Federal water impoundments. Most of the national forest land, as well as land controlled by federal agencies, is managed for game production by the Department of Fish and Wildlife.

Special Regulations

Army M-1, .30 carbine prohibited for deer, as are full jacketed- and tracer-bullet ammunition.

Further Information

Department of Fish and Wildlife Resources, State Office Building Annex, Frankfort, Kentucky 40601.

Kenya

Lying across the equator, in east Africa, the country covers nearly 225,000 square miles, rising from the coastal plain to a broad, high plateau, of between 3,000 and 10,000 ft above sea level, which is cut by the Rift Valley. The climate is tropical in the coastal plain and warm-temperate in the highlands.

Only about 12% of the total land area is suitable for intensive farming, but this produces a wide range of crops, including tropical fruit and vegetables, wheat, coffee, cotton, coconuts, maize, sisal and sugar cane. Most of the remainder of the country is arid or semi-arid and at best suitable for stock raising although there are about 5,000 square miles under water (part of Lake Victoria lies within Kenya's boundaries in the south-west) and about 3,000 square miles of forest which yields valuable timber. Kenya encourages the tourist trade and as this is based, to a large extent, on the abundant and varied wildlife, the country has much to offer visiting hunters in terms of ample facilities and plentiful game.

Organization

There are several safari companies of varying size, offering a fair range of types of shooting. Typical average rates are about $100 per person per day upwards. This will not include alcoholic drinks, hire of guns, any licences or permits, transport of goods and trophies or air travel. The recommended duration of a safari is at least 30 days. There is in any case a minimum legal duration of safari for those wishing to shoot certain animals: at least 35 days for rhinoceros, and at least 28 days for elephant,

Masai lion and leopard if all three are to be shot. For any two of these three the minimum duration is 20 days, and for any one it is 15 days.

The maximum practical number of hunters on a safari is four as no more than two hunters are allowed in any hunting area at once. A party of four can camp on the dividing line between two hunting areas and two may hunt in each area. There must be at least one professional hunter for every two clients. Hunting areas may be reserved six months in advance, so arrangements for safaris should be made at least this much ahead so that the best areas may be reserved. Seasons are not of special importance. There is no particular breeding season, and the wet seasons, April and May, and November and December, are not excessively wet. The most popular season is January to March, though June to October is also good. The same seasons are good for birds, but some areas have close seasons that fall partly within these dates, so bird shooting must be arranged accordingly. In 1970 a Nairobi-based company was set up to conduct bird-shooting-only safaris, for which special blocks have been set aside.

Special Regulations

All shooting at night, or from a car, or within 200 yds of a vehicle is forbidden. The minimum permitted calibre for lion and eland is .375 magnum. The minimum permitted calibre for elephant, buffalo and rhino is .400 magnum.

Further Information

The Permanent Secretary, Ministry of Tourism and Wildlife, P.O. Box 30027, Nairobi.

Kenya, Shooting in

There is a great variety of shooting still available in Kenya although the diminishing species, such as sable and rhinoceros, are licensed under greater control and more expensively than in former years. Added to the wealth of available game, the Kenya sporting environment is further characterized by pleasant climate and superb light conditions, due to the situation of the country on the equator and the bulk of the land being at an altitude ranging generally from 3,000 to 9,000 ft, the exceptions being the coastal lowlands and Mt Kenya itself.

The sportsman cannot shoot anywhere in Kenya, with shotgun or rifle, without a licence. In all aspects, the Government Game Department is the first authority. In making arrangements to shoot, contact should be made first with the Chief Game Warden in Nairobi and with the local wardens of Districts the sportsmen may wish to visit, unless dealing with a professional 'Safari' company.

There are many varieties of game birds in Kenya. A considerable number of them sleep or nest on the ground, dusting themselves frequently, and so tend to be discoloured, their feathers stained by local soil conditions, particularly the red soils. Among the game birds available are francolin, spurfowl, snipe, pigeon, dove, sand-grouse, guinea fowl, button quail, bustard, teal and other duck and geese.

They are found all over Kenya. Most of them, notably the dove, sand-grouse, francolins and guinea fowl are in the dry areas characterized by the low scrub thorn trees or bush. Where this type of country merges with the open veldt it is the best bird cover in Kenya. Some of the pigeons, for instance

Game Licences—Kenya

Type	Fee (Kenyan shillings)	Limit	Comment
Birds	60		Covers species listed
Dove			
Duck			
Geese			
Francolin			
Guinea fowl			
Lesser bustard			
Partridge			
Pigeon			
Sand grouse			
Snipe			
Private—land			Covers species listed
Bushbuck	Depends on how many are to be shot		
Grant's gazelle			
Impala			
Thomson's gazelle			
Waterbuck			
Zebra (common or Burchell's)			
14-day	500		
Bohor reedbuck	40		
Coke's hartebeeste	100		
Dikdik	30		Covers species listed and the birds listed above
Grant's gazelle	40		
Grey duiker	60	One each	Individual fees for each animal shot are additional to the basic fee of 500 shillings
Oribi (all species)	40		
Steinbok	40		
Thomson's gazelle	40		
Warthog	40		
Wildebeeste	50		
General	1,500		
Bohor reedbuck	40		
Coke's hartebeeste	100		Covers species listed and the birds listed above ; valid for one year
Dikdik	30		
Grant's gazelle	40	2 of each	Individual fees for each animal shot are additional to the basic one of 1,500 shillings
Grey duiker	60		
Oribi (all species)	40		
Steinbok	40		
Thomson's gazelle	40		
Warthog	40		
Wildebeeste	50		

Type	Fee (Kenyan shillings)	Limit	Comment
Special	Fee in brackets represents additional cost for each animal shot		Only obtainable by holders of general licence. Only one special licence may be taken out for each species, except for those noted.
Bongo	500		
male	(1,000)		
female	(2,000)		
Buffalo	100 (200)		Four licences may be taken out
Bushbuk	30 (60)		Two licences may be taken out
Crocodile	75 (150)		Three licences may be taken out
Duiker, blue, red or Harvey's, Foster's or Hook's black-fronted	30 (60)		
Eland	200 (400)		
Gerenuk	250 (500)		
Hartebeeste, Coke's	50 (100)		
Impala	50 (100)		
Klipspringer	60 (120)		
Kudu, greater	500 (1,000)		
Kudu, lesser	200 (400)		
Leopard, male	1,000 (2,000)		
female	1,000 (4,000)		
Lion	300 (600)		
Masai lion	600 (1,200)		
Monkey, blue or Syke's	30 (60)		
Monkey, putty-nosed	50 (100)		
Monkey, red or patas	50 (100)		
Monkey, black and white colobus	120 (240)		
Oryx, fringe-eared and beisa	200 (400)		
Ostrich	100 (200)		
Reedbuck, Chandler's mountain	40 (80)		
Rhinoceros	2,500 (5,000)		
Suni	60 (120)		
Topi	180 (360)		
Waterbuck, common and defassa	50 (100)		
Zebra, common or Burchell's	50 (100)		Three licences may be taken out
Zebra, Grevy's	250 (500)		
Elephant	2,000 for each shot	2	Plus a variable charge based on tusk weight

he olive and the bronze-naped, are found in dense forest. Others, like the green pigeons, are usually in fruit-bearing trees in open parkland or by the rivers, particularly in riverine fig trees. The green pigeons are fine shooting because of their rapid flight.

Ducks and geese, of several species, are to be found in the reedy and muddy watery places, from ditch, rivulet and pond to the larger streams and great lakes in and near the Rift Valley. The underparts of the ducks often are stained a rusty brown from the vegetable and mineral matter of the water in which they have been circulating. The yellow-billed duck is the commonest of the surface feeders, swimming high in the water and, at night, flighting out to corn in season, similar to the European mallard. The white-faced tree duck is seen on Lake Rudolf from May until September, a slow, rather tame flyer and on land, standing upright. There are also many European migrant species. The several types of snipe, from the great to the jack, are usually found in swampy places. As in Europe, they are quick, twisty flyers. The jack is not easily flushed without a dog. The button-quail is usually in meadow grass or cultivated areas.

The flights of the Kenya game birds, as already suggested, are both like and unlike their counterparts in Europe. The yellow-necked spurfowl flies similarly to the European pheasant. Grant's francolin 'explodes' like the bobwhite quail ('One barrel for the bush; the second for the bird'). The olive (or rameron) and green pigeons are faster than the European wood pigeon. Geese flock in smaller skeins and tend more to fly individually than when in Europe. The birds in Kenya tend both to squat tighter and run further.

The best hours for shooting birds in Kenya are when they come out: from dawn to 9.30 a.m., and again between 4.00 p.m. and 6.00 p.m.

Due to the clear light, the range is deceptive. The bird is often farther away than the sportsman thinks it is. For a better chance of a shot, he should walk down-wind, since the birds in Kenya, as elsewhere, tend to rise into the wind.

With regard to the type of shotgun to use, anything less than a 20-bore does not give the sportsman much chance. A 28-bore would be all right for children. For general bird shooting, a double-barrelled 12-bore is probably the best; it is easy to obtain cartridges, and it has the required killing capacity. There are times when two guns are required; one gun may break down or get too hot, for instance in duck, pigeon or sand-grouse flighting. (There are virtually no trained loaders available.)

There are many ways of shooting. If in a party, perhaps an adaptation of the German 'riegler' system as practised in Germany and Austria is the best; that is, forming a circle and walking inwards. As most of the Kenya bird shooting is walking-up as opposed to driving or standing, fairly heavy shot is needed. Numbers four, five or six are ideal; and for snipe or sand-grouse, seven. To have a biddable dog is to have more fun and see more birds whether it be retriever, pointer, or indeed a dachshund. The real danger for dogs is from colobus monkey and baboon; and for both man and dog, from pigs, snakes and leopards.

When a shotgun is fired, anything may be put up from a rhino to a mouse. The civets, jennets, other small wild cats and hares, can all be killed with the same shot as used for

Firearms Permit—Kenya

When a safari booking is confirmed an application form for a firearms certificate will be sent to the visitor wishing to take his own firearms. A full range of firearms may be hired in Kenya. The applicant must state ; make, calibre and serial number of each weapon, and the quantity and calibre of ammunition. A maximum of five guns (no automatics or semi-automatics) and generous quantities of ammunition may be imported. Ammunition can be purchased in Kenya. The cost of the firearms permit is 20 Kenyan shillings

birds. On the other hand, for the unlikely arrival of bigger game, it is useful to carry some solid shot, such as 'Brenneker' bullets suitable for the gun in hand. If unable to get solid shot, use S.G.

The range of rifle shooting for big game is very great. The leopard, lion, buffalo and elephant are the most sporting and the most dangerous, none of them to be tackled by a beginner alone. It is also permitted to shoot zebra, eland, oryx, gazelle, kudu and bongo, gerunuk, kongoni, wildebeeste, impala, giraffe, rhinoceros, antbear, waterbuck, wild dog, hyena, hippopotamus, crocodile, warthog and forest hog.

Most of the big game has gone into shade and thick cover by 10.00 a.m. and stays there until about 4.00 p.m., although there are exceptions. Ordinarily they come out at night on to the grasslands to feed.

Guns are a matter of personal preference and confidence. An all-round rifle for use against most game is a .375, either double for

bush and heavy cover, or magazine for open country. For the largest game, a .450 or even, for elephant, a .475 is desirable. All should be express. For small antelope, a .280 is recommended.

Nowadays all game in the shooting areas is wary. This means the sportsman must move quietly (on crepe soles), make use of wind, have sharp eyesight, as well as take plenty of time and be thoroughly fit. He must be prepared to run 'like a stag' to outpace a moving herd of elephant, buffalo, zebra or smaller game. Buffalo, rhino, leopard, not necessarily lion, when in thick cover are very apt to charge on sight and go straight for the sportsman without any warning; usually such charges are not to be deflected. He must be prepared to shoot fast to kill. In this connection, it is as well to note here that sound has such peculiar echoes that if a gun stands still for some time after firing, he is likely to find game coming towards him having misinterpreted the direction of the shot.

Shots at distances of over 100 to 150 yd should be avoided. A useful motto is: shoot not to wound; long shots wound. It is a *sine qua non* that a wounded beast must be followed up and killed; if not it must be reported to the nearest game warden and the owner of the land.

Suitable clothing is particularly important. Camouflage is essential, as is moving quietly and slowly. Grass seed can be a bother, so wear knee-high boots, under trousers or shorts and a good shooting jacket. Cartridges carried in a belt make less noise; dark spectacles tend to be a disadvantage, a brimmed hat is preferable for protection against the glare of the sun. A good pair of small binoculars is useful. Another good motto is: the gun should move with the sun on his back and the wind in his face.

Protected species—Kenya

Aardvark
Aarwolf
Abbot's duiker
All albino animals
Bat-eared fox
Birds (except game birds and pest species)
Black leopard
Caracal
Cheetah
De Brazza's monkey
Dugong
Elephant with tusks less than 25 lb
Golden cat
Green marine turtle
Hartebeeste (except Coke's)
Hawk-billed turtle
Hippopotamus
Hirola or hunter's antelope
Hyrax
Mangabey
Otter
Pangolin
Potto
Red colobus monkey
Roan antelope
Sable antelope
Serval cat
Sitatunga
Thomas's Kob
Wild dog
Yellow-backed duiker
Zanzibar duiker

The lion is one of the classic African big-game animals which can still be hunted in Kenya.

A greater kudu bull. The males tend to be solitary animals.

The klipspringer is a small antelope found only in rocky hills and mountains in Africa.

Some of the African gunbearers are excellent for tracking, handling the second gun, local knowledge and ability to spot game which would be unfamiliar to the visitor. Practically every form of equipment, from gun, and clothing to a good white hunter – the latter not cheap – is obtainable in Nairobi. E

Klipspringer (Oreotragus oreotragus)

A small and active antelope with thick, brittle, golden flecked hair found in rocky hills and outcrops throughout southern and central Africa as far as Ethiopia in the north. They are known as the chamois of Africa and stand about 34 in with horns about 4 in long, 2 in round the base and with a spread of 3 in. They are usually found in pairs or threes and are browsers, though they may also graze a little. They require careful stalking, some active climbing and accurate shooting.

Kob see under Lechwe

Koorhaan see Bustards

Kudu (Tragelaphus species)

The greater kudu (T. strepsiceros) is found in most parts of Africa south of the Sahara. This large, handsome, dun-coloured antelope prefers thick thorny scrub or woodland, and avoids the open, though not averse to hilly ground. Both sexes are marked with narrow vertical white lines, but only the males have horns. The average height at the shoulder is 52 in and the length of the handsome spiralling horns averages 45 in, though generally larger in the south than in the north. It is principally a browser, but unlike many other antelopes the greater kudu drinks frequently and will generally be found within a few miles of water except during the rainy season. The female may give birth to a single calf in any month of the year. It has large ears, fully 10 in long, and relies on the acuteness of its hearing for protection. It prefers to escape by concealment rather than flight, thus it will stay within a few yards of the hunter when well concealed, rather than move. Hence it frequently requires a snap shot before it escapes into thick cover again; however, it does not need much lead to kill it, being thin skinned. It may require some weeks of hunting to secure a good kudu head.

The lesser kudu, Tragelaphus imberbis, is a smaller version of the greater kudu, standing no larger than a fallow deer. Its dorsal and flank stripes are more clearly defined and it is found chiefly in valleys or flat plains at the base of mountains, though invariably in thick cover. Its habitat is more restricted than that of the greater species. It has the most refined and high-bred head of all the African antelopes and a good trophy has its own intrinsic beauty, nor is it easily secured. It also generally requires a quick snap shot to catch it as it bounds for cover.

L

Labrador *see* Newfoundland

Lebanon *see* Middle East

Lechwe *(Kobus* species*)*
The lechwe *(K. leche)*, red lechwe, *K. leche leche*, and black lechwe, *K. leche smithemani*, are three closely related subspecies of water-loving antelopes found in many parts of central Africa. The lechwe stands about 3 ft at the shoulder, with black markings on the forelegs; the males have lyrate horns about 2 ft 6 in in length with a spread of about 20 in at the tips. The red lechwe has smaller horns and its fore-limb markings do not extend to the shoulder. The black lechwe is altogether smaller, with the males almost wholly black. The females of all are hornless. Their habitat is shallowly inundated flood plains and sometimes the near-by dry ground, where they are found usually in small herds of 10 but sometimes in herds of up to 100, often with the males separate from the females. They are grazers living mainly on flood plain grasses; have a single young annually, generally around July or August, and like the waterbuck they will take to water when chased or alarmed.

The Nile lechwe, *K. leucotis*, or white-eared kob, is a smaller, black-coated, white-eared species found in Ethiopia.

Leopard *(Panthera pardus)*
Distributed over a greater geographical area of the world than any other feline, the leopard is found throughout many parts of Africa and Asia as far as Java. They may vary considerably in size, but the average length of a male is just over 7 ft, including a tail of nearly 36 in, and an overall weight of 115 lb. The female is about 6 ft 4 in and weighs from 60 to 70 lb. They are extremely powerful for their size and expert climbers,

An aerial photograph, taken early in the morning, of the lechwe in the swamps near the Zambesi.

The leopard is a good climber and may sleep all day in a tree.

being first and foremost arboreal, although they are sometimes found in quite mountainous and comparatively treeless areas.

Their typical coloration is large black spots against a yellowish background. A black variety is found in the dark forests of southern India and is sometimes mistakenly called a black panther, although it is nothing more than a melanistic strain and the dark spots are still visible in good sunlight against the darker background. Solitary, and largely nocturnal in habit, the leopard will kill anything from deer or antelope to monkey and dogs, the two latter being considered their favourite diet, though much depends on the local conditions; they have also been known to turn to man-eating but this is, fortunately, exceptional. They either stalk their prey or lie in wait on a branch preparatory to springing down on it. They have the habit of hauling their kill or what is left of it, into a tree where it remains out of reach of jackals or hyenas awaiting their return. Unlike tigers (q.v.), they do not mind unduly if the kill is moved and this, when found, can often be taken to a more suitable place, with the reasonable hope that the leopard will return for it. However, a platform in a tree is no protection against leopards and indeed, may be a positive hindrance, so that it is better to make a hide, on the ground, in a suitable position. With a clear view of the bait or kill the hunter can wait down-wind behind the concealing hide for the leopard to appear. Apart from baiting, leopards may sometimes be shot when still-hunting for deer, or occasionally when driving other game. Such occasions however are rare and the hunter will generally have to take a snap shot. In some parts of Africa it is possible to hunt leopards with dogs, although well trained beasts, which will not press too far forward, but will follow the scent consistently, are necessary. The commonest method of hunting is by baiting. Whatever method is used it is advisable to make a clean kill because following a wounded leopard can be a hazardous proceeding. They are extremely bold and aggressive when wounded and when followed are liable to charge without warning. In these circumstances a dog to give warning of their presence is a considerable asset and the hunter must be ready to shoot as the leopard charges. The skin makes a good trophy.

Lion (Panthera leo)

Once common throughout Africa and Asia in 1800, by 1900 it was almost extinct in north and south Africa and Asia. Although a number of lions are maintained in India as a tourist attraction and are strictly protected, the only part of the world where they continue to flourish in the wild is in central Africa. The mature male measures around 9 ft from nose to tail and stands approximately 3 ft at the shoulder, with a large mane growing from the head, neck and shoulders and a conspicuous tuft on the end of the tail. Its average weight is 400 lb. The lioness is smaller and has no mane, standing about 2 ft 6 in and weighing about 300 lb. The coloration is a sandy-beige with considerable variation, particularly in the manes, some deepening to a near black.

They live in groups, known as prides, of from 3 or 5 to as many as 30, and hunt as a unit, living in a communal territory. Hunting is conducted as a group affair, the males generally driving their quarry in the required direction and a lioness frequently being the one to make the actual kill. The entire pride then take their share. Since they tend to kill the lame, or elderly of any species they fulfil an important ecological role, ridding the herds of their weaklings and ensuring that the antelopes and other animals on which they prey, breed from the strongest. The lioness will generally have from two to three cubs annually, although in captivity they are known to have double this number. They are entirely carnivorous, but do not eat a great deal, seldom killing wantonly; once they have made a kill they stay with it, until they have eaten their fill. They may cause considerable losses amongst domestic cattle and because they are quite common in some areas, and may even appear near large towns, there are times when they must be considered a pest and culled as such. There is little difficulty in stalking them. The greatest danger is in treating them too lightly. The modern tendency is to decry them as rather cowardly, rather than to regard them as the noble 'king of beasts', but the fact remains that they are extremely powerful, capable of felling an antelope with one blow of their paw. They are quite capable of charging a man and killing him. Anyone stalking them should remember that he only has his rifle between him and an animal, or several animals, which are capable of killing him without any difficulty. It should also be borne in mind that when one lion in a pride has been shot at and killed or wounded it is not unknown for another to charge the hunter. A heavy-calibre rifle is desirable and quite deliberate shooting, as with any quarry, essential. The skin makes a good trophy, but it is unlikely that the hunter will wish to have more than one.

Loading Tools see Firearms

Long-tailed Duck (Clangula hyemalis)

A small sea duck, found in many parts of the world, that breeds along the Arctic coasts of Europe, Asia and America, and winters in western and central Europe, the Middle East, the Caspian, Japan, the Great Lakes, south Greenland, North Carolina, and, occasionally, California.

It was given its American name of old squaw by the Cree Indians, because of the breed's incessant calling and chattering. They fly low, frequently in Indian file, over the sea and dive deep, often staying down for periods of one minute or more. Their diet consists mainly of molluscs, crustacea, worms and algae rather than fish, and makes their flesh inedible.

Courtship consists of calling, posturing and pursuit displays by several drakes. After selection the nest is built on a small island or the open tundra, and the average clutch of five to seven eggs takes 25 days to incubate, the drake remaining in attendance.

The drake weighs about one and a half to two pounds and measures between 19 and 22 in. The head is predominantly white and the body brown and white, with the central tail feathers elongated, like a pintail's. The feet and bill are black, the latter ending in a pink tip. The duck has no elongated tail feathers, shows more brown and less white than the drake, and has no pink tip to its bill. Migration south starts in October, and the return to the Arctic breeding grounds is in April.

Longtails are restless birds, rising frequently from the water, and they have a twisting habit of flight that makes them difficult to shoot. They come readily, however, to decoys, should anyone want to shoot them, in spite of their unpalatability.

Louisiana (U.S.A.)

A southern state, its 48,000 square miles consists mainly of the broad, marshy valleys of the Mississippi and Red Rivers, and over a third is taken up by the Mississippi Delta. Most of the coastline is marshy. In the rest of the state the soil is fertile, and sugar, rice, cotton, corn and fruit are grown. The climate is sub-tropical in the lowlands.

Both deer and bear hunting are being improved but the state is primarily famous for its waterfowl. It lies at the end of the Mississippi Flyway, and ducks and geese of many species winter on its marshes and bayous. Turkeys are abundant in the forests, and squirrels, rabbits, quail and doves are shot on the more open lands. It is a favourite wintering ground for woodcock.

Further Information

Wildlife and Fisheries Commission, Wildlife and Fisheries Building, 3400 Royal Street, New Orleans, Louisiana.

Lynx *(Felis lynx)*

This cat is found throughout the forests of North America, Europe and Asia. The Canadian lynx is sometimes regarded as a separate species from the Eurasian lynx, but it is more correct to consider them both as the same. They have a yellowy, brown spotted fur and measure 36 in from the tip of the nose to the end of the short 6 in tail. They have long black ear tufts and two obvious throat tassels, which move when

The European lynx

they hiss with anger. Generally solitary and nocturnal, they prey chiefly on chipmunks, rabbits, rats, mice and hares, but they will also hunt small deer. In deep snow conditions they have been known to attack and kill large prey such as reindeer or moose. The vividly spotted Spanish lynx, *F. lynx pardina*, is now exceedingly rare and is rightly protected.

The lynx is not generally regarded as a sporting animal and is seldom hunted. It is only likely to be encountered and shot when still-hunting in North America or Asia or parts of Scandinavia (the annual bag in Sweden is 40). *See also* Bobcat.

Licence Fees—Louisiana

Type	Status	Fee
General	Resident	$2
General	Non-resident	$25
Deer tag		$2
Turkey tag		$2

Big Game Inventory—Louisiana

Species	Shot	Est. pop.
Deer	38,000	275,000
Wild turkey	350	6,500

Seasons and Limits—Louisiana

Species	Season	Limit	Comment
Deer	Varies between 7 Nov-10 Jan	1 per day, 5 per year	Generally bucks only
Rabbit	3 Oct-28 Feb	8 per day	
Squirrel, gray and fox	3 Oct-10 Jan	8 per day	
Bobwhite quail	26 Nov-28 Feb	10 per day	
Wild turkey	27 March-18 April and autumn season	2 per year	

M

Maine (U.S.A.)

The most north-easterly of the eastern states, it has an area of 33,000 square miles. Much of the north is hilly and unsuitable for farming, and most of it is given over to forests. In the valleys and in the south, however, farming is carried on, and Maine is the largest potato-growing state in the Union. There are about 17 million acres of productive forests, and together with fishing and tourism, lumbering is an important industry.

Most of northern Maine is owned by large lumber companies, and they generally open their lands to hunting, many of them only accessible by air or water. Deer, often very large, and black bear are plentiful, especially in the north; there are a few moose, which are protected, and game birds consist of ruffed and spruce grouse. Waterfowl and woodcock are plentiful, and there is good early-season duck shooting, especially of black duck.

Further Information
Department of Inland Fisheries and Game, State House, Augusta, Maine 04330.

Malaysia

Malaysia is a south-east Asian federation of about 128,000 square miles, divided into two distinct parts. West Malaysia consists of the former Federation of Malaya, lying at the southern end of the Malay peninsula. East Malaysia is made up of Sarawak and Sabah (North Borneo) in the north-east of the island of Borneo, East and West Malaysia are separated from each other by about 400 miles of the South China Sea. Both parts have hilly interiors, and about three quarters of the Federation is covered by equatorial rain forest, as yet undeveloped. The whole region is open to maritime influences and the wind systems that originate in the Indian Ocean and the South China Sea, and the year is commonly divided into the south-west and north-west monsoon seasons. Rainfall averages 100 in per year, but can vary considerably from place to place and year to year. The average temperature varies between 70° and 90° F.

Malaysia is essentially an agricultural country, and is the world's leading exporter of natural rubber, palm oil and tin. Shooting is controlled by an act of 1955, which only applies to West Malaysia. Regulations in East Malaysia are best established on the spot. Both parts of the Federation provide large areas of untouched rain forest, with associated game and shooting conditions, as well as much more open country in the hills of the interior.

Licence Fees—Maine

Type	Status	Fee
Hunting/Fishing	Resident	$7.75
Hunting/Fishing	Non-resident	$33.25

Seasons and Limits—Maine

Species	Season	Limit
Deer	15 Oct-28 Nov in the north, 1 Nov-30 Nov in the south	1 per year
Black bear	1 June-31 Dec	
Cottontail rabbit	1 Oct-31 March	4 per day
Snowshoe hare	1 Oct-31 March	4 per day
Gray squirrel	1 Oct-30 Nov	
Pheasant	1 Oct-30 Nov	2 per day
Grouse, ruffed and spruce	1 Oct-15 Nov	4 per day

Big Game Inventory—Maine

Species	Shot	Est.pop.
Deer	41,000	230,000
Black bear	2,000	10,000

Game Licences—Malaysia

Type	Issued by	Comment
Big game Covers banteng, bear, elephant and gaur	The Mentri Besar in a state or resident commissioner in a settlement	Applicant must produce a firearm with 12-bore minimum calibre or .350 for high-velocity rifles. Further information may be obtained from state game wardens.
Deer Covers sambar or ruga, barking deer, mouse deer, serow	State or settlement game warden	Licence must be returned to issuing officer before fourteenth day after expiry
Mouse deer	State or settlement game warden	
Game bird See game list	State or settlement game warden	
Reserved mammals See reserved list	State game warden	Each state draws up its own list and establishes its own conditions and fees for the grant of licences.

Any mammal not classified as protected, reserved, big game, or deer may be shot or taken at any time.

Certain birds are classified as 'neither game birds nor totally protected birds', and may be shot if an open season is proclaimed for them. Included among them are common pests, such as sparrows, finches and munias, and certain birds of prey. Any bird not so classified and not a game bird is fully protected.

Firearms regulations

Overseas hunters are advised to bring their own guns for hunting as licences for local purchase are not easily obtained.

Firearms permits for certain guns are compulsory; details and conditions of issue are variable, and should be established on the spot.

To obtain a big-game licence it is necessary to produce a firearm with a 12-bore minimum calibre or .350 for high velocity rifles.

Special Regulations

In Game Reserves no animal or bird may be shot or taken without the written permission of the game warden in addition to any other licence required. In a sanctuary no shooting whatsoever is permitted.

Dangerous traps, poison, birdlime, and wire snares, except on cultivated land, are illegal, as is the use of any artificial light or torch for hunting anything except tiger, leopard (or panther), and crocodile. Deer, other big game and game birds may not be shot at night, and game birds may only be shot; they may not be trapped, netted or decoyed. No animal or bird may be shot or taken within a quarter of a mile of a saltlick.

Further Information

The Chief Game Warden, Game Department, 202, Jalan Temiang, Seremban, Negeri Sembilan, Malaysia.

Ministry of Information, 'Angkasapuri', Bukit Putra, Kuala Lumpur.

Mallard (*Anas platyrynchos*)

Probably the best known, the most widely distributed, and the most commonly shot duck in the world, the mallard is the ancestor of the domestic duck, and will often attach itself to tame ducks on ornamental waters. It breeds in northern Europe, Asia and America, over a very wide territory south of the Arctic Circle. Frequently it remains, as a resident or partial migrant, inside its nesting range. Sometimes it will migrate to as far south as the Nile Valley, India or Mexico. In Britain it is, at once, a resident, a passage migrant, and a wintering visitor.

A surface-feeding duck, it is a bird of fresh rather than salt water, and is most frequently found on ponds, streams, marshes and estuaries. It is largely vegetarian, but will, on occasion, eat almost anything from

---

Principal Game Species—Malaysia

Mammals

Banteng
Barking deer
Bear
Elephant
Gaur
Mouse deer
Sambar
Serow

Birds

All gallinacious birds (including peafowl, jungle fowl, and local pheasants, partridges and quails)
Coots, rails and crakes
All wild ducks, (especially teal and shovellers)
All wild doves and pigeons
All hornbills
All snipe, sandpipers, plovers and waders

Protected and Reserved Mammals—Malaysia

Protected:

Binturong (bear cat)
Gibbon
Pangolin (scaly anteater)
Rhinoceros, Javan and Sumatran
Slow loris
Tapir

Reserved

Varies from state to state. Principal mammals include:
Cat (4 species)
Civet (4 species)
Leopard
Mongoose (4 species)
Monkey (5 species)
Otter (3 species)
Pig (2 species)
Porcupine (3 species)
Squirrel (2 species) and flying squirrel (5 species)
Tiger

Game Seasons—Malaysia

Vary from state to state; alternative dates in table refer to seasons in different states

Species	Season
Big game	1 Jan or 2 Jan-31 Dec
Deer	1 Sept-31 Dec
Mouse deer	1 Jan-31 Aug or 1 May-31 Dec
Reserved mammals	1 Jan or 2 Jan-31 Dec
Jungle-fowl	1 July-31 Dec or 1 Aug-30 April
Malay turtle dove and small ground dove	1 Jan-31 March or 1 Aug-30 April
Pigeon	1 Sept-31 Dec or 1 June-30 Oct or 15 Aug-30 Nov
Sandpipers, plovers and waders	Varies between 1 July and 30 April
Snipe	1 Jan-31 Dec or 1 Aug-31 Dec or 15 Sept-30 April
Teal	Varies between 1 April and 31 Dec
Waterfowl	1 May-30 Aug or variable between Aug and April
Other game birds	1 July-31 Dec or variable between 1 Aug and 30 April

---

a frog to an acorn. It flights in to feed at dusk and rests by day, usually on open water. It is a fast and enduring flyer, averaging speeds over 50 m.p.h. during migration flights. It can jump straight up off the water and into immediate flight. The duck has a loud and frequent 'quack', the drake a quiet 'yeeb'. Average weight for both sexes is around $2\frac{1}{2}$ lb and average length of males is 23 in. It is not unknown for interbreeding to take place between it and gadwall, widgeon, pintail or black duck.

In full winter-plumage the drake has a stocking of dark, lustrous green, ending in a thin white collar. The breast is purplish-brown, the underparts are vermiculated gray and white, and the back is brown, also vermiculated. The tail coverts are black, the four central feathers curling upwards and twisting. The tail is white, the wings are gray, and the speculum, in both sexes, is violet-purple with black edges bordered thinly by white. The feet and legs are orange. During the eclipse moult the drake loses most of his colour and closely resembles the duck, which has plain, mottled, brown and buff plumage. His bill, however, remains yellow-olive rather than becoming orange, like the duck's.

Courtship consists of swimming and plumage displays, and of flight pursuit by several drakes at once. After selection the nest is built, generally close to water. It normally consists of a scrape in the ground lined with grass and down. The clutch of 8 to 12 eggs takes 26 to 28 days to incubate, the drake deserting the duck as soon as incubation starts in order to join other drakes and prepare for the eclipse moult. The ducklings can usually fly within 10 weeks, and plumage differentiation starts in autumn, though the young drake will not assume full winter plumage until the second winter. On many modern shooting estates much is done, by providing artificial nests and nesting sites, or by the hatching and hand rearing of ducklings, to improve the local mallard population.

Mallard can be shot off the stubbles just after harvest, they can be flighted, they can be shot over decoys, they can be jump shot off a stream or river. They are always interesting birds both to breed and shoot. They are excellent eating. *See also* Flighting Ponds for Duck; Hides and Decoys; Wildfowl and Wet Gravel Pits.

Manitoba (Canada)

This, the most easterly of the three great Prairie Provinces, covers some 251,000 square miles, but some 40,000 square miles of these are water, as the province contains many large, shallow lakes, such as Manitoba, Winnipeg and Winnipegosis. These are remnants of a large Ice Age lake, which partially dried up, leaving silts and a black, largely vegetable soil of great fertility. On this soil, the great wheat farms of Manitoba have been developed. In the southern part of the province, 17 million acres are farmed. The northern parts of the province, however, are less fertile. They are largely covered with forest. There are over 37 million acres of woodland in the province, and lumbering and mining are the chief industries in the north.

The province is fairly rich in game, though deer are the only big game present in abundance. The annual deer harvest exceeds 10,000, principally white-tailed deer, though mule deer are found in the west, especially in the Duck Mountain area. Moose are found in the north of the province, though they are scarcer there than deer are in the south; caribou and elk are even scarcer. The upland game birds consist almost entirely of grouse and partridge, but, like the other Prairie Provinces, Manitoba, with its many lakes, sloughs and potholes, is the nesting ground for a great number of ducks, as well as being in the flight-path of the migrations to and from the more northerly nesting grounds.

Licences

A Wildlife Certificate, which costs $2.25, is needed, in addition to the correct Game Licence, before either big game or game birds may be hunted. Funds from the sale of these certificates are used to improve hunting facilties, by land acquisition, the planting of game food crops and so on. All residents applying for game or game-bird licences must either have held a similar licence previously, or else must have passed a Manitoba Hunter and Firearm Safety Training Course. It is advised that non-residents obtain all the licences required before arriving in the province. This can be done by applying to Room 1003, Norquay Buildings, Winnipeg. Licences can also be obtained at most ports of entry, and from various sports shops in the province.

Waterfowl Inventory—Manitoba		
Species	Total shot	Per cent
Duck	295,682	
Mallard		50
Pintail		9
Green-winged teal		8
Lesser scaup		8
American widgeon		7
Others		18
Geese	20,062	
Canada		45
White-fronted		41
Lesser snow		13
Others		1

Snow geese, seen here in their white and blue phases, are one of the many species of waterfowl which may be hunted in Manitoba and other parts of North America.

Seasons and Bag Limits—Manitoba

The province is divided into 36 Game Hunting Areas. The seasons and limits vary from area to area and from year to year. The dates given are for the 1971 season.

Big Game

Moose

There is a 'bulls only' season in the northern and central-western areas. The season at its longest (in the northern areas) is 8 September to 27 November. In the western areas it starts 20 September, and in some areas finishes 20 October. The 'any moose' season, in much the same areas, is 29 November to 18 December, but in one eastern area is 20 September to 22 January. Limits : 'bulls only' season, one bull over a year old ; 'any moose' season, one of any age or sex.

Woodland caribou

In the north and north-east the season is 20 September to 18 December. Further south, in predominantly eastern areas, the dates are the same but there is a gap in the middle of the season for most of November. There is a long season for woodland caribou in an eastern area. Limit : one caribou of any age or sex. Barren ground caribou have extended their range eastwards, but because of their importance to the Indians of the north no open season has been declared.

Deer

The season is 26 October to 28 November, or within those dates, in most areas. Two north-central and one south-eastern area have no open season. In some western areas the season is 18 September to 21 October and there is a late season for residents only in early December. Limits : non-residents, one male over a year old ; residents, one of any age or sex.

Elk

May be shot by residents only, in two areas on the western border, towards the south of the province. In one area there is a September/October season and a December season, and in the other area the season is December to February.

Black bear

The fall season is early September to the end of October in the north ; from mid-September to the end of October in the west ; in three other areas the long fall season is mid-September to the end of November. The spring season is 1 May to 28 June north of the 53rd parallel and 1 May to 24 June south of this parallel. Limits : two of any age or sex in the fall season and two adults, excluding females with cubs, in the spring season.

Game Birds

Grouse

The season starts 3, 6 or 17 September (the further south the later), and ends 27 November except in some central areas, where it ends on 18 December. Limit : 6 per day, 18 in possession.

Partridge

The season starts mid-September in the centre-west and late September in the south-west, and ends 28 November. Limit : 2 per day, 6 in possession.

Ptarmigan

In the north, 3 September to 12 February, and in the west, 6 September to 12 February. Limit : 10 per day, 30 in possession.

Sandhill crane

May only be shot in two special areas in the south-west, with boundaries quite distinct from the normal areas. The season is 1 September to 14 September. Limit : 4 per day, 8 in possession.

Waterfowl

The seasons for duck, geese, coot, rail and snipe are : north of the 57th parallel, 1 September to 28 October ; between the 53rd and 57th parallels, 7 September to 5 December ; south of the 53rd parallel, 21 September to 5 December, but 28 September to 5 December for geese. Limits for duck : 8 per day, 16 in possession, of which not more than 1 per day and 2 in possession may be canvasback or redhead, and not more than 5 per day and 10 in possession may be mallard. After 10 October, 2 additional scaup or goldeneye may be taken daily, increased to 4 after 12 October. Limits for geese : 5 per day, 10 in possession, of which not more than 3 per day or 6 in possession may be white-fronted geese. Limits for coot and rail : 8 per day, 16 in possession, except for Indians, Eskimos, professional trappers and hunters who may take up to 25 per day, with no limit on the numbers in possession. Limit for Wilson's snipe : 10 per day, 20 in possession.

Special Regulations

All big game hunters in Manitoba are required to wear a complete outer suit of white extending to below the knee, together with a cap or hat in blaze orange. A belt of the same colour may also be worn. Those only hunting game birds are advised to wear a blaze orange cap. No loaded firearm may be carried in, or discharged from, any power boat, vehicle or aircraft. No shotgun larger than a 10-bore or with a magazine that has not been plugged so as to be incapable of carrying more than two cartridges may be used. No game may be hunted on Sundays or between the times of half an hour after sunset and half an hour before sunrise. No big game may be hunted with a rifle using rim fire cartridges, or metal cased, hard point cartridges. No dogs may be used when hunting big game. No power boats may be used in a marsh frequented by game birds except on channels designated for the purpose. Live decoys and baiting are illegal.

Big Game Inventory—Maryland	
Species	**Shot**
Deer	7,309
Turkey	306

Noted particularly for its waterfowl, Maryland also has opportunities for hunting white-tailed deer.

Further Information

Field Administration, Department of Mines, Resources and Environmental Management, Box 18, 138 Tuxedo Building, Winnipeg 29, Man.

Manitoba Wildlife Federation, 1770 Notre Dame Avenue, Winnipeg 21, Man.

Director of Western Region, Department of Mines etc, 120 1st Avenue N.E., Dauphin, Man.

Director of Northern Region, Department of Mines etc, Box 990, The Pas, Man.

Marmot *see* Woodchuck

Marsh Rabbit *see under* Cottontail and other American Rabbits

Maryland (U.S.A.)

A small, maritime state, its 12,000 square miles are mostly made up of a fertile coastal plain, but there is a narrow extension westwards to the Appalachian Mountains. The climate is moderate in winter and hot in summer, and about one third of the area is farmed. Wheat, maize, and potatoes are the chief crops and there is a considerable amount of stock rearing.

Maryland is primarily famous as a major wintering ground for waterfowl. Canada geese are to be found in great numbers on the Eastern Shore, and Chesapeake Bay is famous for its mallard, black duck and canvasbacks. In the mountainous, western areas there is good grouse and turkey hunting, and in the east there are quail. Deer have become so well re-established that two deer limits are now sometimes possible and antlerless beasts may be shot. The chief drawback to hunting in the state is the amount of posting that has been done, and the number of private clubs that have taken the best waterfowl hunting sites. State forests and some state parks are open to public hunting, and the Fish and Wildlife Administration owns 45,000 acres of hunting grounds, managed for waterfowl in the east and for deer and turkey in the west.

Special Regulations

It is illegal to use any gun on deer except one propelling an all lead, lead alloy, soft-nosed, expanding bullet, ball, or one using cartridges giving a muzzle energy below 1,200 foot pounds.

Further Information

Department of Game and Inland Fish, State Office Building, Annapolis, Maryland 21401.

Massachusetts (U.S.A.)

A small, New England state, of 8,000 square miles which has a temperate climate, but the winters are long and cold. There are over 2 million acres of farmlands and over 3 million acres of forests.

Licence Fees—Manitoba

Type	Status	Fee	Comment
Moose	Resident	$16.00	
	Non-resident Canada	$20.00	
	Non-resident alien	$100.00	This licence includes tags for one male deer over one year old and 2 adult black bears. Must be used by non-resident aliens when hunting deer or bear in moose areas during moose open season.
Woodland caribou	Resident	$20.00	Limited number for each area, often balloted for
	All non-residents	$100.000	
Deer	Resident	$6.00	
	Non-resident Canadian	$25.00	
	Non-resident alien	$40.00	See above for hunting deer in moose areas
Elk	Resident	$20.00	Residents only
Black bear	Resident	$5.00	
	All non-residents	$15.00	See above for hunting bear in moose areas
Game bird	Resident	$2.25	
	Non-resident Canadian	$5.00	
	Non-resident alien	$35.00	
Canada Migratory Game Bird Hunting permit (for waterfowl)		$2.00	Require for hunting waterfowl **in addition** to game bird licence. Obtainable from post offices, or the Postmaster, Winnipeg, 266 Graham Avenue, Winnipeg 1, Manitoba.

Seasons and Limits—Maryland

Species	Season	Limit	Comment
Deer	15 Sept-27 Nov	one per year	Either sex
	28 Nov-5 Dec		Bucks only
Antlerless deer	Usually follows bucks only season		
Rabbit and hare	30 Oct-20 Feb	4 per day	
Pheasant	30 Oct-13 Feb	2 cocks per day	
Ruffed grouse	10 Oct-31 Dec		
Bobwhite quail	30 Oct-20 Feb	6 per day	
Turkey	10 Oct-25 Oct spring season varies	1 per season	

Although small, highly industrialized, thickly populated, and subject to urban sprawl, Massachusetts still provides varied sport, with deer in fair numbers and waterfowl, woodcock, pheasant, quail and rabbits in many areas. Mourning doves, which are plentiful, are protected.

Big Game Inventory—Massachusetts		
Species	Shot	Est.pop.
Deer	1,427	12,000

Special Regulations
Deer and bear hunters may use only shotguns loaded with buckshot or rifled slugs. During the open season for deer, all hunters must wear red or yellow on head, back or shoulders. Rifled extension tubes may not be used on shotguns when deer hunting.

Further Information
Division of Fisheries and Game, 100 Cambridge Street, Boston, Massachusetts 02202.

Mexico

Mexico is a country of some 760,000 square miles. Most of the country consists of a central plateau, of between 3,000 and 8,000 ft (higher in the south), contained between two mountain ranges, the Sierra Madre Oriental and the Sierra Madre Occidental. These ranges converge towards the south where the plateau is crossed, on an east-west axis, by a range of volcanic mountains, just north of the isthmus of Tehuantepec. Both ranges of the Sierra Madre are separated from the sea by low-lying coastal plains. Not included in this general pattern is the peninsula of Lower California, narrow, semi-arid and mountainous, which runs parallel to the north-west coast, and the peninsula of Yucatan in the south-east, which is low-lying jungle country. The rivers are mostly steep, short, and unimportant, with the notable exception of the Rio Grande del Norte which runs east along the northern border.

The climate varies with the altitude. The areas under 2,000 ft are very hot; most of the central plateau, between 2,000 and 6,000 ft, is milder; and any area above 6,000 ft is quite cool. Rainfall is very light in most of northern Mexico, heavier but erratic in the south of the central plateau, and abundant in the coastal areas and the south.

Though now being rapidly industrialized, Mexico has always been primarily an agricultural and mining country, and over half the population is still engaged in farming, forestry or fishing. The climate range means that a wide variety of crops can be grown, with wheat and maize the staple food, and sisal, coffee, sugar and fruit important for export. Ranching is common in the more arid parts of the north, and a great many cattle are reared and exported.

In most of the more popular hunting areas

Licence Fees—Maryland			
Type	Status	Fee	Comment
General	Resident	$6.50	Sold by the clerk of the
General	Non-resident	$25.00	court in each county.
Deer tag		$5.50	
Deer tag		$5.50	

Licence Fees—Massachusetts			
Type	Status	Fee	Comment
Hunting/Fishing	Resident	$8.25	Sold by city and
Hunting/Fishing	Non-resident	$16.25	town clerks

Seasons and Limits—Massachusetts			
Species	Season	Limit	Comment
Deer	7 Dec-12 Dec	One per year, either sex	Special drawings for antlerless permits
Black bear	16 Nov-21 Nov	One	Scarce
Rabbit	20 Oct-Feb		
Hare	20 Oct-Feb		
Squirrel	20 Oct-30 Nov		
Pheasant	20 Oct-30 Nov	2 cocks per day, 6 per year	
Quail	20 Oct-30 Nov	5 per day, 25 per year	
Ruffed grouse	10 Oct-2 Jan	3 per day, 15 per year	

The redhead, or American pochard, shot in Mexico, is easily decoyed.

guides, guns and jeeps may be hired by the day for a fee of about $35 per day ($25 per person for parties of two or more). Longer safaris may be arranged for small parties. They usually last from five to thirty days and cost between $30 and $50 per day.

Game and Seasons
These are not the same throughout Mexico. There are 29 states, two territories and a federal district, and each has its own laws and seasons. While in general it may be said that the season runs from the early fall to the middle or end of winter, organization of hunting is very vague and no clear guidelines can be given. The table lists the chief species shot:

Most of the listed species are to be found in at least north and central Mexico, if not throughout the country, but alligator, tapir, brocket deer, western bobwhite, oceloted

Principal Game Species— Mexico

Alligator
Armadillo
Baldpate
Band-tailed pigeon
Black bear
Black-tailed deer
Blue-winged teal
Brocket deer
Bufflehead
California quail
Canada goose
Chachalaca
Cinnamon teal
Collared pecary
Coyote
Crane
Desert bighorn
Dwarf jungle deer
Fox
Gadwall
Gambel's quail
Green-winged teal
Hare
Harlequin quail
Jaguar
Jaguarondi
Mallard
Mexican wild turkey
Mountain lion
Mourning dove
Mule deer
Ocellated turkey
Ocelot
Parrot
Partridge
Pintail
Pronghorn
Rabbit
Raccoon
Redhead
Ring-necked duck
Ruddy duck
Scaled quail
Scaup
Shoveller
Snipe
Spotted wood quail
Tapir
Tinamou
Tree quail
Upland plover
Western bobwhite quail
White-fronted goose
White-tailed deer
White-winged dove
Yellow-legged plover

turkey and parrot are found only in the south. However, the hunting regulations are such that a species may well be shot all-year in one state, and not at all in a neighbouring state. Nevertheless, as the variety of the species indicates, Mexico has a lot to offer to the hunter. Mexicans themselves do not hunt very much, and most Americans tend to go north for their hunting, to Canada, rather than south. Consequently, despite the proximity to the United States hunting pressures are still slight (which is one reason for the state of the game laws) and the country is relatively unknown and unexploited as a hunting territory.

Licences

Visitors may import two guns of any make or type, except Mauser 7mm rifles and Colt .45 automatics, together with 100 rounds per gun. However the procedure for doing so is not simple. A reference must be obtained from the local police department, magistrate, sheriff or similar authority, and must be sent to the nearest Mexican consulate together with eight passport photos, one signed across the front, and details of the brand name, calibre, and serial number of the gun. The consul will notarize and return the reference for a fee of $16. On entering Mexico the guns will have to be left with the customs while the notarized reference is presented to the commander of the local garrison of the Defence Ministry, who will issue and stamp a firearms permit, which will automatically authorize clearance of the gun or guns from customs. For the casual hunter it will probably be easier to hire guns on the spot. In any case a hunting licence is necessary. It may be obtained from an office of the Federal Department of Agriculture (there is one in most major cities and border towns). Visitors will be required to produce identification, their tourist card (which they must have to enter the country), and two passport-size photos. The fees vary depending on how long the licence is valid and how wide an area it covers, but a typical six-month licence for one region will cost about $20.

Further Information

The best source in the individual states is: Dirección General de la Fauna Silvestre in the state capital of the proposed hunting region.

Sr. Director de la Fauna Silvestre, Sub-Secretaria Forestal y de la Fauna, Aquiles Serdan 28, Mexico 1, D.F.

Michigan (U.S.A.)

The state consists, essentially, of two peninsulas protruding into Lakes Huron, Michigan and Superior. A fifth of the land in the state is national or state forest, park, game area, or otherwise state or federal owned and, as such, open to the public for hunting. Under the 'Williamson Plan' for farmer-hunter co-operation, large areas of private land are also open, without fee, for hunting. In the Lower Peninsula the game normally associated with farming – pheasant, quail, rabbit – is hunted. The Upper Peninsula has the largest deer population (Michigan has one of the largest deer herds in the country) and all the bears, most of the snowshoe hare, and most of the grouse. Wild turkey are increasing in the Upper Peninsula sufficiently for there to be a spring, if not an autumn, season. Waterfowl hunting depends very largely, on the annual migrations, and so reflects, fairly accurately, conditions on the nesting grounds.

Mexican partridges

Licence Fees—Michigan

Type	Status	Fee	Comment
Deer	Resident	$5.10	Sold by county
	Non-resident	$35.10	clerks, sporting-
Bear	Resident	$5.10	goods and hard-
	Non-resident	$35.10	ware stores
Small game	Resident	$3.10	
	Non-resident	$2.00	

Seasons and Limits—Michigan

These vary from zone to zone

Species	Season	Limit	Comment
Deer	15 Nov-30 Nov	One buck per season	Antlerless permits by special drawings
Black bear	10 Sept-14 Sept	One per year	Upper Peninsula only, bear licence required
	15 Nov-30 Nov		Deer licence sufficient
Cottontail rabbit	1 Oct-31 March	5 per day	
Snowshoe hare	1 Oct-1 April		All zones
Squirrel, gray and fox	15 Sept-10 Nov		
Pheasant	1 Oct or 20 Oct-10 Nov	2 per day	
Ruffed grouse	15 Sept-31 Dec	5 per day	
Sharp-tailed grouse	1 Oct-15 Oct		Zone 1 only
Bobwhite quail	1 Nov-20 Nov		Southern counties only
Wild turkey	announced later		

Special Regulations

During the deer season it is illegal to carry a rifle larger than a .22 rimfire, or a shotgun with buckshot or slugs, unless one holds a deer licence. In the Upper Peninsula .22 rimfire rifles may not be used for deer, and dogs are forbidden, state-wide, when deer hunting.

Big Game Inventory—Michigan

Species	Shot	Est.pop.
Deer	100,000	600,000
Black bear	835	8,000
Wild turkey	160	3,700

Further Information

Division of Fish and Game, Department of Conservation, Lansing, Michigan 48926.

Middle East

The Middle East may be regarded as those countries on the eastern and south-eastern edge of the Mediterranean, the United Republic of Egypt, the Lebanon, Syria, Jordan, and Iraq beyond, and those down the Arabian peninsula, of which the largest are Saudi Arabia, Muscat and Oman, Yemen and Aden. The whole area is distinguished by its aridity and the desert or semi-desert nature of the terrain. The only important exceptions are the areas lying along the valley of the Nile and the lower Euphrates, the Egyptian coastline, and the hills of the Yemen and south-west Saudi Arabia, and those of northern Iraq.

The general aridity means that the economy is very largely pastoral, except along the valley of the Nile and in those areas where oil or petroleum has been found. The whole area is predominantly Arab. There is considerable political tension, exacerbated in many cases, by the mineral deposits and the ill-established boundaries. Certain countries of this part of the world therefore actively discourage tourists, and this, together with the adverse nature of the terrain, should be borne in mind by any prospective hunters.

The numbers of game species are also severely limited by the aridity and the terrain. There is a fair variety of carnivores, wolf (in the north), jackal, fox, genet, civet, hyena, wildcat, lynx and leopard, but none in any numbers. Much of their prey is small species, such as hare and hyrax. There are also wild boar in the north and gazelles in the south, as well as the odd mountain goat and feral camel. Inevitably the chief sport is supplied by birds: chiefly partridge, quail and sand grouse in the countries around the Mediterranean. Moreover, as these countries are on some of the flight paths between Europe and Africa, there are vast numbers of waterfowl at certain times of the year, particularly along the Nile valley.

Those who wish to hunt in this area should contact initially the nearest embassies of the countries concerned.

Migratory Bird Treaty Act

This is the Congressional Act, originally of 3 July 1918, and amended in 20 June 1936, which gave legislative effect to the 1916 Convention between Great Britain and the United States for the Protection of Migratory Birds in the United States and Canada, and the 1936 Convention between the United States and the United Mexican States for the Protection of Migratory Birds and Game Mammals.

The signing of these conventions, and the legislation embodying their provisions must be regarded as the first, and probably still the greatest and most successful work on conservation on an international scale. Without it the waterfowl and other migratory game birds of the North American continent would, by now, largely have disappeared, and the migratory insecti-

The Egyptian goose inhabits southern Israel, the entire Nile valley and parts of Africa south of the Sahara.

vorous and other non-game birds have been greatly reduced in numbers.

The Conventions, very briefly, arranged that migratory game birds, including the *Anatidae* (waterfowl), *Gruidae* (cranes), *Rallidae* (rails), *Limicolae* (shorebirds) and *Columbidae* (pigeons) should be preserved by the institution of closed seasons for periods of the year and, in some cases, for periods of years, and that migratory insectivorous and other game birds should be protected throughout the year. Exceptions were to be made for such birds as scoters, auks, guillemots and puffins to be taken for food by Indians and Eskimos. The taking of eggs, or nests, or the export of eggs or birds from any state or province was forbidden.

Minnesota (U.S.A.)

A state of the northern Midwest of 84,000 square miles, its northern parts are hilly, and covered with forests and lakes. The southern part is principally rich prairie land, merging into the wheat belt of the Dakotas in the west and the corn and cattle land of Iowa in the south-east. State and national forests, game management areas, national parks and so on, occupy about one sixth of the land, and most of these are open to the public for hunting.

White-tailed deer are the most numerous of the big game. They have multiplied almost sufficiently to meet the increase in hunting pressures, but their numbers will depend, of course, on the hardness of the winter and the condition and quality of the browse far more than on the number of deer licences taken out in any one year. In 1971, following a severe winter, the deer season was closed entirely. There are a very few mule deer in the north of the state, and a large number of bears. Elk and moose are protected as are quail. Pheasant numbers have dropped steadily under the impact of clean farming methods, and resident waterfowl are decreasing in numbers as potholes and sloughs are drained. Nevertheless, the waterfowl flying the Mississippi Flyway supplement the native population and still provide sport for the duck hunter. The state is first among all 50 in numbers of woodcock shot by hunters.

Special Regulations

No deer may be taken with a rifle of smaller calibre than .23, nor with one that uses a cartridge less than $1\frac{3}{4}$ in in length unless it is .35 in calibre or larger. All cartridges must contain a soft point or expanding bullet, and shotguns must be used with rifled slugs only; buckshot is forbidden. Dogs and high seats are illegal when deer hunting, and the hunter's cap must be entirely red, and his jacket at least 75% red.

Further Information

Division of Fish and Game, Department of Conservation, 390 Centennial Building, 658 Cedar Street, St Paul, Minnesota 55101.

Licence Fees—Minnesota

Type	Status	Fee
Deer	Resident	$7.50
	Non-resident	$50.25
Bear	Resident	$7.50
	Non-resident	$50.25
Small game	Resident	$5.00
	Non-resident	$26.00

Seasons and Limits—Minnesota

These vary from area to area

Species	Season	Limit	Comment
White-tailed deer Mule deer	Starts 14 Nov, ends within that month	One per season	
Black bear	All year	one per season	Protected in 5 counties except during deer season
Rabbit, cottontail and jack Snowshoe hare Squirrel, gray and fox	Starts 26 Sept, end varies with area		
Pheasant	Starts 31 Oct	3 per day	
Hungarian partridge	Starts 31 Oct	3 per day	
Ruffed grouse	Starts 26 Sept	4 per day	
Sharp-tailed grouse	Starts 26 Sept	5 per day	

Big Game Inventory—Minnesota

Species	Shot	Est.pop.
White-tailed deer	103,000	500,000
Black bear	190	

Mississippi (U.S.A.)

A southern state of some 47,000 square miles. Although low-lying and liable to flooding, the lands of the Mississippi valley and delta are extremely fertile, and heavy crops of cotton, rice, corn and cereals are grown. In the north and north-east the soils are rather poorer, and much of the land is given over to forests, which actually cover almost a third of the state. The climate is sub-tropical, though frosts do occur in winter.

There are quail in all counties, and wild turkey has spread to almost every county in

Big Game Inventory—Mississippi

Species	Shot	Est.pop.
Deer	31,578	250,000
Wild turkey	3,764	53,000

sufficient numbers for there to be a spring season. Opossum and raccoon may be run with dogs at any season of the year, and rabbits and squirrels are also plentiful. There is an expanding deer herd, and there is now a general season in most counties, as well as managed hunts in many of the wild-life management areas. Black bears and alligators are protected. Waterfowl are abundant.

Further Information
Fish and Game Commission, Woolfolk State Office Building, Jackson, Mississippi 39205.

Missouri (U.S.A.)

A Midwestern state covering some 70,000 square miles, it lies between two great rivers and straddles the transition zone between prairie and forest. It has, as a consequence, a varied agriculture and a varied game population. North of the Mississippi lie the prairies and the cornbelt, south of it lie the Ozark Mountains, a hilly, heavily forested area, and south of them again is an area of deep silts capable of growing a great variety of crops. However, in spite of its agricultural character, Missouri has over 20 million acres of forests, most of them in the Ozarks, and this influences the distribution of the game and the character of the hunting. Pheasants, for example, will be found mainly in association with the grain fields in the north, turkey will be most abundant in the forests of the Ozarks, as will deer.

Cottontail rabbits are well distributed throughout the state, as are quail, and the great rivers and their tributaries attract large flights of waterfowl, including blue, snow and Canada geese, all of which winter there. There is good early dove shooting before the migrations. Black bears are protected.

Special Regulations
Pistols, revolvers, rifles, spring, air and gas guns are all permitted, but pistols, revolvers and rifles may not be used on game birds. Rifled slugs may be used on deer, but not buckshot, nor a rifle firing a bullet of less than 60 grains.

Licence Fees—Mississippi

Type	Status	Fee
Hunting/Fishing	Resident	$5.00
Hunting only	Resident	$3.50
Deer/Turkey	Non-resident	$25.00
7-day	Non-resident	$10.00
Small game	Non-resident	$15.00
3-day	Non-resident	$6.00
Deer tag		$2.00
Turkey tag		$2.00

Seasons and Limits—Mississippi

These vary from county to county

Species	Season	Limit
Deer	21 Nov-1 Dec, 19 Dec-22 Dec, 26 Dec-11 Jan	One buck with 4in antlers
Rabbit	10 Oct-9 Jan	8 per day
Squirrel, gray and fox	10 Oct-9 Jan	
Bobwhite quail	5 Dec-22 Feb	10 per day
Wild turkey	27 March-11 April 24 April-2 May	One gobbler per day, 3 per licence year

Licence Fees—Missouri

Type	Status	Fee	Comment
Deer/Turkey	Resident	$7.50	Sold at sheriff's offices and sporting-goods stores
Deer/Turkey	Non-resident	$30.30	
Small game	Resident	$4.50	
Small game	Non-resident	$25.30	

Seasons and Limits—Missouri

Species	Season	Limit	Comment
Deer	14 Nov-17 Nov 14 Nov-23 Nov	one per year	Either sex Bucks only
Cottontail rabbit	30 May-1 March	10 per day	
Squirrel, gray and fox	30 May-31 Dec	6 per day	
Pheasant	10 Nov-31 Dec	one cock per day	
Bobwhite quail	varies	varies	
Wild turkey	March and April	one gobbler per year	

Big Game Inventory—Missouri

Species	Shot
Deer	22,649
Wild turkey	1,270

Further Information
Division of Game, Missouri Department of Conservation, Jefferson City, Mo. 65101.

Mongolian Gazelle (*Procapra gutterosa*)

Also known as Indian gazelle, chinkara or ravine deer, it is found throughout the plains of India and Central Asia and derives its name chinkara from the sneezing sound it makes when alarmed (chink meaning 'sneeze'); its other name, ravine deer, indicates it prefers to inhabit bush and thin jungle, intersected by deep nullahs or ravines. It stands about 28 in and is deep fawn in colour on the back, white on the sides, buttocks and belly, with an 8-inch

'The Bear Hunt' by Samuel Howitt from the original sketch by Captain Thomas Williamson, 1806

Licence Fees—Montana

Type	Status	Fee	Comment
Hunting/Fishing (includes black bear)	Resident	$20.25	Necessary before partaking in draw for big-game permits
Big game permits			
Moose, sheep	Resident	$25.00	
Goat	Resident	$15.00	
Deer, antelope, elk	Resident	$3.00	
Grizzly bear	Resident	$1.00	Plus $25 trophy fee
Upland birds	Resident	$2.00	
Turkey tag	Resident	$2.00	
Hunting/Fishing (includes deer, elk, black bear and birds)	Non-resident	$151.00	Necessary before partaking in draw for big-game permits
Big game permits			
Moose, sheep	Non-resident	$50.00	
Mountain goat	Non-resident	$30.00	
Grizzly bear	Non-resident	$25.00	Plus $25 trophy fee
Antelope	Non-resident	$10.00	
Deer, antelope, black bear	Non-resident	$35.00	
Upland birds	Non-resident	$25.00	
Turkey tag	Non-resident	$2.00	

Seasons and Limits—Montana

Montana is divided into 7 game management areas having different seasons, game and limits.

Species	Seasons	Limit	Comment
Deer, white-tailed and mule	18 Oct-29 Nov	One or 2 of either sex	
Elk	18 Oct-29 Nov	one per year. either sex	
Antelope	11 Oct-8 Nov		Special drawing
Black bear	15 March-29 Nov	One per year	
Grizzly bear	18 Oct-29 Nov	One per year	
Mountain sheep	15 Sept-29 Nov		Special drawings in most areas
Mountain goat	15 Sept-29 Nov		
Moose	15 Sept-29 Nov		Special drawing only
Rabbits, cottontail and jack	All year		
Snowshoe hare	All year		
Pheasant Grouse Partridge	Decided annually		

The common shoveller on a lake in North India. This species has a wide distribution in Europe; Asia and North America.

black tail which it wags vigorously when alarmed, often betraying itself by this movement. Usually found in herds of from 3 to 8, solitary bucks are not uncommon. The bucks in northern India tend to have better heads than those in the south, weighing as much as 50 lb. Both sexes have horns, the buck's averaging about 10 to 12 in, whereas the doe's are about 6 to 7 in. They are wary animals and while feeding constantly raise their heads to look around for danger so that stalking requires patience and skill in using cover. They are now protected in India.

Montana (U.S.A.)

The third largest state in the Union, it is split into two distinctive parts by the Continental Divide, the larger, eastern part belonging to the Great Plains, and either farmed or ranched, the smaller, western part belonging to the Rockies and predominantly mountainous, forested and wild.

Montana is essentially a big-game state, with good populations of deer, elk, mountain goat, moose, bear and turkey. Antelope and goat are increasing rapidly and extending their habitat. Only bighorn sheep are in any real danger of declining. Bighorn, mountain goat, elk, moose, grizzly and black bear are found in the west of the state. Antelope are found in the south-east, and mule deer are found everywhere, with a certain number of white-tailed deer in the north-west. Game birds include Franklin's, ruffed, and blue grouse in the mountains, and pheasants, sage and sharp-tailed grouse in the east. Hungarian partridge are found in north-central Montana and some chukar in south-central Montana. Some wild turkey are shot, and their numbers are increasing. Waterfowl are fairly abundant, especially in the north-east, where there are several marshes and potholes.

Special Regulations

The only gun that is illegal in the state is a shotgun larger than 10-bore. For hunting deer, shotguns must be loaded with single ball, 00, or 0 buck cartridges. Red clothing must be worn as a safety precaution.

Big Game Inventory—Montana

Species	Shot
White-tailed deer	25,250
Mule deer	74,500
Elk	16,000
Moose	460
Black bear	1,950
Grizzly bear	20
Pronghorn antelope	11,500
Wild turkey	400

Further Information
State Fish and Game Commission, Helena, Montana 59601.

Moose (*Alces alces*)

Whenever moose are discussed an unfortunate confusion over nomenclature is likely to arise. The animal called moose in North America is called elk in Scandinavia, where it also lives, and what is called elk in America is, in fact, the wapiti. The confusion arose because the early settlers had all heard of, but never seen, an elk, and when they first saw a wapiti they decided that this was the elk. But when they finally came across a true elk, they had no name left to give it, and so used its Algonquin name of Moose.

Moose is the largest deer in the world, and it is distributed in a wide arc through the northern forests of Europe, Asiatic Russia and America. There are three subspecies in America: the Alaskan-Yukon moose (*A. alces gigas*), which is the largest, the Wyoming moose (*A. alces shirasi*), which is the smallest, and Canadian moose (*A. alces americana*), which may be thought of as the typical American moose. It is slightly larger and darker than the European moose (*A. alces alces*), but otherwise it would be difficult to tell them apart.

Moose are essentially deer of the forest and the wilderness. As such they have had to retreat, in both Europe and America, in front of man and civilization. There are few to be found, now, south of the Canadian

This moose, photographed in Montana, belongs to the smaller, Wyoming race.

border, and few to be found in southern Scandinavia. The movement is not, however, entirely one way. Moose are browsers, and they eat, for preference, the leaves of non-coniferous trees and shrubs. Timber extraction and burning off are changing the nature of many of the largely coniferous forests of the north, and secondary timber growths of the willow, poplar, aspen, alder type are appearing which can attract and support moose where none were before. Within living memory they have appeared in parts of British Columbia where they had never been seen before, and these must have pressed down from Alaska and the north. In Newfoundland, once the forests there had been opened up, the introduction of no more than seven moose has led, in fifty years, to a population capable of supporting an annual harvest of up to 8,000. The moose, however, cannot move back beyond certain limits; sooner or later it will come up against, not only Man, but also the ubiquitous white-tailed deer, that will compete with it and defeat it for territory.

In appearance the moose is a long-legged short-bodied animal, with its body sloping backwards from a high shoulder to low quarters. The cow is always smaller than the bull. Both are the same colour – dark brown or brownish-black with gray legs and some gray around the muzzle. The tail is vestigial, and a short, thick neck terminates in a narrow head with large, mule-like ears. The muzzle is exaggerated, with a decided hump and a hairy nasal pad. The upper lip is flexible and prehensile, to help browsing. The teeth include 12 heavy molars on each side, which allow it to chew twigs up to half an inch thick. A bag of skin – the 'bell', which shrinks with age – hangs under the chin; its function is uncertain. The legs are long and thin and the feet large and spreading to enable the beast to walk easily in boggy ground. The antlers are, perhaps, the most characteristic appendages. They consist of great palms or 'shovels', wide spreading and curving upwards, with, in the adult bull, a number of points along the outer edge. Smaller brow palms, with three or more points branch out from the main beam and point forward. The antlers do not reach adult pattern until the fourth year, and palmation is not complete until the sixth or seventh. When it is, the space between the points is so filled in that the points merely appear as jagged edges. Antler growth starts in April, the velvet is stripped by September, and the antlers are shed, in mature bulls, by January.

The rut extends from September till late November. The bulls challenge each other and call to the cows by bellowing, and fights will develop. The bull and cow stay together for about a week before the bull goes off to find another cow. Calves are dropped in April and May, usually twins, and they will stay with the dam until the second season.

Though primarily a browser the moose will also graze and eat mosses, lichens, water plants and especially water-lilies. When the insects are biting it will seek refuge in water, where it is a strong swimmer. The latest game census shows some 20,000 moose in Alaska and no other American state with a population larger than 8,000.

The methods of hunting this animal in both North America and Scandinavia are discussed in the entry: Deer of the World and their Hunting.

Morocco

Morocco lies along the Atlantic coast in the extreme north-west of Africa, and has an area of about 175,000 square miles. The dominant feature of the country is the High Atlas mountain range, which runs from south-west to north-east, flanked by smaller ranges: the Anti-Atlas, the Middle Atlas and the Riff. The Anti-Atlas and the southern slopes of the High Atlas are exposed to the dry desert winds, and are consequently arid and desolate for the most part, while the interior plains are intensely hot in the summer. The climate elsewhere in Morocco is generally pleasant and healthy, even humid on the coast, where the rainy season may last from November to April.

The aoudad, or Barbary sheep, is native to Morocco.

Agriculture is the chief occupation. Much of the land not exposed to the desert winds is fertile and cereals, citrus fruits, dates, figs and vegetables are important. Esparto grass is also produced and cork is a very important commercial forest product, with large areas of cork forest on the northern slopes of the mountains, so that there is plenty of good, uninhabited, mixed cover.

Visitors are recommended to shoot on the Arbaoua Tourist Hunting Reserve rather than on private property. It lies on the Rharb basin (80 miles from Tangier, 90 from Rabat), covering some 75,000 acres of moors and swamps, and 25,000 acres of forest. The reserve is restricted to visitors, who may also hunt the so-called 'Complementary Zone' to the north of the reserve. Boar are hunted in two distinct areas within the reserve, in each of which there are about 15 beats a year, with a bag limit of four boars per beat.

Three or four guides and organizers are appointed each year to arrange hunting for tourists, contact provincial authorities on their behalf, obtain necessary documents, and arrange beaters. Beaters are supplied by local 'Chioukhs' (heads of villages) and are usually given a mid-day meal and a bonus, depending on the success of the hunt.

Further Information
The names and addresses of the organizers and further information about them and other hunting matters can be had from: Moroccan National Tourist Office, 22 rue d'Alger, Rabat. There are branches in most of the capital cities of Europe.

Mouflon (*Ovis musimon* and *Ovis orientalis ophion*)
Mouflon are members of the great family of wild sheep that spreads out from Europe, across Asia, to Alaska, Canada and the United States. Two different species of mouflon are found in Europe – *Ovis musimon*, which is the wild sheep of Corsica, Sardinia, and the alpine areas of central Europe, and *Ovis orientalis ophion*, the Cyprian mouflon, which is the only European representative of the Asiatic mouflon, or red sheep (*q.v.*).

The mouflon looks very much like an unusually small bighorn (*Ovis canadensis*) (*q.v.*). The ram stands about 28 in at the shoulder and weighs about 100 lb. The winter coat is dull brown, with a prominent light gray saddle and a black throat-mane. The summer coat is red-brown, with the belly, inside of the legs and rump patches white, and a black streak along the back. The horns are, as in all sheep, hollow, and are triangular in section. There is some variation in curl and spread, some horns lying almost in one plane, and others achieving a normal curl. A good head will measure about 30 in, and a record one over 31 in, with a diameter of about 10 in. The female is generally hornless, smaller in size, and more subdued in colour. Rut normally occurs in November and December, and the lambs are dropped between April and May.

Mouflon are found in Sardinia and Corsica (in very small numbers), in Czechoslovakia where the world record head was shot and over 1,000 are shot in an average year, in the north of Hungary in the Bakony Forest, in the German alps, where the bag in 1969/70 was 893, and in Austria. The Cyprian mouflon is still found inside the Paphos Forest reserve of Cyprus, where its numbers have recovered from about thirty to around three hundred ever since goats and goatherds were excluded from the reserve, so reducing competition from the goats and over-hunting by the goatherds.

Mouflon were once driven towards the passes in Sardinia, and shot as they came through the defiles. In Cyprus where, in mediaeval times, mouflon were found almost everywhere, they used to be hunted with hounds, and even coursed with cheetahs. Nowadays they are almost always stalked, an exercise that presents some difficulty, not only because the terrain is generally mountainous but also because the animal possesses keen sight and even keener powers of smell, and has a habit of lying out just under the lee of a ridge, where air currents meet from each side, warning of the hunter's approach. It is probably easiest to stalk them early in the season (late autumn) before they come down from the higher slopes to the cover of the valleys, but as this is the beginning of the rut, and the rams will be mixed up with the ewes, it will be slightly more difficult to select a good head. In spring, when the rams are once more on their own, selection is easier, but the beasts will not be in such good condition. Mouflon mutton makes most excellent eating when it has been well hung.

Mountain Hare *see* Blue Hare

Mountain Lion *see* Cougar

Mountain Quail (*Oreortyx picta*)
A bird of the Pacific mountain ranges from Oregon to California, it is the largest American quail, measuring up to 12 in and weighing around 9 oz. Attempts to introduce them in other areas have never been successful. Inside their range they are partial migrants, moving down from their breeding grounds in winter for distances as far as 50 miles.

The male and the female closely resemble each other, both having the distinctive crest of two upright black feathers. They are bluish-gray on the upperparts, head and breast, the throat is chestnut, bordered with white, and the flanks are chestnut, barred with white. They feed on greenstuff in summer and grain and seeds for the rest

The handsome mountain quail which is found in greater numbers in California than in other parts of its range.

A bighorn ram, photographed in Ontario

of the year. The chicks need insects, and usually take large numbers of ants. Unlike other quail they need to drink water.

Pairing occurs in early spring and nesting in May and June. The nest is a shallow depression lined with grass and leaves, and the clutch of from 8 to 15 eggs takes about 24 days to incubate. The cock shares in the rearing and the young are difficult to distinguish from adults after 12 weeks. The birds tend to remain in family coveys all winter, and there is very little packing.

They are excellent eating, but difficult birds to hunt, since they prefer to run on into thick cover rather than flush. When they do fly, for short distances only, they are extremely fast.

Mountain Sheep (*Ovis* species)
The mountain sheep of America are related to the mouflon (*q.v.*), and to those other wild sheep distributed, in an interrupted chain, from the mountains of the Mediterranean Basin, through those of Asia Minor and Central Asia, to the mountains and desert country of western North America. Of the seven recognized species two are to be found in America – the bighorn and the thinhorn.

The bighorn are represented by the Rocky Mountain bighorn and the desert bighorn (which are also called California bighorn or cimarrones). They are all alike in being large, or fairly large, brown or gray sheep with white on their bellies, the inside of their legs, and their muzzles. Their small, dark tails stand out prominently against the white of their rump patches. Their hoofs are black, and rubbery pads on the feet prevent slipping. Their eyes are golden and both sexes are horned, the horns consisting of a bony core and an outer sheath that grows. They are never shed and, while in ewes and lambs they are thin and erect, like those of a domestic goat, in the mature rams they grow into massive spirals that complete a three-quarter circle or more. Bighorns are now only hunted as trophy animals, that is only adult rams are taken. As they are polygamous, and the sexes are roughly in balance, hunting is no longer a factor affecting sheep populations. Nevertheless, populations do fluctuate and continue to decline, probably because of competition for winter ranges with domestic and other stock, disease, and, though only in a minor way, predation.

The Rocky Mountain bighorn (*O. canadensis canadensis*) is a bigger animal than the desert bighorn; a mature ram may weigh 300 lb and stand 42 in at the shoulder. It is, primarily, a grazing animal of the high alpine meadows, living as close as it can to the cliffs and scree runs on which it is safe. In winter it may be forced to browse, and to descend to the lower valleys, but the herd range is a limited one and, though there is a limited migration from summer to winter anges, there is no large-scale migration unless a failure of food supplies compels it. Except during the rut the adult rams keep separate from the ewes and their young. The rut is timed to allow the lambs, often twins, to be dropped at a time of maximum grass growth, five months later. Courtship is by pursuit, with several rams pursuing each ewe as she comes in season. In the course of this, fighting will occur, the rams charging each other head-on with great violence, but the fighting seems to be as much concerned with herd dominance as with mating a particular ewe.

There are six recognized subspecies of desert bighorn: the Nelson (*O. canadensis nelsoni*), the Lower California (*O. canadensis cremnobates*), the Southern Lower California (*O. canadensis weemsi*), the Arizona (*O. canadensis gaillardi*), the Texas (*O. canadensis texiana*) and the Mexican (*O. canadensis mexicana*). They are all smaller than the Rocky Mountain bighorn, and are browsers rather than grazers. They do not need, as the Rocky Mountain sheep do, to come to water every day, and can often extract sufficient moisture from cactus and other succulents. Otherwise they are very similar.

The Rocky Mountain bighorn are found in largest numbers in Canada, especially in British Columbia and Alberta. Only Colorado, Idaho, Montana and Wyoming have populations in excess of 1,000. Desert bighorns are found principally in California, Arizona and Nevada, and in Lower California, Sonora, Chihuahua and Sinatoa in Mexico.

The thinhorn are divided into the white, or Dall's sheep (*Ovis dalli dalli*), and the black, or Stone's sheep (*O. dalli stonei*). Dall's sheep are the smallest of the mountain sheep, the rams weighing under 200 lb. Their coats are white both summer and winter, and they are found in the Kenai Peninsula of Alaska, in central Alaska and in the Yukon Territory. Stone's sheep are slightly larger and their colour patterns are similar to those of the bighorns, except for being so dark in the coat as to look black. They occupy a range south of the Dall's sheep stretching down into northern British Columbia. Where the ranges overlap there is some inter-breeding between Stone's and Dall's sheep, but there is no evidence of interbreeding with bighorns. Both sheep have thinner, more flaring horns than the Rocky Mountain sheep, and they are triangular, rather than round or oval in section.

Stalking the rams is, very often, more a test of mountaineering than of hunting skill. It should be undertaken before the rut, while the rams are apart from the ewes. The skill lies in the selection of a suitable ram, and in the approach; the shooting itself is not difficult. A high-velocity rifle with telescopic sights is essential. Because of the

The mourning dove. In the southern states of America the flocks of migrating birds make excellent hunting.

climbing, however, it needs to be both light and efficient. The bullet should be one that shocks as much as possible; a pointed expanding or hollow pointed bullet is suitable, since damage to meat is not of prime importance (although the meat is highly rated for flavour and texture).

Mourning Dove (*Zenaidura macroura*)
Although this small dove is known to breed in every one of the United States except Hawaii and Alaska, it is also recognized as a migrant, and so comes under the protection of the Migratory Bird Treaty. It is also found in Canada, Mexico, Central America and the West Indies. In many of the northern states of the United States it is additionally protected as a song bird, and so not shot at all. In most of the southern states, however, where resident populations are swollen every year by migrations, it is the most frequently shot of all birds, more being killed than either bobwhites or duck. In spite of this its numbers are increasing.

It is light gray on top and pinkish-buff underneath; the gray tail is spotted with white and rimmed with black. The hen differs from the cock only in having slightly duller plumage and a shorter tail. They are seed and grain eaters and highly gregarious. When feeding in flocks they are liable to cause considerable crop damage.

They breed for at least six months and, even in the north, generally have at least two broods. The male is monogamous and shares in the nesting and rearing; the average clutch of two eggs takes 12 to 14 days to incubate, and the young can be turned off within six weeks.

Not easy birds to shoot since they curl, float and dive over the gun, they can be shot at watering holes or coming in to roost. In many of the southern states it is customary to have organized shoots during which several guns surround a field where the doves feed and shoot them as they fly out.

Mule Deer (*Odocoileus hemionus hemionus*)
The mule, with its various, rather localized, sub-species is essentially a deer of western America. It may once have been plentiful on the Great Plains, but hunting pressures and advancing civilization have pressed it back into the mountains, and it is little seen east of the foothills of the Rockies. Recognized sub-species include: the California mule deer, the gray mule deer, the cactus buck, the desert mule deer, the burro deer, the southern mule deer, the plains mule deer and the Rocky Mountain mule deer. The black-tailed deer (*O. hemionus columbianus*) (*q.v.*) is also a sub-species of the mule, although all zoologists do not agree on this.

The mule deer is found in broken, rocky, and hilly country for which its alarm gait, springing stiff-legged off all four legs in great jumps, is very suitable; it is not, however, a gait it can continue for very long.

A buck mule deer in velvet.

It is heavier than the whitetail, and has larger, mule-like ears that give it its name. The buck carries a heavier rack than either the whitetail or the blacktail. The antlers grow upwards, rather than forwards as do the whitetail's, the brow tine is small, and the other tines are formed by bifurcations of the antler, rather than by growing straight out of the main beam, as they do with the whitetail. Weight depends largely on range conditions, but in British Columbia, where conditions are especially favourable, weights of between 300 and 400 lb are common. There is, between the sub-species, some variation of colour in the summer coat, ranging from dull yellow to rusty-red. All have a gray winter coat, however, the result of a growth of the guard hairs, and all have the dark, 'horseshoe' mark on the forehead and the distinctive white rump patch. The most distinctive part is the tail, which is thin, hairless underneath, and white with a black tip on the outside. It is held close to the body when running. The metatarsal gland is, on the average, five inches long, which is considerably longer than in either the white-tailed or the black-tailed deer.

During the rut, which occurs from October to December, there may be fierce fighting between the bucks as they set about collecting their harems, which generally contain five to seven does, but may hold up to fifteen. Antlers are shed in February and March and begin to re-form immediately. Fawns are dropped in May and June – singles for the young does, twins, or even triplets for the older ones. Mules are generally more gregarious than other deer and tend, when breeding is over, to collect in groups and herds, especially in winter. They are primarily browsers, but will also graze, and eat moss and lichens each in their due season. They do not, normally, move far, but, if food supplies become restricted, they are capable of undertaking lengthy migrations.

The most favoured range of the mule deer is the rough country around the Rocky Mountains from British Columbia to Mexico, but they also range from the Pacific in California to as far east as the Dakotas and Manitoba. The 1963 Big Game Inventory placed approximately six million mules in the United States alone, with the heaviest concentrations in Colorado, Montana, Oregon and Wyoming.

The best sport to be had from the mule is when it can be stalked in the open. In the woods, however, still-hunting, or organized drives are the effective procedures. Apart from Man, the mule's principal predators are timber wolves, cougars and coyotes. But all of these combined have far less influence on population size than does the season, the adequacy of the winter ranges and condition of the habitat. *See also* Deer of the World and their Hunting.

Muscat *see* Middle East

N

Nakong *see* Sitatunga

Nebraska (U.S.A.)

Its 77,000 square miles consist principally of open plains, intersected by the Platte, Missouri, Republican and Niobara rivers, and it is primarily an agricultural state, forming part of the Corn Belt.

The landscape is too open a one for Nebraska to be a good big-game centre, but it has some of the best pheasant shooting in the country. It is also one of the very few states where prairie chickens are numerous enough to be hunted legally. Besides these there are quail, sharp-tailed grouse, and eastern and Merriam's turkey. The antelope and deer populations have been re-established sufficiently for both to be hunted. The deer in the east of the state are whitetails, and in the west mules. Antelope are found only in the north-west of the state. There is excellent wildfowling, and blue, snow and Canada geese all fly over the territory. There are 240,000 acres of national forest open to public hunting, and no less than 38 public hunting areas maintained by the Game Commission.

Special Regulations
No rifle delivering less than 900 foot-pounds of bullet energy at 100 yd may be used on antelope or deer. Hand guns of .357 calibre or upwards may be used on deer only. Shotguns of between 10- and 20-gauge may be used on turkey. Rifled slugs and buckshot are legal.

Further Information
Game, Forestation and Park Commission, State Capitol Building, Lincoln, Nebraska 68509.

Nepal

Nepal is a Himalayan country of some 54,000 square miles. Sikkim lies along part of the short eastern border, and Tibet to the north, but otherwise India surrounds the country. It is primarily mountainous, but includes the Terai, a strip of heavily wooded country between the Himalayas and the Gangetic plain. For a full description of the type of terrain and the game species to be found see the Himalayan section of India. Rice and other grains, jute, hides, livestock and timber are exported and industry, based mainly on hydro-electric power, is growing.

Of the species found the chief ones hunted are leopard, bear, sambar, ghoral, wild boar, hog deer, thar, barking deer, serow, blue bull, bharal and crocodile. There is organized hunting but rates and conditions differ with the type of game. Typically, general hunting, mostly based in the Terai, will cost about $100 per hunter per day (about $50 for non-hunting guests), with a minimum of 10 days. Mountain game hunting is cheaper, about $50 per person per day, but the minimum is about 25 days, extended to 45 days for bharal, only found in particularly remote areas.

Big Game Inventory—Nebraska

Species	Shot	Est. pop.
White-tailed deer	5,536	25,000
Mule deer	6,988	30,000
Antelope	1,429	6,500
Wild turkey	663	4,000

Seasons and Limits—Nebraska

Vary in different Game Management areas.

Species	Season	Limit	Comment
Deer, white-tailed and mule	14 Nov-22 Nov	One per day and one in possession	
Antelope	26 Sept-4 Oct		Special drawing in some units
Rabbit, cottontail and jack	All year		
Squirrel	1 Sept-31 Jan		
Pheasant	Starts 7 Nov	2 or 3 cocks per day	
Bobwhite quail	Starts 7 Nov	6 per day	
Sharptail grouse	Starts 3 Oct	2 per day	
Prairie chicken	Starts 3 Oct	2 per day	
Wild turkey	31 Oct-14 Nov	one per day and one in possession	

Licence Fees—Nebraska

Type	Status	Fee	Comment
Antelope, Deer	Resident	$10	Sold by clerks and sporting-goods stores
	Non-resident	$30	
Turkey	Resident	$5	Plus $1 tag
	Non-resident	$15	
Small game	Resident	$1	Plus $1 upland bird stamp
	Non-resident	$25	Plus $1 upland bird stamp

Further Information
Nepal Wildlife Adventure Company, Ramshah Path, Katmandu, Nepal.

Chief Conservator of Forests, His Majesty's Government of Nepal, Singha Darbar, Katmandu, Nepal.

Nesting Boxes (for Waterfowl) *see* Wildfowl and Wet Gravel Pits

Netherlands

The Netherlands, generally known as Holland, is a small country (about 13,500 square miles) of north-west Europe. The country is renowned for its flatness, with only a few hills rising to about 1,000 ft near the German border. Much of the land has been, and is being, reclaimed from the sea and is heavily intersected by canals, rivers and river estuaries.

Despite the intensive exploitation of the land there is still plenty of game, but shooting is not readily available to foreigners. Visitors can only obtain shooting if they are invited by a Dutch friend or if they rent a shoot for six years as the Dutch have to.

Further Information
Royal Netherlands Hunters' Association, Joz. Israelslaan 20, The Hague.

Nevada (U.S.A.)

A south-western state covering some 110,000 square miles lying between the Rocky Mountains and the Sierra Nevada. Most of it lies within the Great Basin, a semi-desert region where ranges of hills running up to 10,000 ft separate valleys which often hold salt lakes. The south of the state slopes down to the Colorado River. The climate is dry and, except where irrigation is practised, ranching is the only form of agriculture possible. There are, however, about 5 million acres of forests.

The big game of the area is not plentiful, and most of it has to be drawn for, with non-residents seldom allowed to participate. Only about 20 permits are available for elk and up to 100 for bighorn sheep. Chukar is the most important game bird, and it is generally found at heights between 4,000 and 8,000 ft. There are pheasant and waterfowl around the irrigated land of western Nevada, together with Hungarian partridge and California quail. Sage and blue grouse and mountain quail are found in the north of the state.

Special Regulations
Shotguns, hand guns and .22 rim-fire rifles may not be used on big game, nor any rifle exerting less than 1,000 pounds of energy at 100 yards. No steel, steel-cored, metal-jacketed, tracer, or incendiary bullets may be used.

Further Information
Department of Fish and Game, Box 10678, Reno, Nevada 89502.

Seasons—Netherlands	
Species	**Season**
Duck :	
Mallard	24 July-31 Jan
Shoveller	18 Aug-31 Jan
Teal	
Others (except those listed below)	1 Sept-31 Jan
Geese :	
White-fronted	1 Sept-31 Jan
Graylag	
Bean	
Coot	18 Aug-31 Jan
Snipe	
Golden Plover	1 Nov-31 Dec
Partridge	1 Sept-31 Dec
Pheasant hen	15 Oct-31 Dec
cock	15 Oct-31 Jan
Hare	15 Oct-31 Dec
Woodcock	15 Oct-31 Jan

Protected duck
shelduck, goldeneye, red-crested, pochard, white-headed, ferruginous, goosander, red-breasted merganser smew, common eider, scoter, long-tailed

Licences—Netherlands
A Dutch shooting licence, required in order to import firearms, can be obtained from the local police through a Dutch intermediary. The fee is 45 Dutch florins per week, or Fl.100 per season.

Big Game Inventory—Nevada		
Species	**Shot**	**Est. pop.**
Mule deer	20,387	200,000
Pronghorn	193	3.000
Elk	7	260
Bighorn	32	2,500

New Brunswick pays an annual bounty on the bobcat, illustrated here, bears and porcupines.

Licence Fees—Nevada			
Type	**Status**	**Fee**	**Comment**
General	Resident	$5	Necessary before obtaining
	Non-resident	$50	obtaining specific tags
Bighorn sheep	Resident	$25	Specific game tags are
	Non-resident	$125	generally only valid in specific areas, and seasons and limits vary from area to area
Cougar	Resident	$1	
	Non-resident	$50	
Antelope, elk	Resident	$15	
Deer	Resident	$5	
	Non-resident	$30	
Upland birds	Non-resident	$10	

Seasons and Limits—Nevada

Species	Season	Comment
Mule deer	10 Oct-8 Nov (shorter in some areas)	Special drawings for non-residents
Antelope	22 Aug-7 Sept	Special drawing for residents only
Elk	21 Nov-13 Dec	Mainly Clark county, special drawing, residents only
Cougar	10 Oct-31 March	Limit: one per season
Bighorn sheep	Nov-Dec, (2 weeks in Dec in 2 units)	Special drawing for 5 non-resident tags
Jack rabbit	All year	
Pheasant Grouse, sage and blue Quail, Gambel's, California and mountain Partridge, chukar and Hungarian	Seasons for these species vary each year	

Game Inventory—New Brunswick

Species	Shot	Most productive areas
Deer	28,000 (10-year average)	Victoria, Restigouche, York, Charlotte and Queens counties, and Grand Manian Island
Bear	1,000	
Moose	858	Northumberland county Albert county
Grouse	145,000 (10-year average)	York and Northumberland counties
Duck	60,000	
Canada geese	2,351	
Snipe	2,341	
Woodcock	17,819	

New Brunswick (Canada)

An eastern province which also includes the islands of the south-west – Grand Manan, Campobello, Deer and West Islands.

The terrain, except in the south-west, is fairly flat and heavily wooded. There are many rivers, including the St John, the St Croix, the Miramichi and the Tabusintac, and several lakes, the biggest of them being the Grand Lake. The soil is deep and fertile, and there are nearly 700,000 acres under the plough. The most important crops are potatoes, oats and barley. There are large fisheries, and the chief industry is timber and its derivatives – pulp and paper. Mining, however, is becoming increasingly important.

Big game consists, principally, of white-tailed deer, moose and black bear. The only important upland game birds are grouse – ruffed and spruce – and woodcock. Waterfowl shooting is good in coastal areas.

Licence Fees—Newfoundland

Species	Status	Fee
Caribou	Resident	$15
	Non-resident	$100
Moose	Resident	$15
	Non-resident	$75
Black bear	Resident	$10
	Non-resident	$10
Snowshoe hare	Resident	$1
	Non-resident	$5
Game birds	Resident	$2
	Non-resident	$5

Special Regulations

When hunting deer, or any other big game, the non-resident hunter must be accompanied by a licensed guide – one to every two non-residents. The Department of Tourism will provide a list of outfitters able to supply guides. Class 1 and Class 3 Licences can be issued only to persons over 18 years of age, and Class 2 and Class 4 Licences to persons over 16 years of age.

Revolvers and other firearms capable of being concealed may not be carried, nor may a rifle or shotgun be carried on Sunday, or during the closed season, or in a Provincial Park. No shotgun is allowed that carries more than three cartridges unless it has been plugged down. Silencers are illegal. Deer and moose may not be hunted with rifles firing rim-fire cartridges, but, during the month of December, no rifle capable of firing a cartridge bigger than .22 rim-fire may be carried, nor may shot larger than Number 2 be used. Dogs may not be used to hunt deer or moose, and special permission is needed from the Director, Fish and Wildlife Branch, to use dogs or hounds on rabbit, foxes, wildcat and raccoons. A deer hunter must tag his kill immediately, and present it for registration at the first registering station on his route. It is suggested that all hunters wear bright coloured clothing, preferably red, yellow, or orange.

Further Information

Fish and Wildlife Branch, Department of Natural Resources, Fredericton.

Department of Tourism, 796 Queen Street Fredericton.

Newfoundland (Canada)

This is the newest of the Canadian provinces, since it only voted itself into the Confederation in 1949. It consists of the island of Newfoundland, which covers about 42,000 square miles, and Labrador, which is, for this purpose, the coastal part of the Labrador peninsula. Both the island and mainland parts of the province are wild, mountainous, and often barren lands, encompassing forests, tundra, lakes, rivers and swamps. The coastline is deeply indented and has many offshore islands.

The non-resident sportsman visits the province principally to fish or to hunt moose, caribou and black bear which are found, in varying densities, all over the province, not all of which is open to hunters because of lack of access. Newfoundland moose are descended from an original introduction of six animals in 1878. Since then they have spread over the entire island, and the present moose population is estimated to be between 40,000 and 50,000, with an annual legal harvest of around 8,000. Caribou were once more plentiful, their numbers having been reduced by illegal hunting. The largest surviving herds are now probably in

Seasons, Limits and Licences—New Brunswick

There are five deer-management zones : zone 1, the north ; zone 2, the centre ; zone 3, the south ; zone 4, all islands except Campobello ; zone 5, Campobello.

Species	Zone	Season	Limit	Type of Licence	Fee	Comment
Deer	1	1 Oct-30 Nov	one per season (either sex)	Residents-Class 3 Non-residents-Class 1	$4.50 $35.50	
	2	26 Oct-30 Nov				
	3	9 Nov-30 Nov				
	4	1 Oct-11 Nov				
Moose	1, 2 and 3	21 Sept-26 Sept		Residents only, special licence by ballot	$15.00	
Black bear	1, 2 and 3	1 Oct-30 Nov and 15 April-30 June	2 per season (either sex)	Class 3 or class 1, plus bear permit for residents Non-resident bear permit	Bear permit, free $10.00	Female with cubs may not be shot during spring season. The carcass of bear shot must be shown to a Forest Ranger for examination and tagging within 48 hours of being killed.
Rabbit	All	1 Oct-31 Dec	No limit	Residents-Class 4 Non-residents-Class 2	$2.50 $25.50	Can also be shot under Class 3 licence Can also be shot under Class 1 licence
Bobcat, porcupine cormorant, crow, Fox, ground hog, raccoon and skunk	All	1 Oct-31 Dec 1 Oct-31 Nov	No limit No limit	Any Any		Night hunting of raccoon is encouraged, but hounds must be licensed for the purpose.
Grouse	All	1 Oct-14 Nov		Any		

There are four waterfowl zones. These do not correspond with the Deer Management zones, but are those laid down in the Migration Birds Convention Act : zone 1, southern coastline west of Saint John ; zone 2, the islands ; zone 3, the northern and western counties ; zone 4, the southern and eastern counties.

Species	Zone	Season	Limit	Comment
Duck	1 and 2	19 Oct-7 Nov 23 Nov-9 Jan	6 per day, 12 in possession	Limit exclusive of mergansers, not more than 2 on any day may be wood duck.
	3 and 4	1 Oct-12 Dec		
Sea duck (scoter, eider, old squaw, and mergansers)	1 and 2	1 Feb-27 Feb	10 per day, 20 in possession	In addition to a Class 1, 2, 3, or 4 licence the hunter must have, for migratory birds, a Canada Migratory Game Bird Hunting Permit. This costs $2, and is obtainable from post offices.
Geese	1 and 2	19 Oct-7 Nov 23 Nov-9 Jan	5 per day, 10 in possession	
	3 and 4	1 Oct-12 Dec		
Brant	1 and 2	19 Oct-7 Nov 23 Nov-9 Jan		
	3 and 4	1 Oct-12 Dec		
Wilson's snipe	1 and 2	19 Oct-7 Nov 23 Nov-9 Jan	10 per day	
	3 and 4	1 Oct-12 Dec		
Woodcock	1 and 2	28 Sept-21 Nov	8 per day, 16 in possession	
	3	21 Sept-14 Nov		
	4	28 Sept-21 Nov		

northern Labrador, though there is still a sizeable population of them in central New-foundland. Bear are found in some abund-ance in all the moose areas. The only common game bird is the ptarmigan ('par-tridge'), but spruce grouse are found in Labrador. Ruffed grouse have recently been introduced to Newfoundland, and there is now an open season for them. Rabbit (snowshoe or varying hare) are plentiful, but Arctic hare may be hunted only in Labrador. Except for sea ducks, waterfowl are not abundant, and non-residents are not encouraged to hunt for them.

Licence Regulations

Caribou licences can be obtained only from the Department of Mines, Agriculture and Resources at St John's, which issues them on a quota system and a first-come first-served basis. Regular moose licences can be bought from licensed vendors in most important centres, as well as from the Department of Mines, but licences to hunt in the Moose Management Areas are limited by quota, and are also issued on a first-come first-served basis. Non-residents holding either a moose or a caribou licence may shoot ptarmigan (as well as rabbits) without taking out a small-game licence.

Non-resident hunters must be accompanied by licensed guides, never in a less proportion than one guide to every two hunters. When hunting big game, dogs are illegal, as are .22 rifles and those using ammunition with a muzzle energy of less than 1,500 foot pounds. Shotguns of smaller gauge than 20-bore, or larger gauge than 10-bore are illegal, as are automatic rifles and shotguns not plugged down to three cartridges in all. Big-game licences must be handed into the nearest appropriate

---

Caribou, Moose and Bear Seasons—Newfoundland

Caribou

Shot in five caribou areas along the south coast. In four, the season is 5 September to 24 October; the fifth area, the Avalon peninsula, has a season running from 12 September to 26 September, open only to residents. In every area the bag limit is one (male in the Avalon peninsula).

Moose

The island is divided, for the purpose of moose management, into both zones and smaller moose-management areas. The season in all five management areas (four in the centre and one in the south-west) runs from 5 September to 19 December. The bag limit is one moose of either sex. The season varies in the zones : in three it runs from 5 September to 24 October ; in the others there is a November-December season. The bag limit in all zones is one moose of either sex.

Black Bear

The areas and seasons for black bear coincide with those for moose, and the bag limit is one of either sex.

---

authority within seven days of expiry, and all successful big-game hunters must hand in the appropriate licence within seven days of the kill. Successful grouse hunters are required, by law, to send the wing tips and the two central tail feathers of all birds killed to the Wildlife Service Building, 810 Pleasantville, St John's. In Management Areas or Zones, where only male moose or caribou may be taken, the antlers must be left on the skull of any kill as a proof of sex, and in moose management areas the lower jawbone of any kill must be submitted to the local wildlife office for the purpose of statistical research into herd composition.

Further Information

Tourist Development Division, Department of Economic Development, Confederation Building, St John's.

Wildlife Division, Department of Mines, Agriculture and Resources, Confederation Building, St John's.

New Hampshire (U.S.A.)

A small, New England state of about 9,000 square miles. Much of it is mountainous and heavily forested, and dairying is the main form of agriculture. Since it lies close to large centres of population and is a favoured holiday resort hunting pressures are heavy, and game management has to be of a high standard to maintain hunting at its present levels.

Small Game Seasons and Limits—Newfoundland

Species	Area	Season	Limit	Comment
Ptarmigan	Newfoundland Brunette Island Labrador	19 Sept-28 Nov 1 Oct-10 Oct 1 Oct- 30 April	50 per season	
Spruce grouse	Newfoundland Labrador	No open season 10 Oct-30 April	No limit	
Ruffed grouse	Newfoundland Labrador	19 Sept-28 Nov 1 Oct-30 April	25 per season	
Snowshoe hare	Newfoundland Avalon peninsula Labrador	1 Oct-31 Dec 1 Oct-27 Feb 1 Oct-31 March	No limit	
Arctic hare	Newfoundland Labrador	No open season 1 Oct-31 March	No limit	Recently introduced to Brunette Island, it is illegal to hunt them there.
Duck (except scoter, eider and squaw)	Northern Labrador Southern Labrador Newfoundland Coastal region of Newfoundland	1 Sept-21 Nov 1 Sept-21 Nov 7 Sept-21 Nov 7 Sept-21 Nov	6 per day exclusive of mergansers	No limits in any area on the number of migratory game birds in possession
Geese Wilson's snipe			5 per day 10 per day	
Scoter Eider Old squaw	Northern Labrador Southern Labrador Newfoundland Coastal region of Newfoundland	1 Sept-5 Dec 14 Oct-13 Jan No open season 2 Dec-10 March	} Total of 25 per day Total of 12 per day	

New Hampshire has an autumn season for gray squirrel, with a limit of 5 per day.

Big Game Inventory—New Jersey		
Species	Shot	Est. pop.
Deer	8,682	38,000

Deer are now found almost everywhere, although any-sex harvesting is the rule, but ruffed grouse have come under pressure and increasing numbers of pheasant are released every year to reduce that pressure. There is not enough arable farming in the area to allow the pheasant to become indigenous. Waterfowl do not overfly the state, but there are a certain number of nesting species, principally black duck, wood duck and American mergansers. Nesting and migrating woodcock may also be found in large numbers in the many alder coverts.

Special Regulations
No .22 rim-fire rifles or semi-automatics holding more than five rounds may be used on deer.

Further Information
Fish and Game Department, 34 Bridge Street, Concord, New Hampshire 03301.

New Jersey (U.S.A.)
A small, heavily populated, highly industrialized state, New Jersey still manages to provide hunting and hunting grounds. The Department of Fish and Game maintains 38 public hunting grounds in addition to more than 200,000 acres of state forests that are open to hunters. In addition it runs four game farms at which pheasants and quail are raised for release throughout the state.

Rabbits, pheasant, quail, squirrels and waterfowl provide most of the sport, and deer have increased sufficiently to provide hunting in most counties. Geese, brant, black duck and scaup provide good shooting, and great flights of woodcock cross Cape May during the migrations.

Special Regulations
Rifles may not be used for taking game animals, though they may be used on woodchuck. No shotgun larger than 10-bore or capable of holding more than two cartridges may be used, and no shot smaller than buckshot may be used on deer.

Further Information
Division of Fish and Game & Shell Fisheries, Box 1809, Trenton, New Jersey 08625.

Big Game Inventory—New Hampshire		
Species	Shot	Est. Pop.
Deer	13,619	45,000
Black bear	199	1,100

Licence Fees—New Hampshire		
Type	Status	Fee
Hunting/Fishing	Resident	$7.25
	Non-resident	$30.50

Seasons and Limits—New Hampshire		
Species	Season	Limit
Deer	10 Nov-1 Dec	One, either sex
Black bear	1 Sept-1 Dec	No limit
	With dogs : 1 Sept-14 Nov	
Rabbit	1 Oct-15 March	5 per day
Hare	1 Oct-15 March	3 per day
Gray Squirrel	1 Oct-1 Nov	5 per day
Pheasant	1 Oct-9 Nov	2 per day, 10 per year
Ruffed grouse	1 Oct-1 Dec	4 per day, 25 per year

Seasons and Limits—New Jersey

Species	Season	Limit
Deer (with 3-in antlers)	7 Dec–12 Dec	One per season
Deer (either sex)	20 Dec	
Bear	7 Dec–12 Dec	One per season
Cottontail rabbit	7 Nov–5 Dec, 14 Dec–6 Feb	4 per day
Gray squirrel	7 Nov–5 Dec, 14 Dec–6 Feb	5 per day
Pheasant	7 Nov–5 Dec, 14 Dec–2 Jan	2 cocks per day
Ruffed grouse	7 Nov–5 Dec, 14 Dec–6 Feb	3 per day
Bobwhite quail	7 Nov–5 Dec, 14 Dec–6 Feb	7 per day

Licence Fees—New Jersey

Type	Status	Fee
General	Resident	$5.15
General	Non-resident	$15 15
Special deer (either sex)		$2.00

Licence Fees—New Mexico

Species	Status	Fee
Barbary sheep	Resident	$20,00
	Non-resident	$100.00
Elk	Resident	$15.00
	Non-resident	$50.00
Antelope	Resident	$10.00
	Non-resident	$40.00
Deer/bear/squirrel/turkey	Resident	$7.50
Bear	Non-resident	$25.00
Deer/squirrel/turkey	Non-resident	$50.25
Deer, special drawing	Resident	$3.00
	Non-resident	$6.00
Deer tag	Either	$2.00
Cougar	Resident	$10.00
	Non-resident	$100.00
Upland birds	Resident	$5.00
	Non-resident	$17.00

Big Game Inventory—New Mexico

Species	Shot
Mule deer	25,800
Wild turkey	2,192
Pronghorn	1,349
Elk	1.285
Black bear	253
Barbary sheep	60
Bighorn sheep	4

The principal big game consists of deer (mule and whitetail), elk, antelope, javelina, bear, bighorn and Barbary sheep, an introduced species. Game birds include pheasant, grouse, quail, turkey and sandhill crane. White-winged and mourning doves are abundant. New game birds recently introduced include Afghan pheasant, and black and gray francolins, and new big game animals include Siberian ibex and African oryx.

Special Regulations
Deer may be taken with buckshot during the special season. Otherwise no fully automatic rifles, M1 carbine, or rifle not using centre-fire cartridges may be used. Cartridges that are used on deer must have at least 55-grain bullets, and have a rated muzzle energy of at least 960 foot-pounds, for elk at least 87 grains and 1,000 foot-pounds.

Further Information
Department of Fish and Game, State Capitol, Sante Fé, New Mexico 87501.

New Mexico (U.S.A.)
A largely desert state of the south-west, its 122,000 square miles are mostly mountainous, lying at an average height of 5,700 ft and running up, in the north, towards the southern foothills of the Rockies. The climate is dry, with an average rainfall below 15 in and, except where there is irrigation, ranching is the commonest form of agriculture. The low rainfall is a limiting factor for game populations as well as for farm crops, and an important part of the Department of Game's work is providing water and watering places for the various forms of game.

New South Wales (Australia)
New South Wales covers 309,453 square miles and is entirely situated in the temperate zone, with a healthy and equable climate. The coastal regions on the east are naturally well watered, and form the most populous and urbanized area of the state. They are bounded on the west by the Tablelands (part of the Great Dividing Range), which rise to over 7,000 ft, the western slopes of which form a distinct section, watered in the south by the Snowy river, diverted westward through the mountains. The Western Plains are watered by the Murray-Darling river system, with immense reservoirs and numerous artesian wells.

There is considerable mining, but, sheep, for which the climate is ideal, are still extremely important. There is also plenty of arable farming and a considerable timber industry. Nevertheless, despite the varied and mostly unspoilt terrain, the shooting of native fauna is very limited and it is only the introduced species that provide any variation in the bag.

Licences
A firearms licence is not required for shot-

Seasons and Limits—New Mexico

The State is divided into zones, regions and special areas, many of which have different seasons and limits.

Species	Season	Limit	Comment
Deer, white-tailed and mule	7 Nov-8 Dec		Special drawing in some areas.
Antelope	3 Sept-11 Oct	One per season	Special drawing for permits
Elk	26 Sept-24 Jan		Special drawing in some areas
Cougar	20 Nov-28 Nov (without dogs) 29 Nov-31 March (with dogs)	One over one year old, except for females with kittens	
Black bear	8 Aug-27 Dec		
Bighorn sheep	19 Sept-18 Jan	19 Sept-18 Jan	Special drawing, residents only
Barbary sheep	6 Feb-14 Feb		Special drawing
Rabbit, cottontail and jack	All year		
Squirrel	12 Sept-20 Sept		
Pheasant	28 Nov-29 Nov		
Quail, Gambel's, scaled and bobwhite	Starts 28 Nov, end varies		
Blue grouse	12 Sept-20 Sept		
Prairie chicken	12 Sept-20 Sept		Sometimes no open season
Wild turkey	7 Nov-20 Dec, 17 April-15 May		
Sandhill crane	Set from year to year		Shot in Charez country

guns or rifles, except .303s. However, a game licence is required for those shooting duck or quail. The licence covers both species, and may be obtained for $4 from all Court Houses. Approximately 10,700 licences are issued annually, but only a small proportion of their holders are regular quail shooters.

There are six private and two state Game Reserves where hunters may shoot for a fee. Otherwise all hunting is on private property and the consent of the landowner or occupier must first be obtained. Hunters may shoot ducks in the State Game Reserves (at Llangothlin Lagoon, Guyra, and Lake Innes, Port Macquarie) provided they have a permit issued by the National Parks and Wildlife Service, which controls the numbers visiting the area, the duration of each visit, and the conduct of the hunters in the reserve. During the close season the Game Reserves are used for wildlife conservation and the study of wildfowl and their habitat. The six private game reserves have only very recently been established, their clientele is local, and they are not at present looking for additional shooters.

Special Regulations

No hunting or firearms are permitted in 'Wildlife Refuges', National Parks, State Parks, Historic Sites, or Nature Reserves. The National Parks and Wildlife Service employ Law Enforcement Officers to enforce these and all other regulations concerning hunting in every section of the state.

Further Information

There is only one firm in New South Wales at present offering guide and hunting services:

High Country Safaris, Messrs Gregory & Leighton, Sunny Corner, N.S.W. 2795. Additional information from:

N.S.W. Field and Game Association (Hon. Secretary, G. Rabbidge, Box 4178, G.P.O., Sydney).

N.S.W. Branch, National Sporting Shooters' Association (Hon. President, L. Morton, 22 Gladys Ave., French Forest, N.S.W.) is primarily for those interested in rifle shooting (deer, pig, goat, fox, rabbit).

National Parks and Wildlife Service, A.D.C. Building, 189-193 Kent Street, Sydney, N.S.W.

New York (U.S.A.)

This state, which covers about 50,000 square miles contains the Adirondack and Catskill Mountains, and the Hudson, Mohawk, Susquehanna and Upper Delaware rivers. In spite of its large cities and dense population it is still a predominantly agricultural state, with dairying and market gardening among its important industries. The whole state is timbered, and there are over 11 million acres of commercial forest. In addition to these, many of them open for hunting, there are the forest preserves of the Adirondacks and the Catskills, together with over half a million acres of public lands, all of them open to the public, which account for the excellent hunting still available in spite of the hunting and population pressures.

Deer are plentiful enough to cause damage to farm crops, and farmers are issued, from time to time, permits to take offending deer, and open seasons for antlerless deer have to be declared. The north-east of the state has a well established population of Hungarian partridge, together with excellent woodcock and ruffed grouse. There is good pheasant hunting in central New York, where a considerable acreage of cereals is grown, and a growing wild turkey population in the south-west and the Catskills. There is good duck shooting on the northern lakes, and the coastal marshes are open to the public and offer black duck, green-winged teal and brant.

Special Regulations

In some counties only shotguns may be used on deer. Except during the deer season it is illegal to have cartridges bigger than .22 or shot shells larger than Number 4 in the field. Only shotguns may be used on turkey. Dogs may not be used on deer.

Seasons and Limits—New South Wales

Of the native fauna, only duck and quail have open seasons ; introduced species may be shot all the year.

Species	Season	Limit	Comment
Duck : black duck, chestnut teal, hardhead, mountain duck, gray teal, Australian shoveller, wood duck and pink-eared duck	Penultimate Saturday in Feb—last Saturday in April	10 per day (varies with season)	A specified number of ducks damaging rice crops may be shot by special authorization from the National Parks and Wildlife Service
Quail : brown quail and stubble quail	First Saturday in May—last Saturday in July	25 per day, maximum of 50 in possession	
Kangaroos and wallabies		Only a specified number	May only be shot when damaging crops and improved pastures. Special authorization from the National Parks and Wildlife Service
Deer, red and fallow Feral dog and dingo Feral goat Feral pig Indian mynah Javan rusa Sparrow Starling	All year	No limit	

Big Game Inventory—New York

Species	Shot	Est. pop.
Deer	91,993	375,000
Black bear	387	4,000

Licence Fees—New York

Type	Status	Fee
General	Resident	$3.25
General	Non-resident	$35.00

A cottontail at the entrance to its burrow. New York has an open season for this small-game animal.

Further Information

Department of Environmental Conservation, Albany, New York 12201.

New Zealand

New Zealand consists primarily of two large islands in the South Pacific Ocean, North Island and South Island, separated by the Cook Strait, and Stewart Island to the south of South Island as well as several widely dispersed small outlying island territories. New Zealand proper covers about 103,000 square miles. The two chief islands are mountainous, the principal range being the Southern Alps, which stretches much of the length of South Island and includes the highest point in New Zealand, Mt Cook, over 12,000 ft. There are subsidiary ranges and some very large glaciers among the higher peaks. In North Island there is nothing to compare with the Southern Alps, but there are several smaller mountain ranges, noted in particular for their volcanoes, of which there are at present three active, and for the geysers and hot springs of the Rotorua district. The only extensive area of flat land is the north-west peninsula of North Island, culminating in Cape Maria van Diemen, though there are small flat coastal strips on the east and south of South Island. Rivers and lakes are numerous, the former being short and mostly unnavigable.

The climate is moist-temperate marine, with a small annual temperature range which permits vegetation growth all the year. Rainfall is moderate, generally slightly heavier in North Island, but the western, and in particular the south-western slopes of the Southern Alps have a very heavy rainfall, approaching 300 in per annum.

The soil is fertile and agriculture remains the chief industry. Sheep and dairy farming are particularly important; wheat, oats and barley are the main crops and fruit and vegetables are also grown. Of special interest is the venison export market, which is supplied by extensive commercial deer shooting. The official government policy is one of extermination, all deer being considered pests. While this is true of red deer it seems a shortsighted attitude towards the minor deer species, in particular moose and wapiti.

Noxious Pests

Certain species, listed in the table, are classified as 'noxious pests' and may be shot at any time. They are the most interesting category as far as the hunter is concerned. Where possible a rough indication of their distribution is given.

Of those listed moose and wapiti both appear to be diminishing rapidly; moose because they are trapped within the inhospitable and unsuitable Dusky Sound area by the surrounding ring of mountains; wapiti, though less firmly trapped, are suffering badly from interbreeding with red

Seasons and Limits—New York

Vary from zone to zone

Species	Season	Limit	Comment
Deer	25 Oct-1 Dec 2 Nov-31 Dec	One buck with antlers at least 3in	Northern zone Southern zone No open season on Long Island, in Westchester county and Southern Delaware areas
Black bear	25 Oct-1 Dec 16 Nov-1 Dec 16 Nov-16 Dec	One per year	Northern zone Southern zone Catskills
Cottontail rabbit and snowshoe hare	1 Oct-28 Feb 1 Nov-15 Feb	6 per day	Statewide Long Island
Gray squirrel	1 Oct-31 Jan	5 per day	
Raccoon	1 Oct-14 March 19 Oct-14 March	No limit	Northern zone Southern zone
Pheasant	1 Oct-15 Nov 1 Nov-31 Dec	2 per day	Statewide Long Island
Ruffed grouse	1 Oct-31 Jan 1 Nov-31 Dec	4 per day	Statewide Long Island
Bobwhite quail	19 Oct-15 Nov 1 Nov-31 Dec	4 per day	Statewide Long Island
Hungarian partridge	1 Oct-1 Nov 19 Oct-1 Nov 19 Oct-15 Nov		St Lawrence county Clinton and Franklin counties Jefferson county
Wild turkey	2 Nov-14 Nov and 10 May-15 May		A special licence, no charge, is necessary

deer. Large areas of Fiordland National Park, however, are denied to hunters because of the presence of the *Notornis*, a large flightless gallinule, previously thought extinct. These areas are perfect sanctuaries for red deer; the cullers cannot get at them, and they continue to breed wapiti out. The government's culling programme does not include moose and wapiti, but this negative attitude is unlikely to provide a satisfactory substitute for a positive management policy that now appears to be the only hope for these two species.

The other species classified as noxious pests are much more numerous. Between 150,000 and 200,000 are shot each year by an estimated hunting population of 20,000. The only limitation on deer-shooting is for wapiti. These have been shot on a block system, with New Zealanders balloting for the blocks and some set aside for visitors. However, the future of the block system is in some doubt, and it is uncertain what will take its place. For trophy purposes deer are best shot between March and September as the antlers are in velvet from October to February.

The thar and chamois breeding season is

Seasons and Limits—New Zealand

The season is variable, but usually starts on the first Saturday in May, with three weeks for waterfowl and six to eight weeks for other species (including swan). Licence fees and bag limits vary with seasons and districts. The average licence fee is NZ$5 per season. Average daily bag limit for ducks is between 10 and 25 ; Usually no limit for pheasant, quail and swan. Landowners and occupiers do not require a licence on their own land.

A nilgai bull in open canopy forest, India

Game—New Zealand

Australian (brown) quail
Black swan
Californian quail
Canada geese
Chukar partridge
Gray duck
Gray duck hybrids
Guinea fowl
Mallard
Mallard hybrids
Paradise duck
Pheasant
Pheasant hybrids
Pukeko
Spoonbill duck
   (New Zealand shoveller)
Virginian quail

Partially Protected Species— New Zealand

If damaging land or property the following may be shot by landowners, occupiers or their agents :
Black-backed gull
Bush hawk
Sea hawk
White-eye

The following may be hunted or killed only if so decided by the Ministry of Internal Affairs :
Gray-faced petrel
Little shag
Mutton bird
Pied shag
South Island weka
   (on Chatham Island only)
Stewart Island weka
   (Stewart Island and islands of the Fouveaux Strait only)
Black swan
Gray duck
Gray duck hybrids
Mallard
Mallard hybrids
Pukeko
   (The latter 6 species on Chatham Island only ; elsewhere considered as game).

Noxious Pests—New Zealand

Species	Distribution
Axis deer	Generally considered extinct, possibly a few survivors
Chamois	Higher areas of central Southern Alps
Fallow deer	One area in North Island, and two areas in the south of South Island
Goat	Southern, western and eastern corners of North Island, and north-east and south-central South Island
Himalayan thar	Highest areas of central Southern Alps
Japanese (sika) deer	One area on edge of Lake Taupo in central North Ialand
Javan rusa	One area on the River Wanganui in North Island
Moose	Dusky Sound in extreme south-west of South Island
Opossum	
Pig	Much of higher ground of North Island, and north-eastern, southern and south-eastern South Island
Red deer	All South Island, especially south Southern Alps, and most high areas of North Island
Sambar deer	Rotorua district and some coastal areas of North Island
Virginian (white-tailed) deer	Stewart Island and with fallow deer on edge of Lake Wakatipu in South Island
Wallaby	
Wapiti	Fiordland National Park in the south-west of South Island

April, May and June, and winter is good for shooting as their coats are at their best then, there being of course, no seasonal variation in their horns. For many visitors the shooting of these two animals represents the peak of achievement as the hunters must have mountaineering ability, good long-range marksmanship, and considerable stalking skill; moreover the animals can provide world class heads. All the deer family produce a proportion of trophy racks with 12, 14, 16 or more points each year. In many cases, owing to the nature of the terrain, they can provide much more sporting and exciting shooting than in their native countries. In order to obtain good heads of any species it is necessary to work away from the easily accessible areas; this may involve terrain and conditions such as are found in the south-west corner of South Island, which is 'extremely arduous, precipitous, very remote, and in a high rainfall area'. Only very fit and experienced hunters should venture into such country, and even they face hardship and some danger.

Organization
It is difficult, particularly for visitors, to hunt alone. They are, therefore, advised to use a professional guide, who can ensure success, and to spend not less than a week on a hunting trip, preferably between 14 and 30 days. Permits are necessary to hunt on most lands (they may be obtained from the Forestry Department, National Parks Offices, and the Lands and Survey Department) and guides will arrange these, as well as supplying necessary equipment, tents, sleeping bags, transport, four-wheel drive vehicles, arranging skinning and taxidermy and so on. Clients should provide their own clothing, and in particular boots. Guides' fees vary considerably, generally they are between NZ $20 and NZ $60 per day.

The most popular all round calibre in New Zealand is.30–06, followed by calibres such as .270, 6·5 mm and 7 mm. Guides, if necessary, can usually supply rifles, but the formalities for importing them are simple. A police officer meets all aircraft and ships, records the number of rifles, and issues an entry permit. The rifle must be then registered at the nearest police station (registration fee: NZ $1 per rifle).

Special Regulations
Revolvers and pistols are illegal. Bows and arrows are legal and there is no separate season. Shotguns only may be used on species classified as 'game'. Shooting is permitted in certain parts of National Parks, but not in wildlife sanctuaries nor in wildlife refuges without specific authorization.

he lesser kudu is smaller and more graceful than the greater species; its distribution in Africa is smaller.

A yearling spiker. Deer are considered pests in New Zealand, and may be shot at any time despite their decreasing numbers.

Further Information

Hunting and Fishing Officer, Government Tourist Bureau, P.O. Box 527, Rotorua.

Nigeria

Nigeria is a West African country of some 356,000 square miles, divided into 12 states. There are three main topographical zones. Along the coast lies a belt of mangrove swamp forest, bounded in the north by a much wider region of tropical rain forest. The third region occupies the rest of the country to the north and is known as the Guinea Savannah belt. It is characteristically an area of open woodland and savannah, but in the north is dry, almost desert, and in the south merges with the 'high forest', with large sections burned annually to keep down the fire-tender forest flora. There are few mountains, but in the north the central plateau rises to an average elevation of about 4,000 ft. The main rivers are the Niger and its tributary the Benue, which form a massive 'Y', embracing the entire northern two thirds of the country. The climate varies considerably with the terrain and the type of country. Temperatures are high everywhere, however. On the coast they are much more constant and less extreme than in the north, but on the other hand the humidity is considerably greater. There are three chief seasons, rather less marked in the south. The rainy season lasts from May to October/November, with a short gap in August. There is a dry season from November to February, characterized by a cold dust-laden wind from the north, known locally as the 'Harmattan', and a dry hot season from late February to May/June.

Though oil is fairly important Nigeria is mainly agricultural. Palm oil and palm kernels, cocoa, cotton and ground nuts are by a long way the most important produce for export, but there is a wide range of crops for home consumption, as well as a large number of cattle, raised particularly for their hides. The country is comparatively densely populated, especially in the south, with a total population of over 60,000,000.

Nigeria's wildlife resources are not as great as those of the East African countries nor can it compare with that of many of the nearby West African countries. The high level of population is one reason for this; also a long history of commercial poaching. A more recent setback has been the eradication of the tsetse fly in many areas, resulting in the introduction of domestic cattle at the expense of wild species. Added to these factors are the annual forest burnings which also have an adverse effect, especially when they are conducted late in the year.

Prohibited Species

Certain animals are particularly rare and are classed as prohibited. They are: chimpanzee, dama gazelle, Derby's eland, dorcas gazelle, immature elephant, giraffe, gorilla, manatee, pigmy hippopotamus and rhinoceros. They may only be hunted with specific permission from the minister in charge of animals and forest resources, and permission is not granted except for scientific purposes and essential administrative reasons.

Protected Species

Other species are classed as 'specially protected' or 'protected', and a licence is required to take them, with a bag limit stated on the licence (generally smaller for specially protected species). In the following lists they are designated, when first mentioned, (sp) and (p) respectively.

The Mangrove and Fresh Water Coastal Swamp.

Apart from one or two smaller predators the only major mammals normally resident in this region are the western sitatunga (sp) which is found in the freshwater but not the mangrove swamps, and the hippopotamus (sp). There are two types of crocodile, the Nile and broad-fronted which, as well as the monitor lizard, are widely hunted for food. However most of the mammals classified as 'high forest' types are occasionally found in the marginal swamp areas, particularly when the forest is inundated by the rain.

Lowland Rain Forest. Duikers (p): black, black-fronted, Ogilby's, yellow-backed and Maxwell's, of which yellow-backed and Maxwell's are common, the others relatively rare. The royal pigmy antelope, western sitatunga, harnessed bush-buck (p), forest buffalo (p), hippopotamus, bush pig, giant forest hog, elephants (sp) (some are relatively small and may possibly be a separate sub species), leopard, African golden cat and other minor felines, numerous primates including the specially protected colobus monkey.

The Guinea Savannah (except for the desert north-east). Western hartebeest (p), Senegal hartebeest (p), red-flanked duiker (p), western bush duiker (p), klipspringer (sp), pigmy antelopes, oribi (p), western kob (p), defassa water-buck (p), Nigerian bohor reed-buck (p), red-fronted gazelle (p), western roan antelope (p), harnessed bush-buck, Cameroun giant eland, forest buffalo, hippopotamus, warthog, red river hog (p), elephants, lion, leopard, cheetah (sp), serval and other small felines, side-striped and black-backed jackal, African hunting dog, spotted hyena, dog-faced baboon, 'togo' hare and numerous rodents, hydraxes and aardvark.

North-East Guinea Savannah. Senegal hartebeest, western bush duiker, red-fronted gazelle, scimitar-horned oryx, addax antelope, western sitatunga, forest buffalo, hippopotamus (found with the sitatunga on the fringes of Lake Chad), warthog, barbary sheep, elephants, lion, leopard, cheetah, caracel (sp), spotted hyena, African hunting dog.

As the distribution indicates, the best area is the Guinea Savannah, providing general 'plains' hunting and the highest density of large mammals. The montane and desert areas, the swamps and the 'high forest' each provide specialized hunting.

Game Birds of Nigeria

The chief game birds are as follows:
Ferruginous duck (white-eyed pochard), common pochard, shoveler, common teal, garganey and pin-tail migrate to northern Nigeria. Mallard is occasionally found in parts of the south. Spur-winged goose, Egyptian goose, fulvous goose, knob-billed goose are resident in northern Nigeria. Hartlaub's duck is resident in the high forest. Whistling teal (white-faced duck) and pygmy goose (dwarf goose) are resident throughout the territory. The best wildfowl shooting is in the north-east, on the approaches to Lake Chad, but other swamps and large rivers are also good.
Francolins, including Senegambian double-spurred francolin, Latham's francolin, white-throated francolin, and, less commonly, the Sierra Leone double-spurred, Adamawan double-spurred, Clapperton's and Ahanta francolins.
Butler's stone partridge.
Common or migratory quail, Africa blue quail, African button quail.
Gray-breasted helmeted guinea fowl, African crested guinea fowl.
Sudan bustard, Denham's bustard, Nubian bustard, Senegal bustard, northern black-bellied bustard.
Common snipe and greater or solitary snipe (winter immigrants).
Pin-tailed and four-banded sand-grouse.
Pigeons, including speckled, Bruce's fruit and Gambian green fruit pigeons.
The upland game birds, particularly the phasianids, are generally walked up on farmlands and suitable savannah, though bustard is commonly shot with a rifle.

The black-bellied bustard is one of the many game birds to be found in Nigeria.

Protected Birds
Pelican is 'protected', as are Abyssinian ground hornbill, and vultures, secretary bird, ostrich, great white heron, greater bustard, European stork and crowned crane are 'specially protected'.

Game Bird Seasons
There are no seasons but game birds should not be shot during the rainy season, when mating. The best time of year is late November to March, and the migratory wildfowl add variety at this time.

Organization
Nigeria's wildlife is not exploited for tourist purposes, consequently there is no arrangement for the temporary importation of sporting firearms and there are no professional hunting organizations to assist visiting sportsmen. Visitors are advised to make private arrangements with friends, part-time hunters, or one of the few professional hunters (those who make their living by hunting) still to be found in the mid-Western state. It should, perhaps, be noted that the organization of safaris for visitors is at a much more advanced stage in the neighbouring French-speaking countries. The best time for all round shooting in West Africa generally is between the savannah burning (about the end of December) and the start of the heavy rains (June/July), except in the 'high forest', where the best conditions are immediately after the heavy rains (November/December).

Further Information
There is no organized source of information for visitors about hunting, and those interested will have to make their own arrangements. Some helpful information may be obtained, however, from: A. P. Leventis, Iddo House, Iddo, Lagos.
Mr John Charter, Federal Forestry Department, Ibadan.

Nilgai *(Boselaphus tragocamelus)*
The blue bull is found throughout India, though rarer in the north and south. The name 'Nilgai' means blue cow, but the cow is brownish in colour and only the bull has a bluish coat. The largest of the Indian antelopes, it stands 54 in at the shoulder and can weigh up to 700 lb. Its short cone-like horns average a mere 8 in and make an insignificant trophy, so the nilgai is largely ignored by sportsmen, although in parts of Madhya Pradesh holders of licences are asked to shoot it because of the damage it does to growing crops. The cows produce one or two young, annually, and in many parts of India they are held to be sacred. Very easily shot, the nilgai's main enemy is the tiger.

Nilgiri Ibex *see* Nilgiri Thar

Nilgiri Thar *(Hemitragus hylocrius)*
Locally misnamed Nilgiri ibex, this species

is found in the mountains of southern India, particularly the Nilgiri hills and those of Cohin, South Coimbatore, Travancore and Madura. Their favourite habitat is the grassy highlands close to steep precipices where they are usually found in herds of four or five up to as many as sixty. Slightly larger than their close relative the Himalayan thar they stand 42 in at the shoulder with horns averaging about 14 in long and 8 in in girth. The Nilgiri thar breeds once a year, and usually one, though sometimes two kids, are born. The old males are nearly black with a distinctive white marking behind the shoulder from which they get the nickname 'saddlebacks'. Only one may be shot on licence. Spying for them and stalking them in the early morning or evening, when they are out grazing, in magnificent scenery and a pleasant climate above 8,000 ft, within sight of the Arabian Sea, makes a memorable day, quite apart from the trophy. Excessive poaching has greatly reduced their numbers, but it is felt that little harm can be done in permitting licence holders to continue shooting the saddlebacks, which are useless from a breeding viewpoint and the presence in the hills of official licence holders, it is hoped, may deter the poachers and thus protect the diminishing numbers.

North Carolina (U.S.A.)

One of the largest eastern states, its 52,000 square miles consist of a coastal plain, giving way to the rolling uplands of the Piedmont Plateau, which, in their turn, rise to the mountainous country of the Appalachians. It is an agricultural state, the chief crops being cotton, maize and tobacco. Nearly two thirds of the state are forested.

Big game is found mainly on the coastal strip and in the mountains, with deer, wild boar, bear and turkey in both areas. Quail are found on the uplands and ruffed grouse in the mountains. There is excellent waterfowl hunting all along the coast, with geese especially plentiful on Lake Mattamuskeet, duck on Currituck Sound and brant in the Hatteras and Ocracoke areas.

Special Regulations

Rifles of .243 calibre or larger may be used on deer, as well as shotguns of 20 gauge or larger, loaded with rifled slugs, though buckshot is permitted in some Game Management Areas. Rifles of .22 calibre may be used on all small game except migratory birds.

Further Information

Wildlife Resources Commission, Box 2919, Raleigh, North Carolina 27602.

North Dakota (U.S.A.)

A large midwestern state of 70,000 square miles. The eastern half of the state forms part of the Central Lowlands, and consists of a flat and fertile plain with ample rainfall for arable farming. West of this it rises to the Great Plains where, at 3,000 feet and with little rainfall, corn crops give way to ranching. West of this lie the Black Hills, outliers of the Rocky Mountains. Several large rivers run through the state, including the Missouri and Red Rivers, and much of the small game is found in these river bottoms.

There are white-tailed deer throughout the state, but mule deer are only met in the woods and hills of the west. Antelope are also to be found in the west, and there are ruffed, sharp-tailed and a few sage grouse in the mountains. Hungarian partridge are

---

Seasons and Limits—North Carolina

Vary in different Game Management areas.

Species	Season	Limit	Comment
Deer	12 Oct-2 Jan	One per day, 2 per season	Antlered males only
Black bear	12 Oct-21 Nov, and 25 Dec-2 Jan	One per day, 2 per season	Permits by special drawing
Wild boar	12 Oct-21 Nov, and 25 Dec-2 Jan		
Cottontail rabbit	14 Nov-13 Feb	5 per day, 75 per season	
Squirrel	12 Oct-2 Jan	No limit	
Bobwhite quail	14 Nov-27 Feb	8 per day, 100 per season	
Ruffed grouse	12 Oct-27 Feb	3 per day, 30 per season	
Wild turkey	19 Nov-13 Feb, and 12 April-1 May		

Licence Fees—North Carolina

Type	Status	Fee
General	Resident	$5.50
General	Non-resident	$22.00

Big Game Inventory—North Carolina

Species	Shot
Deer	38,000
Black bear	430
Wild turkey	220
Wild boar	400

Licence Fees—North Dakota

Type	Status	Fee	Comment
Basic registration	Resident	$50	Sold at county auditor's offices
Basic registration	Non-resident	$50	
White-tailed deer, mule deer and antelope	Resident	$6	
	Non-resident	$50	
Small game	Resident	$2	
	Non-resident	$35	
Predator stamp	Non-resident	$15	
Turkey tag	Resident	$3	
Deer tag	Resident	$1	
Mule deer tag	Non-resident	$1	

Big Game Inventory—North Dakota		
Species	Shot	Est. pop.
White-tailed deer	12,000	80,000
Mule deer	1,850	20,000
Antelope	2,100	5,000

Seasons and Limits—North Dakota			
Species	Season*	Limit	Comment
Deer, white-tailed and mule	6 Nov and 15 Nov	One buck per year	Drawings for mule deer and special antlerless whitetail permits
Antelope	18 Sept and 27 Sept		Special drawing, residents only
Rabbits, cottontail and jack	All year		
Snowshoe hare	All year		
Squirrel, gray and fox	19 Sept and 31 Dec		
Grouse, sharp-tailed and ruffed	19 Sept and 13 Dec		
Hungarian partridge	19 Sept and 13 Dec		
Wild turkey	21 Nov and 29 Nov		Special drawing, residents only

*The dates given are those within which the seasons are decided

common in good breeding years, and wild turkey have become well established, especially along the Missouri. Pheasant have declined so markedly in recent years that there is no longer an open season for them. Mourning doves, both resident and migrant, are plentiful, and waterfowl, after a good hatching year, can be abundant, the resident numbers being swollen by the flights south from the Canadian prairies. Bighorn sheep have recently been introduced from British Columbia.

Further Information
State Game and Fish Department, 103½ South 3rd Street, Bismarck 58501.

Northern Ireland *see* United Kingdom of Great Britain and Ireland.

Northern Territory (Australia)

The Northern Territory covers an area of 523,000 square miles, most of which lies in the tropics. There are three main types of terrain: the low-lying, heavily wooded coastal plains; the jagged and eroded scarps and mountain ranges of the Barkly Tableland in the north-east, and the Macdonnell ranges of the south; and the broad, semi-desert plains that cover the rest of the country. The lowlands of the centre and south are semi-arid, but the coastal region receives heavy monsoon rainfall from November to April, which also affects the high country of the south to a varying and unpredictable degree. The 'dry' is warm and pleasant, with very little rain anywhere and quite cold nights in the south. The 'wet' is humid and unpleasant in the north and extremely hot, day and night, in the south.

The chief pastoral activity of the territory is beef cattle raising, but mining and tourism now produce more revenue, and there is a growing fishing industry. Despite the vast open spaces, there are numerous and complicated restrictions on shooting, as the Northern Territory Administration has an active conservation policy. Moreover, before shooting on private property, permission must be obtained from the owner, and this is not as readily forthcoming as it once was, owing to irresponsible shooting and consequent stock losses.

All animals are protected, unless they are specifically classified as 'game', 'partly protected', or 'pests'.
Special Regulations
Certain areas are classified as sanctuaries or as protected areas (the latter include all aboriginal reserves). No one may take or kill any animal within these areas, nor may they carry a firearm or trap there, unless they are on a public road, or have authorization, and can prove they have not used the firearm or trap, or that the road by which they entered was not posted.

Penalties for infringement of these regulations are up to $400 or 12 months' imprisonment. Maps of existing sanctuaries and protected areas are available for public inspection at every police station and Animal Industry branch.

Firearms may not be discharged within 2 miles of the post offices in the major towns, or within the Greater Darwin area (extending about 11 miles south of the city).

The estuarine, or saltwater crocodile is the larger of the two Australian species. It is found along mangrove-fringed mudbanks in northern Australia.

Game, Partly Protected and Pest Species—Northern Territory

Game

The following may be shot from 1 July to 31 October:
All ducks and geese except magpie geese, which may be shot from 1 Aug to 31 Dec, and pygmy geese and burdekin duck, which are completely protected.

Partly Protected

May only be taken or killed under a licence issued by the Chief Inspector of Wildlife.
Parrots and cockatoos:
red-collared lorikeet, varied lorikeet, red-tailed black cockatoo, white cockatoo, galah, corella, little corella, cockatiel, red-winged parrot. Port Lincoln parrot, mulga parrot, Bourke's parrot, budgerigar.
Finches:
zebra, banded, black-ringed, chestnut-breasted, yellow-tailed, pictorella, star, crimson, long-tailed, black-tailed, masked, Gouldian.
Marine crocodile
Buffalo
Red kangaroo

Pests.

May be destroyed at any time within the stated area:
In the whole Northern Territory: feral rabbit, feral donkey, feral pig, feral camel, feral cat, feral goat, fox, dingo and wild dog, black rat, Norway rat, house mouse, little reddish fruit bat, Gould's fruit bat, all snakes.
In Alice Springs Pastoral District (except Trephina Gorge area): wedge-tailed eagle.
North of the 15th parallel (except the Arnhem Land aboriginal reserve): agile wallaby.

Licences

All firearms must be registered, but pistols and 'high-powered firearms' require a special licence, the issue of which is severely restricted. However, sporting needs should be amply catered for by those firearms that do not fall into the 'high-powered' category. These are: shotguns; rifles with the striker or firing pin not situated centrally in the breech face; rifles with a calibre of .310 in; rifles commonly classed as .32/40, .25/20, .44/40, .32/20, .38/40, .38/55, and .45/70 (the decimal point and first two figures indicate the calibre in inches, and the last two figures indicate the weight of the propellent charge commonly used, in grains).

Visitors carrying firearms must report to a police station within two days of entry and register/licence their firearms.

Further Information

Animal Industry and Agriculture, Northern Territory Administration, Darwin, Northern Territory 5790.

Northwest Territories (Canada)

These territories, comprising one third of all Canada, constitute the Canadian Arctic. They cover an area of 1,300,000 square miles and contain a total population of around 33,000, two thirds of it Indian or Eskimo.

The area can be divided, climatically, into sub-Arctic and Arctic zones, that is, those parts where the average daily temperature will, in the hottest month, exceed fifty degrees, and those parts where it will not. The topographic division is between areas of tundra and forest. Tundra predominates in the east, and along the Arctic Ocean coast, whilst forest predominates in the south and the west. There are, besides the vast Great Bear and Great Slave Lakes, numerous smaller lakes, and a great number of rivers, including the Mackenzie River system which, together with the tributary Athabaska River, runs for 2,500 miles. Some parts of the alluvial plain of the Mackenzie River basin are capable of growing cereals and vegetables, but farming is, for obvious reasons, limited. Mining, fishing and fur trapping are the principal and almost sole occupations. Transport is mainly by air or water, but the Mackenzie Highway is now beginning to open up parts of the south to motor traffic. It is an ambitious system of gravel roads running from Grimshaw in Alberta north to Yellowknife, and from Fort Resolution in the east to Fort Simpson in the west. Near Fort Simpson lies the beginning of Zone 12, which, together with Zone 19, constitutes the vast Mackenzie Mountains hunting area, lying along most of the western border, which has only recently been opened to non-resident hunters. Similarly, National Highway No 5 runs south from the south-eastern spur of the Highway, and through the Wood Buffalo National Park to Fort Smith. Wood Buffalo

Park is the largest national park, and contains the largest surviving herd of bison in the world. Hunting is, of course, prohibited inside the park, but the bison population in contiguous areas is now high enough for carefully limited hunting to be possible, and Zones 3 and 5, lying on the centre of the border with Alberta have, accordingly, been opened to non-resident bison hunters.

The government of the Territories insists, correctly, that the indigenous population of Indians and Eskimos, whose whole economy and style of life are still closely bound up with hunting, should always have the first claim on all the game resources of the area. Because of this only certain game zones have been opened to the non-resident hunter, and a strict bag limit is enforced for almost all forms of game. The zones of greatest interest to the non-resident are Zones 12 and 19. These cover some 60,000 square miles of almost virgin hunting country in the Mackenzie Mountains that have recently been opened to non-residents, and they contain Dall sheep, mountain goat, grizzly and black bears, moose and caribou. The non-resident may also shoot a bison in Zones 3 and 5 close to Fort Smith, and big game may be shot in Zone 7, which has only recently been opened to non-residents. Polar bear hunting has also been recently opened to non-residents. It is carried out from Eskimo settlements on Banks Island and Cornwallis Island in spring, and from settlements on Southampton Island in autumn. These hunts are arranged through the settlements, the community associations acting, in these cases, as the licensed outfitting agencies. Licences for both bison and polar bear hunting are strictly limited, and applications should be made early, as they will be handled on a first come, first served basis. Apart from the Zones already mentioned, non-residents are not permitted to hunt big game anywhere in the Territories.

Special Regulations

Except when hunting only game birds and water fowl, a non-resident hunter must be accompanied by a recognized guide; if hunting either polar bear or sea mammals that guide must be an Eskimo. (It is almost essential for a non-resident hunter to place himself in the hands of an outfitter, Eskimo or otherwise, who will arrange guides, accommodation, transport and licences.) No one may hunt big game with a rifle loaded with a cartridge designed to produce less than 1,000 foot-pounds of energy at a distance 100 yd from the muzzle, or with a tracer or fully metal-cased, non-expanding bullet, or with fully automatic firearms. For waterfowl shotguns must be 10-gauge or smaller and not capable of holding more than three cartridges. Before entering the wilderness all hunters are requested to file their itineraries with a Game Officer or a member

Type	Status	Fee	Comment
Licence Fees—Northwest Territories			
Big Game (includes black bear, grizzly bear, moose, caribou, mountain sheep and mountain goat)	Resident Non-resident Canadian Non-resident alien	$10 $100 $150	Licences sold by game officers at Yellowknife, and other major settlements
Bison	Resident Non-resident Canadian Non-resident alien	$50 $75 $150	
Polar bear	Resident Non-resident Canadian Non-resident alien	$50 $150 $250	Polar bear cannot be shot if accompanied by cubs
Game bird	Resident Non-resident Canadian Non-resident alien	$2 $5 $10	
Migratory game bird permit	Any	$2	Must be held for migratory game birds in addition to game bird licence. Obtainable from post offices.

of the Royal Canadian Mounted Police. It is illegal to shoot from, or carry a loaded firearm in, a motor vehicle, aircraft, power boat or sailing boat, excepting that a power boat may be used when hunting sea mammals. Dogs may be used when hunting game birds, but not when hunting big game of any sort. Game birds and big game meat may be kept up to the bag limit, but any not used must be given to local residents. Up to 25 lb of seal and 50 lb of whale meat may be re-tained, but the rest must be given to the Eskimos. Proof of sex must not have been removed from any game exported from the Territories, and an export licence is required. All kills must be entered in the affidavit on the back of the licence, and this must be sent to a Game Officer for recording.

The Northwest Territories form a hunting area that must always be reserved, very largely, for the indigenous population. For the non-resident, hunting in this vast area

Aerial view of caribou in the Northwest Territories

Seasons and Limits—Northwest Territories

Species	Zones	Season	Limit
Big Game :	12, 19 and 7	1 Aug-30 Nov	
Black bear		1 Sept-30 Nov	One either sex over one year old, when not accompanied by cubs.
Grizzly bear			One male over one year old.
Moose			One male with no less than $\frac{3}{4}$ curl.
Mountain sheep			One either sex over one year old.
Mountain goat			One male over one year old.
Caribou			
Bison	3 and 5	15 Sept-31 Dec	One any age or sex
Polar bear		1 Oct-31 May	One either sex
Duck		1 Sept-31 Oct	Residents, 25 per day ; non-residents, 8 per day, 16 in possession.
Geese		1 Sept-31 Oct	Residents, 15 per day ; non-residents, 5 per day, 10 in possession, of which not more than 2 per day and 4 in possession may be white-fronted geese.
Rail and coot		1 Sept-31 Oct	Residents 25 per day ; non-residents, 8 per day, 16 in possession.
Wilson's snipe		1 Sept-31 Oct	Residents 10 per day ; non-residents, 10 per day, 20 in possession. (No limit for residents of the number of migratory game birds in possession).

of the Canadian Arctic will be a difficult undertaking, even though now, with a partial recovery in game populations, large hunting areas have been opened up to him. The distances to be covered are immense, the means of transport limited, the expense very considerable and the dependence on local knowledge, local guides and local help is almost complete. A hunting expedition will only be as successful as the hunters' outfitter, guide, pocket and stamina allow it to be.

Further Information

Northwest Territories Tourist Office, Centennial Towers, Ottawa, Ontario.

TravelArctic, Yellowknife, N.W.T., Canada.

Frank E. Laviolette, Bison Big Game Outfitting, P.O. Box 163, Fort Smith, N.W.T. Canada.

Norway

Norway occupies the whole of the northern and western edge of the Scandinavian peninsula, with an area of over 125,000 square miles. The entire country is mountainous, and as the border with Sweden runs down the main mountain range, which is rather to the west of the centre of the peninsula, except in the south the country is little more than a narrow corridor on the western slopes of the mountains. The extensive coastline is deeply indented by numerous fiords, and is fringed by countless rocky islands. The rivers are mostly short and rapid, running down deep, narrow, valleys between high, barren tablelands. The climate is however much warmer than normal

for the latitude as the Gulf Stream washes most of the coastline.

Agriculture is important, though only about four or five per cent of the land is under cultivation, and the warmth means that crops such as barley and oats can be grown. Forests cover about a quarter of the country, and are also one of the chief industries, but the remaining area is highland pasture or uninhabitable mountain. Fishing is also very important, again aided by the Gulf Stream, which brings the cod and herring shoals into the fishing grounds. Despite the inaccessibility of much of the terrain, Norway can provide fine sport as the habitat is excellent for a wide range of predominantly northern game species.

The animals shown in the table are the most important game species. There are many others that are either less important, or vermin, or lie somewhere between. They include wolverine, bear, lynx, otter, fox, squirrel, marten, polecat, weasel, ferret, gulls, hawks and other birds of prey, corvids, and pigeon. The regulations and seasons concerning these are varied and variable and should be checked on the spot by visitors.

The local game boards ('Viltnemda') control the numbers of both elk and red deer that may be shot. Only a certain number may be shot for a given area. The minimum area required for permission to shoot one animal varies with the locality, the size of local stocks, and the damage they are doing. As a general rule the minimum requirement per elk is between 1,200 and 2,500 acres, and for red deer between 125 and 275 acres. In many areas there is a complete

A lithograph by Archibald Thorburn of blackcock being shot, 1900

'Leopard Shooting in India' by Samuel Howitt from the original sketch by Captain Thomas Williamson, 1806 (overleaf)

Seasons and Game Inventory—Norway

Species	Seasons	Average Annual Bag
Elk	27 Sept-10 Oct	7,000
Red deer	15 Sept-14 Oct	3,500
Reindeer	1 Sept-25 Sept	8-10,000
Roe deer	1 Oct-23 Dec	8-10,000
Hare	15 Sept or 1 Oct-23 Dec Jan and Feb additionally in the north	75,000
Blackgame	15 Sept or 1 Oct-23 Dec	100,000
Capercailzie		40,000
Hazel grouse		10,000
Ptarmigan		
Wildfowl		
Willow grouse		500,000
Woodcock		5-10,000

Licences—Norway

All hunting rights belong to the landowners, unless leased out to others. Some hotels have hunting rights over certain areas, on which guests may shoot on payment of a fee. However, all visitors, in common with Norwegians, must obtain a licence, available from post offices. The licence is valid for a full hunting year (1 April-31 March) for a fee of 50 kroner.

Everyone intending to shoot large game animals must pass a marksmanship test, which consists of six shots at a standard 1 x 1 metre 10-circle target at a range of 100 metres. The firing position is optional, but no support is permitted.

All visitors importing firearms must produce, at the customs, a gun licence issued by their native country. In addition they must complete, in duplicate, a written declaration, giving name and address, name of authority issuing the gun licence and the number of the licence, age (if under 21), kind of gun, calibre, make and number of gun, quantity and type of ammunition, purpose for which the gun is to be used, and where it will be used. This declaration is countersigned by a customs officer who keeps one copy. The other is retained by the owner of the gun, and serves as a gun licence for a period of three months.

The gemsbok, an antelope now inhabiting the drier regions of south-west Africa, has longer horns than the other species of oryx. It may be shot in Botswana.

cessation of small game shooting during the elk season. Elk are hunted with a dog, either free ranging or on a leash, or are driven towards butts or hides, which is the most common method for red deer, dogs rarely being used. Reindeer, on the other hand, are normally stalked, though sometimes hunters lie in wait close to the trails the animals are known to frequent. Wild reindeer are found only in the south of the country, nearly all those in the north being domesticated. There are three principal regions: the Snøhetta region in the Dovre range, the Hardanger moors, and Njardarheim Veidemark just north of Kristiansand, with an estimated total head of about 40,000. Permission to shoot wild reindeer must be obtained from the Directorate of Hunting, Game Preservation and Freshwater Fishing. The pursuit of roe is not carried out nearly as systematically as that of other deer, and is very often combined with the hunting of smaller game. Capercailzie, blackgame and hazel grouse are shot with pointers early in the season, but later the use of dogs becomes more difficult. Shotguns only are permitted. Pointers are also generally used for willow grouse, but seldom for ptarmigan, while hare is shot both with and without the help of dogs.

Special Regulations

No automatic shotgun may be used into which more than two rounds can be loaded.

Expanding bullets must be used for reindeer, elk and red deer.

No shooting is permitted from a power driven boat under 2 km (about 1¼ miles) from land (including islands), on either salt or fresh water.

It is prohibited to fire from a motor vehicle or aircraft, or to use it to distract the attention of game from a hunter.

All hunting is prohibited from 23 December to 31 December inclusive.

Hunting by artificial light is prohibited.

There are special regulations for reindeer hunting: rifles must have a calibre of at least 8 mm, but special dispensation may be granted on application for other calibres, provided the ammunition is considered suitable. Applications for dispensation should be addressed to the Directorate for Hunting, Game Preservation and Freshwater Fishing. In addition repeating and automatic rifles may only be used if the magazine or repeater mechanism has been put out of action and sealed by the police so that only one shot can be fired each time the action is cocked.

Further Information

Erik Myhres Travellingbureau A/S, N. Vollgate 19, Oslo 1.

Direktoratet for Jakt, Vilstell og Ferskvannsfiske (Directorate for Hunting, Game Preservation and Freshwater Fishing), Elgeseter Gt. 10, Trondheim.

Norway, Hunting in

The Norwegians tend to take shooting more seriously and professionally than the Danes because there is little agriculture and for generations the population has partly depended on hunting and shooting for its very existence.

As in Finland and part of Sweden shooting is mostly over dogs. These are not usually the well-known gundogs, but 'stovare' or elk-hounds, which are really a type of harrier, and 'drever', originally known as 'dachsbracker', a cross between a basset hound and a braque, for roe deer, fox and hare. The Norwegian sportsman only uses pointing dogs for ptarmigan and willow grouse, then mostly setters and pointers.

In addition to the big game, there are large predators such as brown bear, lynx and wolverine and about a thousand miles north of the North Cape it is even possible to find polar bears in the pack-ice.

Elk are shot with the aid of elk-hounds, gray Spitz-type dogs like huskies, and in some southern parts of Norway, particularly on the large estates, or state-owned hunts, beaters are sometimes used. Elk are shot both before and after the rut; bulls, cows and calves are all legal.

Although the Norwegians mostly hunt for venison they can appreciate a good palmated pair of antlers and due to more selective hunting methods there are relatively more good trophy heads to be had in Norway than in Sweden.

The most popular sport is reindeer shooting in September in the high plateaux of the Hardanger Vidda and also the Dovre Fjell further north. This is a real challenge, for the hunter sometimes has to wait several days for the right wind to bring the extremely wary reindeer herds within shooting range. The Norwegian law forbids any reindeer carcase being left on the fjells so that the hunter is faced with a strenuous downhill climb with the venison packed on his back; horses or sno-tracs are rarely available for this task. Of late, too many reindeer have been shot and the Game Department is restricting licences.

An unforgettable experience for any shooting man is a willow grouse or ptarmigan hunt over pointing dogs in the mountains. The scenery in September is beautiful and many hunters from Denmark and Sweden go there every year. Norway has the largest annual harvest of black game, capercaillie and hazel fowl and shooting them in these fascinating surroundings provides not only great exercise, but splendid shooting much appreciated by all who have experienced it. In addition to the use of pointing dogs and barking dogs, the birds are also simply walked up. During the autumn, woodcock are also shot in small numbers, but there is nothing like the craze for them there is in Denmark.

Since 1953 small boats specially equipped for a ten- to twelve-day Arctic cruise with from one to six people on board have been sailing from Tromso to shoot polar bears. Previously the polar bear was only hunted by professional hunters, seal catchers, whalers and personnel stationed in Spitzbergen and although the blame was laid on the 'tourists' the fact was they shot too many. Not more than 35 to 45 polar bears were shot annually by these foreign sportsmen, but from 1971 onwards all polar bear shooting was restricted by licence. The number of licences for 1972, which will probably be the last season any are issued at all, is strictly limited to foreigners and professional Norwegian hunters.

A few brown bears are taken in Norway, mostly by the Lapps, who are also responsible for most of the lynx and wolverine shot. Unfortunately there is still a bounty for wolverines, although the Game Department now wishes to abolish it. By an old law the Lapps are privileged in Norway, Finland and the northern part of Sweden to kill predators whenever they find them attacking their reindeer, their sole source of livelihood. They often kill wolverine in the closed season, but so far from human habitation as to be impossible to control; the result has been heavy poaching.

Due chiefly to the rough weather conditions, wildfowling is not greatly practised in Norway.

Although the Norwegian is considered much more tight-lipped and cool in temperament than other Scandinavians, a visiting shooting man will be welcomed by the local people and will find a friendly atmosphere if he shares a cabin with them or joins in a moose hunt. PM

Nova Scotia (Canada)

This is an eastern province of Canada, jutting out into the Atlantic Ocean. It consists, essentially, of two parts: Nova Scotia proper, a peninsula connected to New Brunswick by the narrow isthmus of Chignecto, and Cape Breton Island, which is separated from Nova Scotia by the Gut of Canso, now crossed by a causeway. The total area of the province is 21,425 square miles, and over two thirds of it is forest land. Agriculture tends to be intensive, with fruit, dairying and poultry farming popular.

Big game in the province consists of moose, deer and bear. There is a sufficient moose population, scattered on the island to sustain an annual harvest of around 300. Hunting is for residents only, and licences are issued by ballot, 1,000 being so issued in 1969. Deer have increased enormously in the province from a small original importation made many years ago, and an annual harvest of around 20,000 may now be expected. The best hunting is in the eastern counties and Cape Breton Island. Bears are to be found throughout the province; the harvest, in 1969, was 218, with the heaviest kills in Annapolis, Digby and Queen Counties. Fur-bearers are treated as game animals in the province, in addition to being trapped professionally, and beaver, mink, otter, muskrat, lynx, fox and raccoon are all found. Of the game and migratory birds, ruffed grouse are the most plentiful, 67,914 being shot in 1969, with the heaviest kills in Colchester, Cumberland and Cape Breton counties. The harvest that year for pheasant was 8,756, of which 2,269 were shot in the Annapolis Valley Preserve. Until 1965 no pheasants were shot outside this preserve, so that the increase demonstrates the spread and adaptability of birds descended from reared stock. Some 2,661 Hungarian partridge were shot in the 1969 season, with the best hunting in Kings County and the Minas Basin. Woodcock are plentiful and are shot along the coast and in the alder thickets. The population is made up of migrant as well as locally nesting birds. In 1969 the woodcock harvest was just under 11,000, and just under 8,000 Wilson's snipe were also shot. Willow ptarmigan have very

Top, the wolverine is shot in Norway by the Lapps to protect their reindeer.

Centre, a well-camouflaged European woodcock – a popular Norwegian game bird

Bottom, A female eider. There is a special winter season for sea ducks in Nova Scotia, including scoter, eider, old squaw and merganser.

Licence Fees—Nova Scotia			
Type	**Status**	**Fee**	**Comment**
Big game	Resident	$4	Sold by Department
	Non-resident	$40	of Lands and
Small game (includes game birds)	Resident	$2	Forests in Halifax, rangers and agents. No one may buy more than one licence of the same type in one season.
Small game (includes game birds)	Non-resident	$15	
Pheasant	Any	$1	Sold at the Pheasant Preserve
Moose	Residents only	$15	By ballot

Game Inventory—Nova Scotia	
Species	**Shot**
Duck (all)	98,319
Blackduck	36,442
Sea duck	25,427
Others	36,450
Geese, Canada	165

recently been introduced to the province, but are not yet sufficiently established to be hunted. Waterfowl consists principally of black duck, sea ducks, and teal.

Special Regulations

No automatic firearms may be carried, and no rifle loaded with tracer, full-jacketed, hard-nosed or service ammunition. No shotgun may be loaded with any shot larger than AAA. No .22 rifle firing rim-fire cartridges may be used except between 16 November and 15 February. No shotgun holding more than three cartridges may be used. All deer must be promptly and properly tagged, and the Report Card attached to the licence must be posted within seven days of the end of the season, whether it was successful or not. A permit is required to keep the meat of moose or deer after the end of the season. Non-residents may only hunt if accompanied by a licensed guide or by a resident aged over twenty-one who has written permission from the Minister to act as a guide.

Further Information

Department of Lands and Forests, Wildlife Division, Box 516, Kentville, N.S.

Nyala (Tragelaphus angasi)

A spiral-horned medium-sized antelope found in various parts of Africa. There are two sub-species, the mountain and the plains nyala, with little real difference between them. They are shy animals, found chiefly in light scrub or woodlands. Distinctively long-haired with white stripes on their grayish black flanks, their necks are covered with a growth or mane of long brownish hair and they have lyrate-shaped spiral horns. In the mating season the rams perform an unusual courtship dance. Principally grazers they may browse; one young is born annually. They may be shot in several areas, but their numbers are decreasing throughout Africa.

Seasons and Limits—Nova Scotia

Species	Area or County	Season	Limit	Comment
Deer		15 Oct-15 Nov	One, any sex	
Bear		15 Oct-15 Nov	No limit	
Moose	Cumberland, Colchester Picton, Guysborough and Antigonish	30 Sept-10 Oct	One, any sex	Residents only, by ballot
Pheasant	Annapolis, Kings and Hants	1 Nov-15 Dec	2 cocks per day, 4 in possession	
	Rest of the province	1 Oct-15 Dec		
	On pheasant preserves	15 Sept-28 Feb	No formal limit	
Varying hare		16 Nov-15 Feb	No limit	No licence needed
Ruffed grouse		1 Oct-15 Dec	5 per day, 10 in possession	
Hungarian partridge	Annapolis, Kings and Hants	1 Nov-15 Dec	5 per day, 10 in possession	
	Rest of the province	1 Oct-15 Dec		
Mink, otter, muskrat, lynx and fox		1 Nov-15 Jan	No limit	
Raccoon		All year	No limit	Night hunting, by special permit
		1 Sept-31 Dec	No limit	
Woodcock		1 Oct-16 Nov	8 per day, 16 in possession	
Wilson's snipe		1 Oct-16 Nov	10 per day, any number in possession	
Waterfowl are shot in two principal areas:	Area 1 includes Cumberland, Colchester, Pictou, Antigonish, Hants, Kings, Annapolis, Inverness and Victoria.			Area 2 includes Guysborough, Halifax, Luneburg, Queens, Digby, Sheburne, Yarmouth, Cape Breton, and Richmond.
Duck	Area 1	15 Oct-23 Dec	6 per day, 12 in possession	No more than 1 per day or 2 in possession may be wood duck.
	Area 2	15 Oct-24 Oct, and 26 Nov-20 Jan		
Sea duck, (includes scoter, eider, old squaw and merganser)	Coastal waters only, (includes Bras d'Or Lakes)	5 Oct-20 Jan	10 per day, 20 in possession (of the four species combined)	After 1 Nov in Area 1, and 28 Nov in Area 2, 2 extra scaup per day and 4 in possession are allowed.
Geese	Area 1	15 Oct-23 Dec	5 per day, 10 in possession	
	Area 2	15 Oct-24 Oct, and 26 Nov-20 Jan		

Ohio (U.S.A.)

Most of the state's 41,000 square miles consist of a low plateau of fertile soil suitable for arable farming. Forests have been decreasing in the west of the state as fresh farmland has been opened up; at the same time new forests have been established in the hilly country of the east and, because of these changes, the game distribution patterns have also been changing. There are now more pheasants in the west than before, and more deer and grouse in the east.

Deer and pheasant are, in fact, found in most counties, quail are abundant in some of the central counties, and squirrels and rabbits are found everywhere. Heavy flights of woodcock come in during the migrations, and there is good waterfowl hunting around Lake Erie. Wild turkey have only recently been re-established in sufficient numbers for hunting, and Hungarian partridge have almost disappeared.

Special Regulations

Only shotguns loaded with single ball or rifled slug are permissible in deer hunting.

Further Information

Ohio Division of Wild Life, 1500 Dublin Road, Columbus, Ohio 43212.

Big Game Inventory—Ohio		
Species	Shot	Est. pop.
Deer	1,379	22,000

Oklahoma (U.S.A.)

A south-western state, its 70,000 square miles consist of an upland prairie, highly fertile in the east and rising towards semi-arid mountains in the west. Most of the fertile areas are devoted to arable farming, and corn and cotton are the principal crops.

The Department of Wildlife Conservation is extremely active both in acquiring fresh land for public hunting and in game management. Deer and turkey have had their ranges greatly extended and their numbers increased, and reservoirs and lakes have been so managed as to encourage waterfowl. Cottontails and bobwhites are still the mainstay of the hunting season, but white-tailed deer, a few mule deer, pheasant, turkey, prairie chicken and scaled quail are all hunted. In 1969 the numbers shot were: 3,244,547 quail, 842,729 squirrel, 524,782 rabbits and 172,652 ducks, in addition to deer, elk and turkey.

Big Game Inventory—Oklahoma	
Species	Shot
White-tailed deer	5,359
Mule deer	60
Pronghorn	30
Elk	20
Wild turkey	3,181

Licence Fees—Ohio		
Type	Status	Fee
General	Resident	$4.35
General	Non-resident	$20.35
Special deer		$5.35

Seasons and Limits—Ohio

Vary from zone to zone.

Species	Zone	Season	Limit	Comment
Deer	1 and 3	29 Nov-3 Dec	1 buck with	Special drawings in
	2	29 Nov-1 Dec	5-in antlers	some counties of zone 1
	4	29 Nov-8 Dec	per year	for antlerless deer
Cottontail rabbit		13 Nov-30 Jan	4 per day, 8 in possession	
Squirrel	On private land	10 Sept-13 Nov	4 per day, 8	
	Public hunting areas	10 Sept-25 Dec	in possession	
Pheasant and Hungarian partridge	Public hunting areas	15 Nov-29 Jan	2 per day, 14 in possession	Also shorter, split season on private land
Ruffed grouse		9 Oct-27 Feb	3 per day	
Bobwhite quail	On private land	15 Nov-1 Jan	6 per day,	
	Public hunting areas	15 Nov-29 Jan	12 in possession	
Bearded turkey	14 counties only	3 May-6 May and 10 May-13 May	One per season	Drawing for 2,000 free permits

Seasons and Limits—Oklahoma

Vary from area to area

Species	Area	Season	Limit	Comment
Deer		20 Nov–28 Nov	Buck only, with antlers at least 6in or with one fork	Special hunts for either sex with shotgun or rifle depending on area
Elk	Comanche and Kiowa counties only, in lieu of a buck		one either sex	Also special elk hunts, with drawing for permits, in Nov and Dec, in Wichita Mountains Wildlife Refuge.
Cottontail rabbit		2 Oct–15 March	6 per day, 12 in possession	
Swamp rabbit		2 Oct–15 March	2 per day, 4 in possession	
Jack rabbit		2 Oct–15 March	No limit	
Greater prairie chicken	North-east only	31 Oct–1 Nov, and 7 Nov–8 Nov	2 per day, 4 in possession	
Lesser prairie chicken	North-west only	31 Oct–8 Nov	2 per day, 4 in possession	
Quail, bobwhite and scaled		20 Nov–15 Jan	10 per day	
Pheasant	Beaver, Cimarron and Texas counties	4 Dec–12 Dec	4 cocks per day 12 in possession	
	Alfafa and part of Ellis county	20 Nov–16 Jan	1 cock per day, 2 in possession	
Squirrel, gray and fox		15 May–1 Jan		
Wild turkey	Some areas only	6 Nov–14 Nov 29 April–14 May	One gobbler per season	

Special Regulations

No rifle normally holding a bullet of less than 75 grains and having less than 1,000 foot-pounds of muzzle energy, no automatic rifles, and no steel-jacketed or hard-pointed bullets may be used on deer or elk. Shotguns firing a rifled slug may be used in certain areas only. Hunters must wear red or yellow hat or jacket.

Further Information

Department of Wildlife Conservation, 801 North Lincoln, Oklahoma City, Oklahoma 73105.

Old Squaw *see* Long-tailed Duck

Oman *see* Middle East

Ontario (Canada)

This eastern province of Canada, once known as Upper Canada, occupies an area of over 400,000 square miles, some 11% of which consists of water. The climate is typically continental – hot in summer and cold in winter. There are many lakes and forests, but otherwise the land is open and rolling. Forest and tundra prevail in the north, but much of the south is remarkably fertile, and under the plough. The farmed area is over 7 million acres, and the main crops include cereals, sugar beet, potatoes and fruit. Lumbering is important, and over one

Oklahoma does not have a closed season for cottontail rabbits.

Licence Fees—Oklahoma

Type	Status	Fee
Deer	Resident	$5.00
	Non-resident	$25.00
Small game	Resident	$3.25
	Non-resident	$15.00
Special turkey		$3.00

third of the province is forests, principally spruce, pine, birch and poplar.

In spite of the largely uninhabited areas in the north, the province, as a whole, is more heavily populated and industrialized than any other in the Dominion. Consequently, population pressures, urban sprawl, pollution, deforestation and land

Game, Seasons, Limits and Licences—Ontario

Deer

Primarily white-tailed, though elk can also be found in the western part of the province. The greatest number of deer is in the west, around the Lake of the Woods and Rainy River, and especially in the areas around Fort Francis and Kenora. They are also abundant in the south-east along the northern shores of Lakes Erie and Ontario. The season varies from year to year and area to area. It also varies as between residents and non-residents. For most of the province, and in a normal year, the season generally runs from either the first or last week of October to 15 December for residents, and to 15 November for non-residents. A non-resident can obtain a licence to shoot deer, bear, fox, game birds, rabbit, raccoon and squirrel for $40 ; if moose is added the price increases to $125. The bag limit is one deer per season.

Moose

Found throughout the north of the province, especially in the areas around Sioux Lookout, Kenora, and Cochrane. Guides are obligatory for non-residents in the Rainy River area. The season varies in the same way as does the deer season. In most years and in most of the province it generally runs from 15 September to 15 December for residents, and to 15 November for non-residents. Certain areas are closed to non-residents for moose hunting.

Black bear

Resident hunters shoot most of their bears while deer hunting. Non-residents, however, now come to the province specifically for bear hunting. The total number of bears shot in the province in 1968 was 820, of which one quarter were shot around Chapleau and Sudbury. A Bear and Deer Licence costs a resident $10, ($5 if he is a farmer). A Bear Licence for non-residents, valid from 1 September to 30 June costs $15, but bear may be shot in the winter under one of the general licences available for non-residents. These all expire by 28 February, and are not valid for the spring hunting, which has become increasingly popular. The best month for this is early June. The bear season is from 1 September to 30 June. There is no bag limit for residents, but non-residents are allowed only one bear per season.

Raccoon

There is no bag limit, and no closed season. They can be hunted at night by residents only with a special licence, and specially licensed hounds. Non-residents can hunt raccoon by day under any one of the three general licences available to them.

Fox and coyote (brush wolf)

There are no bag limits and no closed seasons for either of these animals. They are generally hunted with hound and gun.

Gray squirrel

They are most abundant in the south-west of the province, from where they are spreading. The season varies from area to area, but is generally either 26 September or 3 October to 15 December. The bag limit for two areas in the extreme southwest is 5 per day. Elsewhere the limit is 10 per day and in possession.

Rabbit (cottontail, varying hare, European hare)

The season, again, varies from area to area, but generally extends between September and March. There are no bag limits for the hares ; the limits for cottontail are 6 per day. Non-resident general licences are not valid for hunting rabbits in the counties of Kent and Essex in the extreme south-west and, in many of the southern townships, an extra licence is required to hunt rabbit or pheasants.

Ruffed grouse

These are found in most parts of the province, and are generally shot walking up with dogs. The bag limit for both ruffed and spruce grouse is 5 per day in aggregate, and 15 in possession.

Sharp-tailed grouse

There are two sub-species in the province, the prairie sharptail found on Manitoulin Island in Lake Huron and in the Kenora, Rainy River area, and the northern sharptail, found in the blueberry bogs and secondary timbers growths of the Hudson and James Bay areas. A good breeding season, however, will send the northern sharptail spreading southwards, as far as the Geraldton and Kapuskasing areas. Bag limits are 5 per day and 15 in possession. The season for all grouse runs from 26 September to 15 December, but sharptail and ptarmigan may be shot in the districts of Cochrane, Timiskaming, and Northern Kenora up to March 31. North of Georgian Bay the season opens on 15 September, and in the southwest on 3 October.

Woodcock

These are found in the alder thickets of southern Ontario, though they are also found east of Lake Superior. The season runs from mid-September to mid-December, and the bag limit is 8 per day. In 1968-69 it was estimated that about 56,000 woodcock were shot in the province.

Rail, coot and gallinule

The season for all runs from mid-September to mid-December. The bag limit is 5 per day in aggregate.

Wilson's snipe

The season for these runs from mid-September, to mid-December. The bag limit is 10 per day. A total of 8,645 snipe were shot in the province in 1968-9.

Ring-necked pheasant

The severity of the winter limits the breeding range of this bird to a narrow strip along the northern shores of Lakes Erie and Ontario. Few pheasants will be found in areas with over 50 in of snowfall a year. The Department of Lands and Forests rears and releases chicks and poults on both private and public shooting grounds. In 1968 it turned out 41,000 and 14,000 respectively. The season and bag limits vary from year to year and area to area, but the normal season runs from 6 September to 15 December and the normal bag limit is 3 per day ; in some areas all must be cocks. The hunting hours vary slightly, but in general they run from half-an-hour before sunrise to half-an-hour after sunset.

Bobwhite quail

The season runs from the beginning to the middle of November, and the bag limit is 5 per day.

Hungarian partridge

These are plentiful in the eastern counties of the province. The season varies from area to area, but generally runs from 26 September to 21 November. The bag limit is 8 per day, 16 in possession.

Waterfowl

Their hunting is controlled by the Canadian Government under the Migratory Birds Convention Act. Hunters must have a Migratory Game Bird Hunting Permit, price $2.00, in addition to whatever provincial licence they hold. Unless varied, the seasons for duck and geese in Ontario are :

Northern District : 15 September to 15 December.
Central District : 26 September to 15 December.
Southern District : 3 October to 15 December.
In the extreme south-west 3 October to 15 December, but to 31 December for geese.

The bag limits, for all districts, are 5 duck and 5 geese per day, with 10 of each in possession, but not more than one redhead and one canvasback and 4 wood duck may be taken daily. After 10 October 2 additional scaup or goldeneye may be taken. Hunters living more than 25 miles from James Bay may not kill more than 15 geese per season. There is no open season for geese in the counties of Wellington and Waterloo. During the 1969 season approximately 800,000 duck were shot in the province. The species shot were, mallard (29%), black duck (15%), wood duck (12%), the other species included green- and blue-winged teal, ring-necked duck, common goldeneye, and bufflehead. In the same season over 25,000 geese were shot, of which the various sub-species of Canada goose formed 94%.

rosion have all had their effects on the game population. In spite of this, Ontario still has large and varied supplies of game, and a Department of Lands and Forests expertly interested in conserving, increasing, and correctly harvesting them. In the north, where the pressures on wildlife are fewer, there is a great deal of big game – deer, wapiti, moose and bear. In the south there are deer and bear, and the area is richer than the north in small game and upland game birds.

Perhaps the best goose shooting of all is to be had from one of the Cree Goose Camps in the James Bay area. These have been placed on the main migration routes and are open to hunters from 15 September to 18 October. The Cree Indians are justly famous for their skill in hunting; they are excellent guides when duck or goose shooting and their ability to call down the geese is well known. There are, at present, about 15 camps open to visitors, varying from elaborate to primitive, and further information about them can be obtained by writing to the last pair of addresses below.

Further Information

Department of Land and Forests, Parliament Buildings, Toronto.

Canadian Wildlife Service, Post Office Buildings, Aurora.

Cree Goose Camps, Box 1000, Cochrane.

Tidewater Goose Camp of Ontario, Box 100, Moose Factory.

Opossum *(Didelphis virginiana)*
Opossums are rather primitive marsupials. The typical species of North America is described here.

It is an arboreal and nocturnal animal, weighing about 10 lb and measuring about 30 in from nose to tail. The tail itself is naked, scaly, and prehensile, and about 12 in long. The ears are large and erect, the feet each have five toes and all, except the first toes on the hind legs, end in sharp claws. The muzzle is long and sharp, the legs are short, and the fur is grizzled, becoming yellowish-white on the top of the head. Pelts are of low value, nevertheless they are taken in great numbers every season.

The opossum dens in a hollow tree or log; in the winter it may, without actually hibernating, 'den up' for a week or two. It is omnivorous, eating anything from fruit to carrion. It climbs well but slowly, and is most commonly found along wooded streams. If cornered it will feign death.

In the south of the country it will generally produce two broods, but only one in the north. The young, of almost microscopic size, will pull themselves into the pouch, fasten on to a teat, and remain there for around two months, when they will be the size of mice; as there are only 13 teats, any more young born must die.

They are hunted at night, by hunters

A buck mule deer, photographed in Ontario

armed with a rifle or sticks, and a dog capable of finding, treeing, and baying a possum. As soon as the baying is heard the hunters find the tree, and, by the light of their torches, either shoot, or shake or club the possum out of it.

Marsupials, also called opossum, are found and sometimes hunted in Central and South America and Australasia.

Oregon (U.S.A.)
A west coast state, it has an area of 100,000 square miles. The Cascade Mountains, running north and south, divide the state into a western section, which has a mild climate and a soil of great fertility, and an eastern section which is mainly dry plateau country rising up to the Blue Mountains. Oregon is the most heavily forested of the states, and timber of great size flourishes.

Licence Fees—Oregon

Type	Status	Fee	Comment
General	Resident	$5	Sold by county clerks and sporting-goods stores
	Non-residents	$35	
Elk tag	Resident	$10	
	Non-resident	$35	
Bighorn tag	Resident	$10	
Cougar tag	Resident	$10	
Antelope tag	Resident	$5	
Deer tag	Resident	$2	
	Non-resident	$15	
Turkey tag	Resident	$2	

Seasons and Limits—Oregon			
Species	**Season**	**Limit**	**Comment**
Mule deer	3 Oct-10 Oct	1	
Black-tailed deer	3 Oct-17 Oct	1	Also early and extended seasons in some areas
Black bear	1 Sept-31 Dec 15 April-20 May	1 per year	Special drawing, residents only
Antelope	15 Aug-19 Aug	1 adult buck with horns longer than ears	
Rocky Mountain elk	31 Oct-18 Nov	1	North-east only
Roosevelt elk	14 Nov-22 Nov	1 antlerless	North-west coastal range
Bighorn sheep	28 Sept-2 Oct	1 ram with not less than ¾-curl	Special drawing, residents only, in Hart and Steens Mountains only
Cougar	1 Dec-31 Dec	1	Special drawing, residents only
Rabbit, cottontail and jack, and snowshoe hare	All year round		
Gray squirrel	1 Sept-3 Nov	5 per day, 5 in possession	No limit, no closed season in north-west area
Partridge, Hungarian and chukar	3 Oct-24 Jan	8 per day, 12 in possession	
Grouse, blue and ruffed	5 Sept-27 Sept 3 Oct-25 Oct	3 per day, 6 in possession	East Oregon West Oregon
Sage grouse	5 Sept-7 Sept	2 per day, 4 in possession	Limited area
Valley and Mountain quail	17 Oct-22 Nov	5 per day, 10 in possession	West Oregon
	17 Oct-24 Jan	10 per day 20 in possession	East Oregon, except Klamathy county
Pheasant, cock	17 Oct-22 Nov	2 per day, 4 in possession	West Oregon and Klamathy county
Wild turkey	21 Nov-24 Nov	1 per season	Special drawing, residents only

Big Game Inventory—Oregon		
Species	**Shot**	**Est. pop.**
Mule deer	89,210	458,000
Black-tailed deer	62,170	466,000
Elk	9,140	55,000
Black bear	2,900	10,000
White-tailed deer	70	
Mountain goat	5	70
Bighorn sheep	3	175
Wild turkey	45	2,000

Agriculture is the principal industry, and fruit growing is of considerable importance.

Almost half the land is Federally or state owned, and most of this is open for hunting. Since this is largely forest land it contains most of the big game. There is an unusually high big game population, with black-tailed deer west of the Cascades and mule deer east of them, the largest surviving elk (wapiti)

A gemsbok in a South African game reserve

herd in the country in the north-east and along parts of the coast, and some antelope in the south-east. Game birds consist of pheasant, quail, partridge and grouse, and waterfowl are abundant, especially on the Southern Lakes and along the Snake River. The state lies along the line of the Pacific Flyway.

Special Regulations
No buckshot, pistol or revolver may be used on big game, nor semi-automatics holding more than five cartridges, nor rifles under .25 calibre and developing less than 1,220 foot-pounds of energy at 100 yd. Dogs must be used when hunting upland birds, but not when hunting big game.

Further Information
State Game Commission, Box 3503, Portland, Oregon 97208.

Oryx *(Oryx gazella)*
The beisa, *Oryx gazella beisa*, or true oryx, stands about 4 ft high and is heavily built, being found principally in Ethiopia, where it may still be shot in the wild. The tail is long and black and the coloration gray with black markings on legs, croup and flanks. The horns, carried by both sexes, are long and black and the coloration gray from the base and sharply pointed. Those of the female are longer than those of the male, being over 3 ft with a circumference at the base of about 7 in and a spread at the tips of about 10 in. They are grazers and seem independent of water. One young is born annually. They are said to be able to defend themselves against lions with their formidable horns and if wounded require approaching with great caution.

The gemsbok, *Oryx gazella gazella*, now only found on game ranches in southern Africa, where it may be shot under special licence, is very similar to the above except that its black flank-bands are broader. It also has longer horns, approaching 4 ft in length.

Ovis Ammon *see* Great Tibetan Sheep

P

Paauw *see* Bustards

Paca *(Cuniculus paca)*
Also called spotted cavy, this animal is found throughout South America between Paraguay and Mexico. It is a shy, forest-dwelling, spotted rodent with a large stocky body. It lives in burrows in riverbanks or similar swampy regions. Generally found in pairs, it has one or two young annually. It is hunted in much the same way as the capybara *(q.v.)*, and when hunted always tries to take to the water. The Indians regard its flesh as a particular delicacy.

Painter *see* Cougar

Pakistan
Pakistan consisted of two distinct geographical units. West Pakistan lies to the north-west of India and covers about 310,000 square miles, occupying most of the basin of the Indus, the mountains of Baluchistan to the west and part of the Western Himalayas to the north. East Pakistan (now the independent country of Bangladesh) lies to the north-east of India, about 1,100 miles away. It covers the lower basin of the Brahmaputra and the eastern half of the Ganges delta, with a total area of about 55,000 square miles.

Agriculture is the main occupation in both provinces. West Pakistan is a great wheat-producing area, but cotton, barley, millet and rice are also grown in the artificially irrigated plains of the Indus. Fruit and dates are grown in the mountainous west, and cattle, sheep, goats, horses and camels are reared. Bangladesh is important for its jute production, with rice, sugar cane, tea and tobacco the other chief crops. Bangladesh has little industry that is not based on jute, but Pakistan produces cotton and woollen fabrics, and mines coal, and a little iron, in the north-west.

On the whole Pakistan does not encourage hunting. There are, however, some professional hunters who can organize what shooting there is for visitors. A list may be obtained from the Department of Tourism. The chief big game species are ibex, urial and markhor. Certain species are strictly protected: elephant, clouded leopard, snow leopard, wild ass, Marco Polo sheep and crocodile. No information is available about any other shooting.

Further Information
Department of Tourism, Central Hotel Building, Club Road, Karachi, West Pakistan.

Licences—Pakistan

Firearms are dutiable and a 'possession licence' is required to import them. The licence may be obtained from the District Magistrate at the point of entry. Firearms will not be cleared through customs except on production of the licence. Certain calibres are prohibited : .303 rifles, .410 shotguns, pistols and revolvers with a bore of .30 or more.

Palla *see* Impala

Panther *see* Leopard

Paraguay
Paraguay is a landlocked South American country of 157,000 square miles. East of the River Paraguay is a series of plains intersected by abrupt hill ranges, not rising much above 2,000 ft. West of the river is the area known as the Chaco, a flat plain rising uniformly to over 1,000 ft in the west, which suffers badly from both floods and droughts. Most of the plains are covered with grass, and the hill slopes with dense forest. In large areas the soil is marshy and liable to floods during the heavy summer rains, notably in the south-east, in the angle formed by the confluence of the Paraná and Paraguay rivers. The climate is tropical to sub-tropical.

About three quarters of the population are engaged in agricultural or pastoral pursuits, cattle breeding being the most important industry. Cotton and grapefruit are grown for export, and sugar, rice, manioca, maize and tobacco are the most important crops for home consumption. The forests are at present only exploited for cedar and the better known hardwoods.

For game *see* South America, Shooting in

Further Information
Consult initially the nearest Paraguayan consulate.

Partridge Biology and Management in Britain
In Britain the gray partridge *(Perdix perdix)* and the red-legged partridge *(Alectoris rufa)* are both living near the edge of their climatic range and their numbers are subject to dramatic annual variations. Although the ultimate cause of these fluctuations is variation in weather conditions, game biologists are still trying to unravel the precise effects of weather on chick survival. Abundance of partridges in the autumn depends on both spring breeding densities and chick survival rates; it is primarily variations in the latter which cause the fluctuations in partridge numbers.

Of the two species the gray is considerably smaller, with cocks and hens averaging 380 gm and 370 gm respectively. Cock red-legged partridges average 520 gm while the hens are only 450 gm. The predominantly dark brown plumage of the gray shows little sex differentiation except in the scapular region where the hen's feathers have transverse cream-coloured bars in addition to the cock's median longitudinal type. In the red-legged partridge no plumage differences can be recognized between the sexes and the presence of knobbly spurs on the legs does not always indicate a cock.

Although the gray partridge occurs as a breeding bird throughout the British Isles it is most numerous in the drier arable areas of southern and eastern England. The light, well drained, cereal-producing soils developed over chalk are particularly suitable and from Hampshire and Wiltshire in the south to Lincoln and Norfolk in the east high partridge densities have been associated with the chalkland type of agriculture. The red-legged partridge, introduced in the seventeenth century but not becoming firmly established until the eighteenth century, is most numerous in East Anglia. In spite of many releases it has so far failed to establish itself in Scotland, Wales and the northern and western counties of England.

From June until January partridges are unique in grouping themselves in coveys. These may consist of the two parent birds with their young or, at the other extreme in a year of low chick survival, may be made up entirely of pairs of adults or single cocks. Between these two extremes a wide variety of covey structure has been observed but whether it is a family group or a number of unrelated adults, the covey formed in July or early August maintains its individuality until the time of covey break-up. Only occasionally will severe reduction in numbers – by shooting or some other cause – result in the amalgamation of small groups of survivors. Otherwise there is no interchange of members between different coveys. By observing large numbers of individually marked birds in different coveys it has been proved that the old theory that shooting 'breaks up the coveys' is a false one. Within a few hours, surviving members of coveys driven over a line of guns, regroup in their original covey formations.

Throughout January the gray partridge coveys gradually break up, but the rather looser covey formation of the red-legged partridge may persist until early March. In the unlikely event of both members of a pair of gray partridges surviving for a second season they will almost certainly remain together. Young cocks are usually the first to move away from the covey and may travel considerable distances (up to nine miles has been recorded) in search of a hen from another covey. No brother and sister matings have been observed and the exchange of eggs with other estates to offset the disadvantages of 'inbreeding' appears to be quite unnecessary. Although very cold weather may retard covey break-up for several days, pair formation is usually completed by the middle of February and territories firmly established by mid-March.

With optimum field size (30 to 40 acres),

good hedges and suitable crop distribution partridge pair density can be as high as a pair to four acres. On well-managed partridge shoots in East Anglia such breeding densities have been maintained for several years in succession. At that time of the year gray partridges are extremely sedentary and dusk to dawn watch on marked pairs has shown that flying-time is usually only a matter of seconds each day.

By the end of April each gray partridge hen will have scratched out one or two saucer shaped 'scrapes', selected the most suitable one and laid her first egg. Before leaving the bare 'scrape' a few leaves and grass stalks will be placed over the egg and since this is repeated with each egg laid the clutch is soon well camouflaged with material gathered from the vicinity of the nest site. When the clutch is almost complete the hen spends a considerable amount of time on the nest. With beak and claws she manages to raise the eggs and work the nesting materials – augmented by feathers from the brood-patch – into a surprisingly compact mat on which the eggs lie. Frequently one more egg is laid after the eggs have been 'uncovered' and the average clutch of 15 eggs completed in about 20 days shows little annual variation.

Incubation involves a period of 25 days and since both fertility and hatchability of the eggs are high it is rare to find more than one unhatched egg left in the nest. Only the hen gray partridge incubates but when the eggs are about to hatch the cock may sit beside the nest and brood the first hatched chicks. The red-legged partridge hen may lay two clutches (of about 10 to 11 eggs) one of which may sometimes be incubated by the cock. This has occurred in penned redlegs and also in wild birds where the

Here both the cock and hen gray partridge may be seen brooding their eggs

ock has been marked with a plastic tab
o allow recognition in the field.

Between six and seven weeks may elapse
rom the commencement of laying until the
hicks leave the nest – usually the day that
hey hatch. During this period the eggs, as
vell as the sitting hen, are vulnerable to a
vide variety of predators. Egg thieves –
ooks, crows, magpies, hedgehogs, rats,
toats and weasels – may steal some or all
f the eggs at any stage of incubation. If the
oss occurs before incubation begins, or
ven during the first 10 or 12 days of incuba-
ion, renesting will almost certainly occur,
he hen laying a somewhat smaller second
lutch (10 to 12 eggs). But a bird that loses
ts newly hatched brood (or even its clutch
uring the last week of incubation) will not
ake a second attempt. Predation by foxes
nd feral cats, although perhaps less fre-
uent, is much more serious since not only
re the eggs lost but the sitting hen is killed.
arming activities – particularly grass
utting in areas where alternative nesting
ites are scarce – may also cause a signifi-
ant number of nest losses and on the
verage well-keepered partridge shoot nest-
ng success is unlikely to exceed 70%.

Most partridge nests hatch when the days
re longest and in an average year well over
alf the nests will hatch between June 10–20.
gg thieves, forcing renesting to take place,
elp to spread the hatching period and so
educe the chances of one spell of severe
veather conditions wiping out the greater
art of the year's chick production.

For the first few weeks after hatching
artridge chicks are extremely vulnerable –
o food shortage and predators as well as
he direct effect of bad weather. The high
rotein diet necessary during this period
an be obtained only from animal foods –
nainly insects. The abundance of this type
f food is partly controlled by the sequence
f weather during April, May and June but
lso by the type of crops grown and the
nethods of cultivation. Unless there is an
bundance of available insect food when
he partridges hatch, chick survival is
ikely to be low even if weather conditions
n the post-hatching period are favourable.
ed-legged partridge chicks are less de-
endent on an insect diet and this, together
vith their wide-ranging feeding habits, may
ccount for their better survival in recent
ears.

Even when the essential insect food is
resent the effect of three consecutive days
vith low day-temperatures (not rising above
6°C) and wet vegetation can adversely
ffect the survival of the down-covered
hicks. The effects of the continuous use of
erbicides in cereal crops is now being felt.
he lack of weeds (and the insects they used
o support) means that the partridge chick
nay now have to travel five times as far as
ts predecessors only 10 to 15 years ago to
btain its fill of insects! Under these con-

The nesting materials form a compact mat
on which the eggs of the gray partridge lie.

Six-week old partridges, hatched under a
broody hen, almost ready for release

ditions the June weather becomes an even
more critical factor than it has been in the
past.

Some of the nest predators, particularly
stoats and weasels, will also prey on the
partridge chicks before they can escape by
flying (at two to three weeks). In an average
year in which nest losses reduce the number of chicks hatched per pair to 10, subsequent predation, disease, accident, weather
and starvation will further reduce the
number of surviving six-week-old young to
only four birds. In Britain's best partridge
survival years an average of between eight
and nine young birds has survived, but in
several recent years the survival figure has
been less than two! If however an average
of four young per pair are produced then
approximately one third of the partridges
present in the autumn can be shot without
impoverishing the following year's breeding
stock. Another third will disappear – either
as a result of death or emigration – and the
remaining third would form the breeding
pairs.

If, after a season of relatively high chick
survival, no shooting takes place, there
may be a slight increase in breeding density
the following spring. But 'winter loss' – i.e.
the birds that disappear between September
and the following March – would be
unusually high. Food shortages, resulting
from the early ploughing-up of stubbles,
may cause local emigration, and although
the land might be capable of carrying a
larger breeding stock in the spring, un-
favourable winter habitat may become a
limiting factor.

Although at one time the red-legged
partridge was viewed with disfavour on
many a partridge shoot – due to the fact that
when partridges were 'walked-up' instead

of being driven the red-legged partridge would often run ahead and eventually rise out of range of the guns – it is now equally esteemed and management for the two species is similar.

Essentially this consists of ensuring a high nesting success by the reduction of nest predators, the provision of safe nesting cover and finding and protecting as many nests as possible. The latter is achieved by the skilled keeper in various ways – by the use of strong-smelling substances in movable containers, suspended tins or other 'strange objects' hung in the vicinity of nests to temporarily deter potential nest predators. Some of the early clutches may be picked up before incubation begins so that the hatching period will be extended by enforced renesting. The eggs picked up in this way, together with those from dangerously sited nests and from large clutches that the keeper has reduced to 14 or 15 eggs, are hatched under broody bantams for rearing and subsequent release when six or seven weeks old.

Nest protection however will avail nothing if food is scarce when the chicks hatch. The shooting man, who is also the farmer, has a great advantage here since, by planning his crop distribution so that there is an interspersion of grass, root and cereal crops, he will help to ensure an adequate food supply within each brood-range during the summer, and reduce loss from emigration during the winter months.

On the larger estates where only driven partridges are shot there is usually little danger of overshooting the stock. But on shoots both large and small a precise knowledge of the numbers of partridges present at different times of the year can be a great help to successful management. Census methods developed by research workers can be easily adapted for the use of shoot owners. Breeding pairs of partridges may be censused in March during the first two hours after dawn and the last two hours before dusk. With the aid of binoculars, and preferably from a car, partridge pairs are readily seen on the bare ground and their positions plotted on a sketch map. Approximately 300 to 400 acres can be censused in this way during each census period. In early August, when a proportion of the corn has been cut, a ride around the stubbles – again in the early morning or late evening – will allow an estimate of the breeding success to be made. In each covey seen the number of young and old birds is noted and when approximately 30% to 40% of the old birds have been seen, young and old are totalled and a young/old ratio worked out. From this sample figure and the March census an estimate of partridge numbers can be made and, allowing 30% to 40% for 'winter wastage' the number of birds that can be shot without endangering next year's breeding stocks is easily estimated. TB

Partridges see Chukar Partridge; Gray Partridge; Hungarian Partridge; Red-legged Partridge (French Partridge)

Peccary see Collared Peccary; South America, Shooting in

Pennsylvania (U.S.A.)

A north-eastern state of 45,000 square miles. Although now primarily an industrial state there is still a considerable amount of grain growing and dairy farming and some 15 million acres under forest, of which two million belong to the state and are open to the public for hunting, as are over a million acres of hunting land owned by the Game Commission.

There is a large and well-spread whitetail population; turkey are found in many of the woods, and black bear in the central and northern counties. Ruffed grouse populations are usually low because of overbrowsing by the deer herd, and pheasant are found in the southern farming areas. The state is, however, only marginally suitable for bobwhite quail. There is some waterfowl hunting on Lake Erie, along the Susquehanna and Allegheny Rivers, and the marshes of the Delaware, and woodcock may be found in many of the alder woods and carrs.

Licence Fees—Pennsylvania

Type	Status	Fee	Comment
General	Resident	$5.20	Sold by County Treasurers
	Non-resident	$25.35	and Department of
Antlerless deer tag		$1.15	Revenue, at Harrisburg.

Seasons and Limits—Pennsylvania

Species	Season	Limit
Deer, antlered	30 Nov-12 Dec	One per season
Deer, antlerless	14 Dec-15 Dec	
Black bear	2 days in late Nov	One per season
Cottontail rabbit	31 Oct-28 Nov, and 26 Dec-16 Jan	4 per day, 20 per season
Snowshoe hare	26 Dec-2 Jan	
Squirrel, gray and fox	17 Oct-28 Nov, and 26 Dec-16 Jan	
Pheasant	31 Oct-28 Nov	2 cocks per day, 8 per season
Ruffed grouse	31 Oct-28 Nov, southwestern area, 26 Dec-16 Jan northwestern area	2 per day, 10 per season
Bobwhite quail	31 Oct-28 Nov	4 per day, 20 per season
Wild turkey	31 Oct-21 Nov, and 8 May-15 May	One per season

Big Game Inventory—Pennsylvania		
Species	Shot	Est. pop.
White-tailed deer	141,874	350,000
Black bear	218	1,800
Wild turkey	17,300	45,000

Special Regulations

No big game may be shot with automatic, semi-automatic, autoloading rifle, shotgun or pistol; .22 rifles firing rim-fire cartridges may not be used, nor may silencers. No more than five may form a party to hunt small game, and parties hunting big game must keep a roster giving names, addresses, etc.

Further Information

Game Commission, P.O. Box 1567, Harrisburg, Pennsylvania 17120.

Peru

Peru lies on the west coast of South America, covering about 530,000 square miles. There are three main zones: the Sierra, or mountain ranges of the Andes, the coastal belt, known as the Costa, and the Montana or Selva, which is a large area of jungle stretching eastwards from the Andes. Lake Titicaca lies across the border with Bolivia. The Amazon and its tributaries water the Montana, which is very hot. The Sierra is cooled by its altitude, and the Costa by the Humboldt Current.

Agriculture is one of the chief industries, employing a large proportion of the population. The coastal strip, though producing cotton and sugar, is not generally fertile, but the eastern slopes of the Andes produce livestock and crops such as rice, sugar and coffee, while maize, potatoes and wheat are grown in the mountain valleys.

For game *see* South America, Shooting in.

Further Information

Consult initially the nearest Peruvian consulate.

Pheasants *(Phasianus* species)

There are fifty-nine species of pheasant divided into twelve genera, of which the genus *Phasianus*, which contains the true pheasants, is the largest. These are all birds without a crest and with long tails composed of 18 feathers, the middle pair being very much longer than the outside pair. It is possible to recognize two geographical types – those with white rings around their necks, which are northern types, and those without white rings, or with only traces of one, which are southern types. There is considerable hybridization, so that clear cut distinctions are often difficult to find, for, of the twenty species of true pheasants, sixteen will interbreed and produce fertile offspring. These include:

Common Pheasant *(P. colchicus)*

This was the pheasant introduced into most countries of the Roman Empire by the Romans, and still found wild in Asia Minor and Transcaucasia. In most countries, and certainly in Britain, it is now almost impossible to find a true-bred common pheasant, because of repeated hybridization with subsequent imports of other species. The adult male has a green head and neck shading into purple on the sides and front of neck. The chest and flanks are fiery orange, the feathers being edged with purple. The feathers of the upper back and scapulars are mottled black, buff, orange-red and purple. The lower back, rump and upper tail covert feathers are red-maroon glossed with purple-green. The wing coverts are sandy-brown, the middle of the breast and sides of belly are dark purplish-green, and the rest of the underparts are dark brown mixed with rufous. The tail feathers are olive, edged with rufous and glossed with purple, with narrow, wide-set, black bars. The length of the tail is approximately 21 in, and its overall length 37 in. The adult female will be of a generally sandy-brown colour, barred with black. The feathers of the side and back of the neck are tinged pink with green or purplish margins, those of the mantle, sides of breast and flanks are chestnut with black centres, and the tail feathers are reddish-brown shading into olive. Tail length about 11 in, overall length 24 in.

This is a description of a bird that is now difficult to find. The English common pheasant, for example, is almost certain to have a white collar or traces of it from hybridizing with Chinese and Mongolian pheasant importations.

A melanistic mutant which has been given the name of *P. colchicus tenebrosus* is a game bird of considerable importance. It generally breeds true.

Pheasants are polygamous, though there in some vague evidence that they were once monogamous. The cock will mate with up to five hens, and will fight other cocks at breeding time. The hens are indifferent mothers, frequently deserting the nest, or their broods at the first sign of danger. When leaving the nest the hen generally covers the eggs with leaves, and goes and returns on the wing, in order to leave no tracks. The call of the cock is a repeated, rattling, 'or-ork' and is heard at sunset and in the morning, and all day during the pairing season. In Britain they have become dependent on artificial feeding and probably present populations could not survive a hard winter on natural foods alone. Their natural diet includes grain, seeds, berries, green leaves, mast, insects and grubs. Though essentially ground birds they frequently roost in trees, and are among the fastest flying of birds. *See also* American Ring-necked Pheasant.

Persian Pheasant *(P. persicus)*

Distinguished from *P. colchicus* by having the lesser and median wing coverts nearly

An English ring-necked pheasant

233

white. Its total length is 35 in. It is found in the regions south-east of the Caspian Sea, and is a hardy and shy bird that flies extremely well. The hen closely resembles *P. colchicus.*

Zerafshan Pheasant (P. zerafshanicus)
Its dark brown scapulars and narrow purple margins to the breast feathers distinguish it from the related Prince of Wales pheasant *(P. principalis)*. It is found in the highly cultivated Zerafshan Valley, and although living in reed beds, it feeds in the fields.

Mongolian Ring-necked Pheasant (P. mongolicus)
Resembles *P. persicus* but has a broad white ring, interrupted in front, around the neck; mantle, chest and back are bronzy orange-red glossed with purple or green, the rump is dark maroon shading into purple, the throat is purplish bronzy-red, the breast and flank feathers are tipped with very dark green, and the breast and sides of belly are dark green. A large bird, its overall length is about 36 in. This is one of the best and most sporting of pheasants, flying fast and high, and it has frequently been introduced into Britain. A sub-species of it is Svertzov's ring-necked pheasant *(P. semitorquatus)*.

Chinese Ring-necked Pheasant (P. torquatus)
The general colour of the lower back, rump and upper tail coverts is greenish or bluish-slate colour, the mantle and flanks are bright orange-buff, and the breast has a purplish gloss. There are wide black bars on the basal part of the tail feathers. Its length is 35 in. It is found in Manchuria, Korea, Mongolia and northern and eastern China to as far south as Canton. It was introduced as early as 1513 to St Helena, and was, at various times, introduced, together with *mongolicus*, to America (*see* American Ring-necked Pheasant), and New Zealand. Just as there are probably no pure-bred common pheasants left in Britain, and indeed, Europe, so also are there probably no pure-bred Chinese or Mongolian pheasants, not in captivity, the three sub-species having cross-bred so much that it is almost impossible to decide which strain predominates. However, in the resultant stabilized hybrid, they have produced a larger and more sporting bird than any of these three species alone could have provided.

Japanese Pheasant (P. versicolor)
The adult male is easily distinguished from all other true pheasants by having the whole of the underparts a uniform dark green. The mantle is dark green shot with purple. The rump is uniform greenish-slate with no rust-red patches on the side. Its length is 29 in. The hen has strongly marked black bars on breast and flank. They are found throughout the islands of Japan except for Yezo. It is an extremely hardy bird, and was imported into Britain by the Earl of Derby

in 1840, and when crossed with either *torquatus* or *colchicus* excellent sporting birds of great size were produced. They are reputed to stray less from coverts and to take wing more readily and to fly more strongly than any of their parents.

Soemerring's Copper Pheasant (P. soemerringi)
A generally copper-coloured pheasant with large chestnut tail barred with black. Its length is 50 in. The hen has a blackish crown and the upperparts are largely black and buff. The chest is pale gray-rufous spotted with black and the rest of the underparts buff. The tail feathers are chestnut. They are found on the Japanese islands of Hondo and Kiu-siu. Both cocks and hens are extremely pugnacious and will, in captivity, destroy each other.

Top, the common pheasant hen

Above, Reeve's pheasant was once introduced to Scotland, but proved very quarrelsome and strayed great distances.

Reeve's Pheasant *(P. reevesii)*
This is the finest of all true pheasants, with a tail 5 ft long and an overall length of 6' ft 6 in. It is a very hardy bird and flies well, but it has rarely been treated as anything but an ornamental pheasant. It has a white crown, surrounded by a black band, white chin, throat and nape, cinnamon upperparts with each feather bordered with black to give a scaled appearance, white wing coverts, chest, breast and flanks, the last with chestnut margins, the rest of the underparts black. The hen has a reddish-brown crown, buff head and neck, upperparts mottled rufous, buff and gray, chest, breast and sides, rufous mottled black and gray, tail feathers mottled sandy, buff and black. They are found in the mountains of northern and western China. If turned out in Britain they chase common and ring-necked pheasants away, nor will they interbreed. Lord Tweedmouth turned some out in Inverness-shire in 1870, but they were found to fly for distances of over 30 miles, and to be impossible to approach.

Of pheasants other than true pheasants there are few that need interest the shooting man in Europe or America. Golden pheasant *(Chrysolophus pictus)* and Lady Amherst's *(Chrysolophus amherstiae)* have, from time to time, had some popularity among enthusiasts and been turned out as game birds, never with any success. Though beautiful birds to look at, they are quarrelsome, chase the native cocks away, and rarely fly well enough to be shootable.

The other genera all provide birds that offer sport in their native habitats in the Himalayan Mountains or China or Malaya, but they are so unlike the true pheasants in flight, or so localized and unsuitable for introduction anywhere else, that discussions of them, though of great interest to keepers of aviaries and breeders of ornamental fowl, are of little interest to those who breed, rear and shoot the common, Chinese, and Mongolian pheasants, or, more accurately, the stabilized hybrids descended from them.

Pheasant Management in Britain
History
The pheasant's first claim to fame was as a highly-prized delicacy at Roman banquets in the middle of the first century A.D. The River Phasis in the Caucasus, where the Greeks discovered them at a very early period was – according to historians – 'stripped of its birds to supply the luxury and extravagance of the dwellers in ancient Rome'.

It seems likely that pheasants were introduced to Great Britain by the epicurean-minded Roman army of occupation. These would have been blacknecks *(colchicus)*. At the same time they were gradually being taken to many other European countries. In the United States, Chinese and Mongolian birds *(torquatus* and *mongolicus)* were not imported until the 1880s, but they soon became successfully acclimatized in most states.

There are fifty-nine species of pheasants, including both the game and ornamental varieties, and the common ringneck of the European hedgerows is a hybrid of many pure species which have been imported by sportsmen and naturalists over the years. It is a tough, adaptable bird, and whilst not as large as the Mongolian, as prolific an egg-layer as the blackneck, or as beautiful as the Chinese or Melanistic Mutant *(tenebrosus)*, it is a 'good doer' and probably the best strain for the shooting man in Northern Europe.

Since World War 2 the pheasant has displaced the partridge *(Perdix perdix)* as the sportsman's commonest quarry, for intensive farming has hit the partridge harder than the pheasant, and we have not been able to make good these losses – as we have with pheasants – by restocking with *reared* birds. Redleg partridges *(Alectoris rufa)* are a different matter.

Biology
Before we consider the management of a typical British pheasant shooting estate, we should understand something of the biology of the species. The ideal habitat would comprise mixed woodlands of not too large a size, dotted about on mixed farms. But pheasants also thrive in wetlands and scrub country: they will happily jug on the ground in reedbeds or they will roost in trees, if available. They can be shot on treeless fens or out of crops of kale grown at 1,000 ft on hill farms. Their food is very varied indeed, but from the survival point of view it is important to realize that, like partridges, the young chicks need the high protein of an insect diet for the first few weeks. And on a modern farm, with sprays, clean crops, much soil disturbance and so on, insects can be lacking in sufficient numbers.

The laying period shows a much wider bracket than the gray partridge and extends approximately from 21 May to mid-June. The average clutch would be 12 – 13 eggs; the incubation period 24 (+) days; hatchability over 80%. Nesting success on an average busy farm is probably little over 50%; production rate very seasonal indeed, but should average 3 – 4 poults per hen. Pheasants are, of course, polygamous – the harem size varying, but in a good habitat three hens per cock should be attained.

Habitat
When considering management the four factors to take into account are habitat; food; predation; farm hazards.

Pheasant habitat can for our purpose be divided into two: woodlands and farmlands. If the landowner does not provide what amounts to 'homes' for the pheasants, he can

The artichoke is one of the many valuable game crops which can be grown on a farm.

forget about all the other subtleties of conservation, because there won't be any birds to conserve. The first consideration is to get the general pattern correctly balanced: the right proportion of woods to crops and open spaces. The pheasant range should have a reasonable network of hedgerows or belts, if possible. The all-important cover should provide nesting facilities, shelter from the weather, protection from natural enemies, roosting accommodation and some of the food. Obviously the better these 'services' are divided up over the ground, the heavier will be the density of wild birds. Two 10-acre woods a quarter of a mile apart are better than one 20-acre plantation. Four 10-acre blocks of kale, with another crop in between, provide better conditions than one 40-acre field. It will repay the owner to plant up all the old banks, pit holes, rough corners and similar untillable areas with suitable trees, shrubs and crops. It will also beautify the farm and benefit many other forms of wildlife.

Planning actual pheasant coverts is a specialized job, but if the owner just remembers that he should aim for mixed ages and mixed species, that the wood should basically do two things – keep the wind out and let the sun in – he will have the ideal environment. Obviously the commercial block of well-ordered spruce won't suit pheasants, and the *perfect* pheasant spinney won't suit the Head Forester. But the Game Conservancy in Britain has shown that a sensible compromise is possible, one which will provide good timber and quality pheasants. A good shoot can bring in £2 per acre for the sporting rights, so in places the pheasant crop can be more valuable than the timber crop.

When beautifying a woodland with berried shrubs, a lot of money can be wasted buying the wrong shrubs, which may perhaps be more palatable to fieldfares than pheasants. The best are *Cotoneaster distichus*, *Cotoneaster frigida*, *Crataegus prinufolia*, *Sorbus aucuparia* and *Viburnam opulus*.

Out on the farm in addition to the ordinary crops, if a little space can be found for crops particularly favoured by pheasants, it will be worthwhile considering them. Popular game crops include: artichokes, Brussels sprouts, buckwheat, fodder radish, seed kale, maize, mustard, oil poppy, sunflowers and mixed food patches. The latter vary from region to region but most would include: sunflowers, maize, canary seed and buckwheat, with smaller proportions of caraway, sweet clover, marrowstem kale and Nida rape.

Feeding

As the stubbles get ploughed in, the kale fed off, the beet lifted and so on, natural food will become scarce. Additionally a great number of shooting estates rear birds and therefore carry a larger number than can be supported without supplementary feeding until the coverts have been shot two or three times. This means feeding by hand and by hopper.

The hand feeding will consist of scattering corn along the woodland rides, half in the undergrowth, so that the birds have to hunt for it; or alongside a hedgerow or a crop. Some feed rides will benefit by being strawed so that the birds have to scratch amongst it for the grains. The straw must be fresh every season, or fungus disease may develop. The feeding should take place at the same time every day, and accompanied by whistling or calling. The hoppers can be home-made from old oil drums, placed on two bricks, with suitable slots punched in the sides to allow the grain to be pecked out. The most efficient hoppers will be hung or set-up off the ground, having a feeding grille of netting *underneath*, so that only the pheasants will take the food and not crows, pigeons, finches and other scavengers.

Other self-feed receptacles, such as miniature silos made of straw bales and filled with tail corn, weed seeds and so on, or deer cribs lined with chaff and grain which will be pecked out slowly, can be sited all over the shoot, preferably in sheltered places.

Water containers, such as old motor tyres cut in half to provide two circular shallow drinking troughs, will be necessary if any reared birds are released, and they will also serve wild pheasants.

Predation

Partridge keepers in particular know that they *must* control the 'vermin' or they will lose at least a third of the surplus that would otherwise be available in the shooting season. Many modern pheasant keepers tend to think more about rearing extra bird than about protecting those they have.

Many years ago, the then editor of *The Field*, Mr Eric Parker, wrote 'The wood is far fuller of enemies for the pheasant than

Feeding pheasants from hoppers is necessary when keepering staff is limited.

An open pheasant-rearing field

the field is for the partridge'. Not everyone would perhaps agree, but there is no doubt that if the pheasant's enemies are not controlled, the stock will suffer enormous losses.

To protect both pheasant and partridge a network of tunnel traps (using the humane Fenn trap) will control stoats, weasels, rats and other small mammalian predators. Additionally, rat-baiting points containing 'Warfarin' in polythene sachets should be maintained all over a shoot. All the corvids are clever egg thieves, and should be controlled by means of funnel-entrance cage traps baited with eggs, white bread, maize or with decoy birds, placed on flight lines, near poultry pens or in other suitable places. They must be capable of being moved from one site to another, as required. In some countries – though not in Great Britain – phosphorus bait-eggs can be put out in safe places for crows, and are deadly effective.

First and foremost the pheasant's greatest enemy is the fox, followed by the feral cat. Having said this, it must be stressed that no one country sport would wish to upset another. If foxes are not all that common and can be dealt with by the local hunt, so much the better. If not, the pheasant-shoot manager will be wise to do this himself. Gassing the earths with a cyanide powder is at least humane and deals with vixens and cubs together. Shooting at fox drives must be accurate and at short range only, otherwise a pricked animal may die of gangrene. Snaring is effective, though precautions must be taken to avoid catching domestic stock, roedeer using woodland paths, and so on, but it cannot be said always to be sufficiently quick to be humane.

Farm Hazards
Modern agricultural machinery and some toxic chemicals can take a severe toll of pheasants. Almost any operation from forestry work in the breeding season to the silage cutting of the green crops can destroy nests, sitting hens and poults. It is important for all the farm staff to be aware of the value of the game crop, and for the foreman to be given a gun and encouraged to take an interest! Silage cutting is probably the biggest single killer. It will help if vulnerable fields can be cut from the centre outwards or, if not, the last vital patch in the middle can be left overnight so that the birds can draw out themselves. 'Dogging' will also assist. Flushing bars with steel tines – not weighted chains – will help, but only if the tractor driver is interested in what he is doing.

Farm chemicals tend to be more specific and less dangerous than they were some years ago. Perhaps after the losses caused by the chlorinated hydro-carbon seed dressings, like dieldrin, and the organo-phosphorus sprays on the brassicas we have learned caution. Apart from selecting the chemicals with care, using only the correct quantities, and leaving no residues about like concentrated puddles of poison, it is wise to complete weed killing before too many young pheasants go foraging in the crops. If kale is to be sprayed, it should be done before harvesting so that the standing corn can provide alternative safe cover.

Rearing birds
One aspect of management that is important on many shoots is rearing. The techniques are now very well understood. We have come a long way since Palladius, the Roman, told his husbandmen to feed young pheasants on barley meal, locusts and ants' eggs sprinkled with wine! Pellet foods are complete and foolproof: equipment is mostly predator-proof. And if the methods used are not too intensive, disease problems will be minimal.

But there remains one rather weak link in the game manager's chain – the technique of naturalizing or liberating his poults into the wild, so that they can feed and protect themselves properly. The make-up of the cover in the release pen – trees, shrubs and sunning areas – is one of the most important points to which priority should be given; also protection from foxes. Finally to be considered are the feeding and management of the home coverts, into which the young birds will be released.

But whether the stock is predominantly reared or wild, the professionalism of making a good pheasant shoot lies mainly in producing high, fast and testing birds. Better show one hundred 'screamers' than five hundred routine targets destined mostly to swell the game book total. CLC

Philippines
The Philippines are a group of over 7,000 islands lying just north of Borneo. The total area is about 115,000 square miles, of which over 100,000 are made up by the eleven largest islands. The islands of the main chain are traversed from north to south by a range of mountains with several volcanoes. Forests cover over half the land surface. Timber, bamboo and vegetable oils are important products, and coconuts, sugar, rice, maize and hemp are the chief crops. Though the country is predominantly agricultural there are mining and growing industrialization.

All species may be hunted in the Philippines, and the only limitations on shooting are in and around urban areas. There are no hunting clubs as such, but some organized hunting is arranged by local gun stores (the address of the principal one is given below).

Further Information
P. B. Dionisio, 552 Rizal Avenue, Manila.

Pigeons and Doves (*Columbidae*)
There are over three hundred species of pigeons and doves found throughout the

Philippine duck

Licences—Philippines

Applications for gun licences should be made to The Secretary, Department of National Defence, 4 Aguinaldo. Quezon City, Philippines, giving details of the firearms to be imported.

world with wide variations in coloration and size. Their nesting habits, however, are fairly uniform; the nests are generally flimsy affairs of twigs carelessly put together and only one to three eggs are laid; both sexes incubate the young. Their food may consist of grain, seeds, fruit, and insects. Their flesh is generally quite edible, though seldom highly rated. Some species are scarce and protected in various parts of the world, but the commoner species are generally so numerous as to be pests. They are usually fast fliers and despite their loose feathers can take a lot of shot, providing some very good sport. Owing to the large number of species only those principally shot have been dealt with separately.

Pigeon Shooting around the World

In all parts of the world, even remote island groups where few of the typical gamebirds or waterfowl are found, pigeons of the 300 recognized species are hunted for food and sport. Two of the most heavily harvested of all birds fall in this group: the woodpigeon of Europe and the mourning dove of the United States.

The larger species are usually called pigeons and the smaller doves, but there is no clear dividing line. Most breed and roost in trees, feeding on the ground, but the fruit pigeons are entirely arboreal.

Various types of green fruit pigeons are the principal sporting bird in several tropical countries, including the West Indies, parts of West Africa, South-east Asia, and elsewhere. Often rolling in fat, these rather sluggish birds make excellent eating. Strong fliers, once on the wing, despite their slow movements in the trees, fruit pigeons are usually shot as they flight in to favoured feeding sites.

Three pigeons are regarded as gamebirds in the United States. These are the white-winged dove (q.v.) of the arid south-west, the larger band-tailed pigeon (q.v.) of western mountains and the widespread mourning dove (q.v.), which breeds in all states except Alaska and winters south to Mexico.

Although small, weighing about $4\frac{1}{2}$ oz and measuring 12 in overall, the mourning dove is eagerly sought out by gunners from coast to coast. It is a challenging target, fast and agile, usually shot by hunters waiting at feeding areas or waterholes. Many thousands of birds may be drawn to small-grain fields on the main migration routes in autumn.

The population of this dove has been favoured by the planting of grain close to shelter belts, a combination which has also encouraged the European woodpigeon. Winging their way southward on migration, averaging about 15 miles a day – although able to exceed 40 mph in short bursts – these great waves of doves offer more widespread hunting opportunities than any other American species.

Pigeons and Doves

Band-tailed pigeon *
Barbary dove
Bronzewing
Collared dove
Emerald dove
Green pigeon
Imperial pigeon
Mourning dove *
Red-eyed dove
Ringneck
Rock dove *
Stock dove
Topknot
Turtle dove
White-crowned pigeon
White-winged dove *
Woodpigeon *

The turtle dove, although protected in Britain, is heavily shot in Europe.

More than 20,000,000 mourning doves are killed annually in the United States – more than all waterfowl species combined.

In Florida, the white-crowned pigeon finds its only foothold in the United States. This bird, with striking plumage of slate-black and a contrasting white top to the head, is a major game species in the Bahamas and the West Indies.

The rock dove (q.v.) or feral pigeon is found in various forms, some semi-domesticated, in most parts of the world. This was the bird used for live pigeon shooting, the forerunner of clay target shooting, and is still killed in these events in several U.S. states, Spain, Italy, Central America, the Middle East and North Africa. Where these pigeons have gone wild, they give excellent sport, especially when flighting in to feed from their nesting sites in cliffs, ruins or caves. This pigeon, the ancestor of domestic racing pigeons, is extremely fast on the wing, maintaining speeds in excess of 60 mph for quite long distances, which makes it among the swiftest of shotgun targets, vying with the big geese, ducks and grouse.

In Europe, Asia and Africa, several species of collared dove and turtle dove are abundant locally and give good shooting. The non-migratory collared dove has extended its range rapidly north-westwards from Asia Minor during this century and has now colonized the British Isles. It is still largely protected, but likely to be declared a pest species – and therefore a gunner's quarry. The turtle dove is protected in Britain, but heavily hunted on migration in Europe.

Millions of woodpigeons (Columba palumbus) (q.v.) are shot in Britain and Europe. Regarded as an agricultural pest as well as a game resource, this pigeon is shot all the year, in addition to being reduced in numbers by narcotics, nest-destruction and even netting on some of its migration routes. British woodpigeons are largely sedentary, but Scandinavian and East European birds move south and west during the early winter.

The woodpigeon is a heavily built bird, measuring about 16 in and weighing $1–1\frac{1}{2}$ lb, gray in colour, with white patch on either side of the neck and a broad white band across the wing. Feeding on grain, fruits and greenstuff, a large flock of pigeons can do a great deal of damage in fields of grain, young kale or turnips, and other crops. This bird is found almost everywhere in Europe where there are agricultural crops and some trees or tall hedges.

Woodpigeons are usually shot by a lone gun over artificial or dead-bird decoys at a feeding site or by groups of guns at roosting areas in woodland. This pigeon decoys very effectively and some very large bags have been achieved – several times exceeding 500 birds shot by one gunner in a day.

Despite this hard shooting, often sub-

Setting up shot pigeons as decoys

sidized by pest control groups, the wood-pigeon continues to be abundant over all of its extensive range in Europe.

Often found in association with the wood-pigeon is the smaller stock dove, a similar bird with even more rapid flight, no white markings and a broken black wing-bar.

Some pigeons appear able to withstand almost unlimited shooting, while others have to be carefully protected by close seasons and bag limits. Among the list of the world's extinct species are many pigeons, mainly ground-nesting types (including the dodo) which have been destroyed by predators introduced to remote islands, but also including the once-abundant passenger pigeon of North America, wiped out by thoughtless over-harvesting for market consumption. WAN

Pigs (*Suidae* and *Tayassuidae*)
Like goats, the pigs have been spread throughout the world by man, but some species such as the wild boar, warthog and bushpig, also, though not true pigs, the peccaries of Central and South America, have never been domesticated. Omnivorous and tusked they will root for food. Found frequently in herds and generally shy and nocturnal except where seldom hunted, they

---

Principal species—Pigs
Bushpig*
Collared peccary*
Giant forest hog
Warthog
Wild boar*
White-lipped peccary

---

will readily go feral from a domesticated state. One of the classical beasts of the chase, they may be hunted with hounds, or on horseback with a spear, or shot, but in various parts of the world they are still tackled on foot with hounds, spear or knife in the time-honoured fashion. Their flesh is strong tasting, and the tushes make a notable trophy.

Pig Shooting *see* Australia

Pink-footed Goose
(*Anser brachyrhyncus*)
This gray goose is probably the most plentiful of the wild geese that come as winter migrants to Britain, and is found, often in large flocks, all along the east coast and, in smaller concentrations, on the west coast as well. It rests in marshes and estuaries and moves inland to feed, grazing on grass and corn, and showing a special liking for potatoes. It is the goose most commonly associated with farmland and farm crops.

Pinkfeet are gregarious and noisy, the call consisting of either a two- or a three-syllabled honk. They are migratory, nesting in Greenland, Iceland and Spitsbergen and wintering in Britain, Germany and the Low countries, and occasionally vagrant to Ireland, Italy, Yugoslavia and the Baltic. They arrive in Britain with some regularity towards the end of September.

They resemble the bean goose (*q.v.*) in appearance, but are slightly smaller, measuring between 24 and 30 in and weighing about 7 lb. Their upperparts are pale blue-gray, with a very dark head and neck, pink legs and small, pink and black bill. They have blue shoulder patches, not as light as those in the graylag. The nest is built on the ground or on a cliff ledge, and the clutch of four or five eggs is laid in May and June, incubation takes 28 days, and is done by the goose only, though the gander helps with rearing the goslings, which are able to fly after eight weeks.

Pinkfeet are frequently shot in Britain, and are hunted by much the same methods as those used for graylag (*q.v.*).

Pinnated Grouse
(*Tympanachus cupido americanus*)
The sharp-tailed grouse, *Pediocetes phasianellus* (*q.v.*), is also sometimes called prairie chicken, but the name properly belongs only to the pinnated grouse. It is a bird of the open grasslands and, so long as the prairies remained unploughed, it was a common bird in most states east of the Rockies and west of Kentucky. There was even an eastern race, now extinct, called the heath hen that was found in the New England states. Since the prairies have been ploughed its numbers have dropped enormously. It is still found, however, though more thinly distributed, from Saskatchewan to Colorado, and from North Dakota to Texas.

During the spring and summer it is largely insectivorous, and during the winter it lives on grass and flower seeds, hips, mast and berries. The pinnated grouse is about the same size as the ruffed grouse but, since it has a shorter tail, it is actually a heavier bird. The upperparts are yellowish-brown barred transversely with darker brown. The head feathers are buff, those on the crown being mottled with black and capable of being raised into a crest. On either side of the neck are the pinnae (whence 'pinnated') – tufts of stiff brown, black-tipped feathers, about three inches long, capable of being raised over the head like horns. Below these the cock has orange air sacs. The underparts are white barred with brown, the primaries are brownish-black, as is the tail, which is short and round. The legs and feet are feathered. The hen resembles the cock except for having shorter pinnae and no air sacs. The birds are gregarious and at least partially migratory, gathering into large packs before migrating.

Mating takes place between March and May after elaborate courtship displays, during which the cocks assemble to boom by inflating and deflating their air sacs. This they do competitively, in order to attract the hens. The nest is made in a slight hollow in the ground and the clutch of 8 to 12 eggs takes around 24 days to incubate.

Prairie chicken may, early in the season, hold well to the point, flushing only within gunshot. They rapidly learn caution, however, and soon learn to flush at extreme range. Before the turn of the century they were so unwary of man that the market hunters could ride out on the Great Plains, behind a screen of dogs and, dismounting, shoot prairie chicken by the wagon load.

Pintail (Anas acuta)

A surface feeding duck closely related to and almost identical with the American pintail, *A. acuta tztzihoa (q.v.)*.

It breeds in the northern parts of Europe and Asia, and winters in North Africa, Nigeria, the Nile Valley, Abyssinia, Kenya, Uganda, India, Ceylon, Thailand, Burma and southern China. It has been known to be a partial migrant in Belgium, France and Spain, both breeding and wintering there, as it sometimes does in Scotland and East Anglia.

Plovers (Charadriidae)

A large family of 63 species, many of which can be classified as waders (*q.v.*) but only a few of which are commonly shot. They are widely distributed throughout most of the ice-free parts of the world. They are plump birds, distinguished from the rest of the waders by their short bills, which are slightly enlarged near the tip. They are mainly black, or brown, and white and are found principally on beaches, sand and mud flats, and open fields. They are divided into two

Top, the pintail drake is easily recognized by its long tail.

Centre, the lapwing, or green plover, is still shot in some countries.

Bottom, the masked plover of Australia

main groups – the plovers proper and the lapwings. The former are mostly members of the genus *Charadrius*, all of which have white underparts and bands of black or gray across the upper breast which gives them their name of ringed plover. They include the ringed plover (*Charadrius hiaticula*), the little ringed plover (*C. dubius*), the Kentish plover (*C. alexandrinus*), the gray plover (*C. squatarola*), the golden plover (*C. apricanus),* the American golden plover (*C. dominicus*), the dotterel (*C. morinellus*), and the black-bellied plover (*C. squatarola squatarola*).

Most of them breed as far north as the Arctic tundras and migrate south of the Equator in winter. Only the golden, gray, black-bellied and the American golden plover are commonly shot.

The lapwings (*Vanellus* species) are inland birds, slightly larger than the true plovers, found in all temperate and tropical countries except America. The commonest is the lapwing of Eurasia, which breeds from Britain to Siberia. It is now generally a protected bird, but it used to provide the 'plovers eggs' of the epicure, and indeed, still does so in Belgium and the Netherlands. Several of the lapwings have spurs on the bends of the wings, with which they fight. These include the masked plover of Australia and the 'blacksmith' group of Africa.

Plovers tend to circle and return to the sound of a shot or even whistle, and may thus often be easily brought within range of the gun.

Pochard (Aythya ferina)

A fairly common European diving duck. The drake has a uniform dark chestnut stocking, black breast and pale gray body. The duck has a brownish head and forepart with a pale patch around the bill and chin. Both have black bills with a pale blue band.

They like large ponds, lakes and other open water, but are seldom seen on the sea. Their diet is mainly vegetarian, consisting of aquatic plants and their seeds. When feeding they dive deep and are able to stay under for up to one minute. They swim low in the water and need a run on the surface to take off, but are fast straight flyers. They are not extremely vocal, the duck's call being a guttural k-r-r-r and the drake's an asthmatic wheeze.

Display includes head jerking and inflating and deflating the outstretched neck. The nest is built in reeds at the water's edge. The pochard breeds in northern Europe from Holland to as far as Lake Baikal, also in the Balkans, on the Black Sea coast and the Kirghiz steppes. It is a partial migrant, wintering in the south of some of its breeding range, but also migrating to the Nile Valley, India, Burma and South China. Not as edible as the American pochard, it is not greatly hunted.

The pochard of Europe in flight. It is closely related to the redhead of North America, but unlike the latter, not particularly good eating.

See also Redhead (American Pochard); Ferruginous Duck (White-eyed Pochard).

Poland

Poland lies in central Europe, its 120,330 square miles being part of the Great European Plain. It is mostly undulating, but towards the south it rises to the Sudeten, Tatra and Carpathian Mountains. There are many rivers of which the most important are the Vistula, the Bug, the Oder and the Warta.

In the west, the old German provinces of Upper and Lower Silesia, there is considerable industrialization. However, a third of the population is still dependent on agriculture, and over a quarter of the country is under afforestation. Combined with the river systems this means that even the flat central parts of the country hold considerable game, though most of the hunting grounds are concentrated in the mountainous terrain of the south, or the lakes and waterways of the north-east.

High ground animals, such as chamois and mouflon, are not found in Poland, but two species deserve particular mention, even though they may not be shot at all. There are about 300 European bison living in the wild in the Bialowieza and Borecka Forests, and the Bieszczady Mountains, and there are about 400 elk in the almost inaccessible swamps of the Masurian Lake District and the Kampinos Forest.

Hares may not be hunted by groups of under six.

Licences

All visiting hunters must have a special gun licence. This must be obtained from a Polish consulate before the trip, and states the bearer's name and surname, number, date of issue and office of issue of the passport, type and bore of firearms, amount and calibre of ammunition, list of spare parts, if any, and the term of validity, which will be up to 14 days.

Hunters must have a valid licence in order to take their guns out of Poland. It is therefore very important for those wishing to stay longer than a fortnight to report to the nearest Voivodship Militia Headquarters where they may renew their special gun licence.

Polish third party insurance is compulsory for all hunters. It may be obtained from the office making the arrangements for the hunting trip, at a fee of $1·41 for thirty days.

Hunters may import duty free all their necessary firearms, up to 100 cartridges, one telescopic sight, one pair of fieldglasses, and their dogs (provided they have a veterinary certificate). If two or more guns are carried they must be entered on the customs declaration.

Estimated game population—Poland

Species	Est. pop.	Shot*
Red deer	54,400	
Fallow deer	3,800	
Roe deer	281,000	
Wild boar	59,000	
Hare	Up to 4,500,000	460,000
Lynx	480	
Partridge	Over 3,000,000	300,000
Pheasant	350,000	
Blackgame	26,600	
Capercailzie	10,000	
Hazel grouse	13,000	

*Figures available for two species only

Seasons—Poland

Seasons may vary from year to year

Species	Season
Red deer (stag)	21 Aug-10 Feb
Red deer (hinds and calves)	1 Sept-10 Feb
Fallow deer	1 Oct-10 Feb
Roe deer (buck)	21 May-20 Oct
Roe deer (does and fawns)	1 Oct-10 Feb
Wild pig (boar)	1 May-10 Feb
Wild pig (sows and piglets)	1 Aug-10 Feb
Lynx	1 Nov-31 March
Wolf	All year
Fox	All year
Hare	1 Nov-10 Jan
Rabbit	1 Oct-10 Jan
Capercailzie	15 March-20 May
Blackcock	15 March-20 May
Hazelcock	21 Aug-10 Feb
Pheasant	1 Oct-20 Feb
Partridge	11 Sept-20 Oct
Woodcock	1 Aug-31 May
Duck (female) and bald coot	1 Aug-30 Nov
Duck (drake)	1 March-20 April
Snipe, great, common and jack	1 Aug- Migration
Corncrake	1 Aug-Migration
Ruff	1 May-31 May
Goose	1 Aug-30 April

Special Regulations

Visitors are requested to observe the following simple hunting regulations:

Only rifles of 6·5 mm plus may be used on deer and wild pig.

Only shot may be used on capercailzie and blackcock.

Wild pig may only be hunted with dogs and beaters from 1 October to 10 February.

Deer may not be shot while hunting wild pig with dogs. They may be shot during silent drives.

Capercailzie and blackgame may only be shot on mating grounds. Woodcock may only be shot in flight.

Further Information

Hunting trips may only be arranged through one of the three following offices:

Sports-Tourist, Warsaw, 84-86 Marszalkowska St.

Foreign Tourists' Office of the Polish Motor Federation, Warsaw, 6-14 Krucza St.

'Orbis' Polish Travel Office, Warsaw, 16 Bracka St.

There are 'Orbis' branches in Paris, Brussels and London, and agents in all the major cities of Europe, from whom further information may be obtained.

Polecat *see* Ferrets and Ferreting

Pollution and Game

Game, like other forms of animal life, and like man himself, both suffer from, and themselves give rise to, pollution. The pollutions caused by game are simple ones and arise, in nearly all cases, from the introduction of new species or the dying out of old established ones, causing changes in the vegetation, the condition of the soil and, ultimately, in the whole eco-system. A well known example of this is the introduction of the rabbit into Australia, which profoundly affected the flora and fauna of an entire continent. The over-hunting of lions in Africa led to a large increase in the zebra herds, over-grazing, and the subsequent degradation, if not destruction, of large areas of African savannah. The introduction of myxomatosis into Britain has led to the uninhibited growth, in areas not under cultivation, of such things as brambles that the rabbits once used to keep close cropped, with a consequent change in the ecology.

If the pollutions that game cause are simple, the pollutions they suffer from are many and frequently complicated, and most of them are man-made. They suffer in several ways – from direct poisoning arising from contact with, or ingestion of, noxious materials; from indirect poisoning via the food chain; from the destruction of essential foods; from interruptions of the breeding cycle either because of a lowering of fertility or because of a loss of breeding ranges; from introduced predators and diseases; from the pollution of water supplies, or from induced drought caused by a local over-extraction of water; from changes or destruction of habitat.

There are many forms of direct poisoning, and most of them are, by now, well known. They range from the organo-phosphates used in sprays and seed dressings to nickel and mercury poisoning caused by mining and industrial wastes. A well known example of indirect poisoning via the food chain has been the accumulation of D.D.T. in the bodies of predators such as hawks and eagles placed at one end of a long food chain, each member of which has been contaminated with some amount of the D.D.T. that man, in his understandable anxiety to control malaria, has rashly scattered around the world. These accumulations of D.D.T. have led to infertility in the eggs and a decline in the numbers of raptors. Essential foods that have disappeared, to the detriment of one or more species, include the over-hunting of deer in Florida which led directly to the almost complete disappearance of the Florida cougar which lived on it, and the eel-grass blight, which was possibly caused by oil pollution, and led to the rapid decline of many *Zostera*-eating waterfowl.

Oil pollution, itself, has greatly affected all animal life, by direct poisoning, by clogging the plumage of seagulls and waterfowl, and by destroying much of the marine animal life on which they existed. The breeding cycles of whole families of duck were interrupted, and, in some cases, destroyed when the prairies of Canada and the Middle West of America were ploughed and drained to enable the farmers to grow corn. Drainage destroyed many of the potholes and swamps around which the waterfowl bred, and to which, soon after the hatch, the ducklings had to be led. Ploughing destroyed many of the nests themselves. Since these are the nesting grounds on which many of the waterfowl of an entire continent are bred, the interruption has been a dangerous one, undoing much of the good done by the Federal Migratory Birds Convention Acts. At the same time, the reduction of flow in the rivers because of over extraction of water, and the pollution, with industrial effluents and wastes, of the remaining flow, have profoundly affected game populations. Introduced predators include the cat, which, in both domestic and feral form has had considerable influence on game-bird populations, the mink, which, escaped from captivity has, in a number of countries, become a new and dangerous predator on fish and game, and, perhaps the most dangerous introduced predator of all – man himself. In the past, and, one hopes, only in the past, man had destroyed whole game populations by over-hunting. It is true that hunting-man has always striven, to a certain extent, to conserve, as well as to destroy game. But it was, from the forest laws of Canute to the deer parks of the eighteenth and nineteenth century, an attempt to conserve by limiting, not the amount killed, but the numbers of people who could be allowed to kill. It is, perhaps, only in this century, when hunting-man has finally realized that he has come close to gutting the world, and to emptying the continents of game, that firm attempts are being made at a form of conservation that is based, not on ability to pay, but on a determination to match the game crop to the game resources, and to do nothing that can weaken the seed stock, and so the future, of any species.

Oil pollution apart from clogging the plumage of seabirds and waterfowl, destroys much of the marine life on which they feed.

It is ironic, therefore, that, at a time when man has begun to realize the degree to which, as a hunter, he has polluted the animal kingdom, he has also embarked, as industrial man, on a pollution even more dangerous, a pollution that threatens to poison, not only the game animals, but the entire environment in which all animals, including ourselves, have to live. DG

Portugal

Lying on the west coast of the Iberian peninsula, it covers a total area of approximately 35,500 square miles, including the islands of Azores and Madeira. The terrain is mostly fairly mountainous, with several parallel ranges running from north-east to south-west, bisected by the valleys of the main rivers, the Minho, the Douro, the Tagus, and the Guadiana. The climate is nevertheless very temperate, as no part of the country is far from the sea.

Portugal is still mainly agricultural, the chief crops being cereals, citrus fruits, potatoes, olives, almonds and wine. However, the timber industry is perhaps the most important, especially cork (Portugal supplies most of the world's cork). The more mountainous areas are mostly scrub and pine, but the emphasis on timber and tree crops, such as olives, almonds, peaches, etc, very much affects the nature of the cultivated areas. The ground crops tend to be planted around the trees, rather than vice versa, giving a parkland effect (except for the Alentejo, which is a strong wheat-growing area). The value of the trees as cover is thus spoilt by the constant cultivation around them. Consequently, though Portugal has a good variety of game, total populations are not large, except for partridges, for which Portugal is famous.

There is a diversity of game available almost everywhere in Portugal. Wolf is of course confined to the mountains, and hare, the bustards, and wood pigeon are more abundant south of the Tagus.

Wolf-shooting with beaters tends to become a local fiesta. Partridge shooting, however, is highly organized, with numerous beaters, and usually 12 guns. Although such shooting is available for visitors through organizations catering especially for them, within Portugal only the very large landowners can afford this type of sport.

Typical prices for visitors are around 800 Escudos per day per person, when hunting in groups for all game except wolf and partridge. No fixed rules apply to wolf hunting, but partridge are expensive, rising from Esc. 2,000 per day per gun, depending on the amount shot. Charges are greater for those wishing to hunt individually.

Further Information

The following organizations can supply shooting for visitors:
'Retur', Rua Rodrigo da Fonseca, 56-1, Lisbon.
'Star Travel Agency', 4A, Avenida Sidonio Pais, Lisbon.

In addition there are Portuguese National Tourist Offices throughout Europe.

Licences—Portugal

A special visitor's firearms licence must be obtained from the customs at the point of entry. The licence is valid for six guns, and allows up to 400 rounds of ammunition for 60 days. Extensions may be obtained at local police stations. To obtain the licence, visitors must deposit 1,000 escudos. This will be refunded on departure, provided the visitor leaves by the same point of entry. Should he leave by another route the deposit will be refunded later. Travel agencies can deal with licences, insurance, etc, in advance.

Seasons—Portugal

Species	Season
Partridge, red-legged	15 Oct-15 Jan best: 15 Nov-31 Dec
Hare	
Rabbit	
Great bustard	
Little bustard	
Woodpigeon	15 Oct-15 March
Turtle dove	15 Aug-30 Sept; best: Sept
Snipe	1 Sept-15 Feb; best: 15Nov-31 Dec
Duck (special regulations in different regions)	15 Aug-15 Feb; best: 15 Oct onwards
Quail	1 Sept-15 Feb; best: 15 Oct-31 Jan
Woodcock	15 Oct-15 Feb
Wolf	In winter, when available

Prairie Chicken, Prairie Hen *see* Pinnated Grouse

Predator Control

In most European countries, and especially in Britain, a sound knowledge of predator control is considered essential for effective game management and preservation. The first requirement is the ability to recognize the kills of the various predators and learn their habits. Thus the peregrine falcon leaves his riven or headless corpse in the centre of a ring of feathers as unmistakable proof of his handiwork. The fox leaves the wings shorn from the body, or sometimes the remains of the half-eaten corpse partly buried in the ground. The cat is likely to leave only the beak, claws and a few scattered feathers as evidence of its kill. The stoat and the weasel will each leave their victim with a neat puncture mark in the neck where the blood has been sucked from the still warm corpse. Where the teeth marks only are visible it is probably the work of a weasel, but where a portion of the body has been eaten it is generally the work of the stoat. The otter may take one large bite from its victim, generally in the shoulder, as it does with a fish, and leave it lying by the river bank or in rushes. The badger will turn the skin of a rabbit neatly insideout like a glove or sock, though if it encounters a nest it is likely to leave a mass of smashed eggshells. The more tiresome winged predators such as the hooded or carrion crow, the greater black-backed gull, magpies, jays and jackdaws are less likely to leave traces of their work, except for sucked eggs scattered around the area, mute evidence of the damage they have caused.

The marten and the true wildcat are both rare in Britain, but along with the polecat are uneasy neighbours for good game management. Rats, uncontrolled, can be amongst the worst predators of all. The sight of their runs and holes anywhere should be warning to the preservationist. All-out war should be waged against rats, but in general, it is not necessary always to kill predators, more especially any that are rare, although it is desirable to maintain a suitable ecological balance.

Where the predators are too numerous it may well be necessary to thin them out a little. Culling of predators as with culling of weak, sickly or aged game which will not breed, or is likely to breed poor progeny, in itself a form of artificial predation, is part of the sound biological management of game stocks. In big-game management on a large-scale this can generally be left to the natural processes, in a small area this cannot always be left to nature. Inevitably, breeding game on any scale unbalances the ecological environment and then the game preserver, if he is doing his job correctly, must maintain an artificial balance. This is not always easy. Sound assessment of the balancing factors involved is the prime factor in good game management. The whole process is a form of hunting and detection in miniature which can provide enormous fascination and satisfaction to those so minded. The sight of rather more stoats and weasels in a given area than normal should not at once trigger off a determined trapping onslaught upon them. Rather than having the effect of increasing the game birds in a given area, it might well have the opposite result, since the observed increase of mustelids might have been due to a build up of the local rat population resulting from a fire, flood or other natural phenomenon in a neighbouring area. Thus with the stoats and weasels out of the way, the rats finding no predators to keep them at bay might well end by robbing more nests and killing more young birds than if the ecological balance had been left undisturbed. Such a situation is fortunately rare and the average game preserver watching his ground carefully and studying the tell-

Left, above, a squirrel pole being used to poke out a crow's nest — one method of controlling the predator.

Left, wild cats are fortunately uncommon in Britain, but they can make game management difficult in some areas.

Right, pheasant shooting in England

A male red-crested pochard, a large diving duck with erectile crown feathers and a red bill

tale signs left by the numerous animals under his control is able to assess quickly whether any predators are having a harmful effect on his game stocks. He will learn to ignore the occasional mishap and concentrate on the serious inroads caused by determined predation of one sort or another.

In the setting of traps, in the decoying of predators to the gun by calling with a piece of grass between the thumbs, imitating the cry of a rabbit in distress, or by trailing the bloody entrails of a rabbit along a ditch to a suitable point, or the sex glands of a female stoat or weasel, he will be able to practise outwitting the wild in a form of miniature hunting every bit as interesting in its way as that on a larger scale. He will find also that his game stocks remain constant or increase to a point whereby his sport is greatly improved. In thus learning the habits of the predators he learns more about the habits of the game itself. Trapping the larger predators in cage traps and transporting them to other areas where they will do less harm may help defray his shooting costs since what is one man's poison is generally another man's meat. Through studying game preservation and the trapping and control of predators the

sportsman will learn more about his sport than he ever will by simply going out with a gun. He will learn far more about the ways of the wild and he will have the satisfaction of observing the young birds whose nest he saved from being raided by the carrion crow earlier in the season, providing good sport for his dog and his friends later in the year. MWB

Prince Edward Island (Canada)

This is the smallest but the most densely populated of the Canadian provinces, and consists of a long, narrow island, some 2,000 square miles in area, in the Gulf of St Lawrence. The climate is maritime and mild. The surface of the island is gently undulating, and nowhere higher than 500 ft. The soil is a sandy loam over red sandstone, fertile, and intensively farmed. Potatoes and bacon pigs are the most important agricultural products. There are several marsh and dune areas attractive to waterfowl. Before the eel-grass failure in 1933 this used to be a famous goose shooting area. Now only the Canadas use it as a staging post.

Prince Edward Island is not, primarily, good hunting country. It holds no big-game animals, except, perhaps, for an occasional bear. Most of the land is farmed and in private hands, though permission to hunt is seldom difficult to obtain, and arrangements for non-residents can usually be made by the Department of Tourist Development, Charlottetown. Foxes, raccoons and rabbits are plentiful, but there is no tradition of hunting them with hounds. Similarly, although woodcock are plentiful during the breeding season, they migrate early and are seldom hunted because there are few good woodcock dogs in the province. Snipe are plentiful, both in the salt marshes and the alder carrs. The principal game bird is the ruffed grouse, with the Hungarian partridge, first introduced in 1927, taking some of the shooting pressures off the former. Pheasants have been introduced on several occasions, but never with sufficient success for there to be an open season for many years running. Today, pheasant hunting is confined to the Earnscliffe-China Point Co-operative Shooting Preserve which had, in 1970, a 71-day season from 3 October to 26 December, in the course of which 644, or some 59% of all birds released, were shot.

Further Information

The Fish and Wildlife Division, P.O. Box 2000, Charlottetown, P.E.I.

Pronghorn *(Antilocapra americana)*

This is not an antelope, although it is sometimes so called, nor, in spite of its Latin name, is it really a 'goat-antelope'. It is the only surviving representative of a family that has always been unique to America. It resembles the *Bovidae* in being

---

Licence Fees—Prince Edward Island

All hunters must possess a Provincial Licence, $2 for residents and $10 for non-residents. These can be bought from authorized vendors, or from the Department of Tourist Development in Charlottetown. If waterfowl are to be shot, a Canadian Migratory Game Bird Hunting Permit is necessary, $2 from Post Offices.

Game Inventory—Prince Edward Island

Species	Shot	Per cent
Duck	19,395	Green-winged teal 49% Black duck 24% Blue-winged teal 18%
Geese	6,041	Canada goose 100%

Seasons and Limits—Prince Edward Island

Species	Season	Limit
Snowshoe hare	2 Nov-30 Jan	5 per day
Fox	1 Oct-13 Feb	No limit
Raccoon	No closed season	
Ruffed grouse	1 Oct-30 Nov	3 per day, 6 in possession
Hungarian partridge	1 Oct-31 Oct	3 per day, 6 in possession
Duck (other than black and wood duck)	1 Oct-12 Dec	6 per day, exclusive of mergansers, and not more then 4 may be black duck; 12 in possession of which not more than 8 may be black duck
Geese and black duck	14 Oct-12 Dec	5 per day, 10 in possession
Wood duck	No open season	
Woodcock	1 Oct-28 Nov	8 per day, 16 in possession
Wilson's snipe	1 Oct-28 Nov	10 per day, no limit in possession

'Antelope Shooting' from *North American Indian Portfolio*, 1844, by George Catlin

horned rather than antlered, but those horns are branched and at least partly deciduous, the outer, pronged sheath being shed in early autumn, even though the bony, fibrous core remains.

Its survival as a game species represents a genuine triumph of game management over hunting pressures. It was estimated in 1925 that no more than 30,000 pronghorns were left in the whole of North America. Since then, strict and intelligent control of hunting has led to a situation where the annual legal kill, in the United States alone, can safely exceed 75,000, and the estimated population in Canada, the United States, and Mexico is in excess of three-quarters of a million and steadily increasing.

Pronghorns are primarily browsers, with a special liking for low growing shrubs such as sage-brush. They choose open country where such shrubs can be found and where they can use their great turn of speed. In summer this will be on higher land, but in winter the snows may drive them down into the valleys. During the winter they will be found in large herds, but except during the breeding season, they spend the rest of the year in small, single age, single-sex groups. Herds are found as far north as Alberta, Saskatchewan and Manitoba, and as far south as Chihuahua and Sonora in Mexico. The largest populations are in Wyoming (350,000) and Montana (220,000) but there are quite large herds in Colorado, South Dakota and New Mexico, and some population in seventeen different states in all.

The male pronghorn is 45 to 56 in long, 35 to 41 in high, and weighs between 100 and 140 lb. The female is smaller, and weighs between 80 and 100 lb. The belly is white, the rest of the body tan, buff, and dark brown, the throat is marked with white bars, and there is a prominent white rump-patch, the hairs of which, being erectile, flash when the animal turns to run. The record horns measured 20 in, and 17 to 18 in is common. The feet lack dew claws, and the animal is probably the fastest land mammal on the continent, reaching speeds of over 60 mph. Its powers of sight are highly developed.

Sexual maturity is reached during the second year, and the rut takes place during September and October. The bucks may fight whilst collecting their harems, which may include up to 15 does. Gestation takes 230 to 240 days, and the does leave the group in May to drop their kids – singles with a first birth, twins generally thereafter. The young can run with the group very soon after birth.

Pronghorn are best stalked, however difficult this may be because of the animal's sharp and almost telescopic sight. In some, but not many states, it is still not illegal to chase them on horseback or in an automobile, dismounting to take snap shots. Even during the most careful stalk, longer shots than usual may be necessary, and it is important to use a flat trajectory, long-range rifle with telescopic sights and firing a bullet of 100 to 200 grains.

Ptarmigan (*Lagopus* species)

These are the smallest of the grouse, averaging between 15 and 20 oz in weight and measuring around 14 in. They are represented, in Europe, by the European ptarmigan *(Lagopus mutus)*, the willow ptarmigan or willow grouse *(Lagopus lagopus)* and the red grouse *(Lagopus scoticus)* (*q.v.*). This last bird must not be included in a collective description of ptarmigan, not only because it differs from them in several ways, but also because it is one of the most important of all game birds. Other ptarmigan, are, generally speaking, birds of the tundra and the high mountains and other inaccessible places, and therefore are seldom encountered and shot. But the red grouse (*q.v.*), even though it is only found in the north of Britain, attracts shooting men from all over the world. The ptarmigan of North America include the willow ptarmigan, together with its subspecies Alexander's ptarmigan *(L. lagopus alexandrae)*, the various subspecies of white-tailed ptarmigan *(Lagopus leucurus)* and the rock ptarmigan *(Lagopus rupestris)* and its subspecies. It has been suggested that there is no real distinction between the European and rock ptarmigan, and it is, indeed, true that the differences between the various species and, even more, between the various subspecies of ptarmigan, are very small, and are confined almost entirely to differences of range, habitat and size. It is, in addition, difficult to distinguish clearly between species of birds all of which (with the exception of red grouse) have three moults and two colour changes every year.

In the winter months all ptarmigan assume pure white plumage, though in some species there may be some black on the tails or bill. In the summer they change back to plumage of various browns, reds and grays, all with black barrings and mottlings, adapted to conceal them against their particular background of stone or vegetation. But even in their summer plumage they all retain considerable white on their underparts and underwing feathers. Their legs and feet are well-feathered to help movement across the snow and they are all, unusually for grouse, monogamous. There is generally little courtship display but the cocks will fight, quite fiercely, for hens and for territory. Nesting is on the ground and the clutch, which will vary in size from one species to another, takes around 21 days to incubate. The cock remains by the nest during this period and helps with rearing the covey. There is a certain amount of packing in autumn, especially with willow grouse, who may form, under certain conditions, into very large groups and undertake what amount to quasi-migrations, taking them well below the treeline. Otherwise ptarmigan tend only to move down, in winter, to the lower levels of their range, and the white-tailed ptarmigan, which is a bird of the higher Rockies, remains on the heights consistently. Ptarmigan seem to be as seriously affected as other grouse by the well-known grouse cycle, and to undertake, under pressures that cannot always be explained, quite large movements in range.

Most of them live, in summer, on a variety of insects and green foods that are replaced, later in the year, by grass and ling seeds. In the winter they will survive on lichens and mosses, whilst the willow grouse will eat the buds of willows and alders. They have harsh, rattling calls, even during courtship, and the alarm call is a repetitive 'owk-owk-owk'. Once flushed they fly well, and for longer distances than other grouse, but they often crouch and depend on protective camouflage rather than flight to save them. In winter they are difficult to pick out against the snow, and in summer they resemble amazingly the rocks and stones they crouch among.

The European ptarmigan is found throughout Norway, in northern Finland, in the Russian tundras, in Iceland, northern Scotland, the Pyrenees and the French Alps, but always on the higher slopes and never below the treeline. Willow ptarmigan, however, live at a lower level, since they need willow and alder stands for winter foods. They are found throughout Scandinavia, the eastern Baltic, the north of Russia and Siberia, and in the North American tundras from the Aleutian Islands to Greenland. The rock ptarmigan, which lives at about the same level as the willow ptarmigan, is found in Alaska, the Yukon and northern British Columbia. The white-tailed ptarmigan is found only very seldom away from the higher slopes of the Rocky and Cascade Mountains, from Alaska to as far south as north Montana.

Willow and rock ptarmigan, as well as European ptarmigan, may be specifically hunted, but even they, and far more the white-tailed ptarmigan, are generally encountered when hunting other game – highlying red grouse, for example, or Rocky Mountain goat. In either case they will

Willow ptarmigan, photographed in Canada

always be difficult birds to hunt and shoot. Early in the season, when they are still in their small family coveys and the percentage of young birds is high, they will lie well to the dog. Later in the season they will be more difficult to approach, and will tend to run on in front or else flush early and fly straight off one mountainside to the next. It is important, at that stage, to have a dog, sufficiently well trained not to attempt to follow them.

Pudu *see* Deer of the World and their Hunting

Puku *(Kobus vardoni)*
This member of the antelope family is found in parts of central Africa and is very similar

to the lechwe, except that its horns are smaller and it has no black markings on the forelegs. Unlike the lechwe it has face glands and well developed inguinal pouches and glands. Its habitat is similar, though it does not like the extensive flood plains favoured by the lechwe and is sometimes found in light woodland. It is found in herds of from ten to a hundred, sometimes associating with lechwe, but more often with impala. The sexes are often found in separate herds. It is mainly a grazer, perhaps browsing occasionally. A single young is born annually from May to September. Twins are rare.

Puma *see* Cougar; South America, Shooting in

A female puku, a central-African medium-sized antelope, rarely found far from water

Q

Quail (*Coturnix coturnix*)

The common or migratory quail is a small, partridge-like bird, partially migrant in Europe as some winter in southern Spain, Italy and the Balkans, but otherwise only a summer migrant to Europe, south of the Baltic and, now, a rare visitor to the British Isles. Vast numbers of these birds used to move southwards in September to south Africa and India, returning in March and April. They were snared, netted, trapped and shot in their millions as they left and returned to southern Europe, and there has been a marked reduction in their numbers. Nevertheless they are still plentiful, provide excellent shooting, and are highly prized by epicures.

The female is very similar to the male in appearance. Both are sandy brown birds measuring about 7 in, with buff shaft stripes and black bars and markings. The chin and throat are white, the chest rufous-black, and the rest of the underparts pale gray. The cock has a black, anchor-shaped mark down the middle of its throat that is missing in the hen, whilst the hen's chest is thickly spotted with brownish-black.

Quail are monogamous and nest on the ground in cover. The nest is a small scrape with little or no lining, and the clutch consists of 8 to 12 eggs. They are slower flyers than partridge and, except during migrations, are solitaries. The cock has a typical trisyllabic call which is heard day and night, the hens call being a bisyllabic 'queep-queep'.

Quail

Asia
Black-breasted (rain)
Blue-breasted button
Gray

Australia
Australian* (stubble)
Australian swamp
Brown (Common)
King

Europe
Quail* (Common)

New Zealand
Californian

North America
American
Bobwhite* (Virginian)
Californian (valley*)
Desert* (Gambel's)
Harlequin (Mearn's)
Masked
Mountain*
Scaled*

The common quail is the only species of quail found in Europe.

Quails

Quail are small, shy partridge-like ground-nesting birds divided principally into old world and new world species. Often highly coloured, crested and plumed, they generally form coveys and sometimes pack in the winter, often being found in arid conditions. Among the best game birds to shoot over dogs, they are particularly prized both in North America and Australia. There is only one species in Europe. Their flesh is generally excellent.

Quail Shooting around the World

Quail are among the most important of gamebirds around the world. Nearly 100 species – some as big as partridges, others as tiny as sparrows – figure in the bag in such widely scattered places as Australia, South America, Africa and Europe. Two of the best known species are the bobwhite (*Colinus virginianus*) of the United States, West Indies and Central America, and the migratory quail (*Coturnix coturnix*) of Europe, Asia and Africa.

The bobwhite, which is resident throughout the eastern and south-eastern States, and also in the north-west, is almost legendary as a quarry for the hunter who enjoys a combination of interesting dog-work and tricky shooting. The birds, named after their cheery 'bob-white' whistle, weigh 6 to 7 oz and measure 8½ to 10½ in. Their plumage is an intricate mixture of browns and buffs, with a noticeable white eyestripe and bib in the male.

Bobwhites are found in coveys averaging 15 birds during the non-breeding season, frequenting farmland, open pinelands and the fringe of brushy woods. They lie well to pointers and setters, bursting into the air in a 'bouquet' when flushed and heading for cover unpredictably at all points of the compass. This explosive energy makes the selection of safe shots, which will not connect with dog or companion a matter of quick judgment, and is one reason why it has been said that 'like a honeymoon, bird hunting is built for two'.

Single birds are usually followed up after a covey is flushed, but in parts of the Deep South, where plantation quail-shooting has been raised to a fine and gracious art, hunters may follow their relays of bird dogs in a mule-drawn buggie, dismounting for each new covey and leaving the singles to re-form for another day.

The bobwhite can withstand habitat changes and heavy harvesting which would reduce the numbers of many less adaptable

birds, and there is still a long quail-hunting season over most of its range in the U.S. Even so, in districts near big cities it is no longer found in great enough numbers to satisfy hunting pressure and is the subject of 'put and take' shooting on private preserves.

Under this system, artificially-reared bobwhites are released into suitable cover a few hours before the arrival of pre-booked parties of hunters. Each member of the group, which is accompanied by a guide and pointing dogs provided by the preserve, usually pays a fee for a 'reasonable chance' to shoot, say, eight quail. At its best, the system takes pressure off over-harvested wild populations and provides sporting shooting. At its worst, it can be a travesty of a fine field sport.

The bobwhite has been nominated 'King of American Gamebirds', but the migratory quail of the Old World was long regarded only as a table delicacy fit for netting and trapping. It was found in such abundance that quail shooting was looked upon almost as a chore, particularly when vast numbers reached northern India during the autumn migration. Col Tickell wrote during the 19th century that it 'is usual to be provided with two or three guns, to be loaded as fast as emptied, by a servant. A tolerably good shot will bag 50 to 60 brace in about three hours.'

In some districts of India, the custom is to draw quail into grain fields by siting call birds in cages atop poles. The birds are then flushed by walking guns or beaters.

The migratory quail is small (4 to 5 oz, 8 in long), but it is known as a gourmet's delight over its entire, vast range. The presence of this quail is often revealed by its distinctive call, a staccato triple whistle, usually rendered as 'wet-my-lips'. The birds flush singly and fly fast on surprisingly long and narrow wings. The flight path is usually direct, 5 to 15 ft up, and they are not particularly challenging to the gun.

This quail formerly bred north to Britain, but changes in climate and farming methods, combined with heavy over-harvest of the birds at migration bottlenecks in southern Europe, have greatly reduced their numbers. It is now completely protected in Britain. It is still an important gamebird in Asia, the Middle East and Africa, while of the closely-related Australian stubble quail, Gould noted that 'it lies well to a pointer and has from the first settlement of the colony always afforded considerable amusement to the sportsman'.

The Japanese race of the migratory quail has been domesticated and is the most productive of gamebirds – fertile eggs have been reported from birds only 36 days old. With maturity at 50 days or earlier and machine-like production of more than 300 eggs a year from the females, it is not surprising that efforts have been made to

The male bobwhite quail. The bobwhite has a wide distribution in North America.

mass-produce this quail for sport. However, the Japanese or Pharoah quail has almost lost the brooding instinct during 900 years in captivity, although still retaining its migratory urges. These factors, combined with an unwillingness to be flushed, have prevented the bird from achieving any popularity so far.

A melanistic race of this quail, imported from Italy and named the 'percolin' in the erroneous belief that it was a partridge quail-bobwhite *(perdix-coturnix-colinus)* hybrid, was marketed for some time in Britain as a gamebird but is now used by only a few dog trainers and as an ornamental bird.

Apart from the bobwhite and the true quails of Eurasia, the name 'quail' has been applied to many other species, almost as indiscriminately as 'partridge'.

In the western U.S., five quail are of particular importance: they were the only upland gamebirds until the introduction of the chukar. These are the Californian or valley, Gambel's, mountain, blue-scaled and harlequin or Mearn's quail, all of which are found in rather arid habitats. From the shooting viewpoint they are not classic quarry, tending to run rather than fly, but the Californian quail in particular has been a mainstay of shooting in the Pacific Coast area, extending its range into irrigated districts.

The bush-quail of India, wood-quail of Central and South America, and button quail or hemipodes of Europe, Asia, Africa and Australia, all provide sport in their native areas to some extent. Some species such as the 5 in-long painted quail of India and south-east Asia, are too small to be taken seriously, and others, found in thick jungle, are almost unshot, preferring to hide or run rather than take to the wing even when pressed by dogs. WAN

Quebec (Canada)

This, the largest of the Canadian provinces has been known at various times as Canada, New France, Quebec, and Lower Canada. It covers nearly 600,000 square miles, including the Ungava territory and the Iles de la Madeleine and Anticosti Island.

The terrain is varied. Two large mountain ranges run along the St Lawrence Basin, the Laurentian Mountains to the north of the river and the Mountains of Notre Dame to the south. There are a great many lakes and rivers, and it is heavily wooded, 350,000 square miles being under forests, two thirds of them productive. There are large areas of tundra in the north and of fertile farmland in the south, where over 7 million acres are under the plough. The principal crops are cereals, hay, roots, fruit and buckwheat.

Big game consists of caribou, deer, moose and bear. Caribou can only be shot in Zone 0, most of which lies north of the 52nd parallel. The non-resident, therefore, can only hunt there whilst using the services of an outfitter. The zone, however, is far too large for close supervision of the hunters, and there is some fear that the caribou is being over-shot. It has been suggested that the zone may be split up, for the purposes of caribou hunting, into smaller zones, more easily controlled, one of which will be opened each year.

White-tailed deer is shot only in the south and east as the population levels are too low elsewhere, and moose is not shot in certain southern and western zones.

The polar bear is protected, but the black bear can be shot during the fall, and also during a spring season when its coat is at its most valuable.

Licence Fees—Quebec

Type	Status	Fee
Deer, bear and small game (except Anticosti Island)	Resident	$5.25
	Non-resident	$27.50
Deer, bear and fox (Anticosti Island only)	Resident	$5.75
	Non-resident	$28.00
General	Resident	$13.50
	Non-resident	$103.00
Bear	Resident	$5.25
	Non-resident	$12.50
Small game and game birds	Resident	$4.25
	Non-resident	$17.50
Migratory birds	Resident	$4.25
	Non-resident	$17.50
Plus Canada Migratory Game Bird Hunting Permit (necessary for all migratory birds, including water fowl)	Any	$2.00

Seasons and Limits—Quebec

Vary from Zone to Zone

Species	Area	Season	Limit
Caribou	Zone O	27 Aug-27 Sept	One per season
White-tailed deer		30 Oct-early Nov	One
	Anticosti Island	1 July-31 Jan	2
Moose	Some south and west zones	Protected	One
	Elsewhere	1st half of Oct	
	Zone O	Early autumn	
Black bear	Zone O	27 Aug-11 Oct	No limit
	Elsewhere	18 Sept-1 Nov; Beginning May-end July	
Hare		11 Sept-29 Feb	No limit except in southern zones where it is
	Zone O	11 Sept-31 March	5 per day.
Wolf Coyote Bobcat Fox Skunk Raccoon Woodchuck		All year	No limit
Grouse, spruce, ruffed, and sharp-tailed, and Hungarian partridge	Zone O	11 Sept-31 Dec 27 Aug-30 April, spruce grouse only in Zone O	5 per day, 15 in possession each. All possession after 6 Jan is illegal.
Ptarmigan	Zone O	27 Aug-30 April	10 per day, 30 in possession
	Elsewhere	11 Sept-29 Feb	
Woodcock		12 Sept-15 Nov	8 per day, 16 in possession
Wilson's snipe	Start varies within Sept, earlier in north, later in south, season ends, 13 Dec		10 per day, no limit on possession
Rails, coots and gallinules			6 (total) per day, 12 in possession
Duck, including eider, scoter and old squaw			6 (total) per day, and 12 (total) in possession (excluding mergansers) of which not more than 4 may be wood duck. After 10 Oct, 2 more scaup or goldeneye may be included, and 2 more eider, scoter and old squaw.
Geese, including brant			5 (total) per day, and 15 (total) in possession of which not more than 10 may be of species other than greater snow goose. (In the James Bay Area the seasonal limit is 5 times the daily limit of duck and 3 times the daily limit of geese, except for residents of over 6 months standing)

Game Inventory—Quebec

Species	Shot	Per cent
Duck (excluding sea duck)	300,000	Black duck* 26%
		Green-winged teal 15%
		Mallárd 13%
		Blue-winged teal 11%
		Pintail 6%
		Others 29%
Geese	13,000	
Woodcock	28,000	
Wilson's snipe	21,000	
Gallinules	645	

*The Department of Tourism, Fish and Game is becoming concerned by the decreasing numbers of black duck, and further restrictions on its shooting are probable.

Special Regulations

No hunting is allowed half an hour after sunset until half an hour before sunrise. No electrical or mechanical bird calls are allowed. No baiting is allowed for big game.

Deer, moose, and caribou 'yards' must not be disturbed. No low velocity rifles, shotguns or 44/40 rifles may be used on either caribou or moose. Each licence will specify the arms that may not be used. Automatics are illegal. Tags must be attached to moose and deer as soon as they have been killed and the kill must be reported within the specified time limit. Dogs may not be used when hunting big game. Hunting in parks and reserves is generally prohibited except for certain organized moose shoots held in certain parks for residents only.

Further Information

Department of Tourism, Fish and Game, Hotel du Gouvernement, Quebec.

The Department publishes a list of outfitters, as well as the names and addresses of all game wardens.

Queensland (Australia)

Queensland consists of the whole of the north-east corner of the Australian continent, covering an area of approximately 67,000 square miles. The Great Dividing Range, rising to over 5,000 ft, runs down the east, with a narrow slope to the Pacific coast and a long and gradual slope to the west and the central plains. The west is divided into a northern and southern by the watershed of the Selwyn range. The climate is mostly tropical, but not unhealthy, the coastal regions being fairly moist, though rainfall in the west is very scanty.

The main crops are cereals, fruit, cotton, sugar and tobacco; forestry is increasing, there is considerable dairy farming and the western regions are devoted mostly to cattle and sheep rearing. Most of the land is still state owned or leased. Queensland provides several species of game in fair numbers. Large areas are still relatively unsettled. For legislation and organization purposes the state is separated into six faunal districts, roughly three each side of the Great Dividing Range.

There are three main classifications of fauna in Queensland: permanently protected fauna; protected fauna; unprotected fauna.

The permanently protected species are koala, platypus and echnida. They are protected in perpetuity, and penalties for taking, shooting, or otherwise contravening the regulations concerning them are heavy.

Protected fauna is by far the largest category. Species within this category may be taken by special permission if they are dangerous, are damaging property, crops, or livestock, or are causing trouble on an airfield. All species for which open seasons are proclaimed fall within this category, and a royalty is charged per head. Unless otherwise stated, seasons apply to all six faunal districts.

The pest fauna, shown in the table, may be shot or taken at any time of the year unless otherwise stated.

Fauna Sanctuaries

There are over 400 sanctuaries in Queensland, covering about 16,500,000 acres. They include all islands, State Forest Reserves, and National Parks. Details are available from the Department of Primary Industries in a publication entitled 'Queensland Fauna Sanctuaries'. Within a sanctuary landowners and their authorized agents may take or shoot pests on their own property. No protected animal may be taken, whether an open season has been declared or not.

Special Regulations

No hunting is permitted on stock routes, or roads, or on private, leasehold or Crown land without consent of the owner, occupier, or authority controlling the land.

The use of cyanide, or adhesive substances, such as bird-lime, is prohibited. Other poisons, materials or appliances may be prohibited from time to time. The use of flashlights, torches or any artificial light is also illegal.

A pair of wolves in the snow (left)

Pest Fauna—Queensland

May be shot at anytime

Australian goshawk
Bee eaters (only in certain areas)
Collared sparrow hawk
Cormorants (shags)
Crows and ravens
Dingo
Eastern swamp hen (bald coot)
Falcons (except nankeen kestrel)
Flying fox (only in certain areas)
Fox
Grey (white) goshawk
Hare
Pied currawong
Rabbit
Rose-breasted cockatoo (galah)
Silvereye
Sparrow
Starling
Turtle dove
Water buffalo
Wedge-tailed eagle
White cockatoo
Wild pig

Certain guns are prohibited, including any over 16 lb, or with more than two barrels. Single-barrelled guns must not exceed 8-bore or a barrel weight of 8 lb. The equivalent figures for double-barrelled guns are 10-bore and 14 lb.

No barrel may be longer than 42 in, and all guns must be what are normally termed 'shoulder guns'.

Fauna conservation legislation is enforced by all members of the Police Force, 'Forest Officers', and all officers of the Department of Primary Industries or the Department of Public Lands. Certain honorary protectors with suitable credentials may be appointed in any locality. Honorary protectors have only powers of interrogation, but fauna officers have extensive powers of entry and search, investigation and enquiry, and confiscation of appliances and fauna. Only members of the police force have the power to arrest.

Further Information

The Director General, Department of Primary Industries, William Street, Brisbane, Q. 4000 (for information on flora and fauna conservation, including sanctuaries, research and legislation).

The Conservator of Forests, Department of Forestry, Ann Street, Brisbane, Q. 4000 (for information on National Parks, State Forests and Scenic Areas).

The Secretary, Department of Lands, George Street, Brisbane, Q. 4000 (for information on 'The Stock Routes and Rural Land Protection Acts' under which certain fauna are declared as vermin, and on the 'Rabbit Acts').

The Secretary, Police Department, 43 Makerson Street, Brisbane, Q. 4000; or District Police Stations (for information on the use of firearms).

Whip-tailed wallabies are shot in Queensland all year round.

Seasons and Royalties—Queensland

Species	Season	Royalty, per animal (Australian cents)
Marsupials, including: gray kangaroo, red kangaroo; eastern (dusky) wallaroo, North Queensland Wallaroo; red-necked, scrub (eastern brush), black-striped, whiptail, gray-face (pretty face), black-tailed (swamp) and sandy wallaby; red-legged pademelon	All year	20c
Water rat	All year	10c
All introduced birds, including: Java sparrow, non-pareil finch, nutmeg finch, strawberry finch, gold finch, all rosellas, all budgerigars	All year	10c; rosellas, 20c
Finches: black-throated, chestnut-breasted (bull), diamond firetail (diamond sparrow), banded (double-bar), long-tailed (grass), masked, plum-headed, red-browed (red-head), star (red-faced) and zebra	1 July-30 Sept	10c
Snipe: Australian and pin-tailed; knot, great knot, sandpiper, stint, tattler and whimbrel	14 Nov-15 March	Nil, except when taken under special permit during close season when it is 50c
King parrot, rainbow lorikeet (blue mountain parrot) and red-winged parrot	1 May-30 Sept	20c
Cockatiel (cockatoo parrot or quarrian)	1 May-30 Nov	20c
Brush (scrub) turkey	1 June-30 Sept	Nil, but close season special permit rate is 50c
Quail	Varies between June and Sept	50c
Duck, includes: black duck, wood duck (maned goose) gray teal, hardhead (white-eyed duck) pink-eared duck, plumed tree duck, whistling tree duck (water whistling duck)	6 June-29 Aug in 2 southern districts, 4 July-26 Sept in remainder	Nil, but close season special permit rate is 50c Limit: 15 per day
Unprotected species	Any time	
Deer	protected	
Crocodile	May soon be protected	

Licences—Queensland

Open season fauna-permits are required for all those hunting protected fauna for which an open season has been declared. Permits for personal use cost Australian $2; for fauna taken for sale permits cost $5. Permits do not authorize entry to private land. Licences will not be granted without a list of holdings on which applicants have permission to hunt. Permits are not required to shoot duck or quail during the open season.

R

Rabbit (*Oryctolagus cuniculus*)

The European rabbit is a familiar small, brown, long-eared furred mammal generally found living in burrows throughout Europe. They may also live above ground and their breeding is limited only by climate, time and the available food supply. They are vegetarian in diet, grazers and occasional browsers. They are polygamous and generally weigh between 2 to 3 lb. The number born in a litter may vary from 2 to 11 and the phenomenon known as double oestrus or second fertilization, as in hares (*q.v.*), is not uncommon. The young are generally born in a short blind burrow known as a stop. They are born naked, blind and helpless unlike the young of the hare which are born fully furred and with their eyes open. The gestation period is 6 weeks and they are unable to look after themselves until about 3 weeks old. Thereafter the mother may desert them and conceivably have another litter.

The rabbit thumps the ground with its hind legs when alarmed and at this signal all other rabbits in the vicinity will dash for their burrows. It has only its speed and wariness to save it from its predators, but an old rabbit will often face up to a weasel and the latter usually attack only the young and inexperienced. The spread of the disease myxomatosis has very greatly reduced the rabbit population in most countries, but they have by no means disappeared. They provide good sport with a ferret (*q.v.*) and nets, or with a gun and dog (especially spaniels which bustle them out of cover).

Rabbits (*Leporidae*)

Generally living below ground in complex tunnel systems known as warrens, rabbits are prolific breeders. Their young are born blind below ground. They were introduced to Australasia where they rapidly became a pest. Shot, ferreted, netted, trapped and gassed, they are regarded as pests in most areas, but can often provide good sporting shooting for the shotgun enthusiast or for the rifleman with light rifle and telescopic or open sights. Their flesh is light coloured and good eating.

See also Hares

Raccoon (*Procyon lotor*)

An omnivorous, plantigrade mammal with several sub-species showing differences of colour, size and habit, probably reflecting differences in habitat. The raccoon is a medium-sized animal with short legs, a thick, gray-black, grizzled coat, and a bushy,

The European rabbit is no longer as common as it once was due to the spread of myxomatosis.

Rabbits

Cottontails * :
  Brush rabbit
  Forest rabbit
  Marsh rabbit
  Mexican cottontail
  Pigmy rabbit
  Swamp rabbit
Rabbit *, European

black-ringed tail. The face is lighter coloured, except for a black mask and a black streak on the forehead. Adult weight can vary between 15 and 30 lb, the average is 25 lb. It is largely arboreal, generally lives in a hollow tree, and rarely ranges more than one mile from its den. Most of its movements are by night, since it is largely, though not solely, nocturnal. Though it does not truly hibernate it does lie dormant for long periods in winter.

It generally feeds at night, its diet being variable, and including nuts, fruit, grain, insects, crayfish, mice, frogs and bird eggs. It is monogamous, breeds in January and February, the gestation period being 63 days. Litters are born in April and May and the litter average is five, with a range of from three to seven. The young raccoon becomes sexually mature at about one year, and will then settle several miles from the home den. The pelt is of commercial value and is known as 'Alaska Bear' and 'Alaska Sable'.

Raccoon multiply and colonize rapidly, and are now found in most states of the Union, as well as in Mexico and Canada. They can easily over-multiply and become pests, and, since they are predators of waterfowl, many states have no closed season for them.

Raccoon are hunted, generally at night, with hounds. These may be silent, giving tongue only when the quarry has been treed, but, more commonly, they will give tongue as they run, and so allow the hunter to follow the course the hunt takes through the night. If the hound is a cold trailer then hunting will be possible in daylight, but it is more usual to follow a hot trail by night. This is done in one of two ways. One is to allow hounds to range freely over country, the hunters following behind on foot. The other is 'roading' – that is the hounds are run down a road until they hit a crossing scent, the hunters following behind in a car, dismounting only when hounds leave the road. The most important duty of all, for the hound, is to 'tree' the raccoon, and this involves pressing it hard. When hunters come up the treed animal can be pushed or shaken down for the hounds to break up, or it can be shot with whatever firearms the State permits for the purpose. This, besides being kinder and more certain, may well spare the hounds injury, since a large raccoon can cause considerable damage. A 'coon hound has emerged as a distinct breed which has some claims to be specially suited to 'coon hunting. It is a large black

There are several sub-species of raccoon, the one shown here was photographed in Michigan.

Right, below, the red deer is the largest quarry commonly encountered in Europe.

and tan hound, descended from the fox-hound, but with considerable bloodhound crossing in it.

Raccoon Dog (*Nyctereutes procynoides*)
A small wild canine found in eastern Asia, particularly in China and Japan, which has been introduced into the U.S.S.R. compara-tively recently. It is about 32 in long with a thickly-furred body, a sharply pointed nose and a short bushy tail. It is compara-tively easily bred for its fur. The general coloration is black or dusky yellow and it is much more like a raccoon than a dog. It hunts in packs and is chiefly nocturnal, feeding on rats and mice or, in the winter, on fish. It is also said to hibernate. It is shot in Japan.

Rails *see* Waders

Red-crested Pochard (*Netta rufina*)
A less common duck than the pochard (*q.v.*) of Europe, the drake is distinguished from the drake of that species by having a red bill and white flanks. Its chestnut head looks larger than it is because the crown feathers are erectile. The neck is black, the upper-parts dark brown and the neck and breast black. The duck is drab brown with pale cheeks. It has a blackish bill with an orange-red tip and no white on its flanks.

Its feeding, flying and nesting habits are similar to the pochard's. It breeds in Europe and Asia from Spain to southern Russia and from the Kirghiz Steppes to western Siberia. It is a partial migrant, wintering in the Mediterranean Basin, but it also migrates to India, Burma and China. It is only a rare winter vagrant to Britain.

Red Deer (*Cervus elaphus*)
Distributed throughout Europe and Asia, it is most highly regarded in Britain and the European continent, where it is by far the largest commonly encountered quarry. A full grown red deer stag stands 48 in at the shoulder and the antlers may attain a length of about 32 in and an inside width about 30 in, although, since antler growth is largely dependent on available food, this may vary enormously from area to area throughout its range. Similarly their weight may vary from as much as 150 lb to 300 lb, with local variations both very much above and even below these weights. The hind does not have antlers and is generally a good deal smaller and lighter than the stag, averaging about 42 in at the shoulder and weighing only about 112 lb, but again such averages are subject to local conditions. Their coloration is a rich reddish-brown as implied by their name, but during the winter this turns to gray. The short tail is surrounded by a conspicuous light-coloured patch. The young, spotted with white, are born in May or June, generally only one, though twins are not unknown. The rutting

season is in September and October when the stags may be heard roaring and seen fighting for possession of the hinds. Each mature stag will gain his small following of hinds and after a gestation period of eight months the fawns are born in May or June. Very exceptionally, after a mild winter, the stags have been known to seek the hinds again and fawns are then very occasionally dropped in the autumn, but such calves are, of course, at a very severe disadvantage during the following winter, being too young to cope with adverse conditions. Although basically grazers, red deer are also browsers whenever feeding is avail-able. Thus the red deer in a 'deer forest' in the Scottish Highlands, which may consist of nothing but bare hillside or mountain, are at a considerable disadvantage com-pared with those in the fine afforested re-gions of mainland Europe, or even the well-forested part of East Anglia, England. In such conditions they can always find feed-ing which will provide them with plenty of nutrition and shelter during the hardest winter. In these conditions the red deer may have fine spreads of antlers and weigh over 300 lb, sometimes exceeding 450 lb in parts of Germany and Hungary.

This 8-pointer red deer stag was shot in New Zealand. Introduced from Europe, they are now the most plentiful of New Zealand's big game.

The red deer in Europe and Britain has, for centuries, been regarded as one of the principal beasts of the chase when hunted by hounds. In Britain this has been so since the days of William the Conqueror, but now there is only one pack of hounds, the Devon and Somerset Staghounds, which continue to hunt them in the traditional way with a pack of hounds and mounted followers. Otherwise, the only methods of hunting the red deer in Britain are by stalking in the Highlands of Scotland or by still-hunting in the forests of the south. In France the red deer is still the principal beast hunted by hounds as it has been since the days of the Frankish Kings. It is also stalked or still-hunted, the latter being by far the most common method. In eastern Europe and France hunting by encircling an area with shewelling and driving to the waiting guns is also employed, especially for culling hinds, but as there is very little chance of selective shooting it cannot be regarded as a sound method of culling weak stock.

Culling the weak hinds is the best method of maintaining good red deer stock, particularly when allied to leaving the good heads or finest stags to breed and reproduce. Red deer stock management is one of the most difficult problems of wild game management, as the requisite knowledge of each forest, the numbers and quality of the deer in it, can only be gained by the man on the spot, who is frequently ill-educated as to what comprises a sound management policy. In Britain, especially, there is no coherent planned policy for breeding and in France very much the same problem arises because hunting with hounds is the principal method, and hind culling is very ill-organized. Selectivity is more carefully considered as a national policy both in Germany and the central European countries, such as Czechoslovakia and Hungary. Quite apart from the fact that they appreciate the value of good heads as an attraction to visiting hunters there is little doubt that their forest management is very successfully linked with the management of red and roe deer stocks. The serious management of afforestation in conjunction with deer has attained a higher standard there than elsewhere in Europe. The culling of hinds in the late autumn and early winter is not left to deer drives or similar haphazard methods, or to the decisions of employees with no scientific background, as is invariably the case in Britain or France. On the contrary the foresters and rangers undergo a thorough training before qualifying and know their ground and every beast on it, so that their advice regarding the shooting of stags and culling of hinds is rightly regarded as all important. Additionally, the subject is treated on a national basis rather than in small and individual units. It is for these reasons as much as for their better feeding that the heads of the red stags in central Europe have consistently bettered those found in Britain or France, or for that matter Asia. In Australia, where the red deer has been introduced, there has been little interest in them as a quarry and in New Zealand they are regarded as a pest. There, however, their close relative the wapiti or elk of North America has also been introduced and interbreeding between the two may, in the future, produce record red deer heads, for the wapiti has a much larger and heavier head than the red deer.

Red and Fallow Deer Stalking

In America, when anyone goes out with gun or rifle, be it after deer, rabbit or fowl, it is invariably called hunting – in Britain this word generally implies riding with hounds after fox, hare or deer. On the other hand, when after deer with rifle the activity is invariably referred to in Britain as 'stalking', and while this is undoubtedly the best description for coming to terms with a creature of the bare mountains and open moorland which is the habitat of red deer in Scotland, hunting – or still-hunting – is, in my opinion, a more apt term for the chase of any woodland creature such as roe and fallow deer. Stalking implies awareness for, perhaps, several hours of a quarry which has been previously spied from long distance, followed by a stealthy approach, much of which may be in full view, until a shot can be taken. Still-hunting, on the other hand, requires a very slow and quiet approach through woodland, the hunter unaware for most of the time that any deer is at hand but always hopeful that if he is quiet enough a shootable beast may eventually be seen feeding on a ride or in a clearing, completely unaware of his approach.

Deerstalking, such as we know it, has only been practised in Scotland for about two centuries, for according to Patrick R. Chalmers in *Deerstalking*, 'stalking came into general practice only after the deforestation of Scotland at the end of the eighteenth century'. He records that in September 1745, Cluny Macpherson 'was the first Highland gentleman to stalk a stag on the open hill' and thus initiated a great sport. Prior to that date it was the custom to shoot the deer at the *tainchell*, at which many hundreds of men and dogs took part so that a large number of animals could be driven to concealed marksmen, who took considerable toll of the deer.

The main principles of deerstalking are first to find a shootable beast and then make an approach to within about 100 yards of it before talking the shot. Nowadays most people have a telescopic sight fitted to their rifle, and it has been suggested by some that this makes deerstalking too easy, and is therefore a trifle unsporting. If such statements mean that it is easier to take

Spying for deer in Dalness Forest, Argyllshire, Scotland

long shots, then I agree, but this is *not deerstalking.*

Deerstalking is a test of field craft and not marksmanship and the latter act should, if possible, be made so easy that any possibility of a wounded beast escaping is reduced to an absolute minimum. A telescopic sight does not make a sportsman shoot any straighter, but it does enable him to see the quarry more clearly and even in poor light he is able to place the bullet where it will do most damage. In woodland stalking the telescopic sight enables one to see more clearly when the vital area is clear of any twigs or foliage, and also enables shots to be taken at dawn and dusk when the light is too bad for the open sight to be used.

On open ground, once the deer have been located, it is best to try an approach from above rather than below, for deer, normally wary creatures, expect danger to come from the valley, relying on scent to give warning of danger from above. A crawl or slide from above is also a far easier manœuvre than a long uphill crawl in full sight of the deer, and distances are also far shorter when it is necessary to cut off a moving herd.

In late afternoon, in sunny weather, it is often possible to use the sun's rays to dazzle the deer while an approach is made over some open ground. On the other hand, if the sun is behind the deer, any movement on the hunter's part will be more easily detected. It also should be remembered that towards evening any *natural* movement of deer will be directed downhill rather than up, for it is to the valleys that they go for their evening feed.

Although it is easier to pick out deer with binoculars, a telescope is preferable for open hill and long range work, for if a long detour and arduous climb is to be undertaken, it is useful to know what *sort* of beast you are going to find at the end of it. In other words, with binoculars you can find deer but with a telescope you can identify and select.

In woodland stalking, however, where ranges are never very great, a telescope is more of a handicap than help, and in such terrain a pair of binoculars of perhaps 7 × 50 is an essential piece of equipment. It is best to keep off those of really high magnification for they are hard to keep steady and are a strain on the eyes.

In woodland stalking, be it after red, roe or fallow deer, one can either 'still hunt' as already mentioned or wait for the deer to come to some favourite area for feeding or rutting. If the area in question cannot be overlooked from some conveniently placed high ground, the normal practice is to erect a 'high seat', and these perches are becoming a regular feature in many British woodlands which are inhabited by deer.

Generally speaking, results from the high seat are more rewarding in the evening than morning, mainly because one can be in position before the deer leave cover, whilst in the morning they are already out and will probably be disturbed as you make your way to the seat, to which there should always be as quiet an approach route as possible.

Fortunately, even during a dry spell of weather which makes woodland stalking among dry leaves and twigs extremely difficult, an overnight dew will, for a short time at dawn, dampen the undergrowth and with reasonable diligence make stalking possible. For woodland stalking, therefore, the best results are probably obtained by watching from a high seat at dusk, and a 'still hunt' at dawn.

During the rut, both red deer stags and roe bucks can be drawn to the area by calling – the former either by the 'roar of a challenger' or bleat of a hind – and the latter by an imitation of the doe's call. For this purpose imitation calls are available. For fallow deer, however, no such imitation seems successful, but at all times of the day, provided wind conditions are right, and the undergrowth not too dry, excellent sport can be had stalking the sound of a 'groaning' buck during the rut.

On the Continent, in areas of open woodland such as in Denmark and the Netherlands, hunting deer with the aid of a horse-drawn carriage is often practised and produces far more successful results than still-hunting over a carpet of crisp leaves and twigs. Deer are accustomed to vehicular traffic, particularly that of the woodmen, and take little notice of a carriage passing within about 100 yards of them provided it doesn't stop. On such occasions, therefore, the sportsman can slip off the moving carriage while passing a convenient tree, or in dead ground, when the deer's attention is directed to the departing carriage.

For control purposes, deer are often driven to concealed rifles, but this form of sport can never be very selective, and is normally employed to effect a hind or doe cull. GKW

A horse and trap used for deer stalking in Denmark.

Red Fox (*Vulpes vulpes*)
This species has the widest distribution of any of the *Caninae*, being found in Europe, Asia, north Africa and North America; it has also been introduced into Australasia. They vary considerably in size and to some extent in coloration; a big dog fox may weigh as much as 25 lb whereas a vixen in the same area may be only 12 lb to 15 lb. Their pointed noses, ears, bushy tails and rufous coat are easily recognized. Black or white markings or points may be occasionally found. They are extremely adaptable and cunning, relying on hunting nocturnally for their food, though quite often seen during the day. They are virtually omnivorous, eating frogs, insects, berries, mice and larger prey, such as chickens or other birds, domesticated or wild. They also eat carrion. The vixen generally has a litter of from four to six cubs in the spring. The dog fox will usually assist to feed and teach the cubs to hunt until they can fend for themselves.

Although its lair is usually a burrow or earth below ground, some foxes prefer to spend their lives above ground. The cubs, however, are almost invariably born below ground, although with such an infinitely adaptable animal it is inadvisable to be dogmatic. Traces of their presence may be seen in the shape of the wings of their kill, neatly shorn off and left, and sometimes a half-buried half-eaten corpse; outside the earth a few bones are often to be seen. The unmistakably musky odour of the fox at close quarters also makes its presence plain.

Their strong scent makes them ideal for hunting with hounds and their ability to confuse their trail by taking to water, running on hard roads, which do not retain their scent well, or doubling back on their tracks, are evidence of an inherited instinct for survival. They are among the few animals for which distinct breeds of hounds have been bred specifically for hunting them, and in Britain foxhunting has been an important sport since the seventeenth century. Generally followed on horseback, although also on foot, packs of these foxhounds, each specially bred for its own particular district, have been developed to follow the fox by scent at speed, but with the spread of motorways, electric railways and increasing urbanization the sport has naturally been circumscribed in some areas. A considerable number of packs however still exist both in Britain and Ireland. Similar packs with mounted followers are also to be found in France and in North America, but both there and elsewhere in Europe foxhunting is more often carried out on foot with a mixed pack. Alternatively, the fox may be still-hunted or called and shot. Decoying a fox within reach of the rifle by calling it is a favourite Australian sport and 'barking' a fox within reach of the gun in wide open country is by no means as hard as might be imagined.

In spite of the fact that in many areas they are either trapped, poisoned or gassed, as well as shot, foxes are still common in most wooded or mountainous countrysides in their range. The use of hounds, whether followed on foot or on horseback, whether by one man or a dozen, whether with two hounds or more, is still the most fascinating of sports to anyone understanding the work of a hound and the reactions of a wild animal. Well trained hounds and an efficient and knowledgeable huntsman are still among the best ways of killing foxes and there is little doubt that a fox killed by hounds dies more humanely than if trapped or gassed. A clean shot at close range with a shotgun, or at a suitable range with a rifle, is also a clean death if the shot is accurately placed, but a fox's thick coat will carry a lot of shot and its stamina will keep it going unless hit in a vital spot. A good dog is still desirable to ensure that none get away wounded.

Red Grouse (*Lagopus scoticus*)
This is the only game bird unique to Great Britain and is by far the commonest member of the grouse family in Britain. Its habitat is entirely on moors or the edges of moors and it is found throughout suitable country in Scotland and Yorkshire. Although its principal food is the young shoots of ling heather it will also eat blaeberries, cranberries and most other berries, as well as insects, oats, other cereals and even turnip leaves. It always requires a very considerable quantity of grit which is taken into the crop and gizzard and remains there for some time, aiding the digestion. It is reddish-brown or buff coloured, either spotted or barred, but there is very considerable local variation in plumage and coloration and even in size. The chestnut-red feathers are generally more distinct on the breast, throat and chin of the cock birds. The average size of the cock bird is about 15 in and $1\frac{1}{2}$ lb in weight, although Yorkshire birds often weigh up to 2 lb. The hens are slightly smaller, but sexing can be very difficult except during the mating season. Their call is a throaty gurgle, closely resembling the words 'go-back, go-back', but they are notable for their often silent flight, rising soundlessly in front of a line of guns and giving no warning of their presence before they are out of range.

They are territorial birds, pairing in December, and are the first of the indigenous British ground-nesting birds to start nesting; they generally commence to lay in early April. The nests are little more than scrapes in the heather and clutches generally from 6 to 11 eggs, though as many as 17 have been known. The incubation period varies from 24 to 27 days. Both the eggs and the young are hardy; they have been known to hatch after having been waterlogged for several days. The young are able to flutter within three or four days and within a fortnight they are capable of making short flights.

A great deal is still to be learned about the biology of red grouse and it is still not clear why there are good and bad seasons although conditions seem almost identical. It is, however, certain that young grouse require plenty of insect life, and prolonged wet conditions or hard frosts killing the young heather and insects at a critical period, are bound to have their repercussions. The red grouse themselves are extremely hardy birds, but they are affected by the mysterious 'grouse cycle', as it is termed, and however good the moor management may be there are inevitably some disappointing years. It is now accepted that grouse do migrate from moors on occasions and a number of reasons have been suggested for this, namely: bad weather conditions on the home moor, drought, shortage of grit or some other essential feeding. Eagles and hawks, or undue disturbance, may also be sufficient to make grouse leave their home ground, at least temporarily. Whatever the reason, there is little doubt that sometimes migration can temporarily empty one moor and double the grouse population on another. Distances of such migrations are uncertain, but ringed birds have been found over 20 miles away.

The grouse are shot either by walking up over pointers or in line or by driving with beaters over guns sited in butts made of stone, heather or wicker, at approximately gunshot distance from each other across the moor. Advantage of the natural lie of the land is generally taken to site such butts below a shoulder or rise in the ground to provide a clear field of fire, but sometimes they are placed, apparently arbitrarily, in the centre of a flat expanse of moor. To those unaccustomed to this form of shooting the sudden appearance of a covey of grouse coming over the moor without warning can be quite unnerving. The grouse may suddenly appear only 40 yards away and be past before the gun is aware that they were even there. They often have a bobbing flight, apparently sinking into the heather at intervals, which makes them difficult targets even for an experienced shot. Alternatively, they may sometimes come as dots in the sky approaching with such rapidity that it is extremely hard to estimate either their height or speed due to the lack of any landmark, such as trees, with which to compare them. They may be past before a shot has been fired, or else both barrels may have been discharged only to hit the birds behind those being aimed at, or else to find only empty air. Hesitation at driven grouse-shooting is fatal and very often may result in dangerous shooting; it is easy to swing past the danger zone and fire into the neighbouring butt. Snap shooting is almost the only method in such cases.

As the grouse tend to pack in October and are very much stronger on the wing than the birds in August or September, shooting them at that time can be a very different matter. The young grouse in August are often hardly worth shooting, whereas the October grouse are strong on the wing and take a lot of killing. When a large pack is driven over the butts it is easy for a beginner to lose his nerve and fail to pick his birds, firing 'into the brown' and thereby failing to kill any, though possibly mortally wounding several which will either fail to breed or will go on to die in the heather, lost to the bag and to future sport. For those who prefer dogging there are always some moors on which driving cannot be successful and there great sport can often be had over pointers or setters. In some places falconry is still practised. The grouse themselves, especially when young, make excellent eating.

Redhead *(Aythya americana)*

This is the American pochard, a diving duck closely related to the pochard (*q.v.*) of Europe. But, unlike that bird, it is highly edible, and, since it comes easily to decoys, its numbers have been greatly reduced, first by market hunters, then by general over-hunting, and finally by ploughing and drainage in the southern parts of its breeding range. As with the European pochard the drake has a short body, a round, chestnut coloured head, black breast and tail, gray back and flanks, and white belly. The eclipse moult merely dulls its plumage without changing it. The duck is a dull brown and white.

The drake is slightly larger than the duck and weighs between 2 lb and 3 lb and measures from 17 in to 23 in. It is a fast flyer and flies in V-formations, taking to the wing with the splashing and water treading common to most diving duck. It is almost entirely vegetarian, and can dive deeply for the wild celery roots it prefers.

The nest is usually built among reeds at the water edge, and is lined with down, more down being plucked as incubation proceeds to provide warmth and camouflage for the eggs. The clutch of 10 to 15 eggs takes between 24 and 28 days to incubate. The breeding grounds cover the Canadian and American prairies and the wintering grounds lie along the Pacific coast down to the south of Mexico, and from Alabama all round the Gulf of Mexico. The redhead is occasionally seen along the Atlantic coast, usually flying with larger flocks of scaup.

Red-legged Partridge *(Alectoris rufa)*

This partridge, a native of south-western Europe from Belgium to Madeira and the Azores, is also called the French partridge. It was introduced into Britain over a century and a half ago. It is, like its congeneric partridges, a strong runner, and, because of

The red grouse, pictured above, is unique to Britain.

Left, a red fox

this, it is traditional to condemn it as a game bird. It is said that it is not very good for driving because it will always run rather than fly, and is even worse for dogging as it will never hold to a point, but will run-on in front of the dog, putting other coveys out as it does so.

However, now that the gray partridge has declined in numbers, and so in importance, it has become possible to appreciate the redleg better. It does, in fact, drive perfectly well given adequate hedges to drive it to. It comes over fast and rather higher than the gray partridge, not, it is true, in swirling coveys, but as a straight flying single bird. Nonetheless it is a good bird to shoot in front, and no one need be too ashamed of missing. It must be admitted that the bird will occasionally fly up a tree, and it is pugnacious at breeding time with redleg and gray cocks alike, nevertheless its reputation for running in front of dogs is almost as exaggerated as its reputation for refusing to fly, and, altogether, the shooting field would be a much poorer place without it.

It is a small, plump bird, rather larger than the gray, weighing just over 1 lb and measuring between 13 and 15 in. The hen is slightly smaller but otherwise difficult to distinguish. Redlegs are, like most partridges, birds of arable and cultivated lands. They feed on stubbles and grass seed as well as on berries, fruit and insects and greenstuff. They show a marked preference for dry localities and in England are most commonly found on brecks and chalk downs. They seem to prefer hedgerows and the edges of plantations, roosting and nesting on the ground. The nest is a hollow scratched in the ground under a hedgerow or in long grass and the clutch varies between 10 and 18. Incubation takes from 21 to 26 days.

Although, at a distance, the red-legged partridge resembles the gray partridge it is easy to separate them, closer up, by the former's red bill and legs. It has a gray crown with a long, white streak above the eye, a black-bordered white gorget, lavender-gray flanks prominently barred with chestnut, black and white, a bright, rufous-buff belly, and a dark chestnut tail.

Other red-legged partridges are:
Rock Red-legged Partridge (*Alectoris graeca saxatilis*), a rather larger bird, which is sometimes also called the Greek partridge and Bartavelle. It is found, mainly, in the mountainous areas of southern Europe, such as the Pyrenees, Alps, Carpathians, Apennines and in the Balkans. It is probably found on the Greek mainland, though this may be the chukar partridge, which is very similar, and is certainly the partridge found in the Greek islands. The rock partridge sometimes interbreeds with both the common and Barbary redlegs.

Chukar Red-legged Partridge (*Alectoris graeca chukar*) resembles the rock partridge but is slightly smaller and has white instead of black lores. Its range lies east from the Greek Islands to the Himalayas and China. It exhibits considerable differences in colour and size over this large range which includes vastly different temperatures and heights varying from sea level to 16,000 ft. The chukar has been successfully introduced into the United States from the Himalayas and is being introduced into France, not from its native Himalayas, but from the United States. *See also* Chukar Partridge.

Barbary Red-legged Partridge (*Alectoris petrosa*). This is a partridge with a limited range in north-west Africa, Sardinia, and the Canaries.

See also Partridge Biology and Management.

Red Sheep (*Ovis orientalis*)
The gad of Baluchistan, the shapu of Ladakh and the urial of Afghanistan and the Punjab are all closely related varieties of wild sheep which are found in many parts of Asia. Covered with reddish-brown hair instead of wool, with white markings on the lower part of the body and legs, they stand about 36 in at the shoulder and their semi-circular annulated horns are about 29 in long. The old rams are darker in colour and bearded from chin to chest with a darker brown saddle-patch on the back. They are distinguished from each other by colour variations and by the size and shape of the horn. The older shapu rams have fine ruffs of gray and white. The urial have more luxuriant ruffs which become quite white with age. The horns of both are strongly wrinkled and set close together. These sturdy sheep are alert and wary, keen sighted and restless, requiring careful stalking. The rams live apart from the ewes except during the breeding season. To find them is comparatively simple, but stalking them may be more difficult. Though not such a fine trophy as the great Tibetan sheep (*q.v.*), they are only obtained after an arduous climb and hard stalk.

Red Squirrel (*Sciurus vulgaris*)
An arboreal squirrel, found throughout Europe and northern Asia from Ireland to Japan, and from Lapland to northern Italy, though there are different races inside this very wide range, the differences being principally those of colour and size. The squirrels of northern and western Europe are bright red, those of southern Europe a deep blackish-gray, and those of Siberia a clear pale gray. Adults have long tufts of hair on their ears in winter, losing them in summer, when the colour of the tail also becomes lighter.

It can race from branch to branch with surprising speed, and can, if necessary,

A red-legged partridge in the act of calling — beak and eyes closed, throat distended

Red deer, a plate from *British Mammals* 1921, by Archibald Thorburn

jump from treetop to ground, rolling itself into a ball to do so. The tail is used, in a still unexplained manner, to assist in this. It lives in a nest or 'drey' which it either builds or takes over from a rook or magpie, but, when breeding, builds a different drey, which is spherical and has a side entrance. This is lined carefully with moss. Its food consists of nuts, forest mast, berries, pine kernels, and mushrooms. It will also rob nests of their eggs, and even eat young birds. Food is constantly hidden, either in the ground or in holes in trees, against the winter months, during which it does not truly hibernate, but may become torpid for a while. The breeding season is from January to May, gestation takes about 30 days, and from three to five young are born, blind and naked.

The squirrel is hunted in Scandinavia and several other European countries. It is generally shot with a .22 rifle. Considerable patience is needed to get a shot, since a squirrel will race away at the first sight of man.

In Britain, the gray squirrel (*q.v.*) of America has chased out the native red squirrel in many parts of the country, but has not yet invaded Europe. In America, however, the red squirrel, even though it is a smaller animal, is reputed to chase and even kill the gray.

Reedbuck (*Redunca* species)

There are several species and subspecies of reedbuck or reitbok, found throughout central and southern Africa. They have curving black horns, a bare glandular patch under each ear, and may vary in size from about that of a roe deer to that of a fallow deer and in coloration from reddish-brown to yellowish-gray. In general they prefer open country near water, but may also be found in mountainous grassland. They are mostly encountered in pairs, threes or in groups of up to a dozen, often associated with other game. Mainly grazers, they have a single young born each year at any time, though twins have been recorded.

The common reedbuck, *Redunca redunca*, or bohor is found in Ethiopia and South Africa, and is reddish-brown. Chandler's reedbuck, *Redunca fulforufula*, or mountain reedbuck, is found in Ethiopia and Tanzania. The southern reedbuck, *Redunca arundinium*, found in Zambia and Tanzania, is yellowish-gray in colour.

Reindeer *see* Deer of the World and their Hunting; Caribou

Revolvers *see* South America, Shooting in

Rhinoceros *see* Black Rhinoceros

Rhode Island (U.S.A.)

The smallest state in the Union, its 1,200 square miles are densely populated, heavily industrialized. It has less than 150,000 acres of farmland, and less than 25,000 acres of state forests and game areas open to the public. Most of the rest of the state is posted. In spite of this the public can get some hunting, with a few deer, a good rabbit population, pheasant and quail whose numbers are kept up by breeding and releasing birds every year, and fair waterfowl hunting along the comparatively long coastline.

Special Regulations
The only firearms allowed are shotguns and .22 rimfire rifles. Deer hunters are limited to buckshot. In 1968 there were 50 white-tailed deer shot from an estimated population of 1,200.

Further Information
Division of Fish and Wildlife, 83 Park Street, Providence, Rhode Island 02903.

Hunted in several European countries, the the red squirrel, right, is here running down the underneath of a branch to avoid the twigs.

The red fox, introduced to Australia, where t now provides excellent sport for rifle and shotgun.

Big Game inventory—Rhode Island		
Species	**Shot**	**Est. pop.**
White-tailed deer	50	1,200

Licence Fees—Rhode Island		
Type	**Status**	**Fee**
General	Resident	$3.25
	Non-resident	$10.25
Deer tag	Resident	$5.00
	Non-resident	$20.00

Seasons and Limits—Rhode Island

Species	Season	Limit
Deer	16 Oct-22 Oct 18 Dec-19 Dec	One any sex per season
Cottontail rabbit	23 Oct-15 Feb	5
Snowshoe hare		2
Gray squirrel		5
Pheasant	23 Oct-31 Jan	2
Ruffed grouse		3
Bobwhite quail		4

Seasons—Rhodesia

Species	Season	Comment
Game animals	1 May-30 Sept	Persons holding a land-holder's licence may shoot the game to which it applies at any time of the year
Duck, geese and snipe	1 Nov-28 Feb	
Quail	All year	
Other game birds	1 May-30 Sept	
Unprotected species	At any time	

'Shoot a gemsbok' an illustration from the 19th century book, *African Hunting* by William Charles Baldwin

Rhodesia

Rhodesia is a country of about 150,000 square miles in southern central Africa. The main physical feature is the Great Dyke, a ridge of high veldt, between 4,000 and 6,000 ft above sea level, that runs for about 350 miles from north-east to south-west, roughly between Salisbury and Bulawayo. Elsewhere this slopes down to low veldt, only about 1,000 to 2,000 ft high. The main river is the Zambesi, which flows out of Lake Kariba along the border with Zambia. The Zambesi valley is a tsetse fly area, but otherwise is pleasantly modified by the altitude.

The chief crops are maize, groundnuts, kaffir corn, cotton and tobacco, which is particularly important, with cattle, except along the Zambesi valley, and goats as the main livestock. There are large numbers of typical African big game and plenty of shooting is available, though generally it is more expensive for visitors than for residents.

Organization

The government runs several controlled hunting areas, one at Wankie in the north-west, one at Tuli in the south, and 11 in the Zambesi valley. Those wishing to shoot in these areas must apply well in advance. Visits are for set 10-day periods (except for the Wankie area, where they are 14-days) and for a limited number of hunters, usually two, but in some cases four. Up to six non-

Unprotected Species—Rhodesia

A licence is not required for hunting these species. Mammals and birds not listed, apart from those designated game animals, are fully protected, and may not be shot.

Mammals	Birds
Baboon	Black-headed weaver
Bat	Black-throated canary
Civet	Blue-spotted wood-dove
Genet	Bully canary
Hyena	Cape rock
Jackal	Darter
Mole	Emerald-spotted wood-dove
Monkey	House sparrow
Porcupine	Indian mynah
Serval	Laughing dove
Squirrel	Layard's bulbul (toppie)
Wild dog	Masked weaver
Wild pig	Mennell's seedeater
	Mourning dove
	Mozambique canary (yellow-eye)
	Namaqua dove
	Pied crow
	Piscal shrike
	Red-billed quelea
	Red-eyed dove
	Red-faced coly (mousebird)
	Reed cormorant
	Ring-necked dove
	Rock pigeon
	Speckled coly (mousebird)
	Streaky-headed seedeater
	Tambourine dove
	White-breasted cormorant
	White-necked raven

Game Licences—Rhodesia

Type	Number that may be shot	Resident	Non-resident	Comment
		(in Rhodesian dollars)		
General game licence, includes:	total shot must be no more than 12	$20	$50	Valid for one season
Bushbuck	1			
Duiker	4			
Impala	4			
Kudu	1			
Sharpe's grysbok	1			
Steinbuck	1			
Warthog	2			
Wildebeeste	2			
Zebra	2			
Landholder's game licence, includes:				Granted to owners or occupiers of land resident in Rhodesia, or their managers, or in special circumstances, to others, subject to the approval of the National Parks and Wildlife Management to shoot, only on the land in question, mammals during year of issue and game birds in appropriate open season.
Bushbuck				
Buffalo				
Crocodile				
Duiker				
Impala				
Kudu				
Leopard				
Lion				
Ostrich				
Reedbuck				
Grysbok				
Steinbuck				
Warthog				
Wildebeeste				
Zebra				
Game birds				
Supplementary game licence, includes:				Applicants must hold a general or landholder's game licence. Supplementary game licence authorizes the shooting of a specified number of animals *only* on land specified in licence. Fees given are cost *per animal*. Licences expire on last day of open season in the year of issue.
Bushbuck	1	$6	$10	
Buffalo	4	$20	$30	
Crocodile	1	$10	$20	
Duiker	4	$1	$2	
Eland	1	$30	$50	
Elephant (male)	2	$60	$100	
Elephant (female)	3	$30	$50	
Elephant (tuskless)	3	$20	$30	
Hippopotamus	1	$60	$100	
Impala	4	$4	$6	
Klipspringer	1	$20	$30	
Kudu	1	$10	$20	
Leopard	1	$60	$80	
Lion	1	$60	$80	
Oribi	1	$20	$30	
Ostrich	1	$10	$14	
Reedbuck	1	$10	$14	
Sable antelope	2	$30	$50	
Grysbok	1	$2	$4	
Steinbuck	1	$2	$4	
Warthog	2	$1	$2	
Waterbuck	1	$20	$30	
Wildebeeste	2	$6	$10	
Zebra	3	$10	$20	
Game bird licence, includes:		$4	$10	Unnecessary for those holding a landholder's licence.
Duck				
Teal				
Geese				
Snipe				
Francolin				
Guinea fowl				
Sand grouse				
Quail				

hunting companions are permitted (eight at Wankie). Applications for the same period at a given camp are treated on a lottery basis, Fees vary, depending on the facilities at the hunting area camp and the permitted number of hunters, but in all cases they are additional to the licence fees, which are detailed above. There is a set quota of animals that may be shot for each group staying at a camp, and usually a bag limit per hunter. There is of course no such set structure for privately run hunting areas.

Special Regulations
No hunting is permitted in National Parks, Game Reserves, private game reserves or non-hunting reserves. Hunting by night or from motor vehicles or aircraft is forbidden, as is using fire to drive or round up game.

The landowner's permission must always be obtained before hunting on private land. All kills must also be registered, within 12 hours, on the back of the game licence. This applies to animals killed by accident or in self defence, and a detailed explanation will have to be given. It is particularly important to register elephant kills and ivory trophies, as there are drastic penalties for not doing so.

Wounded animals must be trailed and killed, particularly dangerous animals, i.e. buffalo, elephant, hippopotamus, leopard and lion. If a wounded animal is not killed it must be reported immediately to the nearest police station, District Commissioner's Office or officer of the Department of National Parks and Wild Life Management.

When hunting buffalo and elephant a rifle of not less than .375 magnum calibre must be used. Duiker, leopard, lion, steenbuck and Sharpe's grysbok may be shot with a 12-bore shotgun or a rifle of not less than .23 calibre. All other game, except birds, may only be shot with a rifle of over .23 calibre. Crossbows are illegal.

Further Information
The Department of National Parks and Wild Life Management deals with every aspects of hunting, game conservation and the issue of landowner's game licences etc.

Department of National Parks and Wild Life Management, P.O. Box 8365, Causeway, Salisbury, Rhodesia.

See also Southern Africa, Conservation and Shooting in

Rifle *see* Firearms

Ring Dove *see* Woodpigeon

Ring-necked Duck *(Aythya collaris)*
For a long time this species was thought to be the same species as the European tufted duck *(Aythya fuligula)*, which it closely resembles. It does not, however, have a true crest, but loosely growing head feathers which can look crest-like.

The drake weighs about 2 lb and is be-

The roan antelope buck, the largest of all African antelopes, is never found far from water.

tween 16 and 17 in long. It is black all over except for a white band around the bill, a chestnut collar, a white breast and gray flanks. In his eclipse it looks like the duck, which is brown with a white breast. They are largely vegetarian, and make good eating.

Nesting is usually among reeds near fresh water. The nest is made of grass and reeds and is lined with down. The clutch of 8 to 12 eggs takes 23 to 26 days to incubate. The young drake develops full male plumage by December. The main breeding ground is in the Prairie Provinces of Canada, though it stretches also into Minnesota and Wisconsin.

The main wintering grounds lie along the east coast of the United States from North Carolina to Texas, but it also winters on the Pacific, along the coast of Oregon and northern California. Some ringnecks breed in their wintering grounds, but most migrate north in spring.

Ringtail *see* Raccoon

River Hog *see* Bushpig

Roan and Sable Antelopes
(Hippotragus equinus and *Hippotragus niger)*
These antelopes have sufficient in common to be dealt with together. Each is found in many parts of central Africa. Each is large with a fine sweep of curving annulated horn carried by both sexes. Each is chiefly a grazer, but also browses. Each is found generally in herds of 15 to 30 or more in light woodlands or scrub, occasionally in mountainous country. The bulls are sometimes solitary, calving is mainly in the dry season and a single calf is born. Each is strong and full of vitality requiring a heavy calibre shot in the right place to kill it and is capable of travelling a long way even with a mortal wound. Each is also armed with dangerous horns and if wounded may charge the hunter. It is necessary to approach with caution when they have been shot.

The roan antelope stands two or three inches larger, about 4 ft 8 in, and has very noticeably long ears, but its horns are smaller, averaging about 30 in over the curve. In coloration both sexes are reddish-bay. The herds may associate with zebra, hartebeest or sometimes other game and the solitary bulls may also join with other species. Roan antelope is also more often found in plains which the sable avoids. Finally, the roan is found in Ethiopia whereas the sable is not.

The sable stands only about 4 ft 6 in with smaller ears, but the horns are longer, about 40 in or more over the curve. The coloration of the old males is black above, of the females and young, chestnut to dark brown. They do not as a general rule associate with other species.

The rock dove is the ancestor of the domestic pigeon.

A roe deer, feeding on winter seed in Denmark

Rockchuck *see* Woodchuck

Rock-dove *(Columba livia livia)*
Found generally in rocky coastlines around Britain and parts of Europe, seldom venturing far inland, it is distinguished by the two black wing bars and a whitish patch on its rump. It is a smaller, darker bird than the woodpigeon (*q.v.*), but its nesting and laying habits are very similar. When shot from a boat beneath cliffs, or in a quarry close inland, they can also provide very interesting sport. In windy weather especially, the sudden up and down currents close to the cliff face can have most disconcerting effects on their flight. They are not particularly good eating.

Rock Red-legged Partridge *see under* Red-legged Partridge

Rocky Mountain Goat
(Oreamnos montanus)
This is a goat-antelope, whose nearest relation is, perhaps, the serow of Asia, and it is the only member of the genus *Oreamnos* in North America. It is found in the higher mountain ranges of Alaska, the north-west Rockies, and as far south as Idaho. It is most plentiful in Alberta and British Columbia, but it is also numerous in Washington and Montana, and has recently been successfully introduced into Oregon. It is generally hunted under special permit, but hunting pressures are light, for its meat is largely inedible, and the trophy has to be climbed for.

It is a large, white, shaggy coated animal with a beard and a hump rather like a miniature buffalo's. Weight varies between 150 and 400 lb; it is about 4 ft long and stands about 3 ft at the shoulder, slightly less at the rump. Hoofs, lips and horns are black. The feet have what are, in effect, suction pads as an aid to climbing. The horns are hollow, bend back slightly, are needle sharp and average about nine inches in length. There is an oil-producing gland behind each horn. Sight and hearing are poorly developed, but the sense of smell is acute. It is primarily a browser, but will eat moss and lichens in winter, when it might come down to the lower slopes. It is probably the best climber in the animal kingdom, pulling itself up from ledge to ledge with its short foreleg. It has few predators, and has been known, with its sharp horns, to kill a bear. Except during the rut it is a solitary.

The goat is polygamous, and rut begins in November, the kids generally being dropped in April and May and remaining with the nanny for two years.

Only solitaries should be shot, since they are most likely to be males, which are difficult to distinguish, otherwise, from nannies. A great deal of climbing is generally involved in stalking them, but they are not particularly cautious and, if alarmed, will only depart at a walk. Because of the large amount of hair, hide and fat carried they are hard to kill.

Roe Deer and their Stalking
The roe deer, *Capreolus capreolus*, a Palaearctic mammal, is widely distributed in Europe, parts of northern Asia, Persia, Russia and Scandinavia. It may be encountered as far west as Portugal, and its limit appears to be the terrain bounded by the Japan Sea to the east. There are no roe deer in the Americas, Australia or New Zealand. In India, south of the Himalayas, the animal is unknown. It is not to be found in Ireland, although it is now numerous in many parts of England and Scotland. Wales appears hardly to be favoured at all by the roe. In central Asia (Altai and Tian Shan Mountains), westwards to the Urals and the Volga, is a larger subspecies of roe deer known as *Capreolus capreolus pygargus*. This is an interesting animal to the sportsman as its range is still uncertain to the north and east. The antlers of this roe are longer, more harp-shaped and good specimens have heavy pearling. There are few *pygargus* trophies in the U.K.

The European roe deer, or type species, has for generations been very highly regarded as a worthy beast of the chase. In nearly every country where it is to be found it is accorded protection, and game laws exist throughout Europe for its proper preservation. This was not the case in Britain until a few years ago (1963), when the Deer Act (England) came into force. This act legislates for the type of weapon to be used, and close seasons are specified. In England roe deer does are protected at certain periods whereas roe bucks may be shot all the year round. In Scotland bucks have certain close-seasons. These deer laws are involved, and some say impractical.

Roe are elegant, dainty little deer; rather antelope-like in appearance. A full grown buck will tape about 26 in at the shoulder, and measures approximately 4 ft in length. The females are slightly smaller. Weight lies between 50 to 60 lb for males, the does are some 10 to 15 lb lighter. In summer roe deer are a bright, foxy-red in colour with pale underparts. The summer hairs are short. Those of winter are much longer and a dark donkey-gray in colour. Roe deer in winter look larger animals than in summer. In winter dress roe deer, of both sexes, have large, white caudal discs. These deer have no visible tails. Both bucks and does are frequently vocal, uttering short, sharp barks, not unlike those of a collie dog.

Edward the Second, Duke of York, in the oldest English book on hunting, now called *The Master of Game* (1406–1413), says this of the roe, 'It is a good little beast and goodly for to hunt.' This is certainly as true today as it was when it was written well over 500 years ago!

A high seat from which deer are shot.

One of the great charms of roe-stalking is its infinite variety. One can hunt the roebuck as one would pursue a moose in the Scandinavian woodlands, or a sambar in the forests of India. One can wait for these elusive sylvan animals in high-seats, or butts on stilts, erected in some forest clearing. One can try and call a roe buck with a little plastic, or wooden, whistle, hoping to entice it to within range of the rifle. With the aid of a companion, and perhaps his dog, one can try and move the wily roe buck to where one lies ambushed awaiting his appearance. Roe deer are largely creatures of habit, and they follow their own paths beaten through the woodlands, so that this method of lying in wait for a particular buck is not all that difficult.

In parts of Scotland where roe now have adopted a moorland existence, seldom if ever going into cover, they may be stalked as one now stalks the roe's larger cousin, the red deer of the high hills. In France, roe are still hunted with hounds as are the red deer in Devon and Somerset. Their pursuit in this manner is far more difficult than that of a stag. In the forests of northern England, Land Rovers are used to conduct the sportsman around his block along the numerous forest tracks. As soon as he sees his buck, he jumps from the vehicle to stalk it. Alternatively he may drive to a point in the woods where a buck is known to be, and then it is hunted by the method appropriately known in America as still-hunting. Still-hunting a clever buck in the dawn or at twilight is a splendid sport. In Poland where roe deer frequent open agricultural land in some numbers, a cart or carriage may be used as a form of stalking chariot. Once within range of the desired quarry the hunter descends from his conveyance to shoot the buck provided his aim is sufficiently steady!

In Germany, Austria, Belgium and other European countries the high-seat is still very much favoured. In the warm summer months sitting in these high places watching the wild forest creatures and birds around can be a most pleasant pursuit; but at times it can be a long, perishingly cold business.

The roe buck carries a particularly attractive trophy on his head. The normal head of a buck consists of three points on each antler, with a pair of pearled coronets at the base of the horns where they meet the skull. The buck usually sheds his horns of the year towards the end of October, and the new annual horn growth commences almost at once. By the end of March many bucks are in hard-horn and free of velvet.

Roe buck stalking traditionally, and now by law in many countries, usually starts on 1 May. The horns of male roe deer are of great variety, and this is certainly one of their charms. They can be even, so that one antler exactly resembles the other, they may be twisted, bent, quite pointless, or massively rugose. To see a good collection of such trophies is a delight in itself. The roe-specialist can spend hours examining a roe head, or roe heads, with the greatest pleasure. The cult of the roe head is no new thing. Count Arco-Zinnenberg, a great collector, in the last century, paid fabulous prices for some of his superb roe trophies £60,000 was said to have been spent on his total collection, but this included other species as well.

The worth of the British roe-head has only of recent years been properly appreciated and now that it is realized by sportsmen throughout the world that there are in England and Scotland a considerable number of fine quality trophies, an increasing number of visitors from Europe, Asia and America are coming to Britain in pursuit of the British variety of *Capreolus capreolus*

HT

Romania *see* Rumania

Ruddy Duck *(Oxyura jamaicensis)*

This is a very small, stiff-tailed duck found in North America, the high Andes, the West Indies, east Africa from Abyssinia to the Cape, and southern Australia and Tasmania. In North America its numbers have recently shown some decrease, mainly due to ploughing and draining of part of its nesting range. It is a small, fat bird, almost entirely vegetarian, that makes good eating and shows little fear of man.

It walks only with difficulty and for short distances, but swims and dives well. Its take-off from water is noisy and laboured, but once airborne its wing-beat is so rapid as to produce a buzzing sound, which gives it an American nickname of 'bumble bee coot'. (Another, in more common use, is 'butterball'.)

The drake weighs between 18 and 20 oz and measures about 15 in. In its summer plumage it has a largely chestnut body with a white, vermiculated breast and belly black head with white cheeks, and blue bill and feet. In its eclipse plumage it resembles the duck, which is brownish-gray with lighter coloured underparts. Both have stiff pointed tails.

Courtship display is largely on water, and is elaborate, with much head jerking, neck stretching, inflating of the air sacs in the neck and calling. The nest is usually built among reeds and rushes in a swamp or slough, and the clutch of 6 to 10 very large eggs (the clutch weighing up to three times as much as the duck), takes around 30 days to incubate. The drake remains near the nest during incubation and helps with the rearing. Young drakes only assume full adult male plumage in the following spring.

Ruffed Grouse *(Bonasa umbellus)*

This bird is to the American sportsman very much what the gray partridge is to

is European counterpart – the best known and the most widely distributed of all native game birds. Ruffed grouse are found throughout most of Canada and the United States except in the south and south-west of the latter. The ruffed grouse, however, in spite of the 'grouse cycle', has survived modern farming better than has the gray partridge. This is probably because it is a woodland bird, retreating when the land is cleared, and recolonizing areas where secondary timber growths spring up. It is found, not only in virgin woods, but also in deserted orchards, alder carrs, and willow and poplar stands along the sides of streams.

There are several recognized subspecies including the Canada, Nova Scotia, gray, Oregon and Yukon ruffed grouse, but the differences are mainly ones of colour, size and habitat. In all of them a gray phase occurs.

The adult weighs between 16 and 27 oz and measures about 18 in. The hen resembles the cock except for being slightly smaller and lighter. In both, in the brown phase, the upperparts are chestnut-brown, barred with black and the underparts cream coloured, faintly barred with brown. The ruff, at the base of the neck, is of long, iridescent black feathers, and is shorter and fuller in the hen. The tail feathers are banded with black, the last band but one being wider, uninterrupted in the cock, and broken up with gray in the hen. The legs are feathered and, in winter, the feet have small hairy feathers also.

Young grouse are largely insectivorous; adults are known to eat more than 400 different kinds of plant food, including alder, aspen, beech, birch, blueberry, cherry, clovers, crab-apple, dogwood, grape, hawthorn, hazel, mountain ash, plantain, sedge, viburnum, willow etc. The typical home range covers no more than about 40 acres.

Ruffed grouse are polygamous. Courtship involves 'drumming' but this is also the method by which territory is claimed and defended. The drumming noise is produced by very rapid wing beats forcing the air through the spread primary feathers with a sound like a drum beat. This is done in a clearing, the drumming going on for a few seconds followed by silence before being repeated. If it is answered by another cock, fighting will generally result. If by a hen, courtship will follow.

Nesting is on the ground, and the average clutch of 11 eggs takes 24 days to incubate. The chicks are able to fly after a fortnight and have adult plumage in 16 weeks.

The bird is apt to behave tamely until it has been shot over, but then becomes extremely wary. Because shooting is generally in woodland and the bird normally flies low, close to the ground, snap shooting is necessary. A dog is of little use unless it is very close ranging, since the bird flushes easily and trees will intervene. It settles again fairly quickly, however, so that a second approach to the bird is frequently possible, even after it has been flushed.

Rumania

Rumania lies in south-east Europe, covers an area of about 91,600 square miles and has a widely varied terrain, ranging from the islands of the Danube estuary, and the plains of Wallachia, Moravia and Transylvania, to the heights of the Transylvian Alps and the Carpathian Mountains. Agriculture and stock raising are the chief industries, despite the low rainfall (about 30 in per annum in the mountains, dropping to below 18 in at the coast) and the vicissitudes of the continental climate, with its intense winter cold and fierce summer heat. There are also extensive forests and an important timber industry in the mountain regions. Game is consequently plentiful and

Left, ruffed grouse and nest in Ontario

Licences—Rumania

Hunters are normally permitted to take two rifles, or shotguns, and 100 rounds of ammunition into the country but, depending on the type of game to be shot and the length of stay, the number of rounds may be increased by arrangement with the 'Carpati' agency. Make, serial number and calibre of all guns must be entered in the passport. Automatic and repeating shotguns are permitted, but may not be loaded with more than three rounds. A fine of $10 is automatically incurred by anyone shooting a protected wildfowl.

Seasons and Fees—Rumania

Species	Season	Fee (in American dollars)
Carpathian (red) deer	1 Sept-30 Nov (best, 10 Sept-20 Oct)	Trophy: $100 upwards Deposit: $100 per animal Tracking fee: $200 per animal
Fallow deer	1 Sept-30 Nov (best, 10 Sept-1 Nov)	Trophy: $100 upwards Deposit: $50 per animal Tracking fee: $50 per animal
Roe deer (buck only)	15 May-31 Oct (best, 15 May-30 Aug)	Trophy: $30 upwards Deposit: $10 per animal Tracking fee: $15 per animal
Chamois	1 Sept-30 Nov (best, 20 Sept-30 Oct)	Trophy: $50 upwards Deposit: $10 per animal Tracking fee: $10 per animal
Bear	1 March-15 Jan (best, 15 March-15 May using bait; 1 Oct-30 Nov, using beaters)	Trophy: $500 upwards Deposit: $100 per animal Tracking fee: $200 per animal
Wild boar	1 Oct-28 Feb. Groups of 6 to 8 hunters are recommended	Trophy: $30 upwards Deposit: $10 per animal Tracking fee: $10 per animal
Capercailzie and blackgame	1 April-15 May	Trophy: $25 per cock, $20 per hen Deposit: $5 per bird Tracking fee: $10 per bird

Seasons and Fees—Rumania (Cont.)

Species	Season	Fee
Bustard (cocks only) (certain areas with special authorization only)	10 April-15 May	Trophy : $150 per cock Tracking fee : $75 per bird Deposit : none

The following species have a fixed fee per head.

Species	Season	Fee
Hare	1 Nov-31 Jan	$2 No deposit
Pheasant		$2
Ring dove	1 Aug-31 March	50c
Turtle dove		50c
Partridge	15 Sept-15 Dec	$2
Quail	15 Aug-30 Nov	50c
Snipe	1 Sept-30 April	$1
Wildfowl (in the Danube Delta) Includes :		The hunter may retain up to 10 head of wildfowl. More may be kept on payment of a sum equal to the shooting fee, and a deposit of $5 per hunter per day
Woodcock	15 Aug-20 March	50c
Geese		$2
Duck		$1
Water hen		50c
Cormorant		$1
Crane		$5
Heron		$1
Silcher		$1
Pelican		$100 (Certain areas, with special authorization only)
Swan		$50

For birds shot but not retrieved the normal charge is halved.

Species	Season	Fee
Lynx	May be shot at any time	$200 (Certain areas, with special authorization only)
Pine-marten		$20
Wolf		$10 No deposit
Fox		$5
Wildcat		$3
Badger		$2
Otter		$10
Mink		$20

varied and can provide good if expensive sport.

Shooting methods are much the same as in the rest of central Europe. Big game is still-hunted or stalked, and bustards and tetraonids stalked and/or called. Bear and boar may be driven, as may most small game except wildfowl. Wildfowl may be flighted, and other small game is frequently walked up by varying numbers with dogs.

Organization

Bookings for hunting trips have to be made in advance, either through the Rumanian agency 'Carpati', or through specialist travel agencies. The hunter must pay a deposit on each animal he wishes to shoot in order to have his booking confirmed (with wildfowl the deposit is based on the number of days spent shooting, rather than the number shot). The deposit will only be refunded if the trip is cancelled 30 days or more before the start of the trip (45 days for those hunting bear, wild boar, hare, pheasant or wildfowl). For small game the hunter is then charged a fixed fee per head shot. For big game he is charged for the trophy on a sliding scale based on the C.I.C. system of points classification. If the hunter does not wish to keep the trophy he is only charged the deposit.

It should be added that if the trophy is exceptional the organizer of the shoot is entitled to keep it on the shoot as part of the national collection, unless previously agreed with the hunter.

There is an organization fee of $5 or $10 per hunter per day (depending on the game hunted), except with bear, wild boar, and small field game, when these are driven by beaters. In such cases the organization fee can rise to $150 per shoot.

The value of a trophy according to the C.I.C. formula will normally be established by weighing and measuring 24 hours after boiling and cleaning, or earlier if the hunter wishes.

Hunters may photograph all game in the hunting area, dead or alive, without special permission, as long as they create no disturbance. However those who have not paid shooting fees are charged $50 per day for permission to take photographs of live game. Those filming game within the hunting area are charged $100 per day, and need permission from the Forestry Department.

Further Information

Any Rumanian National Tourist Office.

Carpati Central Agency for International Tourism, Hunting and Fishing Department, Magheru Bd 7, Bucharest.

Rusa Deer *see* Deer of the World and their Hunting

The grey heron is shot in Rumania and other European countries.

S

Sable Antelope *see* Roan and Sable Antelopes

Safety

It can never be emphasized too strongly that a gun should never be loaded unless it is to be fired: loaded guns in vehicles, especially, are extremely dangerous. Whenever a gun is handled it should always be treated as if loaded, even when known to be unloaded. When loaded it should always have the safety catch on unless it is intended for immediate use. When being used care must always be taken that no shot fired could endanger the lives of other hunters, dogs or stock. Bullets and shot may ricochet from hard ground, rocks, trees and water and this must always be borne in mind. Never shoot unless absolutely certain of killing the quarry. No gun, loaded or empty, should ever be handled in a dangerous manner, or fired when there is even a slight obstruction in the barrel.

When shooting any big-game that may be dangerous to man, always ensure that it has been killed before putting the gun down. If in any doubt, put another bullet into the animal to make quite sure. Many hunters have been killed or seriously injured by game which has merely been stunned, but seemed dead, suddenly recovering. Always ensure that the animal has no companion or mate close by which may be ready to charge to avenge its mate or offspring. Remember to reload and put the safety catch on, but do not get caught with an unloaded gun after making a kill.

Sage Grouse *(Centrocercus urophasianus)*

These are the largest grouse and, next to the wild turkey, the largest gallinaceous game birds in America, being very nearly as large as the capercaillie of Europe. They are birds of the sagebrush country which stretches from west of the Great Plains and north of Arizona and New Mexico to south-western Canada. Their summer diet is mixed, consisting of greenstuff and insects, but in winter they exist, almost entirely, on sagebrush leaves. As a consequence older birds are almost always inedible, the sage flavouring them too strongly, and even young birds need to be dressed as soon as they have been shot.

An adult cock may weigh up to 8 lb and measure over 30 in. Its upperparts are gray, mottled with black and brown, and the underparts whitish, marked on throat, breast and belly with black. On each side of the neck there is a prominent tuft of

A male sage grouse in full courtship display

stiff feathers and, in front of each, the bare reddish-brown skin of the air sacs. The tail is long, with each separate feather sharply pointed. The central tail feathers are marbled, and the outer ones are black barred with gray. The legs are feathered down to the toes. The hen resembles the cock, apart from being smaller and lacking the neck tufts and air sacs.

The cocks are highly gregarious, and gather in large groups for the courtship displays, which start in February and may extend into June. In addition to a great deal of strutting and dancing, the displaying cocks inflate their air sacs to monstrous proportions, so that they protrude above, and in front of, the head. The deflation of these sacs produces a croaking noise that attracts the hens to the outskirts of the strutting ground, whereupon mating takes place. The hen nests and incubates alone, generally near water, the clutch of seven to nine eggs taking around 22 days to hatch. The chicks can run soon after birth, but need brooding for some time, the heaviest hatch losses occurring from chilling. The hen and chicks will stay together all the summer, while the cocks remain in separate groups.

Unless they have been heavily hunted, sage grouse are reluctant to flush, and rely on camouflage and crouching to protect them. When they do take wing they do so only slowly, but once airborne, they are strong flyers, and their flights are over longer distances than most such birds can sustain. If they are flushed close they present fairly easy shots, but once on the wing they gain speed rapidly, and their rocking manner of flight presents some difficulties. The best sage grouse shooting is near their feeding and watering areas.

Sambar *(Cervis unicolor)*

This is the largest deer of south-eastern Asia and is common in the more or less hilly jungle country of central and southern India and Malaysia. It has also been successfully introduced in Australasia. The average height of a full grown stag is about 54 in at the shoulder. The horns are large and lengthy but with only one long brow-antler pointing upwards and two terminal tines on each horn, sometimes with a short posterior snag at the bifurcation of the terminal tines. The horn measurement is from about 30 to 40 in. In the Terai and Madhya Pradesh and Madhya Bharat regions they are generally larger than in south India. Their hair is coarse, longish and wiry, particularly about the neck and chest where it forms an erectile ruff which is raised when excited or angry. In colour their coat varies from dark brown to a paler slatey-brown depending on the season and the locality. In the Himalayan regions it is darker and thicker. On the buttocks and belly the hair is yellowish. The hinds and fawns are generally lighter coloured than the stags. The tail is unusually long for a deer and the ears are both big and wide and its hearing is exceedingly acute.

Owing to their very acute powers of hearing and scenting they are not easy to hunt in thick jungle and hunting methods vary from locality to locality, although still-hunting is probably the most usual. Where there is cultivation they frequently raid the crops at night but they withdraw to their chosen retreat long before dawn. They tend to lie up in forms during the day, in the shade of a tree in long grass and are exceedingly hard to spy even after lengthy scrutiny with telescope or field glasses. The best plan is often to move carefully along a hill with another hunter a little below and behind. If the one below disturbs a deer it may bolt uphill giving the other a chance. Otherwise careful movement downhill may be successful. They are often shot by being driven past concealed guns at chosen points, but their sense of hearing is so acute that should the waiting gun make any sound they will turn back through the beaters. Marking a worthwhile beast by either method is no easy matter. A reasonably heavy calibre is recommended.

See also Deer of the World and their Hunting.

A pair of yellow-throated sand grouse, which are African birds more closely related to the pigeon than to the true grouse.

A fine trophy of a sambar deer, with well-formed antlers

Sand Grouse (Petroclidae)

These birds are intermediate in appearance and structure between the pigeons (*Columbae*) and the true game birds (*Gallinae*). There are sixteen species, which, between them, range all over Africa, Asia and southern Europe. They show considerable similarities, all being smaller birds than the red grouse, with a size range between 9 and 14 in, and the hen always smaller than the cock. They are all either three-toed or possess only a rudimentary fourth toe, and their legs and generally their feet are feathered. Their wings are long and pointed and they have extraordinary powers of flight, being both fast and enduring, and covering, during their migrations, great distances at high speeds. There is little plumage difference between cock and hen and plumage is generally mottled, barred or vermiculated to provide camouflage effects suitable to the particular habitat of each species. The head, neck and breast are frequently more brightly coloured.

They nest in shallow scrapes in the ground and the clutch seldom exceeds three eggs. They are sociable birds, feeding and travelling in flocks, the size of which varies from species to species, but will seldom be less than forty or fifty and can sometimes be counted in thousands. Their migrations may, suddenly and inexplicably, change course. Pallas's sand grouse, for example, which is normally only a scarce and sporadic migrant to eastern Europe, had two great migrations, one in 1863 and the other in 1888, during which almost every country in western Europe was not only visited but even used as a nesting ground.

Sand grouse are birds of the deserts, the steppes and the mountains, the Tibetan sand grouse being found as high up as 18,000 ft. They seldom approach closer than the fringes of cultivated land. They are, principally, seed eaters, though they will also eat fruit, insects and greenstuff. They drink early in the morning and in the evening, flying considerable distances to their habitual waterholes, arriving over them in great flocks which will circle before landing. Drinking is rapid, and the first birds will be leaving the waterhole while the last are still arriving.

Though small, they are generally plump, and their flesh, although dark, makes good eating. They are hunted in almost every country they visit, and provide good sport, because they are fast, will take a lot of shot, and will jink and swerve like pigeons when shot at. The general method is to shoot them at known waterholes. The hunter lies out a little distance from the water's edge and stands up to shoot arriving or departing birds. Since the birds must drink they continue to come in, despite the shooting, and will drop down to the water and take wing with all the rapidity of teal. In Arabia and central Asia falcons are flown at them.

Sand Grouse

Species	Distribution
African painted *(Pterocles quadricintus)*	West Africa to Ethiopia
Black-bellied *(Pterocles arenarius)*	North Africa, southern Europe, south-west and central Asia and north-west India
Bridled *(Pterocles decoratus)*	Limited range around Mount Kilimanjaro
Close-barred *(Pterocles lichtensteini)*	North-eastern Africa and south-western Asia through to Sind
Common pin-tailed *(Petroclurus exusutus)*	Senegal to east Africa, from Asia Minor to India and central Asia
Coronetted *(Pterocles coronatus)*	North-east Africa and Asia through to India
Double-banded *(Pterocles bicinctus)*	South Africa
Eastern pin-tailed *(Petroclurus alchatus)*	Asia from Palestine to India, and from Arabia to Transcaucasia
Indian painted *(Pterocles fasciatus)*	India
Masked *(Pterocles personatus)*	Madagascar only
Namaqua pin-tailed *(Petroclurus namquus)*	South Africa
Pallas' *(Syrrhaptes paradoxus)*	Central Asia through to China and north to Lake Baikal. Sporadic migrant to Europe
Smith's chestnut-vented *(Pterocles gutturalis)*	Eastern Africa from Transvaal to Ethiopia
Spotted pin-tailed *(Petroclurus senegallus)*	From southern Sahara, through south-west Asia to north-west India.
Tibetan *(Syrrhaptes tibetanus)*	Most of Tibet
Variegated *(Pterocles variegatus)*	South Africa
Western pin-tailed *(Petroclurus pyrenaicus)*	Southern Europe from Spain through Provence, east to Cyprus, and south to North Africa

The principal industry is agriculture, and of the 62 million acres of farmland about 32 million acres are under cultivation, nearly 18 million of them under wheat. More than half the cereal crop of Canada is grown in the south of the province, and barley, oats, rye, flax and rape are also important. The most valuable natural resource is timber; well over half the province is forested and there are over 30,000 square miles of commercial forest – spruce, pine, fir, birch and poplar. Communications are good except in the north, where one has to rely on gravel roads, rivers or aircraft. The population is just under one million and is concentrated almost entirely in the southern and central areas of the province.

Saskatchewan is rich in game, and has produced many of the record North American trophy heads for deer and moose. One-third of all the duck in the American continent breed around the marshes and lakes of the province. Three flyways traverse it, and the migrating birds come down, in the fall, in their multitudes on to the millions of acres of stubble.

The province is divided into 37 game management zones, and seasons, bag limits, and game available vary from zone to zone, as well as from year to year. Certain species may be shot in some Provincial Parks, usually in the same seasons and under the same regulation as for the zones in which the parks lie.

Saskatchewan does not impose a closed season on several species, among them is the black bear

The different species and their ranges are shown in the table.

Saskatchewan (Canada)

This, the middle of the three Prairie Provinces, has an area of 251,000 square miles, of which 31,000 are water. It has a great number of lakes, the largest of which are Lakes Athabaska and Reindeer, and is crossed by three major river systems, all of which drain into the Hudson Bay. These are the Assiniboine, the North and South Saskatchewan, and the Churchill Rivers. The northern part of the province consists largely of an empty region of muskeg, swamp, rock, and stunted forest. The central part consists of an area of heavy forest and lakes giving way to parkland and long-grass prairie. The southern area consists of short-grass prairie – a rolling, treeless plain of extremely fertile loams and clays. The rainfall is high in the north but low in the prairie area, ranging there between 11 and 15 in. The average snowfall, however, exceeds 50 in, and the winters are long and extremely cold. Even in the south there are rarely more than 130 frost-free days, and the temperature range is from 100° to −50°F.

Seasons—Saskatchewan

Species	Area	Season	Limit	Comment
White-tailed deer		From 15 Nov-11 Dec	One or two, in some areas, three	Many zones open only to residents
	Northernmost	6 Sept-11 Dec		
Mule deer	South-west	Starts 8 Nov		
Moose	North and north-east	20 Sept-9 Oct and 15 Nov-4 Dec or 11 Dec	One, either sex	
	Northernmost	6 Sept-11 Dec		
Woodland caribou	North and north-east	20 Sept-9 Oct and 15 Nov-11 Dec	One, either sex	
Barren ground caribou		15 Nov-11 March		Open only to residents of northernmost zone
Black bear	North	20 Sept-9 Oct	2, either sex	
	Northernmost	6 Sept-16 Oct Also end of March to middle of June		
Antelope	South-west	25 Oct-30 Oct	One, either sex	By drawing, residents only
	East	30 Oct (1 day)		
Elk	Most northern zones	15 Nov-11 Dec	One, either sex	Residents
bull	North and north-east	6 Sept-18 Sept		
Sharp-tailed grouse, ruffed grouse and spruce grouse	Northernmost zone	6 Sept-11 Dec	5 per day, 10 in possession	
	North and north-east	20 Sept-11 Dec	6 per day, 12 in possession	
	Other zones	27 Sept-13 Nov		
Hungarian partridge	South of Prince Albert	27 Sept-13 Nov	5 per day, 10 in possession	

Further Information

Wildlife Branch, Department of Natural Resources, Government Administration Building, Regina, Sask.

Tourist Branch, Saskatchewan Industry Department, 7th floor, Power Buildings, Regina, Sask.

Sassaby *see* Tssesseby

Saudi Arabia *see* Middle East

Scaled Quail *(Callipepla squamata)*
There are three recognized subspecies of this quail, all of them belonging to the arid uplands of the south-western United States and northern and western Mexico.

The most typical race is the Mexican scaled quail *(C. squamata squamata)* which is found throughout northern, central, and western Mexico. The Arizona scaled quail *(C. squamata pallida)* is found principally in Arizona, New Mexico and southern Colorado, and it has also been successfully introduced into eastern Washington. The chestnut-bellied scaled quail *(C. squamata castonagastris)* is found from north-western Texas down to the Rio Grande valley and Mexico.

They are small birds, little more than 10 in long, with erect brown crests tipped with white, which give them their nickname of 'Cottontop'. Their body colours are pale slate and drab brown, and the feathers

Game Inventory—Saskatchewan

Species	Shot	Most productive area	Comment
White-tailed deer	49,075	South-east	4% by non-residents
Moose	6,893	South-east	774 by non-residents. 33% during early season
Woodland caribou	89	North-central lakes	
Black bear	412	Central-eastern zones	55% during spring season
Antelope	2,141		
Elk	352	North-central lakes	
Sharp-tailed grouse	126,796	South-west	Heaviest kill end Sept—beginning Oct
Ruffed grouse	47,577	North-west	Heaviest kill, mid-Oct
Spruce grouse	15,961	North-central area	Heaviest kill, mid-Oct
Hungarian partridge	104,993	West	Heaviest kill, end Sept—beginning Oct
Duck	292,657	Southern half of province	Mallard, 65%; American widgeon, 9%; gadwall, 7%
Sandhill crane	5,670		
Geese	78,762	West and centre	Canada, 43%; whitefront, 39%; snow, 14%; others, 4%

Species	Area	Season	Limit	Comment
Ptarmigan	North Northernmost	20 Sept-29 Jan 6 Sept-29 Jan		Normally only found in extreme north ; late in season may migrate south
Ring-necked pheasant, cock	South and south-west	28 Sept-14 Nov	4 per day, 8 in possession	Residents only
Ring-necked pheasant, hen	One western zone	30 Nov-2 Jan	On per day, 2 in possession	
Duck	North of Prince Albert South of Prince Albert	6 Sept-23 Dec 13 Sept-31 Dec	10 per day (not more than 8 mallard, and one canvasback), 20 in possession (not more than 16 mallard, and 2 canvasback)	
Coot			8 per day, 16 in possession	
Wilson's snipe			10 per day, 20 in possession	
Sandhill crane	A few south-central zones	1 Sept-11 Sept	4 per day, 8 in possession	If whooping cranes are detected in any zone, season in that zone is closed
Geese	North of Prince Albert South of Prince Albert	6 Sept-23 Dec 27 Sept-31 Dec	5 per day (not more than 3 white fronts) 10 in possession (not more than 6 white fronts)	Canada geese are restricted in some south-east zones. Geese only to be hunted from pit-blinds on cultivated land in one western zone.

on their underparts have black edging, which gives them their 'scaled' effect. The Mexican and Arizona quails have buff coloured underparts, and the chestnut-bellied chestnut coloured ones.

They all closely resemble the bobwhite quail (q.v.) in their behaviour patterns, but they rear only one brood per season. Their diet consists principally of weed seeds, grain if they are near crops, cactus, fruit and greenstuff, together with about 25% of animal matter in the form of grasshoppers, beetles and other insects. Only in the most arid areas do they need to visit water, since they can generally survive on the moisture in the food and the dew. They nest on the ground and the clutch of 8 to 16 eggs takes 21 days to incubate. Nesting losses are high, and there is generally no more than a 20% hatch.

Scaled quail are difficult birds to hunt, since they will neither lie to the point nor fly, but run on in front of the dogs, into thick and thorny cover. If finally flushed they will only fly for short distances before coming down and running again. Pointers tend to be spoilt by them, and it is probably best to shoot them when they come down to waterholes.

Scent and Scenting

There are few more constantly variable factors connected with hunting than scent and scenting. All smells or scents are con-

Licence Fees—Saskatchewan

Species	Status	Fee	Comment
White-tailed deer	Resident Non-resident Canadian Non-resident alien	$7 $25 $40	
second deer	Resident Non-resident Canadian Non-resident alien	$6 $15 $20	
third deer	Resident Non-resident Canadian Non-resident alien	$5 $10 $10	
Mule deer	Residents only		Allotted by ballot
Moose	Resident Non-resident Canadian Non-resident alien	$12 $30 $100	
Woodland caribou	Resident Any non-resident	$12 $100	
Barren ground caribou	Residents only	$10	
Black bear	Resident Any non-resident	$5 $15	
Antelope	Residents only	$10	
Elk	Residents only	$12	

continued overleaf

veyed to the olfactory senses by minute particles in the air inhaled through the nose. The smell left by any animal's feet, including those of man, may be termed the ground or foot scent. That left by the passage of the body, or emanating from the body, may be termed air scent. The strength of each depends on a number of factors: the time elapsed since the animal left the scent, the atmospheric and wind conditions at the time the scent was left, the ground or terrain on which the scent was left, also the condition of the animal leaving the scent, whether alarmed, wounded, hurrying or moving slowly, or even trying deliberately to confuse its scent. Another variable factor is the condition of the animal scenting, whether fit and with olfactory senses at their highest pitch, or tired, or with the olfactory senses dulled by a recent meal, or by pungent odours.

Depending on atmospheric conditions both air and foot scent must always be present to a greater or lesser degree. In extremely windy conditions the air scent and, to some extent, the foot scent, may be blown away. Watch the hound following a freshly laid trail across a field and it will often be seen that it is following with head held high some ten or even twenty feet downwind of the exact line. This is the distance which the particles of air scent

have travelled in the time since the trail was laid. Watch it, when the trail has been broken, go on for a pace or two before checking abruptly and casting round in a circle, generally starting downwind, to strike off the line again when it is found. Watch the really experienced hound in such circumstances put its head down and follow the less obvious foot scent, puzzling it out until it strikes the stronger air scent again. Consider how far man's own scent must travel on the wind when walking, alerting game for hundreds of yards downwind. Remember that to the keen-scenting animal each smell, or scent, tells its own story as the result of accumulated experience gained from the moment it opened its eyes and started using its nose. There a fox passed quite recently, moving slowly and probably hunting on its own account. Here was a covey of partridges jukking, which flew off when the fox approached them hoping to pounce. Here was a wounded bird trailing a wing, possibly hit by a motor car. It crossed the scent of the fox and, unable to fly, it must still be close. All these messages and many more can be recorded by the nose of an animal crossing an apparently empty field and the hunter should be able to understand something of the story by his hound's reactions.

Like people, hounds and other animals learn by experience what each scent or smell means; each conveys a separate message. The slightly acrid smell of fear on a rabbit scent combined with the stronger smell of the stoat or weasel may indicate a rabbit hunted by a stoat, the two smells interwoven with each other. The strong scent of the fox may even be smelt by man himself, sometimes by air scent at the height of a man above the ground when the much keener-nosed hound has not yet smelt anything down at its level. Cast the hound in the right direction towards the wind-blown scent and it will soon strike the line at its own level. Consider, however, how the wind may carry scent up a hill, or down a valley, perhaps alerting a bird in a tree, but not the deer beneath.

Precisely what produces the body or air scent is a question which has long been argued. The anal gland or other glands on an animal are the most obvious answer. Even in the human the automatic reaction to fear is a tightening then loosening of the bowels. Thus, any bird or mammal when alarmed generally defecates immediately on rising for flight – perhaps nature's way of removing an unnecessary load on the body. Watch hounds following a scent and see where the fox has pulled up short, alarmed at the unexpected sight of a man standing by a gate with a dog, then see hounds check and remain at fault for several hundred yards before picking up the scent again. Watch the wing-tipped pheasant suddenly check at the sight of a

Pointing. The German short-haired pointer in the rear is backing the front dog which has caught the side scent.

stop or beater close at hand. Watch the gun dog follow the scent to that corner then, temporarily at fault, circle round for some distance before he strikes it off again. It is probable that some of those so-called scentless birds, which fell in full view yet were overlooked by dog after dog and caused anguish at many a field trial, had in fact been hit from behind and their scent glands stopped up or blocked in the most dramatic possible way.

Nevertheless, animals in the wild are masters at the art of confusing their scent to avoid predators. The hare going to its form is often an object lesson in the art of concealing its scent. It will sometimes run twenty or thirty yards back on its own tracks and then leap a massive six feet or more downwind to settle itself at once in its form, curling up tightly to present the least possible surface for scent. By these tactics any predator following by scent will overrun the mark and will then be at a loss to find it. The hare, perhaps most of all animals, is pastmaster of such tactics. It has been seen running at speed in front of a pursuing dog to nudge the backside of another hare lying in its form as if in a game of tag, whereupon the second hare at once dashed off at speed and the first curled up immediately in the vacated form. The dog following by sight, or even some yards downwind by scent, will then continue in pursuit of, or on the scent of, the second hare. Such tactics, not immediately obvious to the hunter, may lead him to conclude that his dog has confused the scents and has taken on a fresh hare by accident; in fact, the dog has merely been the victim of one of the oldest confidence tricks in the world. Sometimes the hunter can use such tricks himself, rather like the hunting lions which will, occasionally, deliberately saunter up wind of a herd of zebra or antelope in order to stampede them past their mate or other members of their pride lying in wait for a victim.

There are always too many variable factors involved to be dogmatic about anything connected with scent and this is all part of the fascination of hunting. The hunter should always be prepared to learn something new on the subject and the best possible way to learn is to watch the ways of the animals in the wild. MWB

Scoters (Melanitta species)

These are all medium-sized, maritime, living ducks resembling, in many ways, that other large family of maritime ducks, the eiders. They are all fast and active flyers, but they have some difficulty taking wing. They normally feed in sheltered bays and shallow waters where the mussel beds are to be found, but, in addition to molluscs, they eat fish, crustacea, and a small amount of vegetable matter. After feeding they rest, at sea, in great 'rafts'.

They are not, outside the United States, of great interest to wildfowlers, partly because they rarely come inland, except to breed, and partly because most people would describe them as being only marginally edible. Hunting pressures, however, have forced the New England hunters to put to sea and hunt scoters and eiders, and, perhaps to justify the exercise, they claim that scoter are edible. Indeed, 'Coot' stew has been elevated into a symbol of New England virility hardly less awe-inspiring than clam chowder.

The common scoter *(Melanitta nigra nigra)* is differentiated from the American scoter *(Melanitta nigra americana)* by small points and separate ranges. The common scoter breeds in northern Europe and Asia and winters along the coasts of western Europe, the Mediterranean, and the Black and Caspian Seas; the American scoter, which is comparatively rare, breeds in Alaska and winters along the Atlantic coast from Maine to North Carolina, and along the Pacific coast from British Columbia to the state of Washington.

The drakes are completely black except for a heavily-knobbed orange patch at the base of the bill, which is otherwise black, and yellow-green legs. They weigh about $2\frac{1}{4}$ lb and measure between 18 and 19 in. The ducks are dark brown with white cheeks and throats, and the immature birds (called gray coots) resemble them but are lighter in colour.

The surf scoter *(Melanitta perspicillata)* closely resembles the common scoter, but the drake has two white patches on its head and a heavy red, white and yellow bill; the duck has pink legs and feet. Their breeding grounds lie from eastern Alaska to the Northwest Territories, and they winter along the Atlantic coast from Maine to Florida, and along the Pacific coast from the Aleutians to Lower California. The adults migrate southwards in September, a fortnight before the immature birds. Wildfowlers generally wait for the 'gray coots', which make better eating.

The velvet scoter *(Melanitta fusca fusca)* is rather larger than both common and surf scoters, and is distinguished from them by a white wing-patch which shows up prominently during flight. The drake has a small white patch below the eye and yellow sides to a black bill. They breed in northern Europe and Asia and winter in western Europe, the Mediterranean, the Black and Caspian Seas, China and Japan. They are sometimes winter migrants to Britain.

The white-winged scoter *(Melanitta fusca deglandi)* is almost identical with the velvet scoter and was, at one time, thought to be the same species. They are the commonest scoters in North America although their breeding grounds are more southerly than those of any other scoter and have suffered heavily from the draining and ploughing of

A male scoter, a species of sea duck with a northern Eurasian distribution.

the Prairie Provinces of Canada. They are the only scoter to nest so far inland. Like all the scoters, however, they lay a clutch of from six to ten eggs which take between 25 and 28 days to incubate. The ducklings all resemble the duck except for being lighter coloured but, by the first winter, the young drakes have begun to turn black.

Scoters are sometimes shot from headlands but it is more common, off the New England coast, to put to sea in a dory, duck boat, gunning float or other craft and, having anchored and put out decoys, to shoot them as they come skimming in low over the gunner's head. Wounded birds tend to dive, and to stay underwater until they drown. Scoter will come equally readily to both block and profile decoys.

Scotland *see* United Kingdom of Great Britain

Shapu *see* Red Sheep

Sharp-tailed Grouse (*Pediocetes phasianellus*)
This is a North American grouse that closely resembles and has much in common with the pinnated grouse (*q.v.*). It, also, is a bird of the prairies and natural grasslands, though with a more northerly range than the pinnated grouse. It, too, has suffered greatly from ploughing and the spread of modern agriculture. Like the latter it is also called prairie chicken, though in this case incorrectly. The cock can be distinguished from the pinnated grouse by its longer and sharply pointed tail and the absence of tufts of feathers on the neck.

The cock's head and neck are buff, and there are orange air sacs on each side of the neck that are concealed by the plumage until they are inflated. The upperparts are grayish-brown with brown and black markings, the underparts are buff or whitish with V-shaped brown pencillings on the breast. The two central tail feathers are longer than the rest and form a point or spike. These are plain coloured in the cock and barred with black in the hen. The legs are feathered to the first joint of the toes. The hen resembles the cock but has a shorter tail and lacks the air sacs. Summer diet includes seeds, berries, insects and greenstuff; winter diet consists largely of sagebrush, grass seeds and tree buds.

Courtship displays take place morning and evening in groups on established dancing floors. The cocks strut, dance, inflate and deflate their air sacs and 'drum' in much the same way as the sage grouse (*q.v.*). The hen nests alone, generally in the open, and the clutch of from 10 to 16 eggs takes 24 days to incubate.

Sharp-tailed grouse are found throughout central and western Canada and Alaska, south of the treeline, but they are not, now,

often found in the United States, though they were once abundant in all the northern states of the Union to as far east as Ohio. They are to be found in natural grasslands with low sage or open woodland, especially in second growth timber around the Great Lakes and the Muskegs of the boreal forest region.

They are excellent game birds, flying well and holding well to pointers except late in the season. Many have adapted themselves to modern farming and are to be found on wheat stubbles and in cornfields, where they may be walked up with guns in line. In brush and wooded country they are best shot over dogs. They make excellent eating.

Sheep *see* Goats and Sheep; Mountain Sheep; Mouflon; Red Sheep

Shorebirds *see* Waders

Shotgun *see* Firearms

Sika (*Cervus nippon*)
The Japanese deer is found in southern Asia and Japan and has been introduced successfully into Great Britain, many parts of Europe, Australia and New Zealand. There is some confusion as there are two closely related subspecies, namely *C. nippon nippon*, originating in Japan, and the slightly larger *C. nippon manchuricus*, from Manchuria, both of which have now spread to many parts of the world and have probably been so interbred that differentiation is sometimes impossible.

In many ways the handsome sika resembles the red deer, although somewhat smaller. The mature stag stands about 36 in at the shoulder and weighs about 120 to 180 lb. The doe stands about 30 in and weighs around 80 to 100 lb. Their coloration is noticeably spotted on a reddish background. In winter their coat turns gray and the spots disappear, but a black dorsal stripe is noticeable throughout the year. The sika has a white rump and the underside of the tail is also white, showing very distinctly from behind when running away. The head is shorter and better balanced than that of a red deer. The antlers lack the brow tine of the red deer and young stags have only six points while mature stags reach eight points, four on each side. There is generally a pronounced spread of about 30 in, making a well balanced head. A noticeable feature is the tufted gland just below the joint of the hind legs. The rutting season is much the same as for red deer, but instead of roaring they make a whistling sound, or else make a sound rather like a donkey braying. Rather fiercer when in the rut, than the red stag, it is also quicker off the mark when alarmed, generally departing at speed with a warning whistling sound. Although faster when alarmed it is probably no warier than the red deer, and stalking or still-hunting is

Top, the sharp-tailed grouse, which are not as common as they once were in North America.

Above, the sika deer has been successfully introduced from Japan into several countries, where it forms a welcome addition to their game fauna.

Lesser snow geese in California

Two jack snipe from Australia compared with a 12-gauge cartridge

The steinbuck is a small antelope inhabiting open plains and light woodland in south and east-central Africa.

conducted in much the same manner. Being more nocturnal in habit, however, it is best hunted at dawn and dusk. A good trophy head can generally be secured and the venison is much preferable to that of red deer.

See also Deer of the World and their Hunting.

Sing-sing *see* Waterbuck

Sitatunga *(Tragelaphus spekei)*
Also called harnessed antelope or nakong, this beast is found throughout central Africa in swamps, marshes and wet reed beds, frequently in small groups of half a dozen or more. It is very nearly amphibious and has notably elongated hooves. It stands about 3 ft 6 in at the shoulder. The bucks are always brown, but there is considerable colour variation in the females. Both sexes are marked with white lines and spots, but unlike the bushbuck the tail is not bushy. The females are hornless but the bucks carry curving horns over 2 ft in length, about 6 in around the base and with a spread of about 16 in at the tips. They live on swamp grasses and are not as uncommon as their limited habitat might indicate. It is extremely difficult to approach without disturbance and hence is not often shot.

Sloth Bear *(Melurus labiatus)*
Found throughout the whole of India south of the Himalayas, it has long, coarse, shaggy hair, especially around the head and shoulders and a yellowish, crescent shaped mark on its chest. The muzzle is a dirty white and it has long claws used for digging up the ground for roots and termites. It also feeds on jungle fruits and honey. The female has from one to three cubs, which she keeps until they are full grown. Both sexes are well known for their uncertain temper and will attack with little provocation. Although short sighted and with poor scenting powers it can climb a tree nearly as fast as a panther. It requires a heavy calibre and straight shooting to stop it when charging. It is usually encountered when still-hunting.

Snipe and Woodcock Shooting around the World
Snipe and woodcock are popular with sportsmen, but much less work has been done on these species than other, less important, game birds because they respond less readily to management. Snipe and woodcock are true products of the wild and the large-scale reclamation and drainage which is helping to solve the world's food problems is, unfortunately, gradually reducing the numbers of these marsh-based migrants. This has been more noticeable in the case of the snipe and its relatives than in the case of the woodcock, which is able to find a living in many areas of commercial woodland.

The common snipe *(Capella gallinago)* is found throughout the northern hemisphere, while the woodcock *(Scolopax rusticola)* and the American woodcock *(Philohela minor)* occupy similar niches in the Old and New Worlds.

The common snipe is known for its fast, zigzag flight – which makes it one of the trickiest of targets as it flashes up with a harsh 'scaap' from the marsh grass – and for its 'drumming' display in spring, during which the bird indulges in fast, shallow aerial dives over its territory, rigid side feathers of the tail emitting a moaning bleat as it does so. It is a highly migratory species in North America, where it is often referred to as Wilson's snipe, the summer and winter ranges overlapping only on a small area of the Pacific Coast. Over much of Asia the pattern is similar, but in Britain and north-western Europe the snipe is found as both a breeding bird and a winter visitor. Large numbers of snipe move southward and westward into Britain, Ireland, France and the Iberian Peninsula during the hardest months of winter, adding to the resident population which tends to disperse locally except in the harshest weather when they, too, may move onward to the southwest.

Similar in form to many other wading birds, the snipe is distinguished by its extremely long, straight bill and the fore-and-aft striping of the head. When flushed, this 10 to 11 in, 4 oz bird is extremely quick off the mark, often towering high into the sky after the initial zig-zag sprint, only to drop down to the marsh again a few minutes later. Members of a 'wisp' or small flock of snipe will flush erratically, some hiding until the sportsman believes that all have gone, only to rise suddenly with their harsh call.

The birds arrive in waves during their southward migration in autumn, marshes which held no birds suddenly becoming alive with snipe, often apparently just ahead of cold weather in October and November. American birds head south to the Gulf Coast as European snipe arrive in their winter quarters in the milder districts of their continent.

Shooting usually takes place with small parties of guns walking the marsh, sometimes using spaniels or retrievers to flush the snipe. Dogs of a retrieving breed are almost essential if shot birds are to be recovered in difficult terrain. In tropical countries, native bearers often do the job with greater efficiency! In some places, snipe are driven off marshes over the heads of waiting guns, but they tend to be too unpredictable for this to be generally successful.

In southern Africa, the common snipe is replaced by the Ethiopian snipe, and in south-east Asia by the pintailed snipe, which is very similar. The pintail and common species are found during winter in India, the former tending to be found in more southern districts. The tiny jack snipe and the larger, slower great snipe provide sport in some places in Asia and Africa. Both are found occasionally in Britain, but the latter is protected.

The curious painted snipe, in which the females are larger and more brightly coloured than the males, is found in India, Africa and Australia. Mainly a resident species, it flies with trailing legs and has been described as 'neither worth shooting nor eating'.

The woodcock of the Old World is found throughout Europe and Asia, breeding in the north and wintering in the south. It is a 14 in bird, rather more dumpy than most waders, and weighs 10 to 12 oz.

Like the snipe, woodcock feed on worms and other invertebrates found in moist soil, but this bird tends to lie up in woodland during the day, feeding at dawn and dusk on marshlands near by. These flight lines to traditional feeding grounds are well known by poachers and a bird or two can often be bagged at twilight.

Woodcock also display in the half light of evening and at dawn, flying a regular route around the woodland territory. With a peculiar slow wingbeat, the bird is very distinctive during this flight and utters a deep grunt, 'waak-wuk-wuk' followed by a chirruping whistle usually rendered as 'twissick'. The flight is known in Britain as 'roding'. In Europe, woodcock are often shot during this display period, the gunner waiting under the well-known flight path at dusk.

Both snipe and woodcock lay an average of four eggs, the former in a grassland nest, the latter among leaves on the woodland floor.

British woodcock are sedentary, but a large influx reaches the country from Scandinavia, travelling down both the west and east coasts. The best woodcock shooting is found on promontories where the birds gather in large numbers on this autumn flight, and in the extreme south-west of Britain, which is a migration terminus.

Woodcock prefer warm, dry coverts with a canopy at about 10 to 15 ft, interspersed with openings where the birds can drop in after their crepuscular wanderings in search of food. Where a covert draws large numbers of 'cock during the migration season, they can be driven like pheasants during the daytime – usually in short drives of 100 to 200 yds. The birds will always fly out of the covert at certain spots, with an uncanny traditional knowledge of the ground.

Spaniels are very useful when driving or walking-up woodcock and the species has given its name to the cocker spaniel. In Europe, the 'bécasse' is, if anything, an even more popular target than in Britain. It breeds throughout northern Europe and

winters in the south and west of the region. The popularity of the woodcock has made a 'right and left' at this bird one of the most highly-regarded of shotgun feats, particularly since the swerving flight of a flushed 'cock through the trees is especially challenging to co-ordination and skill.

The American woodcock looks like a miniature version of the Eurasian bird, 10 to 12 in long and weighing 6 to 7 oz. The female is larger than the male, who performs a strange spiral display flight over an opening in marshy woodland. The timber-doodle, to give the species its very evocative American nickname, is confined almost entirely to the eastern States, summering in the north of the region and wintering south to the Gulf of Mexico and Florida. WAN

See also Waders

'Snipe Shooting' – a print by Samuel Howitt, published in 1796.

Snow Goose

(Anser caerulescens caerulescens)
The only white goose much shot in North America is the lesser snow goose, which is hunted over much of its winter range in Utah, Texas, California and Mexico. The greater snow goose *(Anser caerulescens atlanticus)* is larger and winters along the Atlantic coast from Maryland to North Carolina, and is protected. So, also, is Ross's goose, a much smaller white goose that winters in California.

The lesser snow has a number of other popular names including 'white brant' and 'wavey'. This last name can lead to some confusion, since the white-fronted goose *(Anser albifrons)* q.v. is also known as 'wavey'. The confusion probably originates from the fact that the Indian generic name for goose is 'Wa-Wa'.

Snow geese fly in V or oblique line formation with little apparent wing movement and generally in silence, though their call, if used, is a repeated 'we-honk'. They seem completely white except that their black primaries show, in flight, as a black tip to the wing. The bill is pink with a white nail and black cutting edges to the mandibles. The legs are pink with black claws. They are gregarious and are often associated with other species, most notably the blue goose, *q.v.*, which is thought by many biologists to be a colour phase of the snow goose.

The breeding grounds lie high up in the Arctic on the most northern coasts of North America and north-eastern Siberia. They winter along the Pacific coast from British Columbia to California and along the Gulf of Mexico west of the Mississippi, as well as in Japan. They are seen occasionally, as vagrants, in Great Britain. The nest is a down-lined depression in the ground and the clutch of 4 to 8 eggs takes 22 to 24 days to hatch. The immature plumage is gray with darker markings, but this lightens slowly during the winter, and full, white, adult plumage is assumed after the first summer moult.

Snow geese decoy very easily. They will even come down to scraps of white paper stuck in the ground. They can also be called down with great success by the Cree Indians of James Bay. They are shot extensively from blinds and movable hides in the Californian rice fields and the coastal marshes of Texas and Louisiana.

Snowshoe Rabbit *(Lepus americanus)*
The snowshoe rabbit is more correctly a hare, a fact that is recognized by its alternative name of varying hare. This name is also given to the Scots blue, or mountain hare *(Lepus timidus)* – a much larger animal that also changes coat colour in winter, though not to the extent of the snowshoe rabbit, whose brown coat turns completely white.

A small hare, weighing little more than 4 lb and measuring about 20 in long, it can be distinguished from the cottontail by its coat colour, its larger size, its longer ears and hindlegs, its greater speed, and its habit of running straight across country, instead of in a circle. The snowshoe part of its name refers to its broad and furry feet which allow it to stay on top of soft snow. It is, like all *Leporidae*, a herbivore, living on grasses, weeds and clovers in summer, and twigs and bark, especially of willows, in winter. It is found in the wooded areas of all the northern states of the United States and north from there to within the Arctic Circle.

There is generally only one litter a year, but, if weather and feed conditions are particularly good, a second litter may be produced later in the year. The mating season is in April and May, and gestation takes 30 days. The average litter size is four to six, and the young, like the young of all hares, are born in a form, above ground, already furred and with their eyes open.

The snowshoe rabbit does not hibernate in the winter. It is well adapted for such conditions as its thick coat turns completely white.

The snowshoe rabbit is generally shot with a shotgun, though its habit if sitting makes it a good target for archers. If there are no dogs it will often crouch and hope to be walked over. The best sport is obtained from coursing it with hounds, which it will often lead for a run lasting several hours. In deep snow it will always have considerable advantage over even long-legged hounds, let alone beagles. It can also be still-hunted in the woods in winter.

South Africa
The Republic of South Africa is a large country of about 472,500 square miles occupying most of the southern portion of the African continent. South Africa itself is divided into four provinces: Transvaal in the north, Natal in the east, Cape Province in the south and west, and the Orange Free State in the centre.

Most of the country is occupied by the plateau of the High Veldt, between 3,000 and 4,000 ft, which is a natural grassland. The whole south and east of the High Veldt is fringed by mountain ranges, of which the most important is the Drakensberg, which rises to over 11,000 ft, curving north through western Natal into Transvaal. In the south of Cape Province the mountains mark off the lesser plateaus of the Great and Little Karoo which step down to the sea. In Transvaal the land slopes down through the Bakenveldt to the fertile sub-tropical areas of the Low Veldt in the north and east. Most of the rest of the country has, due to its altitude, a mild temperate climate. The Mozambique Current warms the south-eastern coastal belt in winter. The south-western Cape has a Mediterranean climate with winter rainfall, unlike the interior, where the rain falls mainly in summer. Most of the minor rivers are fairly dry except after rain. The main rivers are the Limpopo in the north, flowing eastwards, and the Orange and its tributary the Vaal, which flow westwards. South West Africa is particularly dry and rather hot. Most of the state is barren upland, giving way to the Kalahari desert in the east, but there is some good grazing in the west.

South Africa has extensive and varied agriculture, producing wheat, maize, barley, Kaffir corn, groundnuts and citrus fruits in large quantities. There are sugar and tea in Northern Natal, and a variety of wines. Cattle and sheep are bred on a large scale and wool is important.

Its minerals, above all, have contributed to South Africa's mixture of wealthy 20th-century cities and untouched bush, which can be very useful for the visiting hunter, in that hunting grounds are never far from modern facilities with good transport and communications. This is tempered somewhat by the government's attitude towards hunting, which is not enthusiastic, mainly as a reaction to the senseless killing of the

Ordinary Game, Natal—South Africa
Bushbuck, male (most districts)
Common quail
Coqui francolin
Crowned guinea-fowl
Egyptian goose
Grey duiker
Greywing francolin
Natal francolin
Redwing francolin
Shelley's francolin
Spurwing goose
Swainson's francolin
Yellowbill duck

Protected Game—South Africa
Black duck
Blesbok
Blue duiker
Blue wildebeeste
Bushbuck, female
Bushbuck, male
   (where not classified as ordinary
   game)
Crested francolin
Crested guinea fowl
Gray rhebuck
Hottentot teal
Impala
Kudu
Nyala
Red-billed teal
Red bush duiker
Red-necked francolin
Reed buck
Reedbuck, mountain
   (only in certain areas)
Steinbuck
   (only in certain areas)
Waterbuck
Warthog
White-faced duck
Zebra

Unprotected Species—South Africa
Black-backed jackal
Black crow
Bushpig
Cape turtle dove
Chacma baboon
Hare
Pied crow
Red-knobbed coot
Rock pigeon
Rock rabbit (dassie)
Vervet monkey

late 19th and early 20th centuries that resulted in the near extinction of many species. Consequently all hunting is privately organized, and no predators may be hunted for sport. South Africa is, therefore, more convenient as a base for expeditions further north, to South West Africa, Rhodesia or Botswana. Nevertheless South Africa can provide some good bird and antelope hunting.

Regulations differ from province to province as each has its own department of nature conservation, which governs hunting and is responsible for game laws etc. The information given below applies to Natal, but it is fairly typical in outline, and differs only in detail from the situation in other provinces.

Licences
There are three classifications of game in terms of the required licence: ordinary game, protected game, unprotected game. Additionally some species are specially protected and may not be hunted for sport in Natal under any circumstances. Ordinary game may be shot by landowners or occupiers on their land without a licence. All other hunters must have an Ordinary Game Licence (cost, 2 Rands), which may be obtained from all Provincial Revenue Offices or from certain private agents such as sporting goods shops or general dealers in small towns. The licence is valid for one season and for Natal only. It must be signed by the holder. The species shown in the table are classed as ordinary game in Natal. Protected game require a separate licence for each species. Licences will only be issued when adequate numbers of a species are

considered to be available in the area to be hunted. A free permit may be issued to landowners and occupiers to shoot certain protected game on their land. Applications for a permit or licence must be made in writing to the Natal Parks Board stating how many of each species the applicant wishes to hunt, and on what land. All permits and licences must be returned, fully endorsed, within 14 days of expiry or of the animals being killed, whichever is the earlier. The table gives those species classed as protected game in Natal.

Licence fees for protected birds are usually 25c. or 50c. per head. For protected mammals the fees range between R1.50 and R5.

Seasons
The open season is the same for protected and ordinary game, and is usually from June to September, though it varies from year to year, and some districts may have special seasons. The season tends to be slightly earlier in other provinces.

Unprotected wild life (see table) may be shot at any time of the year without a licence, though of course landowner's permission must be obtained. There are no regulations concerning methods or weapons, but hunters are advised to follow the same practices as are laid down for protected and ordinary game.

Game Ranches and Safari Companies
The regulations listed above do not apply to game ranches, which are rapidly growing in numbers and popularity. Registered game ranchers are granted an annual culling licence which enables them to 'cull' throughout the year. The simplest procedure therefore is for the visitor to organize his hunting

The warthog is a gregarious animal. It may not be shot in South Africa without a licence.

through one of the local Safari companies, who have arrangements with all the game ranchers. The visitor can then 'cull' at set fees per head, with no seasonal limitations.

Most of the Safari companies also have arrangements whereby clients can hunt other species outside South Africa, such as elephant and the big cats, in East Africa, Botswana, or Rhodesia. In South West Africa, for instance, gemsbok, red hartebeest and cheetah (at present but probably not for long) may be hunted.

Special Regulations
No hunting is permitted at night, from half an hour after sunset to half an hour before sunrise.

Hunting is not permitted in National Parks, public or private game reserves and on or from a road or the area of the road.

Traps, nets, snares, poisons and explosives are illegal, and vehicles, artificial light and veldt fires may not be used directly to hunt game. Hunting game from horseback is also illegal. Any dog not under the control of a lawful hunter, killing or pursuing game may be destroyed by the landowner or occupier or an authorized officer.

Shotguns may be used only to hunt birds and the following antelopes: bushbuck, reedbuck, gray duiker, red bush duiker, blue duiker, and steenbuck. All shotguns must be limited to two rounds per loading.

Automatic rifles and rimfire rifles of .22 calibre or less may not be used for hunting.

Further Information
The South African National Parks Board, P.O. Box 787, Pretoria.

The South African Tourist Corporation, Private Bag 164, Pretoria.

The best source of information specifically on Natal is:

The Secretary, The Natal Parks, Game and Fish Preservation Board, P.O. Box 662, Pietermaritzburg, Natal.

The South African Hunters' and Game Preservation Association, in Pretoria, may also be useful, but they have difficulty obtaining sufficient local hunting for their own members.

South and Southern Africa, Conservation and Hunting in

Africa south of the River Zambesi was once the world's greatest hunting ground. Both large and small game abounded in a variety equalled nowhere else. Today almost all of this game has gone, token herds remaining only in the national parks and reserves.

The development of game conservation, agriculture and hunting have followed a different pattern in southern Africa from that, for example, in North America. This has led to a very sharp division between the reserves, where wildlife is still abundant and only official culling is practised, and the rest of the countryside, virtually denuded of all large game.

Typical Culling Fees— South Africa	
Species	**Fee**
	in Rands
Blesbok	R30.00
Bushbuck	R40.00
Grey duiker	R15.00
Impala	R25.00
Kudu	R1.50
Nyala	R1.50
Wildebeeste	R50.00
Zebra	R1.20

Specially Protected Species— South Africa

Antbear
Buffalo
Bushbaby
Cheetah
Eland
Elephant
Giraffe
Grysbuck
Hartebeeste, red
Hippopotamus
Klipspringer
Leopard
Livingstone's antelope (suni)
Mountain reedbuck (except where classified as protected)
Oribi
Pangolin
Rhinoceros, black
Rhinoceros, square-lipped
Samango monkey
Steinbok (except where classified as protected)
Wildebeeste, black

The steinbuck is a protected species in some areas of South Africa, and may only be shot if there are adequate numbers.

Traditionally the Afrikaans-speaking South Africans have been the main influence on rural life and they have never looked upon game in terms of sporting potential. The Afrikaner shot game to provide food and to protect his crops or open up land for cattle. This attitude extended also into the English-speaking colonies to the north, resulting in the almost complete extinction of game over huge areas during the period 1850–1910.

However, the memory of the great days of big game lingers on, and most efforts of conservationists today are aimed at restoring the numbers of the larger species, as far as possible, and extending their range into new or safer reserves. Meanwhile, the area's potential for small-game shooting has remained almost entirely neglected.

When political squabbles are forgotten and the great growth industry of tourism encourages a new look at southern Africa's rural resources, it may well be found that small game – both birds and mammals – offers important scope for development.

In South Africa itself, over-hunting for commercial and agricultural reasons led to the extinction of the blue buck, the quagga and, combined with trophy hunting, the black-maned Cape lion. The white rhinoceros and the South African elephant came close to extermination but were saved by conservationists' moves to declare game reserves in vital districts.

It is noticeable that the mantle of conservationist did not fall upon the game hunter of southern Africa, in general, until the protectionists had taken most of the glory. The idea of hunters leading the conservation lobby, and thus ensuring the continuation of their sport, as in America, was slow to gain ground. Thus the game parks became total preserves, rather than controlled hunting areas, and laws favoured the landowner and his interests. South African legislation has imposed the less worthy features of European hunting on a landscape which was capable of supporting something much more on the American pattern.

Although Boer farmers, generally speaking, were not sympathetic to wildlife until recent years, the continued existence of two species, the Cape mountain zebra (which now numbers about 200 animals) and a most attractive antelope, the bontebok, was due to protection on enclosed farms. Another antelope, closely related to the rare bontebok, is the blesbok of the Northern Karroo and the High Veldt. The present status of this animal illustrates the problem of South African hunting.

The blesbok, which stands about 4 ft at the shoulder and weighs over 150 lb, is a fine game animal now found almost entirely in herds enclosed on private land. These numbered (according to a 1962 survey) about 9,000 animals in Cape Province,

12,000 in the Orange Free State and 25,000 in the Transvaal. The difficulties in obtaining permission to hunt blesbok in the past have been described as similar to those in getting to grips with a stag in the deer forests of the Scottish Highlands or joining a Missouri duck club! Numbers are culled, but this is usually carried out by professional riflemen for the meat market.

Although it is difficult to give a brief summary of this vast region from the shooting viewpoint, because of the diversity of game and the many types of country encountered – from low-lying tropical forest to high, arid plains and deserts – the best advice is still very simple: don't over-gun yourself, either with shotgun or rifle; stick to familiar weapons (the 12-bore shotgun and the .270 or 30.06 rifle will tackle most quarry other than the specialist items of Royal Game). And get the best local advice that you can find.

In East Africa, organized professional safaris produce the best results in terms of trophies, but under southern African conditions it is often social contact with owners of game-holding land which proves most rewarding. The successful hunter, south of the Zambesi, combines the backwoods ability of a skilled American hunter with the social know-how of the European game shot.

Rhodesia has a rather complex game-laws system, and the reader is referred to the entry for clarification. As with American States, which have low rates for residents and high licence tariffs for non-residents, the game licences are cheap for local gunners but quite costly for the tourist or visitor. Shooting on Crown land is prohibited, except under special permit, and it is brought to the licence-holder's attention that 'possession of a licence does not give the holder authority to shoot on any land. The permission of the owner or occupier of the land must be obtained before any shooting is attempted'.

The hunter from Europe or North America will find the climate of the Cape very pleasant for outdoor activity in every month of the year, but he must be prepared for more difficulty during the hot months farther north, particularly in low-lying districts along the Zambesi in the months prior to the rains, which arrive in November and last intermittently until April. Nights are cool almost everywhere, and frost is common on the High Veldt.

The casual visitor to southern Africa will usually find that the shooting available is limited to gamebirds, duck and the smaller antelopes such as duiker. For these, he will require no additional hunting equipment or skill other than that used at home, although he will have to dress for local conditions, with emphasis on tough boots and cool clothing. If he is not used to tropical conditions, he may also be amused to find that

many Bantu combine the best attributes of guide and gundog!

Francolin (q.v.) are greatly underrated as gamebirds, mainly as a result of disparaging remarks by visiting sportsmen who have expected them to be carbon copies of driven pheasants or grouse. In fact, they can be challenging targets in tricky country, and the skill often lies in forcing them into a position from which they must take wing, rather than creep off into denser cover.

The francolin are a varied group, some being described locally as 'pheasants' and others as 'partridges'. Their calls are a familiar background to early mornings in the bundu and they are often found in surprising density considering the very large number of predators. Experimental work in East Africa has shown that some francolin are present in numbers which are unequalled by any North American or European gamebird under wild conditions and it is to be hoped that this natural abundance can be harvested and managed with care, so that future generations of hunters will find a new meaning for 'the abundant game of Africa'. WAN

See also Rhodesia; South Africa

South America

South America is not well supplied with what might be termed sporting fauna nor are the various governments geared to hunting for sport. The white-lipped peccary is perhaps the most sporting animal. The larger rodents, such as the agouti, capybara, and paca are dealt with separately, as is the Jaguar, and the deer (*see* Deer of the World). The cottontail in various forms also provides sport. Anteater, armadillo, porcupine, tapir, are some of the many other fascinating, but scarcely huntable, animals. The bird life is very varied, but there are no ready fliers, although waterfowl provides good sport in many areas.

See Argentina; Bolivia; Brazil; Ecuador; Guyana; Paraguay; South America, Shooting in; Surinam; Uruguay; Venezuela.

South America, Shooting in

The Weapons

In this area ninety per cent of all game is shot at ranges from 10 to about 60 yd and it is therefore unwise to be over-gunned. Modern magnum rifles are expensive and heavy. The same can be said for their ammunition, which is in scarce supply. From the middle nineties right up to the middle fifties the favourite brush-rifle in this area was the 44.40 Winchester, a rugged little weapon in carbine-style, light, reliable, accurate, without having to rely on very fine sights, up to 120 yd. The low-velocity flat-nosed bullet was a good brush-cutter and carried enough muzzle energy (about 760 foot pounds) to kill any game. It could be safely hand-loaded (in the 1892 model but not in the old '73) to about 1,000

The national emblem of South Africa, the springbok was overshot, but its population is now increasing.

ft lb muzzle velocity. Many of these old weapons are still in use. In the first half of this century there were still many muzzle-loader shotguns for use either with buckshot at close ranges or a round ball in a patch for longer ranges, and very efficient they were, although taking from 20 to 30 seconds to load. Some hunters even used, in these pieces, rifled slugs of European origin, generally the Brenneke with a wad tightly screwed into the base, which were also very effective in 20-bore Remington single-shot rolling block carbines or muskets re-barreled to that gauge.

Probably the best single weapon for all Latin-American brush-hunting is the Winchester or Remington slug-gun pump repeater with a short barrel (18½ in or 20 in) and ordinary open rifle-sights. A peep-sight can be used if considered necessary but the aperture should be large – at least one tenth of an inch – while the best type of foresight is a thick blade. In this kind of shooting where brush is thick and the going hard, it is wise, after zeroing sights, to secure them with solder. In such shooting a long barrel is a liability. The weapon is heavier, more liable to catch in the undergrowth, and more cumbersome to swing on to the target. There is a slight loss of velocity and energy in the shorter barrel but not enough to be a handicap. Any of the modern rifled slugs now made in the United States and various European countries can be used. In a single-barreled gun they are capable of putting all slugs into a 9-inch group at 100 yd, although in the heat of the chase, in heavy brush in a hot country, the diameter of this group could well be trebled. It is, therefore, unwise to take shots longer than, say, 50 or 60 yd if – as often happens – the hunter is hot and out of breath.

As to bore, the 12-bore, carrying rather more punch with a bullet weighing one ounce, is the most powerful. The 20-bore is too light. But the 16-bore is – at least in central Latin America – the most practical. The weapon is slightly lighter and so is the ammunition, more of which can be carried in a given space. Ballistics are slightly inferior to the 12-bore but quite ample for all game likely to be put up. The 16-bore slug is less disruptive on the game and lastly, 16-bore is a more popular gauge in these parts of Latin America than the 12, which is an advantage if the hunter wants to use his slug-gun with shot for flying or small ground game at ranges up to about 35 yd.

For those preferring rifle to slug-gun, probably the best calibres are 30–30 WCF, 32 Special for Winchester or Remington carbines and various other makes, either commercial or hand-loaded to original ballistics. If hand-loaded, flat-point bullets should be used. The advantage of these rifles is that they are lighter than the slug-gun, strong, and capable of bringing down a big swamp deer encountered in the palm-

The largest of the rodents, the capybara inhabits Brazil and the neighbouring countries of South America. It is always found near water into which it plunges when alarmed.

flats which are more or less open, at ranges from 50 yd to about 150 yd. A third choice might be the relatively new Ruger 44, a 5-shot gas-operated self-loading carbine handling the Smith and Wesson 44 Magnum revolver cartridge. The advantage of this carbine is that it is about a pound lighter than the Winchester 94 and, although its paper ballistics are slightly inferior to the 94, the flat-nosed 44-calibre bullet has greater impact at practical ranges and is less liable to be deflected in brush, and, of course, its rate of fire is faster.

The essence of brush-hunting is to waste as little time as possible once the game has been sighted, and therefore the emphasis is on short, relatively light arms and speed of getting on the mark. Also, the range is generally close. Therefore, telescopic sights on brush-guns or rifles, in thick country, are worse than useless. They are costly; they add weight; they are very vulnerable under the rough handling they often get in brush country; and lastly, they turn a man who with open sights is a very good snap-shot into a poker who often hits his quarry in paunch or quarters – or misses it altogether.

As to high velocity rifles and particularly the high-intensity calibres (many of them wildcats) they should never be considered for this type of hunting. Not only do the light, ultra-fast bullets disintegrate on hitting any twig over a quarter of an inch thick or even less, but the ear-splitting report will alert all game within a considerable distance.

The advantage of heavy handguns (for those who can hold them straight) is that they are lighter than a rifle and can be used with accuracy in the heaviest brush. They used to be and doubtless in many districts still are very popular, particularly with ranchers, who always carry them and never

Game—South America

Alligator
Contrary to hunter's tales, these sometimes dangerous saurians are not impervious to leaden bullets. Indeed, a 38-calibre revolver ball neatly placed between the eyes, when all but the eyes are invisible under water, will do the trick quite easily. There is not much sport in shooting them, though they grow to a great size, and commercially only the hides of smaller specimens are acceptable. They can be extremely dangerous on land as they move fast, and with one sweep of their tail can break a man's legs.

Tapir
A heavy beast with a short trunk, allied to the rhinoceros, and not very often seen. If put up by hounds, it goes straight through the thickest brush, as an elephant might, and is almost impossible to follow as it heads rapidly for the nearest water.

Swamp deer
This rather solitary animal is seldom seen in the brush. It is very wary but can be occasionally encountered in more or less open country, offering a shot at between 50 and 150 yd. A heart-lung shot will bring it down instantly but otherwise it may have to be tracked for miles by dogs or Indians, who are expert at this. There are several smaller species of deer, seldom seen in the open but occasionally offering close-range shots in the brush.

Capibara or carpincho
A superb swimmer inhabiting the banks of streams and rivers. The hunter should be in a canoe handled by a local man, while another, with dogs, beats one bank. On being put up, the carpincho rushes for the water, dives in and disappears. Now the reeds in the water are watched for movement and presently a small mark consisting of ears, eyes and the top of its head, appears. This target is no more than about two inches high and three wide — a very difficult shot from a rocking canoe, even at 20 or 30 yd. The meat is unpalatable.

Puma and jaguar
The method of hunting these two cats is much the same. A local man with a few dogs or hounds (the latter not very brave) must be hired, the hunter accompanying him either on foot or horseback. The latter is preferable because after scrambling through brush for half a mile in hot weather accuracy is liable to deteriorate. Eventually the puma or jaguar climbs a tree, the hounds, baying, surround it; the hunter arrives and generally gets a shot in at between 5 yd and 20 yd. Accuracy is essential because the first shot should be an instant killer; a head-shot is best. If a miss occurs, the cat jumps down and attacks, the hounds make off, and the hunter must get in another shot before he is jumped. Nasty accidents and even deaths have occured in this type of hunting, which is one reason why it is regarded as sporting.

Peccary
These gregarious little pigs, living in packs of anything from 6 to 60, are, in the opinion of the writer, the most dangerous beasts to be found in South America, for they are absolutely fearless and if surprised by a hunter, with dogs or with Indians, will nearly always attack. The Indians should, therefore, be allowed to carry, and to use, their own personal weapons – generally consisting of muzzle or breech-loading shotguns, loaded with swan-shot. The range is almost always short, from 2 or 3 yd up to 30 yd or 40 yd, and these pretty little pigs give the most sporting hunting of all. Sometimes the hunter is in as much danger from flying swan-shot as from the peccary, and there are many stories of lone hunters being chased up a tree by an infuriated band of peccary. They surround the tree; he kills as many peccary as he has cartridges, and the survivors patiently await until he falls off his branch from exhaustion or hunger.

---

know what they may meet up with. The best calibres were always the old Colt 45 and 44–40, or the Smith and Wesson 44 special. For all that the latter calibre has long been derided by some of the foremost American handgun exponents, it is a fact that all game mentioned below has been shot with it for over 50 years in standard factory loadings. Indeed, there are many old ranchers and professional hunters who have consistently shot jaguar and puma with nothing heavier than the old 38 Special in factory loads. But they know just where to put their shots.

As to the Magnums, in the opinion of most who have consistently hunted these countries, they are nothing but a nuisance. The recoil is very heavy and hard both on wrist and fork of hand. For this reason aimed fire is slow. It is possible to put five shots from a single action 45 Colt into a small mark in the same time that a 44 Magnum user can only get off three into a larger mark at the same range. Used with cast alloy bullets in a hot country, with or without gaschecks, they lead the barrel – particularly the 357 – which raises pressures and

Licences—South Australia

Gun licences may be obtained by those over 15 years from the Department of Fisheries and Fauna Conservation, or from a police station. The annual fee is Australian $4, or $2 for licences issued after 30 June. In order to obtain a gun licence aliens and those under 18 must first obtain a firearms licence from a police station (fee : 50c). A gun licence is compulsory for all, except landowners and occupiers, or their employees, on their own land.

destroys accuracy. Where they are very useful is when they are handloaded to slightly over standard non-magnum velocities. CWTC

South Australia
South Australia lies in the centre of the southern half of Australia, covering over 380,000 square miles. The terrain is predominantly flat, and about two thirds, in the north and west, is desert or near desert. The four most important physical features are the Spencer Gulf and St Vincent Gulf, the Lofty-Flinder Ranges, and the Murray River. The first three effectively cut off the south-east corner of the state, which is much the most fertile area, and through which the Murray flows. In the western half of the state there is also a series of low ranges, running more or less on an east-west axis. The Warburtons and the Musgraves are the most important of these. The climate is generally temperate in the south-east, warm to hot in the south-west and extremely hot in the north in the summer. Rainfall is low everywhere. Adelaide averages 21 in per year, which is rather higher than the aver-

age for all agricultural areas. The large lakes, such as Lake Eyre in the centre, are really only salt pans, under water only after exceptional rains in their catchment areas to the north and east.

The economy remains basically agrarian, with very few of the holdings devoted to crops or permanently improved pastures. Nevertheless, the state is particularly famous for its citrus fruits and wine, most of which come from the irrigated areas on the Murray. Naturally, however, the climate and terrain are both too limited to permit a great diversity of wild life, and sporting possibilities are to that extent limited.

The landowner's prior approval must be obtained before shooting over private land.

Reserves

There are four types:

Fauna Sanctuaries, which may be over Crown, lease or private land. They are areas primarily dedicated to other purposes than fauna conservation (such as agriculture), but in which shooting is totally prohibited.

Fauna Reserves, which may be over Crown, lease or private land. They are areas perpetually reserved in their natural state for fauna and flora, in which shooting is totally prohibited. Restrictions are placed on further clearance and the purpose for which the land is used.

Game Reserves, which are managed by the Department of Fisheries and Fauna Conservation usually in conjunction with the South Australian Field and Game Association. In these areas attempts are made to improve the yield of game species (usually ducks) while conserving the species native to the area. Shooting is occasionally permitted in Game Reserves for restricted periods during the open season.

Prohibited Areas, which are land and waters (usually breeding areas) where animal and bird life are left completely undisturbed. No one may enter a prohibited area without the appropriate written authority.

Authorized persons may destroy vermin, straying dogs and cats on the above areas. Lighting fires is illegal except in Fauna Sanctuaries. Maps of all restricted areas may be obtained from any office of the Department of Fisheries and Fauna Conservation, and most are posted.

Special Regulations

No gun larger than a 10-bore is permitted.

No hunting is permitted on Sundays.

It is illegal to shoot an animal or bird from a boat moving at over 5 mph. Rifled firearms may not be used at all from vessels on the River Murray.

Duck traps are illegal, as is poison except with permission from the Minister of Fisheries and Fauna.

All Inspectors of Fisheries and Fauna are empowered to enforce the Fauna Conservation Act, as are all members of the Police Force.

Seasons and Limits—South Australia		
Species	**Season**	**Limit**
Duck : wood duck (maned goose), black duck (grey duck), mountain duck (chestnut-breasted shelduck) grey teal, blue-winged shoveller, pink-eared duck, white-eyed duck (hardhead) chestnut teal	20 Feb-26 June	12 per day
Stubble quail	3 April-31 July	25 per day
Kangaroo Island wallaby (Kangaroo Island only)	All year	
Unprotected species	Any time	

Protected and Unprotected Species—South Australia

Unprotected

All introduced species
Australian crow
Australian raven
Budgerigar
Galah
Gray-backed silvereye
Little black cormorant
Little corella
Little crow
Magpie (if attacking any person)
Pied cormorant
Red wattlebird
Wedge-tailed eagle (North of 34.40 S lat)
White-breasted (black-faced) cormorant
Wild dog (dingo)
Zebra finch

Protected

All native Australian species
Blue-billed duck
Freckled duck (monkey duck)
Musk duck

Certain protected species, in particular, kangaroos, possums and emus, may cause damage to crops and property, in which case application can be made to the Department of Fisheries and Fauna conservation to destroy a stated number.

Further Information

There are Inspectors of Fisheries and Fauna throughout the state. The head office is:

The Department of Fisheries and Fauna Conservation, 3rd Floor, Agriculture Building, 133 Gawler Place, Adelaide.

The South Australian Field and Game Association is divided into four regions situated at Adelaide (Central region), Renmark (Riverland region), Goolwa (Southern region), and Mt. Gambier (South-Eastern region).

South Carolina (U.S.A.)

A south-eastern state, of about 31,000 square miles. The coastal strip is marshy, but, inland, the country rises in a series of ridges and valleys to the Piedmont Plateau. South Carolina is, primarily, an agricultural state whose main crops are corn, cotton, tobacco, peanuts and rice. Forestry is also an important industry.

The chief difficulty facing the non-resident hunter is the small amount of hunting ground open to the public. Most of the best deer and turkey hunting is on privately owned land and land controlled by clubs, though some managed hunting is offered on game management areas maintained by the Wildlife Resources Department. Doves are plentiful, as are duck, especially in the coastal districts, where there are 300,000 acres of unposted marshes, and rail may also be shot.

Special Regulations

No .22 rifles and rimfire cartridges are allowed in management areas. Otherwise there are no restrictions on firearms and cartridges other than those laid down by Federal law for migratory birds. Night hunting is not allowed, except for raccoon and opossum, and these may not be hunted by artificial light.

Further Information

Wild Resources Department, Box 167, Columbia, South Carolina.

Licence Fees—South Carolina

Type	Status	Fee
General	Resident	$6.25
	Non-resident	$22.25
3-day hunt		$11.25

Big Game Inventory—South Carolina

Species	Shot	Est. pop.
White-tailed deer	40,000	250,000
Black bear	13	70
Wild turkey	3,000	20,000

Seasons and Limits—South Carolina

There are eight zones. Seasons and limits vary from one to the other.

Species	Season	Limit
Deer	15 Aug-1 Jan	1 to 5 depending on zone
Black bear	15 Nov-1 Dec	One per season
Cottontail rabbit	26 Nov-15 Feb	
Squirrel, grey and fox	15 Sept-15 Feb	10 per day
Ruffed grouse	26 Nov-1 Jan	
Bobwhite quail	26 Nov-1 March	10 per day
Wild turkey	26 Nov-1 March	
	Spring season not yet set	2 gobblers per day, 5 per season

South Dakota (U.S.A.)

A midwestern state, it is 77,000 square miles in area. Much of it forms part of the Great Plains, and there is a considerable amount of treeless, semi-arid prairie. The state is crossed by the Missouri River, and is drained by many of its tributaries. Large irrigation works have been carried out, and the land in the Missouri and James River valleys is extremely fertile. The main crop, however, is still spring wheat grown on a dry farming system. In the south-west of the state lie the Black Hills and the Bad Lands.

South Dakota probably has more pheasants than any other state in the Union, and the annual kill is nearly a million birds. Pheasants are best in the east of the state,

Big Game Inventory—South Dakota

Species	Shot	Est. pop.
White-tailed deer	19,000	130,000
Mule deer	11,925	85,000
Elk	280	2,000
Wild turkey	1,000	7,000
Pronghorn antelope	3,150	18,000

but grouse – ruffed, sharp-tailed and pinnated – are better in the west and southwest. Hungarian partridge are few, but Merriam's turkey is found in the Black Hills. Deer, both mule and white-tail, are plentiful in the east of the state, and some counties schedule 'any deer' seasons to keep numbers down. Waterfowl hunting is good, but is for residents only.

Further Information
Department of Game, Fish and Parks, State Office Building, Pierre, South Dakota 57501.

South-east Asia
On the whole there is very little legal hunting in south-east Asia (though there appears to be much indiscriminate poaching). Burma is the chief exception. Basically the country runs along the Irrawaddy river, with some fairly extensive areas of flat country towards the south. The river is flanked by mountain ranges on the north, east and west, and those on the east are backed by broken-up hill country. Almost the whole area consists of tropical jungle, except where the mountains rise out of it, and there is also a pocket of savannah country just north of the confluence of the Chindwin and Irrawaddy rivers. The rest of south-east Asia presents a similar picture: plains and broken-up hills covered with jungle, except for the odd patches of savannah on some of the plains. Rubber, rice and timber are the main products throughout the area.

In Burma the hunting scene is very similar to that of eastern India, and for most purposes the fauna can be regarded as being the same as that of Assam, though rather less affected, in many areas, by the depredations of man. Elsewhere in south east Asia the fauna approximates to that of Malaysia.

Further Information
Prospective hunters should initially contact the nearest embassy.

Spain
Spain is a country of south-west Europe (total area including the Balearics and the Canaries: about 195,000 square miles), occupying most of the Iberian peninsula. Most of the country consists of the meseta, a rocky plateau sloping slightly to the southwest, crossed by several mountain ranges. To the south it is bounded by the Sierra Nevada, and to the north by the Pyrenees and the Cantabrian Mountains. The main rivers are the Guadiana, Guadalquivir, Tagus, Douro, Minho, and Ebro. The interior has extremes of temperature in summer and winter, and most of the plateau is very dry. The north-west has an equable climate with plenty of rain and the provinces of the extreme south are semi-arid.

Two thirds of the population depend on agriculture, with citrus fruits particularly important, but also wheat, barley, potatoes

Seasons and Limits—South Dakota

Species	Area	Season	Limit	Comment
Deer	Black Hills West River East River	1 Nov-30 Nov 14 Nov-22 Nov 28 Nov-6 Dec	In 'any deer' counties— one either sex ; otherwise one buck	
Antelope	West River East River	3 Oct-11 Oct 24 Oct-26 Oct		Residents only
Mountain goat		10 Oct-31 Oct		Residents only
Rabbit, jack and cottontail		All year		
Squirrel		All year		
Ring-necked pheasant		Starts about 15 Oct, lasts 4-6 weeks	3 cocks per day	
Sharp-tailed grouse		19 Sept-1 Nov	3 per day	
Prairie chicken (pinnated grouse)		19 Sept-1 Nov	3 per day	
Sage grouse		29 Aug-4 Sept	3 per day	
Bobwhite quail		8 Nov-last week in Nov		
Hungarian partridge	West River East River	Starts 19 Sept. Starts 17 Oct	3 per day	
Wild turkey	Black Hills	12 Oct-30 Nov		

Licence Fees—South Dakota

Type	Status	Fee	Comment
General	Resident Non-resident	$1.00 $1.00	Sold by the Office of the Game and Fish Commission, and by county treasurers and their agents
Deer, antelope and mountain goat	Resident	$8.50	
Deer	Non-resident	$35.00	
Upland birds	Resident	$3.00	
Small game (including upland birds)	Non-resident	$25.00	
Turkey	Resident Non-resident	$2.00 $5.00	
Rabbit and squirrel	Either	$2.00	

Seasons—Spain

The following may be shot throughout Spain and in private reserves where available.

Species	Season
Red deer (stag) Fallow deer (buck) Wild boar	12 Oct-3rd Sunday in Feb
Bear Wild goat Chamois Roe deer	2nd Sunday in Sept-1 Nov
Waterfowl	1st Sunday in Oct-1st Sunday in March except in La Albufera, Valencia which starts 1st Sunday in Sept

Other small game :
  Hare
  Rabbit
  Partridge
  Pheasant
	1st Sunday in Oct-3rd Sunday in Jan

and sugar beet. Very little of the country is urbanized or at all heavily populated. Sporting potentialities are consequently good, with state game reserves and innumerable private organizations for preserving game and providing shooting.

National Game Reserves
Seasons in National Game Reserves are not the same as those elsewhere, but usually correspond roughly. The most important differences are that there are additional spring seasons for wild goat, and additional summer seasons for roe deer and wild boar, as well as a capercailzie season from 17 April to 5 June.

Shooting fees in the National Game Reserves vary considerably with the different quarries and the different reserves. There is usually a permit fee and a charge per head shot. Wild goat is the most expensive, at 20,000 pesetas a head, and red deer stag, fallow buck and bear are usually 10,000 pesetas, on top of the permit fee. At the other end of the scale the only charge for waterfowl and capercailzie is the permit fee of 2,500 pesetas.

Further Information
The relevant addresses for the National Game Reserves are as follows:

National Game Reserves—Spain	
Reserve	Principal Game
Somiedo	Bear, boar, roe, chamois and capercailzie
Degaña	Bear, boar and roe
Saja	Red deer stag, boar and capercailzie
Cazorla	Red deer stag, fallow buck, wild goat and boar
Gredos	Wild goat (Spanish Ibex)
Ronda	Wild goat
Picos de Europa	Chamois
Reres	Boar, roe, chamois and capercailzie
La Encanizada	Waterfowl

For the shoots at Reres, Somiedo and Degaña:

Special Delegation in Oviedo, 19 de Julio, 10, Oviedo.

For the shoot at Saja:

Special Delegation in Santander, Pasaje de Arcillero 2, Santander.

For the shoot at Cazorla:

State Forestry Commission, Mayor 83, Madrid.

For the shoots at Gredos, Ronda and Picos de Europa:

Undersecretariat for Tourism, Avda del Generalissimo 39, Madrid.

Also useful may be:

Game Shooting Federation, Plaza de Santa Domingo, 16, Madrid-13.

National Shooting Federation of Spain, Calle Barquillo 19, Madrid-4.

National Game Shooting and River Fishing Service, Goya 25, Madrid.

Spotted Cavy *see* Paca

Springbok (*Antidorcas marsupialis*)
This antelope, whose name can be spelled springbuck, is the national emblem of South Africa and was once very common there. They are protected in many areas. They stand about 30 in at the shoulder, weigh about 70 lb and have a sandy-coloured back and white belly separated by a black flank band similar to that of the Thomson's gazelle. Both sexes have lyrate horns about 12 in long. They are distinguished by an evertible pouch lined with long erectile white hairs lying along the rump. When alarmed this stands erect like a white flag and is particularly conspicuous as the springbok flee from danger in a series of immense bounds from 8 to 10 ft high and as much as 20 ft in length. They are very fast – 60 mph has been recorded. Still found in groups of up to 100, they are grazers and generally inhabit open grassland or arid plains. They do not require

water for long periods, and are often seen in the company of eland, gnu or oryx for mutual protection, hence stalking them can be extremely difficult. One young is born annually late in the year.

Spruce Grouse
(*Canachites canadensis*)
The commonest and most typical grouse of this species is the Hudsonian spruce grouse (*C. canadensis canadensis*), but there are various other, largely localized, sub-species, including Franklin's grouse (*C. canadensis franklini*), Alaska spruce grouse (*C. canadensis osgoodi*), Canadian spruce grouse (*C. canadensis canace*), and Valdez spruce grouse (*C. canadensis atratus*). They are found in various forested parts of Canda and Alaska, though the Canadian spruce grouse is also sometimes found in the more northerly forests of the United States.

The spruce grouse is a rather smaller bird than the ruffed grouse and shows neither ruff nor crest. Its plumage is somewhat darker than that of other grouse, and it possesses a metallic sheen. The male is black and gray above and splotched black and white below, and carries, in the spring, a small red comb. The hen is reddish-brown barred with black; both sexes have square tails barred with red, and feet completely covered with feathers.

Courtship displays are generally performed either on a tree or in the air, and include flying and plumage displays and wing fluttering to produce a drumming noise. Nesting is on the ground, and the clutch of 10 to 12 eggs takes about 24 days to incubate. In the summer spruce grouse feed on berries, insects and green foods. In

In Spain the capercailzie is found in the northern mountains – the Pyrenees and the Picos de Europa.

Licences—Spain

Foreigners need a special 2-month provisional shooting licence. It is issued, after customs' clearance, by the Border Chief of Police for a fee of 425 pesetas. Applicants must show their home shooting licence, stamped within the previous 30 days by the Spanish Consulate or Embassy in the hunter's home country. If shooting licences are not required in their home country the hunter must have reliable references, also stamped. Hunters coming from countries without reciprocal agreements with Spain must have been invited by Spanish associations or individuals. The hosts must send a duplicate of the invitation to the Direccion General de Segurigad, at least 15 days before their guest's arrival, for whom they must take full responsibility. In other cases visitors with valid passports will be allowed into Spain with hunting firearms (not pistols), but they must appear, within 72 hours, before the authority of the town in which they are staying, with two reliable guarantors.

winter, however, their diet consists, almost solely of spruce and fir buds, and at this time of the year the bird's flesh becomes unpalatable. They live, as their name suggests, in spruce forests and tamarack swamps, and in winter they retire to the densest part of the forest for cover.

The spruce grouse is one more grouse that has been given the popular name of 'fool hen' largely because, until it has been heavily hunted, it shows no fear of man – a trait that has led to its disappearance from all settled areas. It will, unless it has already been shot over frequently, sit in a tree and look at an approaching hunter with nothing more than curiosity. Indeed, if a flying shot is wanted, a clod will have to be thrown at it to make it take wing.

Squirrels *see* Gray Squirrel; Red Squirrel

Stalking *see* Red and Fallow Deer Stalking; Roe Deer and their Stalking

Steinbuck *(Raphicorus campestris)*
The steinbuck and grysbok *(Raphicorus melanotis)* are the best known examples of a group of small antelopes found in many parts of central and southern Africa. Sharpe's grysbok, *Raphicorus sharpei*, is also found in some areas but differs little in the essentials. They all stand about 34 in, with short horns about 4 in long and $1\frac{1}{2}$ in girth and with up to a 2-in spread at the tips. They have a small gland pit in the skull. Found generally in light woodland, thick grass and scrub, or sometimes on the plains, they are solitary and both grazers and browsers. They are believed to give birth to one young annually, but twins are also known to occur. There is much confusion between the two species due to the indiscriminate use of the name steinbok.

Stone Sheep *see* Mountain Sheep

Stubble Quail *see* Australia

Surinam
For a description of the territory *see* Guyana, and for game *see* South America, Shooting in.

Further Information
Consult initially the nearest Dutch consulate.

Swamp Deer *see* South America, Shooting in

Sweden
Sharing the Scandinavian peninsula with Norway, and with an area of 173,436 square miles, Sweden is well provided with mountainous terrain, rising to over 6,000 ft. However, the south of the country stretches down level with Denmark, and forms a flattish, fertile area, known as the Skane.

The arctic fox has a circumpolar distribution; Sweden is one of the few countries where it may be hunted.

The far north is completely treeless, but further south there are extensive birch woods, while much of the centre of the country is covered by dense coniferous forest. The whole country is moreover interspersed with lakes and rivers, larger in the south, but more numerous in the north and middle of the peninsula, where they are entirely an east-flowing water-shed. The climate consists of sun in the summer, much rain in the autumn, and snow in the north from October.

Farming is of declining importance as Sweden is one of the leading industrial nations of Europe, because of its abundant raw materials: waterpower, timber (the forests cover over half the country), and minerals. However, the wildness and inaccessibility of much of the terrain provides plenty of hunting north of the Skane. The Skane itself, though providing good farming land, is heavily populated, and contains all the major cities, so that there are already too many sportsmen for the available game in the area.

The hare is the most widely distributed species, being found all over the country. However, the extreme north is the only area in which squirrel, fox, polecat, weasel, ferret, otter, wildfowl (excluding geese), goshawk, blackgame, capercailzie, and hazel grouse are not found, and the northern boundaries of marten, roe deer, woodcock and woodpigeon are only slightly more limited. Moose is almost equally widespread, being found everywhere except in the more mountainous regions. Certain other species have obvious territorial limitations: seal and lesser black-backed gull are found only on the coasts, willow grouse and ptarmigan

Seasons—Sweden			
Species	**Area**	**Season**	**Approx. Annual Bag**
Moose (elk)	North South	Starts 1st Monday in Sept Starts 2nd Monday in Sept. Lasts 2-6 days, except for hunters with special licence, when it lasts one month	35,000
Fallow deer antlered bucks		Oct-Dec Late Aug and Sept	1,100
Roe deer antlered bucks	North and south Centre certain areas	Oct-Nov Oct-Dec All year	48,000
Bear	Varies with area	About Sept and Oct (Female with cubs protected)	20
Lynx	North South	Dec-Feb Jan	40
Fox	North South	July-mid-April July-March	68,000
Squirrel	North South	Dec-Jan Sept-Feb	7,500
Blackgame cock only	North South Everywhere	Mid-Aug-Oct early Sept early Dec	11,000
Capercailzie cock only	North South Everywhere	Mid-Aug-Oct early Sept early Dec	14,000
Hazel grouse	North	Mid-Aug-Oct	12,000
Willow grouse and ptarmigan		Sept or late Aug-Feb	63,000
Lesser blackbacked gull	South	Mid-Aug-April	
Goshawk	North South	Sept-Nov Dec-Feb	2,000
Partridge		Mid-Sept-mid-Oct	
Pheasant		Mid-Oct-Dec (most areas cocks only)	58,000
Raven	Centre South	Sept-Feb protected	
Rook	Extreme south	All year	
Woodcock		Late Aug-Dec	2,000
Woodpigeon	Most areas Extreme south	Aug-Dec Aug-mid-April	73,000
Dabbling and diving duck, coot and snipe		Late Aug-mid-Nov	103,000
Mallard		Late Aug-mid-Nov	78,000
Bean goose	South North	Early Nov Early Sept	1,500
Canada goose		Mid-Sept-mid-Oct	500
Graylag goose		Aug-mid-Sept	500
White-fronted goose		Early Nov	500

in the more northerly mountains, and white-fronted, Canada and graylag geese, rook, fallow deer, badger, pheasant and partridge only in the south or parts of the south (partridge particularly in the coastal areas). Of the remaining species, bear is limited to four provinces, lynx to the inland areas of the north and centre, and bean goose in the extreme north and the extreme south, in contrast to the raven, which is found everywhere except in those two areas.

Shooting rights belong to the landowner, so visitors may only hunt by agreement with the landowner or the owner of the shoot.

Seasons

There is considerable variety of game, but seasons tend to vary from year to year and from province to province. Consequently, the dates and areas given in the table are only approximate and should be checked in advance by prospective visitors. Where not stated bag figures are unavailable.

Licences

All hunters must have a hunting licence, available from any post office for a fee of Swedish Kroner 22. Third party insurance is also strongly recommended. The easiest way to take this out is to join the county hunting association of the proposed hunting area, and pay its fees for the year.

Applications for permits to import firearms and ammunition should be made to the county council covering the proposed point of entry. However, for practical reasons the Swedish host may obtain, sign, and deliver the permit to the customs post in question.

Special Regulations

All bows are illegal. Shotguns and semi-automatic and pump-action rifles must be sealed against loading with more than two rounds. Fully-cased bullets may not be used for any big game; and for moose, all deer (except roe), and bear, a rifle must be used capable of firing a 154-grain bullet with a striking energy of 1,447 foot pounds at a distance of 100 metres (109 yards). A hunter must have a firearms licence in order to hire, borrow, or purchase such a rifle. To qualify for the licence he must pass the Swedish Sportsmens' Association Test, which involves shooting at a moose target, standing (four shots) and running (eight shots), at a range of 80 metres (87 yards). In any case all moose hunters are recommended to take this test, and in certain regions it is obligatory.

Further Information

The following regional tourist organizations supply information on hunting. The first five in the list can also arrange hunting tours or put hunters in touch with agencies that do. Hunting tours are also arranged by Pál Máriássy, Grevgatan 28, 114 53 Stockholm.

Dalslands Turisttrafikforbund, Box 89, 662 00 Amal.

Harjedalens Turistforening, Box 200, 820 95 Funasdalen.

Jamtlands Turistforening, Hamngaten 18, Box 74, 831 01 Ostersund.

Vasterbottens Turisttrafikforbund, Lansmansgaten 5–7, Box 5053, 900 05 Umea 5.

Vasternorrlands Turisttrafikforbund, Storgatan 1, Box 91, 871 01, Harnosand 1.

Gotlands Turistforening, Skeppsbron 20, Box 81, 621 01 Visby 1.

Varmslands Turisttrafikforbund, Kunsgatan 4B, 652 24 Karlstad.

Sweden, Hunting in

Sweden is best known for its large moose population. The annual harvest is about 35,000 and the population is still increasing. There is an open season for between 2 to 6 days, during which anyone who has the shooting rights on his land, however small that area may be, may bag as many moose of any sex or age as he can. The so-called licence season is usually a month, starting on the same day as the short season, but once a licence is taken out for 1, 2, 3 or more moose the hunter is limited to that number. Fortunately this latter method has now become prevalent, as the all-open season, although so short, resulted in degeneration of the moose, shown by a lower weight per animal and a much lower trophy standard. Of course, the small farmers strongly opposed the abolition of the all-open season arguing that moose hunting on licence would turn into a sport for the rich. As the State and some very large lumber companies own a lot of forest area this was an understandable fear, but the lumber companies now allow their workers and personnel to do most of the moose hunting and anybody can lease a smaller block from the State.

The shooting rights belong to the landowner, but unlike Norway and Denmark, Sweden, like Finland, has large forest and fjell areas belonging to the State. Red and fallow deer play a minor part in Sweden's sporting picture. They are mostly found in the south and often in preserves, but roe deer is one of the most popular game animals. They are mostly shot with shotguns during drives by harriers or braques, stovare and drever dogs. In recent years the hunting journals have started a campaign to convince hunters that roedeer should be considered big game and shot only by stalking with a rifle, and in the south, where Danish and German influence has always been strongest, this new trend has had some success.

The Swedes are extremely keen on hare shooting with a driving dog, using both drever and stovare, and are satisfied with a single hare or nothing at all in the bag provided they can hear the hounds giving tongue and enjoy being out in the open all day. From Stockholm northwards it is mostly the blue or mountain hare and in the south chiefly the common hare, with the two

A herd of reindeer in Swedish Lapland

species overlapping, but seldom cross-breeding.

Predators are more or less protected; bear may be shot in two provinces in the north in September and October, but not more than about 20 are bagged each year; lynx are quite abundant, however, and the open season for them is from December to January, even as late as February or March in some parts of the country.

The typical moose area consists of large forests with plenty of moors, bogs and water in them, whereas in the south, where there is more farming, hares, rabbits, pheasants and some partridges are found. Willow grouse and ptarmigan are shot over pointing dogs almost in the same manner as in Norway and Finland, but driven pheasant shooting with beaters has lately become fashionable. Many estates, or tenants of shooting rights on larger areas, have started to establish their own pheasant shoots including rearing, gamekeepers, etc. The largest daily bags equal those in Denmark.

Woodcock is only shot in the fall now, as are upland game birds. The most popular method is still shooting them, with barking dogs as in Finland and parts of Norway, but also in the winter on skis, with .22 rifles and telescopic sights when the capercailzie and blackgame perch on solitary trees. This is a very exciting sport, but it is difficult as the birds are very wary.

Wildfowling is regarded as of minor importance. The discriminating Swedes go to Aland (a group of islands between Sweden and Finland) in the spring. Seal are shot on the coast and foxes both at the earth and by driving with braques. This is quite popular and in many parts a large-scale fox hunt is staged in late February, when about twenty

hunters gather from a game conservation area to cull part of the fox population which they have been unable to tackle with their dachshunds during the year. Such hunts generally yield around 10 to 12 foxes.

It was once a popular sport to shoot crows and other predators over a live eagle owl. However, it is now illegal to use a live decoy, and stuffed or imitation owls are used, but the old enthusiasm for this type of shooting has disappeared. The Swedes are finding their hunting grounds overcrowded and shooting is becoming harder to find and more expensive. Nevertheless, foreigners when they visit Sweden for hunting are assured of a welcome and of good sport. PM

Switzerland

Switzerland, the most mountainous country of Europe, has an area of just under 16,000 square miles. The Alps, ranging from 5,000 ft to over 15,000 ft, occupy the southern and eastern borders and most of the interior, and the Jura mountains rise in the north-west. The Rhine, its tributary the Aar, the

Rhône and the Ticino are the chief rivers. There are numerous large and beautiful lakes. The climate, owing to the nature of the terrain, is distinctly variable.

Lakes, rivers, mountain forests and pastures take up three-quarters of the country. The rest is given over to fairly intensive agriculture, with cereals, tobacco, potatoes and vines. Stock raising and dairying are very important. Though there are few industrial raw materials there is a high degree of industrialization, and tourism, banking and insurance have vital parts in the economy.

The country is not famed for its hunting, but is, of course, rich in Alpine and mountain species, such as chamois.

Further Information

Verband Schweizer Jagdschützengesellschaften, Effingerstrasse 25, 3000 Bern.

Schweizer Bund für Naturschütz, Wartenbergstrasse 22, 4000 Basel.

Syria *see* Middle East

The chamois is protected in Switzerland but may be hunted in the Austrian, French and Italian Alps.

The black swan of Australia is shot in Tasmania, where it is partly protected, and the annual bag is about 4,000.

T

Tahr *see* Himalayan Thar; Nilgiri Thar

Tanzania

The United Republic of Tanzania, in east Africa, has an area of nearly 364,000 square miles. The Central African Plateau occupies the greater part of the country, leaving only a narrow coastal belt, and, of course, the islands of the Zanzibar group. In the southwest the land rises to over 9,000 ft in the Livingstone mountains, and in the north lies Mt Kilimanjaro, at over 19,000 ft the highest mountain in Africa. Parts of two major lakes, Victoria and Tanganyika, are included in the country. Numerous rivers run into the lakes and the Indian Ocean. The climate is equatorial, but in much of the country tempered by the altitude.

The chief commercial crops are sisal, cotton, coffee and oilseeds. There is a flourishing trade in hides and skins, a product of Tanzania's extensive and very varied wildlife. The line between the 'northern' species such as oryx, gerenuk, the gazelles, etc, and the 'southern' species: puku, sable antelope, southern reedbuck, etc, runs through the country and consequently Tanzania offers the widest variety of trophy animals obtainable in Africa.

For each animal which can be shot (see table), there is a maximum number that may be taken by any one hunter (in the Selous reserve and Kilombero area the quota is different from the rest of Tanzania). Hunters may only shoot those animals listed on the permit for the area in which they are shooting. Additional permits may be obtained but the total number of animals shot of any one species must not exceed the permitted maximum. Wounded animals count as shot and must be paid for.

There are three types of hunting area:

1. *Game Reserves*, of which there are only one or two, are closed to all except those who have arranged hunting within them. The Selous is the largest and most important. Bookings can only be confirmed in this reserve for a non-refundable deposit of 4,000 Tanzanian shillings on trophies shot, the balance being payable at the end of the safari. There is also a permit fee of Shs 400.

2. *Controlled Areas* are much more numerous, there being 34 altogether. Only the Shs 400 permit fee is required in advance to confirm bookings. For those wishing to hunt lion or rhinoceros there is an additional fee of Shs 200.

3. *Open Areas* where anyone with a valid licence (including a reserve or controlled area permit) may hunt, and there is no charge for animals shot. Certain animals, for which hunters have to pay in reserves or controlled areas, are classed as vermin in open areas. They are bushpig, hyena, velvet monkey, porcupine and wild dog.

All hunting trips must be organized through Tanzania Wildlife Safaris Ltd. There is a choice of three basic areas for a safari: western Tanzania, northern Tanzania, and the Selous or Kilombero area in the south. The season in northern Tanzania lasts from June to March, but in the other areas is July to December. Safaris in northern and western Tanzania are very often combined, and within those areas can be found every animal listed above except puku, southern reedbuck, Sharpe's grysbok, and Nyasa wildebeeste, all of which are confined to the Selous reserve.

Safaris normally last for between 15 and 45 days (minimum of 28 days for those wishing to hunt lion or rhinoceros), and there is a scale of charges varying from U.S. $2,890 for one hunter accompanied by one professional hunter for 15 days, to U.S. $18,900 for four hunters accompanied by two professional hunters for 45 days. One professional hunter may not accompany more than two clients on any one safari. Additional non-shooting clients, where no extra transport is required, are charged U.S. $30 per day.

Charges include the services of professional hunters and their staff, tented accommodation and requirements, food, medicine, transport and skinning and preservation of trophies in the field. They do not include any licence or permit fees, alcohol, cigarettes, tips, air travel, hotel charges before and after the safari, hire of firearms, ammunition, and transportation of trophies.

A deposit of 30% of the contracted cost of the safari is required on confirmation, balance to be paid before commencement. In the event of cancellation the deposit will be refunded, less 15%, unless cancellation is within six months of the proposed starting date, in which case the deposit will only be refunded if another engagement can be found.

Special Regulations

Young animals and females with young must not be hunted. If a dangerous animal (lion, leopard, elephant, buffalo, hippo or rhino) is wounded it must be reported to the Game Division immediately. As soon as an animal is shot the requisite entries on the hunting permits must be completed before the carcass is moved.

The European scaup is a maritime duck, breeding in northern Europe and Asia, closely linked to the Pacific scaup, which is smaller and breeds in North America.

Licence Fees—Tanzania	
Species	**Fee**
	(Tanzanian shillings)
Baboon	30
Buffalo	400
Bushbuck	200
Bushpig	60
Caracal	200
Crocodile	400
Dikdik	60
Duiker, Abbot's	100
Duiker, blue and red	80
Duiker, common	80
Eland	600
Elephant, with biggest tusk under 60lb	2,000
Elephant, with biggest tusk over 60lb	5,000
Gazelle, Grant's	100
Gazelle, Thompson's	80
Gerenuk	300
Giant forest hog	300
Hare	10
Hartebeeste, Coke's	100
Hartebeeste, Lichtenstein's	100
Hippopotamus	400
Hyena	60
Impala	100
Jennet	60
Klipspringer	80
Kudu, greater and lesser	800
Leopard	2,000
Male lion	2,000
Monkey, vervet and Syke's	60
Oryx	900
Ostrich	500
Oribi	60
Otter	100
Pygmy antelope	60
Porcupine	60
Puku	200
Reedbuck, bohor, mountain and southern	100
Rhinoceros	8,000
Roan antelope	900
Rock rabbit	20
Sable antelope	900
Serval	100
Sharpe's grysbok	50
Sitatunga	200
Steinbuck	60
Topi	150
Tree hyrax	30
Warthog	60
Waterbuck, common and defessa	300
Wildebeeste, Nyasa	150
Wildebeeste, white-bearded	100
Wild dog	200
Zebra	400

Shooting is prohibited in National Parks. No camping or baiting is permitted within a two-mile radius of an air strip, and no animal carcass may be left in this area. All baits in any area must be removed before the hunting party leaves that area.

Hunting by night, with the aid of an artificial light, or from a mechanically propelled vehicle is prohibited, as is hunting within 500 yd of surface water or a salt lick.

Firearms will only be cleared by the police if they have an approval from the Game Division. For dangerous game the minimum permitted calibre is .375 magnum, firing a bullet of not less than 270 grains with a muzzle velocity of at least 3,850 foot-pounds.

Further Information

Tanzania Wildlife Safaris Ltd, P.O. Box 602, Arusha.

There is a branch office at:

P.O. Box 9270, Dar-es-Salaam.

The Chief Game Officer, Publicity Section, Ministry of Natural Resources and Tourism, P.O. Box 1994, Dar-es-Salaam.

Tapir *see* South America, Shooting in

Tasmania (Australia)

Tasmania is an island to the south of the Australian mainland and separated from it by the Bass Strait, which is about 140 miles wide. It covers 26,383 square miles, including the Furneaux Group of Islands, and King Island, both of which are in the Bass Strait. It has a cooler, more temperate climate, and suffers less from hot winds than the mainland. The east is fairly dry, but the west has an overall rainfall varying between 20 and 140 in. The terrain is generally hilly and timbered, with mountains rising to over 5,000 ft. Cattle, and sheep especially, are common; there is extensive fruit growing, as well as grain and root crops.

All small-game shooting is by walking up or over dogs.

Special Regulations

The laws regarding where one may shoot are the same as in other Australian states. A shotgun or rifle may be used to take game during the open season, but bows of any sort, spears or other projectiles are completely prohibited.

Further Information

Tasmanian Field and Game Association, P.O. Box 772, Launceston.

Tasmanian Deerstalkers' Association, 39 Geppe Parade, Moonah.

The Animals and Birds Protection Board, 127 Bathurst Street, Hobart (all questions on Tasmanian wildlife).

Tasmanian Tourist and Immigration Department, Macquarie Street, Hobart (all questions of travel, accommodation, etc).

Licences—Tasmania
Game licences for any of the partly protected species may be obtained at police stations and sporting-goods stores.

Teal *(Anas* species)

A name given, somewhat loosely, to several species of surface-feeding ducks. Between them the species breed and winter in almost every country of the world. They seldom weigh more than 1 lb or measure over 15 in. Nevertheless, they are fast and enduring flyers, undertaking long migrations. They are principally vegetarians, and are generally found on inland waters. They possess the power to spring up vertically off the water into flight. The drakes are generally among the most colourful of ducks, and some of them whistle, though teal are, on the whole, silent. They make good eating and come readily to decoys, so that in many parts of the world they have suffered from over-hunting; the North American species have also suffered from the ploughing and draining of much of their breeding grounds.

Common Teal *(Anas crecca crecca)*

This is the Eurasian teal, breeding in northern Europe and Asia from Iceland to the Aleutians Islands. It has recently been proved that they also breed on the American mainland, and are not merely vagrants there. They winter in Africa as far south as Nigeria in the west and Kenya in the east, as well as in Persia, India, China and the Philippines. Inside Europe they are partial migrants, breeding and wintering in Germany, Holland, France and the British Isles.

The drake has a dark chestnut head with a green patch enclosing the eye, a back vermiculated gray and cream and a breast spotted brown and cream. The duck is speckled brown and buff with lighter cheeks and underparts. Both sexes have a bright green speculum. The drake's call is a low 'krrit', the female has a high quack. The average weight is around 1 lb, and the average length between 12 and 15 in.

Green-winged Teal *(A. crecca carolinensis)*

The American subspecies, which breeds in the prairie regions of the northern United States and central Canada, and winters as far south as Mexico.

Courtship consists largely of aquatic display and pursuit. The nest is a scrape in the ground, close to water, lined with grass and down, and the clutch of 10 to 12 eggs takes 21 to 23 days to incubate.

Garganey Teal *(Anas querquedula)*

This is a slightly larger duck than the common teal, weighing over 1 lb and measuring around 15 in. It has a more southerly breeding range which stretches across northern and central Europe,

Seasons and Limits—Tasmania

Species	Season	Limit	Est. annual bag	Licence Fee (Australian dollars)
Wild duck, includes: black duck, chestnut teal, mountain duck, musk duck, hard-head (white-eyed duck) blue-winged shoveller (rare) wood duck (maned goose), blue-billed duck (rare), pink-eared duck, plumed tree duck (grass whistling duck), freckled duck (infrequent)	6 March-31 May	12 per day	44,000	$2
Brown quail	1 May-31 May	24 per day	2,400	$1
Cock pheasant (King Island only)	5 June-15 June	3 per day, 15 per season	3,000	$3
Yellow wattle bird	17 July-1 Aug	15, 1st day of season; 12 per day, rest of season	6,000	$2
Fallow deer, male with branching antlers	27 Feb-28 March	One per day, 5 per season	1,000	$5
Wallaby	1 April-30 Nov Furneaux Islands: All year	Only Bennett's and Rufous No bag limit	45,000	Crown land licence $2
Water rat	1 May-31 May	No limit		Licence to take and sell—30c
Japanese snipe	3 Oct-31 Jan		800	
Black swan	Not decided		4,000	
Brush possum Mutton bird	May not be shot			
Unprotected species	Any time			

Unprotected Species—Tasmania

Cormorants (all)
Blackbird
Black rat
Brown goshawk
Brown hawk
Brown rat
Coot and bald coot (Eastern swamp-hen)
Crow (Raven)
Feral cat
Hare
House mouse
House sparrow
Indian mynah
Kookaburra
Little falcon
Native hen
Pacific gull (Nellie)
Peregrine falcon
Rabbit
Sparrow hawk
Starling
Swamp hawk (on King Island only)
Wombat (badger)

through Asia to Manchuria and Japan. It winters in the Mediterranean basin, Africa, India, the Philippines, Moluccas and New Guinea.

The drake has a brown head and breast with a broad, curved, white stripe stretching from eye to the nape. The flanks are vermiculated gray and the tail is brown. The blue-gray forewing is prominent in flight. The duck is mottled brown, but rather paler than the common teal. In the British Isles it breeds only in south-east England, generally on grassland, the duck making a nest of grass and down and laying a clutch of about ten eggs.

The Blue-winged Teal (*Anas discors*)
An American teal very similar to the garganey, but having, in the drake, a gray-brown head with a white crescent in front of the eye, while both sexes have powder-blue forewings. They breed on the Canadian prairies and the most northerly of the United States, and winter from Florida along the Gulf of Mexico and down through Central and South America.

Marbled Teal (*Anas angustirostris*)
A resident in the Mediterranean basin and

The Australian wood duck, or maned goose, is one of the waterfowl shot in Tasmania.

north Africa, the Near East, Persia and north-west India. Although a European duck it has never been seen in Britain. The marbled effect is produced by light and dark brown dappling. Seen at a distance both the drake and the duck look gray-brown with a dark smudge through the eye. The drake has a slight crest.

Hottentot Teal *(Anas punctata)*
Found over a range stretching from south Africa to Kenya and Nigeria, it has a dark brown head with whitish cheeks, and the breast is speckled with black. The speculum is green bordered with black and white.

Cinnamon Teal *(Anas cyanoptera)*
A duck found in the western parts of North America, it is uncommon east of the Rockies. Subspecies are found in various parts of South America. It is a partial migrant, with the breeding grounds overlapping the wintering grounds considerably. Migration is more a general movement southwards than a specific migration from one area to another. Breeding takes place from Canada to the Mexican border and wintering is principally in north-western Mexico. It closely resembles the blue-winged teal, but the drake, in full winter plumage, is a dark cinnamon red almost all over, except for the blue forewings. During the eclipse it becomes mottled buff and brown like the duck.

Tennessee (U.S.A.)

A south-eastern state of 42,000 square miles. The Mississippi River runs along its western boundary, and the Great Smoky Mountains along its eastern one. The climate is moderate and, although half the state is still forested, farming is the largest single industry, the principal crops being maize, corn, tobacco and cotton.

The deer herd has been successfully re-established in more than half the counties,

and deer are now hunted on all the states' 22 game management areas. There are bear in the eastern counties, and wild boar in the south, having crossed over from North Carolina. Managed boar hunts are held in the Tellico Wild Life Management Area. The main upland game consists of bobwhite quail, squirrels and rabbits, nearly 2,000,000 of each being killed every year. Wild turkey are found in several counties, chiefly in the Cherokee National Forest and in the Cumberland Mountains. There are ruffed grouse in the mountains of eastern Tennessee, and waterfowl are abundant along major waterways.

Special Regulations
Deer, bear and boar may be hunted only with centre-fire rifles of .24-calibre or larger, or with shotguns loaded with buckshot or larger. Turkeys must be hunted with shotguns loaded with 2-shot or larger. Red foxes are protected with a closed season and may be hunted only with dogs and not with firearms. Permission from the landowner is necessary to hunt on private land whether it is posted or not.

Big Game Inventory—Tennessee		
Species	Shot	Est. pop.
White-tailed deer	6,892	85,000
Wild boar	227	2,000
Black bear	50	450
Wild turkey	214	5,000

Further Information
Game and Fish Commission, 706 Church Street, Nashville, Tennessee 37203.

Tetraonids *see* Grouse

Texas (U.S.A.)

This state has an area of 267,000 square miles. The Rio Grande runs along much of its southern border, and it is watered by the Red, Brazos, Colorado and Pecos Rivers. There are swamps and deserts along much of the coast, with fertile lowlands behind. The country then lifts, through rolling prairies, to the Guadalupe Mountains and the Llano Estacado in the west. The climate varies from the temperate to the sub-tropical and, besides having a great deal of ranching in the more arid areas, it is one of the chief crop-producing states in the country, growing wheat, corn and rice, as well as cotton and fruit under irrigation.

The state has the largest white-tailed herd in the country and there are mule deer in the trans-Pecos district. Hunting, however, is made difficult by the thick brush in southern Texas, where deer are most numerous. There is not a great deal of public hunting land and trespass laws are strict, many ranch owners requiring to be paid for permission

Seasons and Limits—Tennessee		
Vary from area to area		
Species	Season	Limit
Deer	East: 12 Nov-10 Dec Mid-State: 21 Nov-6 Dec West: 21 Nov-6 Dec and 10 Dec-27 Dec	One antlered buck per year
Black bear	1 Oct-31 Oct	One per year
European boar	1 Oct-31 Oct	One per year
Cottontail rabbit	26 Nov-15 Feb	5 per day
Squirrel	29 Aug-18 Nov	
Ruffed grouse	2 Nov-28 Feb	3 per day
Bobwhite quail	26 Nov-15 Feb	8 per day
Wild turkey	One week at end of March, and one week at end of April	Gobblers only

Licence Fees—Tennessee		
Type	**Status**	**Fee**
General	Resident	$5.00
	Non-resident	$25.00
Deer tag	Either	$5.00
Turkey tag	Either	$5.00
Additional permits for management areas :		
Big game		$5.00
Small game		$6.00
Daily permit		$1.50

to hunt. Antelope and javelina are found in the trans-Pecos area and in the Panhandle, javelina being especially abundant along the Rio Grande. Elk are protected except in the north-east and trans-Pecos districts, and then they may be hunted only by special permit. Buffalo may be killed only with written permission from the Parks and Wildlife Commission. Turkeys have been fairly well re-established throughout the

A wild boar surrounded by dogs in Tennessee. This is not a wild razorback, but a descendent of the boars imported from the Hartz Mountains of Germany in 1912.

state, and are most abundant in South Texas. Quail are found everywhere – bobwhite in the better farming areas, and scaled and Mearn's quail in the more arid parts. There is an open season for pheasant in several areas, but chachalacas (Mexican pheasant) may be hunted only in the south-central district. Dove hunting (both white-winged and mourning) is especially popular, and there is excellent goose hunting in some of the coastal districts.

Special Regulations
Antlerless deer, antelope and elk may only be killed on private land after written permission from the owner has been obtained, and this must be on a special form supplied by the Parks and Wildlife Commission. The only limitations on rifles is that .22 rim-fire rifles may not be used on big-game, and no rifle may be used on game birds except turkey. Shotguns must be plugged to hold no more than three shells. A legal buck is, in most of the states, one with hardened antlers protruding through the skin, but in some counties three points on the antler are required.

Licence Fees—Texas

Type	Status	Fee
General	Resident	$3.15
	Non-resident	$25.00
3-day waterfowl (reciprocal*)		$10.00
Shooting resort hunting		$3.15

*Only issued to residents of other U.S. States which permit Texans, as non-residents, to shoot waterfowl on 3-day licences

Seasons and Limits—Texas

Texas is divided into nine game districts, each with its own game laws, seasons and bag limits.

Species	Area	Season	Limit
White-tailed deer		14 Nov-3 Jan	1 to 4 per season
Mule deer		28 Nov-13 Dec	
Antelope	Trans-Pecos, Permian Basin and Panhandle areas	3 Oct-11 Oct	Limited permits
Elk	Gaudalupe Mountains		Special permit only
Black bear		1 Nov-31 Dec	One per year
Aoudad (barbary sheep)	Palu Duro Canyon	14 Nov-20 Nov	Permit only
Javelina		1 Sept-31 Jan	2 per season
Rabbit, cottontail and jack		All year round	
Squirrel		1 March-31 July 1 Oct-15 Jan	10 per day
Pheasant	Mainly north-western Panhandle	12 Dec-20 Dec	
Bobwhite quail Scaled quail		1 Nov-31 Jan	12 per day
Gambel's quail Mearn's quail		Starts 11 Nov	12 per day
Prairie chicken (pinnated grouse)	Certain counties only	10 Oct-11 Oct	
Wild turkey		14 Nov-3 Jan and 24 April-2 May	2 gobblers per year

Big Game Inventory—Texas

Species	Shot	Est. pop.
White-tailed deer	267,475	2,850,000
Mule deer	13,000	170,000
Pronghorn antelope	1,168	15,500
Peccary	1,500	140,000
Bison	9	250
Elk	3	300
Black bear	3	55
Aoudad	33	650
Wild turkey	24,412	575,000

Further Information

Parks and Wildlife Department, John H. Reagan Building, Austin, Texas 78701.

Thar *see* Himalayan Thar; Nilgiri Thar

Thinhorn *see* Mountain Sheep

Thomson's Gazelle *(Gazella thomsoni)*
Found in East Africa in the plains, it is sandy-brown above and white below, with a black streak along the flanks and a conspicuous black tail; the latter is wagged vigorously when the animal is alarmed. They have short lyrate horns about 12 in to 13 in long and a streak of white from the base of each to the nose. They are usually found in small herds of females with one adult male or in groups of young males, often in the company of Grant's gazelle or impala. Mainly grazers they feed and drink invariably in the morning and late evening. One young is born annually, generally during the rainy season. They rely on their speed and eyesight for safety and are usually a sporting stalk. Their flesh is excellent eating, and 'Tommy' steaks are a staple of most safari-camp cuisine.

Tiang *see under* Tsesseby

Tiger *(Panthera tigris)*
Often called the Bengal tiger, it is found in various parts of India, but as the secondary name implies particularly in Bengal. The black-striped body markings on an orange-yellow background are well known, becoming less pronounced and more faded yellow with age. The face is also striped with a pronounced ruff on each side of the head. The whole effect merges perfectly with the light and shadow of the jungle. The mature males average about 9 ft from nose to tip of tail and weigh about 400 lb. The mature female averages from 8 ft to 8 ft 6 in and weighs up to 300 lb. The older a tiger becomes the more pronounced the ridge of bone across the skull, which in an aged beast may be as much as an inch high. The canine teeth, which in a young beast are hollow, become almost solid with age. One of the largest cats, they are exceeded in size by the Siberian tiger (now strictly protected in the U.S.S.R.), which measures up to 13 ft long.

Entirely carnivorous they are capable of killing large game such as sambar deer and bullocks, also at times, turning man-eater. Generally solitary, they are sometimes found in twos or threes. The female usually has a litter of from two to four cubs each year, most frequently in the spring. Due to indiscriminate over-shooting and trapping by villagers intent on protecting their cattle the numbers have been declining. However, licences to shoot tigers may occasionally be obtained if they are known to be man-eaters.

Hunting methods are almost all based on the fact that the tiger is by nature extremely territorial. When beaters and guns are available, suitable cover, where tigers are known to lie-up, may be beaten towards the waiting guns stationed at points of vantage in machans or tree platforms, overlooking a track junction or similar areas where the tiger is known to pass. The tiger, unless much-hunted or a particularly wary and cunning individual, does not generally look upwards for danger; its scenting powers are not outstanding, as its habit is to hunt by sight and sound, stalking prey in the manner of most felines. Baiting with young goats or similar live bait, tethered at a track junction the tiger is known to frequent, the hunter waiting above in a machan, is another commonly used method when beaters and other guns are unavailable. Tigers generally return to their kill if

The tiger has been over-shot by poachers and now is only hunted when it has turned man-eater.

it is not moved, so a third method is to build a machan, with a suitable field of fire, close to a recently made kill.

The tiger will not generally climb trees and a machan 14 ft above ground is usually safe enough, but even so the average hunter waiting for his first tiger, especially a known man-eater, is likely to feel a certain natural trepidation on his somewhat insecure platform. It is particularly important to avoid movement, not always easy in the long, often fruitless, and inevitably cramped waiting period. The usual time to enter the machan is about 4 p.m. As there may be an all-night wait it is important to be comfortable. Even if the tiger does not appear the life of the jungle – sand grouse and peacock coming down to drink should there be water close by, the call of chital or sambur, the bark of the muntjac – is a fascinating experience in itself.

Setting up a figure-4 fox trap, the rabbit will be used as bait; tunnel traps are seen behind.

A vintage animal trap

Topi *see under* Tsesseby

Traps and Trapping

The art of trapping is one of the earliest forms of hunting known to man. Evidence that pits were dug by Paleolithic man to trap large animals may be inferred from the remains in his caves, which included the bones of such beasts as the mammoth, the cave bear, and the woolly rhinoceros, fashioned into tools and weapons. From the Paleolithic Age onwards proof is more positive in the form of cave paintings depicting the use of traps to capture various animals.

The needs of early man were simple. His primary concerns were to protect himself from danger and to find sufficient to eat. Probably his first essays at trappings were the result of copying nature; for example a stag caught by its antlers in tangled creepers may have inspired early nets of plaited vines. Trap design has been handed down the ages and although more sophisticated materials have been used as they have been discovered, the basic blue-prints have altered little. There are few materials which at some time or other have not been used in trap construction.

There are five main types of trap still in use throughout the world today. The simplest and probably the earliest historically are the pitfalls, basically nothing more than pits dug in the well-worn tracks of an animal. The refinements include camouflaging the pit, lining it with logs to prevent escape by burrowing, driving stakes into its floor with points upwards to impale the victim, or partly filling it with water to drown the quarry. More elaborate types of pitfall trap have pivoted lids and the trap may either be baited or not depending on the intended quarry.

Snares have a history almost as long as pitfalls. Few devices could be simpler to make, to use or to carry in large numbers. The basic type of snare is a plain noose with a slip-knot, and materials from which these have been made include, horsehair, animal sinews, rawhide, sealskin, plant fibres and cord, as well as steel and more especially brass wire. Refinements such as stops to catch the victim alive, or swivels and eyelets to ensure smoother working are sometimes incorporated.

Another ancient device still often used by poachers in Africa for taking antelopes, giraffes and other game is the foot trap, a variation of which is the treadle-trap placed in the shallows at waterholes to catch deer by the foot. A common version is made in the shape of a wheel, out of plaited grass or reeds, which form the rim, from which sharp wooden points radiate towards the centre. The trap is pegged down and any animal which puts its foot into the centre of the wheel is held fast by the spokes.

The largest and best known class of traps are the spring type, of which the steel gin, now outlawed in Britain and coming under pressure in other countries, notably America, is the best known example. Before the invention of steel, wooden springs and switches of springy timber often in conjunction with nooses, sometimes set in box traps, activated these engines. The development of metal, however, led to two main types of spring trap; those employing a flat spring and others, like the break-back, which depended on coiled springing. Most of the humane traps now approved by the British government are worked by coiled metal springs.

The only really humane trap is the cage type, designed to capture animals alive. Usually made of wire, they also include the box traps so popular for catching ground vermin on European shoots; their use dates from the Middle Ages.

In addition to these main groups there are also larger, more elaborate trap systems like the boom fishing traps in use in estuaries and rivers to catch migratory fish, and duck decoys, examples of which are still working in Holland and Britain, although the object now is to study and ring the duck rather than to market them.

In some parts of the world traps are still used for original purposes: the provision of food and security against dangerous beasts. The bushmen in south-west Africa still employ most of the traps mentioned to catch all manner of birds and beasts for food. In India and Africa traps for tigers and lions are set outside villages for self protection. Better known, and indeed notorious in some views, are the methods employed by the trappers of the fur trade, especially in North America, Russia and northern Scandinavia.

A less obvious but common use of traps today is in scientific research. Live animals required for a wide variety of special investigation can only be obtained by trapping. In Britain and America particularly, a great deal of live trapping of birds and mammals is conducted in the interests of science and conservation. In addition all manner of traps are still used to control pests and predators, a sector in which governments are usually quick to respond to public pressure against inhumane methods.

Well-set traps, well-placed, will continue to catch animals time after time, and trapping properly conducted can still be more humane than many other methods of hunting for, providing the correct type of trap is used in the right way, it can be selective in its catch. No trap, however, can be more humane than the trapper, for ultimately it is the human agency which is responsible for overseeing the mechanism of the trap. All traps, as a matter of course, should be investigated every twelve hours, or more often if possible, to ensure that no animal is caught and suffering pain.

That uncontrolled trapping can reduce an

animal to the point of extinction has been evidenced all over the world, in Britain by the fate of the wild cat, polecat and marten, in America and Scandinavia by the near extinction of the formerly common beaver. Large-scale commercial trapping and netting of birds and other animals for food and hides, as well as indiscriminate commercial shooting throughout the nineteenth century, led to the extinction of some birds in North America, notably the passenger pigeon and Eskimo curlew, both once common, and the near extinction of many other species.

Elsewhere in the world, diminishing animal populations and the extinction of many species are sad examples of irresponsible trapping and slaughter by commercial hunters. South Africa's loss of the blue buck, quagga and the Cape lion, followed by the near disappearance of the elephant from the Cape district, sounded a warning bell just in time to encourage the formation of conservation departments in all the provinces. In other parts of the same continent the emergent African states have taken South Africa's conservation programme as a model to copy. Yet trapping with wire snares is the most common form of poaching which the game wardens have to combat throughout the continent and inevitably it is taking its toll.

At present there seems little likelihood of reaching universal agreement on whether animal trapping is morally permissible or not. Meanwhile, the best solution is to ensure that only those trapping methods known to be humane are employed. It is good news that in Britain, in Europe and North America, government departments are now giving a sensible and effective lead. They are demonstrating that box traps, cage traps and other humane engines can not only be efficient but at the same time can conserve wild life through selective catching and painless killing. As a means of conservation, to catch predators and remove them from breeding areas in need of protection, traps are still unsurpassed. Even today a knowledge of traps and the various skills required in using them is an essential part of the game preserver's background. The 'Tender Trap' now has a wider and more worthwhile meaning than when it was first coined in the United States of America.
PHW

Trophy Measurement

There is, unfortunately, no standard method of measuring deer trophies throughout the world, but in general, two main systems are used – the C.I.C. *(Conseil International de la Chasse)* formula, which is used for European big game trophies, and the Boone and Crockett formula, which is used for North American trophies. While some of the measurements taken in the two formulas must, of necessity, be comparable (such features as length, span, circumference etc), other factors which include weight, volume and credit or debit points for style etc which occur in some of the formulas of the C.I.C. method, make the two methods entirely different. Moreover, all measurements under the Boone and Crockett system are taken in inches, whereas C.I.C. measurements are in metric. Furthermore, in New Zealand, the Douglas Formula, which is very similar to the Boone and Crockett method, is used for measuring the New Zealand heads, and in Spain a modified system of the C.I.C. formula is used. Space, however, does not permit of these somewhat 'insular' methods being discussed here.

In England, the 'big game' comprise only deer (red, roe, fallow and sika), and until recently the only measurements that have been taken of any deer trophy have generally been length, span, beam, circumference, number of points and sometimes the coronet circumference, particularly with roe heads. More recently, however, British sportsmen have begun to recognize the quality of their roe trophies, and in order to compare them with European trophies, now assess their worth according to the C.I.C. formula.

How does it work? As far as red, roe and fallow deer trophies are concerned, the length of both antlers is taken, and half the average length goes into the assessment column. In red and roe deer the length is taken from the base of the coronet to the extremity of the longest point of the main beam. In fallow deer antlers, however, the length is taken to the highest indentation of the palm – not to the end of the longest point of the palm. In red, roe and fallow, although the span measurement is taken, it has to attain a certain percentage – which differs according to species – of the average lenth of the antler to qualify for any points. For instance, in red deer antlers if the span is more than 80% of the length, three points can be awarded, but if it is less than 60%, then no points will be given. For roe, if the span falls between 45 and 75% of the length, a maximum of four points can be awarded, but if it is less than 30 or more than 75%, no points can be awarded. Span is considered an important feature of fallow antlers and up to six penalty points are given if this feature falls below 85% of the average length, the deductions ranging from one point for 81 to 85% to six points at at 60% or less.

In both red and fallow deer antlers it is necessary to take the circumference of not only the coronets, but also the upper and lower beams – the latter two measurements being taken at the smallest circumference below and above the tray tine. While only the *average* circumference of the two coronets figures in the assessment column, the *total* circumference of both left and right upper and lower beams is entered. In roe antlers, however, no circumference measurement

Assessment of Red Deer Antlers under the C.I.C. Formula

		Left	Right	Total	Average	Factor	Points
1	Length.	114.3 cm	117.2 cm	231.5	115.75	×0.50	57.87
2	Brow.	34.3	32.0	66.3	33.15	×0.25	8.28
3	Tray.	22.9	25.0	47.9	23.95	×0.25	5.98
4	Coronet.	22.0	22.0	44.0	22.0	×1.00	22.00
5	Beam (lower).	14.1	13.6	27.7	—	×1.00	27.70
6	Beam (upper).	12.5	13.0	25.5	—	×1.00	25.50
7	No. of Points.	6.0	7.0	13.0	—	×1.00	13.00
8	Weight.	5.4 Kg. less 0.5=4.9 kg			—	×2.00	9.80
9	Span (3 max.)*	75 cms. $\frac{100\times75}{115.7}$ =64.8%					1.00
10	Crowns (10 max.)						5.00
11	Bays (2 max)						1.00
12	Colour (2 max.)						2.00
13	Pearling (2 max.)						1.50
14	Tine ends (2 max.)						1.50
				Total points without deduction			182.13
15	Deduction (3 max.)						1.00
							181.13

Explanatory Notes on Assessment Nos :
8　0.5 kg. deducted because of full upper skull
9　Span only 64.8% of average length of antlers – see note below
10　4 to 5 points is maximum possible for antlers bearing a total of 7 upper crown points. If the number had been 10 or more well developed points, 10 could have been awarded
11　Bay points only good – not exceptional therefore, instead of 2 points only 1 awarded
12　Colour dark brown – therefore maximum allowed
13　Pearling good on Scottish standards, but not exceptional
14　Tine ends good on Scottish standards, but not exceptional
15　One point deducted for uneven crown points

*Points for span :

Less than 60% of the average length of antlers	0 points
60% to 70%	1 point
70.1% to 80%	2 points
More than 80%	3 points

of any description is taken – in fact, so far as this species is concerned, the length and span are the only physical features measured with a tape. Another measurement which has to be taken for both red and fallow deer antlers is the length of each brow – a quarter of the average length of the two figuring in the assessment column. In the former species also, the length of each tray tine has to be taken and this has the same treatment as the brow; in fallow deer the length and width of the palm on each antler has to be considered, the average of the former and one and half times the average of the latter appearing in the assessment column.

So much for the measurements which have to be taken. It is now necessary to weigh the antlers, and this is a figure which can lead to some inaccuracy for it is normally based on what is known as the normal 'short nose' cut, i.e. the antlers are attached to the skull frontal bone only, which has been cut on a line from the lower tip of the nose through the upper half of the eye socket to the back of the skull. Unfortunately, not all cuts are made in the same place and, in order to 'standardize' the cut, a slight addition or subtraction can be made. For instance, if the antlers are mounted on only a small portion of the skull, then an addition of up to 0·1 kilogrammes may be

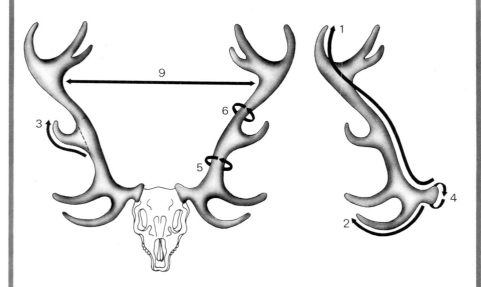

Correct places for measuring antlers :
1　Length of antler
2　Brow tine length
3　Tray tine length
4　Coronet circumference
5　Beam (lower) – smallest circumference between bay and tray tines
6　Beam (upper) – smallest circumference between tray and upper tines
9　Span (widest inside)

Assessment of Roebuck Trophies under the C.I.C. Formula

		Total	Average	Factor	Points
1	Length Left 26.6 cm right 26.0 cm	52.6	26.3	×0.5	13.15
2	Weight 478 grm. add 10 deduct 0 = 488 grm.			×0.1	48.80
3	Volume 228 cc			×0.3	68.40
4	Spread* (0 to 4 points) $\dfrac{10.2 \text{ cm.} \times 100}{\text{Av. length } 26.3 \text{ cm}} = 38\%$				2.00
5	Colour (0 to 4 points)				2.50
6	Pearling (0 to 4 points)				4.00
7	Coronets (0 to 4 points)				4.00
8	Tine ends (0 to 2 points)				1.50
9	Additional points for regularity and appearance (0 to 5 points)				3.00
				Total	147.35
10	Deductions for irregularity and poor appearance (0 to 5 points)				0
				FINAL POINTS	147.35

*Points for Spread :

Less than 30% of the average length of main beams	0 points
from 30% to 35%	1 point
from 35.1% to 40%	2 points
from 40.1% to 45%	3 points
from 45.1% to 75%	4 points
Over 75%	0 points

Additions or deductions for weight according to cutting of skull :

A Frontal bone cut – up to 10 grm may be added.

B Short (normal) nose cut – 0 additions.

C and D Full nose cut – up to 90 grm may be deducted depending on amount of skull present

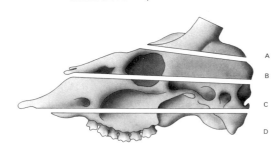

allowed for red deer trophies and up to 20 grammes for roe. On the other hand, if the whole upper jaw is present, or more than the normal nose cut is present, up to 0·7 kilogrammes for red deer, 0·250 kilogrammes for fallow and 90 grammes for roe can be deducted. If all skulls were similar in size this arbitrary adjustment would be easier to assess, but unfortunately this is not the case, and in consequence does lead to inaccuracies. It is, therefore, questionable whether it ought to be included at all in the formula which is concerned only with the measurement of antlers whereas the weight includes both antlers *and* a portion of the skull. In short, antlers of equal size can be attached to two entirely different sized frontal bones, and unless the visual adjustment has been correct one or other will have a superior points score solely due to the fact that this visual adjustment has been incorrectly made.

Antler weight, however, denotes maturity, and it is therefore desirable that it should score heavily if only to encourage the shooting of fully matured rather than more juvenile animals which could well have longer but lighter antlers. It is a pity, therefore, that this section can lead to some inaccuracy of assessment. So far as red and fallow deer trophies are concerned the weight of the antler (taken in kilogrammes)

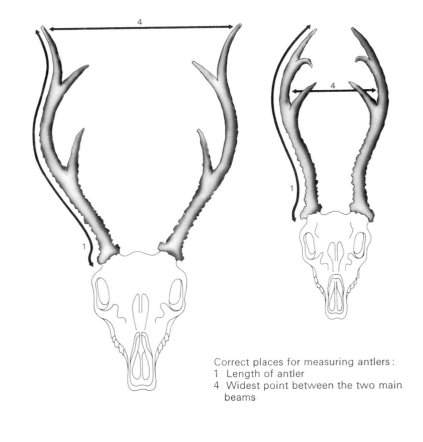

Correct places for measuring antlers :
1 Length of antler
4 Widest point between the two main beams

is doubled in order to arrive at a figure for the assessment column, while for roe a tenth of the *weight* is used.

As regards the latter deer, a good trophy should be heavily pearled – indeed the pearling on some roe trophies is so rugged that individual pearls might be considered small tines. How should this pearling be measured? Under the C.I.C. formula it is done by immersing the antlers, in an inverted position, in water as far as the base of the coronets, but the skull itself must be clear of the water. By this method one ascertains the quantity of water displaced by the antlers, which is, in effect, the volume, and for the points column this figure is then multiplied by 0·3. It is obvious that neither the weight nor volume can be properly assessed if the trophy has been mounted (stuffed), so it is therefore impossible to assess any fully mounted head under the C.I.C. formula.

Finally, apart from the inclusion of the actual number of tines on red deer antlers only, an additional number of points can be awarded for beauty or good style etc,

Assessment of Fallow Buck Trophies under the C.I.C. Formula

			Total	Average	Factor	Points
1	Length	left 61.8 cm right 62.4 cm	124.2	62.1	×0.5	31.05
2	Length brow tine	left 18.8 cm right 19.6 cm	38.4	19.2	×0.25	4.80
3	Length palm	left 39.7 cm right 38.5 cm	78.2	39.1	×1	39.10
4	Width palm	left 18.2 cm right 16.6 cm	34.8	17.4	×1.5	26.10
5	Circum. coronet	left 19.7 cm right 19.4 cm	39.1	19.55	×1	19.55
6	Circum. lower beam	left 12.3 cm right 11.9 cm	24.2	—	×1	24.20
7	Circum. upper beam	left 12.9 cm right 12.2 cm	25.1	—	×1	25.10
8	Weight of antlers	3.66 kilos add 0 deduct 0.1 = 3.56			×2	7.12

Beauty Points:

9	Colour (0 to 2 points)	1.50
10	Tine ends (0 to 6 points)	3.00
11	Bulk, form, regularity (0 to 5 points)	2.50
	TOTAL	184.02

Penalty Points:

12	Insufficient spread*	(0 to 6 points)	1
13	Badly shaped palms	(0 to 10 points)	0
14	Poor pearling	(0 to 2 points)	0.5
15	Malformation	(0 to 6 points)	0 Total penalty points 1.50
			Final total points 182.52

*Penalty points for insufficient spread
When inside spread between
antlers is less than 85% of average length of antlers : 1
80% 2
75% 4 } penalty
70% 3 } points
65% 5
60% 6

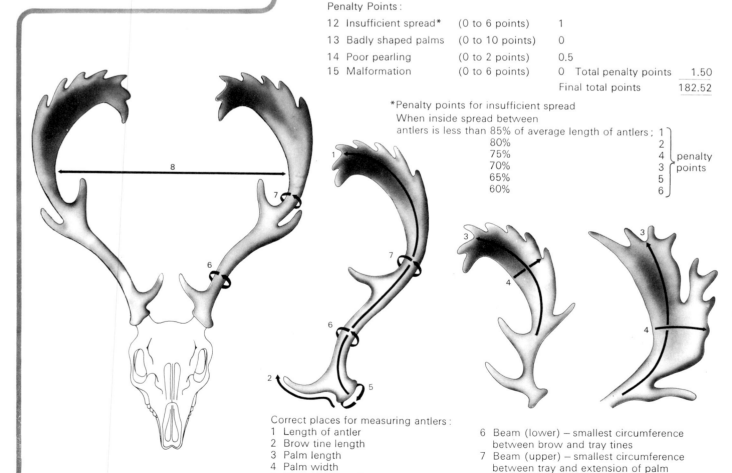

Correct places for measuring antlers :
1 Length of antler
2 Brow tine length
3 Palm length
4 Palm width
5 Coronet circumference
6 Beam (lower) – smallest circumference between brow and tray tines
7 Beam (upper) – smallest circumference between tray and extension of palm
8 Span (widest inside)

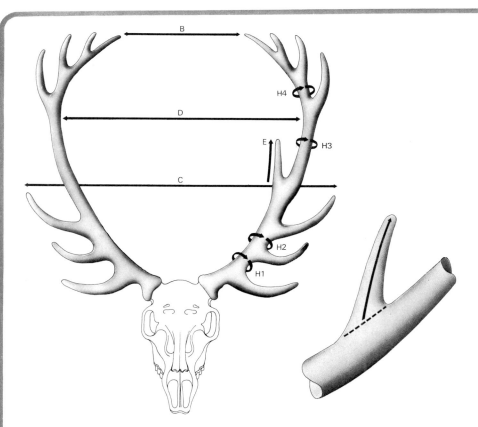

All measurements to be taken with steel tape to nearest one-eighth of inch, and should not be taken within 60 days of the animal being shot.

Correct places for measuring antlers under Boone and Crockett Formula:

B Tip to tip
C Greatest spread
D Span (widest inside)
E Total length of all abnormal points
F Length of antler
G 1 Length of first point (brow)
G 2 Length of second point (bay)
G 3 Length of third point (tray)
G 4 Length of fourth point (royal)
G 5 Length of fifth point
G 6 Length of sixth point
G 7 Length of seventh point
H 1 Circumference at smallest place between first and second points
H 2 Circumference at smallest place between second and third points
H 3 Circumference at smallest place between third and fourth points
H 4 Circumference at smallest place between fourth and fifth points

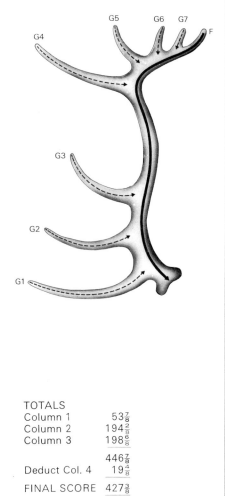

Score Card for Wapiti (under Boone and Crockett formula)

	Supplementary Data Left	Right	Column 1 Spread credit	Column 2 Left antler	Column 3 Right antler	Column 4 Difference
A Number of points on each antler.	7	8				
B Tip to tip spread.		38⅝"				
C Greatest spread.		60"				
D Inside span between main beams. Spread credit may equal but not exceed length of longer antler. If inside span (D) exceeds longer antler length, enter difference.	55		53⅞			1⅛
E Total of lengths of all abnormal points.						2⅝
F Length of main beam.				48²⁄₈	53⅞	5⅝
G 1 Length of first point (brow)				20³⁄₈	20³⁄₈	—
G 2 Length of second point (bay)				25⅝	27³⁄₈	1⁶⁄₈
G 3 Length of third point (tray)				18⅝	20	1³⁄₈
G 4 Length of fourth point (royal)				22⁴⁄₈	21⅝	⅞
G 5 Length of fifth point.				15⁴⁄₈	15⅞	³⁄₈
G 6 Length of sixth point (if present)				11⅞	7³⁄₈	4⁴⁄₈
G 7 Length of seventh point (if present)				—	—	—
H 1 Circum. at smallest place between first and second points				8⁴⁄₈	8²⁄₈	²⁄₈
H 2 Circum. at smallest place between second and third points				7³⁄₈	7⁴⁄₈	⅛
H 3 Circum. at smallest place between third and fourth points				7⁴⁄₈	7⁴⁄₈	—
H 4 Circum. at smallest place between fourth and fifth points				8⅛	9	⅞
TOTALS:			53⅞	194²⁄₈	198⁶⁄₈	19⁴⁄₈

TOTALS
Column 1   53⅞
Column 2   194²⁄₈
Column 3   198⁶⁄₈

446⅞
Deduct Col. 4   19⁴⁄₈
FINAL SCORE   427³⁄₈

amounting to 18 for red deer, 19 for roe and 13 for fallow, with corresponding deductions for malforms, etc, to the extent of 3 for red deer, 5 for roe deer and 18 for fallow deer. These additions or subtractions do not include the credits or debits for span, mentioned earlier.

The example tables, and diagrams, indicating where individual measurements are taken, clarify the method of assessing a red, roe or fallow deer trophy under the C.I.C. formula.

Factors in the assessment of elk antlers include length and breadth of palm, span, beam circumference, and number of tines with penalties amounting to up to eight points for irregular style etc. For reindeer, however, there is no suitable formula, so the Boone and Crockett formula for caribou is used, the measurements being taken in centimetres (instead of inches) and the number of individual tine ends multiplied by 2·5.

In the Boone and Crockett system all measurements are taken with a steel tape – which should also be used when measuring a trophy under the C.I.C. formula – to the nearest one-eighth of an inch. Weight or volume are never taken for any species, nor is there a 'Beauty Section' where additional points can be awarded for good appearance, etc or deducted for malformation. In short, all factors have to be physically measured and none are based on arbitrary assessment, so the final score of this system, even if it does not take into account certain desirable features such as colour, pearling and weight etc, must be more accurate.

For the North American deer: wapiti (elk), white-tailed deer, mule deer, black-tailed deer, caribou and moose, a more or less standard system of assessment is used, except for the last species.

Briefly, the following measurements have to be taken: length of each antler, length of *each* individual tine, which must be at least one inch in length, sprouting from the main beam, circumference of main beam at four different places along its length, and the *inside* spread. If the last named *exceeds* the length of the longer antler then the difference will be entered in a 'difference column' and eventually subtracted from the final score – otherwise the spread distance will be included as a *credit* score. Also, in the difference column will be entered the difference in length between not only the main beams but also all tine lengths and beam circumferences. With caribou trophies the width of brow (shovel) and upper palm of each antler are also taken and entered in the appropriate columns, with the difference in the latter case only being entered in the difference column. The number of tines, also, on caribou antlers is taken into account, but in the other species of deer (except moose) this figure, together with the tip to tip and greatest spread measurements, is

only entered as 'supplementary data', for use in assessing the conformation of the trophy – not in its final score.

The measurements of moose antlers, apart from the greatest spread, are the width and length of each palm, including the brow palm, and the circumference of beam at smallest place. Both measurements are entered in the appropriate column, together with the difference between each pair of measurements which is placed in the difference column for subsequent deduction – as are also the number of abnormal points on each antler.

Non-typical white-tailed deer, mule deer and black-tailed deer are measured slightly differently to typical specimens, the main difference being that the *total* length of all *abnormal* points is added to the final score, whereas in the score card of typical heads this total is entered in the difference column for deduction from the final score.

The wapiti score card will best illustrate how the Boone and Crockett system works, and this should be compared with the C.I.C. formula for red deer, which is a deer of similar type. Score cards for the other American deer are on similar lines. GKW

Tsesseby *(Damaliscus lunatus)*

Also known as sassaby or bastard hartebeest, this is a handsome chestnut or brown-coloured antelope found in parts of central Africa. Its habitat is open plains or light woodland. It stands about 48 in at the shoulder. Both sexes have crescent-shaped annulated horns about 12 in long and 6 in round at the base with a spread, at the tip, of 11 in to 12 in. A grazer, it is found in herds varying in size from 10 to over 100. It has a single calf from June to September.

A related species is the blesbuck or blesbok *(Damaliscus dorcas)* found in parts of central and southern Africa, of the same genus only smaller and much darker in coloration. It stands only about 38 in with slightly longer and thinner annulated horns. It is found more often in woodland and is not as numerous as the tsesseby. A grazer, it also calves once a year. This species, and the topi or tiang *(Damaliscus korrigum)*, which is found in Ethiopia, are rarely shot.

Tunisia

A north African country of about 48,000 square miles. Across the north there are mountain ranges and a fertile coastal strip. South the country reaches down into the Sahara Desert, along the northern fringe of which, at this point, there are salt lakes. In the valleys of the north there are many flocks and herds, and in the fertile areas a wide variety of crops are grown, including cereals, olives, citrus fruits, vines, almonds and dates. There is little industrialization, but some mining of phosphates, lead and iron. Extensive re-afforestation is under way.

Ministre de Tourisme, L'Aménagement de Territoire, L'Avenue Mohamet 5, Tunis.

Turkey *see* Wild Turkey

Turkey

An eastern Mediterranean republic of both Europe and Asia. The bulk of the country consists of Asia Minor, but there is a small section, Turkish Thrace, which lies on the European side of the Bosphorus, the Sea of Marmora, and the Dardanelles, the whole having an area of about 296,000 square miles. The Black Sea lies in the north and the Mediterranean in the south. The interior of Asia Minor is an extensive plateau surrounded by mountains, except in the west, which in the south rise to over 12,000 ft. There are numerous lakes and some large rivers, in particular the Tigris and Euphrates; the Maritsa in Thrace is also important. Rainfall is not great, particularly in the central Anatolian Plateau, and the climate, tempered by the peninsular nature of the country, is very pleasant.

Owing to reckless hunting, and a previous paucity of shooting controls, many species are now scarce in Turkey. These are now protected, and cannot be hunted at any time. Nevertheless, the country still offers varied and interesting hunting, combining European and Asian species.

Special Regulations

Foreigners may hunt anywhere in Turkey,

Licences—Turkey

Foreign hunters arriving individually should apply in advance for their valid hunting permits to, either the Turkish Embassy, Consulate or Turkish Tourism offices. Foreign hunters applying for a permit from the Governor's or district governor's office will need to pay a certain fee and produce proof that they have hired a guide.

Foreigners residing in the country (excluding diplomatic corps) who wish to hunt in Turkey should register as guest members of either a Turkish hunting club of a federal nature, or any local hunting club. Upon production of such a membership, hunting certificates will be issued.

The wild cat is shot in Turkey during a season covering August to March.

except for Thrace, eastern and south-eastern Anatolia, or in special conservation areas. No hunting is permitted in picnic areas, recreational grounds or special conservation forests. However, it is possible to hunt in most forests providing the hunter obtains a permit from the Forest Enterprise Directorate or Forest Regional Directorate. This permit is valid throughout the country, but the hunter must inform the local authorities of his intention to hunt, and abide by the restrictions announced by the local forest administrators.

Hunters wishing to hunt in groups of more than ten should obtain prior permission from the govenor or district governor. This is in order to avoid armed clashes with the resident hunters which have occasionally occurred in the more remote districts.

Foreign hunters may only import shotguns into Turkey; the importation of rifles and pistols is strictly forbidden.

The following hunting methods are forbidden: the use of cages, artificial light, tape recorders, camouflage net, or by setting traps in water, collecting birds in snowy weather or in spring months, using dynamite, poison, lime, fish weed, electric current.

Further Information

Tarim Bakanligi (Ministry of Agriculture), Ankara.

Turizm ve Tanitma Bakanligi (Ministry of Tourism and Information), Ankara.

Seasons—Turkey

Species	Season
Bear Lynx Badger Polecat Wildcat Quail Pigeon Turtle dove Waterfowl Geese Duck	15 Aug-31 March (Bear hunting is banned in the province of Hakkari during this period)
Rabbit Widgeon Gray Partridge Grouse Great Bustard Crane	5 Sept-31 Jan
Otter Rock martin Beech martin	31 Oct-29 Feb
Wolf Hyena Fox Wild boar Crow Magpie	Any time

U

Uganda

Uganda is a republic of central east Africa, lying across the equator. The area covered is about 94,000 square miles, of which some 15,000 are water or swamp. The average elevation is between 3,000 and 4,000 ft above sea level, but there are hills running along both the eastern and western borders which are considerably higher. Lake Kyoga and large parts of Lakes Victoria, Edward and Albert lie within Uganda's boundaries. The climate is tempered by the altitude, but rainfall averages about 50 in, so for much of the year vegetation is fairly lush.

Agriculture is important, with cotton, coffee, sugar and tobacco the main crops. The tourist trade is growing rapidly, and there are extensive tourist facilities, available to hunters as to others. Another feature that recommends Uganda is that there are two distinct groups of fauna: that of the Nile basin in the west, including Uganda kob, topi and sitatunga, and that of the more arid country in the north, with such species as oryx, gazelles and kudu.

Most visitors arrange their hunting through Uganda Wildlife Development Ltd, which organizes all safaris in Uganda. Their clients are only required to pay trophy fees on animals they actually shoot or wound.

The company has arrangements in Tanzania, Rwanda and Kenya should any client wish to hunt there. Safaris of a minimum duration of 30 days are recommended, but shorter ones may be organized if anyone wishes to shoot certain specific trophies in the less remote areas. By law there is a minimum duration of safari for certain animals. For lion, roan and oryx it is 28 days, and for leopard, greater kudu and lesser kudu it is 21 days. Fees, apart from trophy fees, vary very considerably with the number of clients and the number of days. They rise from about $150 per person (hunting) per day. Non-hunting clients or companions are charged about $20 per day.

There is no closed season for hunting even during the wettest period (May and June). However, this can be distinctly uncomfortable, and the best season tends to be December to April in the north and east, and June to November in the south and west.

Further Information

Uganda Wildlife Development Ltd, P.O. Box 1764, Kampala.

The Chief Game Warden, P.O. Box 4, Entebbe.

United Kingdom of Great Britain and Northern Ireland

This political unit forms the bulk of the group of islands known as the British Isles. It has a total area of just over 93,000 square miles divided into four national areas: England, Scotland, Wales and Northern Ireland (Ulster). The Isle of Man, in the Irish Sea, and the Channel Islands, nearer France than Britain, are internally semi-independent. Due to the variety of terrain, surprising in such a small area, it is easier to describe the constituent countries separately.

England

The largest country of the U.K., covers just over 50,000 square miles including the Isle of Wight, off the south coast, and the Scilly

Game Species—Uganda

Species	Trophy fee Ugandan dollars
Mammals:	
Buffalo	43
Bushbuck	21
Bushpig	7
Dikdik	7
Duiker	7
Eland	71
Elephant	214
Giant forest hog	29
Grant's gazelle	21
Hartebeeste, Jackson's	21
Hippopotamus	43
Klipspringer	7
Kudu, greater	107
Kudu, lesser	107
Leopard	214
Lion	214
Oribi	7
Oryx	107
Reedbuck, mountain	14
Reedbuck, common	14
Roan antelope	107
Sitatunga	43
Topi	21
Uganda kob	21
Warthog	7
Waterbuck	36
Zebra	50
Birds:	
Bustard	
Doves	
Duck	
Francolin	
Geese	
Guinea fowl	
Quail	

Protected Species—Uganda

Aardwolf
Black rhinoceros
Cheetah
Chimpanzee
Colobus monkey
Crane (all species)
Giant eland
Giraffe
Gorilla
Great flamingo
Ground hornbill
Heron
Lesser flamingo
Marabou stork
Ostrich
Owl (all species)
Pangolin
Saddle-bill stork
Secretary bird
Vulture (all species)
Whale-headed stork
White rhinoceros
Yellow-backed duiker

Licences—Uganda

Hunters are required to take out a general game licence, and supplementary licences for any game not included in the former. Those who wish to hunt in the 14 game reserves (hunting is occasionally permitted in game reserves), or in controlled hunting areas, of which there are 16, must obtain a special permit from the Chief Game Warden or District Commissioner of the area concerned. A basic charge is made for the permit, plus a per capita fee for each animal taken.

A complete range of guns, including shotguns, is available to clients of Uganda Wildlife Development Ltd (see text). If they wish to bring their own weapons they should inform the company in advance, giving full details of make, calibre, serial number, etc, in order that the necessary import and licensing formalities may be completed before arrival. Revolvers, pistols, automatics and semi-automatics are prohibited.

A warthog in Botswana

Isles, off the south-west tip of the country. It is also the flattest, though with few true plains, the most fertile, the most populous, and the most industrialized. Physically, the hillier regions of the north, west and south-west are distinct from the undulating downs of the south and south-east, and the flat areas of the eastern midlands and East Anglia, where large areas of the 'fens' are under sea level. The main range of hills is the Pennines, which run north-south on the western side of the northern half of the country. North of the Pennines lie the Cheviots, running east-west along the Scottish border, west lie the Cumbrian mountains, with the highest peak in England, and south there are the Cotswolds and in the far south-west the moors. The country is well watered, the chief rivers being the Thames, Severn, Mersey, Tyne, Humber, Trent and the Great Ouse.

Wales
Occupies the peninsula that juts out westwards from the English midlands, with an area of just over 8,000 square miles, including the island of Anglesey in the north-west, one of the few flat areas. The rest of the country is very hilly with the main Cambrian mountain range running from north to south. It includes Snowdon, the highest peak in England and Wales at 3,560 ft. The Severn, and its tributary the Wye, both rise in Wales, and the Usk, Dee and Towy are other rivers.

Scotland
In addition to all the mainland north of the English border, consists of a large number of islands. The greatest number are off the west coast: two in the Firth of Clyde, Arran and Bute, and the rest further north – the Inner and Outer Hebrides. Off the north-east tip of Scotland lie the Orkney islands, and beyond them the Shetlands, the total area of the country being nearly 30,000 square miles. The mainland has three distinct areas: the Southern Uplands along and just north of the border; the Central Lowlands, lying across the country on the Firth of Clyde and the Firth of Forth, and extending much further north in the east than in the west; the Highlands, divided into a northern and southern system by the Great Glen. The southern part of the Highlands contains Ben Nevis, at 4,406 ft, the highest point in the British Isles. The chief river is the Clyde, but the Tay, Tweed and Spey are also important. There are numerous lochs, mostly long and narrow, famed for their beauty. Loch Ness and Loch Lomond are the two largest.

The widgeon, a surface feeding duck of Europe and Asia, is closely related to the American widgeon or baldpate.

Licences—U.K.

No one may take or kill, deer, grouse, blackgame, moorgame, partridge, pheasant, hare, rabbit, woodcock or snipe without a game licence. A full-year licence (1 August–31 July) costs £6. Partial-year licences (1 August–31 October and 1 November to 31 July) are £4 each. There is also a 14-day licence costing £2. A farmer, or a person authorized by him, does not require a game licence in order to kill hare and rabbit.

Permits are required for both shotguns and rifles. Visitors from abroad who are staying in the country for less than 30 days do not require a shotgun certificate. All others must apply for a certificate to their local police station, and supply an attestation by an M.P., J.P., minister, doctor, lawyer, bank official, or person of similar standing. Certificates will not be issued to those under 15 years, to those who have served a prison sentence of three years or longer, or whenever there might be a danger to the public safety. Owners of rifles must obtain a firearms certificate, which is more difficult to acquire than the shotgun certificate. It is granted at the discretion of the local chief officer of police, who will need to be satisfied that the applicant has a sufficient reason for owning the firearm (sport, pest control, target shooting or collecting), that he has a safe place not only to use it, but also to keep it and its ammunition. The firearms certificate costs £3.50, and £2.50 for renewal.

In Northern Ireland the firearms regulations differ; there is only one firearms permit. All hunters must obtain one (cost 50p), unless they already have a permit from Great Britain, which is valid in Northern Ireland. Visitors with shotguns, who have a British shotgun permit, do not need a firearms permit unless they are staying for more than 30 days. They must obtain, however, a certificate of approval from the police in the county in which they intend to shoot (the certificate is valid throughout Northern Ireland).

Ulster
Ulster comprises a small north-eastern area, covering nearly 8,500 square miles of Ireland, the second largest island in the British Isles. For a description of its terrain and climate *see* Ireland. The hunting seasons are shown in a separate table.

The U.K. is very highly industrialized, the chief industrial areas being South Wales, the Midlands and parts of the north and south-east of England, and the Central Lowlands of Scotland. Agriculture is also highly developed, with cereals, sugar beet, vegetables, and fruit the main crops, also stock raising and dairying. There are extensive and increasing coniferous forests in the north of England and Scotland, but the formerly vast deciduous forests, mainly of oak and beech, are shrinking in the south, due to the pressures of over-population, urbanization, industrialization and intensive farming. Despite this there are large areas, mainly in the Highlands of Scotland, that are moor – unpopulated, uncultivated and almost completely treeless.

Special Regulations
No-one under 17 years of age may buy or hire a shotgun or rifle or ammunition for either. Shooting from cars is illegal. It is also illegal to carry a gun (except in a case) on a road or in a public place, or to shoot within 50 yd of one.

Shooting any bird in Scotland on Sunday or Christmas day is illegal and the Home Secretary may extend the prohibition to any county in England or Wales. He may also further restrict the seasons in any area and may restrict them for a particular species because of severe weather conditions.

Further Information
The British Field Sports Society, 137 Victoria Street, London, S.W.1.
W.A.G.B.I. (The Wildfowlers' Association of Great Britain and Ireland), Grosvenor House, 104 Watergate Street, Chester.
The Game Conservancy, Fordingbridge, Hampshire.
British Travel Association, 64 St James Street, London, S.W.1.

United Kingdom, Hunting and Shooting in

In the U.K. the term hunting primarily means foxhunting, which is generally conducted with a pack of hounds and followers mounted on horseback or on foot. Hares are also hunted, either with packs of harriers, when the followers may be mounted or on foot, or with packs of beagles, when the followers are generally on foot. Deer are hunted with a pack of hounds in the West Country only and the followers are mounted or on foot.

Shooting implies the shooting of gamebirds, or ground game (hares and rabbits).

The shooting of waterfowl, or wildfowl as they are generally termed in Britain, is called wildfowling. Deer shooting is either by stalking in the Highlands of Scotland or by still-hunting in the forests further south,

or even from high-seats, is termed, loosely, deer-stalking.

The practice of sport in Britain has developed over the centuries, and during that time sound methods of game conservation and preservation have been evolved. These are excellent in this setting where the sporting rights go with the ownership of the land and there are no large state shooting areas free to all. Within this framework the practices evolved for shooting and hunting are all sound, although they may appear somewhat limited to those accustomed to shoot or hunt where they will in North America, Australia or Africa. Like the terminology which has been evolved with them they suit the particular circumstances.

Britain is a small and highly populated island group and although agriculture is still her largest industry she is very highly industrialized. In these circumstances it is necessary to have all field sports highly organized and a considerable measure of control over them is required. Such control must inevitably come from within, from the sportsmen themselves and from the farmers and landowners on whose land the sport takes place. In effect it is the latter, to a large extent, who are the participants and without their support both hunting and shooting would cease to exist. With their support and co-operation there is no need for the Hunter's Examination as in parts of Europe, and the number of shooting accidents each year is remarkably low.

Roughshooting, that is, shooting without a keeper to superintend the rearing of game, and wildfowling on the foreshore below the high-water mark, which is free, are the cheapest forms of shooting available. Joining a syndicate of guns in a keepered shoot, where game is driven to the waiting guns by beaters organized by the keeper, is more expensive, and varies considerably in cost depending on the part of the country, ease of access to town, etc. Such shoots are generally arranged so that a group of from six to ten guns share the expense of the shoot and expect to have an organized day's shooting once a fortnight or so throughout the season. Each day's bag varies according to the area, the type of shoot, the number of birds bred and the overall costs.

Shooting driven grouse is, perhaps, the most expensive form of this type of hunting, and the sportsmen generally shoot from butts concealed from the approaching birds. In all driven shooting the guns are within gunshot of each other and strict observance of safety rules is expected from all concerned. Before the day starts the landowner, or shoot organizer, will probably explain where the drives are going to take place; each gun then either draws for his number in the line or one will be arbitrarily allotted to him. Thereafter, the normal arrangement is that the numbers change by two each time, so

---

Seasons—England, Scotland and Wales

Species	Season	Comment
Mammals		
Deer : red, fallow and sika	1 Aug-30 April	Males—England and Wales
	1 Nov-28 Feb	Females—England and Wales
Roebuck	All year	England and Wales
Roe deer, female	1 Nov-28 Feb	
Red, fallow and sika	21 Oct-15 Feb	Females—Scotland
fallow and sika	1 Aug-30 April	Males—Scotland
red	1 July-20 Oct	Males—Scotland
Roedeer	21 Oct-28 Feb	Females—Scotland
Roebuck	1 May-2 Oct	Scotland
Hare, brown and blue mountain	All year	
Rabbit	All year	
Pests and predators : fox, wildcat, feral cat, rat, stoat, weasel, hedgehog, mole, mink (feral), marten (rare), feral ferret (polecat), and gray squirrel	All year	Foxes are not usually shot or trapped in those areas where they are 'hunted' (on horseback, or on foot with hounds)
Birds		
Capercailzie	1 Oct-31 Jan	
Blackgame	20 Aug-10 Dec	
Ptarmigan	12 Aug-10 Dec	
Grouse	12 Aug-10 Dec	
Partridge	1 Sept-1 Feb	
Pheasant	1 Oct-1 Feb	
Snipe, common and jack	12 Aug-31 Jan	
Woodcock	1 Sept-31 Jan	Scotland
	1 Oct-31 Jan	England and Wales
Wildfowl : Common pochard, common scoter, gadwall, garganey teal, goldeneye, long-tailed duck, mallard, pintail, scaup, teal, shoveller, tufted duck, velvet scoter, widgeon ; and Canada, bean greylag, pinkfoot and white-fronted goose	1 Sept-31 Jan	Inland
	1 Sept-20 Feb	Foreshore
Waders : Common redshank, coot, curlew (except stone curlew), bar-tailed godwit, golden plover, gray plover, moorhen and whimbrel.	1 Sept-31 Jan	
Carrion crow	Any time	
Cormorant		
Feral pigeon		
Goosander		Scotland only
Greater black-backed gull		
Hooded crow		

Seasons—England, Scotland and Wales (Cont.)

Species	Season	Comment
Waders (Cont.)		
House sparrow		
Herring gull		
Jackdaw		
Jay		
Lesser black-backed gull		
Magpie		
Red-breasted merganser		Scotland only
Rook		
Shag		
Stock-dove		
Rock dove		Scotland only
Woodpigeon		
All other birds	Protected	

Seasons—Ulster

Species	Season	Comment
Deer	No set season	A limited number may be shot on certain shoots
Hare	1 Feb-11 Aug	
All other mammals	As for England, Scotland and Wales	
Grouse	12 Aug-30 Nov	
Cock pheasant	1 Oct-31 Jan	
Partridge	1 Oct-31 Jan	
Snipe	1 Sept-31 Jan	
Woodcock	1 Oct-31 Jan	
Swan	1 Sept-31 Jan	Excluding mute swan
Geese		Excluding brent, barnacle and Canada
Duck		
Golden plover		
Gray plover		
Redshank		
Curlew		
Whimbrel		
Rock dove		
Stock dove		
Shag	Any time	
Cormorant		
Mute swan		
Greater black-backed gull		
Lesser black-backed gull		
Woodpigeon		
Hooded crow		
Carrion crow		
Rook		
Jackdaw		
Magpie		
Jay		
Starling		
Bull finch		
House sparrow		
Feral pigeon	Any time	Only if found damaging crops or property.
Blackbird		
Chaffinch		
Greenfinch		
All other birds	Protected	

that in each drive or beat the guns move along two places, thus each taking in turn the supposedly better centre positions. By this means each gun should and usually does have his fair share of the shooting available. The aim of each drive is to present the birds to the waiting guns so that they are flying strongly and provide the best possible shooting. Where possible, therefore, the guns are often placed in a hollow and the birds are driven over treetops to provide high shots. Many of the shooting coverts in Britain have been planted with precisely this aim in mind.

There is also plenty of shooting over dogs available; the setter and pointer and now the German pointer are often to be found on the moors and may be shot over, as elsewhere in the world. Shooting pheasants or partridges over pointers is less common, though walking them up in line, especially in large-leafed crops, is frequently practised early in the season before the leaves are off the trees, when it is too early to drive them. Partridge driving over the high hedges of East Anglia is also a fine sport but, with the general decline of partridge stocks, is less frequently practised.

Deer stalking takes place principally in the mountainous regions of the Scottish Highlands where the deer 'forests', though so named, have no trees, consisting of seemingly bare and rocky mountainsides. Here the red deer is stalked, generally in the company of a stalker who knows the ground and can aid the 'rifle' in the choice of a stag and the line of country for the stalk. Still-hunting the roe buck or other deer in the southern forests is conducted in the universal manner of the still-hunter, but generally in the company of a keeper who knows the likely ground.

Foxhunting and the other forms of hunting with packs of hounds are to be found in many parts of the country and visitors should make separate enquiries about them. However, there is little chance of the visitor obtaining these sports unless through hotels in a hunting area or through the agency of friends.

United Republic of Egypt *see* Middle East

United States of America *see* Alabama; Alaska; Arizona; Arkansas; California; Colorado; Columbia; Connecticut; Delaware; Florida; Georgia; Hawaii; Idaho; Illinois; Indiana; Iowa; Kansas; Kentucky; Louisiana; Maine; Maryland; Massachusetts; Michigan; Minnesota; Mississippi; Missouri; Montana; Nebraska; Nevada; New Hampshire; New Jersey; New Mexico; New York; North Carolina; North Dakota; Ohio; Oklahoma; Oregon; Pennsylvania; Rhode Island; South Carolina; South Dakota; Tennessee; Texas; Utah; Vermont; Virginia; Washington; West Virginia; Wisconsin; Wyoming.

Urial *see* Red Sheep

Uruguay

Uruguay is the smallest South American republic, covering just over 72,000 square miles. Most of the country is an extension of the Pampas, grassy and undulating plain. There are ranges of hills in the north, which cross the Brazilian border and then extend south down the east coast. The chief river is the Negro, which flows south-westwards into the Uruguay. The climate is reasonably healthy, with summer heat tempered by Atlantic winds, and a mild winter occasionally stiffened by polar winds. Rainfall is fairly regular throughout the year, although droughts sometimes occur.

Various cereals, ranging from wheat to rice, are cultivated, but the chief wealth of the country lies in its cattle and sheep. Industry, though developing, is still largely based on meat, leather and the excellent wool.

For game *see* South America, Shooting in

Further Information
The nearest Uruguayan consulate.

U.S.S.R.

The Union of Soviet Socialist Republics is a vast country, composed of 15 Union Republics, which straddles half Europe and all of Asia, with a total area of some 8,600,000 square miles. The whole area is divided into three regions from west to east: two enormous plains, separated by the Urals (which also form a dividing line between Asia and Europe). Further east there is an irregular succession of mountain ranges intersecting smaller plains and culminating in the peninsula of Kamchatka. From north to south there are three further zones: the Arctic tundra of the North, merging into forests and fertile plains which eventually give way to a desert belt stretching from Mongolia to the Caspian Sea.

The climate is nearly everywhere continental, with extremes of cold in the north and Siberia, and great heat in some of the deserts of the south. The most pleasant climate is in the western areas, particularly round the Black Sea, and in fact most of the hunting grounds open to visitors are in the south-west, by the Black or the Caspian Seas. This area is fairly easily accessible and provides a variety of terrain and shooting.

Shooting for visitors is restricted to a few species of big game and deer: red deer, askania deer, roe deer, bear, boar, tur, and wild goat. The fees, which vary, are shown in the table.

Hunting reserves in the areas of the Black and Caspian Seas are shown tabulated. The only other hunting reserve is in Irkutsk, where bears are hunted from their lairs in November to February. The temperature varies between −20 °C and −50 °C; there is

a 3-4 day tour, allowing 1-3 hunters per tour.

Although not usually shot by tourists, mention should be made of the waterfowl in the central provinces of the European part of the U.S.S.R. There are immense waterfowl migrations to and through this area and consequently considerable shooting, both in autumn and in spring, when the mating birds are decoyed. Also of note is the re-introduction of sable and beaver to areas in which they could not have re-established themselves without assistance; they are at present completely protected, in common with elk and saiga antelope. In Siberia, raccoon dog and fallow deer have been introduced, apparently successfully.

Organization
All hunting tours are organized through Intourist, and visas will only be granted when Intourist has confirmed bookings. Moscow is the starting point, from which hunting reserves are reached by aircraft and car. Fees vary considerably, according to the duration, distance from Moscow, number of huntsmen required (which depends on the type of hunting), and the accommodation, which may vary from a first class hotel to a forester's hut. Certain fees are constant. These include: rent of hunting rifle (with

---

Fees—U.S.S.R.

Species	Kill	Miss	Wounding
		(all fees in Roubles)	
Roe deer	15-300	7	10
Other deer	70 upwards	20	75
Boar	30 upwards	7	25
Tur	75 upwards	10	50
Bear (lair hunting)	700		
Bear (other types of hunting)	600	50	100

Hunting Reserves—U.S.S.R.

Reserve	Species	Comment
Krasny Les	Deer and roe deer	Sept only. 2/5-day tours. No more than 5 per party.
Krasnaya Polyana	Boar and bear	2-day tour. 1 or 2 hunters at a time.
North Ossetian	Tur, roe, bear, boar and wild goat	Tur and roe, Aug-Dec; bear, Oct and Nov; roe, Oct-Dec. 5/6-day tour. Not more than 5 per party.
Gavrilov	Askania deer	Oct only. 5-day tour. Not more than 5 per party.
Kubinsk	Tur	July-Sept. 2/5-day tour. Not more than 5 per party.
Irkutsk	Bears in their lairs	Nov-Feb. Temperature varies from −20°C to −50C° 3/4-day tour. 1-3 hunters allowed per tour.

Big Game Inventory—Utah

Species	Shot
Mule deer	95,161
Antelope	114
Elk	1,352
Moose	14
Bighorn sheep	3
Bison	15
Wild turkey	214
Sage grouse	11,109
Blue and ruffed grouse	32,414
Pheasant	297,752

The red-breasted goose — one of the many species of waterfowl to be found in Russia

10 rounds of ammunition), 10 roubles; transport within the hunting reserve, 25 roubles per car per day; 5 roubles per horse per day; services of individual huntsmen at 5 roubles per day; hunting licences, 1 rouble each. Visitors may take their own rifles and ammunition provided their tourist voucher indicates that hunting is the object of their trip.

Further Information

Intourist Information Offices, situated in most of the capital cities of Europe, Japan, Canada and the U.S.A.

Utah (U.S.A.)

A south-western state, its 85,000 square miles are largely arid, mountainous and infertile, and only a very small percentage of it is under arable crops. Ranching is the principal form of agriculture and there are very large areas of National Forest.

Utah has one of the largest mule-deer herds in the country, and they are found in all counties, though the biggest concentrations are in the south-east. More or less static populations of antelope and elk are maintained, hunted only by residents. There is a small buffalo herd and small moose herd, both hunted under special drawing, by residents only. Bighorn sheep have been introduced, and it is thought that they will thrive in what is a suitable environment. Pheasants are found only in the limited agricultural areas. Grouse – sage, ruffed, blue and sharp-tailed – are found, though in no abundance, and permits are drawn for. Hungarian and chukar partridges are found in some areas, and Merriam's turkey has been successfully introduced. In spite of its desert character, Utah attracts large numbers of waterfowl to nesting grounds on the Bear River Marshes and Ogden Bay. Mourning doves are abundant. The Game Commission maintaines two game farms, which are now producing chukars instead of pheasant, and are being used to study the

possibilities of introducing such exotics as sandgrouse and black and gray francolin.

Special Regulations

All hunters must wear red caps and outer garments. Game birds may only be hunted with shotguns. Aliens may not hunt or carry any sort of gun.

Further Information

Division of Fish and Game, 1596 W. N. Temple, Salt Lake City, Utah 84116.

Seasons and Limits—Utah

Vary from unit to unit

Species	Season	Limit	Comment
Mule deer	17 Oct-27 Oct	One buck per year	Special drawing in some units
Antelope	22 Aug-24 Aug 29 Aug-31 Aug		Special drawing, residents only
Elk	3 Oct-13 Oct		Residents only, special drawing in some areas
Moose	19 Sept-27 Sept		In Uinta Mountains; special drawings, residents only
Desert bighorn sheep	26 Sept-11 Oct		Residents only, special drawings for 10 permits annually
Buffalo	26 Sept-11 Oct		In Henry Mountains, residents only; special drawings
Cottontail rabbit Cougar Snowshoe hare Jack rabbit Squirrel	28 Sept-1 March All year round except that cougar season closes during elk, bighorn, buffalo and moose open season		May be shot without licence
Pheasant	Starts 7 Nov		
Grouse Chukar partridge Hungarian partridge	Starts 26 Sept		

Licence Fees—Utah

Type	Status	Fee
Big game	Resident	$5.00
	Non-resident	$50.00
Small game	Resident	$4.50
	Non-resident	$20.00
Deer	Resident	$5.00
Special deer	Non-resident	$7.00
Special moose, bighorn and buffalo	Resident	$25.00
Elk	Resident	$15.00
Antelope	Resident	$10.00
Turkey tag	Non-resident	$3.00

V

Valley Quail *(Lophortyx californica)*
There are at least three subspecies of this quail of which only the northern one *(L. californica californica)* should properly be called California quail. They were, originally, birds of the coastal plains of Oregon and California, with the southern subspecies found in the drier lands of Nevada and Lower California. They have, however, been transplanted successfully into a number of other states, and even as far away as Hawaii.

They resemble, in many ways, the mountain quail *(Oreortyx picta) q.v.*, and may be found as high as 4,000 ft. They once assembled in great flocks of several thousand birds, but market hunters, and grape growers protecting their vineyards, reduced the size and the number of the flocks. Nevertheless, in the late summer they still pack together in much larger groups than other quail, and stay in the group until pairing starts in the early spring.

They are adaptable birds, not only transplanting well, but also able to take advantage of the fresh foods and altered habitats that modern agricultural methods and irrigation have brought them, and so extend their range. Their principal diet, however, consists of weed seeds in winter and of greenstuff and insects in the summer. They can be bred and reared in captivity with as much success as the bobwhite and, since the hen sometimes raises two broods in the wild, and can lay up to 70 eggs in one season in captivity, the breeding potential, given suitable conditions, is high. Water and predators seem to be the limiting factors. Though the adult can survive on dew it normally has to visit a watering place every day, and the chicks must drink within 24 hours of hatching in order to survive. Ground squirrels are the most dangerous predators, taking more quail eggs than all other predators combined.

Like other quail, valley quail are monogamous, and the cock will assist in incubation and rearing. The nest is usually built in cover, as close to water as possible, and the clutch of 13 to 17 eggs takes between 21 and 23 days to incubate.

Valley quail are slightly smaller than mountain quail, the average weight being between 6 and 7 oz, and the length between $9\frac{1}{2}$ and 11 in. The cock has a curved black crest, its head is barred black and white, and it has brown upperparts, with splashes of white on the sides, light gray underparts with a scale effect and a chestnut patch on the belly. The hen has no crest, a shorter

Licence Fees—Vermont			
Type	**Status**	**Fee**	**Comment**
General	Resident	$2.00	Sold by town and
	Non-resident	$30.50	city clerks
Deer party permit	Either	$3.00	Applicant *must* possess a general licence
Small game	Non-resident	$10.50	

Seasons and Limits—Vermont			
Species	**Season**	**Limit**	**Comment**
Deer	14 Nov-29 Nov	One buck with minimum 3-in antlers per season	In certain areas, deer parties are allowed one additional doe per party
Black bear	1 Sept-30 Nov	One per year	
Cottontail rabbit and snowshoe hare	26 Sept-28 Feb	3 per day	
Squirrel	26 Sept-12 Nov	4 per day	
Pheasant	26 Sept-12 Nov	2 per day	
Ruffed grouse	26 Sept-30 Nov	4 per day	

tail, and is mainly plain brown. Their natural range is a small one and may, in a suitable habitat, exceed no more than a quarter of a mile. They are highly vocal birds, the commonest call being a loud 'cuc-a-coo'.

Left, the valley quail is an adaptable bird, able to take advantage of altered habitats.

Right, the sambar, an Indian species, has been introduced to Victoria, and makes a welcome trophy.

Where they have been extensively shot over, the coveys will tend to run on, so long as there is cover to hide them. If cover is sparse they will generally lie close until flushed. Once flushed they fly well, and often for longer distances than other quail. Once the coveys have been split up individual birds will lie well to a pointer. Indeed a dog will be almost essential to make them flush again. When this happens they will fly for a shorter distance, and will tend not to run on after landing.

Varying Hare *see* Blue Hare; Snowshoe Rabbit

Venezuela

Venezuela is the northernmost South American country. It has a total area of just over 350,000 square miles, centred on the lower basin of the Orinoco, which flows more or less north-eastwards. The basin is flanked on the west by the two arms of the Eastern Andes, where they run into the Caribbean, and on the south-east by other mountain ranges, notably the Sierras Parina and Pacaraima. The coastline is heavily indented, with many lakes and lagoons, including Lake Maracaibo, the largest in South America. In the interior the Orinoco basin is mostly level plain, with occasional trees, but the slopes of the hills are heavily wooded. The climate is tropical, and except where modified by altitude or sea breezes, unhealthy, particularly in coastal regions near lowland streams and lagoons.

Agriculture is not relatively as important as in other South American countries and food has to be imported. Livestock are raised, and the chief crops are cotton, coffee, cocoa and sugar.

For game *see* South America, Shooting in.

Further Information
Ministerio de Fomento Direccion de Turismo, Edificio Sur, Centro Simon Bolivar, Caracas.

Vermont (U.S.A.)

A small, north-eastern state, its 10,000 square miles are still primarily agricultural; mainly dairying, though cereals, potatoes and fruit are also produced. There are large areas of forest, and the Green Mountains run from north to south down its length.

Most of the state is open to hunting, though posting has increased in recent years, and there is a large and well distributed herd of white-tailed deer. The ruffed grouse, especially at the peak of its cycles, provides excellent shooting. Woodcock and wildfowl provide good sport and there are pheasants in some counties.

Big Game Inventory—Vermont		
Species	Shot	Est. pop.
White-tailed deer	14,366	190,000
Black bear	160	2,500

Further Information
Fish and Game Department, Montpelier, Vermont 05602.

Victoria (Australia)

The southernmost and smallest mainland-state of Australia, covering an area of 87,884 square miles. The dominant feature is the Great Dividing Range and the Australian Alps where they turn westward to form the backbone of the state and divide it into a northern and southern watershed. Victoria is the most mountainous state, rising to over 6,000 ft. The southern section has numerous well-wooded valleys, particu-

Unprotected Species—Victoria

Native birds
Australian crow
Australian goshawk
Australian raven
Black cormorant
Galah (rose-breasted cockatoo)
Little black cormorant
Little pied cormorant
Peregrine falcon
Pied cormorant
Wedge-tailed eagle
White-breasted cormorant

Native mammals
Common wombat
All native rodents
(except eastern water rat)

Introduced birds
Blackbird
Common mynah
Goldfinch
Greenfinch
House sparrow
Red-whiskered bulbul
Rock dove
Spotted turtle dove
(Java or lace-neck dove)
Starling
Tree sparrow

Introduced mammals
Black rat
Brown rat
Dingo
Feral cat
Ferret (polecat)
Fox
Gray squirrel
Hare
House mouse
Rabbit

Deer
Fallow deer
Hog deer
Red deer
Sambar deer
(deer may not be shot on any proclaimed sanctuary)

Licences—Victoria

A licence is required by all duck shooters (licence fee : Australian $2). Licences may be obtained from the Fisheries and Wildlife Department, its offices, police stations throughout the state, and Victoria Government Tourist Bureaus. Game licences expire on 31 December each year, and are not available for issue for after the last day of the season. Licences are not required for deer, quail or snipe.

larly in the south-east. The west is good wool and grain country, even north of the mountains, as the Murray river, which forms part of the northern boundary with New South Wales, provides plenty of irrigation. The climate is pleasantly temperate, though it can be quite warm in summer, with an average rainfall of 25 in per year.

Although by far the most closely settled and industrialized part of Australia, with 3% of the land area, 28% of the population and about a third of the gross national product, Victoria is still very strongly pastoral and agricultural. It thus offers good communications and modern conveniences together with much unspoilt country.

There are, at present, 38 wildlife sanctuaries in Victoria (a list can be obtained from the Fisheries and Wildlife Department or its local officers). The sanctuaries are divided into three distinct types: 'game reserves' (20) are for all waterbirds, but duck may be shot during the open season. Otherwise they are closed to shooting. 'Game refuges' (2) are also for all waterbirds, but no shooting is permitted at any time. 'Faunal reserves' (16) are for specific species, or for wildlife generally, and again shooting is entirely prohibited.

Special Regulations
Shotguns larger than 12-bore may not be used.

A pair of mallard. This duck has the widest distribution of any in America and is also the commonest breeding duck in Europe.

Seasons and Limits—Victoria		
Species	**Season**	**Limit**
Duck	Penultimate Sat in Feb-last Sat in April	20 birds on opening day, 10 per day thereafter, not more than 5 of which may be freckled duck (monkey duck), hardhead (white-eyed duck), wood duck (maned goose), pink-eared duck, chestnut teal, blue-winged shoveller or chestnut-breasted shelduck (mountain duck); and not more than 10 of which may be gray duck (black duck) and gray teal
Stubble quail	1st Sat in March-last Sat in March, and 1st Sat in May-last Sat in June	20 birds per day
Jack snipe	Extremely variable. Recent season was 1 July-31 May	No limit
Unprotected species	Any time	
Blue-billed duck, musk duck, plumed tree duck, whistling tree duck English song thrush Skylark Eastern water rat All marsupials (except common wombat)	Completely protected	

Licence Fees—Virginia

Type	Status	Fee	Comment
General (home county only)	Resident	$3.50	Sold by clerks of the courts
	Resident	$2.00	
	Non-resident	$15.75	
Deer	Resident	$2.00	
	Non-resident	$10.00	
Bear	Resident	$2.00	
	Non-resident	$10.00	
Turkey	Resident	$2.00	
	Non-resident	$10.00	

Seasons and Limits—Virginia

Species	Area	Season	Limit
Deer	West	15 Nov-27 Nov	One buck per licence year. In some counties a deer of either sex may be taken on last day only
	East	15 Nov-5 Jan	2 per year. On last hunting day or last 12 days, one may be antlerless
Black bear	Most	8 Nov-31 Dec	One per year with minimum 75lb liveweight
Cottontail rabbit	East	15 Nov-1 Jan	6 per day, 75 per licence year
Ruffed grouse	West	1 Nov-31 Jan	3 per day, 15 per licence year
Quail			8 per day, 125 per licence year
Pheasant		Experimental season to determine distribution on 15, 16 Nov	One cock per day
Squirrel		Varies from area to area	6 per day, 75 per licence year
Wild turkey	West	1 Nov-18 Dec	3 per licence year, of which nor more than 2 may be taken in the autumn, and not more than one a hen (where legal)
	East (except some counties)	15 Nov-18 Dec	
bearded turkeys	All	22 April-13 May from $\frac{1}{2}$-hour before sunrise-11a.m. only	

Big Game Inventory—Virginia

Species	Shot	Est. pop.
White-tailed deer	28,027	170,000
Black bear	342	1,500
Wild turkey	4,707	29,000

A firearms certificate is required for all firearms except shotguns, air rifles, and .22 rifles (pea rifles).

Those under 18 may not purchase any firearm or air gun, but may use a shotgun, and may also use a pea rifle provided thay are over 14 years and have a certificate signed by the officer-in-charge of the local police station.

No one may carry or use a firearm or air rifle across or on land used for primary production, without the consent of the owner or occupier of the land.

No one may carry or use a firearm or air rifle on Sunday, except under special circumstances.

No one may use or carry a loaded firearm in a town or populous place, or on any street, road or lane.

Further Information

The Fisheries and Wildlife Department, 605, Flinders Street Extension, Melbourne, 3000, Victoria.

Virginia (U.S.A.)

A south-eastern state, its 40,000 square miles rise from the lowlands of tidal Virginia to the Blue Ridge Mountains, falls again to the Shenandoah Valley, and then rise slowly, westwards, towards the Allegheny Mountains. Most of the soil is fertile, and three quarters of the state is farmland. There are some 4 million acres of cropland, with corn, tobacco, cotton and peanuts as the most important crops. Virginia has large areas of State and National Forest, and several State Parks in addition to the Shenandoah National Park in the Blue Ridge Mountains.

White-tailed deer and black bear constitute the big-game population. The deer are found in most rural counties, but most abundantly in the south-west, in Dismal Swamp, and in the central mountain areas. Re-stocking of other areas continues. Bears are most common in the Dismal Swamp and Blue Ridge Mountain areas, turkeys are abundant in the Piedmont and the western mountain areas. Squirrels and rabbits are found throughout the state, as are quail. Ruffed grouse are found from the Blue Ridge Mountains westwards. Pheasants have never become well established, but there are large migratory populations of doves, waterfowl, woodcock, rails and snipe.

Special Regulations

No shotgun above 10-bore or not plugged down to three cartridges may be used, and in most counties rifles may be used on all game except migratory game birds, but rifles used for deer and bear must be .23 calibre or larger.

Further Information

Game and Inland Fisheries, 7 N. Second Street, Richmond 23213.

W

Waders
(Rallidae, Charadriidae, Scolopacidae)

It is customary to group, under this comprehensive title, rails, coots, gallinules, curlews, plovers, snipe and woodcock. From the shooting viewpoint, what brings them together is not that they all actually wade, nor that they are all birds of the foreshore, but rather that they are birds that, without actually being either game birds or waterfowl, are hunted and shot in most countries of the world. The most important, to the hunter, are the woodcock and snipe, both members of the *Scolopacidae*.

European Woodcock *(Scolopax rusticola)*

Very similar to, but larger than the American woodcock *(Philohela minor) q.v.*, it is a solitary and nocturnal woodland bird, perfectly adapted, by its plumage, to merge into a background of dead leaves. It lies up, all day, unless flushed, in close cover, emerging at dusk to fly to its feeding grounds, generally in adjoining bogland, returning at daybreak. It measures about 13 in, and has large eyes placed well back in the head, with the ears in front of and below them. It is considerably larger and stouter than even a great snipe, has a thicker bill, considerably less neck, and transverse, rather than longitudinal barring on the head. It is impossible, except by dissection, to tell the sexes apart. It flies, head and bill pointing downwards, and when in trees has a jinking, zigzag habit of flight that makes shooting difficult. It is silent in flight except for an alarm cry of 'tsiwick'.

Its feeding habits are the same as the American woodcock's and, like that bird, it must move to softer soils in front of advancing frost. It is both resident and migratory in Britain and Europe, moving, generally, southwards and westwards ahead of the frosts, so that the heaviest winter populations are found in Devon, Cornwall and Ireland. They are usually shot whilst coverts are being driven, or when wooded, secluded areas are being walked with dogs. On some Cornish and Irish estates, however, there are coverts kept solely, or mainly, for woodcock, or mixed woodcock and pheasant drives.

Snipe *(Capella species)*

There are a dozen recognized species, breeding on all the continents except Australia. (The so-called Australian snipe is really the Japanese snipe, a large species that breeds in northern Japan and winters in Australia.) The snipe of the North American continent is Wilson's snipe *(Capella delicata)*, which

The European curlew inhabits mud-flats and estuaries, and nests on moors.

very closely resembles the European common snipe *(C. gallinago)* and breeds from Alaska to Hudson Bay to as far south as California and winters from the southern states to northern South America. It is recognized as a migratory bird and protected under the Migratory Birds Convention Acts. The snipe of Europe consist of the great snipe *(C. media)*, common snipe *(C. gallinago)* and jacksnipe *(Lymnocryptes minimus)*. The differences between these are principally those of size: over 11 in, about 10 in and 7½ in respectively.

They are all of a brown, black, and buff mottled and rufous appearance, with the great snipe showing some white, the common a little white and the jack no white on the tail. The pale stripes on the crown are all longitudinal, rather than transverse, as with the woodcock, and they have long slender bills with the upper mandible slightly longer than the lower one. The great snipe has a slower, heavier, and less twisting flight than either the common or jack, and flies silently. It breeds in Norway, and east from the Baltic to Russia, and is only an occasional summer visitor to Britain. The common and jack are both residents, and breed throughout the British Isles, as well as having their numbers greatly increased by migrations from Iceland and north-western Europe from September onwards. There is also, as with woodcock, a constant internal migration southwards and westwards in search of softer, frost-free soils. The jack is a solitary, silent during flight except during display, when it has a muffled drumming note. The common snipe generally flies to and from its feeding grounds in small groups or 'wisps', has a markedly zigzag flight, and gives a hoarse rasping cry when flushed. The great snipe prefers, except in the mating season, a fairly dry habitat, and is to be found on heaths, stubbles, in bracken and so on. Common and jacksnipe, however, are birds of wet and boggy lands, and prefer marshes, water meadows, sewage farms, moorland bogs and mosses. They are all nocturnal feeders, flighting to their feeding grounds at dusk, and back from them at dawn.

Snipe can be shot walking up, they can be flighted, occasionally they are driven, and, in very cold weather, they can even be decoyed. They are never easy birds to shoot, but they rarely offer an uninteresting shot.

Curlews *(Numenius species)*

There are at least eight birds in this genus, all long-legged, brown and black birds with long, distinctive, down-turned bills and a gull-like habit of flight. Their normal habitat is on the mudflats and estuaries of the foreshore, but they generally breed inland, on moors and marshes, the nest being little more than a grass-lined depression, often out in the open. They feed by probing in the mud with their long bills for crustaceans and other small marine creatures, as well as grubs, beetles and other insects. Those curlews that are shot are, when still young and fresh from the inland breeding range, quite edible. Later their flesh becomes muddy and unpalatable.

The largest of all is the long-billed curlew of America *(Numenius americanus)*, which measures up to 24 in. They were once abundant along both the Atlantic and Pacific coasts, but their nesting grounds were reduced by agriculture and they were over-shot by market gunners until their numbers were so reduced that they were placed, perhaps too late, on the fully protected list. The European curlew *(N. arquata)* is the largest of all European waders, measuring up to 23 in. It breeds in the British Isles, Brittany, along the Norwegian coast and in Central and Eastern Europe, and is a partial migrant, wintering as far south as the Mediterranean. The whimbrel *(Numenius phaeopus)*, known in America as the Hudsonian curlew, is a smaller bird, measuring about 16 in, with a shorter bill and a boldly striped crown. Its call consists of a rapid 'tit-tit-tit' repeated seven times and ending on a short note. It breeds, generally, in the circumpolar regions, though it has been known to nest in northern Scotland and the Hebrides. The slender-billed curlew *(N. tenuirostris)* resembles a paler whimbrel, but lacks the bold striping on the crown. It breeds on the steppes and winters as far south as the Mediterranean; it is occasionally seen, as a vagrant, in the British Isles. The Eskimo curlew *(N. borealis)* that used to be shot in great numbers by market hunters has now practically disappeared from North America. Its nickname of 'dough bird' explains why it was over-shot. The Madagascar curlew of eastern Siberia winters in Malaya and Australia, and the bristle-thighed curlew of Alaska flies 5,000 miles to winter on the islands of the mid-Pacific.

Closely allied to the curlew are the godwits, of which the bar-tailed godwit *(Limosa lapponica)* and the black-tailed godwit *(Limosa limosa)* may be shot in the British Isles, to which they are passage migrants.

Curlew and whimbrel shooting depends, largely, on a knowledge of local tides and local flight lines. During low water the birds will scatter out along the mudflats, returning to higher sandbanks as the tide rises. When it is high enough to wash them off the sandbanks they will fly inland, and the gunner must meet them on their way to or from the mudflats, concealing himself behind a wall, in a gutter or pit, or under

The bar-tailed godwit is a coastal bird of the tundra regions of Europe and North America.

The whimbrel is similar to the curlew; it is distinguished by being smaller, darker above, and having broad stripes on its crown.

camouflage net, at the right place and right time.

Gallinules

These, together with rails and coots, are members of the *Rallidae*. They are plump, chicken-like birds, living among reeds and rushes in swamps, along lake sides and stagnant ponds. Their large, long-toed feet, which are not webbed, allow them to run about on top of the reed bed vegetation. They are comparatively weak flyers, and dangle their feet as they fly. They find it difficult to take wing from water, making a considerable splash while doing so, and they swim with a characteristic jerking head movement. They have variously coloured frontal shields but are otherwise generally black or drab coloured. These shields are hardened patches, stretching from the base of the bill to the forehead, designed to protect the birds as they thrust through the sharp leaves of a reed bed. The largest of them is the purple gallinule *(Porphyrio porphyrio)*, which is about 19 in long and brightly coloured purple and turquoise on top with red bill, frontal shield, eyes and legs. It breeds in the Iberian peninsula, Sardinia and Sicily and is a vagrant to France, Norway and central Europe. A related species *(Porphyrula martinica)* is found in the United States, south of the Mason-Dixon line, and especially in the rice plantations of South Carolina and in Florida. The moorhen, or common gallinule *(Gallinula chloropus)*, is found throughout the temperate and tropical wetlands except in Australasia, and is almost identical with the Florida gallinule *(G. galatea)*. They are blackish birds with red frontal shields and bills, a white streak across the flanks and white under-tail coverts. They nest in the reeds over water.

None of the gallinules are worth shooting. Their flight is too hesitant and low for them to offer sporting shots when on the wing, and it would be even less sporting to shoot them on the water, in addition to which they are virtually inedible. They are, however, egg eaters, and will chase out nesting mallard and take their eggs, so that it may be necessary to reduce their numbers.

Rails

These include the water rail *(Rallus aquaticus)*, the corncrake *(Crex crex)* and other crakes, none of which are much shot in Europe. In America, however, the Virginia rail *(Rallus virginianus)*, the sora rail *(Porzana carolina)* and the clapper rail *(Rallus longirostris crepitans)* are all keenly hunted. Of these the clapper rail is the largest and the sora rail the smallest. They are all nocturnal, aquatic birds, brown on top and gray or black and white underneath, with curved bills and long legs that dangle in flight. They are low, and comparatively weak flyers, but they swim and dive well and can run on top of the thick vegetation of the fresh-water marshes they live in. They feed on snails and other forms of aquatic life. They are either completely or partially migratory. Although soras live only in fresh-water marshes, the Virginian, clapper and king rails are salt-water marsh inhabitants.

Because they are small, thinly fleshed birds they are hunted for sport only, which has saved them from the market hunters. They are shot along much of the Atlantic coast from narrow, flat-bottomed 'rail boats' which are punted through the tall beds of wild rice with the gunner in front and the pusher and dog in the back.

Coots

The coot of Eurasia *(Fulica atra)* is very similar to the American coot *(Fulica americana) q.v.*

Plovers

Of these only the golden plover *(Charadrius apricarius)* and the Gray Plover *(Charadrius squatarola)* may be shot in the British Isles. *See also* Plovers.

Wallabies *see* Kangaroos

Wapiti *(Cervus canadensis)*

Early settlers in America, who had heard of, but probably had never seen, the elks of Scandinavia, gave the name of elk to these large American deer, called by the Indians, wapiti. Thus they were obliged to give the Indian name of moose to the true elk of America – the *Alces americana*. It is simpler and less confusing to call this animal, wapiti.

The coot has a wide distribution in Europe and North Asia, inhabiting open water.

The wapiti, or elk, is a gregarious North American deer, which in winter migrates to the valleys below the tree line.

The wapiti is similar to, though larger than, the red deer of Europe, and is the only member of the genus *Cervus* to be found in North America. It was once found in most parts for it is a grazer almost as much as a browser, and is therefore at home in open country. However, it came into competition with an advancing agriculture and was, at the same time, exposed to the market hunter who shot it for meat and hides and even, in later years, for its 'tusks' – the two upper canines it was once fashionable to turn into tiepins or watch-chain charms. Pressures like these drove the wapiti back into the forests and mountains, and it is now usually found above the treeline in summer, and never very far from the safety of the forest at any time.

In winter, however, the wapiti still has to come down from the heights to the valleys, where it comes into competition, once more, with domestic cattle and other deer. However much the wapiti is protected now, and it is found in few states and hunted in even fewer, its limiting factor is availability of winter food and winter ranges. Herds must still be culled to ensure that they never outgrow the limited winter ranges available to them, even in National Parks.

Wapiti are now mainly found in the Rocky Mountain states and in southern Canada, but there are also herds in all the Pacific coast states from British Columbia to California. They have been re-introduced, with considerable success, to Alaska, Arizona, New Mexico, and some eastern states, and they were introduced, by Theodore Roosevelt, to the South Island of New Zealand, where they still survive, though in some danger of disappearing because of interbreeding with the local red deer.

The rut occurs in September and October, at which time the older bulls collect their harems of 20 or 30 cows, chasing away, at the same time, the younger bulls. The cows, who start breeding in their second year, generally drop a single calf in April or May. It weighs between 30 and 40 lb and after a very few days is able to run and graze. It will not, however, be weaned until late winter. The bull casts its antlers in March; re-growth begins in April, and the velvet is shed in August. Wapiti are gregarious and, after calving, the cow will rejoin the group which, during the winter, will coalesce with other groups and form a herd of several hundred animals.

A mature bull weighs between 600 and 800 lb, measures up to 9 ft and stands 5 ft at the shoulder. The antlers, which add another 5 ft to its height, are round and widely branching and carry from 12 to 16 points. The cow is considerably smaller and lighter. Both sexes are maned and their coats are tan-coloured with lighter rump patches.

Wapiti are normally hunted in high forest or in alpine meadows above the treeline. Horses and pack animals are essential, the one to allow the hunter to follow a herd that will move large distances in a single day, the other to transport the heavy carcass. They can either be stalked on foot or followed on horse until a shot is possible. Alternatively they can be driven by mounted men towards dismounted guns. In all cases a long range, flat-trajectory, hard-hitting rifle is needed.

See also Deer of the World and their Hunting.

Washington (U.S.A.)

Its 68,000 square miles lie in the extreme north-west. It has a varied topography and climate, with coastal marshes rising to the Olympic Mountains. East of these, Puget Sound, almost an inland sea, cuts into the state, and east of that lies the Cascade Range, which separates the high rainfall coastal areas from dry prairie country split up by the more fertile valleys of the various rivers. Agriculture is the most important industry, and wheat the most important crop, though there is also a great deal of ranching and some fruit growing. Washington is also very heavily timbered, and is, in fact, the second largest timber producing state.

Such a variation of terrain and climate produces a diversified game population. The state deer herd numbers around half a million, the commonest species being the blacktail, with mule, whitetail and Columbian whitetail also present. The blacktail is found in the west and the mule in the east of the state, the Columbian whitetail in a limited area of the south-west, and the Virginian whitetail in the north-east. Elk, both Rocky Mountain and Roosevelt, are found in the coastal areas, and in the south, in the Mount St Helens, Blue Mountains and Yakima-Kittitas areas. The country's largest herd of Rocky Mountain goat is in the Cascades, and black bear are found almost everywhere. There are cougar in the Olympic Mountains; bighorns and wild turkey are both being re-introduced. The commonest game birds are pheasant and California quail; there are also five species of grouse, valley, mountain, and bobwhite quail, and chukar and Hungarian partridge. Waterfowl hunting along the coast is excellent.

Special Regulations

Shotguns firing slugs or buckshot may be used on deer in certain areas, but they may not be used on elk, nor may handguns be used on deer, elk, mountain goat or bear. Rim-fire rifles are illegal for big game. No dogs may be used on deer or elk.

Further Information

Department of Game, 600 N. Capitol Way, Olympia, Washington 98501.

Waterbuck (*Kobus ellipsiprymnus*)

The common waterbuck and defassa waterbuck, *K. defassa* (or sing-sing), are closely related species found throughout many

Licence Fees—Washington

Type	Status	Fee	Comment
General	Resident	$5.50	Sold at hardware and sporting-goods stores
	Non-resident	$35.00	
Bighorn sheep tag	Resident	$7.50	
Elk tag	Resident	$7.50	
	Non-resident	$25.00	
Mountain goat tag	Resident	$7.50	
	Non-resident	$25.00	
Deer tag	Resident	$2.00	
Black bear tag	Resident	$2.00	
Turkey tag	Resident	$2.00	
	Non-resident	$2.00	

Seasons and Limits—Washington

Vary from area to area.

Species	Season	Limit	Comment
White-tailed deer	10 Oct-8 Nov; 21 Nov-6 Dec	One antlered buck	
Mule deer	10 Oct-8 Nov	One antlered buck	
Black-tailed deer	10 Oct-8 Nov	One antlered buck	
Elk	7 Nov-22 Nov	One antlered bull	Drawing for cow permits in some areas
Black bear	1 April-18 Nov	West: no limit east: one per year	
Bighorn sheep	26 Sept-4 Oct		Special drawing, residents only
Mountain goat	12 Sept-1 Nov		Special drawing for 1,000 permits
Cougar	Protected, some areas; all year in others		
Cottontail rabbit	12 Sept-March		
Snowshoe hare	12 Sept-March		
Jack rabbit	All year		
Pheasant	Starts 11 Oct	3 cocks per day	
Grouse, ruffed, blue and spruce	12 Sept-22 Nov		
Sharp-tailed and sage	Starts 10 Oct		
Quail, California, bobwhite and mountain	Starts 10 Oct	10 per day	
Partridge, chukar and Hungarian	12 Sept-9 Oct		
Wild turkey	Autumn and spring season-dates vary	One gobbler per year	

Big Game Inventory—Washington

Species	Shot	Est. pop.
White-tailed deer	12,700	70,000
Mule deer	36,200	185,000
Black-tailed deer	43,200	245,000
Elk	13,000	60,000
Bighorn sheep	11	300
Mountain goat	350	7,000
Black bear	4,100	22,000
Wild turkey	100	2,000

parts of Africa south of the Sahara, the former being slightly the larger, standing about 4 ft; the latter is 3 ft 9 in at the shoulder. The waterbuck has a prominent white ring around the base of the tail, but the defassa has a white rump patch. Both have heavily fringed necks and tufted tails; both have lyrate horns only in the bucks, those of the former being about 2 ft 6 in long and of the latter nearer 2 ft. Both are gray or reddish in coloration and are found in woodlands near water, or occasionally in flood plains. They are generally in small to medium sized herds, but sometimes are associated with larger herds including other species. Both are grazers and possibly occasional browsers. Both may calve at any period of the year and generally only have one calf, though perhaps sometimes twins. When chased or alarmed they take to water.

Waterfowl *(Anatidae)*
This is a large family of closely allied birds popularly classified as swans, geese and ducks – a classification sometimes difficult to maintain taxonomically, largely because there are sometimes blurrings of distinction between true geese and true ducks.

The family consists of 40 genera containing, altogether, 144 species, and many of these are rare, or inedible, or poor birds to shoot, or all of these, and so should not be of any great interest to the hunter as a hunter, though waterfowl are of great interest to those who are naturalists.

It is customary to divide the family into three main groups or sub-families:

1. The *Anseratinae*, which consists of a single, otherwise unclassifiable species – the magpie goose of Australia, which resembles no other species.

2. The *Anserinae*, which includes all the swans and all the true geese as well as the Dendrocygnini – the whistling or tree ducks.

3. The *Anatinae*, which includes all the other waterfowl, most of them called ducks, though some of them are popularly referred to as geese.

The principal differences between the *Anserinae* and the *Anatinae* may be defined as follows: the *Anserinae* are all goose-like, have long necks, walk well, moult only once a year, show no sexual dimorphism of plumage or voice, pair for life, generally share in the rearing of the young, have no elaborate courtship displays, no speculums, and are principally grazers. The *Anatinae* vary in shape and posture, as well as in their ability to walk, they show more or less conspicuous degrees of sexual dimorphism of plumage, generally have elaborate courtship displays, feed on and under the water more than on land, and are frequently eaters of animal foods as well as vegetarians; they are often brightly coloured with metallic speculums, have two moults a year, and the male generally deserts the female at nesting time.

The table lists the most important species; scientific names are given to avoid any confusion that may arise due to the common names not being standardized. Many subspecies have been erected by the authorities, but only those which seem to be important from the wildfowler's viewpoint are included. It should be remembered that what one authority treats as a subspecies may well be given specific rank by another.

Waterfowl of every sort have been chased ever since hunting began. Ancient Egyptian wall paintings show much the same kinds being hunted with nets and throwing-sticks and bows as we hunt today. They are now greatly reduced in numbers, but they still provide the hunter with some of the most difficult, the most rewarding, and above all, some of the most interesting shooting of all. The shooting, itself, is certainly the smallest part of the enjoyment of wildfowling. Pleasure flows from the sight and study of the birds, knowledge of their feeding and flight habits, of the tides and winds that influence their day to day behaviour, and from the generally wild and deserted places in which they are hunted. The hunter will need to be a fast, accurate, almost instinctive shot, able to pick his bird out against a darkening sky, often by sound more than by sight. But the advances of modern civilization and modern agriculture have deprived us of many beautiful and interesting waterfowl, and now none that offer poor sport through being slow to fly or unwary, and none that are rare, or poor eating, ought to be hunted. Enough will still be left to test a hunter's skill.

Waterfowl can be netted in decoy ponds and in other ways (if legal); they can be trapped; they can be shot from the land or from a boat. The boat can be a gun punt or a sneak skiff. On land the hunter can be in a hide, or behind a blind, or in a pit, or crouch under cover along a flightline for pass shooting. The birds can be flighted on or off their feeding grounds or their sleeping grounds, they can be stalked across stubbles, they can be jump shot off a stream, they can be called down or brought down by decoys, live (where legal), block or profile. There are a great many different ways of hunting waterfowl, and all of them demand patience, knowledge and skill.

West and West Central Africa
The area may be considered as comprising all those countries on the west coast of Africa between Senegal and Angola, and two without a coastline, the Central African Republic and Upper Volta. There is a total of 20 countries. At the two extremities they run into desert areas, the Sahara in the north of Senegal, and the Kalahari in the south of Angola. Otherwise they all consist of either tropical forest and jungle, very hot and damp with extremely luxuriant vegetation, or of savannah, hot grassland coun-

Waterfowl

Whistling or Tree Ducks
(Dendrocygnini)
Spotted whistling duck
  Dendrocygna guttata
Plumed whistling duck
  D. eytoni
East Indian wandering whistling duck
  D. arcuata arcuata
Australian wandering whistling duck
  D. arcuata australis
Fulvous whistling duck
  D. bicolor
Black-billed whistling duck
  D. arborea
Indian whistling duck
  D. javanica
White-faced whistling duck
  D. viduata
Northern red-billed whistling duck
  D. autumnalis autumnalis
Southern red-billed whistling duck
  D. autumnalis discolor

Swans and Geese
(Anserini)
Black swan
  Cygnus atratus
Mute swan
  C. olor
Black-necked swan
  C. melanocoryphus
Whooper swan
  C. cygnus
Bewick's swan
  C. columbianus bewickii

Graylag goose *
  Anser anser
White-fronted goose *
  A. albifrons (several sub-species)
Bean goose *
  A. fabalis (several sub-species)
Pink-footed goose *
  A. brachyrhynchus
Snow * and blue goose *
  A. caerulescens caerulescens
Greater snow goose
  A. caerulescens atlanticus
Ross's goose
  A. rossi
Emperor goose *
  A. canagicus
Bar-headed goose
  A. indicus
Canada goose *
  Branta canadensis
  (several sub-species)
Barnacle goose *
  B. leucopsis
Red-breasted goose
  B. ruficollis
Brent goose *
  Branta bernicla bernicla
Black brant *
  B. bernicla orientalis
American brant *
  B. bernicla hrota

helducks and Sheldgeese
(adornini)
outh American sheldgeese
Chloephaga (several species)
byssinian blue-winged goose
Cyanochen cyanopterus
yptian goose
Alopochen aegyptiacus
ustralian shelduck
Tadorna tadornoides
radise shelduck
T. variegata
radise shelduck
T. variegata
uth African shelduck
T. cana
ddy shelduck
T. ferruginea
ommon shelduck
T. tadorna
tagonian crested duck
Lophonetta specularioides

abbling Ducks
ncluding Teal*; Widgeon*)
natini)
rican black duck
Anas sparsa
yssinian black duck
A. sparsa leucostigma
onze-winged duck
A. specularis
allard*
A. platyrhynchos
exican duck
A. platyrhynchos diazi
orida duck
A. platyrhynchos fulvigula
ack duck*
A. rubripes
dian spot-billed duck
A. poecilorhyncha
poecilorhyncha*
rmese spot-billed duck
A. poecilorhyncha haringtoni
stralian black duck
A. superciliosa rogersi
uth African yellow-billed duck
A. undulata undulata
yssinian yellow-billed duck
A. undulata ruppellii
ay teal
A. gibberifrons
stralian gray teal
A. gibberifrons gracilis
estnut teal
A. castanea
ilean teal
A. flavirostris flavirostris
ropean green-winged teal
A. crecca crecca
utian green-winged teal
A. crecca nimia
erican green-winged teal
A. crecca carolinesis

Baikal green-winged teal
A. formosa
Falcated teal
A. falcata
Gadwall*
A. strepera
European widgeon
A. penelope
Baldpate*
A. americana
Chiloe wigeon
A. sibilatrix
Lesser Bahama pintail
A. bahamensis bahamensis
Greater Bahama pintail
A. bahamensis rubrirostris
Chilean pintail
A. georgica spinicauda
Pintail
A. acuta acuta
American pintail*
A. acuta tzitzihoa
Red-billed teal
A. erythrorhyncha
Marbled teal
A. angustirostris
Cape teal
A. capensis
Hottentot teal
A. punctata
Northern silver teal
A. versicolor versicolor
Southern silver teal
A. versicolor fretensis
Garganey
A. querquedula
Blue-winged teal
A. discors
Argentine cinnamon teal
A. cyanoptera cyanoptera
Andean cinnamon teal
A. cyanoptera orinomus
Borreror's cinnamon teal
A. cyanoptera borreroi
Tropical cinnamon teal
A. cyanoptera tropica
Northern cinnamon teal
A. cyanoptera septentrionalium
Red shoveller
A. platalea
Cape shoveller
A. smithi
Australian shoveller
A. rhynchotis rhynchotis
N. Zealand shoveller
A. rhynchotis variegata
Northern shoveller
A. clypeata
Ringed teal
A. leucophrys
Australian pink-eared duck
Malacorhynchus membranaceus
Australian freckled duck
Stictonetta naevosa

Eiders*
(Somateriini)
Steller's eider
Polysticta stelleri
European eider
Someteria mollisima
Spectacled eider
S. fischeri
King eider
S. spectabilis

Pochards
(Aythyini)
Red-crested pochard*
Netta rufina
Rosy-billed pochard
N. peposaca
South American pochard
N. erythrophthalma erythrophthalma
African pochard
N. erythrophthalma brunnea
Canvasback*
Aythya vallisneria
Pochard*
A. ferina
Redhead*
A. americana
Madagascar white-eye
A. innotota
Australian white-eye
A. australis
Ferruginous duck
A. nyroca
Baer's pochard
A. baeri
Ring-necked duck*
A. collaris
Tufted duck
A. fuligula
New Zealand scaup
A. novae-seelandiae
Lesser scaup
A. affinis
Greater scaup
A. marila

Wood or Perching Ducks and Geese
(Cairnini)
Australian wood duck
Chenonetta jubata
Wood duck*
Aix sponsa
Muscovy duck
Cairina moschata
White-winged wood duck
C. scutulata
Hartlaub's duck
C. hartlaubi
Gambian spur-winged goose
P. gambensis gambensis
Black spur-winged goose
P. gambensis niger

Scoters*, Goldeneyes, Mergansers
(Mergini)
European white-winged scoter
Melanitta fusca fusca
American white-winged scoter
M. fusca deglandi
Asiatic white-winged scoter
M. fusca stejnegeri
European black scoter
M. nigra nigra
American black scoter
M. nigra americana
Long-tailed duck*
Clangula hyemalis
European goldeneye
Bucephala clangula clangula
American goldeneye*
B. clangula americana
Barrow's goldeneye*
B. islandica
Bufflehead*
B. albeola
Smew
Mergus albellus
Hooded merganser
M. cucullatus
Brazilian merganser
M. octosetaceus
Red-breasted merganser
M. serrator
European goosander
Mergus merganser merganser
Asiatic merganser
M. merganser orientalis
American goosander
M. merganser americanus

Stiff-tails
(Oxyurini)
Ruddy duck*
Oxyura jamaicensis
(several sub-species)
Argentine ruddy duck
O. vittata
Maccoa duck
O. maccoa
Blue-billed duck
O. australis
African white-backed duck
Thalassornis leuconotus leuconotus
Australian musk duck
Biziura lobata

try with low stunted trees, yellowish-brown in the dry season and reviving in the wet. Along most of this part of the world, particularly in the Congos and Gabon, there are coastal plains backed by broad ranges of low hills, giving way to lower country in the interior. The chief rivers are the Congo and the Niger.

The chief crops of the region are coffee, palm oil, bananas, groundnuts and cocoa. Timber is important, as this area is one of the world's primary sources of hardwoods.

There is little information available about game or hunting. Some countries of the area at present actively discourage tourists. In addition much of the jungle is inhospitable and unpleasantly damp, with none of the compensations of altitude to be found in most of East Africa. The counter advantages are the correspondingly lower hunting pressures, with many species much more abundant owing to their very inaccessibility. The chief species are elephant, rhinoceros, hippopotamus, buffalo, warthog, bushpig, giant forest hog, lion, leopard, hyena, jackal, mountain zebra, giant eland, bongo, greater kudu, sitatunga, bushbuck, hartebeest, tsesseby, tope, sable, roan, addax, defassa waterbuck, Buffon's kob, bohor reedbuck, okapi, and a wide range of duikers.

Further Information

Those interested in hunting in this area should initially consult the nearest embassy of the appropriate country.

Western Australia

Western Australia consists of the whole of the western portion of Australia, covering an area of 975,920 square miles. The greater part of the state is a vast tableland, varying between 1,000 and 2,000 ft above sea level, although large areas, for some hundreds of miles, are hilly with the highest peaks just over 4,000 ft. The climate is remarkably temperate, even allowing for the desert in the far interior, with very small fluctuations in temperature and average annual rainfall.

About two-thirds of the total area is suitable for grazing, and there is also some grain. Forestry is important. The relative uniformity of the terrain, however, limits the variety of game, and even the list of pests is dominated by domestic animals 'gone wild'.

Duck are the chief game species. There are five shooting areas. In 1971 the Eucla Division and the South-West Division, which lie along the south coast and in the south-west corner of the state respectively, had a season lasting from 19 December to 10 January, with a bag limit of 8 per day and 16 in possession (this was a particularly bad year because of drought). The other three areas, the Kimberley, North-West and Eastern Land Divisions, comprise the rest of the state, in which there was no bag limit, either because breeding

was so erratic and irregular that there was no definite season, or, as in the Kimberley season, because breeding occurs during the 'wet' season (November to February) when the area is inaccessible.

Special Regulations

There are special duck shooting regulations which forbid the use of powered boats or rafts, aircraft or motor vehicles, as well as torches or any form of nightlights.

Duck may only be shot with a shotgun of not more than 10-bore. Otherwise gun laws are such that it is extremely difficult to obtain permission for anything more than a .22 rifle.

Further Information

The Department of Fisheries and Fauna, 108 Adelaide Terrace, Perth, Western Australia 6000.

West Virginia (U.S.A.)

About sixty per cent of its 24,000 square miles is covered with forest – a high proportion of hardwoods. The soil is, generally, of low fertility, and agriculture is of a backward, 'hill-billy' type, producing corn, cereals, tobacco, potatoes and fruit.

There are large areas of State and National Forest open to hunting, and the game population reflects the fact that it is a hill and forest area more than an agricultural one. That is, there are deer, bear, squirrels and grouse, but the pheasant population is marginal, and bobwhite quail are numerous only in the eastern Panhandle and along the Ohio River. Turkey re-stocking has been successful, and there are snowshoe hares in the north of the state. Woodcock are abundant in some areas.

Special Regulations

Elk, otter and wild boar are all protected. All hunting except for deer is prohibited on the first three days of the deer gun season. Deer may not be shot with a shotgun using anything more than one solid ball or slug, nor with a rifle using rimfire cartridges.

Big Game Inventory—West Virginia		
Species	Shot	Est. pop.
White-tailed deer	10,500	120,000
Black bear	100	575
Wild turkey	1,700	15,000

Further Information

Division of Fish and Game, Building 3, Charleston, West Virginia 25305.

Whimbrel *see* Waders

White-eared Kob *see* Lechwe

White-fronted Goose (*Anser albifrons*)
A gray goose, smaller than the graylag, it

A plate from Archibald Thorburn's *British Birds*, illustrating tufted duck, bufflehead, ferruginous duck, goldeneye, scaup and long-tailed duck.

Pl. 4.

Tufted Duck. (♂♀)
Ferruginous Duck. (♂♀)
Buffel-headed Duck. (♂♀)   Golden-eye (♂♀)   Scaup Duck. (♂♀)
Long-tailed Duck. (♂♀)

Licence Fees—West Virginia

Type	Status	Fee
General	Resident	$3
	Non-resident	$30
National Forest Stamp		$1

Seasons and Limits—West Virginia

Vary from county to county.

Species	County	Season	Limit
Deer	Most	22 Nov-4 Dec	One buck per season
	Some southern	22 Nov-27 Nov	
Black bear	Eastern only	1 Nov-6 Dec	One bear of 100 lb or more
		13 Dec-25 Dec	
Cottontail rabbit		7 Nov-27 Feb	5 per day, 10 in possession
Snowshoe hare		7 Nov-27 Feb	2 per day, 4 in possession
Squirrel	Southern	12 Sept-2 Jan	6 per day, 12 in possession
	Others	10 Oct-2 Jan	
Pheasant		6 Nov-1 Jan	2 per season
Ruffed grouse		16 Oct-26 Feb	4 per day, 8 in possession
Bobwhite quail		6 Nov-26 Feb	7 per day, 14 in possession
Wild turkey	Some	16 Oct-30 Oct	One, either sex
	Others	16 Oct-20 Nov	
bearded turkey	All	24 April-13 May	One gobbler

The white-fronted goose breeds in the tundra zone round the Arctic Ocean and migrates south in the winter.

Duck shooting from a boat on the River Arun in the south of England

is a frequent winter visitor to the British Isles. It breeds along the Arctic coasts of Europe, Asia and America, and winters in western Europe, the Mediterranean, south Russia, India, China, Japan, the Gulf of Mexico, and the Pacific coasts of the United States and Mexico.

Whitefronts are mainly vegetarians and grazers, and will sometimes visit stubbles and corn fields though they are more generally to be found feeding in swamps and saltings. They are vocal, their call during flight being 'wah-wah-wah'. They breed, sociably, on the open tundra, the nests being built around freshwater ponds rather than by the sea. They consist of scrapes in the ground lined with moss and down. The clutch, normally of five or six eggs, takes about 28 days to incubate, the gander remaining in attendance all the time. The goslings can leave the nest within a very few days, and do not acquire full adult plumage until the second-year moult. During the summer moult the adults, like all other geese, become flightless, and are then subject to predator attack. During their migration flights they fly extremely high in V-formations.

The average weight is about 5 lb and the overall length about 28 in. Its common name

comes from the white band running round the face between the bill and the eyes. The bill is pink turning to orange in the breeding season, and the feet are orange-yellow. The face, neck, chest and back are gray-brown with lighter barrings, and there are irregular dark bars on the belly, giving it its popular name of 'specklebelly'.

It migrates north in March, while the ice is still about, and leaves for its wintering grounds in September. Great collections of whitefronts occur in the autumn, on the Hungarian Plains, as well as on the Vermillion Marshes of Louisiana.

The lesser white-fronted goose (*Anser erythropus*) has much the same breeding and wintering range, though it is seldom seen in the British Isles, and a larger subspecies of the whitefront, the Tule goose (*Anser albifrons gambelli*) winters only in the Sacramento Valley of California.

Whitefronts are wary geese, will not come readily to decoys, and, because they are less frequently seen inland on farm meadows and stubbles, they are more difficult to shoot than either the graylag or the pinkfoot, though often found in company with them.

White-tailed Deer
(Odocoileus virginianus)

This is an American deer, unrelated to any European deer and, except for such importations as have been made, from time to time, into the South Island of New Zealand and Finland, it is found nowhere outside America.

It has survived the arrival and spread of civilization better than almost any other American game animal, and can even be said to thrive from its increasingly close contacts with man, for it is possibly more numerous now than it was when the settlers first arrived. Primarily a browser, it does best not in mature forest, but along the boundaries between forest and farmland, and in the secondary growths and mixed stands that follow timber felling or forest fire. Timber extraction, therefore, which has driven the elk and the moose steadily northwards, has been of benefit to the whitetail. In 1963 the population in the United States alone exceeded seven million, with some two million in Texas, and Minnesota, New York and Arkansas all having herds of near half a million. They are most numerous east of the Mississippi, and comparatively rare west of the Rockies, though they are found right across southern Canada from Quebec to British Columbia. An almost miniature subspecies, the Coue's deer, is found in Arizona, parts of Texas and Mexico. There are several other subspecies scattered throughout America, exhibiting, principally, differences only in size and range.

The factor that makes the whitetail the most important of all the American big-game is its fecundity. Like other deer they are

The most popular big-game animal of North America, the white-tailed deer is widely distributed in the United States and the neighbouring provinces of Canada.

polygamous, so that buck hunting does not necessarily reduce the breeding potential of the herd. The doe will commonly begin to breed at seven months, and will certainly breed at eighteen months. Her life and breeding expectancy, in the wild, will be around ten years and, after her first fawn, which will be a single, under favourable conditions she will probably drop twins or triplets every year. It can be seen, therefore, that the potential for population increase is high, which is why, given good game management and a harvest figure that can be rapidly adjusted upwards or downwards, the whitetail can be expected to continue at least at present levels, in spite of bad breeding seasons, natural disasters, and the pressures of American hunting.

Whitetails vary in average size, the southern ones being, on the whole, smaller than those in the north. Coue's deer, which is found in Arizona, New Mexico, Texas and north-west Mexico, has a weight range between 55 and 85 lb. More normal weight ranges, however, lie between 130 and 250 lb for a mature buck and 120 and 150 lb for a doe. A good-sized buck will measure about 5 ft and stand about 4 ft at the shoulder. The summer coat is thin and reddish-tan, the winter one is heavier, grayish-tan, with a thick undercoat. The winter pelage hairs are hollow, which gives good insulation against cold. The belly, throat, rump patches and underside of the tail are white, and the tail is carried erect when the animal is excited or alarmed.

Only the buck is antlered, the antlers consisting of two main beams that grow upwards and forwards, and carry the tines but do not, themselves, fork. The main beams may measure up to 30 in. The buck reaches breeding maturity in his second year. The rut begins in early September and continues till January. During this period the buck's neck swells and, although otherwise a solitary, it will seek the does, travelling far to find them. Fights over the does are common. The victor will stay with the doe for a few days before seeking out another. Gestation takes about seven months and the fawns are generally born in late spring, the average birth weight being about 7 lb. The fawn is hidden by the doe, who returns to it several times a day. After the first few weeks it follows the doe, and is weaned at about eight months. The buck sheds its antlers in December, regrowth starts in May and the velvet is lost in August. Antler size is more an indication of food and soil condition than of age.

Some states may have any-sex hunting, but most allow only bucks to be shot. There are three common methods of hunting deer: they may be stalked in open country; driven in thick cover; still-hunted. Of these stalking requires the greatest skill and gives the most pleasure. Dogs are usually forbidden, and in some heavily-populated states only

a shotgun firing buckshot or a rifled slug may be used. Where a rifle is permitted, velocity is not, generally speaking, as important as weight of bullet and stopping power. In thick country a short-barrelled carbine is probably best.

See also Deer of the World and their Hunting.

White-winged Dove *(Zenaida asiatica)*
A partially migratory American dove (also called Sonora pigeon) that is found in the southern states of the United States and southwards through Mexico to Panama and to certain areas of South America.

It is rather heavier than the mourning dove *(Zenaidura macroura)*, *q.v.*, has brownish-gray plumage and a pointed tail. There is a large white wing-patch which gives it its name. The female resembles the male but is rather smaller.

They are sociable birds, feeding and nesting in flocks, and rising, when alarned, as a flock, rather than singly. The flocks are largest in autumn, when the groups congregate. They are omnivorous, with a special liking for grain, and they need to visit a waterhole once a day. Partial migrants, they move south within their ranges in winter and return northwards in summer.

They can be shot at the waterhole when they come in to drink, or in woods when they come in to roost. This dove is also shot on organized shoots, when up to 20 men will surround a field in which they are feeding. They are difficult birds to kill, largely because they are faster than they appear.

See also Pigeon Shooting around the World.

Widgeon *(Anas penelope)*
A surface feeding duck, closely related to the American widgeon, or baldpate *(Anas americana) q.v.* The drake is rather smaller than either the mallard or gadwall, measuring about 18 in, and has a chestnut head with a buff crown, a gray body, pinkish breast and white belly. In flight the white 'shoulders' are distinctive. The duck looks like a smaller mallard, but with a shorter neck, more rounded head, and a green rather than violet speculum.

Widgeon breed in northern Asia and Europe, including northern Scotland and Iceland. They may be occasional breeders along the Atlantic coast of America, and are certainly vagrant visitors there, where they are frequently mistaken for the baldpate. They winter in Africa, India, southern China and Japan, and are winter migrant to Britain. They also seem to be breeding in increasing numbers in Britain, and not only in Scotland.

They are, normally, birds of the estuaries and saltmarshes. But as the *Zostera* beds have declined, they have increasingly taken to feeding inland in the freshwater marshes on insects and duck-weed. Nevertheless they are still found resting in great rafts on tidal estuaries, though going inland to breed.

Courtship and display are largely on the water and the nest is generally sited among heather or bracken. They are vocal birds, the drake having a whistling call 'whee-oo' which is unmistakable, whilst the duck has a low, purring call. They fly extremely well, and are fast off the water. They therefore, constitute the best game for the wildfowler and are eagerly hunted. Until the passage migrants arrive in Britain, in October, there are few to be seen except in those parts of Scotland and the south-west of England where they breed.

Wild Boar *(Sus scrofa)*

Although there are large and obvious dissimilarities between them, wild boar and the various breeds of domestic pig are classified as members of the same species. There is, indeed, some evidence that feral pigs begin, eventually, to show certain specifically wild boar characteristics, such as larger tusks and longitudinal striping in the piglets.

The wild boar is found throughout Europe, except for Scandinavia (although a few are still killed in Sweden), and the British Isles, where the last native wild boar was killed towards the end of the seventeenth century. It is also found in north Africa, throughout Asia, and in island forms, in the Pacific Islands, Japan and Formosa.

The story of its introduction into the United States is not without interest. At the end of the last century an Englishman called Moore enclosed a large tract of wild, hilly land near Hooper's Bald in the most isolated part of the Great Smokies, in order to turn it into a hunting preserve. Among the animals he turned out were a few wild boar, supposedly imported from Russia, where the largest of all boars are to be found. These soon escaped into the surrounding countryside and multiplied. Though they were subject, for a time, to uncontrolled hunting by the locals, there are now several thousands of them securely established in the Cherokee National Forest in Tennessee, and the Nantahala National Forest in North Carolina, and hunters come from all over the States to join in the hunting parties organized by the forest authorities. The boars grow to an enormous size and are still known popularly as the 'Russians'.

Although wild boar is one of the four traditional 'Beasts of Chase' it is also classified in many countries as a pest, and it may be shot as one, in France, for example, at any time and by any one. This is because it can, with its rooting, cause considerable damage to farm crops, and farmers and peasants everywhere must be considered its enemies. Nevertheless the wild boar has contrived to survive in the face of advancing civilization and modern agriculture rather better than most other game animals, for a number of reasons. It is a nocturnal forest dwelling animal, and so is seldom seen except by those who have set out to hunt it. It is a prolific and regular breeder and, since it has a life expectancy in excess of ten years, is capable of multiplying rapidly in any suitable habitat. It is strong, ferocious, fearless and dangerous, and so has few predators. In the Indian jungle even the Bengal tiger respects it. Though it has been known to be attacked by wolves its only real enemies are man and rinderpest. Finally, it has the ability to undertake what are, in effect, quite long migrations, away from areas of hunting pressure and into areas of greater safety.

A surprisingly fast runner, it has highly developed powers of scent and hearing. It is omnivorous, and eats enormously, going out to the chosen feeding ground in the evening, and returning to the lair at dawn. It roots the soil systematically, either in discontinuous patches, or else in long, continuing trenches, in search of roots. The same method is used in a field of potatoes or sugar beet, but its preferred food is forest mast, and especially acorns; berries, worms, fieldmice, pheasant poults, rabbits, young fawns, and even carrion, in addition to a wide variety of farm crops, are also eaten. Returning to its lair, which is situated in a fairly open forest glade during the summer, and in thicker growth in the winter, it often has a wallow and visits a rubbing post on the way. The young wild boars lie all together in a thicket, rather than in individual lairs as the older, 'solitary' or sanglier do.

The rut normally starts in the last fortnight in November, and continues till January. During this time the boar will seek out the sows and will be seen travelling the forest during the day. It will fight fiercely with the young boars, driving them away from the sounder herd. When the rut is over the boar becomes solitary again, and the sow, after the normal gestation period of around 115 days, will withdraw from the sounder and farrow. The litter will be of anything up to 15 squeakers, though between 6 and 10 is the normal number, and they are able to follow their dam in a very few days.

An adult boar stands almost 3 ft high at the shoulder; the Indian boar *(Sus cristatus)* is generally slightly taller. It can weigh up to 300 lb, and there have been reports of Russian boars weighing up to 600 lb. It measures over 5 ft in length, and slopes back from high shoulders to drooping quarters and a long and fairly heavy tail. Coat colour varies, being lighter in the summer and when young. The squeakers are born striped, longitudinally, in red and gold. At six months the coat is entirely

Widgeon fly extremely well and are among wildfowlers' favourite quarries.

In many European countries the wild boar is classified as a pest, and may be shot at any time.

dark red, and at a year it is brown and darkening towards black. There is a thick and woolly undercoat beneath the outer bristles. There is little difference between the sexes in size and colouring, but the boar carries longer and heavier tusks. These are developments of the four canine teeth and provide the animal with weapons for rooting and defence. The lower tusks, which are only partly covered with enamel, grow outwards and upwards, reaching a length, in some cases of 9 in or even 10 in. The upper tusks also grow upwards, but more slowly, and they eventually turn inwards slightly and stop growing. They act as a whetstone, against which the lower tusks or 'weapons' may be continually honed, to keep the points and upper edges suitably sharp. To make room for this growth, most of which is external to the mouth, the upper lip is modified so that it can curl over the protrusions. In defence the weapons are used, either as lance with which to stab, or else as a knife with which to slash. Boethius mentions a famous boar killed in Scotland in 1124 that had weapons that measured 12 in.

Wild boar are hunted in a number of different ways. The classical method is on horseback, behind a pack of boarhounds, as is still done in France. Any accepted breed of hound may be used, though the original boarhounds were generally mastiff bred. Today, in New Zealand and Australia, cross-bred mastiffs are generally used when hunting Captain Cookers, or feral pigs on foot. A boar will give hounds a sharp run over a distance of a mile or so, and is able to go through the very thickest cover without slowing down. Sooner or later, however, it will turn and face hounds, and it is thus important to have an experienced pack that will surround and bay the quarry without closing in, for it is then that the boar is most dangerous. It is also important that the hunters, whether mounted or on foot, should be well up with hounds and in a position to kill the boar before it can do much damage to hounds. For this a rifle or carbine is generally used, but the classic weapon is, of course, the hunting knife.

The other weapon classically associated with the wild boar is the spear, and pig-sticking, in some form or other, was once extensively practised in Europe and is still practised in India, where it has been developed to its highest form as a sport that combines all the excitements and dangers of fox hunting, racing and jousting. Where pig-sticking is carried on it is customary not to shoot wild boar for a distance of forty miles around.

In Europe, these days, the boar is often driven towards a line of guns. This requires some skill on the part of those organizing the driving. First thing in the morning the boar must be located, without being shifted. The guns will then be suitably placed, generally downwind, and the quarry will be driven towards them. This will be done, either with a line of beaters, or else with dogs and a few dog handlers. The art, in either case, lies in pressing the boar sufficiently, but not so much that he will turn at bay before the guns are reached.

Perhaps a more sporting method is still-hunting. The hunter will use his knowledge of the boar's habits, and will either wait for it, at dawn, near a known wallow or rubbing post, or he will wait in the evening at the feeding grounds.

In all cases, when shooting wild boar, it is important to have the right weapon and the right dog. The weapon needs to be a rifle capable of firing a bullet of sufficient weight and stopping power to be effective, and it must be remembered that the boar is capable of carrying a great deal of shot. Small-bore and high-velocity rifles are out of place, since most of the shooting will be at close range and in fairly thick country. If the boar is only wounded, then it is essential to have a dog bred and trained for boar hunting, able to follow and bring it to bay. In Germany, and several other central European countries, the German short-haired pointer or similar breeds are used.

Wildebeest *see* Gnus

Wildfowl and Wet Gravel Pits
Creation of habitat in Britain

Gravel extraction in the U.K. as elsewhere is a big and growing industry – an interesting side-effect being the creation of 3,000 acres of new water areas every year. Worked-out pits can be used effectively as wildfowl breeding areas and winter roosts. In this case the planning must be in operation long before the last digger leaves the pit. The ideal is to give thought to the final result even before the first square yard of top-soil is scraped away. A vast, steep-sided square hole, though providing acres of water, will never attract breeding duck, largely because it will lack food and cover. In bad weather there will be considerable wave action which will disturb nesting wildfowl, and may also upset the broods. The big disadvantage is all the wasted space in the middle, which will simply not be used by the vulnerable young ducklings, unless the water is sufficiently shallow to allow escape cover in the form of rafts of aquatic plants – unlikely in a gravel working.

So before considering any subtleties of wild duck management it is first necessary to consider what to do with the basic hole in the ground before the machines leave. It may be difficult to cost how much profit will be lost, if every cubic yard of gravel is not dug out, but equated with the increased duck crop over the next fifty years the loss will probably not be very great. Islands or 'reefs' – solid enough not to be eroded away

Nesting boxes for duck on rafts in an old gravel pit

Collecting wild duck eggs from a nesting raft; note the 'anti-crow' porch on the nesting box

by wind, water, or dibbling ducks – should be allowed to remain wherever possible. They will serve many useful functions, like hedgerows on a bleak open farm, and will greatly add to the beauty of the scenery. Early in the planning stages it may be advantageous to plant a shelter belt or some groups of trees on the windward side; not right up to the water's edge or the cover will provide a jumping-off place for foxes. In any case ducks appreciate a loafing and sunning area near the shore – another use for the islands where the birds can feel safe.

Obviously the pit will be as deep as the gravel beds themselves. If very deep there will be little vegetation – except on the islands and around the edges – and the water will be cold. This will also affect the supply of insects. Deeps in certain places can, however, be used to advantage as they will prevent invasive plants, like reedmace (*Typha latifolia*), from spreading out from the shore. Beyond a certain depth such plants will not survive. The perfect wild-fowl lake would consist of submerged hills and valleys – allowing stretches of open water interspersed with plants – emergent and submergent. Very little useful plant occurs below 10 ft.

The cheapest way to plant up a new pit is to obtain permission to dig up a few clumps of plants that do well locally. Thinning a nearby canal, river, lake or reservoir will not be noticed. Useful specimens include bur-reed (*Sparganium erectum*), sedge (*Carex acutiformis*) and bulrush (*Schoenoplectus lacustris*) for the edges; floating pondweed (*Potamogeton natans*), amphibious bisort (*Polygonum amphibium*), water crowfoot (*Ranunculus aquatilis*) and mare's tail (*Hippuris vulgaris*) for the shallows and mid-water; the duckweeds (*Lemna* sp.) as floating plants; and stonewort (*Chara* sp.) for deeper or stagnant water. If the topsoil has been returned to the floor of the pit, the plant life will get away to a good start.

There are two other rules to apply to the physical structure of the pit. The first concerns the sides of the excavations, which often consist of steep cliffs. It is important to bulldoze these down so that they become gentle shelving beaches. They will then provide warm shallows and allow tiny duck-lings to negotiate the banks easily. They will also grow bankside cover – unlike vertical cliffs. Secondly, the 'geometry' of the water's edge is important: if the pit is round or square with an unbroken shore-line, it will be less attractive to wildfowl than if it is broken up by a number of inden-tations or secluded bays. Where a large number of broods are using a comparatively small area of water, aggression and fighting may occur. The sheltered bays will provide excellent brood harbours and hand-feeding places when required.

Having broadly considered the habitat let us now turn to the wildfowl themselves.

Dutch nesting baskets

The British Game Conservancy's interest in wild duck breeding areas was aroused by a visit to a lake in Holland, about 20 years ago. The Game Conservancy's review de-scribes the scene: 'The breeding lake was 12 acres in extent, surrounded by a fringe of sheltering poplars, alders, willows and other trees. The nearby countryside con-sisted of mixed dairy and corn, intersected by dykes and small irrigation canals. The lake is the home of some 400 nesting baskets – all of which are used – supported on stakes in the water and safe from all predators. At the end of the season the baskets are washed, dried, dipped in wood preservative and carefully stored till the following year. Fresh lining material of short hay is put in every season. If properly maintained the cane baskets last ten years, and the willow ones three to four.

'In the autumn it is no uncommon sight to see two or three thousand duck – mostly mallard – flighting out at dusk from the lake to their feeding grounds.'

The Conservancy were so impressed with the possibilities of the Dutch technique that they returned with a specimen nesting basket and had *exact* copies made by a Wiltshire eel-pot maker, later developing much cheaper wooden nesting boxes of cheap bark timber off-cuts. The measure-ments, especially of the entrance are critical: the *inside* dimensions should be 12 in square and 9 in high, with an entrance 6 in square. If corvids are troublesome, an anti-crow porch or tunnel can be fitted to the entrance, extending 9 in, with a 4 in bottom lip as an alighting board. This will best prevent nest robbing. Although the Conservancy firmly believed their imported basket was new to this country, it was not: John Evelyn in 1665, after a visit to St James's Park, re-corded in his diary that *'there were withy-potts or nests for the wildfowl to lay their eggs in, a little above ye surface of ye water'*.

However, at least the methods of using them were original, for the Dutch ideas had to be adapted to British conditions. In the first place the water levels in British lakes varied much more than in Holland – the home of the greatest hydro-engineers in the world – and baskets on stakes could be awash after heavy rain or standing high out of the water after a drought. It was necessary therefore to develop various types of rafts made from old telegraph poles with plastic fertilizer bags full of waste expanded polystyrene for buoyancy, which would rise and fall comfortably with the water level. With a bed of rotting straw on wire netting the rafts grew attractive clumps of reeds and rushes. Each one housed three or four nesting boxes. Where conditions were suit-able baskets on stakes were still used.

The other major difference between con-ditions in Holland and those in the U.K. concerns the behaviour of the broods after

Mallard nesting baskets on a lake in Holland

hatching. In the Netherlands, the females soon take the baby ducklings away from the main breeding areas to the nearby farmlands, many of which are criss-crossed by drainage ditches, irrigation canals and so on. In some areas there are also extensive reedlands and other lakes nearby, which accommodate the extra broods. The narrow ditches are warm, sheltered and full of food. During the first few weeks of life the ducklings eat aquatic insects, mosquito larvae, crustacea, etc, gradually changing to a more mixed diet including plant food and grain. The dyke-side cover provides good hiding places from sharp-eyed enemies and there the young ducks prosper.

The problems of intensive brood populations
In Britain the young broods hatched from the baskets would usually have no better place to go than their own native lake or gravel pit. Except in a few fenland areas there would be no networks of canals and reedbeds just over the bank. So many more broods than nature can house and feed naturally, begin to live a competitive life in what may be a less than perfect environment. Hence the earlier suggestions about islands, bays and well-dispersed cover. On a bare, open lake food is likely to be scarce. In a well-ordered biotope the ducklings will do well.

As regards the success of adults breeding in baskets the U.K. can match the Dutch figures; in a season or two seventy, eighty or a hundred baskets can be filled with nesting ducks quite easily. But the brood survival is likely to be less good, perhaps averaging one or two young per female, compared with the Dutch figure of five. It all depends on the local conditions. In time – perhaps with the addition of a little artificial feeding for the first few weeks and a better understanding of mallard brood habitat – the U.K. will certainly improve this young survival rate. Meanwhile in the development period the pits and lakes are being made much more productive for the wildfowler – and more beautiful. Furthermore the transformation of the bare pits into 'natural' lakes enormously increases the number and variety of wildfowl species that use these waters as winter roosts. Coot and moorhens – whether desired or not – use the baskets for breeding, as do tufted ducks and pochard. Good mallard management greatly helps other species.

Before taking a closer look at the management of mallard based on the use of hole-nests it is desirable to discuss briefly the dynamics of *Anas platyrhyncos*.

The average wild mallard will lay 12 to 13 eggs in her first nest, usually starting to lay in early March at the rate of one egg a day. If unsuccessful in her first attempt, a repeat clutch of about 10 eggs will be laid. With an incubation period of up to 28 days, the peak hatching period occurs during the first 10 days of May.

More than 90% of the eggs in fully-incubated nests eventually hatch. Nesting success, however, is very variable. While in some well managed area it may be as high as 65 to 70%, in other places the casualties can be very heavy and the hatch well below 50%. From the average successful nest, approximately 10 ducklings are hatched, but before they can fly the brood will have been reduced to five – less where conditions are unsuitable – by bad weather, food shortages and predators.

The main predators, or competitors, in the U.K. include foxes, rats, feral mink, crows, some of the larger gulls, gray herons, pike and coot.

Management of stock
Mallard will often lay eggs far too early in the year for the ducklings to have any chance of surviving in the wild. These early eggs can, however, become a bonus for the wildfowl manager. On the Game Conservancy study areas the basket-eggs laid up to the middle of March are all picked up for hatching and rearing. At 6 to 7 weeks the young duck are leaked out from a secluded release pen built on the edge of the water, and either used for restocking a new area or for building up the stocks on an existing breeding centre. Such duck – hatched from 'basket eggs' – will rapidly become conditioned to using artificial nests, whereas those whose parents have never seen a basket often take a season or two.

Robbing the nesting baskets up to mid-March means the second clutch will hatch out early in May – theoretically the ideal time. And each female duck will have produced two broods, one for the brooder and one for herself. CLC

Wildfowling
Wildfowl, that is to say ducks and geese, have long attracted the attention of man, the hunter, on account of their highly edible qualities and no doubt, over the ages, they have provided a significant source of first class protein. A famous Egyptian tomb painting at Thebes, dating back to about 1,500 BC, shows duck in a clap net, some of which could well be ruddy shelduck and marbled teal. At the Enthronization Feast of William Warham, as Archbishop of Canterbury, on Passion Sunday 1504, teal were served in seven of the courses.

Long before the invention of the firearm, therefore, man was highly skilled at taking wildfowl. Some of his methods are still in use today, as, for instance, the duck decoy, an ancient device in which duck are lured from a secluded pool and made to swim into a netted pipe by a fox-like decoy dog or 'piper', which they follow curiously, as it appears round each successive screen. Decoys were probably in existence during the reign of King John (1199–1216) and this could well have been how the Archbishop secured enough teal for his Feast.

Duck shooting from a camouflaged canoe in Australia

Wildfowl become flightless in summer, when they moult their flight feathers and although in duck the sexes moult at different times and places, in geese the whole population, both adults and young, are all flightless together for a period of about six weeks. Eskimos have long made use of this vulnerable period in their life cycle to round up and salt down large numbers of geese for winter food. Until quite recently Icelanders did the same, taking advantage of a habit of flightless pink-footed geese to run uphill, by building stone corrals on the hilltops into which they herded the pinkfeet, carrying out the round up while mounted on their Icelandic ponies. Peter Scott's expeditions to ring pinkfeet in central Iceland in the 1950s were able to use these same stone corrals, which were still standing, although no longer in use.

Although there are now few places in the world where wildfowl still provide a significant amount of first-class protein, certainly the south shore of the Caspian Sea is one and here the Iran fowlers still practise a traditional method of catching duck with a flare, gong and net. This is carried out on moonless nights on the ab-bandans, wide stretches of embanked fresh marsh, which retain water for irrigation. A flare is mounted in the bows, behind which the first man waits to wield a large net. Another, usually in a second punt, operates the gong, which he strikes to produce a weird, undulating note. Gong and flare combine to mesmerize the duck, which only fly when the punt is almost upon them. At that moment the netsman catches them as they jump. Flight nets and clap nets are also used in Iran but are now becoming carefully controlled.

In Greenland, the Eskimo hunters eagerly await the arrival of the drake king eiders on the west coast coming from the Canadian arctic to moult in mid-summer. Immediately a drake is shot and retrieved, the Greenlander bites off and eats the fleshy knob above the bill – and by so doing he is consuming a valuable source of vitamins A and D, so important for his well-being.

All methods employing nets or decoys could be described as commercial exploitation, which is not to suggest that there is not a great deal of skill and fieldcraft required, because nothing could be further from the truth. None, however, really come under the term wildfowling, as we have come to understand it today.

Wildfowling is the pursuit of wild duck, wild geese and certain wading birds with a shot gun, either on foot or by boat. Wildfowling is a traditional field sport, one which takes the fowler to some of the wildest places left in the world today.

The expert wildfowler plans his shooting on the daily life habits of his quarry species during the open season, which generally means during the autumn and winter. Food

A decoy pipe

and times of feeding vary from species to species throughout the season, as do the times of flighting to and from the roosting and feeding grounds.

As a broad generality, in the Northern Hemisphere geese feed by day and duck by night, flighting taking place at dawn and dusk. On moonlight nights, however, when there is plenty of light, geese will flight back to their feeding grounds from their roosts, which may be on large expanses of inland water or on the open shore or sea. During the few nights around full moon they may even remain in the feeding grounds throughout the whole period if the moon is visible.

Out on the open shore, where duck will also feed a great deal in daylight, four more flights will be added during the 24 hours, as the tide flows and ebbs. The larger the tide and the rougher the water, the more marked will be the flight. The same applies to wading birds, the movements of which are very largely based on the tides, feeding as they do, almost exclusively, on the intertidal zone. Curlew and golden plover are the only quarry waders which regularly flight inland to feed on the pastures, but only the former join the more strictly tidal quarry waders, such as redshank gray plovers and bar-tailed godwits on their night roosts.

In hard weather, with the fresh marshes frozen hard, wildfowl are forced to move to more open areas, often to the nearest coastal marshes and if these then freeze, the birds may rapidly lose condition and become excessively tame. They are then no longer worthy as quarry. Many countries have powers to ban wildfowling in prolonged freezing. Others carry this out voluntarily.

The widgeon is an instructive example of changing food habits both throughout the season and over the years. The bulk of the winter migrants arrive in south-east England from north-east Europe in October and November, when they settle on the estuaries to feed on eel-grass *(Zostera)* and green seaweeds *(Enteromorpha)*, but when the fresh marshes become flooded in mid-winter they flight inland to graze these pastures, returning to the saltings again if during the severe weather the fresh marshes freeze up. In early spring they will move inland again, diligently searching out the 'early bite' for the high protein content of the growing grass before leaving on spring migration. Fifty years ago, before the *Zostera* beds were devastated by disease, widgeon were seldom seen inland, remaining all winter on the tidal marshes.

The expert wildfowler, therefore, is a man of many skills. He must be a naturalist, able to recognize his quarry birds and to understand their habits. For full enjoyment, he will also need to know about the other birds he sees. If an understanding of marsh plants is invaluable, an understanding of tides and weather can be vital for his safety. The complete wildfowler should be capable of handling a boat, whether he is a shoulder gunner, or, in those countries where it is permitted, a punt gunner. Furthermore, a dog is an essential, if inexcusable cripple losses are to be avoided. In North America, he will probably be a great expert in the use of artificial decoys, which he may well make himself.

In general, the quarry species of wildfowl may be defined as those which are good to eat, which in turn implies those which are vegetarian, feeding mainly on fresh or brackish marshes. They must also be abundant enough species to ensure a harvestable surplus. The main quarry species, therefore, are those geese which graze inland, such as the gray and snow geese of the Northern Hemisphere and the dabbling duck.

Animal-eating species, the shovelers, diving duck and especially the sea-duck and 'sawbills' are too strongly flavoured to make them popular for the table, except after special cooking. The exception of this generalization is, of course, swans, which are vegetarian but which are legally protected throughout North America, Europe and many parts of Asia.

The pressing need now, so far as Europe and Asia are concerned, is to rationalize wildfowling methods and seasons throughout this vast area, which must also include the wintering grounds southwards into central Africa, if this monumental task is to be carried out properly.

A shining example of what can be achieved is provided by the North American wildfowl population, where the welfare of the whole breeding and wintering grounds is provided for by treaties between the United States, Canada and Mexico. The administration of this population is much simpler to bring about when only a mere three countries are concerned, compared with the multiplicity concerned with the Eurasian population.

In North America, shooting regulations, length of seasons and bag limits are worked out annually by biologists working for the United States and the Canadian Fish and Wildlife Services, based on winter and breeding aerial surveys, kill statistics (based on questionnaires to wildfowlers), wildfowl production surveys (resulting from duck wings and goose tails collected from wildfowlers) and ringing (banding).

From this massive data programme it is possible to predict population trends and the current bag limits based on the harvestable surplus of each quarry species available annually. Each of the four great migrational routes are administered separately by 'flyway councils' and the season opens progressively as the migrant fowl move southwards from state to state.

The season may be as short as 25 or as long as 95 days and is occasionally closed for some species if their numbers are severely reduced. There is a permanent ban on the sale of all wildfowl, the use of live decoys and electronic calls. No rifles may be used or shot gun larger than a 10-bore. Repeaters are limited to three cartridges and shooting is only allowed from half an hour before sunrise until sunset. The proceeds from compulsory U.S. Federal Duck Stamps of $3 all goes to financing research and habitat conservation, as does the $2 Migratory Bird Hunting Permit in Canada. With nearly 2 million people buying these each year, this is a sound financial basis on which to start!

In Europe and Asia similar responsibilities have been taken on by the International Waterfowl Research Bureau, founded in 1954. The Bureau has initiated research through its specialized groups into wildfowl populations and movements throughout the whole of Eurasia, while endeavouring to evaluate and safeguard wetlands of international significance, a task which reached a climax in February 1971, when the Ramsar Convention on Wetlands and Waterfowl was signed in Iran, but which now awaits ratification by the signatory countries.

Another specialist group of the I.W.R.B. is the Hunting Rationalisation Research Group *(q.v.)*. The massive task of collecting data on wildfowling practices covering Europe, Asia and Africa is now under way, which may ultimately come to form the basis of a further convention.

So far, Dr Teppo Lampio, the co-ordinator of the group, has only been able to report on the European situation, but already it is obvious that a great deal needs to be rationalized. There is a definite tendency to exploit migratory birds rather than sedentary ones, on the assumption that there is no point in leaving them for someone else to shoot in another country. Thus the goose season opens in mid-August in Austria, 1 September in Hungary and 1 October in Czechoslovakia, which cannot be in the best interests of the breeding graylags in Austria or encourage co-operation from the Czechs, while Poland still has a spring open season for the whole of March and April.

There are many other anomalies. The use of rifles is forbidden by law only in Finland, Holland and the U.S.S.R. In the U.K. it is legal, but forbidden to members of the Wildfowlers' Association of Great Britain and Ireland (WAGBI) by a rule of the Association. The use of live decoys is prohibited in Iceland, Denmark, Switzerland, and the U.K. Even artificial decoys are illegal in Denmark and Switzerland and electronic calls in Belgium, Finland, Holland and Switzerland. In the German Democratic Republic, Czechoslovakia and Austria, the use of retrieving dogs is, very rightly, obligatory. Bag limits are in operation in the U.S.S.R.

One could enlarge on this at length, but enough has been said to indicate that a vast amount of work is required of the I.W.R.B. to rationalize wildfowling practices as they affect the Eurasian wildfowl population, basing its recommendations on sound biological facts.

It is only comparatively recently that wildfowlers have come to realize the vital significance of conservation for the future of their sport. In 1937, 'Ducks Unlimited' was formed by wildfowlers in North America to raise money to restore habitat on the Canadian breeding grounds. Since then, over $12 million have been raised and have been used to create some 800 new wetlands with a shoreline equalling that of the entire United States.

In Europe, the lead has been given by WAGBI, operating in the British Isles. The Association and its affiliated clubs now manage over 23,000 acres of wetland reserves and have carried out pioneer research into habitat improvement, based on detailed duck food analyses undertaken in co-operation with the Wildfowl Trust.

The use of hand-reared wildfowl to supplement the wild population has been practised by WAGBI since 1954, birds being released onto reserves, from where they can infiltrate the wild population. The mallard total now exceeds 150,000, all of which have been ringed and the results analysed. This has shown conclusively that mortality rates compare closely to those found in wild birds. Recoveries range from the Arctic Ocean to the Mediterranean and the Black Sea. Similar work is being carried out with other duck and geese. In particular the graylag has now been re-established in many of its former localities in England by WAGBI. A duck production survey based on wing analyses is being operated by

The wild turkey is America's largest game bird, thriving in the cold of Canada and the heat of Mexico.

WAGBI, which is also publishing its own surveys of threatened wetlands.

Other wildfowlers' organizations, particularly the French *Association des Chasseurs Gibier d'Eau,* are becoming interested in conservation. Finland is also carrying out duck production surveys, and Denmark undertakes comprehensive analyses of shooting bags. This is certainly the best omen for the future of a wild, tough and enthralling field sport. JH

Wild Ox see Buffalo, African

Wild Turkey (*Meleagris gallopavo*)
The wild turkey obtained its name, not from any supposed connections with Turkey, but from its call note of 'turc-turc-turc'. There was, however, some confusion for a time between it and the Guineafowl (*Meleagris numidica*) (*q.v.*) because the latter bird, which reached Europe from Africa via Turkey, was often referred to as the 'Turkey' cock or hen, which led contemporary writers to confuse it with the other 'turkey' bird newly brought from the Americas.

The wild turkey is the only native American member of the *Phasianidae,* and the largest member of that family anywhere. There is, in addition to the well-known turkey of the United States and northern Mexico, the ocellated turkey (*Agrocharis ocellata*) of southern Mexico and Central America. The *Meleagris* has several subspecies, including the eastern turkey (*M. gallopavo silvestris*), Florida turkey (*M. gallopavo osceola*), Rio Grande turkey (*M. gallopavo intermedia*), Merriam's turkey (*M. gallopavo merriama*) and Mexican turkey (*M. gallopavo gallopavo*). Of these the Eastern and the Mexican are the most important, though Merriam's turkey is often used when colonizing new areas.

The wild turkey is of course, the ancestor of the domesticated bird and it had already been domesticated by the Aztecs when the Conquistadores arrived and took it to Europe. The early immigrants brought it back to America as a domestic bird, and it is not without interest that in Australia, to which the domestic bird was also taken, there is now a considerable population of feral turkey, which must be well on its way to becoming wild turkey and so completing the cycle.

Wild turkeys are forest birds, and they once populated the American forests from Canada to Mexico. As the forests shrank so did their numbers, and as man, their principal predator, advanced, so they retreated. Timber felling, ploughing and market hunting so reduced their numbers that they completely vanished from a great number of states and became, almost exclusively, a game bird of the southern states. Intensive restocking and game management programmes have now been undertaken in most of the traditional turkey states as well as in areas, such as the far west and Hawaii, well outside their ancestral range. Because of the success of many of these programmes the distribution and number of turkey flocks has greatly improved, and many states are now able to have autumn and spring hunting seasons where none were possible before.

Restocking has never been a simple process, since hand-reared wild turkeys lose their wild instincts, fail to roost, show insufficient fear of predators, breed and rear very few broods and continually attempt to rejoin domestic flocks on the farms. The better method of restocking is to trap wild breeding stock and remove them from areas of plenty in order to release them in areas of scarcity. The reforestation of much derelict farmland has aided the re-introduction of the wild turkey by offering new habitats.

Wild turkeys are gregarious birds and, whether they are in harems, large flocks, or, during the winter, in smaller, single-sex groups, they keep calling to each other in order to prevent scattering. It is this habit of calling and answering calls that is made use of by the turkey hunter. They are fast runners, and can travel considerable distances on foot though they will not readily quit established territory. They fly reluctantly, but well, over short distances. They roost in trees at night, seldom descending to the ground because of their lack of night vision. They feed on forest mast, berries and fruits, and on insects, and are subject to much the same diseases as domestic poultry.

Gobblers are ready for breeding at two years and hens at one. The mating period is usually between April and June, during which time the gobbler will use his courting call of 'gil-obble-obble-obble' to attract the hens. When they appear he puts on a strutting and plumage display, and will fight any other cock for hens and territory. The gobbler rarely feeds during the breeding season, but lives largely off the reserves of fat laid down in its 'breast sponge'. Younger gobblers, unable to form a harem, will form bachelor groups. During the hunting season, therefore, which is in autumn or early spring, a turkey flock may consist of one or several hens with their young, or a group of gobblers two or more years old, or a group of 'Toms' – yearling males.

Once mating has taken place the hen leaves the harem in secret to build a nest and lay an egg; it then returns to the harem, leaving it each day to lay another egg until the clutch is complete and incubation can start. All this must be concealed from the gobbler, who may destroy nest and eggs. The clutch, which varies between 10 and 15 eggs, takes 28 days to incubate, and the young stay with the hen until late autumn.

Wild turkeys resemble the domestic birds except for being less full-breasted. The various subspecies all vary in size but the eastern turkey, which is the largest, weighs anything between 8 and 20 lb for an adult gobbler, with an average of around 14 lb, while the hen, which is always smaller, ranges between 6 and 10 lb. The hen has duller, less lustrous plumage than the gobbler and lacks a beard. This is a long tuft of hair-like feathers hanging from the gobbler's breast that grows in length every year and may, eventually, sweep the ground.

Turkey hunting is one of the most difficult arts. The birds, especially the older gobblers, who are usually the ones hunted, disappear at the first sight or sound of man and, since both their sight and hearing are keen, this is generally too soon. It is very difficult to move towards a turkey with any hope of getting within distance. The art of hunting lies in making the turkey come towards the hunter. This may sometimes be done, in small areas holding many birds, by driving, but such chances are rare. Since turkeys, for all their wariness, always leave signs of their presence, they may be still-hunted, the hunter lying in wait at one of their customary scratching or dusting grounds. They may be shot with a rifle from a distance if snow has fallen in sufficient quantities to provide a white background, but the season closes in most states before snow falls. They may be shot, once again with a rifle, at dusk, out of their roosts. This may not seem a particularly sporting method, but it does involve a careful approach and a nice calculation that will provide enough dusk to conceal that approach and yet leave enough light for shooting. Baiting in front of a hide is, quite properly, illegal in most states.

The classical, and probably the most difficult, way to hunt turkeys is by calling them. This involves finding a flock and then sending in a dog to flush and disperse them. As soon as that has been done the hunter and dog must conceal themselves at the point of dispersal and wait, silent and still, for a suitable interval. The hunter then begins to call the turkeys – using a turkey call and whatever skill he may possess. If he does it well he may eventually be answered, and then visited, by members of the dispersed flock seeking to reassemble. For this method a well-trained dog able to remain quite still is essential.

Theodore Roosevelt described, in the *Encyclopedia of Sport* (1898), coursing a turkey with greyhounds. These followed the flying bird by sight, putting it up whenever it landed until it grew too tired to fly any more. In the more open turkey ranges of the West this has also been done by men on horseback, or even in cars.

If a shotgun is used on turkeys, then it is advisable to have No 4 shot in the first barrel and No 2 shot in the other.

Willow Grouse *see* Ptarmigan

Seasons and Limits—Wisconsin

Species	Season	Limit
Deer	21 Nov–29 Nov	One antlered buck per season
Black bear	21 Nov–29 Nov	One per season
Rabbit, cottontail and jack	24 Oct–31 Jan	
Snowshoe hare	All year	
Squirrel	3 Oct–31 Jan	
Pheasant	24 Oct–6 Dec	2 cocks per day
Ruffed grouse	3 Oct–31 Dec	
Sharp-tailed grouse	3 Oct–25 Oct	
Hungarian partridge	24 Oct–6 Dec	

Licence Fees—Wisconsin

Type	Status	Fee
Hunting, fishing and trapping	Resident	$11.50
Deer and bear	Resident	$5.25
Deer, bear and small game	Non-resident	$50.50
Small game	Resident	$4.25
Deer and bear only	Non-resident	$35.50
Small game only	Non-resident	$25.50

Big Game Inventory—Wisconsin

Species	Shot	Est. pop.
White-tailed deer	126,920	715,000
Black bear	614	7,000
Wild turkey	22	600

The woodchuck lives in burrows over a wide range in North America. In most states it is classified as vermin.

Wisconsin (U.S.A.)

Predominantly an agricultural state of about 56,000 square miles, Wisconsin has over 16 million acres of forests, many of them open to the public for hunting.

There are deer in all parts of the state, but they are especially numerous in the northern and western counties, in many of which there is a two-day, 'hunter's choice', any-sex season before the actual bucks-only season starts. Bear, rabbit, hare and squirrel are the other common game, and pheasant is probably the most common game bird, followed by ruffed grouse; pinnate and sharp-tailed grouse are less numerous. There is good bobwhite hunting along the Mississippi River and in the south-west of the state, and some Hungarian partridge in the east, along the shores of Lake Michigan. There is excellent waterfowl hunting, even though the number of nesting birds has been reduced by the drainage of wetlands, and large numbers of Canada geese are seen in the south of the state.

Special Regulations

No one may hunt deer or bear with a .22 rim-fire rifle or a .410 shotgun, nor may either be carried during, or from five days prior to, the deer season. Nor may any shotgun loaded with other than single ball or slug ammunition be carried during that time. Dogs may not be used to hunt deer, and may only be used to hunt bear under special permit.

Further Information

Division of Fish and Game, Box 450, Madison, Wisconsin 53701.

Woodchuck *(Marmota monax)*

This is a small, American rodent with a maximum weight of 14 lb (average closer to 6 lb), closely related to the marmots of Europe. Marmots, however, are specifically alpine animals, being found only in the French, Swiss and Italian Alps, the Julian and Bavarian Alps, and the Tatra Mountains, whereas the woodchuck can be found almost anywhere in America. There are several species, including the yellow-footed marmot *(Marmota flaviventris)* of the Pacific coast and the rockchuck *(Marmota caligata)* of the Rockies.

They are short-legged, fat, squirrel-like creatures that get even fatter before beginning to hibernate. They only emerge from hibernation after the ground gets soft again. They dig a burrow of considerable extent inside which they live as solitaries, driving out their young as soon as possible. They generally mate in February, producing litters of up to six in late April.

They are difficult animals to shoot since they rarely stray far from their burrows and, at the first sign of danger, they vanish down them. If shot and only wounded they will probably be lost down the burrow. They need, therefore, to be shot from a distance with a high-velocity, flat-trajectory, light rifle, such as a .222 or .243. A telescopic sight of x6 or even x10 is virtually a necessity for shots of over 150 yd.

Woodcock *see* American Woodcock; Snipe and Woodcock Shooting; Waders

Wood Duck *(Aix sponsa)*

This is a perching duck, closely related to the entirely ornamental mandarin duck *(Aix galericulata)* of China, but only found in North America. It was once abundant but, as the forests were felled, it found its habitat shrinking and became dangerously accessible to hunters. Since epicures valued its flesh and milliners valued its feathers, market hunters nearly shot it out of existence. Only complete protection throughout the United States and Canada saved it. It has now recovered sufficiently for it to be shot, under severe bag limits, in several states.

The drake is probably the most decorative of all waterfowl. Its head combines yellow, red, green, white and purple in a most distinctive pattern: its breast is red, spotted with white, and its belly and underparts are white. The sides are buff and the upperparts predominantly blue. The duck is much plainer, being mainly brown and white, but with considerable colour and pattern on the wings. Both sexes are crested. They are extremely vociferous birds, the drake having a loud, whistling alarm call. They are principally vegetarians, eating forest mast and duckweed in addition to small amounts of insect matter. They fly well, and spring rapidly off water, weaving their way through the trees among which they are to be found.

Courtship is on the water and the duck nests in a cavity in a tree. The clutch of from 10 to 15 is incubated in 28 to 30 days, the ducklings fluttering down from the nest almost immediately. The young drakes assume male plumage by November.

The wood duck is principally a bird of the eastern United States, and is rarely found west of the Mississippi, though there is a different but smaller, concentration of them along the Pacific coast from Washington to North California. The main breeding grounds stretch from the Great Lakes to North Carolina in the east and Arkansas in the west. Their wintering grounds form a southwards extension of their breeding grounds, and stretch from the Gulf States up the Atlantic seaboard to as far north as North Carolina, and even Virginia, but many wood duck use the Gulf States as both breeding and wintering grounds. Where they are shot, these ducks come readily to decoys, and are not difficult to kill.

Wood duck populations can be increased by setting up home-made nesting boxes in shallow-water ponds and swamps, as lack of suitable hollow trees is a population-limiting factor. In many parts of the north-

Right, woodpigeons are a serious pest to crops.

Below, the wood duck was over-shot by market hunters in America, but with protection its numbers have increased, and it can now be shot in several states.

Licence Fees—Wyoming		
Type	**Status**	**Fee**
Deer	Resident	$5
	Non-resident	$30
Antelope	Resident	$5
	Non-resident	$35
Elk	Resident	$5
Black bear	Resident	$5
	Non-resident	$25
Grizzly bear	Resident	$25
	Non-resident	$75
Rocky mountain goat	Resident	$25
	Non-resident	$75
Bighorn sheep	Resident	$15
	Non-resident	$75
Moose	Resident	$15
	Non-resident	$75
Rabbit	Resident	$1
	Non-resident	$5
Upland birds	Resident	$2
	Non-resident	$20
Special hunting and fishing (includes 1 antlered elk, 1 deer, 1 black bear, birds and fish)	Non-resident	$125

eastern U.S. these nesting boxes are a familiar – and welcome – sight, and are largely responsible for the come-back of this species, until recently thought to be facing extinction.

Woodpigeon *(Columba palumbus)*

Also known as the cushat and ringdove, this is probably one of the most familiar birds in Britain and much of Europe. They are gray in colour with a white neck mark and a distinctive white barring on the wings noticeable in flight. Britain's resident population is considerably augmented by winter migrants from the European continent. Two eggs are laid in a nest of rough twigs. They take 18 days to hatch and the average pair have some five clutches a year, but suffer a very high predation ratio.

Wary and fast fliers, they have the knack of generally leaving a tree or bush with a flapping of wings on the far side to the approaching gun. They are shot when the hunter is walking round woods and along hedgerows, or whenever he is out shooting. They may also be shot over decoys, when they can provide good sport. Possibly the most exciting method of shooting them is from a platform in a wood over decoys when, coming at all angles and speeds, they can be very interesting shooting. They have a wide range of feed varying from corn, berries and almost any greens to tiny snails. It is always worth opening the crops of pigeons to check the feed and thus possibly locate their main feeding areas, where decoys may then be set up with some confidence. Their flesh is dark in colour and can be quite good eating. A great deal depends on what they have been eating. They should in any event be cropped immediately on being shot.

See also Pigeon Shooting around the World.

Wyoming (U.S.A.)

A Rocky Mountain state of some 97,000 square miles, it is watered by the Yellowstone, Bighorn, Powder and Snake Rivers, and contains the famous Yellowstone National Park. Although primarily a ranching state, second only to Texas in cattle and sheep production, it has some arable farming, mainly on irrigated land in the east and centre of the state. Here corn, sugar beet and vegetables are grown. The state is mainly mountainous and heavily forested, and so offers excellent conditions for forest and mountain game, both big and small.

Mule deer are found throughout the state, but most abundantly in the south-east and in the Bighorn Mountains. White-tailed deer are found in the Black Hills in the north-east. Antelopes are found everywhere on the plains, and the state has the largest pronghorn population in the world. Elk are abundant in the north-west, in the Black

Hills, and in the Medicine Bow Mountains in the south-east. Limited numbers of moose are found in the north of the state, and bighorn sheep are increasing. Pheasant and sage grouse are the most common game birds. Turkeys have now been re-established, and there are ruffed and blue grouse in all the mountain areas.

Special Regulations

A non-resident must be accompanied by a licensed guide when hunting big game. There are no restrictions as to firearms that may be carried. For big game a rifle of at least .23 calibre, chambered to fire centre-fire cartridges not less than two inches long overall, including a soft or expanding bullet normally seated must be used. For birds a shotgun not larger than 10-bore and plugged to hold no more than three cartridges is necessary. Turkey may be hunted with both shotgun and rifle. Dogs may be used on birds and rabbits, but not on big game. Permission must be obtained from the landowner before entering private land, and most landowners charge trespass fees.

Further Information

Game and Fish Commission, Box 1589, Cheyenne, Wyoming 82001.

Big Game Inventory—Wyoming

Species	Shot
Antelope	31,482
Deer	95,119
Elk	18,012
Bighorn sheep	96
Grizzly bear	8
Pheasant	44,063
Chukar partridge	9,023
Hungarian partridge	1,831
Blue grouse	3,522
Ruffed grouse	2,942
Sage grouse	43,376
Sharp-tailed grouse	775
Geese	2,750
Duck	57,360
Cottontail rabbit	164.554

Seasons and Limits—Wyoming

Vary from area to area.

Species	Season	Limit	Comment
White-tailed deer	10 Sept-30 Nov		
Mule deer	10 Sept-30 Nov	Varies from one, any sex, to one buck, or one buck with 4 points or more	50,000 licences issued only
Antelope	Varies between 5 Sept and 15 Nov		30-50,000 permits issued with special drawing for non-residents
Elk	Varies between 10 Sept and 15 Dec	Varies from one, any sex, to one, antlered	5,500 licences available for non-residents
Black bear	1 April-30 June; early Sept-mid-Nov	Residents, 1 Non-residents, 2	Number of licences unlimited
Grizzly bear	Sept and Nov, also a spring season		Special drawing only
Bighorn sheep	1 Sept-20 Nov	One ram with $\frac{3}{4}$ curl or more	Special drawing only
Rocky Mountain Goat	Very small herd—no open season		Special drawing only
Cottontail rabbit	20 Aug-31 Dec	No limit	
Snowshoe hare	All year		
Jack rabbit	All year		
Pheasant	7 Nov-31 Dec	Limits vary	
Ruffed grouse	5 Sept-15 Nov		
Sharp-tail grouse	7 Nov-22 Nov		
Sage grouse	29 Aug-20 Sept		
Blue grouse	5 Sept-15 Nov		
Chukar and Hungarian partridge	3 Oct-31 Dec		
Bobwhite quail	7 Nov-31 Dec		
Wild turkey	1 Nov-30 Nov		

Y Z

Yemen *see* Middle East

Yugoslavia

Yugoslavia lies in south-east Europe, along the east of the Adriatic Sea. The total area is about 98,740 square miles, most of which is very mountainous, the only exception being the fertile lowland area of the Middle Danube and its tributaries, the Drava, Tisa, Sava and Morava. The Dalmatian coast is heavily indented and islanded, but though the islands are low-lying, the mainland rises steeply to the high Dinarske Plateau. The climate is relatively continental, despite the long Adriatic coastline.

Sixty-five per cent of the population is still dependent on agriculture, wheat and maize being the main crops. Timber is important, but industry, though growing fast, is still limited.

Yugoslavia is a federation of the Socialist Republics of Croatia, Serbia (including the autonomous region of Kosova), Slovenia, Montenegro, Bosnia-Herzegovina, and Macedonia. They are similar, in respect of the mountainous and relatively unspoilt terrain, except for the plains of Slavonia, in Croatia, and Vojvodina, in Serbia, where lies Belgrade, the capital. These plains have large game parks, with very heavy deer populations.

Legislation regarding seasons, bag limits, costs, etc differs from region to region, and should be checked in advance, for the appropriate area.

The main species shot and their normal distribution are shown in the table.

Species and Distribution—Yugoslavia

Species	Distribution
Red deer	The plains of Slavonia and the game parks of Vojvodina ; also occasionally in the Bosnia-Herzegovina Forests
Fallow deer	The plains of Slavonia and the woods of Fruska Gora (a range of small hills in the Vojvodina plain)
Roe deer	The plains of Slavonia and the game parks of Vojvodina
Chamois	The Slovene Alps, parts of the Bosnian mountains, and the Sar Planina area in Macedonia
Mouflon	The woods of Fruska Gora
Bear	The Bosnia-Herzegovina forests and some of the mountains of Kosovo and eastern Serbia
Boar	The Bosnia-Herzegovina forests and the middle Danube plains
Wolf	Bosnia-Herzegovina and Kosovo
Fox	Throughout the country especially in Bosnia-Herzegovina and Vojvodina
Badger	Throughout the country, especially in Vojvodina
Marten	Throughout the country, especially in Kosovo
Hare	Throughout the country, especially in Vojvodina
Rabbit	Throughout the country
Grouse	Throughout the country
Pheasant	Throughout the country, especially in Vojvodina
Partridge	Throughout the country, especially in Vojvodina
Wildfowl	All river deltas, especially the Hutovo Blato marshes in Herzegovina, the Obedska Bara marshes in Serbia, and the marshes of Vojvodina

Seasons—Yugoslavia

Vary from region to region

Species	Season
Red deer	Aug-Dec
Fallow deer	mid-May-mid-Oct
Roe deer	mid-May-mid-Oct
Hare	mid-Oct-mid-Jan
Grouse	April-May
Pheasant	Oct-mid-Jan
Partridge	Sept-Nov
Boar	All year
Wolf	All year
Lynx	Protected

Deer are stalked or still-hunted. Pheasants and other small game are shot by driving or organized walking up with beaters. Boar are also shot by organized groups, usually of eight to ten people.

Trophy charges vary with points (measured in conformity with the Madrid Convention). The average fee for red deer is about $500, and for chamois about $100. Roe trophies are $30 upwards. The fees for boar shooting are usually a little over $100 a day. The cost of small game shooting varies so widely that even approximations are not really possible. The normal method is to charge by the day, with an additional fee per head if over a certain number are shot. Up-to-date information should be obtained from the nearest Yugoslav tourist office. Daily charges practically always include guides, ghillies, dogs, etc, as well as board and lodging.

All guns, telescopes, binoculars, cameras, ammunition and other hunting gear must be entered on visitors' passports together with the visa, and everything except used ammunition must be taken out again. Long-barrelled, express rifles are obligatory for big game and deer. For red deer and bear the bore must be over 7 mm, and for roe and fallow over 6 mm. Telescopic sights are strongly recommended.

There are over 100 game parks open to visitors in Yugoslavia, ranging in size from 12,500 acres to 250,000 acres; the average is about 125,000 acres. Visitors may organize their trip through any Yugoslav travel agency, or through the Tourist Association of Yugoslavia, which has branches throughout Europe.

Further Information

Tourist Association of Yugoslavia, Mose Pijade 8, Belgrade.

Yukon Territory (Canada)

Yukon is the most north-westerly province of Canada. It covers an area of about 205,000 square miles and, although some of the terrain is flat, most of it is characterized by rugged mountains with surprisingly wide and gentle valley bottoms in between, in some of which crops can be grown. The climate, however, is a semi-arid one, with a rainfall of no more than ten to twelve inches a year and long and extremely cold winters. Much of the province consists of tundra, some is under a permanent snow cover, but the rest is quite heavily timbered, the principal trees consisting of spruce, poplar, birch, cottonwood and balsam. The chief industries are mining, fishing and forestry, but fur trapping is still an important occupation. Communication is principally by air, but the Alaska Highway has opened parts of the province to wheeled traffic, and water traffic along the Yukon River is still important.

A non-resident can hunt in the province only by employing the services of an outfitter, who will provide the official guides required, by law, for each non-resident; also pack and riding horses, camping equipment, and local knowledge. The usual procedure is to engage the services of an outfitter for a fortnight or more at fees that will average around $100 per person per day.

Further Information

Government of Yukon Territory, Game Branch, P.O. Box 2703, Whitehorse, Yukon Territory.

Zambia

Zambia lies in south central Africa, covering an area of about 290,000 square miles. The whole country is on the central African plateau and, except in the river valleys, has a flat or gently rolling terrain, between 3,000 and 5,000 ft, rising to over 6,000 ft in the north-east, where the country is rather more broken. There are several large rivers, in particular the Zambesi, all flowing southwards, and three large stretches of surface water: Lakes Kariba, Bangweulu, and Mweru. The altitude counters the effect of

Seasons and Limits—Yukon

Species	Season	Limit
Black bear	15 April-15 June	2
	1 Aug-30 Nov	1
Grizzly bear	April-15 June	1 per licence year
	1 Aug-30 Nov	1 per licence year
Caribou	1 Aug-30 Nov	1
Moose	1 Aug-30 Nov	1 — see table of licence fees for restrictions on big-game licences
Mountain goat	1 Aug-30 Nov	1
Mountain sheep	1 Aug-10 Nov	1
Buffalo	No open season	
Deer	No open season	
Elk	No open season	
Musk ox	No open season	
Polar bear	1 Oct-30 May	Eskimos only
Grouse, franklin's and spruce	1 Sept-31 Jan / 1 Sept-31 Jan	10 per day
Ruffed grouse, blue grouse and sharp-tailed goose	1 Sept-31 Oct / 1 Sept-31 Oct / 1 Sept-31 Oct	5 per day / 5 per day / 5 per day
Wilson's snipe	1 Sept-31 Oct	10 per day, 20 in possession
Ptarmigan	1 Sept-31 Jan	10 per day
Pheasant	No open season	
Duck	1 Sept-31 Oct	Non-residents; 8 per day, 16 in possession, residents, 25 per day
Geese	1 Sept-31 Oct	Non-residents, 5 per day, 10 in possession of which not more than 2 per day and 4 in possession may be white-fronted residents, 15 per day
Rails and coots	1 Sept-31 Oct	Non-residents, 8 per day, 16 in possession, residents, 25 per day. There are no limits for the number of migratory birds in possession for residents

Licence Fees—Yukon

Type	Status	Fee	Comment
Game licence	Resident	$5	Entitle holder to kill one male from any two of the following species: moose, caribou (woodland or barren ground), sheep (dall or stone), mountain goat, as well as one grizzly bear (either sex) and black or brown bears, wolves and coyotes without limit. Non-resident licence valid from 1 Aug-30 Nov. Any of the six species, killed in excess of the two allowed will cost an extra 25%
Big game licence	Non-resident Canadian	$50	
	Non-resident alien	$100	
Spring bear-hunting licence	Non-resident Canadian	$25	Valid from 1 May-30 June. Entitles holder to kill two grizzlies and two black or brown bears and wolves and coyotes without limit. Polar bears may only be shot by Eskimos.
	Non-resident alien	$50	
Game bird licence	Any non-resident	$10	Covers ptarmigan, sharp-tailed grouse, franklin grouse, spruce grouse, ruffed grouse and blue grouse
Canadian migratory Game Bird Hunting Permit	Any	$2	For all migratory birds including waterfowl

Zambia's continental and tropical situation and the climate is very pleasant, only hot and humid in the lower reaches of the larger rivers.

Most of Zambia is typical African plains country. The economy is primarily agricultural, with maize, groundnuts, cotton, cassava, Kaffir corn, tobacco, vegetables and livestock. As the population level is low, this country has much to offer in terms of open space and plentiful game.

There are two safari companies: Zambia Safaris Ltd and Luangwa Safaris Ltd. Zambia Safaris are the larger of the two and arrange shooting of the following species (one of each unless otherwise stated) under their inclusive safari licence (licence fee: $1,400): buffalo (two), bushbuck, bushpig, crocodile, duiker, eland (male only), elephant, grysbok, hartebeeste, hippopotamus, hyena, impala (two), jackal, kudu, leopard, lion, oribi, puku, reedbuck, roan antelope, sable antelope, warthog (two), common waterbuck, defassa waterbuck, wildebeeste, wild dog, zebra. By special arrangement rhinoceros, Kafue lechwe, sitatunga, yellow-backed duiker, blue duiker, klipspringer and steinbok may also be shot.

Luangwa Safaris organize shooting of a similar list of species under their inclusive safari licence (fee: $950). The chief differences are that three buffalo, two puku, three impala, five baboon and one monkey may be shot. Sable antelope, hartebeeste, reedbuck, oribi, and jackal may not be shot, and there is a special arrangement only for rhino (fee: $563) and for additional elephant (fee: $141).

The two operate in different areas. Luangwa Safaris on the periphery of the Luangwa Valley National Park; Zambia Safaris have concessions in three areas, two adjacent to Kafue National Park and one at Feira, in the south, near the Rhodesia-Mozambique border. Luangwa Safaris offer the only shooting in Africa of Cookson's wildebeeste, which has exceptionally large horns, while Zambia Safaris offer the equally unique Kafue lechwe. The hunting season is the same for both companies – May to October (the dry season). Neither impose a bag limit on game birds. All species of the following are classed as game birds: duck, teal and geese, francolin, guinea fowl, quail and button quail, sandgrouse, snipe and painted snipe and green pigeon.

Special Regulations and Safari Fees
Dogs may only be used to hunt lion, leopard and game birds. Bows and spears are illegal, as are automatic weapons and explosive missiles or projectiles, including tracer rounds, or any that carry incapacitating chemicals or drugs, all traps of the pit, pitfall or trench type, gintraps or similar traps with a jaw width of over four in, and nets and wire snares.

The calibres required for the game are as follows: elephant and hippopotamus, .375 express; crocodile, leopard or lion, .300 express; game birds, a shotgun, muzzle loader or .22 rifle; other game species, a muzzle loader or .240 rifle. Both safari companies recommend visitors to bring their own firearms, though they may be hired on the spot if necessary. The best combination is a .375 magnum or larger for the big game, a 30.06 or similar for the smaller game, and a 12-bore shotgun. Ammunition should include some solid rounds for the larger rifle. An import permit may be obtained at the point of entry, which will probably be Lusaka. This is in any case the starting point for Zambia Safaris. Luangwa safaris start from Mfuwe or Chipata, to which there are flights from Lusaka. The recommended minimum duration for a safari is three weeks. The fees vary depending on the number of clients and non-shooting observers and the number of professional hunters (not more than two shooting clients to each professional hunter) but generally they are between $150 and $250 per hunter per day with the Luangwa Safari rates being on the whole slightly cheaper than the Zambia Safari rates. A deposit of about 25% of the total fees plus the cost of the licence is required to confirm bookings. In the event of cancellation at least six months before the starting date the deposit will be refunded less 10%.

Further Information
The Chief Tourist Officer, Zambia National Tourist Board, P.O. Box 17, Lusaka.
Zambia Safaris, P.O. Box 2955, Lusaka.
Luangwa Safaris, P.O. Box 72, Chipata.

Zebra *(Equus burchelli)*
Burchell's zebra, found in many parts of central and southern Africa and *Equus grevyi,* or Grevy's zebra, found in northern and north western Africa, are distinct species. Burchell's zebra stands about 13 hands and its body coloration varies from pale sienna to white with thick black and deep chocolate stripes. The head is light and neat, the mane thick and upstanding. Grevy's zebra stands nearer fourteen hands, the body coloration is pure white, but the black and chocolate brown stripes are finely and evenly distributed over the body. The ears are very large. Both are found in plains, mountainous grassland, light woodlands and occasionally in broken, hilly ground. They are found in small herds of a dozen and, during the seasonal aggregations, very large herds of a hundred or more. Mainly grazers, they also browse a little. Unlike antelopes they require water to survive and drink each morning or evening. Foaling is from July to September, though some foals may be born at any time of the year; twins are rare. Zebras are very thin skinned – a shot anywhere in the body is usually sufficient to finish them.

The zebra inhabits an extensive area in central-eastern Africa. There is great individual variation in its striping.